Cape Verde

the Bradt Travel Guide

Murray Stewart

Aisling Irwin and Colum Wilson

edition
6

www.bradtguides.com

Bradt Travel Guides Ltd, UK
The Globe Pequot Press Inc, USA

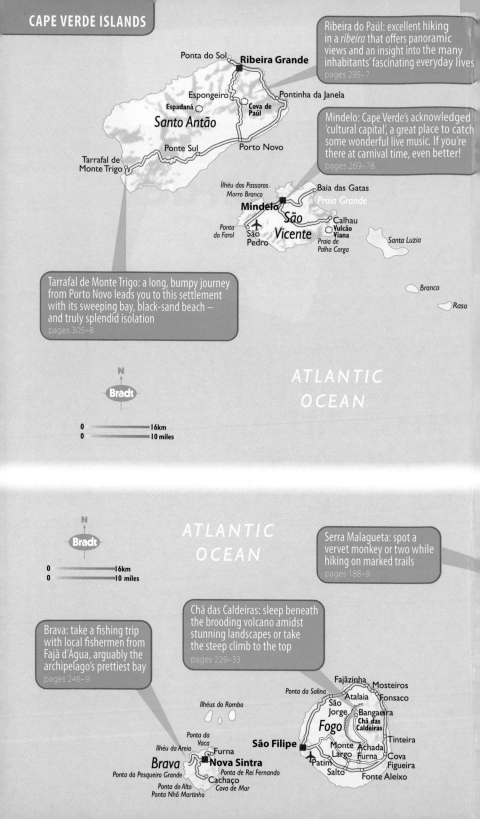

CAPE VERDE ISLANDS

Ribeira do Paúl: excellent hiking in a *ribeira* that offers panoramic views and an insight into the many inhabitants' fascinating everyday lives
pages 295–7

Mindelo: Cape Verde's acknowledged 'cultural capital', a great place to catch some wonderful live music. If you're there at carnival time, even better!
pages 269–78

Tarrafal de Monte Trigo: a long, bumpy journey from Porto Novo leads you to this settlement with its sweeping bay, black-sand beach – and truly splendid isolation
pages 305–8

Santo Antão

Ponta do Sol
Ribeira Grande
Espongeiro
Pontinha da Janela
Espadaná
Cova de Paúl
Ponte Sul
Porto Novo
Tarrafal de Monte Trigo

Ílhéu dos Passaros
Morro Branco
Baia das Gatas
Praia Grande
Mindelo
São Vicente
Calhau
Vulcão Viana
Ponta do Farol
São Pedro
Praia de Palha Carga

Santa Luzia

Branco

Raso

ATLANTIC OCEAN

Bradt

0 ————— 16km
0 ————— 10 miles

N

ATLANTIC OCEAN

Bradt

0 ————— 16km
0 ————— 10 miles

N

Serra Malagueta: spot a vervet monkey or two while hiking on marked trails
pages 188–9

Chã das Caldeiras: sleep beneath the brooding volcano amidst stunning landscapes or take the steep climb to the top
pages 229–33

Brava: take a fishing trip with local fishermen from Fajã d'Água, arguably the archipelago's prettiest bay
pages 248–9

Ílhéus do Rombo

Fajãzinha
Mosteiros
Ponta da Salina
São Jorge
Atalaia
Fonsaco
Bangaeira
Chã das Caldeiras
Fogo
Ponta da Vaca
Furna
São Filipe
Ílhéu da Areia
Monte Largo
Achada Furna
Tinteira
Brava
Nova Sintra
Ponta de Rei Fernando
Patim
Cova Figueira
Ponta da Pesqueiro Grande
Cachaço
Cova de Mar
Salto
Fonte Aleixo
Ponta do Alto
Ponta Nhõ Martinho

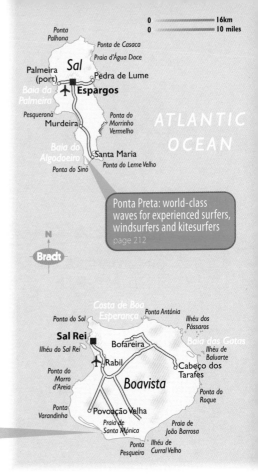
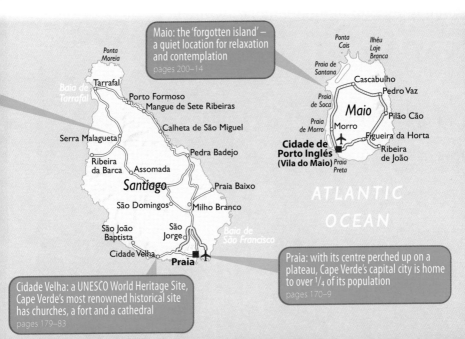

Cape Verde
Don't
miss...

Pico de Fogo
One of the steepest and most
spectacular volcanic cones in
the world, Pico de Fogo is the
highest point on Fogo Island
(S/S) pages 216–18

Watersports
Cape Verde is a popular
destination for windsurfers and
regularly hosts championships
(MM) pages 51–3

Sweeping sand beaches
Some Cape Verdean islands have miles upon miles of beautiful sands, such as here at Santa Mónica beach on Boavista (MM)
page 145

Rich music scene
Music underpins Cape Verdean life and no visit to the archipelago would be complete without experiencing some *morna* or *funaná*
(LH) pages 40–5

Verdant *ribeiras*
The fertile Paúl Valley on Santo Antão is home to thousands of people and lush sugarcane, banana and breadfruit plantations, not to mention a prolific output of *grogue*
(MF/AWL)
pages 295–7

Cape Verde
in colour

above   Inside a ring of mountains lies the Pedra de Lume, a sweeping geometry of saltpans in blue, pink and green depending on their stage of salt formation (MM) pages 128–9

left   The 'Blue Eye' at Buracona, an underground pool connected to the sea by an underground tunnel (MM) page 128

below   With rows of pastel-coloured buildings, Santa Maria das Dores, the lively tourist centre of Sal, remains modest and humble (SS) pages 112–26

above Boavista's white deserts and pretty coastline are dotted with interesting ruins, such as the Igreja Nossa Senhora De Fàtima (MM) pages 154 & 160

right With 14 protected areas that act as breeding grounds for seabirds, endangered turtles and humpback whales, Boavista's biodiversity is of huge global importance (MM) pages 135–9

below The main square in the charming town of Sal Rei — a great place to sit with a beer and watch Cape Verdean life go by (SS) pages 147–54

We're **40**...
how did that happen?

How did it all happen? George (my then husband) and I wrote the first Bradt guide – about hiking in Peru and Bolivia – on an Amazon river barge, and typed it up on a borrowed typewriter. We had no money for the next two books so George went to work for a printer and was paid in books rather than money.

Forty years on, Bradt publishes over 200 titles that sell all over the world. I still suffer from Imposter Syndrome – how did it all happen? I hadn't even worked in an office before! Well, I've been extraordinarily lucky with the people around me. George provided the belief to get us started (and the mother to run our US office). Then, in 1977, I recruited a helper, Janet Mears, who is still working for us. She and the many dedicated staff who followed have been the foundations on which the company is built. But the bricks and mortar have been our authors and readers. Without them there would be no Bradt Travel Guides. Thank you all for making it happen.

Hilary Bradt

AUTHORS

Colum and Aisling's first guide to Cape Verde was published in 1988. Aisling is a journalist and writer, specialising in the environment, the developing world and science. A former *Daily Telegraph* correspondent, she has won several prizes for her feature-writing and has contributed to books on a variety of subjects, including Bradt's guide to solar eclipses over Africa. Colum is a humanitarian worker. He worked for Médecins Sans Frontières and now works for the UK government's Department for International Development. Colum and Aisling have lived in, and written about, a range of countries

including Zambia and Angola. Their other joint book is *In Quest of Livingstone: A Journey to the Four Fountains*, about their retracing of David Livingstone's last journey. See page iv for their authors' stories.

UPDATER/AUTHOR

In 2009, with a new-found ambition to become a travel writer, Murray Stewart turned his back on a 20-year career in corporate restructuring that included receiving a House of Commons commendation for saving a Norfolk pea-processing factory. Drawing on visits to 56 countries, including periods teaching English in Chile and Mexico, as well as working as a consultant in Spain, he has since been published in national travel magazines as well as winning prizes for his online contributions. He updated Bradt's *North Cyprus* guide in 2011

and jumped at the opportunity to update this sixth edition of Bradt's *Cape Verde*. Armed with a crash-course in Portuguese and two words of Creole, he spent two months 'speed-dating' the nine inhabited islands of the archipelago, rejoicing in the the fusion of cultural influences, the diversity of terrains and the monotony of the weather: warm and sunny.

A self-confessed part-time 'pilgrim', Murray has twice walked the Camino de Santiago, raising thousands of pounds for charity in the process. He speaks French, Spanish, German and is currently learning Arabic. And now, thanks to this update, he speaks a little Portuguese. And three words of Creole.

PUBLISHER'S FOREWORD   *Hilary Bradt*

When we commissioned the first edition of this guide in 1997 it seemed an impossibly obscure destination. But once the book was published, word got round that this was one of the best spots in the world for windsurfers and other watersports enthusiasts, and hikers were lured by the remote, volcanic interior. After that, the property market boomed as people sought a second home on an island with guaranteed sunshine. Since the fourth edition, the islands have shifted further still into the limelight. Marketing campaigns have promoted Cape Verde as the new 'cheap Caribbean', and some visitors have expected palm-fringed beaches and an azure ocean. But this isn't the Maldives. The islands are a raw mix of arid interiors, lush sugarcane plantations and clean windswept beaches. This forthright new edition shows you what to expect from each island, so you can pick and choose the best itinerary. Happy travelling!

Sixth edition published June 2014
First published 1998
Bradt Travel Guides Ltd
IDC House, The Vale, Chalfont St Peter, Bucks SL9 9RZ, England
www.bradtguides.com
Print edition published in the USA by The Globe Pequot Press Inc,
PO Box 480, Guilford, Connecticut 06437-0480

Text copyright © 2014 Aisling Irwin, Colum Wilson and Murray Stewart
Maps copyright © 2014 Bradt Travel Guides Ltd
Photographs copyright © 2014 Individual photographers (see below)
Project Managers: Kelly Randell and Laura Pidgley
Cover research: Pepi Bluck, Perfect Picture

ISBN: 978 1 84162 495 2 (print)
e-ISBN: 978 1 84162 792 2 (e-pub)
e-ISBN: 978 1 84162 693 2 (mobi)

British Library Cataloguing in Publication Data
A catalogue record for this book is available from the British Library

Photographs 4 Corners: Reinhard Schmid (RS/4C); Alamy: Jenny Bailey (JB/A), PKlandscape (P/A); AWL Images (www.awl-images.com): Michele Falzone (MF/AWL), Peter Adams (PA/AWL); Dreamstime: Dareon (D/DT); Laurie Hackett (LH); Marco Muscarà, www.marcomuscara.com (MM); Murray Stewart (MS); Shutterstock: Alexandra Giese (AG/S), Axel Lauer (AL/S), Bildagentur Zoonar GmbH (BZG/S), David Thyberg (DT/S), Frank Bach (FB/S), Mark Caunt (MC/S), Mogens Trolle (MT/S), Sundebo (S/S); SuperStock (SS)
Front cover Fisherman at Santa Maria beach on Sal (RS/4C)
Back cover 'Blue Eye' at Buracona (MM); Ponta do Sol (SS)
Title page Maio (AL/S); magnificent male frigatebird (MT/S); Mindelo (PA/AWL)

Maps David McCutcheon FBCart.S

Typeset from the authors' disc by Ian Spick, Bradt Travel Guides Ltd
Production managed by Jellyfish Print Solutions; printed in India
Digital conversion by the Firsty Group

Acknowledgements

Murray Stewart

Any guidebook is heavily dependent on the generosity of others, particularly generosity of time given to the author or updater in assisting them with their task. In every island, I came across those who were happy to assist me in what at times felt like a whirlwind visit, though in fact it lasted nine weeks. I must start my thanks to the Cape Verde people as a whole, as they possess a true kindness of spirit and a hospitable nature that prevents them from being anything other than delightful to spend time with. Thank you to all of you.

Beyond that, special thanks must go to the following: in the UK, to Ian Coates at Archipelago Choice for navigating me through the logistical minefield of covering nine islands in nine weeks and for providing the flights; to Ron Hughes of Cape Verde Travel, for pulling strings to get me accommodation; and to Rachel Fielding and the team at Bradt for giving me the opportunity to fall in love with Cape Verde, which I duly did. Also to Ana Cassis, who taught me enough Portuguese to get by.

Others I met on my travels and who deserve mention are Rosalina and her daughters Rosaline and Rosalita, who welcomed me to Santiago and gave me my first clue that Cape Verdeans are characters who delight; Kenneth Miller of the Millenium Challenge Corporation, who was generous with his time and detailed in his explanations of some of the challenges facing this still young nation; Tommy Melo of Biosfera I for sharing with me his knowledge of the ecological issues facing Cape Verde; for Marijke Katsburg, who got me so close, so quickly, to the people of Brava; Mustafa, who showed me what the Chã das Caldeiras crater is all about; Sarah Litchfield, an enthusiast for Fogo, as if it needed one; Sibylle Schellmann, for an informative lunchtime meeting; Laurie Hackett, for her willingness to give me some excellent contacts on the islands; Stephen and Janette Frankland, for introducing me to Maio; on Boavista, to Savinja Notenbaert and Lloyd Stokes for some useful tips and to Lamine Drame for showing me Boa Esperança; on Sal, to Beverley Chadwick and Moonira Merali for temporarily adopting me and showing me the best of the island; Professor Lucy Durán for her valuable, expert contribution on Cape Verde music; Ana Monteiro for her informative pieces on wind power; vista verde (particularly Sandra and Anne) for their Teutonic efficiency in keeping me up to date with the inevitable changes to internal flights.

I must thank Hotel Avenida on Santiago, Hotel Savana and Pedra Brabo on Fogo, Pensão Paraizo on Brava; Bluebell Hotel, Hotel Paul Mar and the Santo Antão Art Resort on Santo Antão for providing me with free nights' accommodation. Thanks also to others who helped me with the cost, amongst these the Solar Windelo in São Vicente and Blue Banana on Sal, Jardim de Vinho and Rosymar Inn in Praia. Thanks also to Catia Baldan at Porto Antigo on Sal for her help and generosity.

Somewhere, someone will read this and feel they have been left out. I can only apologise. My final thanks go to dear Sara Lister, for doing without me for a couple of months while I bunked off to Cape Verde and researched the book. And an even bigger thank you to her for having me back afterwards.

When Colum and I first visited Cape Verde two decades ago it was, for the British, an obscure destination. The annual number of tourists was a few tens of thousands, of which Brits were an infinitesimal fraction. Now tourism is in the hundreds of thousands and the development of hotels, apartments and condominiums surges ahead. The country is riding a rollercoaster with the added excitement that no-one knows how safe the structure is. I gaze through the estate agents' windows, at the developers' plans, at the construction sites and I try to extract meaning. Who will be living in these fairy-tale condominiums? What corners of the world will they come from? Will there be any Cape Verdeans in there? What will it mean if there aren't – and what will it mean if there are?

Now, when I visit, development has made things easier (though the air and ferry connections between the islands are worse than they were a decade ago). But now I am also finding disappointment among tourists. I have heard complaints about sullen service, about the endless wind, flies, the lack of anything to 'do', and the high cost of living. The main reason for their negativity is that they were oversold their holidays. Cape Verde is – hilariously – being touted as the 'new Caribbean' – when the islands for sale tend to have a barrenness approaching that of the moon.

So I find myself in a strange position now: instead of raving about Cape Verde I find myself sometimes advising people not to go. I've even inserted a small section in each island chapter entitled 'Lowlights' so you know what not to expect. Here is my reasoning: I want you to treasure Cape Verde, and if you're a person who won't find it treasurable, I want you to know beforehand.

So: go, if you love the sea and have a cracking watersports holiday on Sal or Boavista; go, if you love outstanding mountainous landscapes, particularly if you enjoy hiking in them: enjoy Santo Antão; go, if something inside you responds to a barren land with a harsh black coastline pounded by a frothing white ocean; or to a convivial people with the time to strike up a mournful tune over a glass of thick red wine.

I believe, though, that you will have your most fulfilling holiday if a little part of you goes as an anthropologist, interested in whatever the archipelago throws at you. Be like one of my contributors, who responds to notorious Cape Verdean punctuality with the words: 'It's great how these people refuse to be intimidated by time.'

Cape Verde is, at heart, a place not to be consumed, but to be understood.

Aisling's words, written opposite, keep returning to me: 'you will have your most fulfilling holiday if a little part of you goes as an anthropologist'. My two months in Cape Verde demonstrated the inherent truth in those words. Memories reinforce the statement. Cape Verde does not have a wealth of obvious treasures, few museums, no art galleries, a mere scattering of historical sites. So, travel as an anthropologist and little treasures will appear and quickly turn into big treasures – treasures to store in the memory.

I recall the large, matronly lady in Santo Antão who stood in front of the *aluguer* and refused to let it continue its journey until she had finished an impromptu song she was singing. None of the passengers complained. Then I remember the face of the fisherman on Brava, stretched taut – it seemed - with that island's centuries of loss and longing, his emotion heightened by a few too many shots of *grogue,* singing me a *morna* until the tears spilled down his cheeks and those of his three-person audience. Had I understood Creole, I have no doubt I would have wept, too.

Recollections of shared lunch tables, pick-up trucks groaning with an overfill of people and their purchases from the Assomada Market; an uncomfortable, inter-island journey on a chartered fishing boat during which a local woman sitting on the deck simply wrapped (without asking) both her arms around my leg, to steady herself against the effects of the 4m high Atlantic swell …

All of these come back to me, finally allowing me to bundle them together and explain to myself why I love Cape Verde. Yes, the Fogo volcano is stunning. Yes, Santo Antão's craggy peaks steal the breath with their starkness. Yes, the glistening beaches of Sal and Boavista defy you not to curl up your feet and scrunch the white grains gleefully between your toes.

But it is none of these attractions that won me over, rather the gentle patience of the archipelago's inhabitants, their ability to intimately share both time and space with each other (and me), their commitment to live life *communally*. What haunts me is the feeling that the 'developed' countries have lost that ability, and that we'll never get it back. This brings me my own sense of loss and longing, but I can't sing a *morna*. I must simply return to Cape Verde.

Contents

LIST OF MAPS

HOW TO USE THE MAPS IN THIS GUIDE

KEYS AND SYMBOLS

Maps include alphabetical keys covering the locations of those places to stay, eat or drink that are featured in the book. Note that regional maps may not show all hotels and restaurants in the area: other establishments may be located in towns shown on the map. On occasion, hotels, cafés, bars or restaurants that are not listed in the guide (but which might serve as alternative options if required or serve as useful landmarks to aid navigation) are also included on the maps; these are marked with accommodation (⌂), café (☕), bar (♉) or restaurant (✗) symbols.

GRIDS AND GRID REFERENCES

Several maps use gridlines to allow easy location of sites. Map grid references are listed in square brackets after the name of the place or sight of interest in the text, with page number followed by grid number, eg: [103 C3].

Introduction

The flight to the island of Maio was full. As the tiny propeller plane bounced over Atlantic air currents, I was the only passenger to gaze out with a lick of fear at the mighty mid-ocean below. Inside the plane everyone else seemed to have forgotten the sea. All was exuberance, chatter and a roaring laughter. The passengers were young men in polished shoes, expensive trousers and heavy gold jewellery. They spoke in a Creole that was too rapid for me to grasp and I wondered what interest Maio – flat, dry and quiet even by Cape Verdean standards – could hold for them.

A few days later I was driving through the north of Maio, mesmerised by its endless stony red plains where the goats eat rock and the people eat goats. I reached a village – a single street of dust, two rows of parched, single-storey houses. 'This is Alcatraz,' the driver said. The street was quiet apart from a few of the ragged, wide-eyed children who populate the poorer half of the world. Some of the houses were nothing more than bare concrete carcasses while others were painted in greens and pinks and blues and even had glass in their windows.

From the front door of one of the smarter houses a family appeared. I crossed the street and asked if he minded if I took a photo.

'Not at all,' the man replied in perfect English. 'But don't you remember me? I was on your flight.'

My perception jolted and suddenly I saw the urbane passenger, representative of a richer world, gold still gleaming at his neck. And then my world altered again and I saw a poor village, forgotten even within Cape Verde. He must have noticed my perplexity: 'I live in Holland,' he explained. 'I work on the ships… I've come back to see my wife and children.' The woman at his side, uncomprehending, scooped a child onto her hip.

'How long have you been away?' I asked.

'Three years.'

'That's hard.'

'Yes,' he replied. 'But we Cape Verdeans – we have hard lives.'

That is one of the paradoxes of Cape Verde. There is a widespread cosmopolitanism that dates from centuries ago, but it lives side by side with poverty and isolation. For generations the young men have gone abroad – to the USA, to Europe, to the African mainland – because the land cannot sustain them, because their families need money. Back at home their relatives mourn not just the loss of their own sons and husbands but the painful emigrations of generations before. They mourn the peculiar lot of the Cape Verdean, stranded on outcrops in the Atlantic, abused over the centuries not just by the waves but by many nations. They mourn in a particularly beautiful way which I first discovered on Fogo, the volcano island.

I was clinging to the bench in the back of a small truck as it jolted up and down the steep cobbled roads of the old Portuguese town of São Filipe. Every so often the vehicle would halt in front of a house, the driver would shout and a man would appear in the doorway clutching a violin and scramble in beside me.

Soon we had gathered the band back together and we careered up into the foothills of Fogo's dark volcano till we reached the house of Agusto, a blind musician. Inside his white-painted, two-roomed home the men dragged chairs and benches together and I sat in a far corner as the violins made their awakening screeches and the guitars were tuned. Then the music began: sweet melodies and melancholy harmonies. The music was so sad, it was as if the sorrow of generations had erupted in the house.

The Cape Verdeans express through their *mornas* the sorrow of sons lost to the wider world, droughts, famines and relatives drowned at sea. Their music is exquisite, an Atlantic art form with influences from the four continents that surround it. But soon the sadness was done and there came the lively strains of a *funaná*. Now we were celebrating... what, I wondered? I knew the answer, though. We were celebrating the same notion that had just made us cry – *Caboverdeanidade*, the essence of Cape Verde.

I absorbed it all in the dim room with its rough furniture and garish crocheted ornaments. Later I stepped outside where the sun was dissolving into the ocean. As I watched, the music still playing behind me, I thought: this is the reason to visit Cape Verde. There are fine mountains, wildernesses of desert dunes and warm waters. But what makes Cape Verde take hold of your heart is that rare moment, that flush of empathy, when you begin to understand what they mean by *sodade*.

Part One

GENERAL INFORMATION

CAPE VERDE ISLANDS AT A GLANCE

Islands Santo Antão, São Vicente, Santa Luzia (uninhabited), São Nicolau, Sal, Boavista, Maio, Santiago, Fogo, Brava

Location Atlantic Ocean, approximately 1,000km southwest of the Canary Islands, and 460km from the Senegalese coast

Size Ten islands varying in size from 35km^2 (Santa Luzia) to 990km^2 (Santiago), spread over an east–west band of 370km of ocean

Status Independent democratic republic

Government African Party for Independence of Cape Verde or PAICV

Population 510,000 (2014 estimate based on 2010 National Census)

Life expectancy 72 years (UN DESA 2011)

Capital Praia, on Santiago (population around 131,000)

Economy Tourism an increasing earner; bananas most important export; heavy dependence on remittances and foreign aid

Language Officially Portuguese; everyday language is Creole ('Kriolu')

Religion Roman Catholic (85% of the population, estimated)

Currency Cape Verdean escudo (CVE, written as $, after the numeral)

Exchange rate €1=110$ (rate is 'fixed' to the euro). £1 = 133$. US$1= 79$ (March 2014)

International telephone code +238

Time GMT –1

Electricity supply 220V AC, 50Hz. Round, European two-pin sockets

Flag Blue with white and red horizontal stripes and a circle of ten yellow stars

Public holidays 1 January, 20 January, 1 May, 5 July, 15 August, 12 September, 1 November, 25 December. Additionally, each island has its own local holidays – see chapters for details.

1

Background Information

GEOGRAPHY AND CLIMATE

Just a few geographical oddities shape Cape Verde's natural history and economy to a profound degree: a combination of winds and currents that bring heat and cool, dust, dryness and the occasional monsoon. Drought is the key to everything and, as the Cape Verdeans say, 'the best governor is rain'.

LOCATION AND SIZE The Cape Verdes are an arrow-shaped archipelago of ten islands, five islets and various rocks and stacks that poke out of the eastern Atlantic on a band of latitude that runs between Senegal in the east and the Caribbean, 3,600km to the west. They stretch between 14°N and 18°N and 22°W and 26°W. The archipelago is the furthest south of the groups of islands collectively known as Macaronesia. Others in that group include the Azores and the Canary Islands, but the distance between them is great. The Canaries, off Morocco, are over 1,000km away while the Azores, parallel with Portugal, are at a distance of about 2,500km. Even within Cape Verde, its constituent islands are widely spaced. The most easterly is 460km from Senegal and the most westerly is 830km. Santiago, the largest island, is 990km², about twice the size of the Isle of Wight. The smallest is the uninhabited 35km² pinprick of Santa Luzia. Brava is the smallest inhabited island at 64km². The total land area is 4,033km², scattered over 58,000km² of ocean.

The archipelago is popularly divided into two groups. The Barlavento, or windward, islands in the north are Santo Antão, São Vicente, Santa Luzia, São Nicolau, Sal and Boavista. The Sotavento, or leeward, islands to the south are Maio, Santiago, Fogo and Brava.

TERRAIN Another way of dividing the islands is longitudinally: the easterly islands of Sal, Boavista and Maio are extremely flat, while the rest are mountainous. There is extraordinary variation in height: Fogo's peak reaches 2,829m, and you can walk to the top of it, while Boavista musters only a small hill of 390m.

The variation in height reflects the huge age span of the islands and therefore the time available for erosion to take place. Their geological history is still controversial but the most popular theory estimates the flat ones to be up to 26 million years old, dating from the Miocene era. It has been shown that the central islands of São Nicolau and Maio appeared less than 12 million years ago, in the Pliocene. To the west Fogo and Brava, the youngest, have been around for a mere 100,000 years.

The theory is based on the drift of the African Plate, a section of the earth's crust that stretches well beyond the African landmass as far as the middle of the Atlantic. This tectonic plate began a slow drift to the east about 120 million years ago. Underneath it lies a 'hot spot'. As the plate above has drifted, this spot has periodically erupted, poking a series of holes like molehills through the crust. It is thought that the most eroded volcanoes can no longer be seen, submerged by the Atlantic somewhere between Boavista and the mainland. It is even possible that the basalts of Cap Vert, the Senegal promontory, are remnants of the first eruption of the hot spot into the Atlantic.

But some of the islands are more complicated than that. Not all of the magma that erupted from below actually blasted through to the surface. Some of it became trapped within the crust and cooled there, forming large igneous intrusions. The intrusions swelled up and rose within the forming volcanoes, lifting with them the ancient marine sediments that had been deposited on the ocean floor long before any islands developed. The intrusions and the uplifted sediments remained hidden within the volcanoes for millions of years, but the distance between them and the surface has slowly been shrinking as wind and flash floods have eroded the volcanoes away. Now, like slicing the top from a boiled egg, the sediments are revealed, the yolk within. The result is that the flat land of some islands (Maio in particular) is, very roughly, young volcanic rock around the outside and much older sedimentary rock forming an uplifted ring around the intrusions that are exposed in the heart of the island.

The mountainous islands can be very rugged, sometimes with virtually no flat land. Dunes, both still and wandering, are present mainly in the flat islands, most visibly and beautifully in Boavista, where parts feel like true desert.

CLIMATE Caught in the Sahel zone, Cape Verde is really a marine extension of the Sahara. The northeast tradewind is responsible for much of its climate. It blows down particularly strongly from December to April, carrying so little moisture that only peaks of 600m or more can tease out any rain. The high peaks, particularly on Fogo, Santo Antão and Brava, can spend much of the year with their heads in the clouds.

Added to that wind are two other atmospheric factors. First is the **harmattan** – dry, hot winds from the Sahara that arrive in a series of blasts from October to June, laden with brown dust which fills the air like smog. The second factor is the **southwest monsoon**, which brings the longed-for rains between August and October. Often half the year's rainfall can tumble down in a single storm or series of storms. Unfortunately Cape Verde's position is a little too far north for the rains to be guaranteed each year: it lies just above the doldrums, the place where the northeast and southwest tradewinds meet and where there is guaranteed rainfall. The longest recorded time Cape Verde has gone without being watered by the southwest monsoon is 18 years. For 12 years from 1968 there was also a drought.

ANNUAL WEATHER STATISTICS

Jan	Feb	Mar	Apr	May	Jun	Jul	Aug	Sep	Oct	Nov	Dec
Temperature °C day											
24	25	25	25	26	27	27	28	30	29	28	27
Temperature °C night											
8	17	18	18	19	20	22	23	24	23	22	20
Sea temperature °C											
21	20	20	20	21	22	23	24	25	25	24	22
Hours of sunshine											
8	9	10	10	10	8	7	6	8	8	9	8
Days of rain											
0	0	0	0	0	2	3	3	7	4	1	0

In the ocean, the cool stream known as the Canary Current reaches the archipelago from the north and mitigates the heating effect of the northeast tradewind.

Temperature variation on the islands is small – it remains between 22°C and 27°C on Santiago throughout the year. But these figures mask big variations between and even within islands. In the desert centre of some of the flat islands it can reach 40°C between July and September, while on the moist peaks of Santo Antão early in the year it can be as cool as 10°C.

Cape Verde's rainfall figures tell a similarly strange story. A recurring theme is the wide variation in rainfall even between different slopes of the same island – the northeastern slopes are the wettest. On Fogo for example, the average rainfall over 35 years for the northeastern slope of Monte Velha is 1,190mm, while the average on its leeward side is 167mm. Monte Velha's figures also reveal how precious rain can deluge an island over a very short period. In a single month, 20 years ago, 3,000mm of rain fell there. The lower islands, the flat ones, São Vicente and Santa Luzia, receive much less moisture, leaving them almost totally barren.

These chaotic figures can be processed to give mean average rainfalls in the range 10–900mm. Most regions of Cape Verde are classified as arid or semi-arid.

NATURAL HISTORY AND CONSERVATION

Many species on Cape Verde exist nowhere else in the world – the phenomenon known as endemicity. Unlike other islands such as the Caymans, which were once part of a bigger landmass and carry species left over from the greater continent, life here has arrived by chance. Which species completed the extraordinary journey was a lottery and the winners were a peculiar assortment. In addition, these species have had millions of years of isolation in which to branch out on their own, adapting to suit the oddities of the habitat. The grey-headed kingfisher (*Halcyon leucocephela*), for example, in the absence of much inland water in which to live up to its name, dines on insects instead.

The closest relatives of some of Cape Verde's plants are found in East Africa rather than the west. Scientists think that they were borne here from West Africa, which then itself became so dry that they disappeared from there.

FLORA Cape Verde has probably never been profusely covered in greenery. Lack of research and poor early records mean we know little about what it was like before humans arrived. The lower slopes were probably grassy and treeless (steppe) or with low vegetation dotted with trees (savanna). There are a few indigenous trees that still survive: the lovely blue-green, gnarled, flat-topped dragon tree (*Dracaena draco*), fast disappearing except on São Nicolau; the tamarisk palms, known locally as *tamareira* (*Phoenix atlantica*), that fill the lagoons and sunken deserts of Boavista (though some believe that it is just a feral version of another palm tree, *Phoenix dactyl*); the ironwood tree; and perhaps a species of fig tree and one of acacia.

The indigenous plants are adapted to dryness (having small leaves, for example) and are small and sturdy to cope with strong winds.

Over the last 500 years, plants have been introduced from all over the world, and people have tried to cultivate wherever they can. Shrubs and trees have been cleared to make way for arable land. Poor farming techniques and the ubiquitous goat have combined with these forces to oust most of the original vegetation. The result is that, of the 600 species of plant growing in Cape Verde (aside from crops), only a quarter are natural to the islands and about half of those are endemic. Some

1

of the endemic plants, such as *Língua da vaca* (*Echium vulcanorum*) are suited only to ranges of crazily small dimensions, as frustrated botanists will tell you.

Since independence in 1975, people have been making Herculean efforts to plant trees. The roots form a matrix that traps earth so that heavy rain cannot wash them away, and the branches prevent the wind scattering the precious soil. The trees are also supposed to create a moist microclimate. The reafforestation figures have been almost unbelievable: over some periods about three million new trees have been planted each year, or 7,000 a day. The result is pine trees, oaks and sweet chestnuts on the cool peaks of Santo Antão, eucalyptus on the heights of Fogo, and forests of acacia on Maio.

FAUNA

Birds Cape Verde has a dedicated following of ornithologists and amateur birdwatchers who can be found wedged into crevices high up mountainsides or, before new restrictions came into force, trying to secure passages with local fishermen across wild stretches of sea to some of the uninhabited islands. Their dedication stems from the fact that Cape Verde abounds in endemics and some of the seabirds living on cliffs around the islands are particularly important. The archipelago lies on the extreme southwest corner of the western Palaearctic region and is thus the only place in that region where certain species, mainly African or tropical, can be found to breed regularly. There are about 130 migrants for whom Cape Verde is an important stopping point on their long journeys. Some 40 use the islands for nesting. The archipelago is host to three threatened marine bird species: the magnificent frigatebird, brown booby and red-billed tropicbird. The previously endangered Cape Verde shearwater has won a welcome reprieve (see box page 342).

However, as with the plants, much of the natural birdlife has been wiped out, particularly by hungry locals tempted by succulent seabirds or by fishermen treading on their burrows as they search for shellfish along the beaches. Feral cats also pose problems for some species. A more modern threat comes from actual and proposed tourism developments close to important wetland areas, such as Rabil in Boavista and the now-abandoned Salinas development in Maio.

The most prized birds to discover in the islands include the **raso lark** (*Alauda razae*) and the **magnificent frigatebird** (*Fregata magnificens*), both with extraordinarily restricted breeding areas. The population of the former is thought to be around 1,500. The entire eastern Atlantic population of the latter are to be found – all five of them – on the islet of Curral Velho off Boavista, and the extinction of the species seems inevitable. The **Cape Verde petrel** (*Pterodroma feae*), or *ngon-ngon* bird, is disappearing fast and the elegant **red-billed tropicbird**, or *rabo de junco* (*Phaethon aethereus*), with its red bill and streaming white tail, is also plunging in numbers. More common birds include the colourful **grey-headed kingfisher** (*Halcyon leucocephala*) known locally as *passarinha*. It can be found on Santiago, Fogo and Brava, and has a red beak, and orange, black and blue plumage.

You will also see plenty of **helmeted guineafowl** (*Numida meleagris*) on mountain slopes but the distinctive white **Egyptian vulture** (*Neophron percnopterus*), previously abundant at high altitudes, is also fast disappearing, if not actually extinct. Waders frequent the few lagoons and saltpans, on Sal, Maio, Boavista and Santiago. If you miss the **brown booby** (*Sula leucogaster*) – known locally as the *alcatraz* and also an inhabitant of the islet of Curral Velho in Boavista – take a look at the 20-escudo piece. The **Cape Verde red kite** (*Milvus milvus fasciicauda*) is probably now extinct (see page 317) and the **Cape Verde purple heron**, or *garça vermelha* (*Ardea purpurea bournei*), leads a particularly precarious existence in possibly just two trees in Santiago's interior. There are 25 birds in one tree and even fewer in the other (see page 187). The **Cape Verde cane warbler** (*Acrocephalus brevipennis*) (endangered and brownish) lives mostly in Santiago, with about 500 breeding pairs left there, though a significant population was also found in 2004 in Fogo.

Some of the most compelling sites for rare birds in Cape Verde are the islets. On the Ilhéus do Rombo can be found **Bulwer's petrel** (*Bulweria bulwerii*), known locally as *João-petro*. These are known to breed only on Raso Island, which is near São Nicolau, and on Ilhéu de Cima. They are almost totally black with a strip of dark grey stretching along the middle of their wings.

The **Madeiran storm petrel** (*Oceanodroma castro*) is known locally as the *jaba-jaba* or the *pedreirinho*, and breeds only on these islands and on Branco, Raso and islets off Boavista. It is black apart from a white bit just before the tail. The **Cape Verde shearwater** (*Calonectris edwardsii*), once imperilled by a mass annual culling of its chicks (see box, page 342), now thrives again on Raso Island, thanks to the sterling efforts of conservationists.

More information can be found on the partially bilingual website of the Sociedade Caboverdiana de Zoologia (*www.scvz.org/*) and the English-language website of BirdLife International (*www.birdlife.org*).

Other fauna There are no large mammals and no snakes, but several species of bat can be found, and green monkeys inhabit Santiago and can also be found on Brava. There are also many small, brown, endemic reptiles, geckos and skinks. The Cape Verde giant skink (*Macroscincus coctei*) – delicious, sadly – became extinct in the 1940s (see page 342 for more details). Many interesting endemic insects and beetles live on the islands and there are collections of them in the Natural History Museum in London (*www.nhm.ac.uk*).

MARINE LIFE According to the World Wildlife Fund, we are still ignorant of the riches that may lie in Cape Verde's waters. But the marine life here is probably globally significant. There is a high degree of endemism, which is unusual for oceanic islands, and the sea is full of corals – not true reefs but slabs, pinnacles and, importantly, coral mountains reaching up from the ocean floor and providing rare mid-ocean habitats at all depths.

One study concluded that Cape Verde has one of the world's ten most important coral reefs – though that claim has since been disputed by other experts. The highest levels of marine biodiversity are around Boavista, Sal and Maio, which share a marine platform. Meanwhile, despite its aridity, Boavista hosts one of the largest wetlands of the Macaronesia region (see page 136).

So far, scientists have catalogued 639 species of fish including mantas and whale sharks. More than 17 species of whale and dolphin have been reported, including the humpback whale, which breeds in Cape Verde. Five species of turtle frequent Cape Verdean waters, including the loggerhead (*Caretta caretta*) for whom Cape Verde is the third most important nesting ground in the world (see also page 8).

Marine life is more tropical than would be found at the same latitude of mainland Africa, on the coast of Senegal. This is because the archipelago is sufficiently far from the mainland to escape the cold 'winter upwellings', in which the turning of the globe causes water from deep in the ocean to surface at the coast. This would otherwise decrease the temperature of the 21°C waters to about 10°C.

There are several threats to the marine heritage of Cape Verde. One of them is fishing: overfishing by domestic and international commercial boats and the use of destructive fishing methods, such as spear guns, and fishing during spawning seasons, by local fishermen. A second threat comes from coastal development. Many of the most important habitat areas along the coasts are just the places where people want to build hotels and marinas.

The country plans tens of thousands of new tourist beds over the next 20 years. Problems from such developments include pollution, the disappearance of sand as it is siphoned off for construction (entire beaches have already disappeared), the effects of artificial light on turtle nesting and damage from quad bikes and the like roaring across fragile coastal land.

Turtles Marine turtles are some of the most important species on the islands. Cape Verde is an important feeding area for five species. Recent research has shown that Cape Verde is a crucial participant in the life of the loggerhead turtle (*Caretta caretta*), the population being the third largest in the world after the Florida Keys in the United States and Oman's Massirah Island. In the Atlantic, it is the second largest. One estimate states that about 3,000 breed annually in Cape Verde, though the figure varies enormously from year to year. The favoured island is overwhelmingly Boavista, probably followed by Maio, then Sal and all the other islands.

Turtles face two threats. The first is hunting. This dates back possibly as far as 1479, when the French explorer Eustache de la Fosse reported that leprosy was treated locally with a diet of turtle meat and by rubbing the affected areas with turtle blood. King Louis XI, who believed he was suffering from leprosy, dispatched his representative to the Cape Verde Islands to investigate after learning of the cure.

Hunting continues today. Practices vary from island to island: sometimes the meat is cut out of the live turtles, sometimes the eggs are taken, sometimes both. Sometimes the blood is drained and added to wine as a fortifier, while on some islands males are prized for their penises which are added to *grogue* as an aphrodisiac. Meat is often taken from island to island, on fishing boats but also on internal flights. There are nesting beaches where the loss of turtles is 100%.

The threat to habitat is also increasing as land is used for tourism development and sand is removed illegally for building. A report on the effects of tourism on turtles can be downloaded from the Sociedade Caboverdiana de Zoologia website (*www.scvz.org*).

A report by the secretariat for the Convention on Migratory Species called for urgent attention to conserve West Africa's sea turtles. Klaus Toepfer, Executive Director of UNEP, said: 'In the western Atlantic and Pacific oceans, populations of sea turtles have been falling dramatically in recent years. This makes [recent] findings in western Africa doubly significant, given its now undoubted status as a globally important region for sea turtle species.'

The report recommended that conserving nesting sites for the loggerhead turtle on Cape Verde should be a priority. The loggerhead is categorised as endangered. The hawksbill (*Eretmochelys imbricata*), which is critically endangered, feeds at the islands. The green turtle (*Chelonia mydas*), which is endangered, calls at the islands, as do the critically endangered leatherback (*Dermochelys coriacea*) and the endangered olive ridley (*Lepidochelys olivacea*).

A national turtle plan was drawn up in 2008 and has now finally been approved. It is hoped that it will be properly funded and implemented. There are active turtle campaigns on several of the islands, notably Sal (see page 98) and Boavista (see page 137), as well as projects run by communities or city halls on all the other islands. In 2009, a coalition of organisations, called TAOLA, Cape Verde Marine Turtle Network, was formed to synchronise activities and has had some success raising awareness and lobbying parliament.

Whales North Atlantic humpback whales were driven almost to extinction during the whaling exploits of the 14th century. Now there are 10,000–12,000 worldwide and most breed in the West Indies. A few hundred, however, choose Cape Verde. This select group makes seasonal migrations between Iceland, Norway and Cape Verde. The archipelago is where they mate, after which the females travel north to feed, returning around a year later to give birth.

Cape Verde is the only known breeding ground for humpbacks in the northeast Atlantic. March and April are the peak of the breeding season and also the time when the whales can be sighted – mostly off the west and southwest coasts of Boavista, Sal and most other islands. Individuals can be identified from natural markings (ventral fluke patterns). Males sing songs, at least partly to attract females, and also to maintain distance from other males (see also page 138).

CONSERVATION EFFORTS Marine, coastal and inland areas do have friends in Cape Verde. The government has signed up to some key international conventions but implementation takes time and money. There are several programmes, including the National Research and Marine Biodiversity Conservation Programme and the Coastal Zone Management Project, which is establishing policies on how to use and manage coastal areas. The two marine-protected areas in Cape Verde – Murdeira Bay in Sal (see page 98) and the Santa Luzia complex (that island plus the surrounding islets, including Branco and Raso – see page 341) – have management plans. The two areas face threats from very different sources: in Murdeira, it's tourist development, whereas in the Santa Luzia complex it's artisanal fishing. Unfortunately, neither area is patrolled nor properly protected, though NGOs have become more active in recent years.

Crucially – not just for marine and coastal areas but also for inland – in 2002 the government established the General Directorate for Environment – a framework from which environmental care can operate. They have built on a proposal by Cabo Verde Natura 2000 to create a network of 47 protected areas around Cape Verde. The areas were declared in law in 2003 but only one has had its precise boundaries enshrined in law.

Three of the protected areas are part of a UN Development Programme/Global Environment Facility project to develop parks with boundaries, services and income-generation activities for local people, including ecotourism (see pages 164 and 323, respectively). More are in the pipeline, including two on Santo Antão and one on São Vicente.

The government has taken other actions such as banning the removal of sand from the beaches for construction (with patchy enforcement). The Second Environmental Action plan (PANA II) published in 2007, included a proposal that new developments must submit an Environmental Impact Assessment. It's also against the law to build within 80m of the low tide mark.

The Sociedade Caboverdiana de Zoologia (*www.scvz.org*), which was founded with the aim of promoting zoological research in Cape Verde, publishes a scientific journal, and plans other activities such as organising scientific meetings. Descriptions of all Cape Verde's protected areas can be seen on the website (*www. areasprotegidas.cv/index.php*).

1

White lives in big house
Mulato lives in shop
Black lives in hut
Sancho lives in mountain:
But a day will come
When Sancho turn all upside down:
Horribly grimacing
Tail curled up
Sancho drag black from hut
Black drag mulato from shop
Mulato drag white from big house
White run to mountain and there he fall

A *batuque* of Santa Catarina, published in the magazine *Claridade* (1948)
Translated by Basil Davidson, *The Fortunate Isles* (Hutchinson, 1989)

When the first island of Cape Verde erupted from the ocean hundreds of kilometres from the African coast, the archipelago's fate was sealed. For, overwhelmingly, the islands' unique and often tragic history has been the result of their position. Their history is one of use and abuse by nations from the four corners of the Atlantic. The world has changed around them and has found fleeting uses for them: they have served until they are exhausted and then they have been forgotten until another convulsion in world affairs has produced a new use for them.

The archipelago's story has been a sad one but it has begun a hopeful chapter. For now the Cape Verdeans have their own identity, proclaim their own culture and, most importantly, govern themselves. Since the 1970s they have been able to act strategically. At the same time, the outside world has changed and has found new uses for Cape Verde: white beaches to serve the interests of mass tourism, and abundant fish when other seas are severely depleted. Whether the archipelago will be able to exploit these riches for itself, or whether the 21st century will be just another chapter in which it is sucked dry and thrown away, it is too early to tell.

ROCKS APPEAR AND LIFE ARRIVES According to local lore, when God was satisfied with Creation, and brushed his hands together, the crumbs that fell unnoticed from his fingers into the sea formed Cape Verde.

The geological explanation for their existence is just as beguiling. Under the plates of the earth's crust lie 'hot spots' of bubbling magma, one of which is several hundred kilometres west of Senegal. Every so often, when the conditions of heat and pressure are right, this hot spot erupts as a volcano, leaving an island in the Atlantic to mark where it has been. In this way, some 15 million years ago, the island of Sal was created. It was a mountain which has since been the victim of the ocean winds and has eroded away until all that remains is flat, brown rock. The hot spot erupted every few millions of years to make another pimple on the Atlantic. Today it is still putting the final touches to youthful Fogo, which lies in the southwest. The island is 100,000 years old and one senses that brooding Fogo gazes east towards Sal preparing to spend the next ten million years weathering down to a similar fate.

Somehow, plant life found Cape Verde, carried there on winds from mainland Africa or by the ocean itself. Over such a distance there was only a tiny chance of such a voyage culminating in life reaching the islands – but millions of seeds over millions of years transformed that chance to a certainty. Once they had arrived they were cut off from their relatives and evolved into new species, as island life does.

Next came aquatic life. Washed into the Cape Verdean shallows by accident, many species remained to evolve their own identity in the same way as the plants.

RAISING CAPE VERDE'S HISTORY FROM THE OCEAN FLOOR

Divers investigating the shipwrecks around Cape Verde say it is the last great unexplored site in the world. They guess there may be up to 600 boats lost on the archipelago's reefs. Through them, it is possible to build up a vivid picture of the islands' trading history.

Already, after several years of exploration, researchers have a warehouse and museum in Chã d'Areia, Praia, which is stacked with treasures brought up from the sea. Coins and clay pipes help to date the wrecks; hoards of goods such as ivory tusks or silver coins testify to the ships' missions; while the odd treasure has been retrieved that is of great beauty or significance.

Perhaps the most spectacular find by the marine archaeologists – from Cape Verde, Oxford University and the Portuguese company Arqueonautas Worldwide – was a mariner's astrolabe. With the invention of the sextant the astrolabe, which had guided sailors for two millennia, abruptly lost its purpose and many were melted down. The few examples of this marvellous navigational instrument that remain tend to have been found in shipwrecks.

The team found this beautiful example of a bronze and silver astrolabe in a 1650s shipwreck. Despite their detective work, however, they still do not know the identity of the ship. The astrolabe was probably Portuguese, the cannons were Dutch, the coins Spanish.

Sadly Cape Verde no longer has the astrolabe, but only a copy – in 2001, it was sold at Sotheby's.

Piecing together a ship's history, and matching it with a known vessel, requires all sorts of lateral thinking. The cargo provides clues. Sometimes small collections of coins from a variety of countries – perhaps from the pocket of an individual sailor collecting a souvenir from every port – can help plot the ship's route.

'The quality of the cargoes is amazing,' noted Piran Johnson of Arqueonautas Worldwide. A massive batch of ivory tusks – eaten away like long thin pieces of cheese – was brought up from the *Princess Louisa*, a 1743 ship that was on her way between London and Bombay. An intact bottle of wine 200 years old and, more irresistibly, several bottles of cognac, were retrieved from an unknown wreck in the harbour of Praia. One ship yielded huge copper plates that the Swedes once used as an unwieldy currency – the ship went down in 1781 on her way from Denmark to China.

Another ship – the *Hartwell* – contained a collection of watches: 'They were the Ratner's of the day,' says Johnson. 'Gold filigree on top but cheap tat underneath – they were being shipped out to the colonies to buy off the locals.'

Most of the treasures emerge looking most unpromising, in the form of ugly grey concretions formed by the build-up of iron, sand and other substances over the decades. It takes a professional eye to spot the underlying shape; then it takes weeks of painstaking work to remove the concretion without damaging the valuables inside.

To visit the collection, see *What to see and do*, page 179.

Other, more ocean-going species, such as turtles, have found the islands a useful transit point. The story of the birds is much the same.

Legend shrouds the tales of the first humans to arrive at the islands. They may have been Phoenician sea captains who landed there and left no trace except for some enigmatic inscriptions on a rock that survive until the present day. In 445BC, the Phoenician captain Hanno sailed from Cadiz and reported that he passed some small islands which scholars now believe may have been Cape Verde. He named them Hesperias. Once, Hanno wrote that he had seen a large volcano off the West African coast: perhaps it was Fogo. West African sailors may have reached Cape

JEWS IN CAPE VERDE   *Anna Etmanska, Carol Castiel and Murray Stewart*

'See these? Old Jewish merchants' homes,' says Jorge Pires, pointing to the dilapidated edifices on the main street in the town of Ponta do Sol, Santo Antão. Buildings in different stages of decay line the quiet street leading towards the ocean. We get closer to examine a faded sign – Cohen. The once-magnificent house stands in ruin, windows and doors boarded up.

Jorge Pires, an official at the local *câmara municipal*, despairs at the sad state of Ponta do Sol's historical heritage. 'Jews built this town and now our past is left to crumble.'

Mr Pires dreams of turning the old Cohen house into a museum of Cape Verde's Jewish history, and Ponta do Sol into a heritage tourism destination. This area of Santo Antão has more surviving Jewish sites than any other island in the country. The cemeteries in Ponta do Sol and Penha de França already attract curious visitors, and plans are under way by the Cape Verde Jewish Heritage Project to restore them. The village of Sinagoga is just down the road. And in Ribeira Grande, the green mansion of Ruth Cohen de Marçal still occupies the central position in town.

'The old Jewish lady lived there,' explains a local storeowner. And then he proudly adds, 'My grandfather was Jewish, too.'

Though present-day Cape Verde does not have an organised Jewish community, or even any practising Jews, the islanders, like the storeowner in Ribeira Grande, are very much aware of their country's Sephardic heritage.

The two major waves of Jewish immigration left behind them not only names like Benros, Mendes and Levy, or gravestones with Hebrew inscriptions. Thanks to the centuries of intermarriage, the Sephardic culture became an important ingredient in shaping Cape Verde's modern Creole identity.

The first Jewish settlers came to the island of Santiago to escape religious persecution in 15th-century Portugal. Some came willingly, but an even greater number were deported by force, along with other undesirable elements that King Manuel I no longer tolerated in the country. Known as *degredados* (convicts), these Portuguese exiles worked as traders on the coast of Guinea. They lived initially in Praia but, because of their commercial activities, they spread throughout Cape Verde, married African women, and eventually became an integral part of the brand-new, multi-cultural nation.

These Jewish traders acquired the name of *lançados* (outcasts), and quickly became the implementers of the slave trade. Working as intermediaries on the African coast, they traded with whom they pleased and ignored the commercial restrictions imposed on them by Portugal. Yet at the same time, in order to rid Portugal of Jews, the Crown not only allowed, but even encouraged the *lançados's* activities. Of course not all *lançados* were of Jewish origin: the African trade, just

Verde in their sea-going canoes, but they, too, left no trace.

And so the islands lay, effectively undiscovered, until the middle of the 15th century. The reason for their elusiveness is also the very reason why, when they were found, they were to prove so useful. For they lie below the latitude of the Canary Islands, a region into which any ship that dared to venture would never return. Myths surrounded the fate of the ships from the north that vanished beyond the Canaries, but their disappearance has a simple explanation. The prevailing northeasterly wind drove them south but then, like a one-way valve, blocked their return. In the 15th century, this barrier to human ambition fell. The rig was invented, and allowed

like any other profitable occupation, attracted tough men from varied cultural backgrounds. Some of those traders, be they Jewish, Muslim or Christian, became known as *ganagogas*, which in the African Biafada dialect means 'men who could speak many languages'.

By the end of the 17th century, Jewish presence on the islands was an important factor in the success of the colonial economy. However, with the establishment of a branch of the Portuguese Inquisition in Cape Verde in 1672, the Crown forcibly confiscated most of the Jewish trading enterprises. As a result, many of the affected merchants hid their true identities until the frenzy of religious persecution died out in the late 1770s.

In the early 1820s, a group of Jews involved in the Liberal Wars fled Portugal and settled in the mountains of Santo Antão. A few years later, they were joined by economic migrants from Morocco and Gibraltar. Following in the footsteps of their 15th-century predecessors, they also engaged in commerce, such as trading salt and hides, and used their skills to rejuvenate the local economy. And as those before them, they took local wives and successfully assimilated into Creole society. As a result, today the great majority of Cape Verdeans, including the country's former prime minister Carlos Alberto Wahnon de Carvalho Veiga, can claim Jewish ancestry.

Yet the Jewish past of Cape Verde is also a victim of this successful assimilation. While Jewish graves remain in Santo Antão, Santiago and Boavista, on Brava and Maio, they are long gone.

Thankfully, the threat to the continued existence of the cemetery on Boavista, where the Benoliel family is buried, has been resisted. It has now been restored through the persistence of one of the descendants, a Lisbon resident by the name of Rafael Benoliel. Similarly, the Jewish graves in Praia's main Christian cemetery have also been restored and recently rededicated. An additional tombstone was discovered during the restoration work, and work is continuing on signage and walkways.

The initiative of Carol Castiel and her Cape Verde Jewish Heritage Project (*www.capeverdejewishheritage.org*) has been largely responsible for the preservation work in Cape Verde and will hopefully improve the situation in Santo Antão.. Due to the chronic lack of funds, change is slow, and for now, the ambitious dreams of Mr Pires remain just that – dreams. (See *Appendix 2, Further information*, page 352.)

Anna Etmanska is an independent filmmaker and a writer who became interested in the history of Cape Verde Jews after stumbling upon the cemetery in Penha de França on Santo Antão Island. She blogs at www.budgettrouble.com.

mariners to harness the wind so they could sail against as well as before it. It was one of the most significant of all inventions, enabling humans to emerge from their home continents and link every region of the globe. The west coast of Africa was now a prize for whichever nation could reach it first, and it was inevitable that the Portuguese, with the skills and vision of Prince Henry the Navigator behind them, would win.

Several famous mariners pushed ever further south in the 1460s and more than one claimed to have discovered Cape Verde. The debate will probably never be resolved. Perhaps it was the Venetian, Cadamosto, who said he sighted the islands first in 1456. More likely, it was the Genoese António de Noli who may have stumbled on them in 1455 or in 1461. Some reports say he was accompanied by the Portuguese Diogo Gomes.

Whatever the truth, all the islands were discovered between 1455 and 1461 and the credit generally goes to de Noli and to Gomes, for discovering Santiago and the other leeward isles. Diogo Afonso discovered the windward islands of Santo Antão, São Vicente and São Nicolau. The archipelago was named Cape Verde, not because it was verdant, but after the green butt of Senegal that lies across the sea.

It is hard to understand now the value of such a discovery. Venturing over the seas with only the capricious wind for power, with no facility for measuring longitude and with limited water and food, the cry of 'land ahoy' could mean life rather than death.

The Portuguese realised that the islands could be of immense strategic power. And so colonisation began in 1462 when a small group of Portuguese, Spanish and Genoese settled on the most promising island, Santiago. The southern half was allotted to de Noli, who set up in Ribeira Grande on the south coast. The northern half fell to Afonso, who began less successfully in the northwest.

Lisbon wanted to entice talented men to live on the islands and develop them, so Cape Verde was awarded a valuable advantage over other Portuguese colonies. Settlers were given exclusive trading rights along the creeks and shores of the West African coast between Senegal and Sierra Leone. These rivers thus became known as the Rivers of Cape Verde, later to be known as the Rivers of Guinea.

At this time the Atlantic was dotted with Portuguese and Spanish ships making prolific discoveries in the Americas, Africa and beyond Africa's southern tip, as far as India and China. It was the beginning of the expansion of Europe, the spread of its civilisation around the globe and unprecedented mass migration. Over the next 300 years Europeans would emigrate to North and South America and Africa. Africans would fill the Americas, mainly as slaves. The Portuguese and Spanish had begun nothing less than a global redistribution of races, animals and plants and the beginnings of modern mass trade. Meanwhile, the few resources of Cape Verde were put to use, and trading began that would supply the Portuguese Crown with income for centuries.

FROM ROCK TO TRADING POST: THE 1500S The first desire of the colonisers of Santiago was to plant and reap, for which they sought the services of an unpaid labour force. They found what they wanted on the mainland coast of Africa: slaves. Over the next century these captives from the great tribes of west Africa arrived in their thousands, and were soon put to work growing food and cotton in the valleys. By 1582, there were 13,700 slaves labouring on Santiago and Fogo under a regime of 100 white men.

The settlers released goats onto the uninhabited islands where they devoured the scrub pasture and provided meat, hides, butter, milk and cheese, and some cattle were farmed. But barren Cape Verde would never provide enough food for prosperity. Wealth generation was to come from two other activities: resupply of ships, and the slave trade.

Cape Verde lies at the Atlantic crossroads, not just because of its position in relation to the landmasses of the Americas, Europe and Africa, but because of where it lies in relation to the north Atlantic wind patterns and to ocean currents. Both factors drew America-bound ships towards the archipelago. Increasingly, in the latter part of the 16th century, the Portuguese who stopped there were on their way to open up the treasure of Brazil. The Spanish were ferrying goods and people to and from the vast new empire they were creating in South America.

In 1580, Spain and Portugal united to create an Iberian Empire with three powerful realms: the spice empire of the East, the sugar empire of the south Atlantic, and the silver empire of Spanish America. Iberian vessels often found it useful to stop at Cape Verde for food and water, for ship repair and for nautical supplies.

Thus, throughout the 1500s, **ship supply** was the islands' great function, and the most basic commodities – water and food – were its speciality. They charged a high price for fresh water and sold maize, beans and dried or salted goat meat. They also exported horses, donkeys, cattle and goat hides. Cape Verde's other commodity lay in sparkling white lakes on the three flat islands to the east: salt, and enough, it seemed, to supply mankind in perpetuity.

Once there were sufficient **slaves** working on the islands, the Portuguese looked west for new markets. They were in a unique position to sell slaves for labour in South American colonies and so the archipelago became a warehouse for human merchandise. For slave merchants who would otherwise have had to visit the African coast, Cape Verde was an expensive market but a sanitised one. Forays to the mainland could be dangerous and lengthy. Ships were often delayed, sometimes for months. Payment methods were elaborate: tribal leaders often demanded a multiplicity of items – iron bars, cloth, brandy, guns, knives, ribbons and beads. In addition, the land was rife with disease and the creeks and rivers of the coast were tricky to navigate. If a ship became stranded on the shore the local people would claim it for their own.

There were other advantages to be gained from shopping for slaves in Cape Verde. First of all, they had been 'seasoned'. The sickly, unfit and obstinate had been weeded out or had died. Those who remained had given up hope of escape. They had also learned a few Portuguese words so they would understand orders, and they had been baptised. The Portuguese Church argued that a baptised slave was luckier than a free African because the former had achieved the chance of a place in heaven.

Thousands of slaves were Fula. They were victims of Gabu, a tributary kingdom to the Mandingo Empire of Mali. Gabu, founded in the mid 13th century, stretched through most of today's northeastern Guinea-Bissau. Its people were warriors and their battles generated many of the slaves who were then traded on the coast.

Alongside the business of slavery grew trade in other goods from the African coast: ivory, wax, hides, gum, amber, musk, honey and gold dust. Cape Verde took them and became a depot where these products were exchanged for goods coveted by wealthy Africans – Venetian beads and wine from Europe; silver from Spanish America; cloves and coral from the East. Cape Verde itself supplied the African coast with raw cotton, cloth, salted goat meat, horses and cattle.

The important islands in those first years were Santiago, where the settlers built a capital in the green valley of Ribeira Grande; Fogo, a live but fertile volcano; and the lonely salt island of Maio. Ribeira Grande was the first city built by Europeans in the tropics and became one of the highest-yielding cities of the Portuguese kingdom. Visitors praised its comforts and in 1533, it was elevated from the rank of *vila* to *cidade*. In 1556, the Bishop of Cape Verde, whose jurisdiction extended to the mainland, began building his cathedral there, and in 1570, the king agreed to the founding of a seminary. All was optimism and prosperity.

Cape Verde mustered few home-produced goods with one major exception, mentioned above: **cotton**. It was grown by slaves who then wove it into cloth of the finest quality, which was marketed along the west African coast and in Brazil. Its skilful patterns became outstandingly popular amongst Africans and the cloth rose to be the chief currency for trading. This gave Cape Verde a continuing hold on the slave trade even when competition appeared from other nations. English and French ships were forced to stop at the archipelago to obtain cloth for barter on the mainland. Another trade was in the dye-yielding lichen orchil, which was collected in mountainous areas and transformed into a potion of vivid blue.

Thus, positioned between the Old World, Africa and South America, slicing taxes from every import and export, and with a monopoly on trade with the mainland, Cape Verde had become a viable community, with the slave trade its fundamental market and Portugal reaping as much as it could.

During this period the botanical colonisation of the islands was completed as well. As a traffic junction, Cape Verde received plants from everywhere, particularly maize from Brazil, which became a staple, and cassava, which was later planted on the African mainland.

THE ATLANTIC GROWS BUSIER: THE 1600S

Driving the defenders before them they entered the City almost without resistance, where they sacked houses and destroyed them. The authorities fled to the hills and the English, carrying away their spoil, departed to Cartagena and San Domingo.

Contemporary account of the sacking of Ribeira Grande

As the 1600s began, rival nations appeared on the seas. The French, English and Dutch spilled into the Atlantic, and aggression on the ocean became more than the sporadic acts of piracy and smuggling that had characterised the second half of the previous century. Cape Verde became increasingly vulnerable to attack and Portugal foresaw this, responding in 1587 by appointing a governor-general for the islands who was directly responsible to the Crown for Cape Verde and the Guinea coast.

Now France, England and Holland were becoming serious forces in the Atlantic, making their discoveries mainly in North America. As they began to make settlements in their new lands they, too, started to look for slaves. Business across the Atlantic multiplied as the desire for sugar, slaves, salt and fish sent trading ships in a perpetual circle between the four continents.

As international affairs fluctuated so, too, did Cape Verdean fortunes. They fell for a while when the Dutch seized Portuguese slaving sources in west Africa, and when they were sacked and plundered by nations who were at odds with Spain or Portugal. Their fortunes rose after 1640 when Portugal achieved independence from Spain.

Overall, though, the archipelago still made money because the demand for slaves was rising. It was at its peak for Cape Verde during the 1600s and 1700s. Numbers are uncertain, partly because many slaves were not measured in whole 'units'. A 15–25 year old was a *peça*'s worth. A 30 year old in good health was two-thirds of a *peça*. Records are poor but it has been estimated that 3,000 slaves a year left Cape Verde in 1609 and 1610, although these were probably peak years. These slaves earned Cape Verde about £6,500 in import taxes and £1,300 in export taxes over the two years. Nearly three-quarters of the revenue the Portuguese Crown received from Cape Verde was from the slave trade.

Resentment stirs The question that exercised the people of the archipelago was why so much of its profit should go straight back to Lisbon. It was part of a wider question: what was the purpose of Cape Verde? If it was merely an overseas warehouse then the Portuguese were entitled to act as they wished. But Cape Verde was now a place that some called home and they were trying to make a living there in spite of increasingly tight controls from the Crown.

During the first 150 years of colonisation, blacks and whites came together to found the Cape Verdean ancestry, and the core of Cape Verdean society became remarkably stable. Other Portuguese were reluctant to follow as settlers because the islands were perceived as an arduous posting. In particular, few Portuguese women arrived. The black population was similarly stable, with the shiploads of slaves destined for distant lands mere transient visitors, isolated from the static population.

Black and white, isolated from the rest of the world by the ocean, developed complex layers of relationships. Intermarriage produced a race of *mestiços* who had nowhere else to call their motherland and who were not to assert a national identity until the 20th century.

Cape Verdean Creole heritage differed from other Creole cultures around the world for several reasons. The Cape Verdeans emerged in an empty place where there had been no indigenous population. They were the descendants of a smaller number of whites than is the case with other Creole cultures and so the European element was not sufficiently strong to exert cultural dominance.

It was these 'pre-Cape Verdeans' – whites and, increasingly, people of mixed race governing a large number of slaves – who complained bitterly and frequently about the way Lisbon organised the slave and other trades, and in particular about the rise of the Crown monopolies.

The monopolies The right to extract slaves from the African coast was awarded by the Crown as a single, monopolistic contract which lasted for six years. The benefit for the Crown was that the contractor paid a lump sum and agreed to supply a few incidentals including slaves for the king, and some money donated to the Church.

Whoever bought this slaving right then subcontracted it to smaller enterprises. The Portuguese Crown received customs duties when contractors deposited slaves at Cape Verde, and also export duties from those who bought them. The people of Cape Verde were banned from engaging in other trade with non-Portuguese. This rule was resented and widely flouted.

The islanders began to feel seriously undermined in 1675, when the Crown handed out to various companies a series of crippling monopolistic rights over the west African and Cape Verdean trades. The terms seemed to bypass the role of the archipelago as middleman.

Under the rules of the first monopoly, the contractor possessed the sole right to take international products to the Guinea coast for trading: Cape Verdeans were permitted to trade only with home-grown products such as cloth and salt. Santiago's access to Africa, therefore, was deeply threatened. Further decrees were issued by Lisbon. Perhaps the most memorable was that of 1687 which banned anyone on Cape Verde from selling cloth to foreigners, under penalty of death.

The second monopoly was granted in 1690 to a newly formed organisation, the Company of the Islands of Cape Verde and Guiné (Compania Nacional de Cabo Verde e Guiné). Even more restrictive conditions were included in the new contract, and two seemed almost guaranteed to ensure that Cape Verde was bypassed in the international slave trade. Firstly, the contractor bought the right to supply the Spanish Indies directly with slaves, so he had no need to find someone to buy them on the archipelago. Secondly, the Governor of Cape Verde was put in the pay of the new company. By 1700, Cape Verde felt that it had been ousted by the monopoly companies from its role as a slave-trading depot. It was increasingly left to concentrate on the more predictable business of victualling the hundred ships a year that called at Santiago for supplies in the second half of the 1600s.

CONFLICT: THE 1700S The 1700s began with a bang and the War of the Spanish Succession to prevent France gaining control of Spain. Fears that the fusion of the two countries would give them too much power over Atlantic possessions were typical of the concerns of other European powers at the time. The century was to be one of territorial expansion to the west of the Atlantic, consolidation, and the rise of the British as the supreme naval force.

Cape Verde would always be prey to the whims of the rest of the world, successful when exploiting the needs of a diversity of countries and unsuccessful when those needs suddenly changed. When Portugal was drawn into the War of Succession, the slave trade with the Spanish Indies came to a sudden end for Cape Verde but also for the monopoly companies.

That war did not finish until 1714 and was the cause of the sack of Santiago in 1712, a disastrous plunder by the French that robbed Ribeira Grande of all its riches. The people of Cape Verde urged Lisbon to liberalise its trade and finally, in 1721, Portugal relaxed the rules so that the people could trade with whom they wished. Business was reinvigorated, but the central problem remained – Portugal was not prepared to pour money into a string of rocks which could not guarantee much return. The people of the islands were left to live on their wits, thinking only from day to day.

This conflict was behind many of the background problems of the archipelago. Goats chomped inexorably at the fragile vegetation that had taken millions of years to win a hold in the face of Saharan winds. Without sophisticated, long-term land management it was inevitable that famine would increasingly afflict the islands. Every century there were one or two more famines than the century before and, in 1773–76, 44% of the population died.

Lack of investment in proper military protection also led to raids which were a perpetual drain on resources. Like a fleet of marooned ships the islands were unable to flee marauders of the high seas.

THE END OF SLAVERY: THE 1800S Towards the end of the 1700s the seeds were sown in America and Europe for convulsions that would end the 300-year-old Atlantic slave trade and transform life for most nations bordering that ocean. The changes were partly intellectual. The Enlightenment grew in Europe, with its faith in rationality and social progress; with it came concepts of the rights of man and the iniquity of slavery, both of which served to justify the French and American revolutions. After the French Revolution Napoleon's energies were unleashed on the oceans and one of the consequences was that Portugal and Spain were cut off from their colonies in South America. The effect of this was profound. A vacuum arose in 19th-century South America into which grew movements for liberation, followed by the abolition of slavery and, later, the rise of concepts such as African nationalism which would inspire countries such as Cape Verde to fight for independence.

Although slavery continued to flourish for decades in North America, continuing long after its independence in 1783, it was a land of promise that lured millions of emigrants fleeing starvation or unemployment in other parts of the world. The 1800s became an era of mass global migration.

Cape Verde was buffeted by these 19th-century Atlantic storms. One of the most bitter was the demise of its own slave-trading, abolished as a 'business' by the Portuguese in 1854, with private slavery ending in 1876.

During the 19th century the dominance of the sailing ship came to an end, and with it Cape Verde's prime function as a resupplier. But as Santiago suffered, two other islands began to emerge as arenas where profits could be made.

The first was São Vicente. It has a perfect and generous natural harbour, perhaps the safest place to pause in the entire eastern Atlantic. Other than that it is a sterile pile of stones and so it had been of little interest in previous centuries.

This deep harbour was just the place for the new steamships born of the Industrial Revolution to reload with coal on their journeys along the Atlantic shipping lanes. The British, riding the crest of the invention of the steam engine, flocked to São Vicente to set up coaling stations. Mindelo, its capital, grew at an astonishing rate. The second island where epochal events were taking place was a tiny one: Brava. It was at this insignificant dot at the end of the archipelago that whaling ships from New England began to stop and pick up eager crews of young men. The ships offered the prospect of passage to America and in this way Cape Verdeans joined the mass migration to the New World.

They went on emigrating throughout the century and on into the next. In the first 20 years of the 1900s, 19,000 Cape Verdeans set up new homes there. Many of them still regarded the archipelago as their home, which would eventually bring great economic benefit to Cape Verde.

The structure of Cape Verdean society changed in the 19th century as home-grown slavery disappeared. In 1834, a rough count yielded 52,000 free or freed men and women, and 4,000 slaves. Yet for most people the 1870s declaration that, finally, slavery was to end, did not mean a better life, for slaves had to serve further years of forced labour which were to continue in various guises until well into the following century. Another social change occurred as Cape Verde became a place of exile for Portuguese convicts, from thieves to political dissidents. Between 1802 and 1882, according to the English historian Basil Davidson, nearly 2,500 such *degredados* arrived at the islands: 'They were at once absorbed into a population increasingly homogeneous in its culture and way of life, if notably various in the colours of its skin.' Portugal ruled by skin colour. A census of 1856 listed 17 distinctions, ranging from various shades of 'very dark' to 'almost white'. Many lighter Cape Verdeans clung to their rank and despised the darker ones.

SUFFERING: THE BEGINNING OF THE 1900S

The 20th century began with a very different Cape Verde. The cinder heap of São Vicente, not fertile Santiago, was its chief commercial centre. São Vicente attracted a hopeless migration of the desperate from other islands in search of work. But the island had virtually no natural resources and was incapable of sustaining a rural peasant population. So when the shipping business dipped, as it did from time to time, the consequences of drought became increasingly shocking. Some 17,000 died in 1921. In 1922, the Santiago journal *A Verdade* reported:

> 1921 was horrific... yet now follows this of 1922, equally horrific but with the addition that people have spent all they possess, whether in clothes or land, livestock or trinkets, and today are in the last stage of poverty, while emigration is carrying away all whom the steamers can embark.

The rains came in the end. In the 1930s, they were plentiful and the archipelago turned green. Emigrants, fleeing the Depression in the USA, returned to live with their families. But it did not last, and hunger returned in the early 1940s.

Outside the archipelago World War II began. On the islands, anti-Portuguese sentiment surged when Lisbon decided to garrison over 6,000 men amongst the islands' starving population. It is possible that Portugal feared that the British or the Germans were planning to seize the archipelago, and their fears were justified. Winston Churchill had well-developed plans to invade Cape Verde but called them off at the last minute. The matter of who controlled the islands was still of interest to the world.

Peace came in 1945 but for the Cape Verdeans the worst drought they were ever to face was looming. Some 30,000 people died. The hunger was exacerbated by the return of the emigrant Americans a few years before: they swelled the numbers and decreased the remittances.

This hideous cycle of drought and famine raises the question: could it have been avoided? After all, Cape Verdeans do not die of hunger today. The answer is still obscure but it seems certain that an important ingredient of the famines was the way the land was owned and run. It was a system which discouraged peasants from planning more than a season ahead.

Agriculture was mired in a system of inheritance which split land with each generation until people farmed it in splinters in an inefficient way. Land that was not subject to this system was owned in great swathes by a small number of men who rented it out in patches a year at a time. The peasants who farmed this land had no incentive to improve it: they knew that the extra yield would be taken as rent.

So, at a time when the people could have been producing income for the islands by cultivating cash crops such as coffee for export, agriculture stagnated. This, combined with the dwindling of tree cover, imposed deep poverty. Cape Verde was becoming an increasingly unsustainable place. Population control was left to the crude device of starvation.

People escaped not just to America but also to work on other Portuguese islands. They left for São Tomé and Príncipe in their tens of thousands: 24,000

THE SCHOONER *ERNESTINA*

The schooner *Ernestina*, a beautiful, 112ft sailing vessel over a century old, is one of the most famous of the packet ships that connected Cape Verde with the USA in the early 20th century.

She was still working as a packet ship in the 1960s, making her last Atlantic voyage to Providence in 1965 in an era that had long been dominated by the steamship, which itself was fast losing trade to the aeroplane.

The *Ernestina* had many lives. After her launch in 1894 she became a Grand Banks fisher and then an Arctic expeditionary vessel. She sank after a galley fire in 1946, and that was when a Cape Verdean, Captain Henrique Mendes, stepped in. The schooner was raised, restored to seaworthiness, bought by Captain Mendes and then began her new life as a transatlantic packet ship. Her work was to carry passengers and goods between Cape Verde and the USA. Often she took seasonal workers to New England for the cranberry harvest. Hopeful immigrants would also come. Sometimes she would take successful immigrants on rare trips home; more often it was goods she ferried back to the motherland – bought with hard-won money earned on the bogs or in the textile mills of New Bedford.

For ten years this trade continued between Cape Verde and Rhode Island. After her last trip in 1965 she continued to work between Cape Verde and the African mainland. She also worked the islands – one job was to ferry schoolchildren from Fogo and Brava to boarding school in Praia and Mindelo.

But even this work was being eclipsed by other, more modern ships, and eventually it was decided to return the *Ernestina* to the USA. But the trip home, in 1976, was a disaster – a storm dismasted her and she was forced to return to port. There, the government of the new republic had her rebuilt and, six years later, gave her to the USA as a symbol of friendship.

The *Ernestina* then served as a sail training ship, educational vessel and cultural icon until 2005, when the US Coast Guard refused the vessel the certification required to carry passengers, putting at least a temporary end to her many activities on the ocean waves. Sadly, the boat had deteriorated physically. Although significant repairs have followed in the last few years, at time of writing her future as an ocean-going vessel remains uncertain. She lies at rest at the New Bedford State Pier, Massachusetts, where she receives visitors in summer. However, although this grand old lady is in semi-retirement, she does not lack supporters, with various groups active in raising further funds to restore her. For more information on the schooner and a vivid history of the passage of Cape Verdeans to and from the USA, as well as the current status of the efforts to restore her to the seas, see www.ernestina.org.

Cape Verdeans worked there between 1902 and 1922; 34,000 laboured there from 1950–70. In this way these *contratados* escaped starvation, though some said the labourers returned more emaciated than when they left.

Soon Cape Verde's only lingering use, as a coaling station, seemed to be vanishing as well: oil was replacing coal as the fuel for the high seas and, as a result, few ships needed to pause there. When they did stop, resupply with oil was an easier, smaller business than loading coal. There was no need to maintain great companies with armies of staff on the crescent of rock halfway to South America. The world had dumped Cape Verde.

Romantic stories abound of brave Cape Verdean men who risked their lives to sail across the Atlantic and find fortune for themselves and their families in the USA. But these days, many Cape Verdeans in the USA have lost track of their personal family histories. They may have a forgotten great-great-grandfather who toiled on whaling ships on the wild ocean, risking his life to harpoon whales, earn promotion and set up life on the east coast. They may be descended from a couple of lost generations who worked themselves to the bone in the cranberry bogs of New England, returning home with their earnings at the end of each season. You may be descended from a young man who left his sweetheart on Fogo; you may own a stone cottage or great *sobrado* house, now standing forgotten on Brava.

Of all the Africans who went to the USA in the era of mass migration, Cape Verdean Americans are the only ones who can trace their families back to their original villages, according to James Lopes, genealogy expert. This is because there are excellent records of Cape Verdean arrivals in the USA. Those who have made the journey of rediscovery often find they have relatives, or ancestors, from all over the world, including Europe, Asia and South America.

To decipher your family tree, begin by questioning your immediate family, advises Mr Lopes. Write down everything you unearth – in particular the dates of birth, marriage and death of each remembered person, and how they made a living.

Then, when a particularly dim but fascinating figure emerges from the past, there are several sources to help you investigate. For those whose families went to the USA before 1920 the arrival should have been recorded in the passenger and ships lists of the Port of New Bedford. Most Cape Verdeans passed through there, though Boston and Providence were other ports of entry. The voyages of all Cape Verdean whaling ships are also listed, and kept in New Bedford Free Public Library.

One mine of fascinating information is the Old Dartmouth Historical Society at the New Bedford Whaling Museum (*Johnny Cake Hill, New Bedford, MA 02740, USA; www.whalingmuseum.org*). The original logbooks of many of the whaling expeditions that took Cape Verdeans to the USA are stored here. Details of the trip, including how much your ancestor was paid, might be found.

There are several other useful places to begin digging, including the Arquivo Histórico Nacional in Santiago (see *Appendix 2, Further information*, page 355). Staff there will research birth records on request. For more information on where to search, see James Lopes's website, above.

Finally, Marilyn Halter's book *Between Race and Ethnicity* (see *Books*, page 352) gives spellbinding accounts of life in the cranberry bogs and other features of emigrant life.

REVOLT Ideas of independence began to grow in the minds of 20th-century Cape Verdeans as a result of several world events. The consequences of their uprising, when it eventually came, were momentous. It was probably the first time in Cape Verde's history that the rocks made a splash of their own, and the ripples spread far. For it was Cape Verdeans, unique in Portuguese Africa because of their education and cosmopolitanism, who led the foment in other Portuguese African colonies. This in turn weakened Portugal and was the direct cause of the unseating of its fascist dictatorship.

One important force arose from the European 'scramble for Africa', which began in the late 1800s and had allocated most of the continent to colonial rule by the early 1900s. When World War I diverted the colonists' attention, resistance to colonial rule gathered pace, giving rise to the growing feeling that European reins could be thrown away. Cape Verde, unusual in having been subjugated for long centuries rather than mere decades, absorbed these ideas as they emerged in other European colonies. Allied to this was the rise of communism, which leaked into Africa and gave structure to undirected stirrings of antagonism amongst the people towards their rulers.

Another factor was necessary, however, for Cape Verdeans to begin to assimilate these ideas: they needed to hear about them and they needed to be educated enough to understand them. This impetus came, ironically, from the beneficence of Lisbon. Portugal had acknowledged the peculiarity of its Cape Verde colony and recognised its *mestiço* population as closer to its own than were the natives of mainland Africa. As a result, Cape Verdeans were granted a form of Portuguese citizenship, although it is unclear how this benefited most of them. The archipelago was also the intellectual centre of the Portuguese African colonies, with a secondary school which attracted pupils from the mainland, and a seminary.

There arose a small group of urbane, mixed-race Cape Verdeans whom the Portuguese employed as middlemen. They were halfway between black and white and so they could more easily administer the people of Portuguese Guinea, Angola, Mozambique and São Tomé, while being an acceptable interface with the true Portuguese. A select group of Cape Verdeans was thus educated, chosen as a literate class of administrators, and sent to work in diverse outposts of empire. From this group sprang poets and journalists who began to seek to express the nature of Cape Verdeanism. Their political objectives were limited: they prized the privilege of Portuguese citizenship and supported enlightened colonialism, defending the fledgling republic that was born in Portugal in 1910.

Perhaps if the liberalism that accompanied the new Portuguese republic had been allowed to continue, the movement for independence would have come earlier. Perhaps it would have fizzled out. We shall never know, for in 1926, the republic was overthrown by its own military, inaugurating 50 years of fascist dictatorship. Freedom of speech disappeared.

More visible twitchings of nationhood came with the publication of **Claridade**, a journal that called to the nation to realise the essence of 'Cape Verdeanness'. It published the work of some gifted writers in four issues between 1936 and 1941, and in another six after the end of World War II. For 500 years there had been no such race or culture as the Cape Verdean. There were Portuguese, there were slaves and there were *mestiços*. Yet the Cape Verdeans were there, incipient, infused with the knowledge of their African and European roots, endowed with a musical and poetic culture. *Claridade* helped them to see this – to define as Cape Verdean their laments and their poetry, the way they wore their clothes and their craftsmanship. *Claridade* reminded them that they had their own language: Creole.

It was those members of the educated class who were teenagers in the early 1940s who made the crucial step in the evolution of Cape Verdean thought. They were so angered by the mass of deaths in the droughts of that time that they began to believe that Cape Verde could be better off if it was independent from Portugal. **Amílcar Cabral** was just 17, and in his second year at secondary school, when the 1941 famine ravaged the people of Mindelo. His later success in rousing the people of Cape Verde and Portuguese Guinea to rise against the Portuguese, and his effective fighting techniques, have been ascribed by historians to his profound knowledge of these countries and his ability to inspire Africans with a concept of their own nationality.

Numerous categories defined the different elements of Cape Verdean society. *Fidalgos* were the noblemen, representing the king and making money for themselves and for the Crown through a system of royal charters, trade monopolies and land grants. They tended to be Portuguese, though there were some Genoese, Venetians and Spanish. *Capitãos* were military governors appointed by the Crown, with a high degree of local autonomy. *Feitors* were powerful private business agents who had won royal trade monopolies and also represented private mercantile concerns.

The pariahs of the slave trade were the *lançados*. They were, by definition, outcasts, but they were essential middlemen, embedding themselves in the tropical creeks of the West African coast where they channelled the trade in goods and humans. Portuguese, they were often political or religious criminals, and many of them were Jews who had fled the Inquisition. *Lançados* had an ambiguous relationship with the Crown: in theory they complied with royal trade monopolies, but in practice they had a pervasive power that the Crown could not control. They traded with whom they pleased and flouted Portuguese tax and other restrictions. *Ganagogas* were technically Jewish *lançados*, but in practice the term embraced anyone who could speak many local African languages.

Tangamãus were the public interface of the African involvement in the trade, and functioned mainly as translators; the name probably comes from *targuman*, the Arabic for translator. The mercenary bodyguards of the *lançados* and *tangamãus* were the *grumettas*.

Banished from Portugal for criminal or political reasons, *degredados* often became galley slaves in rowing boats. They lived either on Cape Verde or on the African coast, where some became *lançados*. Like the *lançados*, they became an important white ingredient in the founding of the Creole population. *Pretos* were free blacks, while *ladinos* were slaves who had been baptised and given a Latin name.

As slaves escaped or were freed, the peasant population grew. At its core was a group whom the Portuguese despised, as did the later *mestiço* class. These were the Badius, and they clung to their African culture. They were small-scale farmers generally living in the remote central regions of Santiago. *Parcerias* were colonial partnership share-cropping systems; share-croppers usually gave between a half and two-thirds of the crops they grew to their landowner. *Rendeiros* grew subsistence crops for themselves and worked on other people's land, generally for wages.

Later in history came *contratados*, contract labourers who worked in São Tomé and Príncipe and also in the United States.

Born in 1924 of Cape Verdean parents, Cabral grew up in what is today Guinea-Bissau, then Portuguese Guinea, in great poverty, finding the money to attend school from the small profits of his needleworking mother, whom he greatly admired. He had at least 61 brothers and sisters, all sired by his father, Juvenal Cabral. After school he studied agrarian engineering at Lisbon where he graduated with honours. He had a sound colonial career at his feet.

But while he was a student he imbibed from various clandestine sources ideas of communism and liberalism as well as news from the revolutionary intellectuals of other African colonies. After graduating, Cabral's career move must have seemed bizarre to outsiders. He buried himself in the backlands of Guinea, an employee of the farming and forestry service, making the first analysis of its agrarian and water resources. During this time he acquired an intimate knowledge of the country's landscape and social structure.

Cabral's battle was not just against the Portuguese. Cape Verdeans themselves accepted assimilation, and the cycles of drought and emigration, as an unavoidable consequence of the land. Cabral formed a tiny nationalist movement in 1954. He made friends with another product of the Mindelo secondary school, Aristides Pereira, who worked in the posts-and-telegraph office in Guinea. They learned local languages, read literature on uprisings around the world and worked on until Cabral was deported from the country in 1955. The following year, the two formed a tiny party: the **PAIGC (Party for the Independence of Guinea and Cape Verde)**. Other members were educated people with administrative jobs in Portugal, Angola and Guinea. The party pursued peaceful means at first, appealing for better conditions. One of their group, Abilio Duarte, returned to Cape Verde to agitate there amongst the students and the dockers, while Cabral set up a base in Conakry, capital of ex-French Guinea. The **insurrection** stumbled forward, manifesting itself publicly through graffiti at first and then through strikes, which inevitably led to sporadic massacres. A wages strike in Portuguese Guinea left 50 protesters shot dead and the rest sentenced to 15 years' hard labour.

Throughout 1959 and 1960 the activists moved around the world, gaining confidence from news of uprisings outside Portuguese Africa while the islands suffered another drought. This time, however, the loss of life was not of disastrous proportions because of a more compassionate governor. Fighting began in Portuguese Guinea in 1963 and Cape Verdeans made their way to the mainland to join the army. The war lasted for ten years, with the PAIGC, numerically tiny compared with the number of Portuguese troops, employing brilliant guerrilla tactics to lure the enemy into dispersing into numerous garrisons which it could then besiege. Arms from the USSR eventually arrived and by 1972 the PAIGC had control of half of the country, but not the air, where the commanding general, António de Spínola, retained supremacy.

Back in Cape Verde, nothing had happened superficially even by 1971. Abilio Duarte worked both at the Mindelo school, transforming the aspirations of the next generation, and amongst the dockers of Mindelo, more open to new ideas than their inland counterparts. From 1966 a band of 30 of the most talented young men of Cape Verde had been living in Cuba, where they trained for a surprise landing on Santiago and Santo Antão which would begin the war on the archipelago. In fact the landings plan would never be executed, most critically because the group failed to find the transport they needed across the ocean.

It was just as well, because swooping arrests in 1967 eliminated any organised reception the rebels might have hoped for, while the drought of 1968 would have starved any guerrillas trying to survive in the highlands. So, back on the archipelago, there was no war, just the arrests of increasing numbers of suspected rebels. The peasants were waiting with messianic expectation for Amílcar Cabral to come from Portuguese Guinea and liberate them.

But they would never see him. Tragedy struck on 20 January 1973, when traitors from within the PAIGC's own ranks murdered the 52-year-old Cabral on the mainland, just a few months before the victory in Guinea. Anger at his death shook any stagnation out of the guerrilla ranks and this, together with the arrival of ground-to-air missiles from the USSR, triggered the final offensive which was to bring them victory. Guinea-Bissau became a member of the Organisation of African Unity on 19 November 1973.

Cabral had been right when he prophesied in 1961: 'We for our part are sure that the destruction of Portuguese colonialism is what will destroy Portuguese fascism.' Young officers in the Portuguese army in Guinea became convinced that they would never win their African wars. Portugal was becoming overburdened, economically and politically, by these African questions. The officers grouped to form the Armed Forces Movement, returning to Portugal to overthrow the dictator, António de Oliveira Salazar, just five months after Guinea's liberation. Independence followed quickly for some other Portuguese colonies, though for Cape Verde it was far from automatic. Spínola, head of the AMF and new leader of Portugal, wanted to hang on to the strategically positioned islands.

The USA was reluctant to help, fearing that an independent Cape Verde would become a Soviet base. Meanwhile, all the leading militants on the islands were locked up and the remainder were still on the mainland. All Cape Verde had won was an agreement that it could have its own National Council.

Returning from the mainland war in August 1974, the Cape Verdean heroes were given a rapturous welcome. But they arrived in a country where Portuguese authority was not just intact but working overtime under the orders of Spínola. There were those on the islands who wanted to remain with Portugal. Intellectuals from the old *Claridade* movement argued that Cape Verde could never be economically viable on its own and should remain associated with someone, Portugal or the United Nations. They supported the words of Eugénio Tavares, the poet:

> For Cape Verde? For these poor and abandoned rocks thrown up in the sea,
> independence? What sense is there in that? God have pity on thoughtless men!

But most could not bear to remain allied to the country that had caused them so much ill. Rescue came in the form of the democrats in Portugal who overthrew Spínola and were more receptive to Cape Verdean demands. After a transitional joint government, a general election was held at the end of June 1975, and the PAIGC became the new government, a National Assembly proclaiming independence for the archipelago on 5 July 1975. The president was Aristides Pereira, Secretary-General of the PAIGC. Cape Verde and Guinea-Bissau were a joint country.

AFTER INDEPENDENCE Cape Verde was free but it was a wasteland: its resources plundered over centuries, its soil thin and disappearing with every gust of Saharan wind. Drought had come again in 1969 and afflicted the islands for six years. In 1977, the maize and bean harvest was nil. There was no work for wages and exports were almost non-existent. Over half of the islands' imports were of famine food, and emigration surged. The shock of the sudden assumption of responsibility for such a land must have been acute.

One of Cape Verde's few advantages was that it was not riven with tribal rivalries. In that sense it began rebuilding from a metaphorical, as well as a literal, bare ground. Another advantage lay in its good contacts with the outside world. The democrats of Portugal were on friendly terms with Cape Verde, a relationship that continues today.

Help came from many countries: once the USA was convinced that Cape Verde was indeed 'non-aligned' it sent a gift of US$7 million. The World Food Programme dispatched thousands of tonnes of maize, and a variety of countries, including Sweden, Holland and the USSR, also sent aid. Uniquely, the Cape Verdean government insisted that the WFP grain was not handed out as charity but was sold to people who did construction work on water-retention and anti-erosion dykes and on barrages in return for wages.

The government was a socialist one which attracted the interest of the USSR, China and Cuba. There are still strong ties with these countries: Cuba and Russia have been the destination of many Cape Verdean university students, while university links with China are underway. Indeed, the Chinese embassy is the most prestigious building in Praia, and sits opposite Cape Verde's parliament, and China's economic links with the country are growing. Guinea-Bissau, meanwhile, suffered more turbulence than Cape Verde, which led to a coup in 1980 that ruptured the link between the two countries. After that 'The Party', for there was only one, renamed itself the PAICV (Partido Africano da Independência de Cabo Verde).

The PAICV had a political monopoly enshrined in the country's constitution and this went unchallenged at first. One person within the party who objected to the lack of democracy, and also to the centralised control of the party and the limits placed on free enterprise, was one Carlos Veiga, who formed the MpD (Movimento para a Democracia) in 1990. Things moved swiftly and by September 1990 Cape Verde had legally become a multi-party state. Elections the following January swept out the PAICV and handed power to Veiga, who was prime minister from 1991 to 2001. A month later the candidate the MpD supported for president, António Manuel Mascarenhas, was elected. Flagship policies of the government in 1991 were a market economy with less public spending, opening up to foreign investment, and the development of fishing, tourism and service industries. A new national anthem and flag were adopted in September 1992.

A decade later, on 14 January 2001, the PAICV regained control in an overwhelming victory. The people then elected as president (with a margin of 12 votes) Pedro Pires, who had been prime minister of the first government in 1975. More importantly for the PAICV, it won in the Legislative Assembly. In the latest national elections the ruling party, PAICV won a historic victory when it was voted in for a third five-year term.

So the islands survive to face a brighter future than ever before. The land now receives the love it needs. The people are trying to demonstrate that the islands' history has been due to incompetence, greed and neglect, not because of what they once were called: 'bitter bare rocks strung out in mid Atlantic like a crown of thorns floating on the sea.'

GOVERNMENT AND POLITICS

Cape Verde is a parliamentary democratic republic with no political prisoners and a clean human rights record. The oldest party is the PAICV, which won independence for the country in 1975 and ruled it as a one-party state for many years. The MpD (Movimento para a Democracia), devoted to liberal economic and social reform, won democracy for Cape Verde in 1990 and was elected in 1991 and then again in December 1995. A sliver of the MpD broke away to form the Partido da Convergencia Democratica (PCD) in 1994. In late 2000, the PAICV came to power again and was re-elected in 2006 and again in 2011. The current president is Jorge Carlos Fonseca, a law graduate and member of the opposition MpD, who took office in September 2011, and the present prime minister is José Maria Neves of the PAICV, officeholder since that party's election victory in 2001. Elections in Cape Verde have generally been peaceful, though the 2001 election was disputed. Carlos Veiga, of the MpD, claimed that the results were fraudulent

When Cape Verdean cultural icon Cesária Évora (see box, page 45) passed away, one Cape Verdean restaurant owner mourned that she 'was more important than our flag'. And perhaps it's no surprise that the islands' musical *grande dame* should enjoy more affection: after all, she had been around for a lot longer.

With a blue background, ten yellow stars, two horizontal white bands sandwiching one red one, Cape Verde's national flag was only adopted in 1992, some 17 years after independence. In those intervening years, the flag was perhaps more 'African' in character: with the continent's traditional colours of red, green and yellow, it was almost identical to that of Guinea-Bissau. But now the flag is altogether more singular, with its details solemnly described in Article 8 of the islands' constitution.

That blue background represents the sea and sky, both of which are plentiful in Cape Verde. Each island is remembered by one of those yellow stars, so the uninhabited and otherwise neglected Santa Lucia is, for once, not forgotten. The white bands signify peace, whilst the red one stands for effort and endeavour. Together, the three bands represent the building of the island nation.

In a mark of respect to Cesária Évora, the flags on all the public buildings were lowered to half mast after her death in 2011.

and filed a lawsuit, but international election monitors deemed them free and fair. MpD conceded the 2011 elections which PAICV once again won with a small margin on a turnout of 76%. Women candidates were voted in to 21% of the seats. (It is interesting to note that, as of May 2013, seven of the 17 ministerial posts were occupied by women.) Municipal elections were held in 2008 with the majority of seats being taken by the MpD. In many instances this national/municipal power-split has led to a lack of co-operation and a stalemate between central government (PAICV) and local government (MpD), and has sometimes hindered the economic and social development of the islands.

ECONOMY

DEVELOPMENT In the 2013 report for the United Nations Human Development Index, Cape Verde came in at 132 – a lowly rank, but beating the majority of countries in mainland Africa. According to the International Monetary Fund (IMF), Gross Domestic Product was US$3,604 per head in 2012, down from US$3,661 in 2011. Unemployment has reduced from 17% in 2000 to only 10.7% in 2010, according to the official census, though this seems optimistic. On a brighter note, many of the unemployed are occupied for at least some of the time in fishing or farming.

Also according to the IMF, growth has slowed in recent years, slipping from 5.4% in 2010 to 5.0% in 2011, reflecting the reduction in tourism and investment in property due to poor economic conditions in Europe, from where most visitors and investors originate. In early 2013, the IMF were predicting economic growth of 4.1% for Cape Verde, rising to 4.5% in 2014. Reduced, but growth nevertheless. During the post-crisis years from 2008, remittances from Cape Verdeans living overseas also slowed down (according to a US State Department report, these remittances account for 20% of Cape Verde's GDP). Inflation rose to 4.5% in 2011 and was predicted to be 4% in 2013 and 3.3% in 2014.

Cape Verde forged a special partnership with the European Union in 2007, as well as membership of the World Trade Organization, and has been elevated by the UN to 'middle income' status.

In the long term, Cape Verde has extraordinary ambition. It hopes to transform itself into an international financial centre and an investment and transport gateway to continental Africa. The first stage in this plan is to get the money rolling in by the rapid development of tourism, on the back of which a healthy service economy can be developed. For the moment, however, the major inputs into Cape Verde's economy (after tourism and ancillaries) are still foreign aid and remittances from overseas.

AID AND REMITTANCES Foreign aid and remittances together sustain about a quarter of Cape Verde's economy. The islands have been the recipients of one of the highest amounts of international aid, per capita, in the world. Many sources of aid funding were withdrawn from 2007 when Cape Verde was upgraded by the United Nations to the status of 'middle income country' – one of only a handful that have ever achieved this elevation. However, there are still substantial – one might say, enormous – amounts of investment and aid coming from other nations.

One organisation that has stepped into the breach is the **Millennium Challenge Corporation**, a US government corporation that rewards good governance in poor countries with substantial investment in areas that will lead to economic growth. Through the first of two multi-year agreements, with a value of US$110 million and now completed, the MCC provided Cape Verde with support in various key areas, including agricultural development on three of the islands, particularly by improving rainwater capture (and its storage and distribution) and soil conservation. Other areas to benefit were the development of microfinance institutions and building of credit histories, the streamlining of government procurement, as well as port and road improvements.

In the second of the MCC's agreements with Cape Verde, signed in 2012, US$66 million has been committed to assist reforms in water and sanitation, and land management (see box, page 31) – both areas seen as currently harbouring obstacles to further economic growth. In 2008, the World Bank announced US$6 million for the fight against poverty motivated partly, it said, by Cape Verde's inability to secure other sources of funding because of its new elevated 'middle-income' status. Portugal has also continued to contribute significantly to Cape Verde's economy in recent years, and Germany and Luxembourg amongst others have been generous in their assistance. Extraordinarily, Prime Minister Neves announced in 2005 that Cape Verde was considering applying to join the European Union, but this fanciful ambition seems to have disappeared for now.

But the helping hands outlined above are dwarfed by the agreements Cape Verde is reaching with China, an ever-increasing influence in Africa and whose relationship with the country goes back to the early days of independence. Agreements made in 2008 were so vast, embracing shipping, fishing, communications, electricity and construction, that they were dubbed the 'new Chinese wave'. The key project is with the China Ocean Shipping Companies Group (Cosco), one of the world's largest shipping companies, in partnership with Enapor, which is responsible for Cape Verde's port facilities. The investments include several port redevelopments and the building of cargo facilities. Meanwhile there are plans for a major fishing supply centre in São Vicente followed by the conversion of São Vicente into a special economic area. China built Cape Verde its first dam (in Santiago) and has funded the

1

construction of a national stadium (partially completed at time of writing) with capacity for 20,000 people.

Calculations vary but it is believed by some that there may be more Cape Verdeans abroad than at home (see box, pages 32–3), and that between a third and two-thirds of families on the islands are receiving money from relatives overseas. Remittances contributed 20% of GDP in 2009.

FISHERIES Fishing contributes a meagre 1.1% of GDP. The archipelago is at the centre of one of the last great underused fishing grounds of the world, a fact that has not gone unnoticed by China's huge fishing fleet. Tuna and lobster abound, but at present fishing is a trade of artisans, though there is some export of fish and crustaceans. Although the continental shelf area is relatively small, the Exclusive Economic Zone of Cape Verde covers an area of about 789,400km², much of which is not exploited by the national fisheries.

In spite of increased fishing efforts during the past decade, landings have reached a plateau at around 9,000–10,000 per year, and catches of some fish have decreased. However, new fishing agreements are on the horizon, particularly with China and the European Union. New fish-processing facilities will be built in São Vicente.

TOURISM Tourism contributed only 10% of GDP in 2005 but the African Economic Outlook estimated that this had increased, with ancillaries, to 30% by 2012. It thus provides an increasing source of employment – increasing, though probably still only around 5%. Tourism is almost entirely responsible for Cape Verde's recent growth in GDP, and the construction boom has been by far the major component of this. Plans for holiday resorts, condominiums and apartments, abound, some of them fanciful and some of them halted by economic factors. But there's no doubt that tourism is seen as a cornerstone of the archipelago's future economic growth. And the visitor numbers are rising. In 1991, there were a meagre 19,000 tourist arrivals. In 2012, according to official government figures, some 534,000 visitors set foot on Cape Verde, an increase of 12.3% on the previous year. Visitors are attracted primarily to Sal and Boavista, which together account for 73% of guests, mainly due to the existence of the more upmarket and all-inclusive international resort hotels. Inclusive packages operated by Thomson (UK) and TUI (Germany, Nordic) account for a huge number of tourists arriving in Cape Verde, followed by TAP (Portugal). Tourists from the UK now number a staggering 115,000, by far outnumbering those from France (70,000), Portugal (68,000) and Germany (67,000). A mere 4,900 arrived from the USA, with a majority of them favouring Santiago as their destination.

AGRICULTURE 'It is heartbreaking,' says one expat scientist working in Cape Verde, 'to watch a peasant woman patiently prepare the ground and sow, then wait for months while it doesn't rain, then return to break the ground and sow again.'

Only a tenth of the land, 40,000ha, is suitable for cultivation. Of this, 34,000ha are cultivated and less than a tenth of that is irrigated, although this proportion has been rising (see box, pages 34–5). Some 90% of the crop is maize and beans which are often grown together. The beans grow up the maize stalks which act as trellises and offer some shade. Other major crops are bananas, sugarcane, sweet potatoes, manioc and cassava. The only significant exported crop is the banana, although other cash crops are coffee, peanuts, castor beans and pineapples. More than half of the total irrigated land grows sugarcane, most of which is used in the production of *grogue*, the local rum.

With continued development in the tourism sector being the bedrock of Cape Verde's proposed economic growth, it is vital that there are as few obstacles as possible to achieving it. One perceived barrier is the uncertainty that presently exists over land and property rights in Cape Verde. After all, if you don't know 'who owns what,' and boundaries are unclear, how can you sell or buy a parcel of land which could potentially host a new hotel or restaurant? If, as at present, it takes up to two years to establish clarity of good title, potential investors are likely to turn their backs and look elsewhere. The present ownership picture is blurred by illegal settlements, duplicate titles and overlapping borders. One estimate is that there are twice as many titles as there are pieces of land in the archipelago. An additional complication is that so many owners of Cape Verdean land live abroad, especially in the United States. The owners may be many miles away, but they maintain a very close interest in any issues that might impact on their property rights.

To address the current confusion over land rights in the archipelago, the Millennium Challenge Corporation (MCC), an independent US foreign aid agency, is endeavouring to support legal reforms, create a common information system for Cape Verde's land administration institutions, and clarify parcel rights and boundaries in those areas with a high potential for tourism-related investment. An improved land registration process, involving the digitising of titles, is expected to create an administrative environment more receptive to real estate development, increased tourism and ultimately, thousands of employment opportunities.

The MCC's work in this area will last for five years, with the aim of putting in place the necessary reforms and processes that will last far beyond the organisation's involvement. Kenneth Miller, Resident Country Director for MCC, is keen that their work will establish a sustainable platform from which Cape Verde can progress, unaided, particularly in an environment where some NGOs are packing their bags and refocusing resources on other countries with greater perceived needs, and in which 'free' money from abroad is retreating. There is a downside to Cape Verde's welcome and commendable accession to 'middle income' country status.

'The thickness of the envelope is shrinking,' observes Miller, his comment regarding the retreat of overseas assistance neatly capturing the challenges facing Cape Verde.

Historical patterns of ownership have deterred investment in, and maintenance of, agricultural land (see *History*, page 9) but land reform has been very hard to implement. The PAICV's attempts in 1981 were so unpopular that the next government reversed them in 1993. Farming on steep hillsides is another challenge to Cape Verdean agriculture.

There are many devices in the Cape Verdean hills and valleys designed to keep precious water and topsoil from being flushed away. *Arretos* are lines of small stone walls around the hillsides, designed for erosion control. Although they are not supposed to be used for planting, crops grown behind them are producing double the yield of crops grown before the *arretos* were built. Terraces are much bigger walls, properly designed for the ubiquitous shelved farming seen all over Cape Verde.

Check dams of concrete or stone are built in the *ribeiras* to try and slow the

Since the archipelago was first populated, Cape Verdeans have taken to the seas in search of new opportunities abroad. More than 30,000 have emigrated to Portugal since the 1968 drought. Italy has up to 10,000 Cape Verdean immigrants, many of whom went to work there as domestics in the 1970s, a route opened up by the Church and which became self-perpetuating.

Senegal and Angola each have tens of thousands of Cape Verdeans. There are emigrants in Luxembourg, France (10,000–15,000) and Holland (8,000–10,000). There are substantial numbers in Argentina and Brazil, as well as Spain and Sweden.

But the largest group by far is in the United States, where there are approximately 300,000 Cape Verdean Americans. Numbers remain static although unemployment in the archipelago means that arrivals continue, many of whom do not register with the embassy. A new census completed in 2010 showed a significant increase in numbers of emigrants as well as inter-island migration.

Today the community is spread right across the country but the strongholds remain the states of Massachusetts and Rhode Island. The US diaspora has two representatives in the Legislature in Praia. They represent the interests of the entire Americas, including the sizeable Brazilian population. Regardless of whether they are US-born or incomers, however, diaspora members in the US are fully integrated into the American way of life, with many prominent members of the community working in state and federal positions as well as at a grass-roots level.

Yet they have also successfully fought to maintain as many traditions from home as possible – not least the use of Creole (which is taught in several universities, including Harvard) in various media, both print and broadcast, and the celebration of all the usual Cape Verdean festivals. Independence Day (on 5 July, just one day after the host nation) is one of the most important.

Families still get together to eat *cachupa* and drink imported *grogue* and to listen to *mornas* by B Leva and also, increasingly, the newer artists who regularly tour the US. The younger generation in particular has embraced cyberspace and there are a number of electronic fora and blogs that enable cousins on either side

rainwater's progress to the sea. At the moment, when it rains, over 80% of the water is lost. Concreted slopes on the hillside, and sometimes natural rock formations, catch water which then flows into a tank or reservoir at the bottom.

Another major problem for agriculture in Cape Verde is pests. The millipede in Santo Antão devours potatoes and carrots – as a result the island, which is agriculturally the most productive in the archipelago, has suffered an embargo on exports of its agricultural products for decades, although this was finally, and partially, lifted in 2008. Grasshoppers cause devastation on other islands. There is one goat for every two people in Cape Verde. In the villages there are many pigs which forage for scraps, so they cost little and are an important source of meat.

PEOPLE

POPULATION According to the last census in 2010, Cape Verde has a population of 491,000 ranging in ethnicity from virtually white to black: about 70% are mixed race, 1% are white. The actual population figure is probably now closer to 510,000, using the 2010 census figure and the subsequent annual rate of population growth.

of the Atlantic to keep in closer contact than their parents' generation could ever have imagined.

'The importance of the diaspora's contribution to the islands cannot be underestimated,' says Raymond A Almeida, who has lived in the US for many years but who maintains close links with the islands. There is a symbiotic relationship, he suggests, with the remittances from the US a sizeable amount. In addition, the number of charitable associations and friendship groups that provide support, both financial and in kind, is impressive for so small a nation, he says. It is hard to find a school or organisation that does not receive some sort of help from a US-based community initiative.

The political clout, also, cannot be underestimated. It is popularly said that the cliffhanger presidential election in 2001, won by 12 votes, was decided by the diaspora.

The link works the other way, too. In 2008, Patrick Kennedy, nephew of John F Kennedy and the Congressional representative of Rhode Island, visited Cape Verde. There are 80,000 Cape Verdeans in Rhode Island – so it was a constituency visit. He joked that he had come from Cape Verde's tenth inhabited island.

Most American-born Cape Verdeans who return do so to maintain links with family and friends and, increasingly to invest in business, especially in the service industries and in small-scale property development.

'We are way behind the Europeans though,' says John Monteiro, who was born on Fogo and went to the US as a six year old. Almost 50 years later he is looking to build a small hotel but says land prices in the last few years have tripled. 'The only advantage we have over the Irish developers is that we speak the language and some of us have relatives who can help steer us through the red tape. But we're in it for the long term. Those coming from the Cape Verdean community in the US want to see the community on the islands benefit too – we want to see improved education and health care and are prepared to help make that happen. We're not just here to make money. I know a lot of people who have come back from visiting the islands and who say, "We've got to help".'

Women outnumber men because of emigration (51.4% to 48.6%, UNDP 2010), although there are localities where it is the women who are emigrating rather than the men. The lack of men, together with the intermittent returns and lengthy absences, are two of the reasons why marriage, and family units of father, mother and children, are unusual.

Men typically have children by many women and are often married to none of them; the same applies to women. Responsibility for bringing up children invariably falls to the women, who may be dependent on remittances sent back from abroad by the various fathers.

Population growth is 2.1% and the government has campaigned hard to bring it down through birth control, including abortion. The Catholic Church has campaigned hard against the latter. Life expectancy is 68 for men and 76 for women. Some 81% of people are literate, and this rises to over 90% among the young. Cape Verde is a young country in more ways than one: some 39% of the population is under 18 years of age, according to UNICEF figures (2010).

Over half the population lives on Santiago, and of these over 130,000 live in Praia, the capital of Cape Verde. The only other big population centre is Mindelo

Alex Alper and Murray Stewart

'Salt, basalt rock, limestone, kaolin, fish, clay, gypsum.' So reads the finite list of Cape Verde's natural resources, giving insight into the tremendous challenge that existence here has always posed. And yet, in a world where the price of fossil fuels climbs ever higher, Cape Verde has at least been blessed with the need to innovate. Critical deficiencies in water, agriculture and energy are compelling the country to become an innovator, and maybe a leader, in exciting new technologies, from growing plants without soil to capturing water from the fog.

But the difficulties are formidable, and the lack of water is perhaps the most. Rainfall averages 200mm per year, barely enough to replenish the natural springs that supply much of the rural population with water. As the springs slowly dry up, salt water is seeping into the aquifers, contaminating the sources that remain. Desalinisation technologies provide water to the majority of urban residents but are very expensive (see box, page 156).

Agriculture also presents challenges. Throughout Cape Verdean history, severe droughts have caused epic famines, killing thousands and driving many abroad. Erosion, caused by agriculture, grazing, and wood-gathering in a delicate ecosystem, has decreased the quality of the soil, while much of the country was originally sand and rocky mountain slope anyway. Indeed, only 10% of Cape Verde's 4,033km² of landmass is arable, and home-grown food provides only 10–20% of what is consumed. Nevertheless, a large number of Cape Verdeans are still involved in agricultural activities, planting corn, beans, peanuts, squash, sweet potatoes, sugarcane, bananas and other crops each year. Some farmers plant corn only for animal fodder, knowing it will not reach maturity.

The rest of Cape Verde's food is imported, and transportation requires energy – another scarce commodity for a country with no fuel reserves. The country also needs fuel for electricity, for cooking (butane gas) and for desalinisation. Cape Verde spent €54.4 million on petroleum derivatives in 2007 alone, and domestic fuel taxes are high compared with other African nations. When local prices for petrol and diesel climbed to €1.28 and €1.32 per litre respectively in early 2008, *hiace* drivers on Santiago called a strike, protesting at the government's high fuel tax. In the meantime, rural Cape Verdeans rely largely on dwindling forest resources for their cooking needs to supplement expensive butane gas. This constitutes a great pressure on Cape Verde's fragile ecosystem. With rising tourism, and annual population growth of about 2%, the demand for cheap, abundant energy will only continue to rise.

Precisely because of the gravity of these challenges, Cape Verde, with the help of foreign governments and NGOs, is trying to pioneer green technologies. The country promised to achieve 25% renewable energies by 2010, a figure that should rise to 50% by 2020. Cape Verde also hopes to have one island with 100%

on São Vicente, though many of the other archipelago's towns now have 'city' status despite being modest in size. The island of Santa Luzia is uninhabited.

SOCIAL ISSUES

AIDS A recent national study indicated that the prevalence of HIV in the population is 0.8% (1.1% for men and 0.4% for women). This rate is very low for an African country. Rates may increase with the rise in the number of foreigners renewable electricity by 2020, and it is offering tax deductions for expenses related to renewable energies. With 3,000 hours of sunlight per year, Cape Verde has promoted solar energy to pump and heat water, and to illuminate homes in remote areas. The Cape Verdean government and the European Union have begun a campaign to disseminate solar water pumps to 30 rural communities on Santiago. That will go far to help rural Cape Verdeans, most of whom make up the considerable part of the population that still lacks electricity.

In one rural community in Serra Malagueta, a pilot project sponsored by the Protected Areas Programme is underway to disseminate more efficient wood stoves. It aims to reduce wood use among residents who can't afford butane gas for cooking, thereby protecting the endangered forests.

Wind energy is another promising technology (see box, page 263). In consultation with the Danish company Wave Star, the government also began exploring the possibility of wave technology for electrical power generation. Still some years away from commercial implementation, Wave Star's machine consists of 20 half-submerged hemisphere-shaped floats that float upward when a wave passes. Ocean waves offer a more potent and constant energy than wind. Still, wave technology must overcome the formidable challenge of keeping costs low while resisting storms and salt damage over the long term.

The government at one stage did give consideration to a floating nuclear island, which would have supplied 70MW of energy, meeting Santiago and Maio's total energy needs. The nuclear material was to have been provided by the Russian company Rosenergoatom, who would also have been responsible for removing and treating the waste. This proposal was controversial and has not progressed. Cape Verde is innovating in water too, through fog collectors (see box, page 199).

Agricultural innovations are perhaps even more promising, with the advent of hydroponics and the spread of drip irrigation. Drip irrigation, called *gota-gota* or 'drip-drip' locally, utilises a series of plastic tubes running the length of the plant bed. They feature tiny holes that allow water to pinpoint the plant roots alone, bringing water use down by 80% and diminishing weed growth. Materials are somewhat expensive and must be replaced after three to five years. However, the technology allows for year-round cultivation, and local governments and NGOs are helping to fund it, with the result that of the 17% of farming families who use some sort of irrigation, 45% use *gota-gota*.

Soil-less culture, or hydroponics, incurs astronomical start-up costs but cuts water use by 90–95%, land use by 90%, and produces much healthier crops (see box, page 130). Cape Verde is still far from the paragon of green technologies it could be, and may need to become, to deal effectively with rising fuel prices and its own historic lack of resources. Hopefully by 2020 the efforts underway now will be paying off.

coming to the islands. Additionally, the liberal attitude towards long-term, stable relationships presents risks that HIV could become an increasing social issue. The population is young, attractive and sexually active.

Cape Verde has quite a frank attitude towards AIDS, however, so educational programmes have been able to operate openly and it is not unusual to see official 'graffiti' adorning walls of schools and other public buildings, warning of the dangers of the virus.

Drugs When Caribbean and European nations got together a few years ago to crack down on drug trafficking they were so successful that the trade along direct routes dropped almost to nothing. Yet, like water, cocaine will always find a way. It continues to enter Europe in abundance because traffickers switched their routes. They now use 'Highway 10', the 10th parallel transatlantic route from Latin America to West Africa and thence to Europe. Around ten West African countries are thought to be warehouses for cocaine *en route* to Europe, and Cape Verde is one of them. Until recently, its tiny navy and 965km of coastline have left it helpless. Now the international community is stepping in. There has been help from Brazil, and Cape Verde's new partnership with the European Union will give EU navies the ability to help police its waters. In addition the USA, as part of its controversial Africa Partnership Station initiative, is helping to patrol Cape Verdean waters and train and support the Cape Verde coastguards. In 2011, the US government pledged to give Cape Verde US$397,000 to help combat drug trafficking and organised crime. In April 2013, a joint operation between US officials and the Cape Verde police resulted in the arrest off the archipelago of Guinea-Bissau's former naval chief, described as a 'lynchpin' in that country's drug trade. A couple of drug-related murders took place in Praia in 2007–08.

LANGUAGE

In the ethnic mosaic of Cape Verdean slave communities, the speaking of tribal languages was actively discouraged. To communicate with each other, slaves were forced to piece together words from Portuguese and a melange of other sources. It was these fumblings that were the beginnings of the Cape Verdean mother tongue, Creole. It is at root Portuguese, primarily the 15th-century Portuguese of the Algarve, with a simplified grammar. Phonetics and some words have been added from some Mandingo and Senegambian languages, members of the large Niger–Congo family of African languages. Creole was the language in which Cape Verdean writers began to express themselves, sometimes in order to hide their ideas from Portuguese officials but principally as a way of defining themselves. Poems do not always translate easily. Eugénio Tavares of Brava, the legendary writer of *mornas*, was reported by the later luminary Baltasar Lopes to be 'a very mediocre poet in Portuguese but a very good poet in *Crioulo*'. Above all, Creole is the informal, spoken language that everyone understands. It is the language for sharing the Cape Verdean sentiment, the language of intimacy and feeling. The soul of Cape Verde speaks in Creole.

For more information about Portuguese and English usage, basic words, phrases and hints on pronunciation, see *Appendix 1, Language*, pages 343–51.

RELIGION

Cape Verde is a secular state with freedom of religion enshrined in the post-independence constitution. The islands have unsurprisingly been predominantly Catholic from the beginning and most other denominations have had little chance to win many converts. Some 85% of the nation is ostensibly Catholic, though the priests complain that they have lost their influence. Nevertheless, many churches are standing-room only on Sunday. The largest religious minority, less than 1%, is the Nazarene Church. This is a Protestant grouping introduced to Brava in the early 1900s by emigrants returning from the USA. The Nazarenes collaborated with another group, the Sabbatarians, to build two Protestant churches, and they translated the gospels into Creole, the local language. The islands are seen as fertile recruiting grounds by several groups, including the Church of Jesus Christ of Latter Day Saints (popularly known as the Mormons). The Church claims around 5,000 members in Cape Verde. Jehovah's Witnesses proselytise here as well. Also present are the New Apostolic Church and various others. The Jews have a fascinating and formative history in Cape Verde, fleeing there to escape persecution (see box, pages 12–13), though today's population is negligible. There is a new and fast-growing (but still tiny) Muslim population mostly comprising immigrants from the West African coast, with a mosque or two in Praia.

EDUCATION

The government provides tuition-free education for all children from 6–12 years. Education remains compulsory until the age of 11. Secondary education is free only to children whose families have an annual income below 147,000 escudos (US$1,778). (US State Department, 2013).

The University of Cape Verde is an amalgam of three colleges and has only existed since 2006. Although the main campus is in Praia, the Engineering and Maritime Sciences faculties are based in Mindelo. São Jorge dos Órgãos on Santiago is the site for the university's agricultural research centre.

The archipelago's other main university, Jean Piaget, is named after the famous Swiss theorist and is based mainly in Praia with some courses taught in Mindelo. It was established in 2001, partly from an existing research institution, and has around 2,000 students. Other universities are also appearing, such as the Lusophone University in Mindelo.

CULTURE

The faces of Cape Verde are numerous: blue eyes gazing out from above a brown cheek; green eyes below tight curls of black hair with a wisp of blonde; Chinese eyes set in a black face. Race in Cape Verde is not just Portugal mingled with the Rivers of Guinea, but also Italy and drops of Lebanon, China, Morocco and more. Pirates, sailors and merchants from Spain, France, England, Holland, Brazil and the USA deposited their genes here. Senegambians, Mandingos and Fulas gave variety to the African blood that arrived in the form of slaves.

This disorientation of racial types was regarded for centuries as a bastardisation. Then, in the very late 19th century, when the stirrings of nationalism began, the idea arose that Cape Verde had its own identity, not an unholy mixture but an exciting synthesis. This idea marked the emergence of Creole (*Crioulo*) nationhood. The Cape Verdean people have their own history, the result of a unique combination of social and natural forces.

LITERATURE '*Caboverdeanidade*' – 'Cape Verdeanness' – is expressed in poetry, the lyrics of *mornas*, folk stories and novels. The emotion that dominates is a sorrowful one, known as *sodade*. It is often translated as 'nostalgia', though that word has oversentimental connotations in English and does not convey the depth of feeling or the unsentimentality of expression. 'Longing' is a better word. *Sodade* is the longing of the emigrant looking across the sea to the motherland; the longing of mothers for their exiled children. Much Cape Verdean poetry focuses on the sea as the bringer of riches, but also of loneliness and sometimes death: 'Oh gold of the sea, you are dearly earned,' wrote Tavares.

The first Cape Verdean poetry arose in the 1890s and did not directly address the Cape Verdean condition. It followed Portuguese patterns with their rigidity of

1

Portuguese is the official language of Cape Verde. All business is conducted in Portuguese; it is used for correspondence, newspapers, road signs – in fact anything that needs to be written down. But only very rarely will Cape Verdeans speak Portuguese to each other. In the bank, the doctor's surgery, or the barber's, at work or after hours, everyone, be they president or peasant, uses Creole. It is their national language.

Creole (*Crioulo*) is not just a product of Cape Verdean history, it is an index of Cape Verdean identity. During Portuguese colonial rule it was forbidden to use Creole in public situations. Of course, this law was impossible to enforce, and the use of Creole became an act of defiance against the Portuguese.

Creole is now being used in more and more public situations. The DJs on the very popular Praia FM introduce Creole music in Creole. The tagline for one of the campaigns for the February 2001 presidential election was 'Nôs Presidente' – which is Creole for 'Our President'. And yet, despite the fact that many Cape Verdeans feel Portuguese to be an alien and difficult language for them, and despite the fact that the Portuguese of a lot of Cape Verdeans is not particularly good, Creole is perhaps even further now than it was 20 years ago from becoming the official language.

For a start, a lot of people, among them a number of Cape Verdeans, don't consider Creole to be worthy of the name 'language'. It is a dialect of Portuguese, or, as some would have it, badly spoken Portuguese (others counter that French is just a 'dialect' of Latin).

Secondly, Creole is a spoken language only. Written Creole exists, but it is very scarce. A handful of books have been written, among them collections of traditional stories and poems, a grammar, and a structural analysis. Attempts to settle upon a standard way of writing Creole, and more importantly to disseminate Creole texts and get people into the habit of writing Creole, have consistently failed.

The earliest attempt at an alphabet was an 1888 grammar written by António de Paula Brita. This was an etymological version, that is, it was based on Portuguese. The most recent was 1994's ALUPEC (Unified Alphabet for the Cape Verdean Language). In March 1979, a two-week colloquium was staged in Mindelo, and

metre and verse. The movement began in São Nicolau, then the intellectual centre of the archipelago.

Writers produced a literary annual and a book of poetry. This period, known as the Classical period, lasted until the 1930s. Amongst the writers were a very few who did not remain bound within Portuguese tradition. It was then, for example, that Tavares honed and popularised the art form of the *morna*, a combination of music, dance and poetry that expresses *sodade*. Another rebel, whose militant ideas would not be recognised for decades to come, was Pedro Cardoso, who signed himself 'Afro'. He named his journal *O Manduco* (The Cudgel), and he was the first Cape Verdean to try, albeit in a stumbling way, to articulate ideas such as pan-Africanism and Marxism.

With a clarion call in 1936, the Classical period was shattered and a new literary movement began. *Claridade*, a literary review, was published, addressing head-on the nature of Creole culture and the conditions people endured in the islands. Tales of the lives of Cape Verdeans appeared in the classic novel *Chiquinho* by Baltasar Lopes. It is a seminal work, one of the first novels from Portuguese Africa, and the international team of linguists proposed an alphabet which is still the most widely used. But the situation remains that, although the vast majority of Cape Verdeans speak Creole with great passion, wit and intelligence, they are totally unaccustomed to, and even incapable of, reading or writing it.

There are powerful arguments both for and against making Creole the official language. By doing so, Cape Verdeans might finally break the colonial yoke, achieving cultural as well as political independence from Portugal. Thus the language of their folklore, of their poems, stories and songs, might also be the language of their business. The current situation is also damaging for young children. The first language they learn to read or write is not their mother tongue, but a foreign language, learnt in school. Illiteracy is widespread, and if Cape Verdeans want to express their imagination in writing, or conduct any kind of business, they are forced to resort to a foreign language, divorced from the home and the heart.

But, on the other hand, Portuguese is the sixth most commonly spoken language in the world. With it Cape Verdeans have immediate access to 170 million people, plus the possibility of a halting conversation with the world's 266 million Spanish speakers. What use is Creole in the global village?

Officialising Creole would be a mammoth task. It would mean a total overhaul of a whole host of current procedures from the highest levels down. A commission of international linguists would need to be assembled to settle upon an alphabet and a standard form, prepare an official grammar, and develop educational materials for teaching in schools. It would take years. And who would pay?

The most vexed question is that of a standard form. Creole differs greatly from island to island, and even within the islands. Tell someone from Mindelo that the standard form of Creole is Badiu? Or someone from Praia that he must start speaking and writing São Vicente Creole? You might as well tell a cat that it should bark.

Visitors to Cape Verde will communicate successfully in Portuguese. But if they want to participate in something that is unique to Cape Verde, if they really want to impress, flatter, and entertain Cape Verdeans, if they want to approach Cape Verdeans as friends, they will be richly rewarded by using just a few words of Creole.

it was written in Creole. Essays on Creole culture and language poured from the *Claridosos* in their irregularly published journal whose last edition appeared in 1960. Other leaders were Jorge Barbosa and Manuel Lopes. Barbosa introduced a new style of poetry which he thought reflected better the Cape Verdean character, a looser verse for a freer spirit. His book *Arquipélago*, published in 1935 when he was 33, was his pioneering work. It established the central axis of the Cape Verdean tragedy, the desire to leave while being forced to stay, and the desire to stay while being forced to leave.

More recently, literature has become more militant and artists and writers have turned to Africa for inspiration. Onésimo Silveira has written of the 'force which only the black man knows', and Kaoberdiano Dambara has produced some of the first Cape Verdean poems in the Negritude tradition, though these concepts are far less commonly expressed than on mainland Africa.

Some critics believe that Creole is not a sufficiently complex language to be a literary vehicle and that the success of Tavares and Cardoso was an exception. Serious Cape Verdean writers overwhelmingly use Portuguese, albeit the Creole-infused Portuguese of the islands.

Alex Alper

Ethnic conflict may be the story of many countries in Africa today, but the old saying in the title is perhaps the extent of ethnic rivalry in Cape Verde. It compares the Badiu, who inhabit the southern islands, with their northern counterparts, the Sanpadjudu. Both are descended from the mix of African tribes and Portuguese that settled the islands 500 years ago. They speak dialects of the same Creole, root for the same soccer teams, and the Badiu and Sanpadjudu vote for both political parties.

Yet there are notable differences. The quaint farmhouses, the lighter complexions, more lusophone Creole, and Portuguese-influenced *morna* of the north indicate the more 'European' aspect of northern culture. In contrast, the darker complexions, more African Creole, and the thriving traditions of continental origin – from the raw beats of the *batuk* dance to the intricate patterns of the *pano de terra* weaving – denote the vibrant African traditions still alive in the south.

It is said that Sanpadjudus look down on their southern counterparts as less 'sophisticated'. Badius would counter that their culture is more authentically Cape Verdean, pointing out that singers from both regions usually choose to sing in Badiu Creole. ALUPEC, the current Creole alphabet, is modelled on the Badiu dialect.

These time-old stereotypes are rooted in the very origins of the names. Badiu most likely comes from the Portuguese word '*vadiu*' or 'lazy'. It is said that the Badiu slaves ran away from their masters to farm their own plots along the steep ridges. When Portuguese masters would demand their labour, Badius would refuse. Their subsequent label 'Badiu' persists as a proud symbol of defiance, while their alleged 'cracked feet' belie the myth of laziness: in reality there is a truly formidable Badiu work ethic (or lack of sophistication, as the Sanpadjudu might say).

The origins of the word '*Sanpadjudu*' are more obscure. Many think the term comes from the phrase '*são pa' ajuda*' ('they are for helping'). This may refer to those Santiago inhabitants who were convinced to emigrate northward, to populate and cultivate the Barlavento islands. Their 'potato bellies', according to Badiu lore, refer to the only crop that they managed to cultivate.

These stereotypes mostly serve as fuel for good-natured teasing. As Heavy H, a Sanpadjudu rapper sings, '*Sanpadjudu ku Badiu, nos tudo, nos e kul*' ('Badiu and Sanpadjudu, all of us, we are cool').

MUSIC AND DANCE Music underpins Cape Verdean life, gives it continuity and draws meaning from collective, often brutal experience. With perhaps less literature or art to boast about than other cultures, Cape Verde relies heavily on its varied musical traditions to project its culture and history, both within the islands and also onto the world stage. No visitor to the archipelago will go far without experiencing some musical accompaniment at some point, and often the experiences will be moving and memorable. These may be simply a CD being played on public transport, a band playing in a restaurant, a frenzied and spontaneous session in an unlikely location (see box, page 231) or the beat of the *tambour* at one of the many religious festivals. Any visit to Cape Verde will be immeasurably enriched by close contact with the islands' music and musicians.

The slaves on Brava, Santiago and Fogo all wove fine cloth using skills learned on the African mainland. The cloth was in great demand in the 17th century among the upper classes along the Rivers of Guinea and it was also worn by the elite as far away as the Gold Coast and Brazil. The deep blues and beautiful patterns of Cape Verdean cloth were superior to what these people could produce themselves but they were familiar, with a West African aesthetic. It became one of the principal currencies underpinning the slave trade, more in demand than European, Indian or African alternatives.

The demand forced English and French slaving vessels that wished to avoid Cape Verde to call there first for rolls of cloth so that they could barter on the coast. In the late 17th century, a slave was worth 60 *barafulas*, cloths of standard length and width, which in turn were worth 30 iron bars. In the 18th century, Cape Verde exported 6,000 of the 2m-long cloths a year to the mainland.

The cloth was woven on a narrow loom made of cane, sticks and banana leaves, which produced strips never more than 7in wide. Dye was made from urzela, a lichen (see page 16), and from the indigo plant. Female slaves pounded the leaves of the latter, pressed them into small loaves, dried them in the sun and then left them to ferment in a pot with water and ashes.

The standard design was a six-banded cloth (*pano*). Within that strict formula there were many variations. *Panos listrados*, for example, were alternating bands of white and indigo. *Panos simples* were simply white. Others interwove silk with the cotton. *Panos de bicho* interwove white, blue and black threads to make intricate geometric designs including the shapes of leopard and snakeskins and also of Portuguese crosses. The most expensive were cloths of a pure deep blue.

The desirability of such cloth continued for hundreds of years, from the 16th until the early 19th centuries. When the wealthy Diogo Ximenes Vargas died in Cape Verde in 1624, his estate consisted chiefly of hoards of the cloth: 1,800 *barafulas* in 45 large rolls and 840 plain white cloths in 21 rolls. Their value was recorded to be £630.

Today *panos* are worn by women either as shawls or as sashes tied just below the waist.

For more information see www.reisetraeume.de/kapverden/viadoso/c-a4/en00.html.

Traditional and modern musical forms *With thanks to Dr Lucy Durán, Senior Lecturer in African Music, SOAS University of London, formerly BBC Radio 3*
There is some irony in the fact that the dramatic, barren and remote volcanic islands of Cape Verde have given rise to some of the world's most luscious and accessible musical traditions. But maybe it's not so surprising - the archipelago is on the crossroads of the Atlantic, and has absorbed many different styles over the centuries. Cape Verde's music, like its language, *crioulo* (Kriolu), was born in the particular geographies and histories of the islands, a potent mixture of Portuguese and West African culture. Added to that are elements from the Caribbean, Brazil, and further afield, introduced by sailors passing through the country. Plus, mass emigration of islanders to cities like Lisbon, Paris, Dakar, Boston and Rotterdam has also played a major role in the development of their music.

There is now a budding music industry especially on Santiago and São Vicente, with recording studios and festivals, but many Cape Verdean musicians live abroad. They have contributed to keeping the four main traditions – *morna, coladeira, batuku* and *funaná* – alive and constantly evolving.

Morna and *coladeira* are ballroom styles that are quite refined, their melodies and lyrics written by well-known composers and poets, while *batuku* is a simple solo-chorus folk style traditionally sung and danced by women of African descent. *Funaná* is a rough-and-ready dance music for festive days, with frenetic melodies on accordion and metal scraper, fuelled by the consumption of large quantities of *grogue*, alcohol distilled from sugar cane.

Morna is Cape Verde's best-known music. When I went to the islands in 2009 with BBC Radio 3, in order to record programmes for World Routes, time and again I heard the phrase '*morna* is the soul of our people'. It first became famous in the 1990s through the haunting voice of Cesária Évora, Cape Verde's celebrated 'barefoot diva'. Her songs like 'Sodade', 'Mar Azul', and 'Miss Perfumado' captivated audiences around the world. *Morna* has a melancholic feel to it, and is often compared to Portuguese *fado*, because of its minor-key melodies and themes of separation and lost love. But it also has a sensual edginess. Its shuffling syncopated rhythms clearly originate in Africa, but are tempered by the encounter with Portuguese, and recall Brazilian styles like samba.

Morna's langourous melodies are traditionally accompanied on an ensemble of string instruments. One or more Spanish guitars (or *violao*), the *cavaquinho* (small 4-string guitar), which is strummed, the *viola* (ten-string guitar with five double courses of metal strings), and violin, are woven together into a rich tapestry. Piano and wind instruments like clarinet or saxophone may also be added to the *morna* ensemble. *Morna* orchestras and singers can be found on all the islands, from small villages such as Chã das Caldeiras high up in the volcanic crater of Fogo, to the isolated town of Nova Sintra on Brava, shrouded in cloud most of the year. Each place has its own special regional style and composers.

Morna is said to have originated on Boavista in the 18th century, one of the islands that provided salt to the Portuguese Empire. It was popularised by Eugenio Tavares (1867–1930), a poet from Brava, the smallest of the inhabited islands – a place from which many sailors left, never to return. Indeed, *morna* is the perfect soundtrack to this inaccessible spot in the mid-Atlantic whose name means 'wild'. Tavares, who had spent years abroad himself, wrote beautiful songs in Crioulo that are now like anthems for Cape Verdeans – such as 'Hora di Bai' – about the pain of separation from and longing (*sodade*) for loved ones and the homeland.

The concept of *sodade*, so fundamental to *morna*, resonates deeply with the Cape Verdean experience of emigration. In the words of one musician: '*morna* expresses the despair of wanting to stay, but having to leave'. The extreme conditions on the islands, the years of slavery, drought and oppressive colonial rule, and the seafaring way of life, have made Cape Verdean culture what it is. One of the most influential *morna* composers of the 20th century, B Leza (1905–58), whose music is performed by dozens of artists, wrote a song called 'The Sea is the Home of Longing' (Mar e mora di sodadi).

The sea is the home of longing
it separates us from our faraway land
it keeps us from our mothers, our friends
without certainty of meeting again.

'The ocean is very important to us, as a bridge to the world and also a prison', commented Mayra Andrade, a rising Cape Verdean star who is now based in Paris, in an interview with British journalist Maya Jaggi. 'Cape Verdean people need music to feel free.'

However, Cape Verde's music is by no means only sad – Cape Verdeans love to dance. This explains the enduring popularity of the country's second national style, *coladeira*, with its infectious rhythms. The name comes from the Portuguese word 'cola', meaning glue, so called because the dancing couple hold each other tightly, hips swinging together to the two-step beat. *Coladeira* developed out of *morna* sometime in the early 20th century, and shares some of its melodic and harmonic features, but it goes at almost twice the speed. Its lyrics are often humorous and satirical, and include sexual innuendo (eg: 'Sangue Beirona', one of the best known *coladeiras*, says 'if you go to the bottom of the hill, you will find the essence of a woman').

Most Cape Verdean bands have a healthy dose of *coladeiras* in their repertoire, and this is the style you are most likely to hear at clubs and hotel bars whether in São Vicente, Cape Verde's musical capital, or in Lisbon, which has several popular Cape Verdean clubs and dance halls, such as B Leza (named after the composer), where many of Cape Verde's greatest stars have performed. There are also commercialised forms of *coladeira*, such as *cola-zouk* (*zouk* is a syncopated rhythm that was made popular globally in the 1980s by Kassav from Martinique). A much-admired musician from São Vicente who played a tasteful form of *cola-zouk*, was the late Bius (died 2009). A more formulaic and heavily commercialised style, *cabo-love*, was popularised by musicians abroad like Gil Semedo, a Cape Verdean singer based in Rotterdam.

PALOP musicians (PALOP is an acronym denoting the five former Portuguese territories in Africa) often find themselves working together in bands and studios in the diaspora, and their styles inevitably cross-influence each other. Thus *cola-zouk* closely resembles *passada*, a popular dance style from Angola. Cuban salsa is also an important strand in Cape Verde's dance music, as in Cesária Évora's album *Cafe Atlántico*, or Voz de Cabo Verde's album *Voz de Cabo Verde Live*.

Apart from *morna* and *coladeira*, two other genres of Cape Verdean music are well known and can be considered national, even though they originate specifically on the island of Santiago. *Batuku* and *funaná* are rootsy, vibrantly percussive styles associated with the poorer sector of the population, of African descent. Both genres were forbidden at times by the Portuguese colonial regime, feared for their African sound and their rebellious lyrics. But since independence, in 1975, many artists have taken inspiration from these two traditions.

Batuku is a unique type of music performed by women, who beat out interlocking rhythms of two against three on folded cloth or pillows called *txabeta*, held between their knees. As the pounding of the *txabeta* intensifies and gets faster, women take turns to get up and dance, tying a cloth around their hips to emphasise their hips swaying, while sometimes balancing a bottle on their heads. The songs are organised into solo lines with a choral response in typically African fashion.

The word *batuku* comes from the Portuguese '*batucar*', meaning 'to drum'. It is the oldest form of music from Cape Verde, dating back, according to oral tradition, to the late 15th century. 'Slave women used to sing these songs in the back yard of the slave houses, when their men were out working the fields. It was our form of protest,' commented a member of Nos Herança, a professional *batuku* group based in Cidade Velha (the first settlement on Cape Verde, around 1462). Nos Herança is one of many superb *batuku* ensembles from the island of Santiago.

One of the sub-genres of *batuku* is *finaçon*, which features improvised song texts of social critique. The most cherished *finaçon* singer was Nha Nácia Gomi, known as 'the queen of batuku'. Her uncompromising, witty lyrics were much admired by Cape Verdeans, as was her deeply traditional style, reminiscent of the choral singing of the Manjak from Guinea Bissau - undoubtedly one of the principal sources of slaves brought to the archipelago.

Other *batuku* groups like Kultura Speransa from Ribeira da Prata, near Tarrafal in the north of Santiago, are seeking to innovate by adding instruments such as drums, guitar or accordion, and referencing global dance styles. Like many *batuku* groups, Kultura Speransa are associated with a community youth programme. Their songs are hard-hitting; for example, 'Droga mau viciu' laments the pernicious influence of drugs on people's lives. *Batuku* in its traditional form is also widely practised among Cape Verdean ex-pats, both as part of community programmes and as a symbol of female power and solidarity. It was the young Santiago composer Orlando Pantera (who died at the age of 33 in 2001) who first introduced the sounds of *batuku* into popular Cape Verdean music, influencing many young divas living abroad like Lura, Sara Tavares and Mayra Andrade.

Funaná is the other roots style that has made an impact on contemporary popular music from Cape Verde. Like *coladeira*, it is a couple dance, but it is more rural, and goes at lightning speed. In its traditional setting it's played on button accordion, called *gaita* - a generic term for bagpipes in Portuguese – and iron scraper, called *ferro* or *ferrinho* (little iron) - a long thin piece of iron with serrated edges scraped with an iron rod. *Funaná* is celebratory music for feast days such as São João (24 June). Its origins are not well known, but it probably pre-dates the arrival of the accordion to Santiago in the early 20th century. The best-known performer was the singer and accordionist Kodé di Dona (died 2009), from São Francisco village in the plateau above Cidade Velha - a charismatic man for whom *funaná* was a family affair, his young son playing *ferrinho* while the rest of the family joined in on the choruses. *Funaná* was frowned upon during colonial rule, but after independence it was popularised and modernised by a band called Bulimundo. Later generations of singer-songwriters such as Boy Ge Mendes, Tito Paris, Mayra Andrade and Nancy Vieira have included *funaná* in their repertoire, though few, except for the group Ferro Gaita, continue the radical roots style of Kodé di Dona.

There are other lesser-known forms of folk music on the islands, mainly associated with religious festivities. *Tabanka* is from Santiago and is a semi-religious folk theatre, that involves the ritual stealing of a saint and its return, celebrated with processional dancing and the blowing of conches. On Fogo island, *pilão* and *bandera* are songs with percussion performed to celebrate saint days, especially that of São Filipe, Fogo's patron saint. *Pilão* is accompanied by the interlocked pounding of grain in a mortar by several women, a tradition established there by slaves from West Africa. Tcheka, who lives in Praia, capital of Santiago, is typical of the generation of singer-songwriters from the islands whose music is infused with these sounds, but transformed into something completely new. Which is why Cape Verde remains one of the most musical of all African countries.

The international stage Cape Verdean music is flourishing. Cesária Évora, barefoot diva with the mellow, unschooled voice, was the figurehead of the *morna* (see box, page 45), and sold albums in the hundreds of thousands, particularly in France. Her enormous popularity has hardly been interrupted by her death in December 2011.

Other musicians also became increasingly better known on the international stage. In the 1960s, it was the singer Bana – who died in July 2013 - and the Voz di Cabo Verde, who popularised the *morna* in Europe. They were influenced by Latin American and Brazilian rhythms and styles, particularly *cumbia*.

Bands and singers with a long history in the archipelago include Luis Morais, Os

Tubarões and its lead singer Ildo Lobo, Norberto Tavares, Bulimundo and Finaçon. The last three turned the accordion-based *funaná* into its high-energy offspring.

Other well-known Cape Verdean musicians are Paulino Vieira, Dany Silva, Gabrielle Mendes and Tito Paris. The Mendes brothers, emigrants from Fogo, set up in 1976 and have worked particularly with the *coladeira*. They also work with Angolan music, introduced to them by natives of Fogo returning from doing their military service on the mainland. An exciting newcomer is Neuza, whose *Flor di Bila* album is upbeat and danceable.

Commercial Cape Verdean music has often incorporated new ideas from Latin America, and today it is filled with other styles to the extent that purists fear that true Cape Verdean musical culture could vanish. Optimists believe that the Cape Verdean nature, whose essence is to absorb and transform multi-national influences, will ensure that Cape Verdean music remains distinctive and fertile.

FOLKLORE Folklore is rich with tales of Sancho, the mischievous monkey who lives in the mountains and causes chaos wherever he goes. He remained in the hills throughout the Portuguese oppression, waiting until it was time to 'turn all upside down', as the poem on page 10 describes. Sancho's threat of confusion is generally a desirable one, a welcome anarchy upsetting those in power. But sometimes Sancho is purely an agent of trouble. He pops up in proverbs, such as the one reminding the lazy or naughty that they will go hungry if they don't till the soil: 'Beans don't grow where monkeys are.' Another character is Nho Lobo, the lazy wolf, who appears in many cycles of tales in the oral

CESÁRIA ÉVORA

Cesária Évora, the 'barefoot diva' who died in 2011, had a dedicated international following, particularly in Paris. Her enduring appeal lies in the quality of her voice which, in addition to its mellow elements, is untrained, simple and unaffected – the perfect vehicle for expressing the poetry of the *morna*. It earned her the names 'Aguadente' and 'Red Wine'. Évora is also loved because she sang as if she had just stepped into one of the Mindelo bars – lack of pretension, even bluntness, were her hallmarks. She sang the *morna* accompanied mainly by violin, acoustic guitar, accordion, piano, clarinet and the mandolin-like *cavaquinho*.

Évora was born in 1941. It was a friend of Évora's who remarked on her voice when she was a teenager. She joined a band at the age of 16 and sang in the bars of Mindelo, as well as on Portuguese cruise ships. She made no money from it, apart from a little when she performed at Portuguese official functions – but even that source disappeared with independence in 1975. Her humble career seemed to have evaporated and for a decade she refused to sing.

In 1985, at the age of 45, Évora was invited to Portugal by the Organisation of Cape Verdean Women to contribute to a record. She went, but the record was not a hit. However, while she was there she met a businessman, José da Silva, who offered to work with her. Three years later she cut a record, *La Diva aux Pieds Nus* (The Barefoot Diva), in Paris. She went on to make several more albums, including *Destino di Belita*, *Cesária*, *Miss Perfumado*, *Mar Azul* (Blue Sea) and *Cabo Verde*. The album *Voz d'Amor* won a Grammy Award in 2003. For a while she lived in Paris, but retained houses in São Vicente. Having already announced the end of her stellar career due to health problems, she died in December 2011, prompting two days of national mourning.

tradition handed down through generations. A Nho Lobo story generally conveys a moral for children. Bli Mundo is the ox who broke free from the yoke of the *trapiche*, and symbolises liberty. A charming recent children's book is *Do Tambor a blimundo*, available as an English translation (see *Appendix 2, Further information*, page 354).

Speech is also rich in proverbs: 'A scratching chicken will meet its grandmother'; 'A man without a wife is a vase without flowers'; 'A lame goat does not take a siesta'; 'In cooking, eggs show up rotten'; and 'They'll pay you to climb up the coconut palm but getting down again, that's your affair.'

FESTIVALS Traditional festivities are generally Catholic saints' days. They usually begin with church services and include processions, drumming and the eating of specially prepared foods. Many have their own traditions, some of which are described in the island chapters, and most occur in the summer. All the islands celebrate Christmas, Saint John (São João, 24 June) and Carnival (around 16 February).

STARTING YOUR CAPE VERDEAN MUSIC COLLECTION

If you want to buy some recordings of modern Cape Verdean music, here are some ideas to start you off. This list is designed to be small and of course there are many other bands and singers to look out for.

The *grande dame* is of course **Cesária Évora**, with at least ten albums, including *Miss Perfumado* and *São Vicente di Longe*. **Bau**, a musician who plays regularly in Mindelo, has produced *Djailza*, *Tope da Coroa*, *Inspiration* and *Bli Mundo*. Go for the last if you are buying only one. **Bana** is often referred to as the King of *Morna*, and his death was royally mourned in 2013. The 1972 album *Coladeras: The Best of Bana* provides a suitable introduction.

Other, more recent, artists have one thing in common: mixing traditional Cape Verdean music with influences from around the world. **Lura**, whom some critics have suggested is Évora's successor, has been well known since her first album release in 2004. Try *M'Bem di Fora* (I've Come from Far Away). It has a rich mixture of her music, with influences from many of the islands. **Teófilo Chantre** has composed several of Évora's songs, is a top guitarist and has a rich, baritone voice. Try his album *Viaja*, which includes some of his most famous pieces. **Mayra Andrade**, born in 1985, is lauded for her lyrics as well as her music. Try her album *Stória, stória*. **Tcheka**, a guitarist and vocalist, is said to be able to reproduce the feel of all Cape Verdean instruments and rhythms on a single guitar. Try *Nu Monda*. **Cordas do Sol** is a band from Santo Antão whose CD is widely on sale, especially in their home island. In Fogo, **Agostinho da Pina**, the blind violinist who inspired the introduction to the first edition of this book, now has his own CD *Augusto Cego*.

Kamin di Bedju is an album by **Michel Montrond**, highly rated by those in the know. Anything by **Nancy Viera** can be recommended, likewise anything by **Bius**. Two female singers with soulful voices are **Neuza**, who debuted with the upbeat *Flor di Bila* album in 2013, and **Carmen Souza**, who released the equally excellent *Protegid* in 2010.

Finally, for some compilations try *Funaná*, an album dedicated to that musical form. Try also *The Soul of Cape Verde*, for a good mix of some of the bands above. *Travadinha* is a popular instrumental collection. Then there's also *The Rough Guide to the Music of Cape Verde*.

FOOTBALL: EVOLUTION FROM MINNOWS TO BLUE SHARKS

Murray Stewart

Until 2013, any global profile enjoyed by Cape Verde in the world of football had relied almost entirely on the success of those of Cape Verdean origin who had chosen to seek fame and fortune elsewhere. Aficionados of the 'beautiful game' will be very familiar with names such as Nani of Manchester United and Henrik Larsson, formerly of Glasgow Celtic and Barcelona, but not so familiar with their connections with Cape Verde. And why should they be? After all, Nani plays for Portugal's national team, despite being born in the archipelago, and Larsson – whose father was Cape Verdean – won 106 caps for Sweden before his retirement. As the 2013 African Nations Cup approached, surely a nation with a population of half a million was forever destined to remain as minnows, swimming harmlessly in the vast ocean of soccer obscurity?

Not so. After not even bothering to enter the competition 18 times, withdrawing once and failing to qualify for the finals on seven successive occasions, incredibly the 'Blue Sharks' of Cape Verde overcame four-time tournament winners Cameroon to reach the finals for the first time. Nor was the fairy tale over, as two draws and a last-minute victory propelled the Sharks into the unknown waters of the quarter-finals. Finally, the Sharks were sunk by Ghana, courtesy of a penalty and a goal five minutes into injury time. The streets of Praia and other archipelago towns filled with flag-waving fans, eager to acclaim the team's unprecedented success.

And so, with the 2014 World Cup in Portuguese-speaking Brazil on the horizon, the Blue Sharks set about the task of qualifying. By mid-2013, they topped their African qualifying group and seemed set fair to book their place at the world's premier tournament for the first time. But disaster struck. A momentous victory against Tunisia was annulled when it was discovered that the Sharks had fielded an ineligible player. They were duly demoted to second place and an appeal to the authorities failed. The meteoric rise of Cape Verde's stars was at least temporarily halted.

Mirroring Cape Verdeans' wider tradition of seeking opportunity through emigration, the current squad of players earn their day-to-day livings by playing for teams in Portugal, England, Romania, France, Angola, Hungary, the Netherlands, Bulgaria and even China. But despite this scattering of talents across the globe, despite the tragic administrative blunder that cost them a first World Cup Final appearance, 2013 had demonstrated that, once brought back together to represent their country, the Blue Sharks are capable of swimming with the big fish of football.

2

Practical Information

WHEN TO VISIT

The islands are warm and sunny all year round so for many visitors without any special interests, it doesn't really matter when they go. For **windsurfers** the best months are January and February while **divers** will find the calmest waters and peak visibility from June to December; **beach lovers** might wish to avoid the windy winter months. **Fishermen** after marlin should opt for May to October, while tuna fishing is at its best in August. For **hikers**, the mountainous islands are significantly more beautiful during and just after the rainy season of July to December, though flooding can impede some Santo Antão hikes. The heaviest rainfall is usually in August and September. For those concerned about the heat, the peak is in September (with an average daily temperature of 30°C), with the trough being in January (average 24°C). For those who wish to see **nesting turtles** the season is June to October, peaking in mid-July and August. Turtle hatchlings are born from mid-August until the end of November. Whale-watchers will find the best opportunities in March and April, particularly off Boavista. **Photographers** should avoid December to March when the harmattan winds dull the light, and leave deposits of sand. **Party animals and music lovers** might choose February for the São Vicente Carnival, or for that in São Nicolau; August for the São Vicente Baía das Gatas music festival; or May for the Gamboa music festival in Santiago. To coincide your visit with one of the more low-key **festivals**, consult the individual island chapters. Those on a **tight budget** will find hotels cheaper from April to June and in October, and should definitely avoid Christmas and Carnival time. **Peace seekers** might avoid July and August, when Cape Verde is full of both European holidaymakers and *emigrante* families taking their summer holidays back home. As well as Christmas and Carnival times, the whole period from November to March is high season.

HIGHLIGHTS

HIKING Cape Verde is a superb hiking destination – the vistas from the mountains of Santo Antão or from the depth of its gorges, the lonely slopes of Brava and the stunning interior of the brooding volcano crater of Fogo make for a unique experience. Much of the walking on Cape Verde is on the extraordinary cobbled paths that have been constructed in the most unlikely corners and up the steepest of slopes, making the walking much easier than might be construed from the map.

On Santo Antão the classic walks are up or down the *ribeiras*, taking transport at the beginning or end (see page 308). On Fogo, the highlight for many is to ascend the Pico, the 2,829m spectacular volcano cone and, for some, to spend a night or two with the villagers who make their home in its shadow. On Brava there are endless walks criss-crossing the steep 'flower' island where you are unlikely to meet

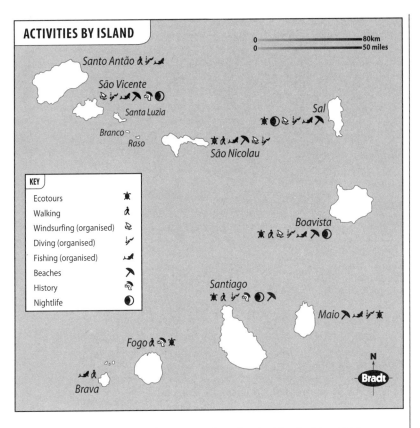

ACTIVITIES BY ISLAND

KEY

Ecotours	🦋
Walking	🚶
Windsurfing (organised)	🏄
Diving (organised)	🤿
Fishing (organised)	🎣
Beaches	⛱
History	🏛
Nightlife	🌓

any other travellers. São Nicolau is a gentle and quiet island with a hidden, green and mountainous heartland filled with beautiful walks, whilst Santiago has its own mountainous spine with some fine walks between it and the coast.

Most of the walks require a certain amount of fitness because they are steep, and a certain elasticity of knee for the descents. In this book each is rated according to a rough scheme:

1 Easy path with little fitness required.
2 Medium fitness, with some bursts of steep ascent and/or the odd slippery stretch.
3 Prolonged steep walking and/or slippery, uncobbled paths.

While we attempt to make our assessments uniform, it is inevitable that our judgements of time lengths and difficulty are a little subjective. Because of this, we have identified the writer of each hike description at the top: CW – fit male, mid-thirties; AI – unfit female, mid-thirties; AH – fit male, 20; HC – unfit female, mid-thirties; MS – fit male, fifties. For those seeking very gentle hikes there are options in Santo Antão and Boavista, but few attractive flat walks on the other islands. You can penetrate quite far by vehicle, however – into Fogo's crater and far up one or two of Santo Antão's *ribeiras*.

BEACHES Cape Verde has miles and miles of virgin coastline, but without the palm trees. Sal, Boavista and Maio have the best white sands. Whether white

- Don't use ferries (except to Santo Antão and Brava) unless you are on a long trip
- If you are on a tight schedule or already know exactly what you want to do, book your internal flights at home
- Visit no more than two islands (in a week) or three–four (two weeks)
- Minimise the number of flights
- Select your islands carefully: they differ wildly and it's hard to change your plans
- If you use a tour operator choose a specialist in Cape Verde

or black sands, the shores are breathtakingly beautiful – and many of them are remote and desolate too. Luxury holiday resorts are now common on Sal and there are a few on Boavista. There are more under construction and some seemingly abandoned projects on Maio and São Nicolau. Beware, though, that some beach tourists complain about the wind and some seem to be plagued by flies, too; others have complained that swimming was not safe in front of their hotel: check before you book.

DIVING *with Jacquie Cozens*

Will Cape Verde soon rival the Red Sea for diving or is it all just hype? The marine life is certainly abundant and there is the novelty of being in the Atlantic yet encountering tropical fish such as parrotfish, angelfish or the occasional whale shark. In addition, flight times from Europe are relatively short, you are never likely to tie up on a crowded dive site and there are exciting seasonal events such as the migration of humpback whales and the breeding of turtles. That said, there are no classic coral reefs, there are occasional strong currents and wind, the water is colder and diving is in its infancy.

Although there are centres on five of the islands, most of the focus is on Sal which has a variety of sites in Santa Maria Bay within ten to 15 minutes' boat ride, a few along the west coast and some less frequently visited places on the east coast. The underground topography consists of rocky ridges, pinnacles and boulders and underwater arches and caves. On Sal there are five wrecks at between 5m and 30m, the latest having been sunk in April 2008 by Manta Diving Center. Sal also offers the opportunity to dive in caves that have been formed by lava in the north of the island. A classic dive is Buracona, a 40m tunnel that emerges at the 'Blue Eye', a pool where you can surface to see the surprised faces of land-based tourists looking down on you.

Dive sites in Cape Verde are usually ridges with big overhangs smothered in bright yellow polyps and populated with large aggregations of surgeonfish, goatfish, parrotfish, Atlantic bigeyes, enormous scribbled filefish and metre-long cornet fish. At certain times *papaguia* (Guinea grunts) form huge balls of up to 1,000 fish. The macro life is also abundant, with numerous nudibranchs, tiny coral eels, sharpnose puffers and frogfish.

Large marine life you may encounter include dolphins and five species of turtles, including loggerheads which come ashore to nest between June and October. Species such as endangered tiger sharks and bull sharks were once common but are now more often seen being gutted on the pier. Sometimes there are nurse sharks, reef sharks and manta rays. Humpback whales visit in the spring.

In general the diving around all the islands is reliably good and, compellingly, it is very underexplored. The potential as a diving destination is huge, as the relative isolation in the middle of a vast ocean is likely to lead to exciting and unexpected encounters.

Water temperatures range from 21°C to 27°C. Diving and courses are available on Sal, Boavista, Santiago, São Vicente and Santo Antão. All the centres have rental gear. Be aware that there is no operational recompression chamber on any of the islands.

FISHING Cape Verde has superlative big-game fishing. Blue marlin, for example, is big both in numbers and in size (fish up to 750lb have been caught here). There are also tiger shark, sailfish, swordfish, kingfish and striped and white marlin. Closer in to shore there are wahoo, albacore, yellowfin tuna, grouper and dorado. Big-game fishing is best from São Nicolau (see page 327) and between São Vicente and Santo Antão (see page 268), though it is also possible from Maio (see page 206). Hiring a boat for the day for such a trip is around €700–1,000 per day, depending on whether it is a local fishing boat or not, while booking an all-inclusive week's trip is around €1,800–2,800, depending on numbers. Around the archipelago it is possible to join local fishermen on their trips, a great experience whether you personally catch anything or not. Often they go out a few hundred metres, drop anchor, and fish for skipjack, grouper, squirrelfish and many other varieties. Some go night-fishing for morays. The locals use harpoons to catch lobster, octopus and parrotfish. As sport fishing grows in popularity, so do less than ecologically sound practices. Many operators with limited knowledge of marine life take undersized fish and target marginal species such as sharks, marlin and other billfish. If you don't want to contribute to this indiscriminate practice look out for a skipper who practices catch and release.

SAILING, SURFING AND WINDSURFING With the trade winds providing a remarkably steady force 5 to 6 in winter falling to a gentler force 3 to 4 in summer, wind is never lacking, and Cape Verde has become an international windsurfing and kitesurfing destination.

Sailing Sailing around the islands is still quite unusual. At any one time there might be 20 boats moored in the main harbour of São Vicente, and a few more to be found in those of Sal and Santiago. A new marina is underway in Praia and may open during this book's lifetime. Facilities are far inferior to the Azores or Canaries, but there are beautiful anchorages at Murdeira Bay on Sal, at the remote Fajã d'Água on Brava and at Tarrafal in north Santiago. In fact, each island has some sort of shelter but it may be a long trek to get provisions and an even longer one if you need spare parts.

There are many day excursions in large sailing boats and powerboats on Sal but less available on other islands. Yachts can also be rented, with or without skipper, in São Vicente. The *Itoma* (*www.itoma.at*) is a 23m (70ft) motor-catamaran with room for 16 passengers; its owners organise cruising, diving and windsurfing tours. (For further information, see page 267.)

Surfing Cape Verde has 965km of coastline, spotted with reefs and points and steady wind throughout the year, and its reputation as an international windsurfing, kitesurfing and surfing destination is growing. The water is warm and the swell from the open Atlantic, during the winter, can be big. It is similar to the Canaries and the Azores in the kind of swell it picks up – but it is warmer. The Barlavento – the islands

Sailing to Cape Verde and spending some time sailing between islands is growing more popular. There is a wide variety of scenery and culture and incredibly friendly people. Many find it a convenient location to stop for a while before an Atlantic crossing.

All islands are suitable cruising destinations but the quality and suitability of the harbours and anchorages vary greatly. The Atlantic swell is all-pervasive and can make any of the anchorages uncomfortable, if not dangerous. A good pilot book, such as *Atlantic Islands* by Anne Hammick, is essential for visiting the less-frequented islands and for guidance on working into some of the more tricky anchorages.

Given the prevailing northeast winds it is best to cruise from north to south and from east to west. The island of Sal makes a good and friendly arrival destination. The port of Palmeira is well sheltered from all but the southwest winds and there are excellent anchorages further south at Murdeira. Santa Maria Bay and Ponta Sino also offer shelter.

Boavista is an easy day's sail from Sal and has an excellent, isolated anchorage in the shallows between the islet of Ilhéu do Sal Rei and the mainland. A short dinghy ride to the rustic town of Sal Rei allows you to sample the outstanding fish restaurants or, surf permitting, you can land the dinghy on the miles of sandy beach that line the west coast or visit the remains of the fort on Ilhéu do Sal Rei.

Tarrafal on São Nicolau is a pretty anchorage where the water is very clear. The island of Maio in the southern group boasts plenty of fish, birds and deserted beaches; it is possible to anchor at Porto de Maio on the southwest side of the island, though the swell often makes disembarking on the pier a bit tricky.

The country's capital, Praia, on Santiago, has good anchorage and a new marina is due to open in 2014. Nearby Fogo is a spectacular island with a good settled weather anchorage on the west coast. Brava is another spectacular and pretty island where it is possible to anchor in the really tiny harbour of Furna; ashore you can visit the capital of Vila Nova Sintra.

As of 2013, São Vicente hosted the only marina in the island chain in Mindelo. Shelter is excellent and a good range of facilities, chandlery and insurer-approved repairs are available for those preparing to cross the Atlantic.

---

in the north – are in the best position for winter surf, while the Sotavento – southern islands – pick up summer, tropical swells and swells from far away in the south Atlantic. The wind is strongest in the winter and calmest from May to September.

The winter swell season runs from January to March and at this time the average deep-swell height is about 1.8m. The swells tend to hit the western coasts of the islands and wrap around into spots heading south. The result is offshore conditions with northeast winds.

The best-known island for surfing is Sal, whose most famous wave is at Ponta Preta – a long, classic right-hand reef with 200m rides. There are also surfing spots on Santiago – Tarrafal, and the coast in the southeast, south of Ponte de Lobo. The surf is mostly reef breaks but there are some beach breaks. Boards are available for hire in Sal and São Vicente.

Windsurfing Cape Verde is a popular destination for windsurfers from Europe to Hawaii, and regularly hosts championships. The two main islands for windsurfing are Boavista (page 143) and Sal (page 104), with São Vicente and São Nicolau offering a lot of potential but little as yet in the way of facilities (pages 278 and 333).

November to the end of May is the windy season. During this time, the winds range from 18 knots to 22 knots and are good for both intermediate and advanced riders. Even during the windiest times there will be days that are good for beginners. If you want to avoid strong winds, the best time to learn is during the summer. Sal has a dedicated kitesurfing bay and also has Ponta Preta, whose huge breakers, kicked up by a strong offshore wind, led to the venue being added to the World Wave Circuit in 2007 and the Professional Windsurfers Association World Cup (*www.pwaworldtour.com*) in 2008, 2009 and 2010. In São Vicente, in the bay of Mindelo, the average wind speed between January and June is 16 knots, with gusts of up to 30 knots. Round the coast in São Pedro Bay, world windsurfing speed records have been set and the current record is over 40 knots.

SUGGESTED ITINERARIES

The most important decision the prospective visitor will make is choosing which island or islands to visit. It is difficult to overemphasise the importance of this. There's nothing more tragic than to meet grumpy tourists at the end of their holidays who, in essence, selected the wrong islands for their tastes. If all you want is mountains and greenery you will loathe Sal. If you are after a bit of luxury by the sea with watersports, you will be frustrated in Fogo or Brava. You can select islands to suit your interests from the map on page 49 and from the list below, which is followed by a few suggested itineraries. Bear in mind, however, the islands' internal flight system is centred on the hubs of Sal (to get to Boavista or São Nicolau), Santiago (to get to Fogo and thus on to Brava by boat, and to get to Maio) and São Vicente (to get to São Nicolau and Santo Antão – the latter by boat); so it might take two flights to get to your island.

CHOOSING YOUR ISLANDS

- **Santo Antão** Mountain walking; scenic driving; one luxury hotel; a limited amount of adventure sports.
- **São Vicente** Barren; nightlife and restaurants in Mindelo, with some buildings of historical interest; one luxury resort hotel by a beautiful beach; game fishing; marina with yachts for hire.
- **São Nicolau** Very quiet; beautiful mountain walking; scenic driving; black-sand beaches; game fishing; one watersports outlet.
- **Sal** Barren, flat interior; superb watersports; large beach resort hotels; nightlife; turtles; best restaurant choice.

GETTING MARRIED IN CAPE VERDE

As the islands develop, demand is growing amongst couples dreaming of a barefoot wedding on a beach. Be warned: unless you can stay on the islands for at least 30 days, getting legally married here is not currently possible for visitors, no matter what you might be told. This kind of tourism is in its infancy, but at present a marriage blessing or renewal of vows is all you can hope for on the beautiful white sands of Sal or Boavista. More information can be found on the Cape Verde Tips website (*www.capeverdetips.co.uk*).

- **Boavista** Flat with desert interior; superb watersports; miles of deserted beaches; a few beach hotels; turtles.
- **Maio** Flat, mostly barren interior; miles of deserted beaches; slow pace; few hotels as yet.
- **Santiago** A balanced mix with no extremes; a capital city with some music and restaurants; one or two nice beaches; craggy mountainous interior with a few good walks; and the country's one major historical sight.
- **Fogo** The spectacular volcano; for sightseers and hikers; some history, *sobrado* architecture.
- **Brava** Very quiet, unspoilt; mountainous with some lovely walks.

SUGGESTED ACTIVITIES

- **Hikers** Make straight for Santo Antão (three+ days) and Fogo (two to three days). If schedules permit, Brava and São Nicolau are also stunning and Santiago has one or two good hikes in its interior.
- **Watersports enthusiasts** Stick to Sal and Boavista. Boavista is quieter and arguably more beautiful but has fewer facilities.
- **All-round sightseers** Choose one of the flat islands (Maio, Boavista or Sal), one of the two extraordinary landscapes (Fogo or Santo Antão) and a day/evening in either Mindelo (if you're heading to Santo Antão) or Praia's Plateau (if you're heading to Fogo) to sample city life.

TOUR OPERATORS

There are a growing number of tour operators and travel agents who claim to understand Cape Verde but in reality have only a shallow knowledge. More than for other locations it is essential to choose an operator who understands the islands with all their peculiarities.

UK

Archipelago Choice 1b Museum Sq, Keswick, Cumbria CA12 5DZ; 017687 75672 (toll free 1-800-490-0446); e info@archipelagochoice.com; www.capeverdechoice.com. Specialises in tailor-made & activity-focused holidays to all Cape Verde islands. See also ad, colour page 9.

Cape Verde Travel 66 Southgate, Pl, Hornsea, East Yorkshire HU18 1AL; 01964 536191; e sales@capeverdetravel.com; www.capeverdetravel.com. Run by Ron Hughes, who has been offering Cape Verde holidays for well over 20 years & knows every island & every hotel inside out. He has done an enormous amount to promote Cape Verde as a destination & to encourage Cape Verdeans to set up their own tourist businesses. He offers a personal service, tailoring trips to your tastes & offering everything from ticket-only to a full package including activities. Welcomes customers from outside the UK. See ad, page 92.

Ramblers Worldwide Holidays Lemsford Mill, Lemsford Village, Welwyn Garden City, HERTS AL8 7TR; 01707 331133; e info@ramblersholidays. co.uk; www.ramblersholidays.co.uk. Runs organised walking holidays to the islands, as well as cruises combining the archipelago with the Canaries & West Africa.

The Cape Verde Experience 3600 Parkway Solent Business Park, Fareham, Hants PO15 7AN; 0845 330 2047; www.capeverde.co.uk. Part of Serenity Holidays, with 20 years' experience in West Africa.

CAPE VERDE

Alsatour CP 33, Paúl, Santo Antão; +238 223 1213; m +992 5875; e alfred@alsatour.de; www.alsatour.de. Based in Santo Antão for the last 20 years, Alsatour specialises in tailor-made trips including international flights. Particularly good with trekking tours in Santo Antão, inhose to remote areas. English spoken.

CaboVerde No Limits Ponta do Sol, Santo Antão; +238 225 1031; m +238 997

9039; e info@caboverdenolimits.com; www.
caboverdenolimits.com. Spanish- & French-run
operator specialising in adventure activities in
Santo Antão. English spoken.
vista verde tours ☎+238 993 0788;
e office@vista-verde.com; www.vista-verde.
com. Well-established & professional travel
agency specialising in social & environmentally
responsible tourism. Arranges small-group tours or
tailor-made holidays with domestic flights, hotels
& excursions. Offices in Fogo, Sal & São Vicente.
Part of the ONE WORLD tour operator group (*www.
kapverdischeinseln.de/*). See ad, inside back cover.

FRANCE
Nomade Aventure ☎0825 701 702; www.
nomade-aventure.com. A specialist company
which offers walking trips & Carnival visits.
Terres d'Aventure e infos@terdav.com; www.
terdav.com. A large operator of adventure holidays,
specialising in walking trips.

GERMANY
Olimar Reisen Unter Goldschmied 6, 50667
Cologne; ☎+49 221 20 590590; e service.center@
olimar.de; www.olimar.de. A big operator doing
mainly package seaside holidays in Sal. Its holidays
can be booked from Britain with a credit card.
Website has an English language option.
Reiseträume Tennentalstrasse 20, 72461
Albstadt; ☎+49 7432 978151; e kapverden@
reisetraeume.de; www.reisetraeume.de/
kapverden-rundreisen.html; ⏰ 15.00–17.00
Mon–Thu. Gerhard & Sibylle Schellmann live in
Calheta in Santiago & have an office in Germany.
They offer hiking tours around the archipelago,
& specialist tours in Santiago. They also speak
English.
Sun & Fun Sportreisen Franz-Josef-Strasse 43,
D-80801 Munich; ☎+49 8933 8833; e anfrage@
sunandfun.com; www.sunandfun.com. A good bet
for watersports, including diving, in Sal & Boavista.

ONLINE BOOKINGS Flights and accommodation can be booked through websites
such as www.travelsupermarket.com, www.lastminute.com, www.thomson.co.uk
or www.tuifly.com. You might find good prices here for a week or two in the sun,
but if you are planning anything more elaborate or complicated, it is advisable to
use a specialist operator.

RED TAPE

Every non-Cape Verdean visitor needs a visa unless they are married to, or are the
offspring of, a Cape Verdean citizen – in which case they need their marriage or
birth certificate. If there is a Cape Verdean embassy in your country you can obtain
the visa from there. The cost varies from country to country.

In the UK, where there is no embassy, you have two options. Whoever books
your air tickets in the UK will probably be able to arrange the visa for you, to be
picked up at the airport on arrival. This is by far the most common scenario. (For
those on package holidays, the cost of the visa is usually included in the package
cost. You simply have to provide the tour operator with all your details in advance
and you will have no delays on arrival in Cape Verde. Note that if you book a flight-
only through a tour operator, the cost of the visa will *not* be included. You will have
to join the queue at the arrival airport and obtain and pay for your visa there, as
detailed below.) The other option for independent travellers is to arrive without a
visa and just buy one on arrival at the airport in Cape Verde. This costs €25, so is
usually cheaper than the other option and is a straightforward operation. Note that
it is payable in euros, so make sure that you have enough handy to pay for it. You will
generally be given a visa for 30 days as this is the norm, but make sure you ask for
the length of time you need. You can extend your visa at the Direção de Emigrantes
e Fronteras during your stay (you will need a passport photo, occasionally a fair
degree of persistence and to pay around 2,000$) and it is much easier to do this
before your visa expires. They have offices in Praia, Mindelo, Sal and Boavista and

the local police will direct you to the office. Fines are often levied on departure if you have overstayed. Visas bought in advance are normally also valid for 30 days.

You are not usually required to show proof of a return ticket to purchase a visa on arrival or to arrange a visa in the UK, but some other consulates (such as the one in Italy) will insist on it. All passengers have to complete an embarkation form which is handed out on the plane pre-arrival. The visa form itself is available at the arrival airport. If travelling from Italy, your travel agent or tour operator should arrange your visa for you. Check with them whether it is pre-paid or whether you will need to pay on receipt. If you are travelling independently, try the Cape Verdean embassy for a visa (for address, see contact details below). (Note that UK citizens *can* obtain a visa in advance through the Cape Verde consulate in the Netherlands, but this carries the risk of committing your passport to the post.)

Anyone planning to visit Cape Verde from West Africa should if possible get a visa before leaving Europe, as it may add time and complications to get a visa in African capitals. In The Gambia, for example, there is no Cape Verdean representation, so organise a visa before leaving home or fly to Senegal.

For a list of additional contact details for embassies and consulates in Cape Verde other than those listed below, see the website www.visahq.co.uk.

EMBASSIES AND CONSULATES
Cape Verdean Embassies and Consulates Abroad

Ⓔ Austria (consulate) Dornbacher Strasse 89, 1170 Vienna; ☎+43 676 549 9114; e kv@meixner.at; www.kv.meixner.at

Ⓔ Belgium (embassy) Av Jeanne 29, 1050 Brussels; ☎+32 2 643 6270; e emb.caboverde@skynet.be

Ⓔ Brazil SHIS-QL 08 Conj 04, Casa 7, 15 Lago Sul, Brasilia: 71620-285; ☎+55 61 365 3190

Ⓔ Canada (consulate) 802 The Queensway, West Suite 103, Etobicoke, Ontario M8Z 1N5; ☎+1 416 252 1082

Ⓔ France Rue Jouffroy D'Abbans, 80, 75017 Paris; ☎+33 1 42 12 73 50; e ambassade-cap-vert@wanadoo.fr

Ⓔ Germany Stavanger Str 16, 10439 Berlin; ☎+49 30 2045 0955; e info@embassy-capeverde.de; www.embassy-capeverde.de

Ⓔ Italy Viale Giosué Carducci, 4-1° Interno 3, 00187 Rome; ☎+39 06474 4678/4596; e elviofernandes@hotmail.com

Ⓔ Luxembourg 117 Val Ste. Croix, L-1371 Luxembourg; ☎+352 2648 0948; e ambcvlux@pt.lu

Ⓔ Netherlands Baan 6, 3011 CB Rotterdam; ☎+31 10 477 89 77; e cons.cverde-nl@wxs.nl; www.conscv.nl

Ⓔ Portugal Av do Restelo 33, 1400-025 Lisbon; ☎+ 351 213 041 440; e emb.caboverde@netcabo.pt

Ⓔ Russia Rubliovskoe Chaussé, 26 APT 180, Moscow; ☎+7 095 415 4503; e Pts287@ipc.ru

Ⓔ Senegal 3 Bd Djilly M'baye, Immeuble Fahd 13ème étage, Dakar; ☎+221 821 1873; e acvc.sen@metissacana.sn

Ⓔ Spain (consulate) Calle Capitán Haya, 51 Planta 4, Of8, 28020 Madrid; ☎+34 91 570 2568; e con.geral-cv@mad.servicom.es

Ⓔ Sweden (consulate) Tellusvägen 16, 135 47 Tyresö, Stockholm; ☎+46 8 742 2927; e miguel.pinto@telia.com

Ⓔ Switzerland (consulate) Rümelinplatz 14, CH-4001 Basel; ☎+ 41 61 269 8095

Ⓔ USA 3415 Massachusetts Av NW, Washington, DC 20007; ☎+1 202 965 6820; e ambacvus@sysnet.net; www.virtualcapeverde.net

Ⓔ USA (consulate) 607 Boston St. 4th Fl, Boston, MA 02116; ☎+1 617 353 0014; e cgcvbost@aol.com (plus satellite office: University of Massachusetts Dartmouth, 800 Purchase St, Rm 109)

Embassies and Consulates in Cape Verde

Ⓔ Belgium (consulate) Avenida OUA 39, Praia; ☎261 2333

Ⓔ Brazil (embassy) Chã D'Areia Nr 2, Praia; ☎261 5607

Ⓔ Denmark (consulate) CP 12, Mindelo; ☎232 1785

Ⓔ France (embassy) CP 192, 7600, Praia;

260 4535; www.ambafrance-cv.org
ⓔ Germany (consulate) Achada Fazenda, Concelho de Santa Cruz, Praia; 269 2925
ⓔ Italy (consulate) Avenida Santiago 57, Praia; 261 9171
ⓔ Netherlands (consulate) Rua OUA 39, Praia 261 2333
ⓔ Norway (consulate) Chã de Cricket 8, CP 970, Mindelo; 232 3464
ⓔ Portugal (embassy) Avenida OUA, Achada Santo António, Praia; 262 6097
ⓔ Senegal (embassy) Rua Abilio Macedo, Praia; 261 5621
ⓔ Spain (embassy) Rua de Espanha 1, Achada

Sano Antonio, Praia; 260 1800
ⓔ Sweden (consulate) Av Andrade Corvo, Praia; 260 8525
ⓔ Switzerland (consulate) Rotunda de Homem de Pedra, Edificio CV Movel, Praia; 261 9868
ⓔ United Kingdom There is no consular representation, but Sal & Boavista are covered by Honorary Consul Tino Mosso (m 593 7383) & the remaining islands are taken care of by Isabel Spencer (232 3512). Both may be able to provide limited assistance in emergencies.
ⓔ USA (embassy) CP 201, Rua Abilio Macedo 6, Praia; 260 8900; praia.usembassy.gov

GETTING THERE AND AWAY

BY AIR Always bear in mind that the airline industry is a fluid one and the services detailed below may change, sometimes from month to month. There are international airports on Sal, Santiago, Boavista and São Vicente. Most international flights land at Sal; however, there is increasing traffic into the other airports. As internal flights are a little unreliable, it can be an advantage to fly to the airport closest to the island of your holiday destination. For example, travellers making for Santo Antão will have a much shorter onward journey if they fly directly to São Vicente, while those heading for Fogo should choose Santiago.

Scheduled airlines flying to Cape Verde include TAP Portugal, the national carrier TACV, Transavia, Bintercanarias, Air Senegal, Royal Air Maroc and TAAG Angola. TACV has been subject to an enormous amount of disruption and although its safety record is exemplary it cannot be recommended as an international link, because of its unreliability. You should, however, check whether the situation has improved. Charter flights come and go. ThomsonFly, TUIfly, TUI Nordic and Jetair are some of the names that operate many flights to Cape Verde from Europe. Direct flights from Europe range from around six hours, from the north, to three hours from southern countries such as Portugal.

Note that a domestic airpass which gives fixed prices on inter-island flights is available but only to tour operators who book their international flights to Cape Verde with TACV. There is no information about this on the TACV website, so enquiry is best made through your tour operator.

British visitors to Cape Verde are easily the most numerous, but none of the many promises of direct scheduled flights from the UK have materialised. This is perhaps because around 95% of British visitors arrive on package holidays, visiting either Sal or Boavista. The number of charter flights servicing these packages means that the independent traveller may be able to find a 'flight-only' deal with, for example, Thomsonfly (see below). For scheduled flights via Lisbon, you can try TAP. There are also other, more roundabout ways for the British to get to the archipelago, by taking a low-cost flight to a mainstream European or even North African destination and then travelling by a different airline to the archipelago from there. For the onward flight, such options include 'starting' your Cape Verde leg in the Canary Islands (Bintercanarias, *www.bintercanarias.com*), in Amsterdam or Paris (both with Transavia, *www.transavia.com*) or even in Morocco (Royal Air Maroc, *www.royalairmaroc.com*), but these may involve long stopovers, sometimes

2

overnight, and will shorten your time on the islands. Aside from the list below, alternatively you can fly from any UK airport to Lisbon, Germany or Belgium and pick up a charter flight to Sal or Boavista.

There have been a few attempts to set up charter flights from Ireland, with none functioning as this book went for publication. The best connections are via Manchester, Birmingham, Gatwick or Lisbon.

From the UK

✈ **TACV** www.flytacv.com. No direct flights from the UK, but you can connect with TACV by flying to another European city, such as Lisbon, Paris or Amsterdam. As yet, you cannot book directly through the airline in the UK or online, but instead through a tour operator, such as Cape Verde Travel or Archipelago Choice (see page 54).

✈ **TAP Portugal** www.flytap.com. Flights from London, via Lisbon, to either Sal, Praia or São Vicente.

✈ **Thomsonfly** www.thomsonfly.co.uk. Depending on the season, flights are either weekly & twice-weekly from Manchester, Birmingham & Gatwick to Sal & Boavista. Geared towards those who book packages with the company, though it is possible to book a standalone flight. It can sometimes be cheaper to book a package but use only the flight

From Italy

✈ **Neos Air** Via della Chiesa 68, 21019 Somma Lombardo (Varese); e linea@neosair.it; www.neosair.it/en. Flies from Milan Malpensa, Verona & Rome Fiumicino to Sal & Boavista. The charter flights can also be booked through Cabo Verde Time (Via Stretta 28, 25128, Brescia; ☎030 370 0167; www.caboverdetime.it).

✈ **TACV** Flights available from Bergamo to Sal; see details above.

From the rest of Europe

✈ **TACV** The national carrier has reduced its flights from Europe in recent years, but still flies direct from France (Paris), the Netherlands (Amsterdam), Italy (Bergamo), Portugal (Lisbon) & Spain (Madrid).

✈ **Jetair** www.jetairfly.com. Flights from Brussels to Sal & Boavista.

✈ **TAP Portugal** www.flytap.com. Connects most major European cities with Lisbon for the daily onward flight to Cape Verde (Sal or Santiago). Also flies directly from Lisbon to São Vicente twice-weekly.

✈ **TUIfly** www.tuifly.com. Flights to Sal & Boavista from 7 German cities, as well as from Basel in Switzerland.

✈ **TUIfly Nordic** www.tuiflynordic.se. Winter seasonal flights from Scandinavian countries to Sal & Boavista.

From North America

Some visitors from North America fly to a European capital and from there to Cape Verde.

✈ **Cape Verde Travel** For contact details, see page 54. Books flights from North America to Cape Verde. See also ad, page 92.

✈ **Neves Travel** 1545 Acushnet Av, New Bedford, MA 02746; ☎508 996 1332; e info@nevestravel.com; www.nevestravel.com. Many years of experience arranging flights & holidays to Cape Verde.

✈ **Sun Travel** 598 Warren Av, East Providence, RI 10914; ☎401 434 7333. Experienced at getting people to & from Cape Verde on any available airlines, including occasional charters at competitive prices.

✈ **TACV** Flies between Boston & Praia.

✈ **TAP Portugal** Flights from New York & Boston to Lisbon, from where you can connect to Cape Verde.

From Africa

✈ **Senegal Airlines** www.senegalairlines.aero. Flights to Praia from Dakar in Senegal with links to Brussels & several African destinations including Bissau in Guinea-Bissau, & Banjul in The Gambia.

✈ **TAAG Angola** www.taag.com. Flies between Luanda & Praia.

✈ **TACV** Operates flights to/from Senegal (Dakar), from Praia.

✈ **Royal Air Maroc** www.royalairmaroc.com. Flies from Casablanca to Praia.

From the Canary Islands

✈ **Bintercanarias** www.bintercanarias.com. Operates twice-weekly flights from Gran Canaria to Praia.

From South America

✈ **TACV** Flies from Praia to the Brazilian city of Fortaleza, on the northeast coast of Brazil, currently once per week.

BY SEA

By ships and cruise Arriving by sea and watching the Atlantic crags materialise from the ocean is an unusual and uplifting way of reaching the islands. Some ships stay for 48 hours, which is plenty of time in which to get across from Mindelo to see the highlights of Santo Antão. An increasing number of cruises are stopping in Cape Verde, mostly in Mindelo. These include **Cunard** (⊙ *0845 678 0013; www. cunard.co.uk*), **P&O** (⊙ *0845 678 0014; www.pocruises.com*), and **Celebrity Cruises** (⊙ *0844 493 2043; www.celebritycruises.co.uk*). Smaller cruise ships, such as the *Marco Polo*, sometimes go to Fogo. **Noble Caledonia** (*www.noble-caledonia.co.uk*) are now offering cruises which involve 'island-hopping' tours to seven islands in the archipelago. For information about passage on a cargo ship to Cape Verde try the following:

🚢 **Arca Verde** CP 153, Rua Senador Vera-Cruz, Mindelo, São Vicente; ☎ 232 1349

🚢 **Atlantic Shipping** Cape Cod, MA 0230; ☎ 508 672 1870. Sometimes offers sailings from the US to Cape Verde.

🚢 **Strand Voyages** 1 Adam St, London WC2N 6AB; ☎ 020 7953 7607; e voyages@strandtravelltd. co.uk; www.strandtravel.co.uk. Very occasionally will have cargo boats that call in at the islands.

By yacht Cape Verde is becoming better known to yachts on the Atlantic run: numbers are increasing, and it is not uncommon to see 20 boats at anchor in Mindelo harbour, a few at Palmeira on Sal and Sal Rei on Boavista, and one or two more dotting bays around the archipelago. One big draw is that pausing in Cape Verde, rather than the Canaries, can reduce the longest leg of the Atlantic crossing by a week.

There are three good harbours and these are on the best-resourced islands (Sal, São Vicente and Santiago). The other islands all have reasonable anchorages, some of them quite beautiful, but at some the safety or comfort depends on the weather.

Cape Verde is short on spares and repair skills compared with ports in the Azores or the Canaries. Boat repair facilities are limited: the best and only real maintenance and spares point is Mindelo. This has lifts for quite large craft and a tradition of woodworking and boatbuilding. There is a chandlery in the new marina in Mindelo with a lot of high-tech equipment for crossing the Atlantic. There is a new marina planned in Praia, due to be completed in 2014.

Food is expensive because it is imported, and it can sometimes be hard to find fresh meat and vegetables. Water and diesel are available on the jetty in Mindelo, but otherwise it can be a case of making journeys to the tap. Water is scarce on Cape Verde and much of it comes from desalinisation plants. Consumption is high in this warm climate so you need to plan your route with care unless you have a water-maker.

You do not need a visa unless you are planning to sleep onshore, or to stay for longer than three months. You must enter and clear at every island you visit.

In the island chapters, brief information is given as to anchorages and facilities. However, the approaches to many of the islands are tricky and it is best to consult the excellent *Atlantic Islands: Azores, Madeira, Canary and Cape Verde Islands* (see *Appendix 2, Further information*, page 352). The most detailed charts are pre-1975 Portuguese; there are also British Admiralty charts but these have errors, sometimes dangerous ones. The British Admiralty Africa Pilot has lots of useful information about weather, sea conditions and currents. All these can be obtained from Hammick and Heath's aforementioned guide.

HEALTH *with Dr Felicity Nicholson*

Cape Verde does not suffer from many of the diseases that are a menace in mainland Africa. There is a limited incidence of malaria and dengue fever – and polio, diphtheria and measles have successfully been combated. With increased immigration from West Africa there have been incidences of yellow fever and hepatitis A and B. Food-borne diseases, from diarrhoea to cholera, are common though, and for the tourist, accidents are a threat. The islands have a good number of doctors, trained overseas.

PREPARATION

Travel insurance Cape Verde's tourism is developing faster than its infrastructure. There are hospitals on São Vicente and Santiago, and there are private medical clinics on Sal and São Vicente, but bear in mind that if you are taken seriously ill elsewhere, the correct treatment may be hard to find as facilities on the less-developed islands are more limited. That's why it's important to take out comprehensive travel insurance.

American travellers should remember that US medical insurance is not always valid outside their country. The Medicare/Medicaid programme does not provide payment for medical services outside the United States. You may need to take out supplementary medical insurance with specific overseas and medical evacuation coverage.

Cape Verde does not have an operating hyperbaric chamber, so divers should take out proper diving insurance, which will include being flown at low altitude to Europe for treatment for the bends.

Immunisations There are no compulsory vaccinations except that if you are going to Cape Verde from countries with a risk of yellow fever transmission then you must carry a yellow fever vaccination certificate. If there are specific contraindications to having the vaccine then a yellow fever exemption certificate should be acquired from a qualified medical professional. Several weeks – or, to be on the safe side, two months – before you go make sure you are up to date with the following: tetanus (ten-yearly), polio (ten-yearly), diphtheria (ten-yearly) which comes as an all in one vaccination (Revaxis). Some countries (eg: Australia and the US) will also cover pertussis (whooping cough). This is not routinely done in the UK for adults but can be obtained on request from some travel clinics. Typhoid and hepatitis A are routinely recommended for most travellers. Hepatitis B vaccinations would be recommended for backpackers or those who will be in close contact with the local population. One dose of hepatitis A vaccine (eg: Havrix Mondose, Avaxim) gives protection for up to one year and can be given even close to the time of departure. A booster dose given at least six months after the first dose provides protection for up at least 20 years, so is well worth having. Consult your doctor before you go, as it may be necessary to have an exemption certificate if the vaccine is deemed unsuitable.

Typhoid vaccine (Typhim Vi) is about 75% effective and lasts for three years. It is recommended unless you are travelling at short notice for a week or less, when the vaccine would have insufficient time to be effective. Oral typhoid vaccine (Vivotif) is a viable alternative for those aged six or more, and who are not immunosuppressed. It provides a similar degree of coverage to the injectable vaccines provided it is taken correctly. Three tablets are taken over five days, and the vaccine is then effective from seven days after that.

Hepatitis B vaccination should be considered by anyone working within a medical setting or with children. It is also recommended for stays longer than four to six weeks. A course of three doses of the vaccine is ideal and can be taken over as little as 21 days (Engerix) for those aged 16 or over. Longer courses provided more sustained protection and must be used in those under 16.

There is no rabies in terrestrial animals in the Cape Verde Islands, but there may be bat rabies. Pre-exposure vaccination is therefore not routinely recommended. However, exposure to bat saliva or neural tissue is considered a potential risk and so advice should be sought as soon as possible.

Immunisation against cholera is not required unless specific outbreaks are reported. There is now an effective oral vaccine (Dukoral) available in the UK. Two doses of vaccine should be taken at least one week apart and at least one week before entry for those over six years of age. At the time of writing, however, there are no specific concerns in Cape Verde. Your family doctor or a commercial travel clinic (see below) can tell you if this list has changed recently.

In the UK the majority of GP practices can provide hepatitis A, typhoid and Revaxis on the NHS. However, it may not always be easy to get an appointment unless you book well in advance. Hepatitis B is not routinely provided free of charge, and if you need a yellow fever vaccine then the surgery must be a designated yellow fever centre. Commercial travel clinics are all registered centres and are able to offer a faster service, particularly when time is short.

Malaria All the islands except Santiago and Boavista are free from malaria, and Santiago and Boavista suffer only from August to November. The current advice is not to take any prophylaxis, but if a fever develops at least seven days into the trip and at least six months on return, it should be investigated promptly.

Dengue fever The year 2009 saw the first cases of dengue fever in Cape Verde following the heavy rains in August and September of that year. Some cases proved to be fatal. The main islands affected were those with the most rainwater, and thus most vegetation – Santiago, Fogo and Brava. There were fewer cases in 2010. There is no immunisation for dengue, so prevention of mosquito bites is the only answer. The mosquitoes that carry dengue fever fly in the day time so remember to use your DEET-based repellents (ideally 50–55%) during the day as well as the evening.

Medical kit Pharmacies are widespread and well stocked but, just in case, bring a small medical kit containing soluble aspirin or paracetamol (good for gargling when you have a sore throat and for reducing fever and pains), plasters, antiseptic, insect repellent and suncream. Many travellers are reassured by investing in a blood transfusion kit, which contains sterile equipment such as needles for use during surgery. Some travel clinics will try to persuade you to take antibiotics but there is no need as doctors' prescriptions and the drugs themselves are readily available. Self-medication should only be a last resort.

Travel clinics and health information A full list of current travel clinic websites worldwide is available on www.istm.org. For other journey preparation information, consult www.nathnac.org/ds/map_world.aspx (UK) or http://wwwnc. cdc.gov/travel/ (US). Information about various medications may be found on www.netdoctor.co.uk/travel. All advice found online should be used in conjunction with expert advice received prior to or during travel.

COMMON MEDICAL PROBLEMS

Travellers' diarrhoea This afflicts half of all visitors to the developing world and can ruin a short holiday. The bacteria are borne on traces of faeces which get into food sometime between when it is growing in the soil and when it arrives at the table. If you are scrupulous you should be able to keep the bacteria from reaching your mouth. Only eat freshly cooked food or peeled raw fruit and vegetables. In particular avoid unpeelable raw food such as lettuce or cabbage and avoid raw seafood. Steer away from fruit juice, unless it is from a sealed bottle, and ice cream – again unless it is a recognised branded carton. Avoid the local water including ice cubes. Tea and coffee should be fine, simply because bringing water to the boil kills 99% of bacteria. Wash your hands after going to the toilet.

If you do fall ill then you should rest, stop eating your normal diet, avoid alcohol and take lots of clear fluids. If you are hungry then eat bland food such as biscuits and boiled rice or potatoes. The idea is to avoid stomach cramps caused by the belly trying to expel food. It is dehydration that makes you feel rotten during a bout of diarrhoea, and dehydration is also the principal danger, so it is of paramount importance to drink plenty of fluid. Sachets of oral rehydration salts such as Dioralyte, Electrolade or Rehidrat give the perfect biochemical mix – so put some in your medical kit. You can make your own such drink with eight teaspoons of sugar, one teaspoon of salt and one litre of safe water. A squeeze of lemon or orange juice improves the taste and adds another vital ingredient: potassium. You can create an approximation to this wonder-drink with flat Coca-Cola and a pinch of salt. Drink two large glasses after every bowel action and more if you are thirsty. If you are not eating you need to drink three litres every day plus enough fluid to compensate for what you are losing through diarrhoea.

Diarrhoea blockers such as Imodium, Lomotil and codeine phosphate are not a treatment and should be avoided: your body is trying to expel poisons, not lock them in. However, it may be necessary to use them if, for example, you are facing long bus rides. If the diarrhoea lasts more than 36 hours you may need antibiotics. Some travellers like to take a dose of ciprofloxacin (one 500mg tablet with a second dose 10–12 hours later works in about 80% of cases). If you are passing blood or slime or have a fever with your diarrhoea you must seek medical advice as soon as you can. If you cannot reach help within 12 hours and you are carrying ciprofloxacin (or norfloxacin or arthyromycin) then you may decide to start treatment whilst still making your way to medical help.

Giardiasis is prevalent on Cape Verde. It can take about ten days to incubate. Stools are loose, greasy and sometimes watery; there can be pains in the upper abdomen, and sulphurous belches from both ends. If you suspect you have it, seek help. The earlier treatment is acquired, the less likely it is to become dormant in your body, only to return from time to time.

Skin infections Any insect bite or cut gives bacteria the opportunity to foil the skin's usually strong defences. Skin infections start quickly in warm and humid climates so they are not such a problem in Cape Verde. Creams do not keep the wound dry so they are not as effective as a drying antiseptic such as Savlon dry, or any other similar product which dries on the skin. If the wound starts to throb, if it becomes red and the redness begins to spread, or if the wound oozes then you may need antibiotics and should seek a doctor. Fungal infections take hold easily in moist parts of the body so wear cotton socks and underwear and shower frequently, drying thoroughly. An itchy and often flaking rash in the groin or between the toes is likely to be a fungus and will require treatment with a cream such as Canesten (clotrimazole). If this is not available then try Whitfield's ointment (compound benzoic acid ointment) or crystal violet.

Insects and parasites

Insect bites There is a slight risk of malaria on Santiago Island, so it is worth protecting yourself against mosquito bites between dusk and dawn by covering up with trousers, a long-sleeved shirt and applying insect repellent containing the chemical DEET (50–55% is the optimum strength). Ideally you should sleep under a mosquito net. Cape Verde's waterless climate keeps insects down but they pop up all year round in odd places where there is stagnant water.

Tumbu flies or putsi The adult fly lays her eggs on soil or drying laundry. When those eggs come into contact with human flesh (when you put on your clothes or lie on a bed) they hatch and bury themselves under the skin. There they form a crop of boils, each of which hatches a grub after about eight days. Once they are hatched the inflammation will die down. Avoid putsi by drying clothes and sheets within a screened house or by drying them in direct sunshine until they are crisp or by ironing them.

Jiggers or sandfleas These bury into bare feet and set up home under the skin of the foot, usually at the side of a toenail where they cause a painful, boil-like swelling. A local expert must pick them out. If the distended flea bursts during eviction the wound should be doused in spirit, alcohol or kerosene to avoid more jiggers infesting you.

Ticks There are several nasty, tick-borne diseases, such as typhus. Avoid ticks by wearing long clothes and repellent, especially if walking takes you into scrubby countryside where you are brushing through vegetation.

Remove any tick as soon as you notice it – it will most likely be firmly attached to somewhere you would rather it was not – grasp the tick as close to your body as possible and pull steadily and firmly away at right angles to your skin. The tick will then come away complete as long as you do not jerk or twist. If possible douse the wound with alcohol (any spirit will do) or iodine. Spreading redness around the bite and/or fever and/or aching joints after a tick bite imply that you have an infection which requires antibiotic treatment, so seek advice. Do not try to burn the tick off or use other irritants such as Olbas oil, this will only encourage the tick to regurgitate its mouth contents. Tick tweezers are easy to use and relatively cheap, so worth carrying with you.

Heat and sun

Dehydration It is easy to get dehydrated, especially in the first week. If you wake up in the morning feeling nauseous and tired that may be the reason. Water requirements depend on temperature, humidity, amount of exercise taken, and the length of time the person has been in the country. Those who get into trouble are people who do not allow themselves to acclimatise, a process that takes up to two weeks. Eager adolescents are particularly vulnerable. In the tropics you need to drink about three litres a day, more if you are exercising. Take it easy for the first week. In Cape Verde it is very likely you could end up on a long, hot and shadeless hike for a day. In those conditions you will need to have drunk five litres by the end of the day to avoid dehydration. If you are going on a day's hike drink plenty before you go, try to carry two litres per person, and fill up again in the evening.

Prickly heat A fine pimply rash on the trunk of the body is likely to be heat rash. Take cool showers and dab (do not rub) yourself dry, finishing off with a sprinkling of talc. If the rash doesn't improve it may be necessary to check into an air-conditioned room for a while, slow down, wear only loose, cotton clothes and sleep naked under a fan.

Sunburn Cape Verde is notoriously lacking in shade so you must bring your own in the form of a broad-brimmed hat, umbrella, or even a windbreak for a day on the beach. The best solution is to cover up: a light-coloured, loose cotton shirt and long skirt or trousers is also cooler than shorts and a T-shirt. Many visitors don't notice the sun burning them because of the cooling effect of the wind. Try and keep out of the sun between noon and 15.00 and, if you must expose yourself, build up gradually from 20 minutes per day. Be particularly careful of sun reflected from water and wear a T-shirt and plenty of waterproof suncream which provides cover for both UVA and UVB (at least a factor 20) when snorkelling or swimming. Tanning ages your skin and can give you skin cancer.

Heat exhaustion and heat stroke Heat exhaustion develops gradually, caused by loss of salt and water through excessive sweating. It is most common in people new to the heat or new to exercise in the heat and in people who have recently had an illness in which they lost fluids (diarrhoea or vomiting). Sufferers have fast shallow breathing and a rapid weak pulse. They may feel dizzy and sick, be pale and sweating, have a headache and have cramps in the limbs and abdomen. Sit or lie the casualty down in a cool place, raise and support the legs to allow blood to flow to the brain. Give plenty of water.

Heat stroke is less common and is most likely to happen as a result of prolonged exposure to very hot surroundings. Symptoms include confusion, swiftly deteriorating to unconsciousness, a strong pulse and slow, deep breathing. The sufferer's skin will be hot, flushed and their temperature will be over 40°C. The essential thing is to cool the person quickly – do this by moving them to a cool place, removing their outer clothing, wrapping them in a cold, wet sheet and fanning them. Call for a doctor immediately.

SERIOUS ILLNESSES

AIDS Although Cape Verde has a low rate of HIV/AIDS, it faces a number of serious challenges to keep it that way. First of all, there is a liberal attitude towards sex and promiscuity, which, at least amongst men, is common. Secondly, the construction boom on the more tourist-orientated islands and especially Boavista has brought an influx of mainland Africans, many of whom have not returned home despite the end of the boom. With them came an increase in AIDS. With the demise of the boom, poverty has led to an increase in prostitution. Sadly, sex tourism is not unknown. Thirdly, Cape Verde has an unusually young population. About 40% of HIV infections in British people are acquired abroad. Bring condoms or femidoms with you. If you notice any genital ulcers or discharge get them treated promptly. The presence of a sexually transmitted disease increases the chance of contracting AIDS.

Cholera This arises sporadically in Cape Verde and in 1995 killed 240 people and sickened 13,000. Avoid it through the precautions described under *Travellers' diarrhoea*, page 62. However, it is very unlikely to affect visitors. The severe form of cholera, which almost never hits travellers, is sudden and copious diarrhoea without any pain, very watery with white flecks in it. There is vomiting but usually no fever. Rehydration is vital – up to 20 litres a day in serious cases. Seek immediate help.

Typhoid Symptoms are fever, headache, loss of appetite, abdominal pain and sometimes pink spots on the skin. The heart rate may slow. Seek immediate help.

Elephantiasis Also known as filariasis, this is spread by mosquitoes and causes massive inflammation of the leg in long-standing sufferers: another reason to avoid insect bites between dusk and dawn.

Trachoma This is a disease of the very poor and not something that travellers get. However, in trachoma-affected countries the risk of travellers contracting ordinary conjunctivitis increases – so a course of antibiotic eye-drops might be useful in your medical kit.

ACCIDENTS Hospitals on the smaller islands can do little and have to evacuate you to São Vicente or Santiago, even for the resetting of a broken leg. The hospital on São Vicente is the best. The inter-island planes always reserve space for medical emergencies.

Vehicles Vehicle accidents – not exotic diseases – are often the biggest killers of visitors to Africa. Cape Verde vehicles are in better condition than those on mainland Africa and many drivers are careful of their investments. Cobbled surfaces and hidden speed bumps conspire to keep vehicle speeds down. But the roads are vertiginous and damage caused by rains is not always repaired in any great hurry – there is plenty of scope for 100m cliff plunges. Make sure your driver has not been drinking alcohol and try not to travel along precarious roads at night, as speed bumps and pot-holes are difficult to spot.

Swimming Swimming accidents are the other danger. The blue waters may be seductive but they are also the wild mid-ocean, abounding with hidden reefs, strange currents and hungry wildlife. The golden rule is to watch what the local people are doing and to ask whether it is safe to bathe (*Não é perigoso tomar banho?* – 'It's not dangerous to take a dip?'), and don't dive from boats that are far from the shore, or you could end up getting nibbled by a shark. In the shallows a pair of plimsolls will protect against coral, urchins and venomous fish spines. The trick after being stung by a venomous fish is to denature the poison by heating it – so stick your foot in a bucket of hot water until sometime after the pain subsides – perhaps 20–30 minutes overall. If the pain returns, immerse the foot again. Then ask a doctor to check for fish spines in the wound.

Hiking Much of the classic walking on Cape Verde is through populated areas or at least on paths trodden regularly each day by local people, but some hikes are so deserted you will meet no-one. On Santo Antão in particular, once off the beaten track it is dangerous, with scree, gullies and landslides and no sign of water or food. It can be easy to leave the path in some of the Santo Antão *ribeiras*, particularly the many tributaries of Ribeira Grande, in which case you could get stuck on a path that has dwindled to a crevice, unable to descend without sliding along the rubble and unable to ascend because there are no footholds – and with the mist approaching. The really remote region is the west of Santo Antão where only experienced hikers should go.

Walking accidents are not uncommon. Cape Verdean terrain – hard, bone-dry soil sprinkled with tiny, rolling bits of grit – can be slippery even for those in good walking boots and even when it is flat. Sometimes you must watch each step, placing the foot on any available vegetation, stone or clear ground and avoiding the mini landslides waiting in the middle of the path. If you break a bone insist on having it set by a qualified doctor rather than a nurse, or you could end up needing it reset later.

If you go hiking don't forget the basic principles: it is essential to wear walking boots with ankle support; plan your route before you set off so that you know which villages to ask for along the way; tell someone who might care where you are going and when you are expecting to be back; drink plenty of water before you go and take two litres of water for a full day away (this assumes you can stock up beforehand and replenish in the evening); bring food – assume you will not find any on the way; take a whistle, as well as a compass or GPS (if you know how to use these tools!); and protect yourself from the sun.

For walks in the Fogo crater and on Santo Antão's peaks take a jumper – it can get cold. Cuts and grazes can be avoided by wearing long trousers.

Animal bites The only mammals to watch out for on Cape Verde are village dogs, cats and monkeys. Dogs are everywhere, sleeping, roaming the streets or engaging in cacophonous barking matches when everyone else is trying to sleep. Some people keep monkeys as guards or pets on long stretches of rope. They are accustomed to being fed and may bite. Terrestrial mammals on Cape Verde are classified as no risk of rabies (WHO, CDC, Nathnac); however, bats may carry rabies and should be considered to do so. Bat bites can be very tiny so if you wake with a bat in your room consider that you have been exposed. Another good reason to sleep under a mosquito net if you are not in an air-conditioned room.

Animal bites do however pose a risk from a whole host of other of bacteria, which can infect the wound. This includes tetanus, which can also be caught from soil getting into wounds. Make sure your immunisation is up to date and clean wounds thoroughly. If you see any signs of spreading redness or pus then seek medical help as soon as possible.

SAFETY

CRIME Although Cape Verde remains a peaceful and safe place with a very low incidence of crime, theft has increased as a direct consequence of tourism. Sensible precautions should of course be taken, but in this respect Cape Verde is no different from anywhere else in the world: carelessness and lack of common sense can bring crime upon visitors – though that does not of course lessen the culpability of the perpetrators. Theft is most common in Mindelo and Praia, as well as at isolated spots on Sal. In Mindelo, tourists can occasionally fall victim to gangs of bag-snatchers, and aggressive begging and pickpocketing are not uncommon, occurring mostly on the waterfront and on the Amílcar Cabral Square (children may follow you until you retreat into a hotel, asking for money but also trying to take it from your pocket). In Praia the speciality theft venue is Sucupira Market, a crowded place and a pickpocket's paradise, but people have had valuables such as laptops snatched from other places in the city. Be particularly careful if using your prized computer in the town squares, where Wi-Fi is often free. In Sal it is Buracona, on the west coast, where the theme is to hide behind a rock and break into cars once their drivers have gone for a walk. In Boavista, in isolated spots, there is an increasing amount of violent crime against tourists. Other islands remain virtually crime-free. In the less populous islands, where everyone knows everyone, the perpetrators are also likely to be known to the police and the locals: this is a massive deterrent in itself.

Recently Cape Verde has had to start to grapple with drug-related crime. Drugs are entering the country as drug-smuggling routes change (see page 36) and it is also said that tourism has increased the problem. A third cause is the US's deportation of criminals with Cape Verdean ancestry back to Cape Verde.

Follow the usual rules. Carry a purse in an inside pocket; when paying, don't open a purse stacked with cash. Keep valuables hidden in money belts, or leave them in the hotel safe where possible. If you are a victim, make a fuss so that people come to your aid. Carrying a whistle on a loose, breakable cord around your neck is also worth considering. Also, it is irresponsible not to report any incident of crime or attempted crime to the police, who are striving to fight crime (also, if you are to claim on your travel insurance you must have a police report).

To sum up, the vast majority of Cape Verdeans you will meet will be scrupulously honest and crime should be no more of a problem than if you were still at home. As a visitor, you are slightly more vulnerable to being targeted by the tiny minority of people with a criminal propensity – a minority which can be found anywhere in the world.

HIKING SAFETY Some of the joys in Cape Verde are the cobbled paths in the mountains, making some walks easier both underfoot and navigationally than they might appear. Nevertheless there are hazards. Dehydration and sunstroke are two: shade is sparse and, on some islands, non-existent, while water sources are scarce.

Another is falls: where the paths are not cobbled they can be shingly, with small loose stones, and it is easy to tumble on the way down. The west of Santo Antão has its own special dangers born of remoteness (see *Chapter 10, Santo Antão*, page 287). Take the usual precautions: strong boots, several litres of water per person, sun protection, a map, and a message left at your hotel about where you've gone.

FOCUS ON SPECIFIC GROUPS

WOMEN TRAVELLERS Females can travel a lot on their own in Cape Verde and never feel threatened, although they might regularly feel mildly irritated. Cape Verdean men will flirt outrageously, as they do with their own Cape Verdean womenfolk. If you're older there's less attention but always a few die-hard admirers hoping to become toy boys. The casual mention of a husband back in town makes most men lose interest pretty swiftly. However, if you reveal that you are childless – whether married, with a partner or single – you will attract huge sympathy, mystification and interest. You will have plenty of offers from potential fathers. If you go to a man's home, or invite him back to your place, he will expect to have sex even if you tell him it is not on the agenda.

Women who stay for a long time in one place – for example volunteers – can have more serious problems (see page 87).

OLDER TRAVELLERS Increasing numbers of older people are holidaying in Cape Verde, and it poses no particular problems for them. There are a few caveats, though. The elderly may find the undulations of steep islands a little hard – there are one or two hotels that can be accessed only by foot up steep paths but these are indicated in the text. Make sure you understand about the distribution of medical facilities: if you keel over anywhere other than Sal, Santiago or São Vicente it will be a ferry journey or a plane ride to the nearest hospital. Most sights are accessible by car, but do bear in mind, if you are in need of a fairly sedentary holiday, that there are not many cultural 'sights' to go and see – just a tiny sprinkling of museums. Travel insurance can be purchased in the UK from Age UK (\ *0845 600 3348*; *www. ageuk.org.uk*) or Free Spirit (\ *0845 230 5000*; *www.freespirittravelinsurance.com*), neither of which has an upper age limit.

FAMILIES Cape Verde is increasingly attractive to families as beach tourism develops. Choose your hotel carefully though: some hotels are built in front of stretches of water in which it is not safe to bathe. Some of the resort hotels on Sal have dedicated children's facilities, such as playground, swimming pool and even activities, but outside of the all-inclusive complexes there are few ready-made, children-orientated facilities. Many hotels are not near the water and the beaches have no shade. If a beach holiday was not what you had in mind, it's perhaps best only to take children if they are old enough to enjoy activities such as windsurfing or hiking.

DISABLED TRAVELLERS As far as we know there are no operators running specialised trips to Cape Verde for disabled people. It would be best to contact a specialist who really knows the islands you want to visit, knows the hoteliers personally and is interested in your quest: they can take the time to craft a journey for you. A good one, if you are visiting several islands, is Cape Verde Travel (see page 54).

The local minibuses are generally very crowded and hard to climb into. There are plenty of taxis in the capitals (Mindelo and Praia). In other towns the taxis may take the form of minibuses or 4x4s which may be even harder to get into. For journeys by car discomfort is reduced by the fact that there are no great distances to cover anywhere in Cape Verde but most of the roads are cobbled, which can be bumpy. Some, non-cobbled, non-tarred roads can be pot-holed and uncomfortable (for example off the principal roads in Santiago, crossing the deserts in Boavista). It is best to take advice beforehand.

Because many trails, particularly in Santo Antão, are cobbled almost all the way, it is just conceivable that a disabled person in a tailored wheelchair could travel on them. One person who achieved this is Jean François Porret and his account of his experience, with some inspiring photographs, is at www.bela-vista.net/Wheelchair. aspx. Travel insurance for those with medical conditions can be purchased in the UK from Free Spirit (\ 0845 230 5000; *www.freespirittravelinsurance.com*). Most insurance companies will insure disabled travellers, but it is essential that they are made fully aware of your disability.

Although the vast majority of people will only want to help you, it is worth remembering that, as a disabled person, you are more vulnerable. Stay aware of who is around you and where your bags are, especially in Mindelo and Praia where bag-snatching is on the increase.

WHAT TO TAKE

Clothing is overwhelmingly casual, though you might want to be smarter for the top restaurants. A sweater is necessary because evenings can be slightly chilly in the cooler seasons, and are always chilly higher up, for example in Rui Vaz in Santiago, or in Fogo's crater. Take walking boots if you are planning to hike.

Even the cheapest *pensão* is likely to provide towels, loo paper, soap and a basin plug. Those using a homestay might sometimes be thankful they brought a sheet sleeping bag and a pair of flip-flops for washing in. For overnight boat trips, which you may spend on deck, you must have a sleeping bag for warmth. The main towns – Santa Maria, Praia, Mindelo – should sell all other basics, including tampons (not necessarily with applicator), hair conditioner, razors, camera film, Imodium and painkillers.

Take suncream – expensive and not so easy to find – and a sunhat. Take insect repellent because there are biters about in the evenings. Although there are few mosquitoes there seems to be an average of one such pest resident in every hotel bedroom, regardless of quality. A few hotels have mosquito nets but if it's very important to you not to be bitten, either take a net, a 'plug-in' repellent available from travel shops, or buy some killer spray on arrival.

Cape Verde struggles with its electricity supply. Some hotels have generators but many hotels of an otherwise good standard do not. Take a torch and consider getting hold of a candle and lighter (remember, this latter item is prohibited in aircraft cabin baggage). Power cuts are far from unknown. The electricity supply is 220V 50Hz, which is standard in western Europe. The plug is a standard European two-pin type so a converter is necessary.

A Portuguese dictionary would be useful. Bring your own reading matter – there is little available in English in Cape Verde. Some hotels have a book-swap scheme. Sal is full of British expats desperate to see a copy of a recent newspaper or magazine from back home. Biros are useful presents for children (but see page 82 for cautions about begging). An ordinary driving licence suffices for car hire.

If you are happy to travel light with only hand luggage you will have the great advantage of whistling through airports much faster than everyone else.

MAPS Most of the best maps of the archipelago and of the individual islands are published by German publishers, particularly AB Kartenverlag and Freytag-Berndt, as well as by ITMB, and are normally available from specialist bookshops such as Stanfords (*www.stanfords.co.uk*) or The Map Shop in Upton-upon-Severn (*www.themapshop.co.uk*) and also from the website www.atlantic-islands.com. AB Kartenverlag's individual island maps, with multilingual legend, include hiking trails. As well as the maps listed below, you may also find copies of out-of-print maps to other islands at the above outlets.

Cabo Verde 1:150,000 tourist map published by Kartenverlag. Cost: €8.80

Santo Antão Hiking map 1:50,000, AB Kartenverlag; €14.80

Fogo & Brava Hiking Map 1:50,000, AB Kartenverlag; €14.80

São Nicolau Hiking Map 1:50,000, Goldstadt €14.80

Santiago Hiking Map 1:50,000, AB Karten verlag €15.80

Boa Vista, Sal, Maio Hiking Map AB Kartenverlag 1:50,000; €12.80

MONEY

The **currency** is the escudo, represented by the $ sign at the end of the number, or by the letters CVE. The escudo is officially set to a fixed exchange rate with the euro, currently €1=110$. In practice, banks and exchange bureaux/*cambios* vary the rates slightly. Rates are also varied by hotels charging in local currency. Note that Cape Verde escudos cannot be taken into or out of the country, so plan accordingly. You will not be able to buy them before departure, nor change any excess escudos after you return home. The euro is increasingly accepted in day-to-day transactions on Sal and Boavista, where prices are often quoted in that currency. This is less prevalent on other islands.

Credit cards are accepted only by some upmarket hotels – it is best to assume that hotels, restaurants and ATMs will not accept them. Visa cards can be used to withdraw funds at Banco Comercial do Atlântico for a minimum charge of 1,000$ with other charges of 0.5% of the amount withdrawn. Rates seem to vary throughout the different islands. **ATMs** can be found at the major banks (BCA, BCN and to a slightly lesser extent, Caixa Economica amongst others) in nearly all island towns and their frequency is increasing. Those on less-frequented islands are occasionally out of operation, but reliability is improving. ATMs display the Visa, Mastercard, Cirrus and Maestro symbols. Each withdrawal from an ATM incurs a transaction charge, typically of between €2–4.

Travellers' cheques are a safe way to carry money around and many of the eight banks will cash them. For many visitors, however, they are a thing of the past, replaced by sensible use of ATMs and credit cards, where accepted. If using travellers' cheques, check the details of fees beforehand because some individual branches make onerous charges – a charge of 1,000$ is normal. (Note also that when you change travellers' cheques, if they are not consecutive numbers, you may have to pay a separate fee for each 'break' in the series.) **Money transfers** can be done very quickly through Western Union to the Caixa Económica and most other banks. High-street banks in the UK will transfer funds to Cape Verdean banks urgently (within two or three days) for a fee of about £20–25.

Given the wide availability of ATMs on Cape Verde, and despite the transaction charges for withdrawals, it's best to arrive with a reasonable amount in euros to buy your visa (if required) and cover the first few days expenditure and then use the ATMs when required to obtain escudos. Although crime rates are not high, it is foolish to arrive with *all* your trip money in cash and carry it around for the duration of your stay. Irrespective of low crime rates, if nothing else, you could simply lose it.

BUDGETING

Many goods and services approach European prices. The good hotels charge €60–200 per night with breakfast for a double room; hiring a vehicle for a day will cost €60–80; a three-course meal in a good restaurant might cost about €18 without drinks; a guide for the day (without car) might cost about €30. At the other end of the scale, a basic hotel might cost about €30 for a double room with breakfast; a more basic restaurant charge around €9 for a two-course meal; and travelling around in the local *alugueres* will cost anything from €1–7 depending on the distance.

Day trips and activities from Sal tend to cost €30–80, while going to another island for an organised day trip (by plane) can cost up to €250. Some tourists on package holidays who have run out of things to do complain that they did not budget for the cost of these entertainments and hadn't realised they would be so expensive.

GETTING AROUND

BY AIR The simplest, most convenient, most comfortable, as well as the most reliable way to travel between the islands, is to fly. Anyone with only two weeks in the archipelago should not consider taking a ferry, though there is no alternative to get to Santo Antão or Brava, neither of which has a functioning airport.

Since the recent demise of their only competitor, Halcyonair, the only practical option for inter-island flights is with the national airline, **TACV** (*www.flytacv.com*). Flights cost from €50 per single journey for a short hop (from Sal to Boavista, for example) to more than double that for longer flights. Journeys take between 20 minutes and 50 minutes. Baggage allowance in economy class for internal flights is 20kg, hand luggage is limited to 5kg.

If you are on a very tight schedule or know exactly what you want to do, it is better to book internal flights before you go. If you leave it until you arrive you may not get the flight of your choice although there may be other options if you are flexible. At certain times of the year (festivals or times when emigrants arrive for their holidays), flights get very busy – it may therefore be worth checking with a local travel agent. Flights are generally cheaper the further ahead you book and there are sometimes promotional fares.

TACV flies to all the islands except Santo Antão and Brava and its flights are orientated around three hubs. From Sal you can get directly or indirectly to São Vicente, São Nicolau, Boavista and Santiago. From Santiago you can get directly to Fogo, Sal, Maio and São Vicente; from São Vicente you can get directly to Sal and Santiago. Popular routes might have two or three flights per day, whereas the flight to Maio is currently every two days. Flights can fill quickly, especially through the

Practical Information   GETTING AROUND

2

summer, so early booking is essential. There is nothing more nerve-wracking than being stuck on a remote island with an international flight looming in Sal and a TACV employee advising you to turn up on standby every day for the next week.

Cabo Verde Express (*www.caboverdeexpress.com*) operates charter day trips, in general from Sal and Boavista to Fogo. Unless you are planning to charter a whole plane, you will need to sign on to a group tour via one of the operators, who advertise everywhere in Sal. You can book a flight-only option if there is availability but this is only possible at the last minute.

BY FERRY These are not the Greek islands; we are in the middle of rough Atlantic waters with great distances between many centres. To reach airport-less Brava or Santo Antão, you have to take a ferry. For other inter-island journeys, ferry trips are difficult to recommend on grounds of comfort and even safety.

If you are hyper-adventurous, or even reckless, ferries do operate between many of the islands, although journey times on potentially rough seas are long and schedules are not always strictly adhered to, so it is essential to double-check the sailing times listed throughout the guide. The following website keeps reasonably abreast of the ferry situations: www.bela-vista.net/Ferry.aspx. In 2008, two ferries sank and before that, two newly introduced catamarans were withdrawn because they couldn't cope with the rough seas. When available, boats cost between €8–35 per single journey. You are unlikely to find a ferry too full to take you, but boats can be delayed for days and journeys are long (typically 14 hours between all but the closest islands). The services between Fogo and Brava, and between Mindelo on São Vicente and Porto Novo on Santo Antão, however, are reliable and enjoy a much shorter journey-time, each around one hour.

A new operator, Cabo Verde Fast Ferry (*www.cvfastferry.com*), started operations in 2011 with an initial route linking the southerly islands of Santiago, Fogo and Brava. The promised arrival of a second ferry has yet to materialise, rumoured to be stuck in Malaysia due to lack of available funds to bring it to the archipelago. The brand-new, custom built ferry is modern and comfortable and has improved the reliability of inter-island travel. Single fares are around €14 between Fogo and Brava, and €35 between Santiago and Fogo.

There is a national propensity towards seasickness, and it is advisable to keep your bags slightly off the floor and keep an eye on the passengers immediately beside you if you want to escape the consequences. Take food and drink and something warm to wear, particularly for night crossings.

BY CARGO BOAT There are sometimes a few cargo boats travelling between the islands, and the ferry ticket offices sell a few passenger tickets on these for reduced prices – typically about two-thirds of the full price.

BY YACHT AND CATAMARAN There are day trips from Sal to Boavista in various different craft (see page 103). There are also yachts available for charter between the islands.

BY BUS *Hiace* minibuses, and open trucks with seating in the back (Hiluxes) constitute the public transport. They are recognisable by the sign *'aluguer'* and on most islands that is what they are called, though on Santiago the preferred term is *hiace* (pronounced 'yazz') (see box, page 74). They are typical African minibuses, often overloaded with people, chickens and packages and trundling along to the sound of happy-go-lucky tinkling music.

Generally, *aluqueres* converge at a point in a town or village which anyone can point out to you; often they drive round town picking up passengers and few leave town before they are full. You shout when you want to get off and you pay after disembarking. *Aluqueres* can be flagged down anywhere along the roads. In Cape Verde, unusually for West Africa, many of these vehicles are in good condition and consequently most of their drivers are careful and reasonably slow.

The great disadvantage for visitors is the timings of the *aluqueres*. With some exceptions (noted in each chapter), they leave outlying villages at 05.00 or 06.00 to take people to town, much to the bewilderment of the visitor. They then leave town for the outlying villages between 11.00 and mid-afternoon. Time and time again tourists pile into the 11.00 *aluguer* only to find they have no way of getting back to town in the evening without chartering a vehicle at great cost.

BY TAXI The term 'taxi' refers both to the cars with meters and taxi signs, found in towns, and to *hiaces* that have been chartered by an individual. Chartering costs about ten times the public fare and you may be forced to do it if you want to go somewhere at a different time of day from everyone else. Sometimes the fares can be bargained down and occasionally an opportunist will try to diddle you, but generally prices are fixed – they're just very high. Drivers in general love to be chartered by a tourist so watch out when they tell you there is no more public transport that day – hang around to check and say you want to travel *colectivo*. Tourists often get together to share a chartered minibus.

BY HITCHHIKING Cars are likely to pick you up, except in Santiago. Offer the price of the *aluguer* fare if it seems appropriate, or ask if the journey is free (*buleia*). In remote areas there may be no traffic all day.

However, women travelling on their own should always exercise caution when attempting to hitchhike.

Murray Stewart

The undisputed backbone of Cape Verde's transport system, the *aluguer* can nevertheless be a source of frustration for some visitors to the archipelago, especially if they have no experience of transport in less-developed countries. Understanding the niceties of using these vehicles, which are either minibuses or pick-up trucks, may help to alleviate any confusion surrounding their operation.

Derived from the Portuguese for 'to hire,' the word *aluguer* is written on the side of the vehicle, on a sign on the windscreen, or on its roof. But even the name can confuse the newly arrived tourist, as on some islands they are referred to in conversation as a '*yasser*', which is a (huge) corruption of 'Hiace', the model name of the most common vehicle. With an *aluguer,* you can choose to travel '*colectivo*,' thus sharing the cost with other passengers, or to hire them as a private-hire taxi. In the former case, you will pay one-tenth of the price of the latter, so it is important to know which way you are travelling before you set off, to avoid a shock when it comes to payment time at journey's end. The easiest way is to enquire of the driver '*Colectivo?*' and get him to confirm it to you, unless of course it is the private-hire option that you want. If you are the only passenger on board when the *aluguer* sets off, the chances are that you are travelling 'taxi-style.'

Travelling taxi-style means that you are in charge of where you go and you will not have to share the vehicle with other passengers; travelling '*collectivo*' means that the vehicle will not set off until it fills up with enough passengers to make economic sense for the driver to do so.

Much is made of tourists across the world being 'ripped-off', but most Cape Verde municipalities issue a printed, laminated list of set fares, from which the drivers should not deviate. Sometimes this is kept in the glove compartment of the vehicle and you can ask to see it if you fear that you are being overcharged. The chances are that you are not: most drivers are honest, helpful and polite. Having said that, they are trying to make a living and so, when business is slow, they will obviously try to persuade you to hire them as a taxi. This way, they are earning money rather than being stuck at the roadside, furiously polishing every part of their vehicle while waiting for their *aluguer* to fill up with passengers. As you almost certainly look like a visitor, you will be targeted more than a local, in the belief that you have more money. And let's face it, you probably have, though you may not want to spend it on taxis. Local people know when transport to or

BY CAR RENTAL This is possible through local chain firms on São Vicente, Sal and Santiago and there are tiny firms on some of the other islands. International firms have opened on Sal and Santiago. For contact details see the relevant island chapters. Book several days ahead if you can and don't expect things to run smoothly – for example, the wrong car might arrive several hours late with no price reduction offered for the inconvenience. Car maintenance standards do not match those you might find in western Europe or North America.

If driving, be on the lookout for speed bumps, which are often poorly marked, wandering dogs, sleeping dogs, meandering goats, careless cows and clueless chickens. Seatbelts are compulsory, though no-one wears them. Your travel insurance may be invalid if you choose not to. The same applies to drink-driving. More than two small beers and you are at risk. Police roadside checks are far from rare. Another dilemma is whether to pick up hitchhikers. As transport on the islands is a communal activity, from is at its most frequent and they time their business in town accordingly, to avoid getting stuck or having to travel 'private hire'.

To varying degrees, drivers are pro-active in finding business, often parading up and down the same street several times, interspersing their drive-pasts with U-turns, tooting their horns, slowing down to shout to anyone who looks like a passenger and to persuade them that it's time to take a ride. Of course, as they usually run set routes (which are sometimes painted on the vehicle doors), they will recognise potential passengers and will know exactly where they live and know the chances of them jumping on board. To visitors from some other countries, the exchanges between driver and potential passengers defy logic, particularly when, on the third occasion, the passenger jumps in, having declined to do so on the first two invitations. Surely, you may ask yourself, they either *want* to go home, or they don't?

If you are the first passenger to board an empty minibus, you will have to be prepared to wait, assuming you are travelling *colectivo*. But rather than be impatient, consider some of the advantages of this type of communal transport. Although the driver's motivation is monetary, waiting for a vehicle to fill before it leaves is also environmentally friendly. Compare this with the 'developed' nations, where car ownership is high and everyone runs around in their own vehicle polluting the atmosphere *ad infinitum*. Travelling *colectivo*-style in an *aluguer* is a lesson in sharing space and time, both of which the Cape Verdeans do exceptionally well.

I have fond memories of my *aluguer* journey in Fogo, down from the crater to Sao Felipe. I counted 24 passengers in our 15-seat minibus, everyone seemed to have someone else's baby on their lap, except for me, whose arm was being dribbled on by a two year old. As we left the village, we stopped to pick up three more passengers, four large, blue barrels and two sacks of goodness-knows-what. As well as carrying passengers, *aluguers* also multi-task as delivery vehicles in many areas, supplying food and drink, car parts, medicines and other essentials – Cape Verde has no postal delivery service.

After a well-ordered rearrangement of offspring, some tying of the mystery sacks to the vehicle roof and creative stowing of the barrels into a previously non-existent space, we lurched off again, out of the village. The three latecomers had to stand for the whole of the hour's journey, by the end of which my arm was thoroughly soaked by infant saliva.

you may feel guilty whizzing past locals who are looking for a lift. If you wish to help them, again be aware that your hire-car insurance or travel insurance may not cover you fully if passengers are injured while you are at the wheel.

BY CYCLING Keen cyclists do take their bicycles to the archipelago and return having had a good time. Bicycles can be transported between the islands on the larger TACV 46-seater planes. You pay by weight, just as with other baggage. Bicycles may be hired on Sal, Maio and Santo Antão.

However, there are several caveats about cycling in Cape Verde. Firstly, many of the roads are cobbled, causing ceaseless, tiring vibrations to the hands as they clutch the handlebars, unless you have a very good bike. Pot-holes can also be a problem. Secondly, the bulk of roads in Cape Verde are utterly devoid of shade and the constant sunshine can be exhausting. Thirdly, some of the most interesting islands have many stretches that are too steep for cycling – in particular, much of Santo Antão and many roads in Fogo. Fourthly, people trying to take their own bike to the islands have run into problems both with bike damage and with the aircraft unexpectedly refusing to take the bike. Fifthly, the islands are full of dogs.

ACCOMMODATION

The hotel star-rating system is an inflated one, internal to Cape Verde. The term 'hotel' implies a place of superior quality, though even this cannot be relied upon. The other terms, *pousada*, *pensão* and *residencial*, are interchangeable. Some establishments use the word *casa* to demonstrate a family atmosphere. At the bottom of the range there are some very cheap, grubby places that are not intended for tourists. No-one will mention them, they will not be marked, and even the proprietors may discourage you from staying for fear you'll complain about the conditions. Above this level, accommodation is almost invariably clean, if basic, and en-suite bathrooms are the norm. Rooms can vary enormously in quality within the same hotel. In particular the windows of inner rooms in older buildings in Praia and Mindelo often open only onto a central shaft, which makes them dark and noisy.

Hotels are listed in descending order of price and are grouped into price categories (for the key, see the inside cover). In May 2013, a tourist tax equivalent to €2 per person per night was introduced for all guests, up to a maximum of ten nights. Prices quoted in this book include the tax, but bear in mind that in response to your telephone or email enquiry, hotels may quote their prices *excluding* the tax, so make proper enquiry when booking, to avoid an unpleasant surprise. There's an increasing number of good-quality and luxury hotels in Cape Verde. At the time of writing this book there were many on Sal, several on Boavista, Santiago and São Vicente, one on Santo Antão and one on Fogo. Rooms in most three-star hotels will have hot water, telephone, fan or air conditioning, and often a fridge and television (often just local channels, though). If hot water is important to you (and it may be less so in a hot climate than at home) then it is worth enquiring in advance. Sometimes the availability of hot water varies throughout the day. Camping is permitted on the beaches, but finding a natural water supply may be difficult.

On Sal, Boavista and Maio there are many apartments to rent and there will be villas. See island chapters for details.

HOMESTAYS On the two great hiking islands, Santo Antão and Fogo, local people are increasingly opening up their homes to walkers. In general you sleep in a spare (or hastily vacated) bedroom and are fed your evening meal as well as breakfast the next day. Sometimes local people have built concrete annexes on to their houses to accommodate tourists. A few homestays provide better facilities. The system has several advantages. It allows trekkers to do more ambitious journeys safe in the

ACCOMMODATION PRICE CODES			
Price of a double room with breakfast, including tax.			
$$$$$ €110+	£92+	US$150+	12,000$+
$$$$ €73–110	£62–92	US$100–150	8,000–12,000$
$$$ €45–73	£38–62	US$63–100	5,000–8,000$
$$ €32–45	£27–38	US$44–63	3,500–5,000$
$ up to €32	up to £27	up to US$44	up to 3,500$

knowledge that they have places to stay along the way. It brings locals and visitors into closer contact – you experience a taste of the rural lifestyle while they derive entertainment and cash from you.

But rural homestays are not for every visitor. Conditions will be basic: perhaps there will be a room without windows, a very old mattress and some sort of shared washing facility without a huge amount of privacy. Although the price will be lower than that of hotels, it may be higher than you expected it to be. This can be because of the high cost of arranging special food for visitors (for example, some homestay hosts in Santo Antão have to spend a day travelling to town and back to purchase food for their guests). For some visitors, a homestay is the high spot of their trip and even a formative experience in their lives; for others it is a disaster from which they can't wait to escape. The key is to abandon your tourist-as-consumer mindset and become a tourist-as-anthropologist for the day, accepting what is given and taking an interest in everything you are privileged to witness. You can take comfort from the knowledge that, as you hand over your money, you are directly benefiting the local people. Contacts for homestays are given in the island chapters.

EATING AND DRINKING

Fish lovers will be in heaven on Cape Verde. The grilled lobster is superb, as are the fresh tuna, octopus and a multitude of other delicacies. The only disappointment sometimes is that no-one seems to have invented any exciting sauces or variations to accompany these freshly caught delights. Vegetarians may find only omelette on the menu but can always ask for a plate of rice and beans. The very few places that welcome vegetarians are mentioned in the restaurant listings.

A speciality is *cachupa*, a delicious, hearty dish that comes in two varieties: poor-man's *cachupa* (boiled maize, beans, herbs, cassava, sweet potato) and rich-man's *cachupa* (the same but with chicken and other meat). *Cachupa* takes a long time to prepare: some restaurants put a sign in their windows to indicate when they will next be serving it. *Cachupa grelhada* is perhaps the most palatable – everything available all fried up together, often for breakfast.

An oddity of Cape Verde restaurants is the apparent default setting of serving your chosen dish with rice *and* potatoes of some variety (chipped, boiled). For many, this is too much stodge, but you may have to be insistent to avoid it happening!

Another minor frustration can be the opening times. The restaurant listings in the island chapters include opening times where there is some degree of confidence that they will be adhered to. However, there is a fairly laid-back attitude to opening times, one which you may choose to adopt. Experience shows that many establishments cannot – or will not – tell you their opening times, or will not stick to them. On Sal and Boavista, this is less of a problem.

RESTAURANT PRICE CODES				
Price of an average main course dish. Drinks and service charge are extra.				
$$$$$	€9+	£7+	US$13+	1,000$+
$$$$	€7–9	£6–7	US$10–13	800–1,000$
$$$	€5–7	£4–6	US$7–10	600–800$
$$	€4–5	£3–4	US$5–7	400–600$
$	up to €4	up to £3	up to US$5	up to 400$

GROGUE

Sugarcane, the sole ingredient of grogue, arrived in Cape Verde with the slaves from mainland Africa. The word 'grogue' is derived from 'grog' – used by English seafarers. At first, the production of spirit from sugarcane was forbidden on the grounds that it presented a risk to public health. However, restrictive laws just drove the distillers underground and by 1866 the authorities relented and introduced a brandy tax instead. By 1900, there was even legislation dictating the safe design of sugarcane presses, or *trapiches*.

The *trapiche* is a large machine traditionally made of wood and driven by oxen or mules, plodding round in a never-ending circle. Men feed cut sugarcane through heavy metal rollers and sugar syrup runs out and is collected in large wooden barrels where it is allowed to ferment for five to ten days. No water is added, and neither is yeast – there is enough naturally occurring on the cane.

The still is partly buried in a loose stone oven, and the fermented syrup is brought to the boil, producing an aroma that wafts up the valley. After an hour, the steam is run through a curly pipe cooled by water, and the clear distilled spirit starts to flow. A skilled eye can tell from the froth in the distillate the point at which a palatable fraction is being produced. That's the theory, at least.

In practice, the grogue drunk in villages will not have been produced under controlled conditions. Distillation is likely to have been carried out in an old oil drum, and the spirit collected in a rusty tin. It will not kill you unless you binge on a particularly dodgy brew, but it may upset your stomach. The rougher distillations of *grogue* cost next to nothing. After 20 years of sustained drinking, the accumulated methanol may make you blind.

For those who are not put off, grogue is an exciting and throaty drink. There are, of course, as many subtleties to grogue as there are distilleries in Cape Verde. To fully appreciate the eye-watering gaspiness of it, it is quite acceptable to sip it, although you may be left with the strange feeling that much of what you were going to swallow has already evaporated in your mouth.

If you find yourself recoiling at grogue's rawness, ask for *ponche* (punch). In this amber-coloured liquid the spirit's kick is muffled by honey. It is also available with flavours such as coconut, masking the inherent harshness of the raw spirit, but making it dangerously quaffable in the process. For those who dislike the cough-mixture sweetness of this, *coupada* ('cut') is the halfway house – a mixture of grogue and punch.

Grogue is something close to the hearts of many Cape Verdeans – an invitation to share a glass in a remote village is not something to be turned down lightly. The drink is an important part of Cape Verdean culture to the extent that the pressing of the cane, with its steady repetitive rhythm, has proved to be a fertile source of inspiration for music. The most famous ballads sung while at work on the *trapiches* are the *abois* or *kola boi*. They dwell at some length on the socio-economic ills which beset the Cape Verdeans. It is said the melodies often reduce the oxen to tears.

Local specialities are the jams (*doce*) and semi-dried fruits. These are often served as desserts along with fresh goat's cheese, making a delicious end to the meal.

Most towns will have local eateries where huge platefuls of rice, chips, beans and fish, or of *cachupa*, are served up for 300–500$; but they may not be open all day though. Look out for restaurants offering *pratos del dia*, often at lunchtime. These 'dishes of the day' give you a chance to fill up very cheaply, usually for around 400$. Restaurant prices are defined in the rest of this book by the average cost of a main meat or fish dish. In most places, these start at 600–1000$. Lobster tends to be 1,800$ upwards, but costs much more on Sal and Boavista. Tea is typically 50$ a cup and coffee 100$. Getting a decent tea or coffee can at times be difficult. Asking for tea can quite often bring an infusion of camomile or blackberry, so bringing a few of your favourite teabags from home is not a bad idea, if it's important to you. The best coffee seems to be available from the larger airport cafes and ferry terminals, or from various Italian establishments on Sal and Boavista.

Food on the streets is fine, if unexciting. There are many women with trays of sweets, monkey nuts, sugared peanuts and popcorn. Sometimes they will have little *pastéis* (fish pastries). Trays of homemade sweets are ubiquitous. The confectionery is very sugary, and flavours are mainly coconut, peanut and papaya. Here and there ladies fry *moreia* – moray eel. Nice, but greasy – just spit the bones out, the dogs will get them.

Cheap picnic lunches can be bought from supermarkets, markets and from bakeries. These exist in every town but they can be hard to track down, due to a dearth of signage. Ask for the *minimercado* if you get stuck and don't be too choosy: often they are more *mini* than *mercado*.

Outside the big towns try to call in at your chosen restaurant about two hours in advance to order your meal or you will be confined to the dish of the day.

Many villages have no eating places, but somewhere there will be a shop – often hard to distinguish from an ordinary house. There you can buy biscuits and drinks. For useful food terms see *Appendix 1*, *Language*, page 343.

Bottled water is widely available and in ordinary shops is cheap (80$ for a 1.5l bottle); prices are inflated at hotels (up to 180$). Some of the wine made on Fogo Island is distinctive and very quaffable and can be found for sale around the archipelago. There are three principal beers. Strela is a domestic brand, brewed in Praia, and has a sub-brand, Strela Ego, which is a high-strength lager (8%). The two brands imported from Portugal are the maltier Superbock and the less-common Sagres. Costs are typically 100$ for local and Portuguese beer and 250$ for other imported brands. On Sal many more familiar brands of imported drink are available, but are usually quite expensive.

The drink that Cape Verdeans literally live and die for is **grogue**. It is locally produced (see box, page 78) and abundantly available – in any dwelling carrying a sign above its door prohibiting children under 18 from entering.

On quieter islands such as Maio and São Nicolau, food shops and restaurants may open erratically and only for short periods. To avoid hours of hunger, always have provisions with you.

PUBLIC HOLIDAYS AND FESTIVALS

Each island has a calendar of festivals, many of which originated as saints' days and all of which offer a great excuse for music and dancing, as well as the downing of *grogue*. The most renowned is the São Vicente Carnival in mid-February. Others of particular interest are described in the island chapters.

The following dates are public holidays, as well as Mardi Gras and Good Friday.

1 January	New Year
20 January	National Heroes Day
1 May	Labour Day
5 July	Independence Day

15 August	Nossa Senhora da Graça (Our Lady of Grace)
12 September	Nationality Day
1 November	All Saints' Day
25 December	Christmas Day

SHOPPING

Shopping outside the towns is almost non-existent. The most colourful market is in Assomada, on Santiago, a flavour of mainland Africa. Most island capitals have some sort of fruit and vegetable market though the only one of touristic interest is on the Plateau in Praia, Santiago.

Local crafts can be bought in Mindelo, in São Vicente, where there have been revivals of skills such as the weaving of cloth and baskets. Baskets and clay figures can also be bought in São Domingos on Santiago. Santo Antão and São Nicolau are also good places to find local crafts and home produce. Locally made souvenirs are becoming increasingly common in the main tourism centres, particularly at Genuine Cabo Verde on Sal (see page 125). For excellent souvenirs of the islands, buy bottles of *grogue* (available in any small shop in a town) or its more exotic variants (try more touristy shops for these), Fogo wine and coffee beans, little bags of the abundant local sweets, and CDs of Cape Verdean music (in Mindelo, Praia and outlets at the airports). More details are given in the island chapters.

Nearly everything is closed on public holidays and on Sundays, and many shops also close early on Fridays. Opening hours tend to be Mediterranean – that is, 08.00/08.30–12.00/12.30 and 14.00/14.30–18.00/18.30 Monday–Friday, 08.30–12.00 Saturday. Banks tend to be open until 15.00, without a lunch break. In the evenings, restaurants generally operate from about 19.00 to 23.00.

ARTS AND ENTERTAINMENT

MUSEUMS AND HISTORICAL SITES Despite the archipelago's fascinating history there is very little to see in the form of buildings or museums. The one exception to this is on Santiago. In the capital, Praia, there is a fascinating museum documenting what is known of the many shipwrecks around the islands; another, general museum and a museum in the Santiago hills is devoted to the *tabanka* musical and dance form.

Cape Verde has one historical site of international stature: the old city of Ribeira Grande (Cidade Velha) on Santo Antão, the first European city in the tropics and a pivotal arena in the transatlantic slave trade. The capital of Fogo, São Filipe, is a fine town full of *sobrado* architecture and now has a new, developing musuem.

Most island capitals have southern European architecture and ambience, and some have a faded Portuguese feel to them with narrow cobbled streets, ochre-tiled roofs and abundant flowers in well-tended public gardens.

MUSIC AND DANCING Music and dancing are the Cape Verdeans' principal means of cultural expression. The music scene is thriving, with an increasing number of bands making the international break and following in the footsteps of the renowned Cesária Évora (see box, page 45), gaining recognition on the world scene. The music is a blend of African, European and more recently, Latin. Music is everywhere in the archipelago: in Fogo crater, in every little village, down the *ribeiras* and of course in the cities of Praia and Mindelo. There are an astonishing number of outstandingly talented musicians for such a small group of islands.

To hear the music in a planned way, spend time in Mindelo (see page 269) and Praia (see page 170). Musicians play every night in Fogo crater and many restaurants in Sal have live music in the evenings. The islands have six or seven key dances and you may be lucky enough to see them all demonstrated by a troupe in Boavista (see page 149). Other than that, you might pick up different dances on different islands, at local nightclubs, for example. *Possada* is a favourite of Mindelo clubs, danced to zouk music; *funaná*, a fast dance done mainly to the strains of the accordion, is a more southern dance form, not really accepted in Mindelo; *cola* (which means 'glue') is a slow and amorous pelvic grind. Nightclubs tend to open at midnight. For more on music, see pages 40–6.

MEDIA AND COMMUNICATIONS

INTERNET Internet access is readily available in almost all towns and is usually high speed and reliable. There are many internet cafés all over the place offering pretty cheap services – which can be triple the price in hotels. If you have your laptop with you, most of the *praças* (town squares) in the main towns have free Wi-Fi access, though the signal here is not always strong enough for Skype and certain other functions. Details are given in the island chapters. The connection for free access is called 'Konekta' and no password or access code is required. All of the international airports have free Wi-Fi (Sal, Boavista, São Vicente and Santiago). You can also buy a dongle from CV Telecom for around 1,000$, which includes credit of 200$. This will give you access almost anywhere and you can top up the credit at CV Telecom branches, as well as many *minimercados* and elsewhere. Make sure to keep safe all of the codes and information you get when you buy the dongle, as you'll need these to top up your credit. On Sal, you can buy vouchers for Wi-Fi access, but this is pricey.

POST OFFICE Cape Verdean post offices are well equipped and it is possible to transfer money, send and receive faxes, make phone calls and often make photocopies there – as well as buying stamps. Opening times vary considerably but tend to be 08.00–12.00 and 14.00–18.00 Monday–Friday.

RADIO AND TELEVISION Local television is provided by **RTC** (*www.rtc.cv*; 12.00–00.00), which broadcasts English-language films and series at weekends. A wide range of satellite channels is available on the main tourist islands, particularly in the top-end hotels and sports bars. These include, as well as all the film channels, BBC, CNN, RAI, French and German stations, Portuguese and even Brazilian soap operas. Voice of America, RDP and BBC (Portuguese and English versions) are rebroadcast on FM radio. The Portuguese channel SportTV shows a wide variety of sports and can be seen in a lot of bars throughout the country. Radio Cape Verde has an office in the cultural centre in Mindelo. Its programmes can be accessed online (*www.rtc.cv*), allowing you to acclimatise to Cape Verdean music, before you visit, and continue to enjoy it after you return.

TELEPHONE It is straightforward to make calls from numerous phone call centres with booths where you phone first and pay afterwards. Most of the island capitals have them. These are cheaper than calling home from the post office, which is punitively expensive (for example, calling to the UK can cost £1 per minute, while costing as little as 16p per minute from a phone call centre). You can also buy cards from the post office to use in the public phones.

2

If you are likely to make quite a few calls in Cape Verde, it's worth buying a SIM card from CV Telecom, or its rival Unitel (formerly TMais (t+)). The latter is not as common as the former. To avail yourself of this service you should get your mobile unlocked back home before your trip, although there are organisations in Praia that claim to be able to unblock phones. SIM cards, including some initial free credit, are cheap, at only 50$ and can be topped up anywhere where you see the relevant sign. Keep all the information that you are given when you buy your SIM, as you need it to top up anywhere other than the phone company's offices. Mobile phones themselves are expensive.

Local calls are cheap but it's very expensive to make and receive international calls on Cape Verdean mobiles. If you have a device which allows Skype, it's worth taking this with you if you want to make free, regular contact with those back home. This is also useful for cheap international telephone calls.

CULTURAL ETIQUETTE

In many practical ways travelling around the islands is a joy, and in general the people are keen to encourage tourism. As one visitor put it: the people have the carefree approach to life of South America combined with the family orientation of Africa. Culturally there is little corruption and bribery.

Cape Verde has a history of cosmopolitanism; people know about the outside world because their sons and brothers live there. Nevertheless, tourism always brings with it crime, envy, loss of dignity, hassle and some despoiling of nature. It remains to be seen what impact widespread foreign ownership of land and apartments will have on local people. An influx of richer people can often send prices soaring in the shops.

BEGGING In a small but growing number of places in Cape Verde – the waterfront in Santa Maria, Mindelo, the streets of Cidade Velha, the Fogo crater – some children have become beggars, pursuing passers-by with persistent demands for money, sweets, pens or photos. Responding to these demands gives the donor a brief feeling of beneficence but does nothing to alleviate poverty. Instead it causes rivalry amongst children, upsets the family balance (in the case of cash gifts) and, worse, instils a vigorous sense among the children that tourists owe them gifts.

Think of the next batch of tourists that will pass through: successful hassle breeds more hassle, which can ruin an otherwise peaceful outing. We suggest you do not hand out money unless it is to people who have earned it – for example through employment as guides. If you would like to help the children, then seek out the local school and give a box of biros or paper to the ill-supplied teachers. Alternatively, consult *Travelling positively*, opposite, for bodies looking for donations for Cape Verdean good works.

There are some effective ways of replying to demands for money – smiles and good humour being the best accompaniments to whatever you say: '*Desculpe* (*deshculp*)' – 'sorry'; '*Não tenho* (*Now tenyu*) *livro/caneta/dinheiro*' – 'I don't have a book/pen/money'; '*Sem trabalho, não dinheiro*' – 'no pay without work'.

One form of apparent begging is children who are merely asking to change the euros they've received from other tourists into useable escudos.

HIRING GUIDES We indicate in the text whether a guide is necessary or not. Where a guide is not absolutely essential, you may still prefer to hire one in order to get to know a local person, embellish the walk with more information and help the local economy.

LANGUAGE Everyone speaks *Crioulo*, an Africanised Creole Portuguese. Portuguese (the official language) is spoken fluently by most townspeople but is not well understood in outlying villages – some people do not speak it at all. Everything official and everything written is in Portuguese. The most common second European language is French, spoken widely by officials, with English third but on the increase.

If you are struggling then keep asking people if they speak English or French (*fala inglês?, fala francês?* – fowle eenglaysh?, fowle frensaysh?). It's astonishing how often such a speaker can be found even in the remotest village. For words and phrases and a discussion of Creole see *Appendix 1, Language*, page 343. Learning a few basics in Portuguese and Creole, such as greetings, as well as 'please' and 'thank you', will endear you to the locals and make for a better experience for all.

LOCAL RESOURCES Water is scarce and has invariably taken toil and money to reach your basin. It is very important not to waste it. There are many endangered plant species on the archipelago (see page 5).

Ultimately, the goats may get them all. Nonetheless, picking flowers is absolutely out of the question. Don't buy products made of turtle shells, coral or other endangered resources.

PROSTITUTES Unaccompanied men may experience some unwanted approaches on the street from prostitutes in Santa Maria on Sal island. Most of these working girls are from the West African mainland rather than Cape Verde. They are rarely aggressive and constitute a minor annoyance.

SCAMS It may be worth giving suspected 'rip-off merchants' the benefit of the doubt in Cape Verde. If you think you are being mistreated it could just be a problem with the language barrier, or the local custom (as, for example, with a two-hour wait in a restaurant), or the fact that prices are genuinely high for everyone (for example, with taxi fares).

STREET SELLERS There have been a lot of complaints from tourists about West African street sellers, mostly in Sal. They've arrived because of the tourists and they operate very differently from the more laid-back Cape Verdeans. (See box, *Street vendors*, page 116, for more information.)

TAKING PHOTOGRAPHS It is best to ask people before you take their photo; smile and say hello, pause, ask to take a photo, offer to take their address and send them a copy. Then, when they are relaxed, you can take the real atmospheric ones. Do not try to photograph the *rebelados* in Santiago, who have scruples about photography; or the hot-tempered market women in Praia. Some old people may have objections as well. Photographing TACV aircraft sometimes provokes an angry response on the runway.

TRAVELLING POSITIVELY

You can give something back simply by venturing out and about, using local tour operators, staying in the many family-run *pensões* and eating in local restaurants.

If you would like to contribute to charitable work in Cape Verde you could contact one of the following. The Peace Corps, who were long established in projects on the islands, withdrew at the end of 2012.

GREETINGS In social situations, men shake hands with men. Sometimes the handshake lasts for as long as the conversation, so a man may hold onto your hand while he's speaking to you. It takes some getting used to, especially for frigid, contact-shy Brits, but go with it. A man and a woman, or two women, generally shake hands plus a kiss on each cheek, even on first meeting.

SMALL TALK This is the name of the game. Conversations tend to run round in circles. Each person will enquire about the other's well-being, the well-being of each member of the other's family, then their colleagues. Then the questions turn to life in general, work, health. Neither will actually answer any questions – they just keep asking each other. So the response to 'How are you?' is 'How are you?'

'TUDU BON?' There are about 50 variations on *'Tudu bon?'* (which means 'everything OK?'). The *tudu* can be followed by *bon, ben, dretu, fixe, em forma, sabi,* or OK, tranquil, cool, fine, nice, and a million others. If you can master just a few phrases in the local language, make it these ones.

NO The gesture for 'no' is a waggle of the index finger with a 'no' look on your face. It seems rude, but isn't.

HISSING If someone wants to get your attention, they will hiss at you. Sometimes this comes out as 'sss', sometimes more like 'pssssyeoh'! This can strike the newcomer as incredibly rude, but it's not meant to be, and it's a lot more effective than 'Ahem, excuse me… ahem… excuse me! Hello, excuse me?'

'OI' This means 'Hi' and is very friendly.

BØRNEfonden www.bornefonden.dk. A member of ChildFund Alliance, this politically & religiously independent Danish NGO has been active in Cape Verde since 1989. The geographical focus at present is on Fogo & Santiago. Working mainly through individual sponsorship of Cape Verdean children, its 4 key areas are education, health, income-generating activities & children & development. More specifically, within these areas, BØRNEfonden provide schoolbooks, materials & construction of school buildings; organise health awareness campaigns & water provision; promote sport & other child development activities; support family self-sufficiency through training & micro-credits. Contributions & child sponsorship are very welcome.
Castelos do Sal m 978 1026/979 7704; e castelosdosal@hotmail.com; www. castelosdosal.com. Based on Sal, this worthwhile organisation has various projects aimed at protecting vulnerable children in high-risk situations. One project seeks to counter children begging on the streets, another to give children basic social, personal hygiene & educational skills. Children receive a balanced meal & medical care, where necessary, in premises provided by the Sal island administration. Contact them in advance to see what help you can give.
SOS Children's Villages www.sos-childrensvillages.org/Where-we-help/Africa/Cape-Verde/Pages/default.aspx. This international social development organisation has 2 SOS children's villages, 1 SOS youth facility & 2 SOS kindergartens on Santiago, & focuses on family-based, long-term care of children who can no longer grow up with their biological families.
SOS Tartarugas www.turtlesos.org. The plight of turtles internationally is dependent largely

on how they are treated at their key breeding grounds, which include Cape Verde. SOS Tartarugas needs money to train wildlife rangers & support grass-roots projects throughout the country. It also needs donations of equipment such as radios & phones (there's a list on the website). You can also volunteer long term or short term & participate as part of your holiday.

The Cape Verdean Society 53 Ty Mawr Av, Cardiff CF3 8AG; ✆ +44 029 2021 2787. This charitable organisation seeks to help with education, relieve need & provide facilities for Cape Verdeans, including expatriates in Cardiff. In the past it has contributed to the upkeep of schools, orphanages, a children's hospital & a malnutrition centre in São Vicente.

ANIMAL WELFARE Treatment of animals in Cape Verde, particularly cats and dogs, has been a long-standing concern. A lack of veterinarians on all the islands resulted in a large population of feral and free-roaming animals, especially dogs, many of which are in dire need of treatment for a variety of diseases and injuries. The government's only answer for a long time was the indiscriminate poisoning by laying strychnine during the night and collecting the bodies the following morning. This led to several concerned individuals setting up shelters and organising neutering clinics with the help of vets from overseas, and coupled with the negative publicity and its potential impact on tourism, the poisoning has now stopped. The focus of campaigning organisations such as Cape Verde Cats and Dogs (see below for details) is now centred on encouraging government to create a compulsory dog registration scheme. Although many dogs have owners, the culture is to let animals run loose on the streets. All animal welfare organisations are desperately short of funds and will welcome donations of money, medicine, tick and flea treatment and even simple things such as collars and leads. If you are a visiting vet, you could do untold good by helping out for a few days. Even if you have no experience most will welcome your assistance for long or short periods. Contact the organisation in question to find out exactly what they need.

Associacão dos Amigos Animais de
Bubista Sal Rei, Boavista; m 992 2864
Bons Amigos Praia, Santiago; ✆ 264 1578; m 984 1339; e info@abacv.org
Cape Verde Cats and Dogs Santa Maria, Sal; m 957 2162; e info@cvcatsanddogs.org; www.

cvcatsanddogs.org
Si Ma Bo Rua Franz Fanon 14, Mindelo, São Vicente; ✆ 231 2465; m 993 7347; e info@simabo. org; www.simabo.org. Offers the opportunity to adopt a pet. Provides accommodation for volunteers.

LIVING AND WORKING IN CAPE VERDE

Cape Verde's diverse population includes communities of expats from many parts of Europe, West Africa and elsewhere. Some of them are retirees; some of them are owners of small businesses, particularly in the service sector. Visitors to the islands may be tempted to join them, or perhaps to purchase a property. The African sun does not give those wishing to settle in Cape Verde any immunity from the obstacles that confront would-be immigrants; nor can this guidebook hope to give detailed advice on settling in a young country where rules and regulations are ever-changing. For some ex-pats, moving to Cape Verde has been all they hoped for and more. For others, especially those who let their 'island dream' overrule their common sense, the experience has been less successful. Some of what follows may seem blindingly obvious, but there are enough disaster stories amongst ex-pats to make it worthwhile writing it. The British Embassy, based in Senegal, issued a useful information booklet in 2012, aimed at British visitors and prospective Cape Verde residents. This can be downloaded from the Cape Verde Tips website (*www.capeverdetips.co.uk*).

FORMALITIES FOR NON-TOURISTS For business travellers to Cape Verde, the same forms are completed for visas (see page 55), but possessing a letter of authority from your employer or Cape Verde business contact is advisable, to avoid any problems. People who wish to become resident in Cape Verde are subject to certain requirements which were under review as of late 2013. Essentially, the would-be resident needs their own private medical insurance and a minimum monthly income level of US$1,300. Up-to-date information can be obtained from the website of the Ministério das Comunidades (*www.mdc.gov.cv*), the *câmara* in Praia (*Rua Cesário Lacerda No 6, Tenis, CP 105 Praia;* ℡ *261 7234/5352;* e *cciss@cvtelecom.cv*), or one of the local *câmaras* on the other islands.

For those wishing to become Cape Verde nationals, it is necessary to have been a (legal!) resident for at least five years, and there are financial requirements – including the payment of a significant capital sum – which were under review at time of writing. In respect of applications for both residence and citizenship, criminal background checks are undertaken.

VOLUNTEER AND DEVELOPMENT WORK Many volunteers and other development workers in Cape Verde have a superb, and sometimes life-changing, time. They can engage with this singular people, impoverished in some ways yet rich in so many others, deeply resilient and formidably artistic. Cape Verde has retained qualities that some feel that Europe and the USA have lost in the stampede for material success. Returning *emigrantes* from the USA, as well as foreigners, enjoy the peace, the relaxed pace of life, and the high value given to (and consequently time invested in) community, friendships, free time, parties and making music.

Trying to work in such a culture can pose problems, however, which are all the more frustrating if your work is designed to help local communities rather than produce a successful business for yourself. Your success is dependent on the enthusiasm and co-operation of the people with whom you work, as well as your own enthusiasm. The ability to motivate and inspire is essential.

'The culture here is a double-edged sword,' says one volunteer. 'They are an island nation, which makes them somewhat isolated and entrenched in their own ways. Yet by African standards they are sophisticated, better educated, and more European.' Some volunteers arrive with an idealistic notion that the people will greet them with 'outstretched arms, waiting for them to teach, train, and show them a better way of life,' he says. It can be a shock to discover indifference – or pride in the current way of life – combined with a reluctance to change.

English teachers may find that pupils lack the docile enthusiasm to learn that is found in mainland Africa and they are also unlikely to have come across educational methods we take for granted in the West. The mere act of learning, never mind the subject matter, can be very difficult for would-be learners. Adaptability on the part of the volunteer is essential.

An invaluable attitude derives from realising that you are in Cape Verde to learn as well as to teach and give. In this way you will derive a deeper understanding of another culture – one that only comes when you spend time in a place and which will be invaluable through life.

Another approach to irritation is to do some mental gymnastics and find something to admire in, for example, the failure to turn up to a meeting. 'My ploy is to think not "Where the hell are they?" but "Ah yes, these people are great the way they refuse to be intimidated by time", says another English teacher.

Above all you must be able to switch off. This does not rule out caring deeply about your work, and putting in more than 100%. But it does mean that when things get beyond your control you can shrug, laugh and say: 'I did my best, and the rest is out of my hands.'

Essential characteristics Consider whether you have the following before you go: linguistic ability, especially the ability to pick up a spoken-only language like Creole, but also the wherewithal to learn a formal written language like Portuguese, used for all official purposes; patience; sensitivity to other cultures and people skills.

Volunteer programmes Historically, many volunteers in Cape Verde were sent by the US Peace Corps, but that organisation withdrew suddenly from the islands in 2012, perhaps evidence of the islands' advancement up the ladder of development. The United Nations (*www.unv.org*) also sends volunteers to Cape Verde.

Environmental projects SOS Tartarugas (Turtle SOS) (m *974 5019*; e *info@ turtlesos.org*; *www.turtlesos.org*) accepts volunteers for its conservation programme from June to December. Language skills are especially valued.

Finding other work Many Europeans disillusioned with life make their way to islands such as Sal and Boavista hoping to be able to pick up work, open a bar or buy a boat. For many who have not done much research, disappointment is rapid. There are very limited opportunities for jobs at a salary Europeans would call a living wage and bureaucracy and language barriers make it hard to start and run a small business. Just like in other countries, to succeed you need to understand the system, follow the regulations and work hard.

TEACHING ENGLISH AS A FOREIGN LANGUAGE (TEFL) The English Language Institute (*Rua Salamansa 17, Palmarejo;* \ *261 2672;* e *elipraia@sapo.cv; www. elipraia.cv*) has schools in Praia, Mindelo and Sal. Lessons are usually business or general English, taught to adults, although there are some classes for children. The pay can sustain a modest lifestyle for some in Cape Verde and the institute is responsive to enquiries from prospective teachers, especially in September and February. They are looking for Celta-qualified TEFL teachers. Some would-be teachers have just walked in off the street with their certificates and secured jobs, but it is probably best to contact them by email beforehand.

WOMEN WORKING IN CAPE VERDE

Unattached women who stay for a long time in one place in Cape Verde report a very different experience from that of female tourists. The concept of an unattached woman is incomprehensible in Cape Verdean society and it seems that some communities just cannot tolerate it, so sexual predation can build up until it is, in some cases, quite frightening. Several unattached expatriate women working long term in Cape Verde have been sexually attacked in recent years. Some ex-pat women report 'kind' offers from local men to 'look after their needs' when they are single, or if their husbands or partners are absent. Meanwhile, local women can become angry with visitors who take a boyfriend from their already limited supply of men. Promiscuity is a way of life: remember that the father of the nation's hero, Amílcar Cabral, was also father to 62 children, which may speak volumes as to some of the prevalent attitudes towards sex on the islands.

Language Link (*CP 68, Praia;* ✆ *262 5101;* m *921 3278;* e *info@languagelinkcv.com; www.languagelinkcv.com*) is another well-established school in Praia, keen to hear from qualified TEFL or ESP teachers. Contracts offered vary between six and twelve months. The school has many corporate clients in the public and private sectors. **High schools** are amenable to approaches by English teachers, so it might be possible to find such work. The pay would be about 50,000$ a month and you are likely to be left to sort out issues such as accommodation and medical insurance yourself. The work can be tiring, with classes of 40, and those who do not already speak Portuguese may have problems with class control. It may also be worth approaching the universities.

It could be possible to give **private classes**, charging 1,000–2,000$ per hour. There are plenty of people who want to learn English for work or to visit the USA, but they might be hard to find until you have links with the local community.

INVESTING IN CAPE VERDE

BUSINESS The stable political situation, a lack of corruption and strong economic growth – at a time when such growth is rare elsewhere in the world – are all valid reasons to consider Cape Verde as an attractive investment destination. Those who can create employment opportunities for locals will be particularly welcome. In 2007, Cape Verde achieved three economic successes: elevation to the status of 'middle income country' by the United Nations; membership of the World Trade Organization and the establishment of special status in relation to the European Union. In 2010, Cape Verde was praised by the Millennium Challenge Corporation for setting a good example in the region through good governance and policy reforms. There is, therefore, a lot of optimism.

On the downside, Cape Verde is still a developing country, with an expensive oil dependency. Not only does Cape Verde have to import all its own fuel for the usual purposes but also in order to desalinate much of its water, a fuel-intensive process. The oil price also affects the price of food, much of which has to be imported.

Infrastructure is still poor, though there are many projects completed and underway to expand ports, improve energy supply, build roads, guarantee water supply and so forth. To fund these, Cape Verde is dependent on foreign aid and foreign investors. And as tourism keeps growing, the demands on the infrastructure keep growing, too. So long as everyone remains confident, the wheel can keep turning.

Incentives Setting up an 'external investment company' which employs a minimum number of Cape Verdeans is an important step in achieving status for a business as an 'external investor', thus qualifying it for various privileges, such as concessions from the otherwise extremely high tariffs on imports and exports of materials.

Foreign businesses also qualify for tax concessions and incentives, some of them sector-specific.

Getting help and advice The first port of call for a foreigner proposing to invest is the state-run Cabo Verde Investimentos (CVI) (*www.cvinvest.cv*), based in Praia, from whom advice, forms and instructions can be obtained. Their website is in English and Portuguese and CVI announced in late 2013 their intention to publish Cape Verde's investment rules in English, French and Spanish 'within six months'. Once contact has been made by a prospective investor, a process of 'due diligence' then takes place, which will require identity checks, a letter from the investor's bank, a business plan. If land purchase is involved, then at some stage surveys and environmental reports will be necessary. CVI can also provide a list of multilingual lawyers and consultants and contacts at the relevent local administration. They also have contacts at the banks, recommending Caixa Economica as they are part-state-owned. Once you have obtained a certificate of external investment (in the case of a tourism facility, *autorização turístico*) you have access to any relevant tax incentives. This can be quite a laborious process. It is useful to cultivate a good relationship with the president of the relevant island's town hall, as they may well become involved at some stage. Cape Verde Investments claim that they are interested in all investments, whatever their size, though some investors have claimed that they lose interest if only a small capital sum is involved. Going forward, an investor's inability to speak Portuguese will make it very difficult to oversee any investment project.

Other suggested contact links:

Banco de Cabo Verde www.bcv.cv. Website of Cape Verde's central bank, in English.
Cabo Verde Telecom www.cvtelecom.cv. Cape Verde's principal telecommunications provider.

Governo de Cabo Verde www.governo.cv. Official Cape Verde government website.

Tips for sucess Cape Verdean culture is complex – at once West African, European, American, cosmopolitan and parochial.

The following are tips from people who have set up businesses in Cape Verde:

* Try to learn the language as soon as possible
* Cultivate a good relationship with the president of the town hall (*câmara*) on your chosen island
* Even small investors should employ a lawyer for dealing with Cabo Verde Investimentos and other bodies
* Customs bureaucracy can delay the release of imported items, sometimes by up to six months
* Cultivate the virtue of patience

BUYING PROPERTY The barren hinterlands of Sal and Boavista serve to contrast dramatically with the nearby, huge-scale developments of hotels and apartment blocks which have erupted in the past few decades. The slowdown after 2008 left many investors high and dry and many construction sites devoid of activity. Some of these *are* still active, now ambling along towards eventual completion; some are dormant, waiting patiently for an improved economic climate; some are practically extinct, seemingly destined to remain half-built for ever. There are still huge areas that are earmarked for massive complexes, especially on Sal, Boavista and Santiago.

Visions and plans are one thing, reality is another. Cape Verde has many natural attractions, but the casual holidaymaker should not allow sun, sea and sand to diminish the habitual caution they would exercise when approaching a property purchase back in their own country. The web forums are full of investors who have had their fingers burned. One scam even involved creating a website with pictures of a luxury development on the archipelago and invited investors to partake, which they duly did. Unfortunately, the development was neither in Cape Verde, nor did it belong to the advertiser. The once-eager investors will not see their money again.

The high-profile sales talk about Cape Verde being 'the next Caribbean' has died down and a second wave of purchasers who have more realistic expectations has arrived. Cape Verde has the potential to be a good, profitable destination (climate,

Many investors buy 'blind', putting down hefty deposits on properties they have never even seen. Sometimes they have not even visited the islands themselves. This is inherently risky, some would say inherently foolish. Here are some essential tips.

GO TO CAPE VERDE The best recommendation before deciding anything is to take a trip or trips to get to know your chosen island, look the developer in the eye, see the proposed development site, check the views, listen to the noise, feel the wind, smell the scent, and see the building progress (if any). Most of all, talk to locals and other ex-pats while you're there. Read the forums on the websites listed at the back of this guide. Then make your mind up.

USE A CAPE VERDEAN LAWYER This is essential. They know the law, they know the language. Charges for checking land ownership, planning, road access and other key issues are usually comparatively modest. It is essential to choose your own lawyer, never one selected by the developer.

CHECK THE DEVELOPMENT FINANCE Many developers can be undercapitalised, putting your investment at risk. Their cash flow relies on a steady stream of deposits from investors to fund the purchase of land and the building of apartments. If this dries up, work may cease.

FIND OUT ABOUT THE LAND OWNERSHIP Land ownership in Cape Verde is complex (see box, page 31). Claims to land ownership have turned out to be false and if they are false, you could lose out. Make your own checks on ownership: white stone markers are placed on plots of land to delineate them – and plans are lodged at the town hall for public scrutiny. Use your lawyer. Some developers do not provide access roads and owners may have to pay for this later.

LOOK FOR THE ROUND STAMP Outline planning permission for development is given by the government. Detailed plans for design must be approved by the town hall on each island, which adds a round stamp to the blueprint. This is not always done.

stability, accessibility, incentives to investors), but now there is an element of investor caution due to the volatility of financial markets.

Many of the agents and property sales companies have moved on, leaving the more experienced developers and agents providing more stability and better advice to clients. Overall the market in the most popular investment island, Sal, has become more professional and organised but there is still a huge amount of property unoccupied. A question mark hangs over whether there will ever be enough tourists to fill it.

Buying in Cape Verde remains speculative, in a market that is flooded with apartments. Land in some islands, such as Maio, is still alluringly cheap, but any future gain in capital value is subject to some major 'ifs' and 'buts'. A real-estate investment in Cape Verde could prove to be lucrative, but it is not recommended for those of modest means or those who cannot afford to take a risk with their capital.

RETURNING *EMIGRANTES* Many Cape Verdeans overseas long to return home one day, either to work or in retirement. On the one hand the flourishing economy is

GET THE CORRECT PAPERS Cape Verde, unlike English-speaking countries, uses a notary system. A buyer receives a sales contract in Portuguese which stipulates when a property will be finished and when stage payments are to be made. On completion, the buyer and vendor meet at the notary`s office, pay the sales tax and sign the deeds. The notary acts as an independent arbitrator and tax collector. Without the correct papers, you are not the legal owner.

CHOOSE YOUR DEVELOPER AND SALES AGENCY WELL Ask around during your inspection visit. Talk to as many people as you can, knock on doors of any neighbouring properties that are already occupied. What is their experience with the developers and the agents?

CHECK THE MANAGEMENT CONTRACT Find out how a property is to be managed and check the contract for onerous clauses. Ideally, annual charges, utility charges, etc and any mechanism for increases in these should be set out in the contract. Is the developer contractually bound to connect water and electricity within a specified period after building completion? If not, your newly completed property may be unusable.

BE SCEPTICAL ABOUT GUARANTEED RENTALS Some developers quote a guaranteed return and a prospective rate of capital gain. Unless this is part of the contract, it is worthless. Some of the figures quoted are very optimistic.

INVESTIGATE MORTGAGE FINANCE This is rarely available on off-plan property until it has been completed. Interest rates from Cape Verde banks can be very high. Cheaper sources of new capital are to borrow against an asset such as your main home.

WHAT IS YOUR LEGAL REDRESS? If the contract is signed in Cape Verde then any arguments are settled in a Cape Verdean court, which is very slow. The law allows for a 7% interest payment by the developer once a building is more than six months delayed, as they often are. Alternatively it provides for a full refund if required, but many developers are loath to comply and it could be difficult to enforce.

creating opportunities, on the other rising land prices and the state of the dollar may make a return financially difficult, if not impossible. Cape Verde Investments reported in 2013 that there was currently very little interest from the US diaspora in investing in the archipelago. Nevertheless, the government are doing their best to encourage the diaspora to get involved. A guide for returning emigrants, entitled *Return to Cape Verde with Success*, is available, online and in English at www.mdc.gov.cv. It contains useful general information about the country, as well as more specific tips for returnees on matters such as finance, job searching, property, starting a business, tax benefits and red tape.

CAPE VERDE TRAVEL

Tour Operator & Retail Agent
Proprietor: Mr Ron Hughes P.Q.R.C
14 Market Place, Hornsea, East Yorkshire, HU18 1AW, England
Tel: 0044 1964 536191 Fax: 0044 1964 536192
www.capeverdetravel.com sales@capeverdetravel.com

Mindelo Office: Carlos Mondlane, Mindelo, Sao Vicente, Republic of
Cape Verde Tel: 00238 9982878 Capeverdetravel@cvtelecom.cv

Specialists in the Cape Verde Islands for 15 years we offer our clients tailor made itineraries to each of the 9 islands as well as the traditional beach holidays.

Discover the Real Cape Verde with its culture and beauty.

Our skills allow us to coordinate travel throughout the archipelago providing many activities such as trekking, rambling, bird watching, diving, deep sea fishing, mountain biking, sailing and other various sports., topped up with wedding arrangements on some of the islands.

We offer the widest range of flights to our country including North and South UK, Europe, USA, Brazil and West Africa including Fortaleza, Gabon, Cameroon, Sao Tome & Principe, Angola and Senegal. We also provide domestic air passes for the local airline.

Accommodation consists of character guest houses, established local hotels and soon to appear are the more internationally recognised hotel chains. All facilities are personally inspected.

Wherever you are in the world, plan your journey with us. Whether it be for business or leisure, contact us.

For more information on flights and holiday reservations please contact our sales team on 0044 1964 536191

Also offering other
adventures to Sao Tome,
Cameroon, Senegal, Angola
and Brazil.

Part Two

THE GUIDE

3

Sal

You live – sleeping mother
Naked and forgotten
Arid, Whipped by the winds
Cradled in the music without music
Of the waters that chain us in…

Amílcar Cabral, quoted in Basil Davidson, *The Fortunate Isles* (Hutchinson, 1989)

There can be nowhere on earth as elemental as Sal. Any mountains, streams or vegetation that may have adorned it in the past have been obliterated by the wind over millions of years. Now Sal is just rock, sand and salt, still blasted by the same winds. On Sal the transience of life – animal or vegetable – becomes very clear.

The arrival at Sal on an international flight is a deliciously depressing descent. For hours the traveller has scanned the Atlantic from the aeroplane window, searching for the lost islands of Cape Verde with a growing sense of their isolation. Then Sal appears: relentlessly brown and featureless, etched with dry cracks through which rain might occasionally flow. Disembarking from the aircraft to cross the heat of the runway you will gaze at the rocky plains in puzzlement, trying to remember why you decided to come. If you've already visited the other less-developed islands, you may think that the airport apron contains more tarmac than exists on the rest of the islands put together, given their penchant for cobbled roads.

Three types of travellers come to Sal: those seeking no more than year-round sunshine, beautiful beaches and blue sea who head for the out-of-town, all-inclusive resorts, the smaller Santa Maria hotels or their own holiday apartments; watersports enthusiasts craving world-class wind- and kitesurfing and diving; and those who use it as a relaxing and comfortable base from which to explore other islands. All three should be satisfied with what Sal has to offer.

HIGHLIGHTS

Sal is a top windsurfing, kitesurfing and surfing destination and also offers good diving and fishing as well as Cape Verde's largest number of organised tourist activities. The beach in Santa Maria is surely world-class and you can sunbathe, snorkel and swim, and enjoy the international hotels with their pools and other facilities. Those based on Sal can get a flavour of other Cape Verdean islands through day trips by boat or plane. You can fill a day by visiting the imposing volcano crater and salt lake of Pedra de Lume (a candidate UNESCO World Heritage Site), the foaming lagoon and Blue Eye at Buracona, see the mirages at Terra Boa or take a boat ride to view whales and dolphins. Other possibilities include taking lonely walks to watch the turquoise sea from its treeless, rugged coastline or crossing the rocky interior with a 4x4 or quad bike. Sal abounds in interesting birds and shells and there are opportunities to watch turtles. The island's resort, Santa Maria, also has the archipelago's best range of decent restaurants, lively bars, live-music venues and nightclubs – enough to satisfy most party-goers.

SUGGESTED ITINERARY AND NUMBER OF DAYS If you are dedicated to a watersport or two, are a real sun lizard, or enjoy the prospect of the resort hotels you should aim to spend at least a week here. If you are a sightseer, or crave mountains or greenery, go for one to two days, maximum.

If you are passing through Sal between flights, we suggest one of the following, all of which are described below: a walk up and around Monte Curral in Espargos (1hr); a trip to Pedra de Lume (2–4hrs); for those seeking some chill-out time between island-hopping, a few hours on the beach in Santa Maria; or an organised excursion around the island (3–6hrs).

LOWLIGHTS

Sal is still developing as a tourist destination and some tour operators and travel agents oversell it as some verdant, undiscovered paradise. If the frenzy that arose a few years ago claiming that this was the 'new Caribbean' has not fully abated, then it needs to. It's not any kind of Caribbean: though its beaches are beautiful, its waters crystal clear, and it has the occasional small mountain, its interior is a brown desert with very little vegetation. Visitors who book under false impressions sometimes return disappointed with the small number of sights on Sal, relatively high prices and the abundant wind. Many others, of course, have had a happy, sunny holiday.

Those who love Sal tend to be sea lovers rather than land lovers. It is not the place for hikers, those in search of beautiful, green scenery or those who seek to immerse themselves in the rustic Cape Verdean way of life. If your goal is to see several islands you may regret having allocated precious days to Sal. Instead, get on with your journey – you can fit Sal into transit times at the beginning and end of the holiday, indulging yourself in this ideal relaxation destination.

BACKGROUND INFORMATION

HISTORY On Sal the living was always marginal, based on whatever demand could be found for its four specialities: sun, sand, wind and salt. Today, for the first time in its history, it is flourishing as the result of three of those commodities. Sand and sun are in demand from beach-loving tourists. And the wind now catches the sails of delighted windsurfers who have discovered one of the best places in the world for their sport.

For the last five centuries Sal's economy has risen (always modestly) and fallen with international demands for its fourth element, the one from which it takes its name: salt. It is thought that even before the island was sighted by Gomes and de Noli in 1460 it was known by Moorish sailors for its rich saltpans.

The colonisation of the rest of Cape Verde had little consequence for Sal for hundreds of years – salt was procured more easily from the island of Maio, closer to the capital island, Santiago. Nothing much disturbed Sal except perhaps the offloading of some perplexed goats in the 16th century as part of the archipelago's drive to increase meat production. For much of the time there were probably also a few slaves on Sal, digging for salt. Early reports from passing sailors reveal that people sometimes hunted marine turtles on the island.

Even by 1683 the passing English sailor William Dampier reported the presence of just six men, a governor… and an abundance of flamingos. There are no longer any of the last – it is believed they disappeared with the rise of the salt industry. The men survived by trading with the odd passing ship – salt and goat skins in exchange for food and old clothes.

It wasn't until 150 years ago, when Cape Verdean businessman Manuel António Martins set up a salt export business, that Sal's population began to grow. A thousand souls came to join the 100 occupants between 1827 and 1882 – 'souls' was the word used by the British businessman from São Vicente, John Rendall, to describe both free men, of whom there were 300, and slaves. The salt business was based at two sites: Pedra de Lume in the east and Santa Maria in the south. Its fortunes fluctuated with the rise and fall of trade barriers in Brazil, the African mainland and even Portugal itself. Eventually the business ceased in the first half of the 20th century and the island returned to desolation. Archibald Lyall, an English journalist who visited in 1936, reported:

Not even the most rudimentary garden is possible among the shifting dunes, and all the landward windows of the houses have to be kept perpetually shuttered against the penetrating yellow grit.

Sal's 20th-century prosperity began when the Italian dictator Benito Mussolini was looking for a site where aircraft could stop to refuel between Europe and South America. Portugal sold him the right to build an airport on Sal, then bought back the resulting facility in 1945. Since then the airport has grown and the town of Espargos has developed with it. Another nation also found Sal a useful refuelling point in the past: South Africa. Throughout the years of apartheid, when other African countries refused to allow its planes to land on their ground, South African Airways stopped in Sal. Responding to the need to house airline crews was Sal's first, tiny step towards tourism.

SAL TODAY Sal draws some income from its airport, its petrol-storage facilities, and the fish-processing factory in its harbour, Palmeira. But it is tourism and real estate where the economic potential is thought to lie, though the financial crisis of 2008 and after has meant that the island may have to wait for the goose to fully finish laying the golden eggs.

Over the last few years, thanks to generous tax concessions and an unquenchable European thirst for virgin destinations, tourism on Sal has surged. Visitor arrivals in Cape Verde in 2012, for example, were up an impressive 12.3% on the previous year, with Sal being the second most-visited island, only slightly behind Boavista. As on Boavista, the tourist numbers on Sal have given the island a more international flavour than the less-visited members of the archipelago: prices here are often quoted in euros, a currency that is readily accepted. If national development plans are followed some 17% of Sal's land will eventually be taken up with tourism developments and services over the next few years.

Echoing this has been a boom in apartment building. The thought of owning a few square metres of real estate in Sal had caught the imaginations of mostly British and Irish nationals who wanted both a place in the sun and a financial stake in what was, at least then, perceived as the 'Next Big Thing'. Following the worldwide economic crisis, many inexperienced speculators had their fingers burned and many developments lie unfinished. For now at least, things have quietened down.

Sal today has a purpose, a place in the world. Its population has soared from just 5,500 in 1970 to around 20,000, with two-thirds of them in Santa Maria. Wander around Sal today and you will find not just the indigenous inhabitants but their compatriots from most other islands; you will find construction workers, trinket salesmen and musicians from West Africa; estate agents, developers, gardeners, plumbers and furniture importers from Britain and Ireland; restaurant owners from Italy, France and Portugal.

But though Sal may be the crucible of Cape Verde's economic transformation, it is in some ways its sacrificial victim. It is providing, in the national government's eyes, the quick economic boost thought to be needed in order both to diversify the economy and fund more sensitive touristic development on other islands.

The danger is that Sal will lose its allure in the longer term unless efforts are made to preserve what makes it unique: thick margins of undeveloped beach, dunes, unique birds, turtles and coral mounts in the sea. Even Sal's celebrated windsurfing spots need a custodian, now that they are jeopardised by new buildings blocking the wind. The government has taken some decisive national protective measures: for example, it has banned the use of sand from beaches for construction; it now insists that potential developers make environmental impact assessments; it is tightening up on what they can build and is proposing to replace freehold purchases with leasehold. Sadly, the enforcement of these environmental laws rarely happens.

The second danger is that mass tourism and unsympathetic development on Sal may have unfortunately set the tone for the rest of the archipelago's sandy islands, with Boavista and Maio perhaps heading along the same road. With some imagination tourism could have been redirected so that it treasures, rather than exploits. A quick trip to certain overdeveloped parts of the Mediterranean would have been enough to show those responsible for safeguarding Cape Verde's future just how the desperate search for a quick buck can lead to ruin as well as riches.

GEOGRAPHY Sal is the most barren of the inhabited islands. Its highest peak, Monte Grande, in the northeast, reaches only 406m. The island is just over 30km long and nowhere more than 12km wide. Its landscape is of brown, stony plains and desert sands deposited by winds from mainland Africa. Around 20,000 people occupy its 216km² and they live almost exclusively in Espargos, the capital in the centre of the island, and Santa Maria, the tourist resort on the south coast.

NATURAL HISTORY

Protected areas The bay of Murdeira has been designated a Marine Protected Area but no monitoring or patrolling has taken place, making it an MPA in name only. Known to some as the 'bay of corals' it is home to diverse life, including around 45 types of small fish, many of them endemic (but no big fish). Although Murdeira is rocky it has very small beaches where some loggerhead turtles (*Caretta caretta*) come to nest, but numbers are dwindling due to development and hunting. For both fish and turtles it is a place to hide and feed, and offers perfect conditions as a nursery for fish stocks. Humpback whales can sometimes be seen in the bay, as can melon-headed whales (*Peponocephala electra*). Widespread throughout the world's tropical and subtropical waters, they often go unseen by humans because of their preference for deep water. In 2005, however, a group became stranded in Murdeira Bay. People managed to guide them back to sea.

The salina of Pedra de Lume is a protected landscape and remains on the 'tentative' (candidate) list for designation as a World Heritage Site. Other protected landscapes are the salina of Santa Maria, Monte Grande (the island's tallest mountain) and the lagoon of Buracona. The natural reserves on Sal are Monte Leão (a small hill at the northern end of Murdeira Bay also known as Rabo de Junco); the southeastern stretch of coast known as Costa da Fragata; the beaches of Serra Negra and Ponta Sino. Morrinho do Açúcar and Morrinho do Filho are natural monuments.

Birds Birdwatchers will find interesting waders in the saltpans including, if they are lucky in Pedra de Lume, the black-winged stilt (*Himantopus himantopus*), known locally as *pernalonga*. This extraordinary, elegant creature has long red legs that extend behind it as it flies, as well as a long, thin beak. It breeds only on Sal. Following the rains in August and September many more birds can be seen in the temporary pools that are left dotted around the island. Species you may see include turnstones, sanderlings, Kentish plovers, greenshanks, egrets, kestrels, ospreys and herons.

Turtles Although it's very difficult to provide accurate figures, one estimate states that around 300 endangered loggerhead turtles (*Caretta caretta*) nest annually on Sal (compared with around 3,000 on Boavista Island), mostly along the southwestern and southeastern coasts. The numbers fluctuate hugely from year to year and SOS Tartarugas (see box, *Saving turtles on Sal*, page 100) reported over 500 turtles nesting on the island in 2013.

Turtles have historically faced two major threats on Sal: from tourism and from hunting. Tourists and turtles have the same taste in beaches, so tourism development has been occurring on exactly those beaches that are important for turtles. Illumination from beachfront hotels and apartments disorientates adults and hatchlings. Although the law stipulates that there should be no construction within 80m of the high-tide mark, some developments have flouted this. And the rising number of tourists is leading to more noise, rubbish and adverse types of beach use, particularly as they have not, until recently, been given any advice on how to minimise their impact. One example of the negative effect caused by the increase in tourism is the undoubted damage caused by the irresponsible use of quad bikes, which historically has crushed a large percentage of the turtle nests laid on Sal's beaches.

Hunting is now more of an issue on Sal's northerly beaches. While there has been considerable success in reducing the problem in the south, those committed to saving turtles are still aware of the threat. While some experts believe that tourism will drive every last turtle from Sal, others believe that tourists offer the only hope of salvation – their interest in the matter may convince all parties to change their behaviour. (For more on turtles, see page 8.)

HAZARDS Take care when swimming: currents are milder than in the UK, but when the wave height is great there can be a powerful undertow. Swimming on the east coast needs care. For unfrequented beaches take local advice.

Theft is common in parts of Sal, mostly of possessions left in unattended vehicles and on beaches. Violent muggings involving theft are very unusual, but use common sense if you go to remote places, and don't walk on unlit streets late at night. In general, there is no reason why you should let safety concerns interfere with your visit.

GETTING THERE AND AWAY

BY AIR Most international flights land in Sal, although there are also international airports on Santiago, Boavista and São Vicente. The arrivals hall at **Amílcar Cabral International Airport** can feel chaotic, with a long queue at passport control, but in reality there is almost none of the hassle commonly found in airports in mainland Africa.

If you already have a visa or have prearranged a visa you should join the main queue for passport control. If you have no arrangements for a visa go to the office to the left of the passport barriers to get one for €25. Some customs officers are used to giving visas for one week but if you state how long you will stay they will usually extend the time to a maximum of 30 days. If that office is closed join the main queue and they'll deal with you when everyone else has been sorted (for more information on visas see page 55).

The airport has two branches of BCA bank, as well as a Caixa Economica. Both banks have an ATM and Caixa has Western Union facilities. There is also a currency exchange kiosk, open until 02.00, useful for getting rid of any spare currency on departure. Airlines with offices are TACV, TAP, Cabo Verde Express (usually charter only) and TAAG, for flights to Angola.

Tour agencies represented are CiTS and Morabitur. The airport has two café/ restaurants, CV Telecom and Unitel outlets, a rental-car agency, several souvenir shops, a branch of the music store, Harmonia. a photography shop and a left-luggage office (100$ per item). You can pay for your taxi from the airport in euros (€10 (day)/€12 (night) to Santa Maria).

FESTIVALS

Festivals, when everything may be closed, are as follows:

19 March	São Jose (Palmeira)
3 May	Santa Cruz (Espargos)
9 June	Santo António (Espargos)
24 June	São João (Espargos)
29 June	São Pedro (Hortela, Espargos)
Last week of July	Santa Ana (Fontona)
15 August	Nossa Senhora de Piedade (Pedra de Lume)
15 September	Nossa Senhora das Dores (Santa Maria)
September	Music festival (date varies)

The common refrain has been that turtles are doomed on Sal. If the locals didn't get them for supper, the quad bikes would crush their nests; and if the bikes didn't get them, hotel and apartment lights would lure them into a deathly inland wander.

SOS Tartarugas (*www.turtlesos.org*), a local NGO, works tirelessly to combat these threats to the turtles' fragile existence. With a dedicated team of employees and a committed corps of international volunteers, the Santa Maria-based organisation has had some notable success, with the hunting of turtles on the island's main nesting beaches virtually under control. But there is much still to be done and Jacquie Cozens, co-founder of SOS Tartarugas, is not yet sure whether the overall battle can be won. Referring to one of the recent beach hotel developments on Sal, Cozens points out on a diagram the huge decrease in turtle nests on that beach since the hotel construction work began.: 'There's been a severe loss of habitat… there's only one part of the beach which is now actually sand. There's light on the beach, there are people on the beach, there are dogs on the beach…' Only five years previously, that same beach had been the prime nesting beach on Sal, with around 30% of Sal's turtle nests. Now, only 10% of the nesting takes place there.

There are fine laws already in existence for the protection of turtles: it's just the implementation that's missing. And implementation needs three things: a willingness on behalf of the authorities, resources, plus manic drive. The willingness is there; shoestring resources have been cobbled together, and the four-strong team running SOS Tartarugas certainly verges on the manic. Since its inception in 2008, it has successfully brought together groups including Cape Verdean soldiers, rangers and monitors to do night beach patrols during the nesting season to prevent turtle hunting. Quad bike trails were developed so that bikers could enjoy themselves without unwittingly going on illegal beach jaunts. SOS has built a good relationship with the local police force, which has been persuaded to take seriously reports of illegal quad biking.

Airlines

✈ **Airport** ☎ 241 1468/1305
✈ **Cabo Verde Express Airport** ☎ 241 2600
✈ **TAAG** Airport ☎ 241 1355

✈ **TACV Airport** ☎ 241 1305
✈ **TAP Portugal** Airport ☎ 241 3129;
e tapreservas.cv@tap.pt

International departures from Sal Get your hotel to obtain updates from the airline about the time of your international departure – better to sit out a delay on the beach than in the airport.

In transit through Sal If you are in transit to Praia Airport on Santiago with TACV then your baggage may well have been checked all the way through. You will, however, have to go through immigration and customs yourself, after which you should check in immediately for your onward flight. If you are in transit to any island other than Santiago you may have to collect and re-check in your baggage. Currently only Sal, São Vicente, Praia and Boavista airports have money-changing facilities so if you are in transit to another island consider obtaining local currency in Sal Airport. If you have a long wait you can leave your luggage at the airport and take a five-minute ride into Espargos or a 15-minute taxi ride to Santa Maria.

Domestic flights TACV flies from Sal to Santiago (about three flights/day); São

Hotels and tour operators are being persuaded to sign up to turtle philosophy – issuing codes of conduct and putting turtle stickers on their bikes. Turtles are also entering the tourist itinerary with the launch of afternoon hatchery visits to see the hatchlings which have been born from relocated eggs. Night trips to witness turtles laying their eggs are also organised by SOS Tartarugas. Unfortunately, a number of untrained and unauthorized 'guides' have muscled in on what is seen as a lucrative 'turtle tours' market, and these irresponsible 'tours' result in disturbance to the turtles and a negative impact on their capacity to successfully nest. A move is afoot to ensure that only properly trained guides can take visitors to see turtles, and hopefully this will be implemented shortly.

Cozens says that one of their more solvable problems is, simply, a lack of awareness. 'I don't think tourists want to destroy turtle nests. And so if we publicise this information I think most visitors will comply. And the government wants to do it: they know they've got a really good resource here; there's little else to do on Sal. That's why I'm so ridiculously optimistic that we can do something here.' As well as the hatchery on the beach in front of the Riu Hotel, SOS Tartarugas runs an education centre in Santa Maria town. These initiatives are doing good work to combat the lack of awareness amongst visitors. The organisation has also been working with developers who look set to infringe the law (for example, those who build beach bars closer than the permitted 80m from the coastline) or to infringe the philosophy (for example, by over-illuminating the beaches they overlook). Problems raised by proposed new developments are probably the most intractable and are generally thought to be what will get the turtles in the end.

'Almost every bit of land on the west coast is earmarked for development,' says Cozens. 'But we do have a big opportunity on the east coast, which is a nature reserve.'

Vicente (two flights/day); Boavista (two flights/day); and São Nicolau (three times/week). Fly to Santiago for connections to Maio and Fogo. If you need to book TACV flights in Sal, it is best to go to the airport office (⊕ 08.00–11.30 & 14.00–17.00 Mon–Fri) or to Barracuda Tours or vista verde tours in Santa Maria (see page 104). Flights can be paid for with Visa or MasterCard. Be warned, however, that flights book up quickly and if you are on a tight schedule it is best to pre-book internal connections before leaving home, through your tour operator or travel agent.

Cabo Verde Express is a charter airline that mostly flies tour groups on day trips to other islands. Enquire at the airport or through tour operators in Santa Maria. Flights only go ahead if the plane is full.

From the airport Most of the big, all-inclusive tourist hotels meet international charter flights with their own buses. Santa Maria is a 15-minute journey from the airport, Murdeira less than ten minutes and Espargos only two minutes. From the airport there are always plenty of **taxis** to Espargos (250$, or 300$ at night) or Santa Maria (1,000$, or 1,200$ at night). You probably won't find **public transport** (an *aluguer*; see page 102 for details) waiting at the airport, but if you walk out of the airport and stand on the main road you can catch an *aluguer* (100$ to Santa Maria); be aware that you may wait some time as most *alugueres* leave Espargos full. Alternatively take a taxi only as far as Espargos and pick up an *aluguer* there. Relying on finding an *aluguer* is not recommended if your flight lands late at night.

BY BOAT Ferries do connect Sal with some of the other islands, but they are not advised if you are on a tight time schedule. It would be misleading to describe them as reliable or comfortable and some people raise questions about their safety. There are two ticket agencies in Espargos and one in Palmeira, which is Sal's port town. Agence Anavsal in Espargos (✆ *241 1359*) sell tickets for services to São Vicente, São Nicolau and Boavista. Also in Espargos, Agence Translogistic (✆ *241 2647*) has tickets for Santiago and Boavista, while Agence Polar (✆ *241 4245*) in Palmeira has tickets for boats to Santiago and Boavista. Tickets can also be bought at the harbour itself. There are day trips by boat to Boavista (see page 104) but you may have to pay for a return fare even if you are only going one way.

BY YACHT Sal is the most upwind of the islands. There is a very good anchorage in the western harbour of Palmeira. It is a useful place for making crew changes because of the international airport. Yachts generally need to fill up with jerry cans. There is a small shipyard where they can do welding. If this is the first island you visit you will be dispatched in a taxi to the airport for an immigration stamp – an easy process. Other anchorages lie in the broad Baía da Murdeira in the west (where a marina may eventually be built); just south of the promontory of Monte Leão; and in the southern bay of Santa Maria, which is a good anchorage except in southerlies.

GETTING AROUND

A tarmac dual-carriageway road links the airport to the capital, Espargos, and runs down the spine of the island between Espargos and Santa Maria. The journey takes 20 minutes by car. The other paved roads run from Espargos to Pedra de Lume, and Espargos to Palmeira. There are many tracks, some of them pretty rocky, criss-crossing the island, and one can drive straight across much of its inland terrain in a 4x4.

BY PUBLIC TRANSPORT *Alugueres* run regularly between Espargos and Santa Maria (100$) and between Espargos and the airport; less regularly from Espargos to Palmeira (50$) and infrequently to Pedra de Lume. A taxi is probably best for this last route. In Espargos the *alugueres* depart from the square across from Hotel Atlântico (see map, page 112); in Santa Maria they depart from near the BCA Bank at the entrance to the town.

BY TAXI Taxis (or public *alugueres* chartered as taxis) from Espargos or the airport to Santa Maria cost 1,000–1,200$; and from Espargos to the airport 200–300$. There is a 30% surcharge after dark. Taxis may also be chartered for a half- or full-day's sightseeing (see page 109).

BY CAR Hiring at the airport is costly and not to be relied upon because cars get booked up quickly. There are several car-hire firms of varying standards: try to get a personal recommendation and check the car's tyres, brakes and lights before setting off.

Prices start at about €50 per day, sometimes with a distance limited to 100km, with a surcharge per kilometre thereafter. Many firms require a deposit of at least €100 in cash, or increasingly by credit card. Make sure you hire a 4x4 or much of

Sal will be inaccessible to you. Take care not to leave valuables unattended in the vehicle as smash-and-grab is a speciality in quieter parts of Sal (some rental cars have the locks disabled in order to discourage you from leaving things in the car and getting the windows smashed). The police sometimes stop vehicles in Sal, checking front-seat passengers are wearing seat belts, documentation is correct (proof of ownership or hire; driving licence), and lights are working. Cars do break down more frequently than in Europe so take basic precautions: water, a hat, relevant telephone numbers and a mobile phone.

Car-hire companies

🚗 **Alucar** Santa Maria; ☎242 1187; m 991 5586; ⏲ 08.00–13.00 & 15.00–18.00 Mon–Sat, closed Sat pm & Sun. A local firm with a good reputation & usually the cheapest prices. A Suzuki Jimny is €50/day but you could probably negotiate a lower rate for more days.

🚗 **Hertz** Santa Maria; m 977 4009; e hertz-sal@cvtelecom.cv. Opposite the Belorizonte Hotel.

🚗 **Joel Evora** Espargos; ☎241 3636; e stand@joelevora.com

🚗 **Luz –Car** Santa Maria; ☎242 1520; m 995 9374

🚗 **Melicar** Espargos; ☎241 1666

🚗 **Mendes and Mendes** Hotel Pontão, Santa Maria; ☎242 8060; e mendesemendes@cvtelecom.cv. Also in Espargos: ☎241 2860.

WHERE TO STAY AND EAT

There are two main places to stay: Espargos and Santa Maria. Espargos is cheaper, near the airport and almost entirely unaffected by the tourism in the south. Staying in Espargos and commuting to Santa Maria, however, carries the added inconvenience and cost of the transport, and if you've come to Sal for your holiday, it is likely that the lure of Santa Maria's beaches and watersports are what have brought you here.

The third option is to take a villa in Murdeira village, halfway between the airport and Santa Maria (see page 126). It's an attractive hideaway with some facilities, but it's still a vehicle trip to the action in Santa Maria or to anywhere with local ambience. With the explosion in apartment-building, there are many self-catering options in and around Santa Maria. Renting an apartment can be a much cheaper option than staying in a hotel, especially if you are in a group. Self-catering in Santa Maria is not always straightforward, however, as it is sometimes hard to find all the ingredients you need for a meal. Renting an apartment for a week starts at around €200.

There are still enormous development plans for Sal, with multitudes of apartments, villas, townhouses and resorts being built in and around Santa Maria. While many of these are complete, many are unfinished and gather dust while their future is uncertain.

ACTIVITIES

EXCURSIONS TO OTHER ISLANDS If you have just a week in Sal, and did not take the preferable step of booking any inter-island trips beforehand, time constraints mean that day excursions are your only sensible option. They will whet your appetite for a return trip to Cape Verde.

There are day trips by plane to Boavista (like Sal but with a slightly prettier interior), Santiago (a microcosm of the rest of Cape Verde), Fogo (dramatic volcano), São Nicolau (gentle, mountainous beauty hard to discern on a day trip) and Maio (tranquil town and deserted beaches). These are group tours and they don't give you too much time to look around by yourself. Costs are around €160–240 depending on the island. They can be booked through the tour operators listed below and the flight is with the charter airline Cabo Verde Express. If you want a tailor-made, private tour with your own local guide, vista verde tours (see below) can set this up for you. Sometimes there are day trips by boat and trimaran to Boavista for around €130; check with local tour operators or your hotels.

LOCAL TOUR OPERATORS AND TRAVEL AGENTS

Barracuda Tours [114 B4] 242 2033 (Santa Maria)/241 2452 (airport); m 983 1225; e geral@barracudatours.com; www.barracudatours.com. Long-established Cape Verdean operator situated just east of the pier that can organise most activities, including trips to other islands & excursions on Sal including island tours (approx €36), boat trips (€40–70), fishing trips, diving, quad bikes & car rentals. They also arrange cookery lessons where you can learn to cook the traditional dish of *cachupa*.

Morabitur [114 B4] At Sal Airport, Espargos & in Santa Maria on the pedestrian road down from CV Telecom to the pier; 242 2070; m 918 7307; e morabitur@morabitur.com; www.morabitur.com. Offers round-island trips, day trips to other islands, fishing, quad bikes, etc.

SalMine Tour Office [114 B3] Outside CV Telecom, Santa Maria; m 983 0712; 09:00–17.00 Mon–Sat. Friendly advice & information & a booking point for all types of land & sea excursions.

Porto Seguro Tourist Office [114 A4] m 959 2030; 09.00–17.00 daily. On the walkway running along the main beach in Santa Maria near the west side of Morabeza Hotel. Excursions on land & sea, including an island tour by minibus (€18), sailing/snorkelling trips (€40), & whale-watching (seasonal, €40). Friendly, helpful service in English & other languages. Formerly called Turtle Shack, it may change its name again.

vista verde tours [114 B4] 242 1261; m 952 5458; e anne@vista-verde.com; www.vista-verde.com; 10.00–13.00 & 16.00–19.30 Mon–Fri, 10.00–13.00 & 16.00-18.30 Sat. In the pedestrian area that connects Santa Maria's pier to CV Telecom. This well-established and multilingual travel agency specialises in social & environmentally responsible tourism. Arranges small-group tours or tailor-made holidays incorporating accommodation, flights, hiking & excursions. Also offices in Fogo and São Vicente. See also ad, inside back cover.

SAILING AND BOAT TRIPS There are many ways to get out on the sea in Sal. Boats including catamarans, traditional wooden sailing ships and powerboats offer whale-watching, cruising, snorkelling and fishing. They leave from either the pier in Santa Maria or the dock in Palmeira. If it is the latter, transport to Palmeira is usually included. Boats come and go so check with a local booking office or your hotel when you arrive.

Fidel Book via the SalMine Tour Office (m 983 0712). Charters available. A 25m Turkish Caicco. Offers daily trips around the west coast of Sal, departing from Palmeira & stopping in Murdeira Bay for snorkelling & swimming. Day trips from €89.

Neptunus m 988 7107; or contact via a tour operator. Day & night trips in a boat with a glass undercarriage that allows you to see the reefs, fish & wrecks in Santa Maria without getting wet. The latest attraction is a statue of Christ (or is it Neptune?) in 6m of water off Porto Antigo. Trips from €33.

SalMine Tourist Office Outside CV Telecom, Santa Maria; m 983 0712. See page 125 for details.

WINDSURFING AND KITESURFING For a discussion of Cape Verde's wind- and kitesurfing potential, see page 53.

Sal is a great destination for these sports and Cape Verde is now included in the Professional Windsurfing Association's competition circuit. Winds can be strong from November to May, however, and beginners need to be careful. For surfers, the best surf comes between November and the end of March. All kite, wind and surf locations are deep-water locations; there are no shallow areas for kitesurfing here. All schools have rescue boats and a rescue will cost you €30–50.

Sal is favoured by many because it has five major locations all within a 15-minute drive from Santa Maria. A wide range of conditions can be found between these five locations including waves, flat water, offshore winds and onshore winds. There are a number of places along the west coast for more advanced surfers and windsurfers. (For further information, see www.surfcaboverde.com). Spares and items such as leashes, helmets and fins are not usually available, so bring your own. The main spots are:

Santa Maria Bay Some 3km of white sandy beach and no rocks. The most convenient spot because it's likely to be walking distance from your accommodation and it's where the kite- and windsurfing schools are. The water is generally flat with gentle swells but the wind can gust a bit close to shore. Near the pier is suitable for beginner windsurfers, the middle of the bay for all levels of windsurfers, and the far end (Ponta Sino) is popular with kitesurfers. Ponta Sino also has a lovely wave when the swell is right. Schools teach kite- and windsurfing in this area, where the wind is more side offshore at the start of the bay and side onshore at the end. Further out, the wind becomes stronger and more steady; nowadays, the wind closer in to shore is more gusty due to the increase in construction. For this reason, more advanced windsurfers prefer Lembje Beach or round the corner in front of the RIU Hotel.

In front of the RIU Hotel A three-minute taxi ride from Santa Maria, this area is growing in popularity with kitesurfers and windsurfers. The area in front of the hotel offers some of the strongest side offshore winds on the island and the sea becomes wavier the further out you go. More advanced kite- and windsurfers enjoy this location as the wind is more consistent, but from January to March there can be a strong shorebreak. Surfzone have a base there and can take you there or rent you equipment once you are there.

Punta Lembje Many windsurfers start out in the bay and make their way to this point at the eastern end of Santa Maria. Lembje is great for more advanced windsurfers; the water is flatter on the inside of the bay and wavier outside. There are some rocks (more in the wintertime) when entering the water, so shoes are advisable. When there are waves at this beach, they are great clean waves. It is also a good spot for more advanced kitesurfers, as it is difficult to enter the water from this beach, because of the rocks and the gusty wind (once you are out in the water the wind is more constant).

Kite Beach Formerly known as Shark Bay, this 2km stretch of nature reserve on the southeastern coast has stronger and more constant side onshore winds but gentler waves. It's shallow for hundreds of metres out to sea. There is a small reef providing a stretch that is useful for beginners and intermediate wave riders, and a deeper area further south for the more advanced (but watch for the occasional rock). It is growing in popularity with windsurfers, but at present mostly kitesurfers are seen here.

It's a bit too far to walk but you can get there in 15 minutes by taxi from Santa Maria (€10 round trip). There are no schools at Kite Beach but the schools in Santa Maria will often allow you to rent equipment to take there. There is a small shack that sometimes sells drinks.

Ponta Preta Now on the world wave-jumping circuit, Ponta Preta is suitable only for the experienced with huge, hollow, perfectly formed waves, which can reach 6m in height. Ponta Preta presents a number of challenges including an offshore (or side offshore) wind, waves breaking mostly onto sharp rocks (though finishing on sand), and strong undercurrents. There are no schools here or rescue boats and it is rare that a school will rent you equipment to take there, since the risk of damage is so high. Ponta Preta has a restaurant (see page 126).

There are several schools offering equipment hire and/or tuition. Sample prices are: kitesurfing introductory lessons €90, full course €345 (11 hours), one day's rental €60; windsurfing lessons: one hour €40, one day's rental €15, one week's rental €345; one hour's surfboard rental €10.

Angulo Watersports Praia António de Sousa; 242 1580; e joshangulo@mac.com; www.angulocaboverde.com. Close to the now-closed Hotel Sab Sab, in the east of Santa Maria, it offers windsurfing, kite rentals, private tuition & island trips. The website has good location information.
Bravo Club At the Vila do Farol Hotel; e bcfarol.recep@renthotel.org. Offers windsurfing.
Club Mistral/Escola de Kitesurf +351 93 833 2245; e info@escoladekitesurf.com; www.escoladekitesurf.com. On the beach near Hotel Belorizonte, this centre offers tuition & equipment

hire for kite- & windsurfing, but it spends the summer in Portugal.
Surf Zone 242 1700; m 982 7910/997 8804; e info@surfcaboverde.com; www.surfcaboverde.com; ☉ 09.00–17.00 daily. Located outside the Morabeza Hotel & on the beach at the RIU Hotel, this friendly, multilingual outfit offers kitesurfing, windsurfing & surfing; instruction & kit hire. Its website has excellent information for independent kite- & windsurfers on the most popular spots on the island.

SURFING Surfing in Cape Verde is discussed in *Chapter 2, Practical information*, page 51. The surf is mostly reef breaks but there are some beach breaks too, and there are breaks suitable for all abilities, but it is particularly good for advanced surfers. The big waves tend to be between January and March. In Santa Maria Bay the area beside the pier is one of the major wave spots for surfers. This wave, like all the waves on the island, are dependent on an ocean swell and when the waves do come in they average in size from 1m to 2m and offer a great ride. The other wave spot is at Ponta Sino at the far end of the bay. For equipment hire see the listings above for contact information.

FISHING For a description of Cape Verdean fish, see *Chapter 2, Practical information*, page 51. Fishing is best done between July and October, but wahoo is available almost nine months of the year. There is a good wahoo fishery about 20 minutes away, by sea, from Santa Maria. Big-game fishing (for tuna, shark and blue marlin; €250–400 per boat for half a day), trawl fishing (for wahoo, tuna, barracuda and bonito; about €250 for a boat) bottom fishing (bonita, sargo and more), pier fishing, and surf casting (about €30 per person for two hours) are available from the Santa Maria-based companies below. In addition, local fishermen at the pier might be recruited more cheaply for interesting fishing trips.

Club Odissea/Sal Sport Fishing m 988 7107/999 1062; e caboverdeaquasport@hotmail.com; www.salsportfishing.com. Offers big-game fishing & bottom fishing. You can also book your trip on *Neptunus* (glass-bottomed boat) here.

Fishing Center 242 2050; m 993 1332; e caboverdefishingcenter@yahoo.it; www.caboverdefishingcenter.com. On the promenade running along the main beach, by the Atlantis restaurant. Trolling, jigging & big-game fishing with a long-established Italian-owned centre.

DIVING Diving in Cape Verde is discussed in detail on page 50. There are some exciting dives on Sal, including five wrecks. There is the 1966 freighter *Santo Antão* sitting at a depth of only 11m but full of large, colourful fish, and the Russian fishing trawler *Kwarcit* (known locally as 'Boris' as its real name is difficult to pronounce!), which was confiscated after being caught transporting illegal immigrants from Africa, and which now sits at 28m. Manta Diving Center, in conjunction with the Oceanário de Lisboa, has developed a project called 'Rebuilding Nature', which aims to create artificial reefs as a means of increasing fish life and developing sustainable tourism. The latest wreck sunk as part of this project is the *Sargo*, a decommissioned Cape Verdean naval vessel. The artificial reefs are being evaluated to determine their role in improving biodiversity and raising awareness of threats to the marine environment.

Within the bay of Santa Maria and along the west coast there is a range of reef dives suitable for all levels. A highlight is Cavala (40m), a dramatic wall dive ending in a large cave. There are several cave dives in the north, including one at Buracona where, 20m down, you swim into lava tubes and journey through caves for about 80m until the tunnel turns upwards, revealing a chink of light. Following it further you reach a huge, open-topped cave, 10m in diameter, where you can surface to the surprise of land-based tourists looking in from the top. There are also good dives at the many other small caves and inlets north of Palmeira (10–15m drops). Salão Azul, 200m off Pedra de Lume, is a reef with a wall that stretches to a depth of 45m, peppered with recesses full of marine life, but the northwesterly winds mean it is rarely dived.

Dive centres based at Santa Maria's hotels are also open to non-guests and all the dive centres offer PADI (Professional Association of Diving Instructors) courses including try dives. Manta Diving Center is a BSAC (British Sub Aqua Club) centre as well. All have equipment to rent. Prices are around €90 for a two-tank dive including equipment, €100 for a try dive, and €380 for an Open Water course.

Cabo Verde Diving m 997 8824; e info@caboverdediving.net; www.caboverdediving.net. PADI resort behind the Djadsal & Crioula hotels; Italian-run, offering PADI courses & guiding in English & other languages. Will help find accommodation.

Manta Diving Center Between hotels Novorizonte & Belorizonte; 242 1540; e info@mantadivingcenter.cv; www.mantadivingcenter.cv. Visits Buracona & Palmeira on a big boat. Also runs snorkelling trips from Palmeira (€40 inc refreshments).

Scuba Caribe At Hotel Riu Funana & Riu Garopa; 242 1002 (town office); 242 9060, ext 8235 (dive centre on beach); www.scubacaribe.com Offers a full range of diving excursions, plus other watersports.

Scuba Team Cabo Verde On Santa Maria Beach near the Morabeza Hotel; m 991 1811; e info@scubateamcaboverde.com; www.scubateamcaboverde.com. 20 years of experience on the island. Offers guided dive trips in small groups & PADI courses, as well as equipment rental.

SWIMMING There are plenty of lovely swimming areas on Sal, but it's not by any means uniformly safe. The swell and the shore breaks vary depending on the time of year, so ask at your hotel for advice. The *câmara municipal* has employed members of the civil guard to work as lifeguards on some beaches. The beaches east of the pier including Praia António de Sousa are often calm when the west coast is rough. Igrejinha, at the far eastern end of Santa Maria, is a 20-minute walk or a few minutes in a taxi and has a small lagoon, a lovely beach which is perfect for children, and a bar. Ponta Preta has a wide beach and stunning dunes as well as a restaurant. Calheta Funda, north of Santa Maria, is favoured by locals and is good for swimming when it is calm (see *Cycling* below for directions). The small coves north and south of the residential complex at Murdeira usually offer calm conditions and clear water.

SNORKELLING There are a couple of good spots for snorkelling but the sea floor off the main beaches is mostly sandy. Look for areas that have rocky outcrops but take care if there is surf. The area directly east of the pier and around Porto Antigo and Papaia's Restaurant in Santa Maria are good spots (there is an underwater statue 50m straight out from Papaia's). Further out of town Calheta Funda and Cadjatinha are local favourites. Some of the boat excursions will also include snorkelling, most notably with Manta Diving Center who organise snorkelling excursions to Palmeira (see page 107 for contact information). Other boat excursions may take you to Murdeira Bay (a Marine Protected Area) where the fish life is good, but they often anchor in a deep part and you will have to swim to the reef – ask where to go before you jump in or you might be disappointed. You can also snorkel in Murdeira Bay from the shore; there are good beaches north and south of the residential complex ten minutes' drive from Santa Maria.

SHARK-WATCHING South of Pedra de Lume is an area where it is possible to see nurse sharks (*Ginglymostoma cirratum*) in 2–3m of water. You can get in the water with these relatively docile, toothless species which have more in common with stingrays than great white sharks. Some tour companies organise excursions but you could drive yourself there if you get good directions.

CYCLING Some people say that Sal is an excellent place to train for cycling or for triathlons. You could do a fairly relaxed trip from Santa Maria past the RIU and up to the restaurant at Ponta Preta, all on good roads. If you wanted to carry on you could cycle on the main road until you reach Murdeira and then turn off and follow a small road and then a track around the bay to Monte Leão (a half-day trip).

A trip following the road through Santa Maria to the east, past the defunct Sab Sab Hotel will take you on a good track that follows the coastline to Igrejinha (little church), a favourite barbecue spot for locals. You will find a small lagoon protected from big waves by a line of rocks. There is no longer a bar here, but there is plenty of shade.

Carrying on from Igrejinha you could find the track behind the dunes and pass by the old salina on the way to Kite Beach (less than one hour). After Kite Beach there is a dry, dusty, rocky, red sand track that will take you all the way to the beach at Serra Negra (two hours approximately). Follow the coastline so you don't end up on the track heading to the town dump.

A trip to Calheta Funda, where you could swim and snorkel in the protected cove, could make a pleasant half-day excursion. Alternatively you could visit Calheta Funda and then head a little further south to the residential complex of Murdeira where there is a restaurant, bar and pool. To get there, head north from Santa Maria towards the airport until you reach the roundabout with Calheta Funda signposted to the left. Head west along the dirt track (you will appear to be going through private property; it is in fact a cement factory and the road is a public road). Keep heading straight on until the road turns to the left to run alongside the coast. Calheta Funda is a small bay that is signposted.

Bikes can be rented from **CV Bike** (📞 *242 1022*; 📱 *980 3636*) who will deliver your bike to you, or from **Be Be Beach** (📱 *939 1711/970 1303*). There may be others; ask a tour operator or your hotel.

HORSERIDING Fairly recently introduced, this can be organised through the SalMine Tour Office (see page 125). Costs are around €25 per hour. Note that the company providing the service is not insured, so make sure that your own travel insurance will cover you in the event of a mishap.

YOGA If you fancy something a *tiny* bit more energetic than sunbathing, there's the opportunity for indoor or outdoor yoga in Santa Maria.

Sal Yoga 📱 954 1630; 📧 info@salyoga.com. Small group classes take place in the gym of the Hotel Dunas de Sal, at the Morabeza or overlooking the beach at Angulo Watersports (see page 106). Phone to reserve, as classes can fill up quickly.

TURTLE WATCHING The only authorised turtle walks on Sal are run by the charity **SOS Tartarugas** (📱 *974 5020*; 📧 *info@sostartarugas.com; www.turtlesos.org;* ⏰ *mid-Jun–late Sep*). Book at their office in front of CV Telecom, through your hotel or at vista verde tours. Some local tourist guides are also licensed, but were awaiting training at the time of writing. The walks are guided by a biologist or biology student, for groups no larger than ten people, and begin around 20.30 with a short talk about turtles followed by a two-hour period on the beach (or longer, depending on laying time). The walking is not strenuous but you should be able to walk 3km on soft sand. It is not suitable for young children who can find it hard to be still and quiet on demand. The cost is approximately €20, which goes straight into turtle conservation and booking in advance is advised. Many unauthorised and untrained guides will also want to take you to the beach at night but as this has the potential to disturb turtles and may be dangerous, it is strongly discouraged.

There are also hatchery visits on the beach outside the Riu Hotel (⏰ *1 Jun–30 Nov 16.00–18.00 daily; no charge*). There may be the opportunity to see hatchlings being released mid-August–mid-November. Please report any sightings of turtles or tracks on the number above.

SIGHTSEEING BY CAR OR QUAD BIKE There are organised island tours by vehicle for a half day (approximately €20) or full day including lunch (approximately €40). These take in the two key sights of Buracona and Pedra de Lume, and other points of interest. Contact local tour operators (see *Local tour operators and travel agents*, page 104). To see the island you have a number of options: rent a car and see the island in a day without a guide, taking in Pedra de Lume, Buracona, Espargos and perhaps Palmeira and one or two remoter locations described below (for information on car hire, see page 103); charter a taxi for €25 for half a day; or take a round-island tour in a pick-up – the local guides are popular and usually receive good reviews. The

> **HIKING**
>
> You can go for lonely long walks virtually anywhere on the island. See pages 130–1 for details of suggested hikes.

pick-ups are normally marked *Volta ilha* or can be found outside your hotel (from €20 per person for a half day). If you don't fancy bouncing around in the back of a pick-up, minibus tours may be available.

Some tour operators offer a tour of Santa Maria, but the village is so small and safe it hardly seems worth it. A few combine this with a visit to a school in order for you to donate small items such as pens and books.

You can rent a quad bike (€70/day, €40/half day) or take an organised tour (€45–65). It is possible to take a quad-bike tour around the southern part of the island through some interesting terrain that would not be possible by car (€60–70). It is illegal to drive on any beach or dune, so stick to the road or tracks. For more details, check out **Discovery Cabo Verde** (*Behind the Pirata disco; m 996 8271; ⏱ 08.30–12.30 & 14.30–18.00 Mon–Sat, closed Sun*).

ESPARGOS

Poor Espargos has an undeserved reputation for dreariness. In fact, it is just an ordinary town of middling size, with no great attractions but no major hassles for the visitor either. There is no reason to visit it but then it didn't invite you: you are meant to be in Santa Maria. Still, Espargos has an increasingly bustling feel thanks to Sal's economic growth. It has a few good restaurants and at night it is pleasantly lively with locals in the main square and around Bom Dia.

Espargos draws its unlikely name from the wild, yellow-flowered, red-berried asparagus bushes that are said to grow on sandy parts of the island. There is nothing touristic to do in town except perhaps walk up Monte Curral, the mound covered in communications equipment, where you can circle the outside wall for a 360° panorama that will eloquently impart some understanding of the island. To get there, go east from the landmark (but tatty) Hotel Atlântico, straight across the roundabout and then take the left turn immediately after the church. Head uphill, passing a sign for the *miradouro* (viewpoint). All listings below are located on the map, page 112.

WHERE TO STAY

Residencial Santos (15 rooms) Morro de Curral; ✆ 241 1900; m 992 3850; e residencialsantos@hotmail.com. Modern & in good condition; very large rooms & upper terrace. No restaurant, though b/fast included. **$$$**

Hotel Atlântico (80 rooms) CP 74, Rua Amílcar Cabral; ✆ 241 1210; e hotelatlantico@ cvtelecom.cv. This is Espargos's only true hotel, but looks like a cross between a motel & an army barracks. Adequate rooms have TV, but no AC. The price is not much above the other options in town, but it has a 'last-chance saloon' feeling to it. The grounds are barren & in a state of neglect – & they have been for some time. The restaurant is closed & the staff sullen. **$$**

Pousada Paz e Bem (16 rooms) CP 161, Rua Jorge Barbosa; ✆ 241 1782; e pensaopazbem@cvtelecom.cv. West of the main square in a fairly modern building, all rooms are en suite with hot water; some have AC, some have balconies. **$$**

Residencial Central (12 rooms) CP 27, Rua 5 de Julho; ✆ 241 1113. On Espargos's main street, facing the square; the entrance is down a side road. Decent rooms, some with AC, some with fan, all with hot water & TV, arranged around a courtyard. Some with balconies, some are gloomy with only internal windows. **$$**

Residencial Monte Sentinha (13 rooms) Zona Travessa; ✆ 241 1446; e barviolao@ cvtelecom.cv. Towards the northern end of town, this has large, good-quality rooms, all with AC, TV, private baths & hot water. Restaurant Amelia on the ground floor (see below). Rooftop terrace for breakfast. The owner speaks English. **$$**

Casa da Angela (19 rooms) Rua Abel Djassy 20; ✆ 241 1327; m 997 7440; e casangela20@ hotmail.com. Friendly, slightly disorganised, simple place in a quiet location towards the north of town. Small en-suite rooms with fans, hot water (extra cost) & TV. Some rooms have a fridge & spare bed. There's no restaurant, but the bar next door is under same ownership. **$**

✕ WHERE TO EAT AND DRINK

✕ **Amélia** Zona Travessa; ☎ 241 1446; ⏰ lunch & dinner Mon–Sat. A pleasant setting below Residencial Monte Sentinha with the same owner, who is from São Nicolau & sometimes plays music here at weekends. **$$**

✕ **Restaurante Salinas** Rua 5 Julho; ☎ 241 1799; ⏰ 08.00–00.00 daily. Airy 1st-floor restaurant serving 'fresh' fish (which may have been frozen!) & spaghetti dishes. **$$**

✕ **Restaurante Sivy** Praça 5 Julho; ☎ 241 1427; ⏰ 11.00–02.00. Traditional local menu; eat in the cool inside or out on the square. **$$**

💻 **Esplanada Bom Dia** ☎ 241 1400; ⏰ 07.00–00.00 Mon–Sat. Just east of the Hotel Atlântico, this café-bar has a large outside seating area & serves snacks & ice cream & is extremely popular with round-island tours, which take over the place at certain times. **$$**

💻 **Tanha Fina** Rua 5 de Julho; ☎ 241 2822; ⏰ 08.00–00.00. A snack bar with good coffee. **$$**

🍷 **Bar Ziquipa** On the square, serving drinks. ⏰ 10.00–02.00. Lively in the evenings. **$$**

ENTERTAINMENT AND NIGHTLIFE The **Millennium Nightclub** (⏰ *23.00–06.00 weekends*) is several minutes' walk east from the Hotel Atlântico, on the roundabout. The most happening place in town. **Lagoa** (⏰ *23.00–06.00*) is in Hortela.

OTHER PRACTICALITIES

Airlines
Major airlines have offices at the airport rather than in Espargos.

Banks
Espargos has five banks, all with ATMs: Caixa Económica, Rua Jorge Barbosa; BCA, on the roundabout to the east of the Hotel Atlântico; Banco Interatlantico, BAI and BCN on Rua 3 de Agosto. All are open 08.00–15.00 Monday–Friday.

Ferries
When they are running, they depart from Palmeira, to the west of Espargos. Each ferry is run by a different company that sells its tickets separately (See *Getting there and away*, page 102).

Hospital
The **Hospital do Sal** (☎ *241 1130*) was fairly recently opened and is out of town on the road towards Pedra de Lume. There is a small government-run clinic on Rua Albertino Fortes (☎ *241 1130*; ⏰ *08.00–17.00*) and a private clinic, Sahida Consultorio (☎ *241 2551*; ⏰ *08.00–17.00 Mon–Sat*), across the street from CV Telecom. There are two more private clinics with reasonable facilities on Sal (see listings for Santa Maria and Murdeira), and many of the large hotels will be able to find you an on-call doctor.

Internet
There are several internet cafés, including one on the corner by the church in the centre of town and Snack Bar Cyber Pretoria, Barrio Novo. Free Wi-Fi is available in the Praça 5 de Julho.

Laundrette (*Lavandaria*)
With Residencial Santos on the right, turn right and follow the road round to the left.

Optician
Optico Nho São Filipe Rua 3 de Agosto; ☎ 241 8142; ⏰ 09.00–12.00 & 15.00–18.00 Mon–Fri

Pharmacy
Alianca Zona Centro; ☎ 241 1109; ⏰ 08.00–18.00 Mon–Sat

Farmácia Ivete Santos Rua 3 de Agosto; ☎ 241 1417; ⏰ 08.00–20.00 Mon–Sat

Police
With your back to the Hotel Atlântico, follow the main road to the right for ten minutes (going straight on at the roundabout). The **police station** (☎ *241 1132*) is on the right almost at the bottom of the road.

Shopping
JDM in Espargos and Genuine Cabo Verde in Santa Maria are two of the few souvenir shops in Sal that sell strictly Cape Verdean products, including wine

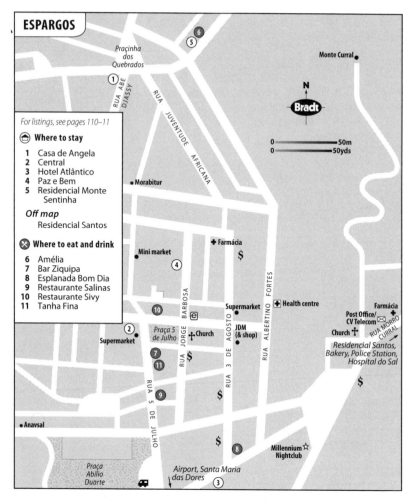

ESPARGOS

For listings, see pages 110–11

⌂ Where to stay
1 Casa de Angela
2 Central
3 Hotel Atlântico
4 Paz e Bem
5 Residencial Monte Sentinha

Off map
Residencial Santos

✕ Where to eat and drink
6 Amélia
7 Bar Ziquipa
8 Esplanada Bom Dia
9 Restaurante Salinas
10 Restaurante Sivy
11 Tanha Fina

Praçinha dos Quebrados

Monte Curral

RUA ABEL DJASSY
RUA JUVENTUDE AFRICANA

N

Morabitur

Farmácia

Mini market

Supermarket

Health centre

RUA BARBOSA

RUA JORGE

RUA 3 DE AGOSTO

RUA ALBERTINO FORTES

Post Office/
CV Telecom

Farmácia

Church

RUA MORRO CURRAL

Residencial Santos,
Bakery, Police Station,
Hospital do Sal

Praça 5
de Julho

Church

JDM
(& shop)

Supermarket

RUA 5 DE JULHO

Anavsal

Millennium
Nightclub

Praça
Abílio
Duarte

Airport, Santa Maria
das Dores

0 ——— 50m
0 ——— 50yds

---

from Fogo, *grogue* and *ponche* in their endless variations, salt from Sal, and assorted handicrafts. *Minimercados* are to be found opposite the church, just off the main square, and under Residencial Santos, in the southeast of town. There is a supermarket under Residencial Central and another on the east side of Rua 3 de Agosto, halfway up. There are two bakeries. Sabores do Sal (m 594 5008;

⊕ 07.00–13.00 & 15.00–20.00) in Barrio Novo has Portuguese-style breads and pastries.

Travel agencies

There are two agencies in Espargos: Morabitur, Rua Toi Pedro (⤳ 241 3372; ⊕ 09.00–12.00 & 14.30–18.00 Mon–Fri); and Trans-Toda Hora, Barrio Novo (⤳ 241 3424; ⊕ 09.00–12.00 & 15.00–18.00 Mon–Fri).

SANTA MARIA DAS DORES

For all the international hype about Cape Verde, Santa Maria das Dores – 'Saint Mary of the Sorrows' – its key tourist town on the main tourist island, remains small and unassuming. Its coastal road and those just behind it are lined with low pastel-coloured buildings housing restaurants, bars, hotels and souvenir shops and the occasional home – lively, but nevertheless often struggling in the shadow of the giant, all-inclusive resorts that lure most of Sal's market. In 1938 Archibald Lyall, the English journalist, reported:

> Never was a place better named than these two or three dozen little houses by the sad seashore. There is no vegetation and nothing to do but steel oneself against the unceasing wind which blows the sand into food and throat and clothes. At night, when the red-eyed people retire to their shuttered, oil-lit houses, the great white crabs come out of the sea and march through the streets like a regiment of soldiers.

But Santa Maria is considerably more cheerful now. The big thing has happened: tourism, and Lyall would struggle to recognise it. And instead of crabs it is tourists that walk the streets at night.

HISTORY While the bay at the south of the island was probably frequented over the centuries by salt diggers and sailors, Santa Maria only officially came into existence at the beginning of the 19th century, when Manuel António Martins of Boavista arrived to exploit the saltpans that lie behind the village.

Martins's workforce scraped away the sand to the rock beneath. They guided seawater inland along little trenches and then pumped it by means of wooden windmills into the rows of broad shallow pans. The water would gradually evaporate leaving white sheets of salt which were dug into pyramids. These were loaded into carts which were pulled by mule, along the first railway tracks to be built in Portuguese Africa, to a newly built harbour. Around 30,000 tonnes of salt were exported each year from the port of Santa Maria and much of it went to Brazil until the late 1880s when that country imposed a high customs tax to protect its own new industry.

In the early 1900s, several new ventures with European companies collapsed, forcing the people of Sal to leave in search of work on other islands. Just a few peasants were left, making a living from salting fish and exporting it to other islands.

Santa Maria's fortunes surged again in the 1920s, when a new market for salt opened up in the Belgian Congo and some Portuguese companies revived the business. By the mid-1900s, Sal was exporting 13,000 tonnes a year and there was enough money to build the Santa Maria of today but, as always, international events were to snatch away whatever prosperity they had bestowed. Independence for the Belgian Congo, changes in Portugal and then independence in Cape Verde brought an end to the business. By 1984, even the routine maintenance of the saltpans ceased.

Santa Maria had a small but significant role to play in Cape Verde's liberation. In September 1974, hearing that Spínola, the new Portuguese ruler, was secretly to visit Sal, Cape Verdeans immediately hired whatever planes and boats they could find. They arrived in Sal and picketed him, daubing slogans on the road from the airport and braving threats that they would be shot. In return an embarrassed Spínola sacked the Cape Verdean governor on the spot and ordered a stronger one to the colony.

Testimony to how tourism has wrought the changes in recent times, the town's modest 1990 population of 1,343 has now grown to an estimated 13,000.

ORIENTATION The bay of Santa Maria takes up most of the southern coast of Sal. The town of Santa Maria begins roughly at a point in the middle of this coastline, and extends to the east. To the west of this midpoint is a line of bigger hotels, connected together by a cobbled dual-carriageway, and interspersed with half-built developments and a couple of closed hotels which failed to survive the recession.

Santa Maria town has three 'layers': hotels make the topping, lining the beach; affluent locals live along parallel streets behind, where there are also many restaurants,

3

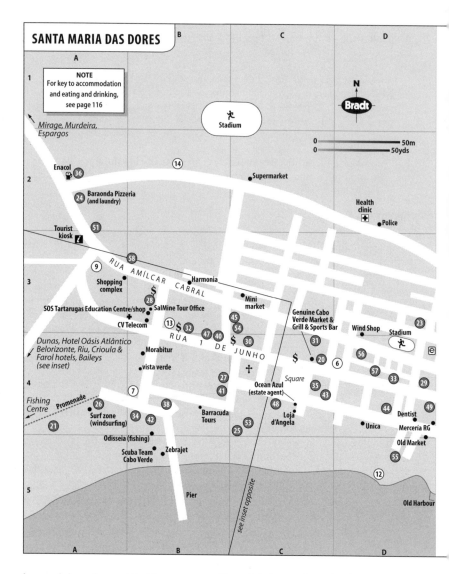

SANTA MARIA DAS DORES

NOTE For key to accommodation and eating and drinking, see page 116

Mirage, Murdeira, Espargos

Stadium

N

0 — 50m
0 — 50yds

Enacol 36

Supermarket

24 Baraonda Pizzeria (and laundry)

Health clinic

Police

Tourist kiosk 51

58

9 RUA AMÍLCAR CABRAL

Harmonia

Shopping complex

Mini market

28

SOS Tartarugas Education Centre/shop SalMine Tour Office

Genuine Cabo Verde Market & Grill & Sports Bar

Wind Shop

Stadium

CV Telecom

13 32

45 54

23

Dunas, Hotel Oásis Atlântico Belorizonte, Riu, Crioula & Farol hotels, Baileys (see inset)

47 40 30

RUA 1 DE JUNHO

31

56

Morabitur

$ 20 6

vista verde

57 33 29

27

Square

Ocean Azul (estate agent)

35 43

Fishing Centre Promenade

7

41

26 Surf zone (windsurfing) 34 42

38

Barracuda Tours

48 Loja d'Angela

44 49 Dentist

21

25 53

Unica

Mercería RG

Odisseia (fishing)

Old Market

Scuba Team Cabo Verde Zebrajet

55

12

Pier

Old Harbour

see inset opposite

---

bars and shops; beyond that the poor part of Santa Maria stretches inland. Here people live in half-finished and unpainted houses made of breeze blocks. To the east there is a new district (Zona António Sousa) of smart apartment buildings being bought by Europeans, tourists and investors which are also available for rental. This district also has a couple of hotels, but still lacks a bit in infrastructure and facilities.

The heart of the town itself consists of three main roads running east to west and centred on the main *praça* and the pier; the main hotel zone is to the west of the village, and to the north and east are the residential districts where most of the self-catering accommodation can be found.

WHERE TO STAY Most of the big, upmarket resort hotels lie on the road running parallel with the beach, west from Santa Maria, and currently all but two are

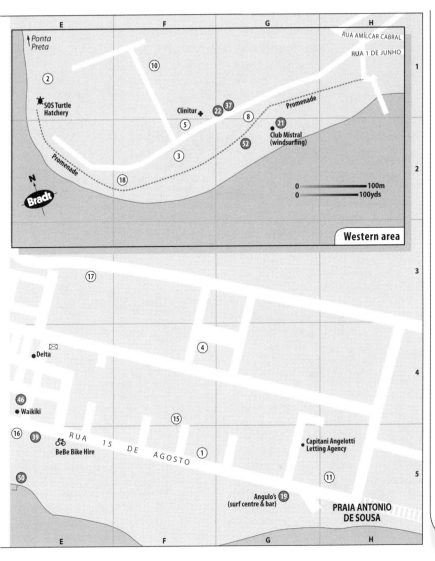

beachfront. There are plans for another international brand hotel in this area, as well as a casino. Most of the other hotels, ranging from budget to boutique, are in town, at varying distances from the beach, though Santa Maria is still so small that nowhere is more than five minutes' walk from the sea. The weekend nightspots in the centre can be late and noisy, so bear this in mind when choosing your accommodation, if you go to bed early. Many new hotels and apartment blocks are still planned but the boom is over for the time being. Santa Maria has a glut of accommodation, though mainly in the mid-range and luxury brackets, while cheaper options are harder to come by. For an explanation of the $ rating, see the inside front cover. Increasing numbers of tourists, particularly watersports enthusiasts, are choosing self-catering apartments, which tend to be at the eastern end of town and can be cheaper. Bear in mind, however, that food shopping in Santa Maria is not that straightforward: food

'Cape Verde – No Stress!' adorns many a T-shirt and is the motto of nearly every souvenir shop in Santa Maria. But for the unwary who venture into one of these emporia, stress could be exactly what you *do* get. Tourism has attracted many types to Santa Maria including souvenir vendors from West Africa whose tactics some Europeans find disconcerting. Their methods differ greatly from the laid-back approach of local Cape Verdeans, who at times seem indifferent to selling you *anything*. The trick to dealing with them is to reteach yourself the art of saying 'no,' without getting upset or wound-up.

Often, the more persistent of these (mainly) Senegalese curio sellers will latch on to you the minute you set foot outside your hotel, and may follow you for some time. If you are not interested in their wares you need to give a firm but polite 'no,' perhaps accompanied with a smile, and avoid being drawn into conversation. Keep walking and resist invitations to follow them to their stall at the local market or into their shop. If you do succumb, then once inside the shop, you may feel intimidated, especially at the point when you decide you really don't want to buy anything. The vendors' tactics can include blocking the door, putting a hand on your shoulder and offering a furious reduction in the price of anything in which you have expressed the slightest interest. Do not allow a vendor of African souvenirs to adorn you with a sample piece of jewellery. Some of those 'priceless' pieces don't unfasten. Even if you are interested, this is one place where you should definitely bargain down the price initially quoted. You can shop for products from Cape Verde at your own pace and without hassle at Genuine Cabo Verde (for more information, see page 125).

SANTA MARIA DAS DORES
See map pages 114–15. For listings, see pages 117–23

Where to stay

1 Aparthotel Santa
   Maria Beach.................F5
2 Club Hotel Riu
   Funaná/Riu Garopa....E1
3 Crioula Hotel....................F2
4 Hotel da Luz...................F4
5 Hotel Dunas de Sal........ F2
6 Hotel Les Alizés.............D4
7 Hotel Morabeza.............B4
8 Hotel Oásis Atlântico
   Belorizonte....................G1
9 Hotel Pontão...................A3
10 Hotel Sabura................. F1
11 Leme Bedje.....................H5
12 Odjo d'Água...................D5
13 Pensão Nha Terra...................B3
14 Pensão Porta do Vento........B2
15 Ponta Preta Apartments......F4
16 Residencial Porto Antigo.... E5
17 Sakaroule................................ E3
18 Vila do Farol Hotel................. F2

Where to eat and drink

19 Angulo's Beach Bar......G5
20 Ao Caranguejo...............C4
21 Atlantis....................A4, G2
22 Bailey's...........................G1
23 Bar Di Nos......................D3
24 Baraonda Pizzeria.........A2
25 Barracuda.......................C4
26 Beach Club..................... A4
   Belorizonte..............(see 8)
27 Blu Bar............................ B4
28 Bombay Brasserie.........B3
29 Café Creolu.....................D4
30 Calema............................C4
31 Chez Pastis.....................C4
32 Chill Out.........................B3
33 Compad...........................D4
34 Crêtcheu Pizzeria..........B4
   Crioula..................(see 3)
35 Cultural Café....................C4
   Dunas..........................(see 5)
36 Enacol............................A2
37 Geko Gourmet................G1
38 Gelataria Sol Doce.........B4
39 Gigi's Manera Café........E5
40 Giramondo......................B4
41 Hexedes Café.................B4
42 Kiosque Beach Bar........B4
43 Lanchonete Angela.......C4
44 Le Privé..........................D4
45 Leonardo's......................C3
   Market Grill & Sports Bar
   (see Genuine Cabo
   Verde Market) C4
46 Marlyne's Restaurant.....E4
47 Mediterraneo..................B4
   Morabeza.................(see 7)
   Nha Terra....................(see 13)
48 Ocean Café.....................C4
   Odjo d'Água..............(see 12)
49 Padaria Dâdo.......................D4
50 Papaia's..............................E5
51 Pirata...................................A2
52 Praia....................................G2
   Sal Beach................(see 53)
53 Sal Beach Club...................C4
54 Sapo Com Fome..................C3
55 Snack Bar Bilu....................D5
56 Tam Tam's..........................D4
57 Uhuru Reggae Bar..............D4
58 Zum Fischermann............... B3

Off map
   Mirage..................................A1

116

is expensive and the range is limited. The following hotels are to the west of Santa Maria and are somewhat isolated from the town itself. As many of them are all-inclusive, you may not feel the need to venture into Santa Maria, but if you do, you'll probably need to take a taxi unless you are a keen walker. All listings are located on the map, pages 114–15, and grid references are on the key opposite.

Hotels west of Santa Maria village

Riu Funana/Riu Garopa (500 + 500 rooms) \242 9060/9040; e clubhotelfunana@riu.com, clubhotelgaropa@riu.com; www.riu.com. Twin resort hotels enclosed behind vast walls beside the beach about 1.5km west of Santa Maria with assorted restaurants, pools, spa & watersports centre. The lobby area is impressive, the grounds less so. Accommodation is in a series of buildings. They provide entertainment & a wide variety of activities & excursions. Heated children's swimming pool. Caters mostly for a variety of Europeans (including British) on all-

---

A HOTEL WITH HISTORY   *Murray Stewart*

As you walk down the pedestrianised path from the CV Telecom building in Santa Maria, heading towards the start of the pier, you will be met by a short column bearing the bust of one Georges Vynckier. Look to your right and you'll notice that the street is named after him too.

In fact, you've already passed the Vynckier family's most lasting legacy: the Hotel Morabeza. It was back in the 1960s when Georges's father Gaspard and his wife Marguerite Massart decided to overcome their dislike of their native Belgium's weather by constructing a house in the then sleepy fishing village of Santa Maria. The house was finished in 1967, and soon afterwards it became accommodation for aircrews whose planes were making stopovers in Sal. In particular, South African Airways used the island, due to the embargo on their planes landing in the African mainland. Eventually, thanks to the drive and determination of Georges's wife Geneviève, the 'house' became an acclaimed 140-room hotel with an excellent reputation. As global events unfurled – and aircraft became more capable of longer flights – the Sal stopover became less popular, but the dwindling needs of aircrew were quickly replaced by the increased accommodation demands of tourists, first from Portugal and Germany, then France and Belgium. Today, many visitors favour the elegant hotel as *the* hotel to stay at in Sal, if not *the* hotel in Cape Verde.

But there is more to the Vynckier dynasty than just managing hotels. The family were true pioneers in the use of renewable energies, making use of two of the few natural resources in Cape Verde, namely sun and wind. Gaspard Vynckier installed a solar-powered seawater distiller on Sal; his son Georges introduced the first solar panels for producing hot water, as well as wind-harnessing equipment that at one time produced 60% of the hotel's electricity needs. The electricity produced by the wind ran a desalination operation through the process of reverse osmosis, the wind supplanting the sun as the energy-giver for the desalination process. Sadly, time has now moved on again, and water and electricity are now simply bought from the local suppliers.

So, doff your sunhat to Georges Vynckier's noble bust, before your feet touch the white sands of Santa Maria. The management of the elegant hotel has been passed down to his daughter, Sophie Vynckier Marcellesi. Likewise, many of the existing staff members are the grandchildren of some of Gaspart's very first collaborators – a true dynasty in a young country.

inclusive package holidays. The buffet restaurant has an enormous variety of food as the Riu tries to cater for its many nationalities of visitor. You either love it or hate it. They do not accept casual, walk-up guests, so book directly on the website or as part of a package with, for example, Thomson Holidays. From Sal, just go to the sales office. All-inclusive rate only. Day-passes are available for approximately €80. $$$$$

Vila do Farol Hotel (236 rooms) ☎242 1725; e farol.recep@hotels.alpitourworld.it; www.villaggibravo.it (in Italian only). Large Italian all-inclusive resort, mainly Italian clientele, big gardens, swimming pool & watersports facilities, including dive centre. $$$$$

Crioula Hotel (242 rooms) ☎242 1622/15; e booking@crioula-clubhotel.com. A 4-star hotel lying to the west of town, of pleasant, muted terracotta & stone architecture with quiet rooms arranged around gardens. It has a large freshwater pool, plus the usual array of excursions & entertainments, & can be booked on a B&B, HB or all-inclusive basis. Wi-Fi at extra cost. $$$$

Hotel Dunas de Sal (48 rooms) ☎242 9050; e geral@hoteldunasdesal.com; www.hoteldunasdesal.com. Located on the landward side of the road that runs west of Santa Maria, this is a designer hotel & the design is minimalist. A stylish hotel with a good restaurant. In addition to the usual facilities, including massage & beauty centre, it also has a gym, yoga classes, diving centre & Wi-Fi (extra charge). $$$$

Hotel Oasis Atlântico Belorizonte (363 rooms bungalows) ☎242 1045; e belorizonte@oasisatlantico.com; www.oasisatlantico.com. Just beyond the Morabeza, this is a refurbished package hotel with a mixture of rooms – bungalows or conventional rooms arranged around 3 pools, with mature planting. Some connecting rooms are available, plus 2 bungalows suitable for wheelchairs. It also has 3 restaurants. There is a vast array of entertainment & watersports, as well as children's activities & a children's pool. Wi-Fi at extra cost. You can book B&B, HB or all-inclusive. The previously named Hotel Novorizonte, which is next door, is now merged as one under the Belorizonte banner. $$$$

Hotel Sabura (40 rooms, 8 suites) ☎242 1515; e direccion@hotelsabura.com; www.hotelsaburacaboverde.com. Opened in 2009, rooms in this bright modern hotel are centred on a lush

garden & swimming pool. The rooms don't have numbers but instead are named after musicians & composers. Suites are only slightly larger than standard rooms. All rooms have AC, minibar, safe, veranda, TV & Wi-Fi (extra cost). Restaurant open all day (vegetarian meals available). $$$$

Hotels in Santa Maria village

Hotel Morabeza (140 rooms) CP 33; ☎242 1020; e info@hotelmorabeza.com; www.hotelmorabeza.com. Built as a private house in the 1960s, long before tourism hit Sal. Centrally positioned, a 4-star hotel with long-serving, loyal staff. Combines a host of facilities with a colonial ambience & has the advantage over other top-end hotels of having the town on its doorstep. Recent developments include the creation of 2 new swimming pools (there are now 3). Elegant reception with pleasant artwork. Attractively laid out, each room has a veranda with sea or garden views. The facilities include a games room with full-size snooker tables, massage, archery, mini-golf, watersports, table tennis, tennis & yoga & even traditional dancing & the Creole language. There are 3 restaurants & 3 bars, including a rooftop venue serving international dishes, including Cape Verdean cuisine. This is a sought-after hotel with a great reputation & is a good choice for location, beach & resort facilities. See ad, colour page 17. $$$$$

Odjo d'Água (50 rooms) ☎242 1414; e reservas@odjodagua-hotel.com; www.odjodagua-hotel.com. Down on the shore to the east of the pier, this is a quiet & pretty hotel with a personal feel, with well-planted gardens & a restaurant practically on the waves. There's a small but attractive pool above steps leading down to what feels like a private beach, & a terrace bar provides an alternative venue for admiring the view. All rooms have balconies but only some face the sea. TV with international channels. Wi-Fi (extra cost). Many satisfied guests & popular with several package-tour operators. See ad, colour page 18. $$$$

Hotel Les Alizés (10 rooms) CP 74; ☎242 1446/1008; e lesalizes@cvtelecom.cv; www.pensao-les-alizes.com. In the centre of Santa Maria, this is a charming hotel in a traditional Cape Verdean building with attractive rooms, each with a balcony (with sea view), TV, fan. B/fast is on a terrace overlooking the sea. The French owners are English speakers & knowledgeable about travel in the islands. $$$

🏠 **Sal4Rent** Rua 1 de Junho, Santa Maria; 📞 242 1715; e info@sal4rent. com; www.sal4rent.com. Rents holiday apartments by the night, as well as offering long-term rentals, property management, keyholding service & commercial units. See ad, page 131.

🏠 **Cape Verde Holidays** m +44 701 008 3058; e book@cape-verde-holidays.net; www.cape-verde-holidays.net. UK-based, with a number of private villas for rental throughout Cape Verde.

🏠 **Pamela Stanley** 📞 242 2045; e pamela@cabo-direct.net; www. cabo-direct.net. Long- & short-term rents, many suitable for watersports enthusiasts. Office on the main square & also in the east of town.

🏠 **Capitani Angelotti Lda** 📞 242 2717; m 993 4930; e willytruck@gmail. com; casa.lda2010@gmail.com. Have more than 100 properties to let, from €100 per week. Includes some in the now completed adjacent Leme Bedje complex, some of which are very well appointed. English, Italian, French spoken.

🏠 **Hotel Pontão** (36 rooms) 📞 242 8063; e ctpontao@cvtelecom.cv. At the western edge of Santa Maria town, opposite the Pirata Nightclub & thus near the main street & a few mins' walk of the beginning of the western beach, the balconied rooms are en suite with AC & TV. There's an unexpected garden with a pool of reasonable size. Wi-Fi (extra cost). Good value. **$$$**

🏠 **Pensão Nha Terra** (25 rooms) Rua 1 de Junho; 📞 242 1109; e nhaterra@hotmail. com; www.caboverde.com/pages/421109.htm. Conveniently positioned at the western edge of town, this airy hotel is bright & cared for with balconied rooms, all en suite & with AC, TV & hot water. It has an attractively planted pool though it's in full view of passers-by on the main street. Bar & restaurant. Better than other hotels at this price. **$$$**

🏠 **Pensão Porta do Vento** (15 rooms) 📞 242 2121; m 991 7877; e info@portadovento.com. In a quiet part of town in the northwest of Santa Maria, rooms are of a good standard with fans, TV, fridge & imaginative décor. Some have balconies. English spoken. **$$$**

In the eastern district (Praia António de Sousa and Zona Tanquinho)

🏠 **Aparthotel Santa Maria Beach** (31 rooms) Praia Antonio de Sousa; 📞 242 1450; m 994 3410. Reservations in France: 📞 +33 1 43 00 87 32. Along the coastal road out to the east, the en-suite rooms in this hotel are mostly

balconied, some with sea views, & have TV. A good mid-range hotel given its quiet location close to the beach. Most rooms have AC, some with fans. All have hot water. Triples & family rooms available. **$$$**

🏠 **Hotel da Luz** (38 rooms) Zona Tanquinho, north Santa Maria; 📞 242 1138; e hoteldaluz@ hotmail.com; www.wix.com/hoteldaluz/sal. Basic hotel but a popular choice amongst those on a budget. Rooms with/without AC. All have private baths, balconies, hot water. Quiet location, small swimming pool, restaurant. **$$**

🏠 **Sakaroule** (7 rooms) m 992 6820/993 5841; e sakaroule1999@yahoo.it; www.sakaroule.com. Tucked away at the back of Santa Maria, just east of the police station, this colourful Italian-owned residencial is a traditional Cape Verdean building with an interior courtyard that has been expanded & improved. Some of the rooms have kitchens & balconies. Has a place to store wind- & kite-surfing equipment. An excellent price because of its location; some love it because it's not in the tourist areas. **$$**

Self-catering apartments

🏠 **Residencial Porto Antigo** (90 apts) 📞 242 1815; e portoantigoreservas@hotmail.com; www.portoantigo.com. This pretty, beautifully planted apartment & villa complex on the edge of the sea. Smart 1, 2, & 3-bedroom apartments with living room, kitchenette & balcony, plus AC, Wi-Fi & TV with international channels. Good buffet breakfasts (extra cost). The complex is run like a high-class hotel, with daily cleaning services.

B&B & HB are available. Booking is directly with the management company. Attractive pool, & the scenic old harbour in front provides a small, almost private beach with snorkelling opportunities. Weekly or daily rentals. See ad, colour page 19.
$$$$

🏠 **Ponta Preta Apartments** (23 apts) Praia Antonio de Sousa; ☎ 242 9020; e info@pontapreta.

info; www.pontapreta.info. In the east of town, with its office a block back from the beach, all apartments are spacious & have balconies with a view of either the sea or the garden. All have satellite TV, phone & Wi-Fi (extra cost), safe, AC, bed linen, towels & cleaning service. Good value & good location. Some apartments can accommodate up to 8 persons. **$$**

✗ **WHERE TO EAT AND DRINK** There are many restaurants in Santa Maria, but most visitors stick to a favourite few along Rua 1 de Junho. It is, however, worth hunting out some more of Santa Maria's 50 eating establishments. Indian and Chinese cuisines are both available, as are fish and chips, but fresh fish and seafood dominate as they do elsewhere in the archipelago. There is a strong Italian presence in town, which means some high-quality pasta and pizza and excellent coffee. If you're British and are homesick for the UK, you can console yourself with a Sunday roast dinner. Although on some of the other islands you can find nothing but local fare, here you'll actually have to hunt it down, certainly in the main tourist-centred streets.

Most of the upmarket hotels – the **Crioula**, **Hotel Oasis Atlântico**, **Belorizonte**, **Dunas** and **Morabeza** – have restaurants that welcome non-residents. If you wander along the beach in front of them you will find several restaurants on the shore. Most of the bars have happy hours at differing times, therefore potentially you could drink cheaply for most of the evening.

The Morabeza's chic bar has a happy hour between 18.30 and 19.30 when *caipirinhas* and beers are very cheap and Blu Bar has a happy hour that lasts almost all day on a Sunday. The most popular tourist restaurants and the upmarket hotels that line the beach have live music most nights in high season. Fresh bread can be bought from early morning from **Padaria Dâdo and Minimercado RG**. All listings are located on the map, pages 114–15, and the map key on page 116.

Best for watching sports
Cape Verdeans love sport, especially football, so there is always somewhere to watch a game. Apart from the national station, sports can be watched on three Portuguese channels as well as British satellite, African, French and Brazilian services. A well-chosen spot on the beach will let you watch the endless live beach volleyball or beach football matches taking place. Or you could join in.
- **Enacol petrol station** [114 A2] Believe it or not, there is a terrace where you can eat and drink cheaply and watch television as well as getting your car filled.
- **Sal Beach** [114 C4] A British favourite, pints and breakfasts and live sports
- **Market** Grill [114 C4] Cheap beer and eats in the open air.
- **Zum Fischermann** [114 B3] Has satellite sports channels, though may favour German matches.

Best for vegetarians
Choices are fairly limited in Cape Verde but you can always get an omelette or plate of rice and beans. In Santa Maria you can always get pizza or pasta, but a few places do something different.
- **Ao Caranguejo** [114 C4] Try the *ortalano*, packed with fresh vegetables.
- **Bombay Brasserie** [114 B3] Several vegetable and chickpea dishes. The owner is vegetarian and will often have something special available. Ask in advance if you want something different.
- **Papaia's** [115 E5] Quesadillas and falafel with hummus are just two options.

Restaurants and cafés

Beach Club 242 1020; ☺ lunch 12.30–15.00. One of Hotel Morabeza's 3 restaurants, it's on the beach with both conventional seating & sunloungers. Excellent service, fairly cheap drinks but pricier food. $$$$$

Geko Gourmet Djadsal Moridias. Opposite Belorizonte Hotel; 242 5109; m 978 5595. A newcomer, serving Spanish tapas & paella, plus other fish & meat favourites. Extensive Italian wine selection. Evenings only in low season. Enthusiastic Spanish owner. $$$$$

Leonardo's Off Rua Amílcar Cabral; m 981 0057; ☺ 18.00–22.30. This upmarket Italian restaurant has had mixed reviews. Some expats swear by it, but it is pricey. $$$$$

Le Privé Rua 15 de Agosto; 242 1299; m 992 3392; ☺ 18.30–23.30. Global cuisine that enjoys praise from locals. Pleasant courtyard, occasional music, excellent food. A good place for that special meal. $$$$$

Odjo d'Água Beside the hotel of the same name. A wonderful, invigorating location almost overhanging the sea. Specialises in grilled fish. Weekly live music. You can get a fisherman to catch you a fish & the restaurant will barbecue it. $$$$$

Praia On the beach in front of the Hotel Belorizonte; ☺ 12.00–15.00 daily. Serving sandwiches & grills; bar open all day. $$$$$

Ao Caranguejo Rua 1 de Junho; 242 1231; m 997 1216; e caranguejocv@yahoo. it; ☺ 19.00–late Tue–Sun. Dingy corridor entrance opens up into a courtyard bedecked with fairylights. Enjoy delicious pasta & great pizza under the stars. Good vegetarian options. Take-aways available. $$$$

Atlantis On the beach outside Hotel Oasis Atlântico; 242 1879; e wcv.pat@ gmx.net; ☺ 10.00–22.00 daily. Open-air fish restaurant with good sea views. A blend of Italian, French & Creole cooking. $$$$

Bombay Brasserie Next to BCA Bank on the road running south to Hotel Morabeza; m 994 4878/991 8666; ☺ 12.00–15.00 & 18.00–23.30 daily. Indian dishes. Good for vegetarians. $$$$

Chez Pastis Rua Amílcar Cabral; 984 3696; ☺ 18.30–23.00 daily. Good reviews for this tiny place, though some say reputation has slightly lost its podium place since ownership change. Offering mostly meat & seafood dishes. Book ahead. $$$$

Crêtcheu Pizzeria 242 1062; ☺ 10.00–22.00 daily. At the bottom of the pier. Pasta, pizza & grilled fish from a pleasant terrace with a view of the sea, the pier & boats moored nearby. $$$$

Dunas de Sal On the western hotel road; 242 9050; e geral@hoteldunasdesal.com; www. hoteldunasdesal.com. Worth the taxi ride out to dine in elegant poolside surroundings. A varied menu & daily specials. $$$$

Mediterraneo Rua 1 de Junho; m 979 8219. Italian restaurant with tables on the street. $$$$

Papaia's Porto Antigo Hotel; m 973 3482; ☺ 08.00–23.00 daily. Refurbished & rebranded, this has a wonderful setting at the edge of the water. Homemade bread & cakes, attractive buffet breakfast & a diverse menu including meals for kids & vegetarians. $$$$

Baileys Djadsal Moradias; m 951 4761. Undergoing renovation at time of writing, but when finished will once again offer pints & British food as well as curry nights & other themed evenings for the growing expat community in the western part of town. There is also a Chinese menu available. $$$

Baraonda In the parade of shops on the left after Enacol; m 985 9350; ☺ 18.30–23.00 daily. Colourful pizzeria. $$$

Barracuda Restaurant 242 2154. Beachfront location just east of the pier; ☺ Tue–Sun. It has a wide choice & a well-earned good reputation. $$$

Café Creolu Travessa Patrice Lumumba; 242 1774; m 995 3690; ☺ 12.00–15.00 & evenings Mon–Sat. Small, busy, established venue with a veranda & a varied menu; proud of its homemade yoghurt. $$$

Compad Av Amílcar Cabral. Perennial favourite with locals. Pleasant, simple food, served quickly. $$$

Cultural Café Main praça; 242 2154; ☺ 08.00–00.00, closed Tue in low season. Hip venue, of mixed Cape Verdean/European design, tumbling out onto the square in the centre of Santa Maria. Promotes a lot of local foods & drinks such as punches, grogues, cakes & a classy cachupa (they will also teach you how to cook it). $$$

Gigi's Manera Café Excellent pizzas from this newcomer next to Porto Antigo. A quiet place, away from the town centre. $$$

Lanchonete Angela Now relocated to the seafront, this diner remains popular with residents due to no-nonsense food at decent prices. $$$

🍴 **Ocean Café** ☎ 242 1895; www.oceancafe.com. By the beachside of the main square, lively bar/restaurant popular with visitors. Live music every night, tasty pizzas. Also serving burgers, omelettes, etc. Ambitious owners have a constantly updated website with features relevant to Cape Verde. Plush suites to rent upstairs. **$$$**

🍴 **Sal Beach Club** On the beach just the east of the pier. Pints, breakfasts, reliable big screen sports. Has sunbeds & small swimming pool. An expat favourite. **$$$**

🍴 **Sapo Com Fome** m 930 3989; Next to Leonardo's, open early until late with pleasant & friendly staff, outside tables, tasty & decent-priced food. Usual fish & other dishes, plus jacket potatoes, sandwiches & for homesick Brits, excellent fish, chips & even mushy peas. Well-priced house wine by the glass. **$$$**

🍴 **Zum Fischermann** m 991 7500; ⊙ 18.00–23.00. Large building with a huge sign just to the east of Pirata, this restaurant is German owned & some say it has the best fresh fish available. German beers. **$$$**

🍴 **Nha Terra** Downstairs at Pensão Nha Terra on Rua 1 de Junho; ☎ 242 1019; ⊙ 08.00–23.00 daily. Sit poolside & watch the world go by as you enjoy pasta & fish dishes. Also does delicious pancakes & muffins for b/fast & sandwiches for lunch. Inexpensive dish of the day. **$$$–$**

🍴 **Bar Di Nos** Recommended budget choice. Limited range of grilled meat & fish, outdoor tables, popular with residents & good value. **$$**

🍴 **Hexedes Cafe** Next to Blu Bar, a newcomer which serves a wide selection of quality coffees, pasta dishes & snacks. Recommended place for a full British breakfast, croissant, fresh orange juice. Terrace & indoor seating. **$$**

🍴 **Marlyne's Restaurant** Near Porto Antigo m 952 3430. Marlyne is an enterprising Guinean offering good-value dishes including fish & filet mignon, Sun roasts & English b/fasts. Friendly & unpretentious. Indoor & outdoor tables. **$$**

🍴 **Padaria Dâdo** Rua 1 de Junho; ☎ 242 1516; e padariadado@yahoo.com.br; ⊙ 07.00–01.00 daily. Mainly a local haunt, this is an excellent venue for inexpensive b/fast, *cachupa* & cakes. **$$**

🍴 **Enacol petrol station** As you enter Santa Maria; ⊙ 08.00–22.00 daily. Perhaps not the most scenic place to eat & drink, but you can't do better

than a prato de dia of chicken, rice & salad for 350$. The café & little terrace beside the shop is a popular choice for a quick, tasty meal. **$**

🍴 **Kiosque Beach Bar** To the west of the pier; ⊙ 09.30–20.00 daily. Simple, cheap food & drinks sitting on the beach watching the world go by. **$**

🍴 **Market Grill & Sports Bar** At the Genuine Cabo Verde Market off the main praça; ⊙ 07.00–23.00 daily. Simple, quick food with a worthy reputation. The burgers are particularly recommended & the cheapest in town. **$**

🍴 **Snack Bar Bilu** ⊙ daytimes only. Down the side road as you leave the Hotel Odjo d'Água, this unmarked restaurant serves Cape Verdean food & continues to be popular. Very good value for the budget-conscious. **$**

🍴 **Gelataria Sol Doce** Beside the pier; ⊙ 07.00–19.00 daily. Café serving Portuguese pastries, crêpes, sandwiches & coffee. **$**

🍴 **Giramondo** Rua 1 de Junho . The best ice cream in town. Also serves coffee, smoothies, slices of pizza & pastries. A popular meeting point. **$**

Entertainment and nightlife

🍸 **Angulo's Beach Bar** [115 G5] An open-air bar/restaurant at the very eastern end of Santa Maria, on quieter Praia Antonio de Sousa, in an area which lacks choice.

🍸 **Blu Bar** [114 B4] At the main square end of 15 de Agosto; www.blubarcapeverde.com. Smart cocktail bar with live music Thu–Sat & great atmosphere. Ladies' Night on Fri (buy 1 get 1 free – that's the drinks, not the ladies) & possibly the longest happy hour on the island (16.30–21.30 on Sun). Available for private parties.

🍸 **Calema** [114 C4] Rua 1 de Junho. Famous, popular late nightspot with live music.

🍸 **Chillout** [114 B3] At the end of Rua 1 de Junho. Very chic, with outside seating area.

🍸 **Cultural Centre** [114 C4] Behind the Cultural Café, this often has free (but poorly advertised) events such as concerts, plays or capoeira displays. You can check the notices on its door.

🍸 **Mirage** [114 A1] Las Vegas meets Santa Maria. Disco, restaurant, pizzeria, brew-pub, cinema, poker tables. A little out of town, on the road to Espargos, but the owner promises a free bus to bring his customers from Santa Maria & home again.

🍸 **Pirata** [114 A2] Near Enacol petrol station; ⊙ late night–early morning at w/ends nightclub.

Has something of a mixed reputation & high prices. Entrance fee.

♀ **Tam Tam's** [114 D4] Rua Amílcar Cabral; ☺ 08.00–01.00 Mon–Sat. A bar frequented by European expats. May be closed in low season.

♀ **Uhuru Reggae Bar** [114 D4] Rua 1 de Junho ☺ 18.00–02.00 daily. Booms out loud, exclusively reggae music from its rooftop location. Gradually becomes a disco as the night progresses.

SHOPPING Souvenirs can be bought at shops dotted all over town. The vast majority of these souvenirs are imported from Senegal and other parts of West Africa, but if you look around you can find a few products made in Cape Verde. One of the best places to go is Genuine Cabo Verde [114 C4] (see box, page 125, for more information), an open-air market with a laid-back approach. Centro de Artesanato, on Rua 1 de Junho, where many of the items are made on the premises, is also recommended. If you fancy some original art, depicting typical Cape Verdean scenes, there are a few possibilities. Perhaps the best way to experience it is to take a reasonably priced guided walking tour, which will introduce you to local and locally inspired painters and sculptors in their workshops and let you talk to the artists. Tours take around two hours and guides are English-speaking: contact Bev (979 1835; e bevchad@hotmail.co.uk) or Moonira (979 3078; e moonira.merali@gmail.com). The artists include Eliseu, who works from a tiny studio at the back of his shop and who has done a stunning mural over one of the arched entrances at Porto Antigo 1. He has smaller and more transportable paintings for sale in the shop. Another artist, Tonih, can be found beside the beach bar at the Odjo d'Agua hotel. Music can be bought at a number of places, including national chain Harmonia (242 1998) on Rua Amilcar Cabral, near BCA bank, and at the airport shop. Fruit and vegetables can be bought from street vendors opposite the bakery, at the new Mercado Municipal in the north of town or on Rua Amílcar Cabral. Surf clothes, accessories and a few boards are for sale at Angulo's [115 G5]. Suncream and other toiletries can be found in often unmarked Chinese stores (*lojas chineses*), where you can also find cheap clothes, shoes and household items. If you want to buy snorkelling equipment, try the SalMine Tour Office or one of the surf shops: they sell far better quality than the poor quality, overpriced alternatives offered in some of the souvenir shops.

By archipelago standards, there is a wide range of good-quality food available in *minimercados* on Sal but availability varies. Many of the *lojas chineses* have also started selling food cheaply. A few shops (see page 125) usually have a good supply.

OTHER PRACTICALITIES
Airlines
Book internal flights directly with the airline at the airport. At its office you take a queuing ticket, but you should still keep an eye out for queue-jumpers. In Santa Maria try vista verde tours, Barracuda or Morabitur (see page 104 for their contact details and further information).

Banks (All have ATMs & ☺ Mon–Fri)
$ **BCA** Opposite Nha Terra; ☺ 09.00–15.00
$ **BCN** Rua 1 de Junho ☺ 09.00–15.00.
$ **Banco Interâtlantico** Rua 1 de Junho; ☺ 09.00–15.00.
$ **Caixa Económica** Rua 1 de Junho; ☺ 08.00–15.00.

Beauty therapy/hairdressers
Waikiki Spa [115 E4] Rua 15 de Agosto; m 977 6178; e waikikispa@gmail.com; ☺ 09.00–19.00 Mon–Sat. Manicure, pedicure, waxing, massage.
Unica [114 D4] Rua 15 de Agosto; 242 1596; ☺ 09.00–20.00 Mon–Sat. Beauty therapy & hairdressing.

Dentist
Dra Carla Rocha [114 D4] Rua 15 de Agosto, just down from entrance to Porto Antigo.

Hospital Clinitur [115 F1], a large private clinic, is on the road from Santa Maria to the resort hotels (242 9090; m 988 7075; ☺ 08.00–15.00

During the summer months, from August onwards, each Cape Verdean island celebrates its music with a lively festival. Each festival is different, some featuring international bands, others just concentrating on the extraordinary talents of local musicians. Perhaps the most famous of the festivals is the Baia das Gatas on São Vicente, which grew from a tradition of a few musicians jamming annually around the August full moon.

But Baia das Gatas is by no means unique. On Sal, the Santa Maria festival is held annually, in September – but in true Cape Verdean fashion, no-one knows the exact date until a couple of weeks in advance, and the line-up is usually announced only a week or so before the event! In the past, the festival has featured top international artists including Alpha Blondy, Youssou N'Dour, Steel Pulse and Ky-mani Marley, plus Cape Verde's own legendary Cesária Évora and many highly talented musicians from Sal island itself.

Until recently, the festival was held on Santa Maria Beach, but due to the frenzied development of recent years, it has been moved: in 2012 it was held on the southernmost tip of the island (Igrijinha), and for 2013 was scheduled to take place on Ponta Preta Beach. This was a disappointment for most people as the traditional venue for the festival had been hugely popular for all of Sal's inhabitants. However, to the rescue came the turtles… due to concerns about their welfare, it was decreed that the festival should move back to Santa Maria Beach!

When I first heard about Santa Maria festival, I was cynical as to whether our sleepy little village would actually get a music festival together, but I have to say I was hugely impressed when a stage with full PA systems and lighting – which would easily compete with Glastonbury – was built on the beach a week beforehand. The beach gets completely transformed, and lots of tiny little stalls are rented out to anyone who wants to sell food and drinks, and create their own 'music' between festival sets. As a result there is a marvellous mix of eager vendors, from individuals selling cold beer and local drinks and delicacies (including *ponche*, *grogue* and *moreia* (moray eel)) right through to the more upmarket town bars, who set up on the beach for the weekend. All around you will be the eclectic music of Cape Verde, West Africa, Brazil and elsewhere, escaping from the many sound systems all over the festival site.

Everyone comes to the festival, pouring in from the island's three main towns and further afield. Whole families will turn up for the weekend, some with tents, and children and babies will sleep contentedly on the beach. Most hardcore festival-goers will arrive on the first day and not go home until the end. Fishermen – perhaps too full of *grogue* – will be found asleep under the stage and the many local characters come out in force to entertain and amuse. It really is a wonderful community event not to be missed.

Depending on which way the wind is blowing, local residents and tourists in hotels may (or may not) get any sleep for the duration, but that is the whole point... after all, it is festival time!

Mon–Sat (on call for emergencies)). Murdeira has a medical centre (241 2451; m 592 3464; ⊕ 09.00–13.00 & 15.00–20.00 Mon–Fri, 09.00–12.00 Sat) with services ranging from gynaecology and physiotherapy to dentistry. Alternatively, try the

Posto Sanitário de Santa Maria (242 1130); or the new hospital just outside Espargos (see page 111).

Internet There are several cafés on Rua 1 de Junho, and on Rua Amílcar Cabral. Santa Maria has

Wi-Fi in most places provided by Cabocom (*www.cabocom.cv*), though this is expensive. Vouchers to access this service from your own laptop or mobile device are available from their office and various outlets, such as some *minimercados*. A voucher for one hour is €3. There is free internet in the town square which can be picked up in the bars and restaurants nearby. A couple of the beach restaurants may offer free Wi-Fi.

Laundry
Serilimpo, next to Baraonda [114 A2] on the left-hand side as you come into Santa Maria (m *995 3494*; ⏰ *08.00–17.00 Mon–Sat*).

Pharmacy
[114 A3] Just around the corner from the CV Telecom building.

Police
[114 D2] (☎*242 1132*). The new building on the tarmac road; northern Santa Maria.

Post office
[115 E4] (⏰ *08.00–12.00 & 14.00–17.00 Mon–Fri*). The large, pink building to the east of town.

Food
Delta [115 E3] Eastern end of Rua Amílcar Cabral; ⏰ 08.00–20.00 Mon–Sat. Owned by the large food importer that supplies many of the big hotels, this shop occasionally stocks British foods & has a range of cheeses & European & New World wines, but isn't cheap.
Enacol [114 A2] Petrol station at the entrance to Santa Maria ⏰ 08.00–22.00 daily. Has a shop that often has things you won't find elsewhere.
Kazu [114 C2] Just to the east of Enacol petrol station on the big tarmac road. Brand new, large supermarket with the usual tinned foods, plus bread, fresh fruit & vegetables & occasionally some European imports.
Merceria RG [115 E5] Opposite Porto Antigo; ⏰ early until late Mon–Sat. A wide range of tinned, dry & fresh foods, bread & ice cream.
Loja Sintanton [114 D4] Rua Amílcar Cabral; ⏰ 09.30–13.00 & 16.30–20.00 Mon–Sat. A decent selection, of goods, particularly of Cape Verdean wine.
Wind Shop [114 D3] Rua Amílcar Cabral; ⏰ 08.00–20.00 daily. Usually has a good range of fruit & vegetables at reasonable prices as well as butter & cheese.

Furniture and household items
There are a few options for furnishing your newly completed apartment.
Aiga Beach side of the main *praça*; m 918 3330; ⏰ 09.00–20.00 Mon–Sat. Wicker furniture, lights & soft furnishings.
Galaxy Rua Amilcar Cabral; m 987 0369; e www.capeverdefurniturepacks.com. Furniture packs, blinds, curtains, mosquito screens & bedding.
Sal Holiday [115 E4] Near the post office; ☎242 1190; ⏰ 08.30–12.30 & 14.30–18.30 Mon–Sat. Large items of furniture & fitted kitchens.
Veranda On the main road out of town towards Espargos; e veranda@verandafurniture.com. Expensive Italian furniture.

Telephone
The post office has facilities for making international calls at a whopping 110$ per minute. They can also sell you a local SIM card for 50$, though you will have to put credit on it. Calls are also possible from several internet cafés, including the one opposite Relax Café on Rua Amílcar Cabral. You can make calls for 30$/minute to most European countries from

GENUINE CABO VERDE

Fed up with the lack of Cape Verdean products available and growing tired of tourists complaining of being hassled by street vendors claiming that their imported knick-knacks were from Cape Verde, the owner of the Cultural Café found his own solution. Genuine Cabo Verde is an open-air market just off the main praça. Open 09.00–23.00 daily, this charming market only sells Cape Verdean handicrafts, grogue, the best *piri-piri* (hot sauce) in town, and other produce from the islands. Even better, no-one will induce you to buy as this kind of sales technique is anathema to Cape Verdeans. You can also have a drink and eat a burger here (for details, see *Where to eat and drink*, page 120).

Access Net behind the sports stadium. If you are staying for a while or you need to make a lot of calls you could consider buying a local SIM card. These are available from the CV Telecom (near BCA bank, English spoken) for 50$ and include credit. You will need an unlocked phone and your passport.

Tourist information

[114 A3] There is a booth operated by the Câmara Municipal do Sal at the entrance to Santa Maria, slightly inconveniently located near the roundabout with information about hotels and excursions (⊕ *09.00–12.00 & 15.30–21.00 daily*). More central is the reliable SalMine Tour Office [114 B3], situated in front of the CV Telecom building. Although this is an agency for many tour operators of all types, they only deal with properly licensed companies and also act as a helpful, multilingual, informal tourist office.

WHAT TO SEE AND DO Santa Maria is a base for the surfing, windsurfing and fishing that are the chief activities of the island. (See *Activities*, page 103.) Beach basking on its stunning white sands is popular. You can also visit the Santa Maria saltpans – walk inland through the northern part of Santa Maria, and they are on the other side.

OTHER PLACES TO VISIT

These are arranged in clockwise order beginning at Santa Maria, to be of use to those doing a tour of the island.

SANTA MARIA SALINA Located behind Costa Fragata, the salina can be found by walking directly north from the closed Sab Sab Hotel. The salina is still worked by hand by a small community; unfortunately they cannot sell the fruits of their labour since it does not meet required regulations for quality and sanitary control. You can walk between the saltpans and early in the morning it is possible to see a variety of birds.

PONTA PRETA A stunning beach with a restaurant from which to appreciate it, Ponta Preta is a favourite of windsurfers and surfers (see page 106). It is possible to reach the beach by walking for about an hour around the coast from Santa Maria. Alternatively, drive along the road that goes west from Santa Maria towards the resort hotels, turn right opposite Hotel Crioula and go straight ahead for approximately 2km. You will see, after a few minutes, the timber-built restaurant, and a minute after that you will find a rough track leading towards the water.

There is also a little wooden hut, where a man can be seen making handicrafts. Just north of Ponta Preta there is the Melia Tortuga all-inclusive complex on Algodoeiro Beach, home to Cabo Verde Diving and Watersports (m *997 8824;* e *caboverdediving@cvtelecom.cv; www.caboverdediving.net*). Behind Algodoeiro Beach, Hotel Dunas is under construction, with a scheduled 2014 opening, plus the massive Vila Verde villa/apartment development. Some of it is completed; some of it has been stopped in its tracks. Most of it lies unoccupied.

✕ Where to eat

✕ **Ponta Preta** ☏242 1774; m 991 8613; ⊕ 10.00–17.00 Tue–Sun. Large wooden building with a big deck & sunbeds serving salads, snacks, fish, seafood, meat & spaghetti overlooking the beach. Owned by the same people as Café Creolu in Santa Maria. **$$$**

BAIA DA MURDEIRA This bay lies about 8km north of Santa Maria. The coast here is quite rocky, with some smaller sandy areas and a fine, quiet beach and sheltered cove just to the south. There is a resort here – Murdeira Village. It is gated but you can enter and use the beach, pool and so forth if you are a customer of the bar or restaurant. This is a good location if you are a self-contained holidaymaker, otherwise you could feel a bit isolated.

Where to stay and eat

Murdeira Village (40 rooms) Espargos (office); 📞 241 1604; e reservas@murdeiravillage.com; www.murdeiravillage.com. Hotel rooms are high-quality suites with AC, TV & verandas.

Facilities at the resort include a swimming pool & children's pool, snack bar, a restaurant with a sunset view, mini-market & car rental. **$$$**

CALHETA FUNDA A favourite with locals at the weekend, this lovely little beach is usually deserted and is a fine place for a swim, snorkel and picnic. See *Cycling*, page 108, for a description of how to get there.

MURDEIRA TO PALMEIRA A few places of interest or beauty (and sometimes both) lie hidden within the land that stretches, like a vast natural car park, between Murdeira and Palmeira.

Monte Leão At the far northern end of Murdeira Bay there is a dead-end track to the west, which leads to the coastal foot of Monte Leão, the unmistakable 'lion' gazing out to sea. It is known on the maps as Rabo de Junco.

Ponta da Parede There is a small, secluded beach here, about 0.5km before the end of the track to Monte Leão. There's a small blowhole and some pretty rockpools.

Viewpoint After visiting Monte Leão, about 2.5km back along the track, there is another track branching to the north, which later joins a bigger track to the left that leads to this viewpoint which stands some 45m above sea level. There's a good view over Monte Leão and down to Santa Maria.

Fontona This is a pretty, tree-filled oasis that lies about 3km south of Palmeira. It can be reached by following the track from the viewpoint (see above) for a further 2.5km, in a northwesterly and then northerly direction. Alternatively, it can be reached from Palmeira (take the signposted turning to the left off the road into Palmeira).

PALMEIRA Palmeira is a friendly, quiet little place which is on the route of many round-island tours. Other than at these times, it is a peaceful village with a couple of restaurants. You could idle away an hour or two here, waiting for a ferry or lounge at the bar overlooking the water with the locals and watch them frolic in the sea (and join in) on public holidays, or chat to visiting yachties taking a break on their passage across the Atlantic. There are a couple of souvenir shops selling the usual trinkets. Get there by *aluguer* from Espargos (50$) or by walking or hitching. There is an **internet café**, Cyber Internet Patrica, next to Snack Bar Gomes (📞 241 3184; ⊕ 08.00–22.00 daily).

✗ WHERE TO EAT AND DRINK A few closures have limited the choice, but some recently closed establishments may re-open again after renovations.

✗ Cantinho/Por do Sol Off the main road, towards the sea, just past the church serves reasonably priced fish dishes, spaghetti & other standards. **$$**

✗ Minimercado Continental 📞 241 3366; ⊕ 08.00–19.00. **$**

✗ Snack Bar Gomes m 986 5214; ⊕ 08.00–00.00. On the main street on the left as you enter Palmeira. **$**

✗ Rotterdam Restaurant Towards the beach,

centred around a brightly painted sea container (!) Fresh fish & snacks $$

BURACONA This is an exhilarating natural swimming pool encased in black lava rock over which white foam cascades every few minutes. Nearby is the Blue Eye, an underground pool reached through a large hole in the ground. Divers can swim along an underground tunnel out into the sea.

If you are not in a car or taxi, you'll have to walk the 6km from Palmeira. Follow the main road into Palmeira and as the road swings round to the left, follow the sign straight ahead to Buracona. The terrain is about 25 shades of brown (including chocolate, wine-stain and rusted) covered with a few bent-over trees. Superimposed on this is a disused wind farm, a few scavenging goats and the odd anti-litter sign with plastic bags caught round it. The coastline itself is wildly beautiful, a jumble of black lava rock and waves. You pass a lesser pool but walk the full 6km to reach Buracona, which is just before **Monte Leste** (263m). It's a great place for a swim and a picnic (but don't leave belongings unattended).

There are the ubiquitous African craft sellers and a small snack bar selling cold drinks. Unfortunately this has led to an increase in litter and the beauty of the Blue Eye is increasingly spoiled by plastic bags and bottles floating on the surface. Go early if you want to avoid large tour groups.

PEDRA DE LUME This is a spectacular place, and best appreciated in silence, so the poetic should rise early to reach it before anyone else. Inside a ring of low mountains lies a sweeping geometry of saltpans in blue, pink and green depending on their stage of salt formation, all separated by stone walls. You can sit here, listening to the water lapping in the lakes below and the cry of an occasional bird circling the crater rim.

There is nowhere to stay in this area, and the planned Stefanina development is now an ugly concrete half-finished monstrosity marring the previously beautiful vista from the small town.

History Manuel Martins, who developed Santa Maria, had a business here as well. Bags of salt were strapped to pack animals, which had to climb up the slopes of the volcano and down the other side to reach the port. In 1804, a tunnel was cut through the volcano wall, and in 1919 transport was made easier when a businessman from Santa Maria and a French firm bought the salt company and built the tramway, the remnants of which can be seen today. They could then transfer 25 tonnes an hour to the port, from where it was shipped to Africa. But markets shifted and the saltpans fell into disuse by 1985: today they do not even produce enough salt for Sal. Pedra de Lume is still inhabited but it feels like a ghost town except on public holidays.

There is disagreement about how salt water rises into the bottom of this crater – some believe it comes from deep in the earth, but the most orthodox explanation is that it infiltrates through the natural holes in volcanic rock along the kilometre distance from the sea.

Getting there and away The village is off the main Santa Maria to Espargos road. There are no *alugueres* running here, so a taxi is the only option unless you have your own rental car or quad bike. A taxi here and back from Espargos – the driver will wait as you look around – could cost you as little as 800$, including waiting time, but Espargos's taxi drivers might try to charge you as much as 2,000$. Stand your ground, bargain hard. You can try hitching but you might end up walking all the way.

✗ Where to eat and drink

✗ **Cadamosto Restaurant** ☎241 2210;
🕐 09.00–18.00 daily. This large seaside restaurant down by the shore has an inviting terrace, good seafood, pizzas & ice cream. $$$$

📺 **Café** Inside the crater, serving drinks & snacks. $$$

What to see and do When you have looked around the village with its important-looking housing blocks and its little white church you can examine the relics of the pulley system for taking salt from the crater and loading ships. Then turn inland, along a track that lies just after the church, and follow the old overhead cables uphill. After a few minutes the track arrives at a car park. Ahead is the tunnel into the crater.

Entrance fee is €5 for adults and free for children under a certain height. This seems steep, but a lot of development has gone into the site in recent years. Once you pass through the entrance tunnel, there is a café, as well as a shop selling 'the white stuff' and a few other souvenirs. You can take a dip or book a reasonably priced massage or other treatment such as thalassotherapy; antioxidant treatment to face and feet; or an application of water, *salina* salt and aromatic oil, said to be draining and nourishing. Showers and toilets are available. If you don't fancy paying the entrance fee to go down into the crater, follow the path off to the right of the ticket kiosk and after about 100m you can scramble up the slope for a free look down. You can sit here, listening to the water lapping in the lakes below and the cry of an occasional bird circling the crater rim.

The old wreck Head south from Pedra de Lume following the rough tracks along the coast and you will see the remains of a wreck sticking out of the sea. It is possible to snorkel here although it is a bit of a walk across slippery rocks. Take care as the sea can be very rough on this side. A little further on you will see a small sandbank. At certain times it is possible to spot the fins of schools of nurse sharks (*Ginglymostoma cirratum*) that swim into this area which is less than 1m deep. Further south are some pleasant bays and coves but, ultimately, a dead end.

SERRA NEGRA This is a stunning stretch of coast. Beaches alternate with black rocks lashed by white waves and the cliffs of Serra Negra rise behind them providing a touch of topographical grandeur unusual for Sal. This is a good place for a peaceful day away from the crowds. You can swim here, but note that the northern end of the beach gets cut off by high tide so, in common with the whole of the eastern coast, you should take care. It's a lonely spot, except on public holidays, so take the usual precautions against opportunistic theft. There are no facilities.

Getting there requires a 4x4 or quad bike and is hard (but not impossible) to navigate, over slightly tricky terrain, if you've never been there before. The driver must negotiate the sparse network of rough tracks and rocky ground that lies between the main road and the east coast. Coming from Santa Maria, turn right at the roundabout just before the chapel on the hill onto a dirt track. Follow the track as it forks to the right and head for Restaurant Demiflor (signposted but now closed); there will be another fork to the right, marked with painted rocks, which you should follow (going straight on will bring you to the town dump). When you are past the restaurant, turn left and follow the coast. You will cross some dry *ribeiras* which look steeper than they actually are. You will see a sign when you have reached Serra Negra. (See also *Hikes*, pages 130–1.)

COSTA DA FRAGATA This wild coast is hardly visited, most people preferring the calmer western and southern beaches. Its designation as a nature reserve should ensure some degree of protection for the important dune ecosystem. It is home to

3

CUCUMBERS IN THE DESERT *Alex Alper*

Deep in the heart of Sal's waterless moonscape, cucumbers, tomatoes, lettuce, peppers and other crops are being harvested year-round thanks to hydroponics.

Hydroponics is soil-less culture. Developed by Germans in the 1860s, it uses nutrient solution in place of soil, which increases yields and greatly reduces water use. While hydroponics is practised widely in Europe, the Americas and the Middle East, it is nascent in Cape Verde. There are farms in São Francisco (Tom Drescher's 'VenteSol Cultura Hidroponica e Turistica') and São Domingos on Santiago in addition to Sal. A popular method is the Nutrient Film Technique (NFT). A shallow stream of nutrient-rich water flows constantly along a slightly tilted trough, which holds the plants. A non-soil medium like gravel may be used to anchor the plants. Usually a mesh encloses the crop, retaining moisture and protecting against insects.

The advantages are tremendous. Water input is reportedly between 5% and 10% of that necessary for normal agriculture, even less than what is used by drip irrigation. That's because no water is wasted through soil absorption or excess evaporation, and because water can be recycled through the trough. Hydroponics also uses only 10% of the land required for normal agriculture and there is no need for weeding or ground preparation. Crops are usually healthy and mature quickly, because the microbes that cause weak plant growth reside only in soil.

Start-up costs are high. One farmer estimates having spent €6,000–7,000 to set up his 500m² farm. And the method requires constant energy as the water must keep flowing to prevent rapid plant death. Nevertheless, monthly yields were so good that he claims to have recouped his investment after only seven months.

---

many native plants and an important turtle-nesting area. (See below and opposite for a description of where to start and finish.)

HIKES *Jacquie Cozens (JC)*

Hikers can go more or less anywhere on Sal – the important thing is to take plenty of water and a hat. Even on the very quiet beaches it is rare for muggings or theft to take place, but take minimal possessions and ask for advice. A good, 1:50,000 map is published by Goldstadt (see page 70). For more details on hiking in Cape Verde and abbreviations used below, see pages 48–9.

1 SAB SAB HOTEL (CLOSED)–IGREJINHA
Distance: 2km (circuit); time: 1 hour; difficulty: 1 (JC)
Follow the instructions for the bike trail (20 minutes) (see pages 108–9). You can make this a circuit by continuing north to the start of the beach on Costa Fragata, turning left and walking through the dunes back to Santa Maria (20 minutes).

2 COSTA FRAGATA
Distance: 6km (circuit); time: 1 hour; difficulty: 1 (JC)
Costa Fragata is a natural reserve and in theory is protected from development. Along the wildest coast, subject to strong northwesterlies and with attractive dunes and some birdlife, walking one-way will take around one hour. In the summer you will see many turtle tracks, and in the winter dozens of sails of kitesurfers flying in the sky. Start at the eastern end of Santa Maria, where the development peters out or take

a taxi to Kite Beach (500$) and walk southwards along the coast to Santa Maria. Don't rely on getting a taxi back from Kite Beach unless it is during the windsurfing season.

3 SERRA NEGRA

Distance: 1km (one-way); time: 30 minutes; difficulty: 1 (JC)
To many, this is the most beautiful beach on Sal. It consists of three secluded bays surrounded by tall cliffs. Other than at weekends in the summer it is deserted. The area is home to many types of birds including the red-billed tropicbird (*Phaethon aethereus*), known locally as Rabo de Junco, and is an important turtle-nesting beach. It is possible to walk to Serra Negra from Santa Maria but it is a dry, dusty and rocky walk. Much better to drive to the start of the beach and then take a walk to the end (30 minutes) – to reach the last bay you need to walk over a rocky area. You can also drive along a track around the back of the cliffs, park and walk to the top for a magnificent view of the coastline. There is a bit of scrambling to get to the top, so you need to be in reasonable shape to do this. At the top you will see cairns and tributes built from stones and shells to friends, family and lost loves.

4 SANTA MARIA PIER–PONTA PRETA

Distance: 4km (one-way); time: 1½ hours; difficulty: 1 (JC)
A big favourite with locals and resident expats alike, this is a delight first thing in the morning. Heading west out of Santa Maria, this takes you past all the big hotels and on to Ponta Sino, a long, unspoilt nature reserve with Sal's only lighthouse. Turning north you will pass the RIU Hotel; continue up past the dune until you reach the Ponta Preta Restaurant. You can either return the same way or walk beside the road directly inland from the restaurant, where you can easily stop a taxi or *aluguer*. The alternative is to take transport towards Espargos, asking the driver to drop you at Ponta Preta and do the walk in reverse.

5 MONTE LEÃO

Distance: 2km (circuit); time: 1½ hours; difficulty: 2 (JC)
Follow the trail to the top of Monte Leão at the northwestern end of Murdeira Bay for an amazing view of the surrounding area (one hour). Eagles and their nests are frequently seen here. You will need a rental car or hire a taxi driver to reach Monte Leão.

4

Boavista

Mornas Dancing
In the sensuous bodies of the sensuous girls
In the dyspnoea of the brave waves
Dying in the sand
In the rolling of the
Languid and gentle waves,
Boa Vista,
The unforeseen
Scenery
Of sands marching on the village
                    Jorge Barbosa

Boavista is the siren island. For many seafarers down the years, it was the first sight of land for months. The white dunes, like cusps of icing, must have been an alluring sight but Boavista's beaches have drawn many to a watery grave. It is ringed by reefs and its iron-rich rock formations send ships' compasses spinning. Over 40 ships have foundered here, within sight of land.

Beyond the idyllic beaches another story unfolds. The bleached land has a terrible beauty but it will leave you feeling parched and a little crazed by the sun. The only forests are petrified remnants on the shores: aeons ago, Boavista was a moister place.

In many parts the struggle for existence has become too much. Villages are abandoned, and sand drifts across the floors of their empty houses.

HIGHLIGHTS AND LOWLIGHTS

Go for walks along deserted, searingly beautiful beaches, drifting dunes and desert oases; go for wind- and kitesurfing and go for game fishing. There is diving, though currents and wind can make it hard to explore many of the shipwrecks and can impair the clarity of the water. Go for fledgling ecotourism centred on birds, turtles, corals and whales. Or just go for unashamed sunbathing on pristine white-sand beaches, cooling yourself with some swimming in crystal-clear waters.

However, don't expect any mountain walking. If the landscape or the watersports do not appeal then the only other reason to come here is sunbathing: there is little in the way of conventional tourist 'attractions' to visit.

SUGGESTED ITINERARY AND NUMBER OF DAYS You can see Boavista in a day by 4x4, although you will be hot and exhausted by the end of it. Three full days would be an ideal period in which to do a more relaxed vehicle tour that encompasses some of the remoter beaches; do a hike, perhaps to the north and/or a quad-bike expedition, maybe to the Viana Desert, with a watersports session or an eco trip thrown in as well. Add a few more days if you want to relax on those beaches.

BACKGROUND INFORMATION

HISTORY With little to offer but salt, Boavista, like Sal, did not receive much attention after its discovery on 14 May 1460. It was named Saint Cristovão until, it is said, a storm-tossed sailor's triumphant cry: *'Boa vista!'*, the equivalent of 'Land ahoy!', led to its present name.

Island life has been punctuated by shipwrecks – tragedies that were often fortuitous for the starving islanders who would clamber over the rocks after a stormy night to retrieve food and goods from the debris. It is said that in times of starvation the people would tie a lamp to a donkey's tail and send it in the darkness along the coastal reefs in the hope of luring ships to their doom.

Most ships were wrecked by a strange conflation of circumstances. A strong and gusty trade wind combined with a powerful current pulled sailing ships towards the island. Flat, and often shrouded in a dusty haze, Boavista could be invisible until those boats rammed into the hidden rocks of its northern and eastern coasts. Meanwhile, maps and charts consistently placed Boavista several miles to the west of where it actually is.

Against this background, modern life began very slowly. It was visited early in its history, in 1498, by Christopher Columbus on his third voyage. By then the island already had a few inhabitants and was also used as a leper colony for well-to-do Europeans. After three days Columbus left, made a brief stop at Santiago and went on, reporting that the islands had: 'a false name... since they are so barren that I saw no green thing in them and all the people were infirm, so that I did not dare to remain in them'.

Apart from that, little happened on the island for the first 150 years after its discovery except desecration by goats. In 1580, there were only 50 people living there and by 1619, there was just a group of hunters chasing the goats.

Then English sailors discovered Boavista's high-quality salt and an economy began in about 1620, based at Povoação Velha – its first village. By 1677, Boavista even had a priest, but periodic sackings shook its economy. English sailors attacked the island in 1684, taking chalices from the churches to trade on the African coast. There was another attack in 1697, and by 1702, the population of Povoação Velha was routinely armed.

Nearing the 1800s, Porto Inglês (now Sal Rei) became the most important town on the island and salt production was increasing, reaching its zenith in the first half of the 19th century. But the pillages continued in 1815 and 1817. The final desecration came in 1818 when the town was razed. As a result a fort was built on the Ilhéu do Sal Rei, and with this protection Boavista began an era of relative prosperity, becoming an important cultural centre. In 1834, it was even argued that the town should become the capital of Cape Verde. The Luso–British anti-slavery commission made Boavista its base in 1843.

The fortunes of even the prosperous dwindled, however, when the building of the port at Mindelo transformed the island of São Vicente into the new trading centre. When Charles Thomas, chaplain to the American Africa Squadron (an anti-slavery police) visited in 1855, he found the inhabitants to be starving and the cattle 'with sad faces and tears in their eyes, walking solemnly in cudless rumination over grassless fields'. The chief amusements of the people, he reported, were 'fishing, salt-making and going to funerals'. Fortunes changed again towards the end of the

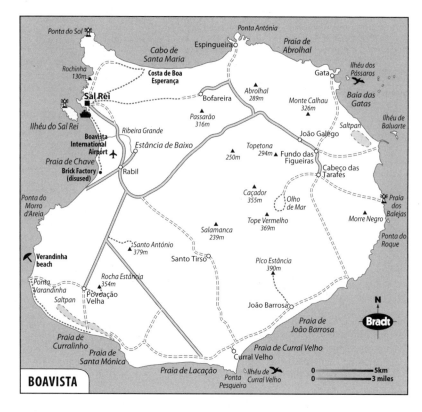

BOAVISTA

19th century with increasing business in lime, clay tiles and castor oil. Over the last hundred years or so the island has been the victim of drought, famine and grasshopper infestation which has led to emigration.

Perhaps the island's most famous son is Aristides Pereira, the 12th son of the priest of Boavista, who became the first president of Cape Verde in 1975 and who now has the island's international airport named after him..

Boavista today Boavista is an island marked by tragedy and struggle. There is little in its history, though, to guide it through the pressures it faces today. On the one hand it is poised to participate, for the first time, in international prosperity, through mass tourism. On the other it seems ready to fall headlong into destruction – plundered by the same industry and with little to show financially as a result.

Boavista's beaches have an almost traumatic beauty. In these days when so many bewitching landscapes have been consumed by tourism, and the European palate is jaded, Boavista has allure. Exploiting this, most people seem to believe, means to build, build, build massive hotels and streetfuls of apartment blocks and condominiums, hence the surely fanciful prediction that this island of just over 6,000 people could be welcoming a million visitors a year by 2020. This is the rationale behind the planned construction of 15,000 hotel bedrooms at Santa Mónica Beach; 18,000 in total for Chaves Beach; nearly 3,000 for Morro de Areia: in total a possible 50,000. The coast from Sal Rei to Curral Velho could be filled with hotels and apartments. Many foreign businesspeople, particularly Italian retaurateurs, have already invested here in anticipation of a continuing upward curve in visitor numbers. What Boavistan,

archipelago° choice

EXPLORE
CAPE VERDE

Walking

High volcanic craters, fertile valleys and quiet coastal hideaways – enjoy the best of the islands on our guided and self-guided walking holidays.

Wildlife

With so much to see, why not try whale watching, bird watching, or even lend a hand with Cape Verde's turtle conservation on our wildlife and conservation holidays.

Watersports

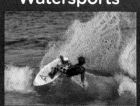

Whether you're a beginner or a pro, Cape Verde's crystal clear blue sea and sunshine make it the ideal holiday destination for diving, kitesurfing, windsurfing and sailing.

Step into your own tailor made adventure

YOUR HOLIDAY.
YOUR ADVENTURE.

above On Brava, as on many other islands, fishing is a key part of the local economy (MS) page 242

left Known as the 'wild' island, Brava's discouraging slopes hide a hinterland that is at times moist and fertile, filled with the potential for cultivation (SS) pages 242–3

below A tiny village at the foot of the mountains, Fajã d'Água is quite possibly Cape Verde's most beautiful bay (JB/A) pages 248–9

above A mural on the plateau, Praia, celebrates a true Cape Verdean hero, Amílcar Cabral (MM) pages 23–6

right Surrounded by rich *ribeiras* in which you can discover ruins of the Portuguese Empire, Cape Verde's Cidade Velha is well on its way to becoming a truly delightful town (PA/AWL) pages 179–83

below left Head to Assomada's vibrant and typically West African market, where you can buy a chicken, dead or alive, whole or in pieces (PA/AWL) pages 186–7

below right Fort Real do São Filipe in Cidade Velha was built in the 1500s to defend the island from overland attack (D/DT) page 181

top Precariously perched on the side of a mountain, the fairy-tale village of Fontainhas can only be reached via a winding cobbled path (PA/AWL) page 304

above left Fish market, Ponta do Sol (SS) page 303

above right Santo Antão has the largest cultivated area of any of the islands (FB/S) pages 286–7

below Local women carrying goods on the road to Ponta do Sol, one of the oldest Barlavento settlements (SS) pages 301–4

above São Vicente's capital, Mindelo, has an air of importance about it and attracts a wealthy clientele (FB/S) pages 269–78

right Cape Verde's most renowned and exuberant festival takes place in Mindelo, São Vicente — the outlandish Carnival is held in mid-February (SS) pages 260 & 264

below A colourful mural highlights Mindelo's generally accepted status as Cape Verde's cultural capital (PA/AWL) pages 276–7

above On Maio, even the children get
& inset involved in the fishing
(AL/S and MS) pages 201–2

left Fogo's capital, São Filipe, is an
attractive town peppered with
striking Portuguese architecture
(SS) pages 223–9

below Hiking opportunities are
plentiful on Fogo–as well as
the big climb up the Pico,
there are other rewarding
walks to be had around the
crater (SS) pages 234–8

above São Nicolau is a joy to visit, with several outstanding walks in the mountains offering an opportunity to get up close and personal to Cape Verdean village life (P/A) pages 338–41

below A pretty town with houses of ochre, green and blue, Ribeira Brava is wedged into the side of a *ribeira* (LH) pages 328–31

above left — The magnificent frigatebird (*Fregata magnificens*) is one of three threatened marine bird species found in Cape Verde (MT/S) pages 6, 139 & 157

above right — Spot a red-billed tropicbird (*Phaethon aethereus*) on the rugged coast of Santiago (DT/S) pages 6 & 164–5

left — The common and colourful grey-headed kingfisher (*Halcyon leucocephala*) is known locally as *passarinha* (AG/S) page 6

below left — The Egyptian vulture (*Neophron percnopterus*) is fast disappearing on the archipelago, and may already be extinct (MC/S) pages 6, 139 & 309

below right — The Cape Verde purple heron (*Ardea purpurea bournei*) is particularly evasive, possibly living in only two locations on Santiago (BZG/S) pages 6, 164 & 188

laden with an ancestry of famine and isolation, could fail to be dazzled by all this proposed activity?

But over the last few years some voices have questioned Boavista's direction. There is the economic question: how much does an all-inclusive resort hotel under foreign ownership, built under generous tax concessions, actually make for Boavista? Then there is the more subtle question: might Boavista's 'progress' destroy its very capital and thus, ultimately, extinguish itself? And of course, there are environmental questions.

One group that has spoken out about this is the World Wildlife Fund (WWF), concerned mainly about Boavista's role in the international fight against species collapse. 'The planning process lacks transparency,' said Ricardo Monteiro in 2006. 'Nothing has been done to assess the potential effect of land speculation, inflation, and increased immigration to the island. And, it does not address the likely negative impact on the natural beauty and biodiversity of the island.' 'The plans for Boavista,' added Arona Soumare, WWF's Marine Protected Areas Programme Officer, based in Dakar, Senegal, are 'massive, destructive, operations.'

To develop a vision for Boavista and regain some control, the government formed the Society for the Development of Boavista and Maio (*www.sdtibm.cv*), a state-owned company with the power to decide who gets to invest in what, within the tourism development zones. 'We don't want to make the same mistakes as were made in Sal,' said a society representative in Boavista. 'We want quality tourism and benefit to the local people.' The society, launched in 2005 and rejigged in 2007, has strict criteria to apply to developments.

Since then, however, development has taken place on yet another beach, Lacação, where a massive hotel complex has appeared. This huge new all-inclusive RIU Hotel has already had a significant impact on this important turtle-nesting beach, while further building phases could eventually mean there is no untouched land on this section of the southern coast. It seems that the island's government is merely ushering Boavista towards its own destruction. At least the economic crisis has given everyone time to ponder, with many developments stalling at an early stage without so much as a brick being laid. But another international hotel chain has designs on the stunning beach at Santa Monica and it seems only a matter of time before development begins.

GEOGRAPHY Boavista is the closest island to the African mainland, and 50km from Sal. It is the third largest, at 620km^2, but sparsely populated, with only 6,000 inhabitants. The island is very flat with the highest point, Pico Estância, at only 390m. The barren, stony landscape is covered in many areas with white sand and drifting dunes, which pile up on its western coast. The dunes have swallowed various buildings and covered the once-busy saltpans just outside Sal Rei, as well as at one time infiltrating one of the all-inclusive hotels – without an identity wristband, would you believe.

There are 55km of white beaches and, in the centre, Sahara-like oases filled with date palms. Since independence, environmental measures have been taken such as the building of catchment dams and planting of trees.

NATURAL HISTORY Boavista's biodiversity is of global importance as it includes endemic species of plants, birds and insects, as well as marine species. Its shores provide important nesting sites and feeding grounds for endangered marine turtles. Humpback whales come here to breed. A broad swathe of eastern Boavista is a hugely important coastal ecosystem, encompassing wetlands and nesting sites for thousands of loggerhead turtles. It is scattered with temporary wetlands all the way from Curral Velho at its southern tip to Ponta Antónia in the north. There are breeding colonies for a variety of seabirds along this shore and its offshore islets (Pássaros, Baluarte and Curral Velho). Corals grow in small bays and coves of the north and northeast coasts, protected from high swell and strong currents. These quiet and warm inshore waters are often frequented by nurse sharks (*Ginglymostoma cirratum*), juvenile hawksbill turtles (*Eretmochelys imbricata*) and green turtles (*Chelonia mydas*).

Protected areas In 2003, a law was passed approving 47 protected areas across the archipelago, including 14 on Boavista. The technical work carried out to delineate these areas has not, however, been approved, which has left them vulnerable.

After 2003, the government published its zones for integrated tourist development (ZDTIs). Land that was part of the protected areas was reallocated to ZDTI areas – most notably the coastal part of the Morro de Areia area in the southwest of the island and much of Praia da Lacação, the beach to the east of Santa Mónica: an ominous sign, perhaps, of future priorities.

The protected areas are Curral Velho, Monte Caçador and Pico Forçado. There are nature reserves at Boa Esperança in the north and Ponta do Sol at the northwest tip, Tartaruga, and Morro de Areia on the southwestern coast. An expanse of the northwest has been made into a natural park. Many of these areas will be affected by roads designed to link the island's villages. National monuments are: Monte Santo António, Monte Estância, Rocha Estância and Ilhéu do Sal Rei (the islet opposite Sal Rei). The islets of Baluarte, Pássaros and Curral Velho are Integral Nature Reserves (RNIs)

UNEP-GEF and the Ministry of Environment of Cape Verde have committed to support and co-finance a project named 'Consolidation of Cape Verde's Protected Areas System.' This project is being implemented over a period of four years, with the focus on BoaVista primarily on the island's east coast which contains marine reserves, integral reserves, a natural reserve, a natural park and landscape protected areas. The east shore of Boavista harbours the most important loggerhead turtle nesting beaches in the whole country, several feeding habitats for juvenile green and hawksbill turtles, as well as other significant natural resources of the archipelago (seabird breeding colonies, coral areas, etc).

Ramsar sites Given the aridity of much of the island, it may seem counterintuitive that Boavista has one of the largest wetlands in the Macaronesia region. It stretches from Curral Velho, at its southern tip, up to Ervatão, and this region has been designated a Ramsar site – that is, a wetland of international interest.

It's not wet all the year round – just over the rainy season and during extreme spring tides. But this is enough for it to be an important host to many migratory birds coming from Europe and west Africa.

A second Ramsar site is Rabil Lagoon, which acquired this status in 2005 and is also categorised by BirdLife International as one of 12 Important Bird Areas in Cape Verde. This site seems doomed, however, by the noise of aircraft arriving at the new international airport, quad bikes tripping through the area, quarrying and general developments on the coast.

Marine Boavista shares with Maio and Sal a single large marine platform that harbours the country's highest levels of marine biodiversity. The nearby João Valente seamount, an underwater mountain between Boavista and Maio, hosts

Cape Verde has the world's third-largest loggerhead turtle nesting population, and 90% of the archipelago's loggerhead nesting takes place on Boavista. The number of nests fluctuates each year according to climatic factors such as water temperature. In 2009, over 20,000 nests were recorded on Boavista; two years later there were a mere 5,000. Happily, preliminary data shows that 2012 was a record year for nest numbers. The nesting season takes place primarily between June and October and researchers gather on Boavista to study the loggerhead turtles (*Caretta caretta*) that nest at Ervatão Beach. They want to understand the status, distribution and numbers of the turtles. It's a night job, and as soon as volunteers spot a turtle coming ashore they lie on the ground and crawl towards her. After she has laid her eggs and is on her way back to the sea, they put a chip in the turtle and ID attached with tags on the flippers. Turtles equipped with satellite transmitters send information about their migratory routes and feeding areas back to scientists. Meanwhile, hatchlings are counted, weighed and measured before being released into the sea.

A history of poor law enforcement and a lack of vigilance has allowed the threats to loggerheads to continue, despite the full protection afforded to all turtle species by the Cape Verde environmental legislation. But progress has been made, with the approval of the Marine Turtle National Conservation Plan and the establishment of TAOLA as the umbrella organisation for turtle protection being significant recent achievements. Ana Liria Loza, President of CV Natura 2000, reports that they have had success in reducing the number of turtles killed for meat, at least according to the data they can collect from carcasses on the beaches. They are now turning some of their attention to the illegal 'fishing' of turtles, caught by boats even before they reach the shores. The effects of incidental catch ('by-catch') by industrial and artisanal fishing is awaiting further research and assessment. Data for that is harder to monitor than land-based slaughter.

Since 2008 another group, Turtle Foundation (*www.turtle-foundation.org*), has also become active on five beaches, concentrating on preventing the slaughter of the turtles as they nest. Patrols by international volunteers and Cape Verdean soldiers are made through the night on Canto, Boa Esperança, Norte and Lacação. A third NGO, Bios, is also now involved, covering some of the other beaches.

The growth of tourism is bringing increasing problems for the endangered loggerhead species through loss of habitat, light pollution and increasing numbers of cars, quad bikes and dune buggies driving on nesting beaches. With the developers on one side, and NGOs on the other, battle has well and truly been joined.

Boavista BACKGROUND INFORMATION

4

a particularly rich biodiversity. Seamounts are known to fishermen for high concentrations of fish, and to researchers as rare and unique habitats.

Turtles Thousands of loggerhead turtles (*Caretta caretta*) nest on Boavista's east coast and especially its southeastern beaches annually, making it the second most important nesting site in the Atlantic Ocean and the third most important in the world, after the Florida Keys and Oman's Massirah Island. The key stretch for turtles is from Curral Velho in the south to As Gatas in the northeast.

The mother turtles crawl up the beaches between mid-June and late October. Once they have laid their eggs they disappear, leaving the hatchlings to fend for themselves. When the baby turtles emerge from their eggs in late August to late December, they make a frenzied dash for the sea. It is thought that the glimmering surface of the ocean is what attracts them – hence the problem that lights from houses and hotels could lure them in the wrong direction.

But development is not the only threat to turtles. There remains a strong local culture of turtle consumption, and dead turtles, the relics of this, sometimes litter the beaches. This is not done out of hunger, says Professor Luis Felipe Lopez Jurado, who has studied turtles in Boavista since 1998, including for the NGO Cabo Verde Natura 2000. 'The people killing turtles have big cars and jobs,' he says. 'They come down on a Friday night. Nobody needs the meat of the turtle to survive.'

Whales Sal Rei is the bay of choice for many humpback whales as a place to give birth and nurse their young. They arrive from December onwards, although March and April are probably the best months for sightings, which can sometimes be experienced as late as June. The giant mammals nurse their calves in a shallow haven free from waves, and then depart for the deep ocean (for more on whales, see *Natural history and conservation*, page 9).

Sharks The quiet bays and coves of the north are often frequented by nurse sharks (*Ginglymostoma cirratum*).

WHALES

Interest is growing in the whales that frequent the waters around Boavista and other islands, and a consolidated team of international whale researchers has been created, supported and funded by various organisations. Over the last decade Beatrice Jann, a biologist from the University of Basel in Switzerland, has been documenting sightings of humpbacks and other species. Sometimes Pedro López Suarez, a naturalist who has been living in Boavista for a decade, gathers what information he can for her during the whale-watching trips he organises for tourists. Other groups such as the Irish Whale and Dolphin Group have organised research trips to try to uncover a link between the Cape Verdean whales and the whales sighted around Ireland. Their website (*www.iwdg.ie*) has a useful report on humpbacks off Cape Verde.

Whales are identified by the undersides of their tail flukes, each underside being unique to that whale. Their shifting patches of black and white look like an ink-blot pattern. The shape and scarring of the dorsal fin is also used in the photo-identification process. The photographs are sent to a store at Bar Harbour in Maine, USA, where there are now 'fingerprints' of 5,000 whales. 'It's sort of an Interpol of the humpbacks,' says Beatrice. By matching observations, scientists can piece together the whales' migrations. They have found whales photographed in Norway turning up in the Dominican Republic, and whales from western Canada appearing in Japan. For the visitor, Boavista presents great opportunities to see these mighty mammals, with over 5,000 people taking whale-watching trips in 2013. In season, sightings are almost a certainty.

Birds The emblematic species of Boavista are the white-faced storm petrel (*Pelagodroma marina*) and the magnificent frigatebird (*Fregata magnificens*), sadly now nearly extinct. Other sought-after birds are the cream-coloured courser (*Cursorius cursor*), and the Egyptian vulture (*Neophron percnopterus*), the latter of these approaching extinction. There are also breeding colonies of red-billed tropicbirds (*Phaethon aethereus*). The Cape Verde sparrow (*Passer iagoensis*), one of four endemic Cape Verdean birds, is found in Rabil Lagoon.

For the non-specialist the most eye-catching birds to watch for are perhaps the magnificent frigatebird, black with a 2m wing span and a long beak, hooked at the end. Males have a scarlet throat pouch which inflates in the breeding season. It is estimated that this species will have disappeared within five to ten years. Secondly, look for the red-billed tropicbird, white with its eponymous red bill and a long, streaming white tail following behind. The population of this species is also under threat, having declined by 40% in the ten years to 2013.

Overall there are more than 20 species of bird breeding on Boavista. The areas of most interest are perhaps Ilhéu de Curral Velho, Ilhéu dos Pássaros, and the wetland areas, both fresh water and salty.

Flora The tamareira (*Phoenix atlantica*) and the date palm (*Phoenix dactilifera*) fill the lagoons and *ribeiras* of the island (see page 5, for more information on palm trees in Cape Verde).

ECONOMY Apart from the growing business of tourism, there is some business exporting dates and fishing (limited because of lack of investment in the large boats needed to withstand the stormy seas). An unusually poor soil thwarts agriculture. Villages across Boavista are supplied with water by tanker from a desalinisation plant in Sal Rei. Some water is drawn from the ground by windmills (many of which are broken) but this is brackish and not suitable for drinking. It is used for washing, and also for agriculture, although the salt content constrains the type of vegetable that can be grown. Salt production ceased in 1979.

HAZARDS

Crime Unfortunately robberies, some of them violent, became increasingly frequent on Boavista as tourism advanced. Many of these incidents took place on remote beaches with tourists being violently robbed in the dunes along Chaves Beach or in the vicinity of the wreck of the *Santa Maria*. There have also been instances of mass robberies of quad tours.

The City Hall of Boavista responded by calling in the army to work with the police and are working on the development of a programme of safe tourism. Locals say that this has stabilised the situation. Take basic precautions – don't go walking alone in these areas and don't carry valuables with you. Also, try asking around about the current security situation, because it would be a shame to restrict yourself unnecessarily.

Hiking Boavista is a parched landscape, bereft of shade, which could cause serious dehydration or sunburn for the unwary, particularly hikers. Kit must include several litres of water (as many as five for a full day's walking); boots for dealing with the stony ground and frequent, short hilly scrambles; and sun protection. The interior is empty: most folks gave up on the possibility of living there many years ago. Learn from them and take at least a map and preferably a compass or handheld GPS. Swathes of Boavista have, however, no mobile-phone coverage.

Driving If you rent a 4x4 or quad bike remember that it is illegal to drive on beaches and dunes; stick to the tracks. If you become stranded, help may be hard to find. Carry food, water and a spade – and leave details of your journey at your hotel. Quad biking on your own in remote areas is not recommended.

Swimming Offshore winds and swells in the north make swimming periodically hazardous. In places (for example stretches of Chaves Beach or north of Espingueira) the beach slopes steeply and there can be a strong undertow. Check before you dip.

Near the wreck of the *Santa Maria,* the beach attracts debris which can cut an ill-placed foot, so keep your shoes on.

GETTING THERE AND AWAY

BY AIR There are direct international charter flights from the UK, Italy, Germany, Belgium, Switzerland and Scandinavia. You can also fly scheduled airlines with TACV and twice-weekly flights with TAP from Lisbon began in October 2013. Otherwise, flights from Portugal involve a stop in Praia or Sal, or both. There is at least one, sometimes two, daily flights to and from Sal, with TACV. As with all internal flights it is best to book well in advance in order to get a seat.

Boavista International Airport The airport (☏ 251 9000) is 6km south of the capital, Sal Rei, near to the town of Rabil. It's an attractive place, as airports go, with laid-back architecture and an endearing welcome notice in the arrivals hall: 'This airport loves you. We hope you love us too.' Not very airport-like at all,

FESTIVALS	
1 January	New Year (whole island)
6 January	Twelfth Night (João Galego and other northern villages)
3 May	Santa Cruz (Rabil slave liberation)
	Parades, drumming and whistling
4 May	Pidrona (Rabil)
8 May	São Roque (Povoação Velha)
Last weekend of May	Cruz Nhô Lolo (Estância de Baixo)
	Horse racing, *coladeras*, goat fighting
13 June	Santo António
	Procession to a church near the deserted Rock of Santo António
24 June	São João Baptista (northern area)
	Procession and offerings
4 July	Santa Isobel (Sal Rei)
	Boavista's most important feast day, attracting visitors from around the archipelago
15 August	Nossa Sra da Piedade (João Galego)
16 August	Saint Roque (Rabil) Praia da Cruz festival
	A week after the Baía das Gatas festival in São Vicente, this beach festival attracts national and international musicians.
8 December	Imaculada Conceição (Povoação Velha)

really. Facilities include a bar/cafe, bank and two ATMs, souvenir shops, a branch of Harmonia music store, car hire and two tour-operator offices (Morena and Barracuda). TACV also has an office (✆ 251 1415). There is also an information desk for tourists, which opens to coincide with flight times. There is free Wi-Fi access if you have your own device.

Some hotels meet their clients with a minibus. *Hiaces* and *hiluxes* wait outside and can be hired as taxis. The charge to town is 700$; the fare to the Marine Club (see page 148) is higher.

Transport back to the airport from Sal Rei can be found by loitering in the main square, though getting a collective *aluguer* is a hassle and risky if your flight is imminent. Better to bite the bullet and go 'private hire.' You can always ask your hotelier to arrange a vehicle.

BY FERRY Ferries come and ferries go. At the time of writing there is no regular and reliable ferry service to Boavista. The Anavmar agency (✆ 251 1730) is based in the northeast of Sal Rei town and handles the ferry services from Sal Rei to Sal and Praia, but they unashamedly have no timetable. The journey times – assuming you can even find a boat – are four and nine hours respectively. Cost will be around 2,500$ to Sal and 4,000$ to Praia.

It's unlikely to be very comfortable and some people advise against ferry travel on safety grounds. The other ocean option therefore, is a day trip from Sal – either by catamaran (faster, which maximises time on the island) or by boat (slower but also cheaper).

BY YACHT The waters off Sal Rei offer a very good anchorage. Most people anchor between the southern end of the islet and the shore. Harbour officials are generally on the pier. There are few facilities for yachts, but you could ask around at the port.

GETTING AROUND

BY PUBLIC TRANSPORT *Alugueres* run frequently between Sal Rei and Rabil (100$). To other destinations they generally leave Sal Rei in the afternoon, and do not return until the following morning, arriving in Sal Rei at about 07.00. Information is particularly difficult to come by from anyone in town. Don't get stranded. Buses for the northeast leave from the west side of the main square in Sal Rei at about 13.00. Those heading south depart from the south of the square.

BY TAXI In the form of chartered *alugueres*, these can be hired for about ten times the public fare (eg: to Rabil 500$; to Santa Mónica 5,000$; to Morre Negro 6,000$; one day around the island 9,000$). To do a thorough tour of Boavista it is essential to have a 4x4.

BY CAR Most of the hotels can put you in touch with a car-hire firm and driver. A 4x4 is recommended. Prices start at around 7,000$ per day, self-drive.

🚌 **La Perla** ✆ 251 2293; m 997 4863; e info@laperlaboavista.com; www.laperlaboavista.com. On the main square.

🚌 **Mendes and Mendes** ✆ 251 1982; e mendes&mendes@cvtelecom.cv

🚌 **Olicar** Largo Santa Isabel; ✆ 251 1743. On the main square.

4

The origins of the *morna* are obscure but it is said to have emerged on Boavista, named after the English word 'mourn' or perhaps the French word 'morne', meaning 'sad'. There are a multitude of theories as to how its characteristic melodies arose. According to the Cape Verdean historian António Germano Lima, one theory is that it came from the sound of fishermen's oars hitting the water on their long journeys, and their marking of the rhythm of the rowing with the call 'vo-ga... vo-ga'. Others say it came from a mixture of musical types, such as the medieval Portuguese ballad, the *cancioneiro*, the Portuguese–Brazilian *modinhas* and the priests' liturgical chants. Lima himself favours the idea that the melancholy music must have been born from the hearts of slaves longing for home.

The modern *morna* was developed by Eugénio Tavares (see box, page 247). Boavistan *mornas* are much livelier than Tavares's tearful versions. They can be full of satire, caricature, ridicule and dreams of revenge.

WHERE TO STAY AND EAT

Unless you have opted for an all-inclusive, most accommodation, including all of the cheaper places, is in the capital Sal Rei. There are a few hotels some kilometres to the south, along Chaves Beach. There is one hotel 2km north of Sal Rei, along the coast. And there is one, remote luxury hotel in Espingueira. The massive Riu Touareg is in the far south and there are plans for many more hotels along Chaves Beach and along Santa Mónica Beach. As in Sal, hotels on Boavista are more expensive than in the rest of the archipelago. There are an increasing number of apartments available for long- and short-term rental. Try asking tour operators or rental agencies such as Blue Banana (for contact information, see page 151).

To be within walking distance of any external facilities, such as local restaurants or the watersports establishments, it's best to stay in Sal Rei. A hotel along Chaves Beach such as the Parque das Dunas (see page 158) is a beautiful and isolated option but it is too far (and, at certain times of day, potentially dangerous) to walk to Sal Rei, so you will be reliant on the hotel shuttle or a taxi (1000$).

ACTIVITIES

EXCURSIONS TO OTHER ISLANDS There are day trips to Santiago, Fogo and Sal on offer. These are not cheap and won't allow you much time on the island but will give you a flavour. The companies listed in the following sections can assist with tours and activities on the island.

If you want to see a different side to Sal Rei, thought-provoking, a little distressing yet uplifting, a walking-tour of the Boa Esperança township (see box, page 148) is to be considered. Lamine Drame (m *594 4600*) speaks French and English and can act as guide and interpreter to this interesting community.

LOCAL TOUR OPERATORS

Barracuda Tours Av 4 de Julho, Zona de João Cristovão, Sal Rei; ☎251 1907; e geral@ barracudatours.com; www.barracudatours.com; ⏰ 09.00–13.00 & 15.00–18.00 Mon–Fri, 09.00–13.00 Sat. Southwest of town on a road running towards the beach from opposite the fuel stations.

Offers half- & full-day trips around the island, quad tours & buggy tours, as well as a day trip to Fogo.

Clamtour Av 4 de Julho; ☎ 251 2121/1982; m 918 7351/7352. Offers walks, 4x4 tours, boat tours & day trips to Santiago & Fogo.

EXCURSIONS

Giggling Gecko Adventures m 978 6926; e info@gigglinggeckoadventures.com; www. gigglinggeckoadventures.com. A highly rated tour company, run by an enterprising Scottish couple who support local charities. Tours include island tours, BBQ tours, whale-watching & turtle tours (both seasonal), Sat night sunset tours & many more on offer.

Lloyd Stokes m 931 4059. English guide with 10 years' island experience. Organises tailor-made excursions.

Morena Tourist Agency Largo Santa Isabel; ☎ 251 1445; e boavistapoint@cvtelecom.cv; ⏰ 09.00–12.30 & 16.00–19.00 Mon–Fri. In the north of the main square. It offers day trips to the dunes & further afield to Santa Mónica Beach, horseriding & other activities.

Naturalia ☎ 251 1558; m 994 1070/998 6650; e naturalia.cv@hotmail.com; www. naturaliaecotours.com. Offers whale-watching, snorkelling among corals & nurse sharks, turtle-watching & birding trips. The company, set up in 2008, is one outcome of the EU's Naturalia Project to restore ecosystems & test whether they can be used sustainably & profitably in ecotourist activities. See individual entries below.

Olitour Largo Santa Isabel; ☎ 251 1743. It offers half- & full-day tours into the dunes.

DIVING

See page 50 for a discussion of diving.

⁀ Boavista Diving At the side of Tortuga Beach Restaurant, on the beach; m 596 3737; e info@ boavistadiving.com; www.boavistadiving.com. Multilingual PADI centre, offering single dives at €39 plus equipment for €19. Open Water Courses are €399.

⁀ Dive School Submarine Center Located along the beach south of the Hotel Estoril near Tortuga Beach; m 992 4865/7866; e atilros@ hotmail.com; www.caboverde.com/pages/924865. htm. Atila & Rose have lived on Boavista since 1997 & offer PADI & NAUI courses at all levels, including try dives for adults (€130) & PADI Bubblemaker for kids (€100). They also organise snorkelling trips (€40) & rent windsurfing (€25/hr), surfing (€25/half day) & bodyboard equipment & kite lessons from €50/hr. SUP for €29 per hour. Kayaks available. Plans are afoot to open a bar/restaurant. Between them they speak English, Portuguese, Italian, Spanish & French.

⁀ Watersports Center Scubacaribe Located at RIU Karamboa Hotel, Bahía de Chaves; ☎ 251 9100, ext 9070 (dive centre); 251 1999 (office); e info@scubacaribe.com; www.scubacaribe. com. PADI Gold Palm Resort offering scuba diving, snorkelling, quad tours, fishing trips, kitesurfing & windsurfing in many different languages. Open to all, despite its close connection to the hotel. Prices & reservations available on the website.

WINDSURFING AND KITESURFING The excellent windsurfing potential of Cape Verde is discussed on page 53. Boavista has many great spots but not everywhere is suitable: rescue facilities are non-existent in many places so beaches like Santa Mónica, with a strong offshore wind, are not recommended. The northern shore has a heavy wind swell, and though wind- and kitesurfing are possible there are better places elsewhere. The island is good for independent and advanced kitesurfers, windsurfers and surfers looking for a variety of conditions, but beginners should stick to Sal Rei Bay. For many of the spots you will need a hire car or arrange a pick-up or taxi. Key spots are:

1 SAL REI BAY A long white sandy beach stretching south of town, with the wind increasingly stable as you move south, and the ground increasingly sandy once you have left town behind. The wind is offshore, so make sure you know how you will be rescued. There's a reef with small break waves. Apart from that the water is flat.

2 CHAVES You can windsurf or kitesurf on the beach outside the RIU Karamboa but in the winter this often has a large shorebreak and to find a good place to enter the water you will have to go much further down the beach.

3 BAÍA VARANDINHA Reached by 4x4 overland this remains a lonely place with stable, side-shore winds, beach break waves and sand below. Not suitable for beginners.

4 EAST COAST Out of the turtle season it should be possible to windsurf and kitesurf on many of the beaches here. Again the wind is stable and side-shore to side-on. There is some wind swell out of the protected bay areas. Not suitable for beginners.

Kit hire and lessons are available from the following:

Boavista Wind Club m 596 3870/972 7856; e rest.alisios@hotmail.com; www. boavistawindclub.com. Located at Tortuga Beach on the south side, this long-established club offers windsurfing & rents windsurfing, kayaking & surfing kit. Also offers surf safaris to 'secret' surfing spots on the island. 4hrs of windsurf hire come to just over €50, with lessons at €60 for 90mins. Kayak hire at €10/hr, surfboards at €10/hr. **Dive School Submarine Center** (see *Diving*, page 143). Also rents watersports kit. **Vista Surf** On the beach in front of the RIU. Offers

SHIPWRECKS ON BOAVISTA

A few years ago, divers plunged into Cape Verde's waters on a hunt for shipwrecks, and surfaced clutching a gold coin bearing the date 1760. They believe they discovered the remains of the *Dromadaire*, a French trading ship that sank in 1762, carrying more than £3 million of gold and silver. It is said the crew of the *Dromadaire* only realised their plight when they saw the reef surf under the prow. Some 17 miles south of Boavista lies the notorious reef, Baixo de João Leitão: it has wrecked many a vessel. One man who spent tormented hours battling (successfully) to avoid it was Captain James Cook on his third and last voyage to the South Seas, in 1776.

Old people on Boavista still tell of a legendary cargo of gold brought to their ancestors by shipwreck. This may have been the wreck of the English vessel *Hartwell* on 24 May 1787. The ship suffered a mutiny while on the seas and in the confusion the crew let the boat stray to Boavista's shallows. The reef that sank her is now called the Hartwell Reef and lies at the northeast side of the island – it is partly above water, and extends for about 6km.

Cape Verde's version of the *Titanic* disaster occurred in the 19th century – the tragedy of the *Cicília*. It was the night of 5 November 1863, and the Italian ship was carrying emigrants destined for South America. Their spirits were high and there was a dance going on in the ballroom when the ship foundered near Boavista. When the captain realised what had happened he commanded the door of the ballroom to be locked. He made a great error. According to the poet José Lopes: 'There inside was true horror… a dance of life was transformed into a macabre dance of death…'. Passengers were later found dead in the act of struggling to get out of the portholes; in all 72 died.

The *Santa Maria* was wrecked in August 1968 on the northwest coast. She was *en route* from Spain to Brazil with a cargo of cars, drink, melons, cork and cheese. The year 1968 had until then been a bad one for Boavistans: they spent the next 12 months salvaging booty.

rentals & lessons. However, in winter even though the waves are fantastic, the shorebreak can be very large, making it difficult to enter the water.

At other times it can be a great spot for advanced windsurfing & kitesurfing. Kite lessons are often given in a shallow lagoon near the school.

SURFING Cabral Beach, where the swell is greatest, is the most popular venue for surfers. Surfing is best from November to March in terms of waves and swell, but calmest in May to September. Boards can be hired from the Boavista Wind Club or Dive School Submarine Center (for further details, see page 143).

BEACHES AND SWIMMING The vast strands of Chaves, Curralinho, Santa Mónica, Curral Velho and many others make Boavista into one huge, ravenously beautiful beach. There are endless opportunities for sunbathing, dipping and swimming. Opposite Ilhéu do Sal Rei is a lovely option – the water is never more than 3m deep and it is only 1,000m to the island. Another possibility close to Sal Rei is Praia da Cruz Beach which is just before the beach used by the Marine Club, and is divided from it by a little spit of land (although if more apartment complexes are eventually finished behind it, it may get busy). There are also many protected coves around the island – for example Praia de Ponta Antónia in the north (see page 140).

FISHING
Both line fishing and deep-sea fishing are available.

 Boapesca m 994 1060/991 8778; e luca@ boavista2000.com. Deep-sea fishing. Catch your fish with Boapesca & get it cooked at the Blue

Marlin Restaurant (see *Where to eat and drink*, page 151).

 Morena Tourist Agency (see page 143)

 Olitour (see page 143)

WHALE WATCHING Humpback whales come to Boavista to have their young and to nurse their calves until they are strong enough for the open ocean. Journeying out on a catamaran in search of them, watching their great masses surging and looping effortlessly through the water, and catching glimpses of their signature tail flukes, is a magical experience, as is taking a dip on the way back to shore. You may be accompanied by scientists photographing, recording and collecting skin samples, which adds even more interest to the trip.

Naturalia For contact details, see page 143; available Sep–Apr 08.30–11.00 & 14.00–16.30 approx, several days a week, depending on the

wind & swell; adult/under 12 €50/30 including transfers, although this may differ depending on the number of people.

BIRDWATCHING Local fishermen can be recruited to take tourists to the various islets.

Naturalia For contact details, see page 143; half & full-day tours €35–80, depending on number of participants.

TURTLE WATCHING Watching nesting loggerhead turtles is a night-time experience, with August the peak of the nesting season. There is an 80-minute journey to the southeastern coast. A guide gives a briefing on turtle biology and conservation work in Cape Verde as well as the basic rules to follow to minimise disturbance to the animals. Seeing turtles is guaranteed; witnessing their egg laying is more hit-and-miss as it depends on their finding a suitable nesting site.

Naturalia For contact details, see page 143; available Jul–Oct 20.00–01.00 approx; adult/under 12 €50/20. Book directly or via travel agent.

Turtle Foundation www.turtle-foundation. org. The foundation may be offering tours in conjunction with local travel agents.

CORAL SNORKELLING
Snorkelling takes place at Gatas Bay, on the northeast shore of Boavista, where, in the summer, you may find yourself nose to nose with nurse sharks as well as exploring the corals.

Naturalia For contact details, see page 143; available at high tide; adult/under 12 €40/18 (min

4 people); price includes equipment & transfers.

HORSERIDING
Perhaps this is the perfect way of seeing Boavista. Treks go mostly along the beach or inland to oases.

Morena Tourist Agency For contact details, see page 143. Around €30 for 2 hrs, weight limit of 75kg.

QUAD BIKING
Motoquad is increasingly popular and a compelling way to see the sights. It is, however, frowned on by some who wish to preserve the peace of Boavista's beaches. It is illegal and irresponsible to take vehicles, including quad bikes, onto the beaches or the dunes.

Clamtours (see page 143) can organise rentals with Boa Quad from €65.

Quadzone ✆ 251 2025; m 992 7306. Organises tours from €65 for 2hrs. Also quadfishing tours.

HIKING
Although Boavista lacks the verdant mountainous scenery of the more traditional hiking islands, its white deserts, pretty coastline and serendipitous oases, combined with its emptiness, make it a rewarding place to explore on foot (provided the hiker is properly shod, hatted and watered – see page 139 for potential hazards).

There are several short hikes around the north of Sal Rei, and three of these can be joined together to make a full-day excursion. There are a couple of short hikes up small peaks in the southwest, near Povoação Velha, and a charming hike down Chaves Beach and around Rabil Lagoon.

For hike descriptions, and further hiking ideas, see page 159.

CULTURE
A small dance group does a rip-roaring trip through the main dance forms of Cape Verde, performing weekly at some of the resort hotels. Some of these performances are open to non-residents (try asking at Marine Club or Royal Decameron; see pages 148 and 158 respectively).

SIGHTSEEING BY VEHICLE
Contact Olicar Rental (*Largo Santa Isabel, beside Olitour; 4x4 rental from €65/day; see page 00 for details*). Alternatively, 4x4 taxis can be picked up at the east end of Largo Santa Isabel.

A popular activity is to join a half- or full-day tour of the island, using one of the tour operators listed on page 142, or to hire your own car, or taxi with driver, for the day. The latter option, of course, has the advantage that you can dawdle where you please. Another option is to hire a quad bike and set out on your own, but if you are new to quad bikes take advice on how to extract yourself from the sand. A possible route is to go south from Sal Rei, northeast along the main road after Rabil, branch off north to see Espingueira and Bofareira and then return to the main road; follow it to Fundo das Figueiras and Cabeço das Tarafes; take the track south to Curral Velho, northwest back up to the main road, then southwest on the main road to Povoação Velha, where a new road has now been built.. Most of the sights along this route are described below. Exercise extreme caution if travelling alone as there have been incidents of violent mugging on deserted beaches. Listen to advice about the current situation before venturing to remote places. Remember that it is illegal to drive on the beach anywhere in Cape Verde; unfortunately, you will still see it done.

Take local advice about the state of the track directly linking Curral Velho to Povoação Velha and, if you are taking a driver, check with him beforehand that he is happy to follow your route. Don't embark on the venture on your own without a good map.

SAL REI

There is a charm about this town that seeps in slowly, as you sit with a beer at the *esplanada* in the main square watching life go by, or drink coffee in thankful shade overlooking the beach. The water is a glorious turquoise and the mounds of sand are a true, desert-island yellow. Men maintain their painted boats and children shout and play around the decrepit ones or hurl themselves into the water from the old pier. From the town, the modest hillocks of Boavista appear like craggy mountains.At night, you may become aware of a canine sub-culture, characterised by ferocious barking matches and brawling in the empty streets. Next morning traces of fur in the square are all that remain.

Sal Rei is quietly busy. Town planners made the cobbled roads wide and planted acacias, their trunks painted a tidy white. The main square is vast, with bandstands, children's play areas, benches, a café and an ice-cream stall.

So far the influx of visitors to the all-inclusive hotels has made little impact on Sal Rei, which has not experienced a sudden boom in restaurants and bars in the same way as the neighbouring island, Sal. But although ownership changes seem frequent, it has not suffered from wholesale closures. There are, however, far more souvenir sellers from west Africa than ever before. In common with every other island, the town has seen an influx of Chinese shops.

 WHERE TO STAY

Those not staying in one of Boavista's massive all-inclusive hotels may find that a spot of relative luxury does not come cheap in Sal Rei. Accommodation is available across the price range, but the cost is higher than on the other islands, apart from similarly tourist-orientated Sal. All listings are located on the map, page 150.

4

THE BOAVISTA ULTRATRAIL

Running for three days through the dunes, beaches and oases of Boavista, testing themselves in the bone-dry heat and under the desert night skies, is the experience of a lifetime for many of the contestants in the annual ultratrail (formerly ultramarathon). Launched in 2000, the 150km race lasts for up to 60 hours, with a hefty entry fee but a prize fund of €6,000. Sleep as you go. For more information, including details of other extreme events, contact Boavista Ultratrail , based in Italy (e *info@boavistaultratrail.com; www.boavistaultratrail. com*). The website is multilingual.

Murray Stewart

On the northeastern side of Sal Rei, far away in geography and equally distant economically from the massive all-inclusives on Chaves Beach, is Boa Esperança – or 'Good Hope' – Boavista's impoverished township.

It may not be somewhere that all the guests at the luxury hotels become aware of during their stay, yet it has many past and present links to those establishments. Boa Esperança's inhabitants are almost entirely foreigners, immigrant workers who came to Cape Verde to construct the vast hotel and condominium developments before the economic crisis of 2008 brought everything to a shuddering halt. Now, engineers from Senegal, architects from The Gambia, construction workers from Nigeria all rub shoulders with each other, living in 'Good Hope' that something's going to change sometime soon.

For the present, many of the township's womenfolk are bussed out to the large hotels every day to perform the menial cleaning and other tasks that Cape Verdeans will not readily do for a monthly salary of €200. Despite the low income, amazingly some of the money is remitted to the relevant motherland, supporting loved ones left behind: after all, this is the reason that many of these people came to Cape Verde in the first place.

Some of the menfolk have set up tiny shops and bars in the illegally constructed township buildings, serving their own community. Right in the centre of Boa Esperança, crowded in by buildings on all sides, is the township's football pitch.

There is no electricity and nearly all the houses lack sanitation. In the rainy season, the township floods, raising the risk of disease. Toilet needs are satisfied in the nearby woods; at night the residents do not even bother to walk that far. Prostitution and drug abuse are problems, though the police have had success in reducing the latter. Ironically, within sight of the township, are the abandoned 'Casa para Todos' ('Houses for Everyone') developments. For the moment, it's houses for nobody.

Despite the poverty and its associated problems, the atmosphere in Boa Esperança is lively and there is a strong community spirit, a spirit born out of shared adversity. Momo, from Senegal, smiles and shakes his head when I ask him if he believes the talk of a new hotel being built on one of the southern beaches, something that might offer to make good use of his skills as an electrician and bring him some income. And yet, amidst the roaming dogs, the piled-up litter, amidst the waft of human waste that blows through the township on the warm wind, hope – whether misplaced or not, whether 'Good' hope' or mere desperation – somehow sustains the thousands of people crammed together. Boa Esperança has its own bars and restaurants, shops and entertainment – it seems to look after itself, in a fashion. It is truly Sal Rei's lesser-known, 'all-inclusive' resort.

Hotels

🏠 **Marine Club** (60 rooms, 39 villas) 📞251 1285; e booking@marineclubresort.com www. marineclubresort.com. A 20min walk along a straight cobbled road that leads from the north of Sal Rei. The oldest resort in Boavista, occupying a prime position overlooking the water. Marine Club's mature planting & chalet-style layout give it a village feel. Used mainly by Italian package holidaymakers. All-inclusive packages are the norm, B&B & HB are options. The all-inclusive is 'soft': all alcohol is charged extra. As well as the rooms there are 2- & 3- bedroom villas. Only 'superior' rooms & villas enjoy a sea view. There's a beautiful pool & small playground, & the hotel makes use of the adjacent small beach. There is a buffet restaurant open to non-guests for a set price of €20 (lunch) or €24 (dinner). Non-guests can also pay to spend a half day enjoying the facilities (€30). Entertainment includes a Fri performance by Cape Verdean musicians & dancers, also open to non-resident diners. **$$$$$**

🏠 **Hotel Boa Vista** (34 rooms) Rua dos Emigrantes, CP 40 Sal Rei; 📞251 1145; e hotelboavista@cvtelecom.cv. Positioned on the right as you enter Sal Rei from the airport. Large, bright, mostly balconied rooms have private baths with hot water, AC & TV, fridge & with a communal terrace offering views over Sal Rei to the sea. Back rooms have no sea view & can be a bit dingy & dark. A bit overpriced. **$$$$**

🏠 **Hotel Luca Kalema** (20 rooms) Av Amílcar Cabral, CP 30 Sal Rei; 📞251 1225; e reception. kalema@riu.com; www.riu.com. Previously called Hotel Dunas, this Riu Group hotel is a recently modernised, tasteful, bright, spacious hotel on the seafront, with most mod cons. Its modernisation has moved it upmarket. The courtyard restaurant serves only breakfasts. **$$$$**

🏠 **Guest House Orquidea** (10 rooms) 📞251 1041; e domorguidea@hotmail.com. A charming, upmarket guesthouse only a few metres from the sea featuring delightfully decorated rooms, each with bathroom (hot water), balcony, fridge, TV & safe. There is also a gym, internet & laundry service. Upstairs rooms have a wonderful sea view. Buffet b/fast is served in a shady courtyard & the welcoming owners, long-term residents of Sal Rei, will arrange all the excursions you could want. A safe & comfy place to base yourself while exploring Boavista. **$$$$**

🏠 **Migrante Guesthouse** (5 rooms) Av Amílcar Cabral, CP 80 Sal Rei; 📞251 1143; m 995 3655; e info@migrante-guesthouse. com; www.migrante-guesthouse.com. On a road to the west of the main square, this is the most atmospheric guesthouse in town, a traditional house set around a courtyard, lovingly restored & tastefully decorated. Many people are captivated by its charm, but some complain that the rooms are too hot. Rooms are en suite with hot water & fan. English spoken. There's a bar (🕐 08.30–22.00

daily), & dinner is available if requested in advance; there is also Wi-Fi. **$$$$**

🏠 **A Paz** (9 rooms) Av 5 de Julho; m 978 9431; e info@apazboavista.com; www.apazboavista. com. Near the main square, this small, Italian-run house has been decorated with some charm & much bamboo. Comfortable enough, all rooms are en suite with hot water & a fan, & some have a sea view. B/fast is on a roof terrace. **$$$**

🏠 **Hotel Estoril** (20 rooms) 📞251 1078; e estorilboavista@gmail.com.To the southwest of town. Refurbished in parts & has had mixed reviews in the past. Pleasant rooms with fans, satellite TV, hot water. Restaurant next door. Also has apartments. Could be good value if new management deliver. **$$$**

🏠 **Pensão Santa Isobel** (9 rooms) Rua dos Emigrantes; 📞251 1252; m 992 7990; e gildaevora2003@hotmail.com. Centrally positioned on the inland side of the square & renovated. All rooms with fan, private bath & TV. **$$**

🏠 **Residencial Salinas** (14 rooms) Rua Bom Sossego; 📞241 1563. Simple, clean rooms with large bathrooms near the salinas in the northern part of Sal Rei. Fans & TVs in all rooms & a bar & restaurant downstairs. Good budget option. **$$**

🏠 **Residencial Boa Esperança** (7 rooms) Rua Tavares Almeida; 📞251 1170. In the road east of the main square. Proud to be by far the cheapest in town, this establishment is definitely just a place to lay your head & is becoming increasingly run-down. Some rooms have shared bathrooms. **$**

🏠 **Residencial Bom Sossego** (7 rooms) Rua de Bom Sossego; 📞251 1155. In the block behind the church – the lively, English-speaking owner lives at Bar Sossego around the corner. A couple of bedrooms have verandas. **$**

🏠 **Residencial Rosa Crioula** m 992 7854. Good-value budget option with private bathrooms, TV & fan. **$**

Apartments

🏠 **Casa Nicola** (28 apts) 📞251 1793; e info@ canicola.com; www.canicola.com. Attractive, stone-faced block built around 2 courtyards & just 50m from the water, with a panoramic view from its rooftop terrace. Serves b/fast & snacks. Reception can organise tours. This is in a good location very close to the windsurfing & diving outfits on Estoril Beach but also very close to Sal

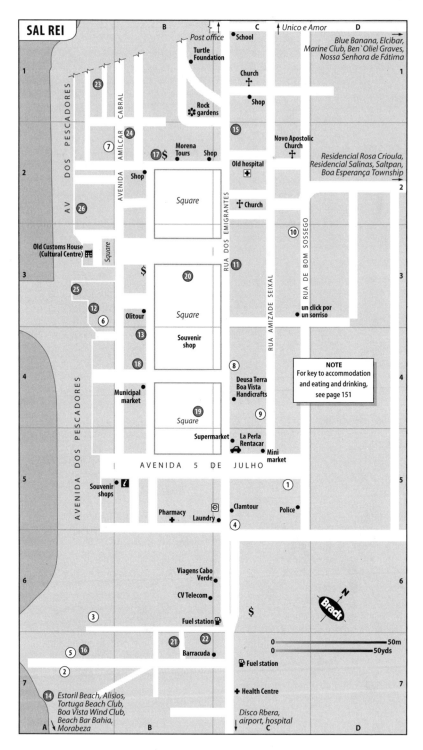

SAL REI

Post office

Turtle Foundation

School

Unico e Amor

Blue Banana, Elcibar,
Marine Club, Ben`Oliel Graves,
Nossa Senhora de Fátima

Church

Shop

Rock gardens

15

Novo Apostolic Church

7

17 $

Morena Tours

Shop

Old hospital

Residencial Rosa Crioula,
Residencial Salinas, Saltpan,
Boa Esperança Township

Shop

Square

Church

26

10

Old Customs House
(Cultural Centre)

Square

11

25

20

Square

un click por
un sorriso

12

6

Olitour

13

Souvenir shop

18

8

NOTE
For key to accommodation
and eating and drinking,
see page 151

Deusa Terra
Boa Vista
Handicrafts

Municipal market

19

Square

9

Supermarket

La Perla
Rentacar

Mini market

AVENIDA 5 DE JULHO

Souvenir shops

1

Pharmacy

Laundry

Clamtour

Police

4

Viagens Cabo
Verde

CV Telecom

$

Fuel station

3

0 ————————— 50m

0 ————————— 50yds

21

22

5 **16**

Barracuda

Fuel station

2

Health Centre

14 Estoril Beach, Alisios,
Tortuga Beach Club,
Boa Vista Wind Club,
Beach Bar Bahia,
Morabeza

Disco Rbera,
airport, hospital

Rei. Pleasantly decorated & with verandas, all apartments have kitchens & living rooms. Wi-Fi & laundry (both extra cost) **$$$$**

🏠**Hotel Estoril Apartments** (For more details, see page 149) **$$$**

🏠 **The Blue Banana Group** 📞251 2698; 📱 974 2349; e bluebananaholiday.cv@gmail.

com. Offers spacious, well-equipped apartments for short- or long-term rental as well as maintenance & management. At Cabral Beach, which they manage, guests have use of a good-sized pool & children's pool, plus a bar that serves food. See ad, colour page 20. **$$$**

✕ WHERE TO EAT AND DRINK

Island specialities include *chicharro assado* (saurel fish coated in olive oil and roasted); *canja de capado* (boar broth) and *botchada* (sheep or goat stomach). Apart from that, fresh fish abounds and the strong Italian community comes to the fore with fresh pasta everywhere. On Estoril Beach and the northern end of Chaves Beach, several of the beach restaurants have sunbeds and parasols for the use of their clients. Some are free, some are not, so it's worth asking before you order your meal. The restaurants of several hotels are open to non-residents – for example the buffet at the Marine Club. You can also buy fresh bread from the *padaria* east of the Bom Sossego Bar in the mornings, and generally cheese and vegetables from the women at one corner of the square or in the *Mercado municipal*. All listings are located on the map opposite.

✕**Alisios** Estoril Beach; 📱 987 7881; 🕐 09.00–18.00 Mon, Tue & Thu, 09.00-22.00 Fri, Sat, Sun, closed Wed. Spacious, colourful café on the beach with a large deck. Features breakfasts, snacks, lunch & dinner. **$$$**

✕ **Beach Bar Bahia** 📱 951 4288/981 7191. 🕐 17.00–21.00 daily. At the southern end of Estoril Beach & thus in a beautiful location. Italian-run, friendly,with imaginative fish dishes, carpaccios, pasta. Sunset party on Sun. **$$$**

✕ **Beramar Restaurant** 📱 974 6514; 🕐 10.00–18.00 daily. Fish & other specialities, plus some innovative dishes & tasting menus.

Vegetarian options, salads & snacks. **$$$**

✕**Boavista Social Club** 🕐 10.00–20.00 daily. Pleasant outdoor venue on Estoril Beach, bar/restaurant during the day, when it's a popular stop-off for adventurous all-inclusivers. Lobster dinners on Thu until midnight. **$$$**

✕ **Blu Marlin** 📞251 1099. This small restaurant & bar is on the main square & popular with locals & expats, serving traditional Cape Verdean dishes, especially freshly caught fish & seafood. **$$$**

✕ **Café del Mar** 🕐 all day. Serving mainly local & Italian cuisine, including pasta that is handmade on site, the restaurant can be found beside the

Hotel Estoril, under the same management. It's open air, but there's not much of a view. $$$

✘ Cocoa ⊕ 07.30–00.00, sometimes later. Newly reopened & run by an enterprising New Zealander, offers good coffee, a long cocktail list, salads, carpaccios, dish of the day, cachupa. Homemade cakes. Popular buffet breakfast at weekends. Plans for blues & jazz nights. A pleasant place at the northwest corner of the main square. $$$

✘ Restaurant Ca Luisa m 981 7191. Located on the road that runs towards Estoril Beach after the fuel station, this is a happy Italian concern serving pizza. Another good place for vegetarians. $$$

✘ Restaurant Chandinho m 986 0718; ⊕ 19.00–late, closed Wed. Up the hill behind the northwestern end of the main square. Fish, meat dishes, tasting menus & homemade bread. Hosts live music nights $$$

✘ Tortuga Beach Club/Café m 981 7192. This is an open-air, Italian-run restaurant on the beach just south of town & serving mainly Italian dishes, meat & fish cooked on an open-air grill. You can rent a sunlounger & parasol on the beach just in front of the restaurant. $$$

✘ Bar Naida ✆251 1173; m 993 4804. A simple, local establishment on the north side of the main square which has been running for over a decade & may be the oldest restaurant in Sal Rei. Varied food served in a whitewashed yard with a banana-leaf roof. Book in advance. $$

☐ Cabo Café m 917 8076. Cape Verdean & international seafood restaurant with a terrace lounge bar. Occasional live, Cape Verdean music. $$

✘ Dom Pincho's Italian cafeteria-style eatery with tasty daily dishes, sandwiches, snacks & salads. $$

✘ Elcibar m 994 2360/953 5995; ⊕ 09.00–until late Tue-Fri, 09.30–late Sat & Sun. Along Praia Cabral, 10mins walk northeast of town. Wide variety of snacks, b/fast dishes, full meals, all

served around a good-sized swimming pool, which can be used by customers. Happy hour 18.00–20.00. A pleasant, quiet alternative to town. $$

✘ Esplanada Municipal Silves Largo Santa Isabel; ⊕ day & night. A refuge from the sun. Popular café serves snacks & drinks during the day & hosts music & dancing at night, with local traditional music on Fri. $$

✘ Morabeza m 595 4631. The most southerly of the beach bar/restaurants, a recommended stop if you're heading along Chaves Beach. Reggae nights, Cape Verdean nights, African Drum nights. Lobster dinners. Sunset parties. German & English spoken. $$

☐ Rosy Bar/Café Close to the Migrante Guesthouse. This is popular, & used by some day-tripping groups from Boavista. Advance booking compulsory. $$

✘Témanché A pier restaurant serving straightforward, basic dishes. Lounge here in the shade & watch the local children diving off the pier & playing in the water, or welcome the odd fishing trip come in, or conduct your local business. Lively on Sun. Service is pretty slow. $$

☐ Unico e Amor ✆251 2096; m 930 1069; ⊕ 18.00–until late, closed Wed. Breezy bar & café with sofas & great views over the bay towards the Marine Club. Simple food such as fish & pasta. Themed nights such as Ladies' Night, Latin Night & live music. $$

☐ Wakan m 978 2656. Boat-shaped kiosk close to the pier where you can sit in the shade & watch the fishermen's daily activities. Simple food including sandwiches, burgers, fresh fruit salads. Good selection of quality teas, good coffee. Happy hour with cocktails. Pleasant Italian management. $$

☐ Pastelaria Doce Vida ✆251 1533. Open early for Italians seeking good coffee & b/fast. Good-value pizzas & sandwiches, croissants as well as Italian specialities such as cakes & focaccia. Near Estoril Beach. $

ENTERTAINMENT AND NIGHTLIFE

Apart from the discos listed below, there is nearly always something going on, be it live music in the square or at one of the town restaurants, or sunset parties on the string of beach bars just south of town.

♀Boavista Social Club [150 A7] Friday is disco night until 05.00. For dining options, see page 151.

☆ Crystal Disco Rabil ⊕ 22.00–02.00 Sun. Transport to this Rabil disco generally materialises in the main square of Sal Rei at about 23.00–00.00. The *aluguer* drivers will sell you an all-in-one ticket to take you there, get entry, & transport you home afterwards. Cape Verdean music & disco.

☆ **Disco Rbera** [150 C7] ⊕ 00.00–05.30 Wed

& Sat; 400$ entry which includes free transport to & from Sal Rei. A wooden structure, 3km out of Sal Rei on the road to Rabil. Mixture of music including Cape Verdean, hip hop & disco.

SHOPPING Traditional Boavista crafts include hats made from palm leaves (a speciality of Povoação Velha) and ceramics (from Rabil). There are a few small craft and souvenir shops in the backstreets of Sal Rei, for example one street north of Rua dos Emigrantes, near the old hospital. There's also a complex of shops selling the ubiquitous West African souvenirs down by the southwest of the main square [150 A5], a Cape Verdean souvenir shop in the middle of the main square (⊕ 08.00–19.00 daily) and Deusa Terra [150 C4] on the square's eastern side.

A good, ethical option for your souvenirs is the rather quirky shop of Un click per un sorriso (*www.unclickperunsorriso.it*) an Italian project which supports various good children's causes in Boavista. The crafts they sell are all made in Cape Verde and all the sales revenue stays within the project. You can find their shop just off the main square [150 C3]. Original artwork can be bought from the stall that backs onto the Cultural Centre [150 A3]. The artist, Mora (**m** *959 2233*), is actually from Senegal, but draws his inspiration from Cape Verde. His work can be seen on the walls inside the Cocoa bar [150 A3] and you can commission work from him on a couple of days' notice, roll it up and take it home. He speaks French, but his English is limited.

There is a *minimercado* on the southeast corner of the square. Maps, including the AB Kartenverlag 1:50,000 map of Boavista (see *Maps*, page 70) can usually be bought at the Shell garage in Sal Rei and Morena Tourist Agency [150 B2] in the main square.

OTHER PRACTICALITIES
Airlines
TACV (*At the airport;* ⊕ *08.00–12.00 & 14.30–17.00 Mon–Fri, 09.00–11.00 Sat*).

Banks
BCA and BCN (⊕ *08.00–15.00 Mon–Fri*) are both on the main square. Caixa Economica and Banco Interatlantico are near the fuel stations on the road to the airport. All have ATMs.

Hospital
Just out of town on the way to the airport.

Internet
A few options & opposite Hotel Boa Vista [150 C5].

Pharmacy
[150 B5] Farmacia Dias (☏ *251 8094*) in the street that faces the Hotel Boavista.

Police
Av 5 de Julho [150 C5] (☏ *251 1132*). Round the corner from Residencial A Paz

Post office
[150 B1] (⊕ *08.00–15.30 Mon–Fri*). Up the hill to the north of town.

WHAT TO SEE AND DO For activities, see page 142. In Sal Rei itself there is little to do of a non-sporting nature except soak up the quiet atmosphere, or bask on the beach south of town.

However, there are quite a few places to visit within walking distance of Sal Rei (or walking plus a short spell on public transport). These are listed below and can be visited individually or put together into hikes.

Cultural Centre Near the pier is the charmingly refurbished old Customs House [150 A3]. It sometimes has exhibitions of handicrafts and hosts art shows.

The Ben'Oliel graves These lie directly in front of the main entrance to the Marine Club and have resisted all pressure to remove them. Happily, they have now been restored with a wall built around them and their future in the present location looks assured. Follow the signs out of the northeast of Sal Rei and along the road that runs the length of Cabral Beach. The walk is perhaps 2km in total, with only the Elcibar, halfway, to provide refreshment.

The graves are of the Jewish Ben'Oliel family, who fled here from the Moroccan persecution of the Jews in 1872. There is also the tomb of a young English woman, Julia Maria Pettingall, daughter of Charles Pettingall, who was one of the administrators of the Luso–British Commission. Julia was the 19-year-old victim of a plague of yellow fever that struck Boavista in the 1840s. She left with her family to the safety of another island, but her father later decided the threat had receded and returned to Boavista. He was wrong. Julia died in November 1845. While on board the boat returning to São Nicolau after her death, Pettingall himself died, and later his daughter's fiancé died too.

Igreja Nossa Senhora de Fátima This is a little hike – 15 minutes from the Marine Club, or 45 minutes from the centre of Sal Rei. (See *Hiking*, page 160, for a description.)

Islet of Sal Rei This islet is nearly 2km at its longest, and up to 700m wide. It was the site of the fort of the Duque de Bragança, though all that remains of the 19th-century construction is some circular stonework and some cannons. In the north of the island there are also some ruins and a lighthouse. It is uninhabited apart from crabs, lizards and litter left by previous visitors. Along the western side are little sandy coves, while to the east there are views over the anchored boats. Looking back, there are beautiful views of Sal Rei and down Chaves Beach.

You should be able to persuade a fisherman to take you out there for a fee (about 2,000$). Alternatively, if you are a strong swimmer, you could swim the 1,000m: locals say the water is never deeper than 1.5m.

OTHER PLACES TO VISIT

The rest of the island is described in a clockwise order, beginning at Sal Rei.

COSTA DE BOA ESPERANÇA This long and beautiful, windswept and deserted beach stretches from the lighthouse in the northwest (Ponta do Sol) to Ponta Antónia in the northeast. Along it is the unmistakable wreck of the *Santa Maria* (see box, *Shipwrecks on Boavista*, page 144). At its western tip is Ponta do Sol, where there is a lighthouse reachable on foot (see *Hikes*, page 159). This area is usually deserted and has been the scene of many muggings. Be wary and do not take valuables with you.

BOFAREIRA AND ESPINGUEIRA These villages can be reached by hiking northeast from Sal Rei along a track marked on the map, or by 4x4 along a road from Rabil. After leaving Sal Rei, bear left at the fork south of Rabil and take the road to João Galego. After about 11km turn left at the small, incongruous shrine to the Virgin Mary at the side of the road. Stay on the cobbled track and after 20 minutes you will emerge at the tiny village of Bofareira. This place is serviced by a daily *aluguer* but there is not much else happening – there's a shop and a telephone box. The focal point of the village is the standpipe, when there's any water (it all has to be tankered in from Sal Rei).

From the Bofareira road it is possible to get to the shore: about 4km from the village take the rough track, signposted to Spinguera, which resembles the bed of a river. This leads to the coast and the ruined village of Espingueira, now partly transformed into a hotel. There is a small fishing camp out on the Ponta Antónia and, just east of the point in a semicircular cove, lovely snorkelling – if you're lucky, among nurse sharks (*Ginglymostoma cirratum*). Looking west along the beach there is a good view of the hulk of the *Santa Maria*.

Where to stay and eat

Spinguera (12 rooms) ◖ 251 1941; **m** 997 8943; **e** info@spinguera.com; www.spinguera. com. The ruined cottages of an abandoned village inspirationally transformed into the designer chalets of a small hotel. This is a deeply quiet, lonely & evocative stretch of coast & the hotel has been created by an artist in a sparsely beautiful style that echoes its environment. Free Wi-Fi in lounge bar & reception, no mobile-phone network. Electricity is produced by solar power & generator. Accommodation includes an apartment & 2 villas – the latter can be a self-catering option & ingredients for cooking can be ordered from the owner. There is also a bar, open to non-guests, & a restaurant, which must be booked in the morning. The owners can organise activities. The hotel is about 500m from the coast. Swimming is not recommended in the winter. **$$$$$**

JOÃO GALEGO, FUNDO DAS FIGUEIRAS, CABEÇO DAS TARAFES Accessed along the road that leads south and then east from Rabil, these three villages are strung out at the fertile end of a *ribeira*. After the flat, dry plain you have crossed from Rabil, it is refreshing to be near vegetation again. The villages are centred on the most agriculturally productive part of Boavista and enjoy modest renown as the source of delicious goat's cheese. Rather less commendable is the villages' taste for turtle meat, something that has traditionally been a delicacy here on festival days and at special occasions. João Galego has a smattering of shops and two nightclubs. In Fundo das Figueiras, a few kilometres further on, there are shops, the Bons Irmaos snack bar and the Nha Terra Restaurant. You should phone ahead to ensure you get something to eat (◖ *252 1114*).

What to see and do

Baía das Gatas The bay is a 15-minute drive by 4x4 along a reasonable track 7km from Fundo das Figueiras. It is named after the tiger sharks that have been seen from the point. There is a small, semi-permanent fishing camp here, with racks of salted fish hung out to dry. The fishermen will let you have a piece very cheaply – it is probably best to strap it outside the vehicle on the way home. You can see dolphins here. The largest of the islets in the bay is Ilhéu dos Pássaros, home to the white-faced storm petrel or *pedreiro-azul* (*Pelagodroma marina*). Travel to the islets is prohibited.

Morro Negro Lighthouse The most easterly point of Cape Verde, this lighthouse sits on a 150m-high promontory accessed along a track southwest from Cabeço das Tarafes. It offers a great panorama of the east coast.

Oasis of Santo Tirso This is the greenest part of the island, where you will find coconut palms, acacia and baobab trees. If rains have been good in the previous few years, it is a nice shady spot for a break.

Olho de Mar A small natural pool overlooked by a cliff with a remarkably human face. It lies to the southwest of Cabeço das Tarafes, along a track and then a path.

A SIP OF THE SEA — *Alex Alper*

Salt water is fast becoming a widespread source of drinking water for Cape Verdeans. Desalination plants on Sal, Boavista, Santiago, Maio and São Vicente – managed by Electra, the state-owned energy company, and Aguas da Ponta Preta, a private enterprise – produce roughly four million m³ of water annually. That supplies almost 30,000 Cape Verdeans.

The most common technology used in Cape Verde is reverse osmosis (RO). Osmosis is a natural phenomenon in which the substance dissolved in the water (in this case, salt) naturally moves from an area of high concentration to an area of lower concentration through a semi-permeable membrane, equalising its distribution between the two. During reverse osmosis, the salt water is pressurised so that the salt moves towards an area of high concentration. What's left behind is clean water. RO is cheaper, but more high-tech, than vapour-compression distillation and multi-effect distillation, two other technologies used in Cape Verde. Still, it is far more expensive than other water-collection methods, such as drilling or rainwater harvesting. The most energy-efficient RO plants still require between 2kWh and 3kWh per m³ of water. For a 1,000m³-capacity plant, that's about US$600–900 a day.

Moreover, it is possible that the highly saline leftover 'brine' dumped back into the ocean is harmful to marine life.

Other forms of desalinisation are being tested to address these problems. Two volunteers are working with students at Assomada's technical school to develop solar stills that use sunlight alone to convert seawater into fresh water through evaporation. Construction costs are low and materials readily available – but so far the prototype produces only about two litres a day.

Nevertheless, Cape Verde is counting on desalinisation for the future. Two new RO plants are under construction in Santiago's interior, while if the rash of promised private golf courses ever materialises then they will have to build and run their own plants. If all goes according to plan, underground water sources will be left exclusively to agriculture and Cape Verdeans will drink seawater every day.

Ponta do Roque and Praia dos Balejas From the lighthouse, the path continues to the south to this point and to the dolphin graveyard. Here lie the bones of nature's equivalent of the Boavista shipwrecks. They litter the sand near Morre Negro, which is alleged to have magnetic properties that draw the creatures to their deaths.

PRAIA DE CURRAL VELHO This beach is glorious but exposed and remote. Come prepared for a day in the desert. At 15km from the nearest civilisation, it is probably too far to attempt by foot. Curral Velho is, however, accessible by 4x4 from Povoação Velha, from Cabeço das Tarafes, or directly across the heart of the island from Sal Rei. This last route is 43km from town and takes just over an hour by jeep. On the road south from Rabil, bear left at the fork towards Fundo das Figueiras, and after about 1.5km, strike right on a track. For the next hour or so, you will feel as if you are driving across the surface of the moon, and then at last you will reach a T-junction near the coast. Turn right and, after about 300m, take the rough track down to the left through the deserted village of Curral Velho. Then head round to the right of the salt lagoon until the track runs out at the back of the dunes. Beyond is a blindingly white beach, with extensive, Sahara-like dunes to your right, providing the unwary motorist with ample opportunity to get stuck.

There is only one islet in the whole of the eastern Atlantic where the magnificent frigatebird or rabil (*Fregata magnificens*) deigns to breed. You can see that islet ahead: Ilhéu de Curral Velho. Watch out for the bird with its long, slim, black wings that have a span of around 2m. The female has a white breast and the male's is red. But you will be lucky: experts now say that there are only two left.

PRAIA DE LACAÇÃO This can be reached by following the track from Santa Mónica. This impossibly beautiful beach is the chosen location of the new RIU Hotel, now open. This massive development has occasioned the building of a new tarmac road and has changed this remote area into a destination for all-inclusive mass tourism – and that is only the first stage.

PRAIA DE SANTA MÓNICA This beach is well worth a visit, but do come prepared, particularly if you are walking. You will need food, suncream and loads of water (see *Health*, page 63). In a 4x4, follow the road through Povoação Velha. After 6km a very rough track deposits you on the beach, named after the famous Californian strand. The Boavistan version is undeniably magnificent but a good deal bleaker. Swimming is possible here because of its southern aspect. At present, there are no facilities. A huge new all-inclusive hotel is planned.

PRAIA DE CURRALINHO This is a beautiful beach and, like Santa Mónica, is reasonably accessible – a two-hour walk from Povoação Velha. Don't expect ice-cream kiosks – the most Curralinho Beach offers is the possibility of shelter from the wind in the lee of rocky outcrops. Bring your own shade.

As you enter Povoação Velha on the main road, turn right by the bright-green school and head towards the hill that looks like a large slag heap. The track is uncobbled, but the surface stays good for 4–5km until you reach the sand. This is not the beginning of the beach – you are still about 3km away. Beyond the dunes there is a dusty flat land, pockmarked with a reafforestation programme. Then, at last, is the sea. The shore is steep, so take care when swimming. No facilities.

POVOAÇÃO VELHA In the words of a Povoação Velha landlord: 'It's a slow place, this.' It doesn't look much, but a settlement has endured here for almost 500 years and today it has a sleepy appeal: old folk ruminate on doorsteps, dogs scratch in the sun and donkeys twitch their ears on street corners.

There are two main, parallel streets with a handful of souvenir shops. The Bar António will prepare food on request; they need about two hours' notice so you could place your order before you ascend Rocha Estância, and return to the village as the meal arrives on the table. At the very far end of the village, the Fon Banana (🌙 251 1871; m 982 4213; ⏰ 10.00–19.00 Mon–Sat) is a pleasant restaurant option. On Tuesday, Thursday and Saturday, they do a good Cape Verdean evening for €40 including live music and return transport. You can reach Povoação Velha from Sal Rei by *aluguer* – there's one at 13.00 and one at 16.00 – and hope to hitch back later in the day. *Alugueres* from Povoação Velha to Sal Rei go only very early in the morning. To ascend Rocha Estância or Pico Santo António see hiking information on page 161.

VERANDINHA BEACH An exposed beach with fantastic conditions for wind- and kitesurfing (though not for beginners). Another attraction is the caves behind the beach. Reach them along a track heading west from Povoação Velha. Much to the locals' dismay the area has become a racing track for quad tours, ripping through the village of

Povoação Velha and destroying crops on the way to the beach. If you drive yourself there, take care as the dunes constantly change and require a 4x4. There are also caves here.

RABIL This was the capital of Boavista until the early 19th century. It is a bit short on attractions, but has a pottery open to visitors and a couple of bars to refresh yourself. Look inside the imposing church of São Roque, built in 1801, the oldest church on Boavista. You can visit Rabil by *aluguer* (see page 141) or as part of the hike on pages 160–1. The canyon east of town is very Saharan in scenery, with palm trees and the dunes to the northeast enhancing the atmosphere.

✗ Where to eat and drink

✗ **Restaurante Sodade di Nha Terra** ☎251 1048; closed Mon. A large building with a flight of steps in front, this is a happening place serving local food including the renowned Boavista goat's cheese & much-praised lobster & goat. Some consider this the best restaurant in Boavista. $$

Entertainment and nightlife

☆ **Crystal Disco** For details, see pages 152–3.

What to see and do A much-praised desert to the northeast of Rabil, **Viana Desert** is beloved for its fine white sands and its oasis filled with coconut and date palms. This is a vast place covering about a quarter of the island and extending for about 15km north–south and 10km east–west.

CHAVES BEACH One of the most exhilarating beaches of Cape Verde, Chaves lies to the south of Sal Rei and stretches forever down the coast. The walk from Sal Rei is wonderful although the return journey can be a bit sand-blown.

🏠 Where to stay and eat

A long walk from town, but then most visitors here will be at the Riu or the Royal Decameron, so the incentive to leave the hotel may be low.

🏠 **ClubHotel Riu Karamboa** (750 rooms) ☎251 9100; e clubhotel.karamboa@riu.com; www.riu.com. Vast, all-inclusive resort hotel stretching like a desert palace along Chaves Beach, 7km from Sal Rei. It offers the usual resort facilities including 4 restaurants, children's & adults' pools, spa, a daytime activity programme for children & sports from tennis to scuba diving, nightclub & so forth. Inclusive packages only. $$$$$

🏠 **Royal Decameron** (300 rooms) ☎251 1407; www.decameron.com. Previously the Venta Club, this is an all-inclusive resort hotel on Chaves Beach. The stunning panorama & the stepped construction of its rooms means that each one has a private terrace with sea view. The food is pretty good & varied, with 3 restaurants & 3 bars. There are tennis courts, activities for children & various

sports & entertainments, several pools, spa & a beauty centre. $$$$

🏠 **Parque das Dunas Village** (28 rooms) ☎251 1283/1290; e info@parquedasdunas.com; www.parquedasdunas.com. Being renovated at time of writing, so check website for changes. Located at the southern end of Chaves Beach, south of the brick-factory chimney, this is a quiet retreat with shady trees & an airy bar/restaurant area with a large pool. Although the rooms are not really luxurious (& have no TV, AC or phone) the hotel's position on the beach, & the setting of the terraced chalets, many patios of which open directly onto the shore, create a peaceful & evocative atmosphere. Sea bathing is often dangerous (see *Hazards*, page 140). Free shuttles to Sal Rei depart at 10.00 & 19.30; return at 12.00 & 22.30. Internet access is also available. $$$

✗ **Parque das Dunas Village** ⊕ lunchtime & 19.45–late. Bar; light snacks 07.00–23.00. $$$$

What to see and do The **brick factory** is an eerie building that is slowly being submerged by the dunes. It takes just over an hour to walk to it from Sal Rei down

Estoril Beach to the south, crossing Rabil Lagoon after about 35 minutes and continuing towards the chimney, which you will see poking out of the sand. There is a track leading inland from the factory to Rabil from where you can travel back to Sal Rei. Ribeira do Rabil is the main watercourse on the island and its water content varies through the year – sometimes dry, sometimes brackish pools, sometimes a good stream.

Rabil Lagoon itself has water all year round. It's a pretty lonely, place surrounded by shifting sand dunes and popular with birdwatchers for its wintering migrant waders and for the Iago sparrow (*Passer iagoensis*). In fact, BirdLife International has designated it one of 12 Important Bird Areas in Cape Verde and it is a Ramsar site – a wetland of international importance. The area stretches from the airport road to the sea. The quickest way to reach it is to take an *aluguer* destined for the airport and ask to be deposited at the bridge (*ponte*), after about 3km. From the road, however, the lagoon looks rather uninviting, so it is better explored from the beautiful beach end. You can do this by walking down from Sal Rei (see hike on pages 160–1).

HIKES   *Aisling Irwin (AI); Colum Wilson (CW)*

In the northwest of the island is a triangle of hikes: Sal Rei–Ponta do Sol Lighthouse (7km); Ponta do Sol Lighthouse–wreck of the *Santa Maria* (5km); and Sal Rei–wreck of the *Santa Maria* (7km). Combining them yields a satisfying hike of 21km, which should take at least six hours and requires several litres of water per person as well as hiking boots and sun protection.

1 SAL REI–PONTA DO SOL LIGHTHOUSE (FAROL)
Distance: 7km; time: 2 hours; difficulty: 1 (AI)
The first part of this walk is not particularly scenic. Walk along the road to the Marine Club until you are 200m from it, at which point fork right along a road that runs for just over 2km to the cemetery. Just after the cemetery the road becomes an ascending track and bends to the left. Continue for 500m until you reach a fork: straight on leads to the church of Nossa Senhora de Fátima; branch to the right instead, and continue uphill. The view of old rubbish dumps is not edifying – but look on the bright side: they enhance the magnificence of the end of the walk. Stick to this track even, after 2.5km, when you pass another that forks to the left and appears to be a more direct route. Less than 1km after that fork you will come to Chã de Agua Doce where the path turns left for the lighthouse (or right for the wreck of the *Santa Maria*). Continue for another 2km, through Curral Preto and its further litter dumps. Finally, you ascend to the etiolated structure that passes for a lighthouse. It's a lonely, atmospheric place.

2 PONTA DO SOL LIGHTHOUSE–WRECK OF THE SANTA MARIA
Distance: 5km; time: 1½ hours; difficulty: 2 (AI)
The first 2km of this walk are a reversal of the final 2km of the previous walk. Follow the track from the lighthouse, through Curral Preto, and on to a fork. The right track leads back to Sal Rei. The left track takes you down, past lime kilns and onto the beach. You have a choice of following this track to its bitter end – it bends inland and then out again in a 'U' shape – or descending to the beach as soon as you have reached white sand. The two routes take about the same amount of time. After this the hulk of the wreck can be your guide.

3 SAL REI–WRECK OF THE SANTA MARIA
Distance: 7km; time: 2 hours; difficulty: 1 (CW)
The old hulk of the *Santa Maria* dominates the beach to the north of the island,

though the wreck is now crumbling so badly that it is becoming barely recognisable as a ship. It is within walking distance of Sal Rei. Looking northeast out of town from a high point you will see a ridge – it lies over that.

Head south out of town towards Rabil and just past the small houses at the edge of town you will see the old road to Rabil (signposted Via Pitoresca) branching off on your left. Follow the old road for about 2km until a left turning. Take this rough track for about 7km. You will pass through Floresta Clotilde, an oasis filled with various species of palm including the endemic *tamareira* (*Phoenix atlantica*), and then through Boa Esperança. At times now the road is almost entirely obscured by sand but the route is straight. About 1.5km after leaving the oasis the paving gives way to sandy track. Just keep going until you hit the beach where you cannot miss the wreck – though due to deterioration, this may change.

Following this route in the other direction (ie: starting at the wreck), the track is signposted; in the oasis avoid a track branching off to the left: keep right.

4 SAL REI–MARINE CLUB–IGREJA NOSSA SENHORA DE FÁTIMA
Distance: 2.5km; time: 45 minutes; difficulty: 1 (AI)
Walk northeast out of Sal Rei on the straight road that leads to the Marine Club. At the front of this hotel there is a vehicle barrier. Don't go through this but instead take the little path that has been built down the left-hand side. This takes you around the coast, at first on a nicely crafted passageway. At the end of this walkway it becomes a rough little path and then a track along a pretty coastline including a sandy beach that would fit perhaps one person. By this time you will be able to see the ruins of the chapel and the path towards it. Beside it there was once a house with steps leading down to the beach.

5 SAL REI–ESTORIL BEACH–RABIL LAGOON–ESTÂNCIA DE BAIXO–RABIL
Distance: 10km (18km if done as circular walk); time: 3 hours (circular walk: 5 hours); difficulty: 1 (AI)
This walk begins down the beach and over high dunes with views over the sea, inland up a bird-filled lagoon and up a silent *ribeira* filled with *tamareira* trees and surrounded by sand hills. There's a hill to ascend up to Rabil but in general it is a flat and easy walk. At Rabil it should be possible to organise transport back to Sal Rei – the alternative is to walk. (Guard against sun and theft, however – see pages 139–40 for information on hazards.)

Go to the beach at Sal Rei and turn left (south), following the coast. After ten minutes you'll pass Tortuga Beach Resort, where you can pick up a drink and watch people skidding across the bay.

Set off again south, walking up the dunes until you reach a disorientating world composed of nothing but expanses of hard-packed white sand. From those high dunes there is a vertical drop to the beach below and superb views of the cobalt sea and the islet of Sal Rei. There are often whales in the bay, in season, and you may spot turtles on the beach. Further on you will see the black masts of a shipwreck poking out of the water.

Half an hour from the windsurfers is the lagoon. All you can hear is the waves, the wind on the dunes and, increasingly, the tweets of a multiplicity of birds who thrive on the salty water. The mud is covered in millions of their footprints.

Walk inland up the side of the lagoon. If you choose the left side then ascend a great beer-belly of a dune and after that follow your instinct – there is no path and sometimes you must leave the lagoon edge out of sight in order to find a way between the thick trees. After 20 minutes there is a rough track to the main Sal Rei–Rabil road. Follow the road south as far as the bridge and then clamber down into the *ribeira* on the landward side and follow it inland. It is a broad, dry riverbed full of *tamareira* trees (*Phoenix atlantica*), a speciality of Boavista. After the rain it is lush, full of grass and small plants. The *ribeira* is hauntingly quiet except for the sounds of goats and the occasional child on a donkey collecting water.

The *ribeira* broadens and turns to the right; at times it must be 200m wide. Soon you are between two ridges – inland the hills look as if they are covered in snow with just the tips of plants poking through. Always stay where the trees are thickest. To the left appears a cliff with the village of **Estância de Baixo** on top. Keep well away from that side of the *ribeira* and stick to the right until, eventually, you see Rabil Church, on the ridge; tracks lead up to it.

From Rabil you may find transport back to Sal Rei or you can walk down to the airport (look for the windsock), before beginning the 8km trek back to town, hopefully picking up a lift on the way. If you want to walk back to Sal Rei, it's more scenic to take the old road (now called the scenic route), which begins after the main road crosses the *ribeira*, and goes straight on where the main road bends to the left.

6 SANTO ANTÓNIO (379M)

Distance: approximately 8km round trip; time: approximately 2½ hours; difficulty: 2 (CW)
From the waterfront at Sal Rei, Santo António can be seen on the left. Take an *aluguer* towards **Povoação Velha** and disembark at the point which seems closest to the mountain. The castellation near the summit means that it cannot be ascended from this side, so cross the rough ground to the mountain (past the men breaking rocks) and skirt round its north side, past some small ruins, before beginning the ascent from the east, which is straightforward.

7 ROCHA ESTÂNCIA (354M)

Distance: 3km round trip; time: 1 hour; difficulty: 2 (CW)
From the waterfront at Sal Rei, Rocha Estância is on the right, with the antennae on top. There are two routes to the summit. The first involves a scramble. Go straight out of the back of the village of **Povoação Velha** near the Bar di Africa and strike slightly up to the right towards the saddle. Once on the saddle, head left towards the summit. Alternatively, go towards the church on the low ridge to your right as you are looking north at the mountain, and then follow the shoulder up to the left. It is longer this way but more gentle.

For a less arduous walk around the base of the mountain, continue past the church and go round the *rocha*'s north side. It is not possible to reach the summit from this side.

Boavista HIKES

4

MORE HIKING IDEAS

Armed with a good map (see map information on page 70) it is possible to walk to remote Bofareira in the northeast. There is a round-trip hike from Povoação Velha west to Varandinha and then southeast along the coast to Praia de Santa Mónica, followed by a northern leg back to Povoação Velha. Finally, you can create another trip by hiking from Cabeço das Tarafes west and then southwest, first along a track and then a path, to the pool at Olho de Mar. Some of these hikes are described on www.bela-vista.net/Boa-Vista-Reviere-e.htm.

5

Santiago

The sea
You enlarge our dreams
and suffocate our desires

Jorge Barbosa, born on Santiago Island, 1902

Among the extremes of the Cape Verdean archipelago – the desert islands and the islands so mountainous there is barely a scrap of level ground – Santiago stands out as the normal relation. It is more balanced, more varied – it has a bit of everything. At its heart are craggy mountains cut into exotic outlines and afforested on their lower slopes. Sliced in between are green valleys alive with agriculture. To the south lie irrigated plantations; to the southwest a sterile and gravelly landscape where nothing grows; and in the north and southeast there are some pretty beaches of both black and golden sands.

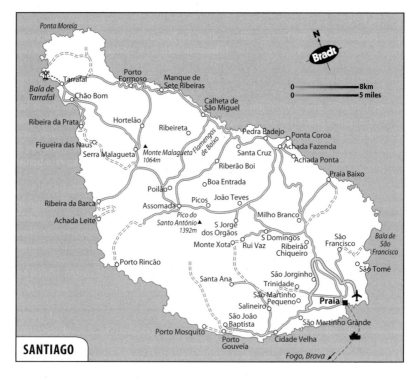

In Santiago the varied ingredients of the archipelago's past are at their most vivid. On the southern shore is the old capital of Cape Verde – Ribeira Grande, now known as Cidade Velha ('Old City') – the first European city in the tropics whose pivotal importance in the Atlantic slave trade is still being uncovered. Up in the mountains, in contrast, the people are as African as Cape Verdeans can be – their ancestors were escaped slaves from the city below.

And of course, this island is where you'll find the majority of the Cape Verde population and Praia, the capital city of the archipelago.

HIGHLIGHTS AND LOWLIGHTS

Cidade Velha, the 500-year-old city, is the most important historic site in the archipelago and is of such international significance that in 2009 it became a World Heritage Site. The landscape in central and northern Santiago, and down much of its east coast is stunning and worthy of exploration at least by vehicle and preferably with a couple of hikes as well. Santiago also gives a good overall sample of what Cape Verde has to offer if you are very limited in time.

Santiago is not the island for those who seek idyllic beaches, nor for the best diving, surfing or windsurfing of the archipelago. It has some beautiful hikes but if that is your only priority, and you are stuck for time, it's best to head straight for Santo Antão or Fogo.

Praia is not a tourist city and some people find it hot, unattractive and – at night, at least – a little threatening. Yet its heart – built on a plateau with sheer sides overlooking the sea, has personality; there are a couple of interesting museums and plenty of pleasant restaurants, many with live music.

SUGGESTED ITINERARY AND NUMBER OF DAYS You could 'do' Santiago in a day and a half – half a day for Cidade Velha and a full day for an organised, round-island excursion. For a richer and more relaxing experience, take two days for the round-island tour, spending the night in either Assomada and visiting its lively market, or Tarrafal. Those with more time and inclination could easily find two or three good hikes to do, spend a day on the beach in Tarrafal or at one of the few hotels with some coastal ambience (eg: Pôr do Sol in Cidade Velha; see page 181), take advantage of some of the excellent remoter accommodation options (eg: Cabo Ned or Pousada de Vassora; see pages 185 and 186 respectively) and visit some of the other attractions covered below.

BACKGROUND INFORMATION

HISTORY Santiago *was* Cape Verde for hundreds of years. It was here that the two discoverers of the islands, António de Noli and Diogo Gomes, together with a small group of settlers from the Algarve in Portugal, set up in 1462. Their town grew and the business of resupplying ships and trading in slaves flourished. The other islands, except for Fogo, remained unexplored or were exploited merely for salt or grazing. Even today, inhabitants of Santiago refer to the island as Cabo Verde – as if it were the mainland – and to the other islands as just that: '*as ilhas*'.

Yet from early on Santiago was also a centre of dissent. Its links to west Africa were strong. The *rebelados* and other African renegades escaped miscegenation and lived isolated lives in the interior where they remembered their ancestral tribes. In the 20th century, rebellion stirred primarily in São Nicolau and São

Vicente, yet Santiago too had its uprisings – and produced the islands' first great poet and dissenter, Jorge Barbosa.

The Portuguese spelling São Tiago (St James) died out early on in favour of the Spanish spelling used today. (For more on Santiago's history see *History*, pages 163–4)

Santiago today Today Praia, the political centre of Cape Verde, is undergoing enormous expansion while its infrastructure struggles to keep up. The south of the island is changing quickly, with a new ring road, a few enormous condominium developments and the general spread of the city and its attendant services, from universities to sewage plants.

New roads have also been completed in the north recently but the island still feels very much at times like rural Africa. Here there is a slower pace of life, permeated with donkeys and carts, pigs, hens, dogs and goats. Much of the economic development of the country is concentrated in Santiago, with many foreign NGOs working on diverse projects designed to stimulate the economy, upgrade the infrastructure and improve the standard of living.

GEOGRAPHY The largest island in the archipelago, at 990km², Santiago has two mountain ranges: the Serra do Pico do António, which rises to a peak of 1,392m, and the more northern Serra Malagueta, rising to a height of 1,064m. There are lush valleys in the centre and several permanent sources of water. Some 290,000 people live here – about 130,000 in Praia, the capital.

The volcanic rocks on Santiago are four–five million years old while the rocks from the sea floor are even older, at 8.5–9.5 million years. An important and distinctive feature of Praia's landscape is the *achadas* (elevated plains) on which the different districts of the city are built. Santiago is the principal agricultural producer of Cape Verde.

NATURAL HISTORY
Protected areas There are two protected areas in Santiago: Serra Malagueta and Serra do Pico do António, both of which are natural parks. Serra Malagueta is one of three protected areas in the archipelago where there is a team (the Cape Verdean government working with United Nations Development Programme (UNDP) and the Global Environment Facility (GEF)) actively working to breathe some life into the protection through a combination of conservation measures and development of local economic opportunities.

It boasts a large number of endemic plant and bird species, including erva-cidreira (*Melissa officinalis*), used to treat a wide range of illnesses, aipo (*Lavandula rodindifolia*) and losna (*Artemisia gorgonum*).

Birds There are five Important Bird Areas on Santiago, as designated by BirdLife International. Three trees – a huge kapok tree in Boa Entrada and two mahogany trees near Banana – constitute two of them. The first tree, a single, huge, 25m-high kapok tree (*Ceiba pentandra*), lies at the heart of a valley near Boa Entrada village. The two mahogany (*Khaya senegalensis*) trees are of moderate height, and also stand at the valley bottom in Santa Catarina.

Here are the only two breeding colonies of the endemic Cape Verde purple heron (*Ardea purpurea bournei*), although it is said that the occupants of the mahogany trees have moved north to Serra Malagueta. Some 8km of rugged cliffs along the southwestern coast of the island of Santiago, from the

15 January	Municipality Day (Tarrafal)
2 February	Nho Fenrero Festival (São Domingos)
Wednesday after Carnival	Ashes Day
13 March	Municipality Day (São Domingos)
15 days after Easter	São Salvador do Mundo (Picos)
April	Kriol Jazz Festival (lasts for four days, exact dates vary)
23 April	São Jorge
1 May	São Jose
May	Music festival (Gamboa Beach) A three-day-long jamboree
8 May	São Miguel Arcanjo Feast (Ribeira Calheta de São Miguel)
13 May	Nossa Sra de Fátima (Assomada)
31 May	Imaculada Conceição
June and July	*Tabanka* processions
15 August	Nossa Sra do Socorro
25 November	Municipality Day (Santa Catarina area)

fishermen's village of Porto Mosquito to Baía do Inferno (Baía de Santa Clara), make the third area, which is known for its brown booby (*Sula leucogaster*) and red-billed tropicbird (*Phaethon aethereus*) populations, among others. The fourth site is made up of two lagoons and their environs south of Pedra Badejo on Santiago, where about 20 species of wader have been recorded.

The final site is the central mountain range including Pico do Santo António, a breeding haven for many endemic birds including Cape Verde little shearwater (*Puffinus assimilis boydi*), Cape Verde buzzard (*Buteo 'buteo' bannermani*), Alexander's kestrel (*Falco tinnunculus alexandri*), Cape Verde peregrine (*Falco peregrinus madens*), Cape Verde swift (*Apus alexandri*), Cape Verde cane warbler (*Acrocephalus brevipennis*) and the Iago sparrow (*Passer iagoensis*).

HAZARDS Bag-snatching and pickpocketing are becoming more audacious in Praia. Take the usual precautions (no visible or accessible laptops, cameras, purses, etc). Sucupira Market is the most notorious for theft and Achada Santo António has a bad reputation, particularly at the northern end. Taxis are everywhere and relatively inexpensive: it's worth hailing one if you're not sure about where you're going.

GETTING THERE AND AWAY

BY AIR
International flights You can fly direct from Lisbon or Paris to Santiago, as well as from Boston (USA), Fortaleza (Brazil), Gran Canaria (Canary Islands) and Casablanca (Morocco). Flights also go twice per week to Senegal, as well as to Angola, via São Tome. For full information on international flights see pages 58–9.

Domestic flights There are TACV flights to and from Sal, São Vicente, Maio and Fogo (for ticket purchase, see page 186). There is a regular day trip from Sal to Santiago with Cabo Verde Express which can be booked through the major tour operators on Sal and involves an island tour. The Cabo Verde Express office at Praia airport will not sell you a ticket, though the office at Sal Airport will.

Praia International Airport
The airport and terminal building are fairly new. Facilities include an ATM and money-changing (⊕ *8.00–15.00 Mon–Sat though times may vary*); international and local car-hire firms; a completely underwhelming and sometimes unmanned tourist information kiosk; a tour operator (Orbitur); free Wi-Fi access; and two cafés. Good coffee is available at the café beside domestic departures.

If you arrive on an international flight and do not have a visa you will need to complete a visa request form, handed out on arrival at the airport (see details on page 55).

Taxis from the airport wait in a mostly orderly queue, though some drivers will approach you inside the arrivals hall. A taxi from the airport to town will cost around 700$, but 1,000$ at night.

BY FERRY A new service operated by Cabo Verde Fast Ferry (*www.cvfastferry. com*) started operations in January 2011 with a service connecting Praia, Fogo and Brava. Other routes were supposed to follow, but as yet there are no additions. Their boat has comfortable seats, a refreshment kiosk and entertainment on plasma screens. This new company has had a significant impact on inter-island travel, offering some much-needed competition to the two domestic airlines. For ferries to other islands and updates, check the latest with the ferry agencies, listed below, with a tour operator in Praia or on www.bela-vista.net/ferry.aspx, a site which updates ferry news regularly.

The port is at the northern end of the harbour. Taxis to the port or back cost 200–500$ depending on the destination.

ANAV Shipping P 58, Rua Serpa Pinto; ☎ 261 7858/260 3100; e anavpraia@cvtelecom.cv
Cabo Verde Fast Ferry Ave Andrade Corvo 35, Praia; ☎ 261 7552; e cvff.info@cvfastferry.com; www.cvfastferry.com
Cabo Verde Shipping Agency ☎ 261 1179; e csa.rai@cvtelecom.cv

Polar Shipping CP 120, Rua Candido dos Reis 6, Praia Plateau; also try Rua Serpa Pinto 141; ☎ 261 7177/5223/5225/7224; e polarp@cvtelecom.cv
Viagens Cabo Verde Also on Rua Candido dos Reis, for shipping; ☎ 231 8016

BY YACHT Praia provides a well-sheltered harbour where yachts are asked to anchor in the west between the two jetties. It is essential to follow all the entry procedures with the port captain and immigration office, whether or not this is your first stop in Cape Verde; on departure get clearance again from the port captain. Yacht facilities are poor, but a new marina should be open in 2014. At time of publication there is no boatyard or chandlery. Fuel and water have to be collected by can, though the new marina will change that. Ask the port captain for a watchman.

The next-best anchorage is Tarrafal, at the north of the island, where yachts are often at anchor. Visit the harbour office on arrival. Another anchorage is at Ribeira da Barca (but there is swell and northeast winds funnelling off the island).

BY PUBLIC TRANSPORT *Alugueres* (on this island, more commonly referred to as *hiaces* and pronounced 'yazz') travel up and down the spine of the island – the road between Praia and Tarrafal – all day and evening. Villages down the west coast are reached on roads extending from this central spine, so catch one of these *alugueres* and change at the relevant junction. *Alugueres* are also frequent along the slower, eastern coastal road between Praia and Tarrafal. They all leave from the chaotic Sucupira Market west of the Plateau. For Cidade Velha there are regular *alugueres* leaving from the far side of the main street across from the *sucupira* market, and from Terra Branca in Praia, southwest of the Plateau. Sucupira Market is a noisy melee of drivers and their assistants trying to get you to choose their vehicles. Pick the one with the most people inside, as they don't leave until they are full.

Many of the roads have been improved with money from the Millennium Challenge, making travel in Santiago more comfortable and faster as well as improving the lives of the residents by providing small communities with better links to main towns. A grey-haired driver is the safest bet.

BY TAXI The taxis in Praia are everywhere, clearly marked and cream-coloured. They will gently beep their horns at anyone vaguely tourist-like, in the hope of a fare. A journey within town costs 150–300$, sometimes more, especially after 23.00. A taxi for the day costs about 8,000$.

🚗 **Various numbers:** ☎ 262 2062, 262 2083, 262 2087; m 994 8720/972 9957. If you need an English-speaker, try Quintino on m 919 6188 /992 6188.

BY CAR There is an enormous choice in Praia and a walk around the Plateau can scarcely avoid the numerous tour agencies which will happily arrange a rental vehicle. Remember that only a 4x4 can take you on the dirt tracks down to the west coast: anything less may limit your ambitions. One day's hire should cost around €50–60, the usual deposit by credit card or in cash is required. It is cheaper to hire a car in town (many companies are in the Prainha area), but not as convenient as picking one up at the airport. There are two rental kiosks at the airport – **Inter-Cidades** (m *999 4353*) and **Hertz** (m *991 7907*) – but they are not always open. June 2013 witnessed the controversial introduction of parking meters to Praia's Plateau – an unwelcome 'first' for Cape Verde.

🚗 **Atlântico** Prainha, close to the Hotel Oasis Praia Mar ☎ 261 6424; m 993 9630; e geral@atlanticorentacar.cv; www.atlanticorentacar.com
🚗 **Avis** At the Hotel Oasis Praia-Mar in Prainha; ☎ 261 8748
🚗 **Classic Auto Rental** Achada Santo António, Praia; ☎ 262 1808; e rentcarclassic@cvtelecom.cv
🚗 **CV Rent a Car** Prainha; m 989 9545;

🚗 **Hertz** At the Hotel Pestana Trópico in Prainha; ☎ 261 4200
🚗 **Inter Cidades Rent-a-Car** Achada Santo António, Praia; ☎ 261 2525; m 994 353; e comercial@intercidadesrentacar.cv; www.intercidadesrentacar.cv

WHERE TO STAY AND EAT

Most people stay in the capital Praia because anywhere on the rest of the island can be reached in a day trip. Here there are two smart international-standard hotels each with a pool and most of the trimmings, and many others encompassing a great range of quality, though none of the latter are places in which to laze for a day.

There are two other hotel centres on the island. The growing city of Assomada has a couple decent hotels, but neither one of them has any real potential for relaxation. Assomada is a growing staging post though – a departure point for hikes, with a craft centre and a vibrant market. The other centre is Tarrafal where, in addition to budget hotels, there are a few choices for those who want to enjoy this quiet seaside town in more comfort.

There are a few enjoyable hotels in odd, interesting places near to Assomada, if you prefer to get away from it all, most notably the inland Quinta da Montanha, Cabo Ned and Pousada Vassora. If you have a vehicle you could comfortably base yourself at these locations and make day trips to other parts of the island.

ACTIVITIES

EXCURSIONS

Try the following operators for guided tours to highlights of the island.

Girassol Tours [174 D3] Rua Serpa Pinto, Plateau, Praia; ✆261 2899; e girassoltours@ cvtelecom.cv. Offers transfers around the island, excursions to Cidade Velha or Achada Leite & a round-island tour, as well as the usual hotel reservations, car rental & national & international air tickets.

G and S Schellmann Esplanada Silibell, Ponta Calhetona, Calheta de São Miguel; ✆273 2078; m 996 7930; www.reisetraeume.de, www. reisetraeume.de/kapverden/viadoso/enindex. html. Gerhard & Sibylle have lived in the islands for years now & specialise in individual & small-group hiking holidays in Santiago. They also operate on an international level, organising your entire holiday in the archipelago including international flights. At their base in Calheta de São Miguel (see page 191), they offer an open-air, sea-view restaurant, bar & tourist information centre & can direct you, for example, to the local hard-to-find accommodation options or to finding out more

about the weaving of *pano de terra*.

Orbitur [174 E3] Rua Cândido dos Reis No 9; ✆261 5736; m 991 8331; e orbitur@cvtelecom.cv; www.orbitur.cv. Arranges tours in Santiago as well as travel to other islands, books flights, ferries, etc.

Praiatur [174 C4] Av Amílcar Cabral ✆261 5746/7; e praiatur.lda@cvtelecom.cv; ☺ 08.00–12.00 & 14.00–16.30 Mon–Fri. This established agency has been running for well over 20 years in Praia. It offers a round-island tour of Praia, does a 1-day tour of Santiago; half-day or full-day tour of Cidade Velha; a trip to Praia Baixo for swimming & lunch. Price pp drops considerably for groups of 5 or more. Guides speak a variety of languages.

VCV (Viagens Cabo Verde) [174 C3] Av Amílcar Cabral; ✆261 8016/7; e vcv.tur@gmail.com. Arranges city & island tours, books flights & ferries. Multilingual.

Zebratravel [174 C2] Av Amilcar Cabral; m 991 4566; e info@zebratravel.net; www.zebratravel. net. Based primarily on Fogo island, but with an office on the Plateau organising excursions, car rentals, hotels & other services.

HIKING The interior of Santiago is filled with spectacular craggy mountains, *ribeiras* and plantations. Though it does not have the breathtaking drama of Santo Antão, or the sheer strangeness of Fogo, it has walks that are both beautiful and rewarding, for which it is definitely worth putting aside some time. Many walks consist of finding a point along the spine of the island and walking down a *ribeira* to the coast (or vice versa). The two, perhaps classic, hikes are to descend from Serra Malagueta down towards Tarrafal (about six hours – you could get yourself dropped off and your luggage taken on to a hotel in Tarrafal) and the hike down Ribeira Principal, towards the east coast.

The biggest hike is to the top of Pico do Santo António – a twin peak that protrudes from the landscape like a canine tooth. Unfortunately the path to the

Pico is not clear, the final ascent borders on the hazardous and knowledgeable guides are hard to find. One option is to stay a few days at Cabo Ned (see page 185), as the owner, Etienne, is a keen hiker and can either advise or accompany you. New hikes are opening up in Serra Malagueta, with the development of the natural park. See page 188 for more details.

FISHING You can link up with local fishermen in almost any village (try Tarrafal or Pedra Badejo) – pay them about 6,000$ per boat for two hours if they take you out on one of their trips. See page 51 for a discussion of fishing.

DIVING Most diving is done in Tarrafal where there are several interesting diving spots all reachable within 15 minutes of Tarrafal by boat. There is also diving off Cidade Velha (interesting for the relics of centuries of ships that anchored there) and at Baixa de Janeia. The dive centre in Praia, based at Hotel Praia Mar, is an on/off affair. Currently it is closed, but may reopen at some point.

⏬ **Divecenter-Santiago** Tarrafal; m 993 6407; e divecenter-santiago@email.de; www. divecenter-santiago.de. The website gives a good description of diving spots off Santiago.

⏬ **King Bay** Tarrafal; ☎ 266 1007; e hrolfs1@ gmx.net. Part of the King Fisher Resort (see page 189). 4 languages spoken. €38/dive.

SURFING There are some reasonable surfing spots on the island, though it is not worth coming to Santiago especially for them – choose another of the archipelago's islands. The swell is best between January and March.

In Tarrafal, a short walk southwest from the main bay, there are some reef breaks, in particular at Ponta do Atum and at Chão Bom. The other well-known spots are in the southeast of the island: the coast south of Ponta do Lobo Lighthouse which marks the easternmost point of Santiago (accessible only by 4x4) and the local bodyboarding beach at Praia itself, just in front of the Plateau. See pages 51–2 for general surfing information.

BEACHES Santiago's beaches fade into insignificance compared with the exhilarating expanses of Boavista and Sal, and the beaches on Maio. Nevertheless there are some to enjoy: Tarrafal has perhaps the best, a pretty cove and white-sand beach, busy at the weekends with local day trippers. Also try Ribeira da Prata, a short journey south of Tarrafal, a long black-sand turtle-nesting beach set in front of lush green palms. The Câmara Municipal operates a turtle hatchery on this beach during the summer. São Francisco is another, currently hard to get to except at weekends when locals head down there from Praia. There is a beach at Praia Baixo and there are several in Praia. You may well find other undiscovered gems if you explore the island in depth.

CULTURE The whole city of Cidade Velha is a museum; Praia has a small general museum on the Plateau and an interesting archaeological museum, which includes many trophies from the diving of wrecks. Heading north, in Chão de Tanque, near Assomada, there's the Tabanka Museum documenting this fascinating traditional dance and music form, and Tarrafal has its more sombre Museum of the Resistance, in the former concentration camp there. You can also seek out the cloth-weaving tradition (see page 177 for shopping and page 168 for excursions), and enjoy traditional and modern Cape Verdean music at Quintal da Música, which has done so much to shepherd and nurture the country's musicians.

SIGHTSEEING BY VEHICLE A one- or, less often, two-day tour of the island by vehicle is a popular thing to do and well worth it, though it leaves a tantalising amount unseen off the main roads. This, however, is inevitable. If you hire your own vehicle or taxi for exploration try to get a 4x4 so you can go down some of the quieter roads, though an ordinary car will easily take you on the main island circuit and to and from Cidade Velha.

PRAIA

Built on a tableland of rock, with the city overflowing onto the land below its steep cliffs, the centre of Praia – its Plateau – is attractive. It has a disorientating feel: it is indisputably African and yet Mediterranean as well.

Praia is undergoing rapid growth and the current estimated population is around 130,000. Infrastructure – from sewage treatment to electricity generation – is finding it impossible to keep pace with this chaotic expansion. Journey to the outskirts of Palmarejo, where there is frenetic building, and you will see an entire hill being gradually, and illegally, hand-mined away. Some of the miners live in little caves in the hillside.

During the day, people of every shade of skin go about their business on the Plateau. At night, though, the Plateau is empty – life continues in the scattered regions beyond. To its south rises another level plain, the Achada Santo António, where the more affluent live in apartment blocks and where the huge parliament building is. Between the two lies Chã de Areia, and, in front of Achada, Prainha, where there are embassies, expensive hotels and nightclubs.

Other districts include Terra Branca to the west and Fazenda district to the north. Palmarejo, separated into the coastal and upper suburbs, is a new, middle-class residential area to the west of central Praia, still under development and with a few decent cafes and a hotel on its Avenida de Santiago. To the northwest is a huge sprawl of half-built houses and burning litter – Cape Verde's version of the urban drift from the countryside.

HISTORY From the early 1600s, Portugal tried both to entice and to force its citizens to make Praia da Santa Maria their capital instead of Ribeira Grande (now Cidade Velha). But the colonisers ignored instructions and stuck to their preferred settlement, 13km away. By ignoring Praia, they left themselves open to attack from behind: Praia, with its poorly fortified beaches, was a place where pirates could land. From there it was an easy overland march to attack the capital.

This happened on two disastrous occasions. Francis Drake used the tactic in 1585 and the Frenchman Jacques Cassard did exactly the same more than a century later in 1712. After the first assault the population built the fort, which survives to this day just outside Cidade Velha. The second sacking signalled the demise of Ribeira Grande as investment was made in the fortification of Praia. Praia's shacks were replaced by permanent buildings and it grew. By 1770, it was the official capital achieving, in 1858, the rank of *cidade*. Today Praia remains the administrative centre while culture seems to gravitate towards Mindelo.

One of Praia's most distinguished visitors was Charles Darwin, who anchored there at the start of his famous voyage on the *Beagle* on 16 January 1832, and spent some time examining the flora and fauna, as well as making forays to Cidade Velha and São Domingos. He reported that he 'feasted' upon oranges and 'likewise tasted a Banana: but did not like it, being maukish and sweet with little flavour'. He wandered through a valley near Praia:

Here I saw the glory of tropical vegetation: Tamarinds, Bananas and Palms were flourishing at my feet. I expected a good deal, for I had read Humboldt's descriptions, and I was afraid of disappointments: how utterly vain such fear is, none can tell but those who have experienced what I today have. It is not only the gracefulness of their forms or the novel richness of their colours. It is the numberless and confused associations that rush together on the mind, and produce the effect. I returned to the shore, treading on Volcanic rocks, hearing the notes of unknown birds, and seeing new insects fluttering about still newer flowers… It has been for me a glorious day, like giving to a blind man eyes, he is overwhelmed with what he sees and cannot justly comprehend it.

He also wrote about the more barren slopes of Cape Verde:

A single green leaf can scarcely be discovered over wide tracts of the lava plains; yet flocks of goats, together with a few cows, contrive to exist. It rains very seldom, but during a short portion of the year heavy torrents fall, and immediately afterwards a light vegetation springs out of every crevice. This soon withers; and upon such naturally formed hay the animals live. It had not now rained for an entire year. When the island was discovered, the immediate neighbourhood of Porto Praya was clothed with trees, the reckless destruction of which has caused here, as at St Helena and at some of the Canary islands, almost entire sterility.

WHERE TO STAY For international, tourist-style facilities with pool choose either the Praia Mar or the Trópico, which also serve the business community. Top of the mid-range establishments, without a pool but with most of the facilities needed for business travellers, are the Hotel Santiago and the Hotel Pérola. All four of these are based away from the Plateau and can be found on the map of Greater Praia (see page 172). Apart from these, and also off the Plateau, there are good mid-range hotels such as Jardim de Vinho and some with an ocean view (for example, the Benfica).

On the Plateau, many hotels are in traditional buildings, erected around a central atrium. As a result the windows of some rooms open only onto a dark shaft or public corridor: it's worth asking to see the room beforehand. One of the best low-budget hotels on the Plateau is Paraiso Pensão, which has the added advantage of being in a quiet neighbourhood, while the Rosymar is full of hostel-like character. All listings are located on the map, page 172, unless otherwise noted.

Hotel Oásis/Praia Mar (123 rooms)
261 4153; e geral@oasisatlantico.com; www.oasisatlantico.com. Attractive, low-rise hotel on the headland of Prainha with plenty of space for terraces & balconies, as well as a swimming pool with pool bar & tennis court, sauna, jacuzzi, gym & massage. It has free Wi-Fi & a basic business centre. Previously had a dive centre, which may re-open. Accepts Visa, MasterCard, Diners Club & travellers' cheques. **$$$$$**

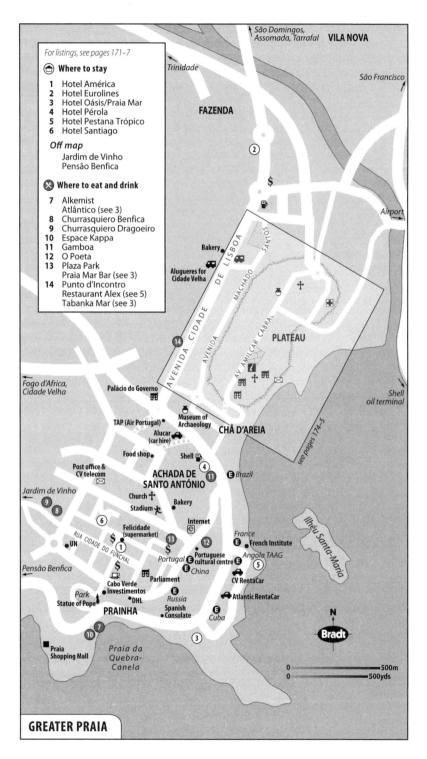

For listings, see pages 171–7

⌂ **Where to stay**

1 Hotel América
2 Hotel Eurolines
3 Hotel Oásis/Praia Mar
4 Hotel Pérola
5 Hotel Pestana Trópico
6 Hotel Santiago

Off map
   Jardim de Vinho
   Pensão Benfica

✕ **Where to eat and drink**

7 Alkemist
   Atlântico (see 3)
8 Churrasquiero Benfica
9 Churrasquiero Dragoeiro
10 Espace Kappa
11 Gamboa
12 O Poeta
13 Plaza Park
   Praia Mar Bar (see 3)
14 Punto d'Incontro
   Restaurant Alex (see 5)
   Tabanka Mar (see 3)

São Domingos,
Assomada, Tarrafal **VILA NOVA**

Trinidade

São Francisco

FAZENDA

Airport

Bakery

CIDADE VELHA
AVENIDA DE LISBOA
MACHADO SANTOS

Alugueres for
Cidade Velha

AV AMILCAR CABRAL

PLATEAU

AVENIDA

Fogo d'Africa,
Cidade Velha

Palácio do Governo

Shell
oil terminal

Museum of
Archaeology

TAP (Air Portugal)

Alucar
(car hire)

CHÃ D'AREIA

Food shop

Shell

see pages 174–5

Post office &
CV telecom

**ACHADA DE
SANTO ANTÓNIO**

Brazil

Jardim de Vinho

Church

Bakery

Stadium

Internet

Felicidade
(supermarket)

RUA CIDADE DO FUNCHAL

UN

Pensão Benfica

France

French Institute

Portugal Portuguese
          cultural centre
          China

Angola TAAG

Ilhéu Santa-Maria

Cabo Verde
Investimentos

Parliament

Russia

DHL

CV RentaCar

Atlantic RentaCar

Park
Statue of Pope

Spanish
Consulate

Cuba

PRAINHA

N

Bradt

Praia
Shopping Mall

*Praia da
Quebra-
Canela*

0   500m
0   500yds

GREATER PRAIA

🏠 **Hotel Pestana Trópico** (93 rooms) ✆261 4200; e reservas.tropico@pestana.com; www. pestana.com. On the coast road in Prainha, the Trópico is the most luxurious hotel in town. Part of an international chain, refurbished rooms are stylish. Rooms are arranged around the seawater pool which is very relaxing with an overlooking bar, a health club & gym, & the hotel feels more peaceful than its cousin up the road. Business-wise, there is a conference room, free Wi-Fi & an internet terminal. Accepts Visa & Mastercard. **$$$$$**

🏠 **Hotel Pérola** (20 rooms) Chã d'Areia; ✆260 1440; e reservas@hotelperola.cv; www. hotelperola.cv. Smart & comfortable, some rooms with generous balconies overlooking the harbour. Also a fine business option, one notch down from the Praia Mar & Trópico. Free Wi-Fi. Accepts Visa. English spoken. **$$$$**

🏠 **Hotel Santiago** Avenida Figueira da Foz; ✆262 4618; e info@hotelsantiago.cv; www. hotelsantiago.cv . New business option, away from the Plateau but handy for government offices etc. 2 bars, decent facilities, roof terrace. **$$$$**

🏠 **Hotel América** (17 rooms, 7 suites) A little out of the way, in the peace of Achada Santo António; ✆262 1431; e hotelamerica@ cvtelecom. cv. It is a bright & modern hotel, all rooms with fridge, TV & AC. Internet & Wi-Fi available. **$$$**

🏠 **Hotel Eurolines** (14 rooms) Av Cidade de Lisboa, Fazenda; ✆260 3010; e eurolines@ cvtelecom.cv. Very large, en-suite rooms, many with 2 beds, with AC, hot water. Restaurant serves European & Cape Verdean food. Shuttle to airport available. Very good value. **$$$**

🏠 **Pensão Benfica** (20 rooms) Palmarejo de Baixo; ✆ 262 9313; e pensaobenfica@cvtelecom. cv. Situated in the emerging, bourgeois area of Palmarejo, this is quite far from the Plateau but is one of the few hotels with ocean views. Adjacent restaurant is much more sophisticated than the *churrasqueiro* of the same name, with live music at w/ends, which is under the same ownership. Rooms have AC, hot water, TV & internet. **$$$**

🏠 **Residencial Santa Maria** [map page 174] (15 rooms) Avenida 5 de Julho; ✆261 4337; e reservas@girassol.cv. Offers good standard, en-suite rooms with satellite TV, hot water, AC, fridge. Accepts Visa & Mastercard. **$$$**

🏠 **Jardim do Vinho** (5 rooms) Achada Santo Antonio; ✆262 4760; m 970 6849; e ojardimdovinho@gmail.com; www. ojardimdovinho.com. Away from the Plateau, a good standard, secure establishment with spacious rooms & shared bathrooms. Pleasant patio to enjoy a glass of wine. Run by charming, friendly & knowledgeable French couple: they may offer you a glass of wine, or play you some music. **$$**

🏠 **Pensão Paraiso** [map page 174] (14 rooms) Rua Serpa Pinto; ✆261 3539. In a quiet setting at the northern end of the Plateau, this is a good mid-range choice, with decent-size rooms, all en suite and many with both bath & shower. **$$**

🏠 **Rosymar Inn** [map page 175] (10 rooms) 15 Rua Tenente Valadim (Madragoa), Plateau; ✆261 6345; m 916 3112; e info@rosymarinn. com; www.rosymarinn.com. Owned by a characterful returned US citizen, Rosalina, this is one of the longest-established hotels. Convenient location directly behind Pão Quente. Rooms have fans & are en suite. Hot water is sporadic. **$$**

🏠 **Residencial Sol Atlantico** (16 rooms) ✆261 2872; e residencialsolatlantico@sapo.cv. Overlooks the Alexandre Albuquerque Square, but with no sign, it's difficult to find. Go up 2 flights of stairs, next to the pharmacy, & ring the bell. Probably the cheapest acceptable choice in town. **$$**

WHERE TO EAT AND DRINK All listings are located on the map, pages 174–5, unless otherwise noted.

On the Plateau

🖥 **Pão Quente de Cabo Verde** ⊕ 06.30–21.30 daily. A wide variety of delicious cakes, snacks & sandwiches in a busy, spacious European-style café. Part of a small chain, look out for other branches around town. **$$$$**

✗ **Quintal da Música** Av Amílcar Cabral; ✆261 1679; ⊕ from 08.00 to around midnight Mon–Sat, with live music every night. One of the classic places to spend an evening in Praia, this restaurant was founded by musician Mario Lucio along with the Cape Verdean band Simentera to promote traditional music & stimulate local musicians. Its courtyard & little stage make an evocative place to while away a Praia evening & the food is good. Can

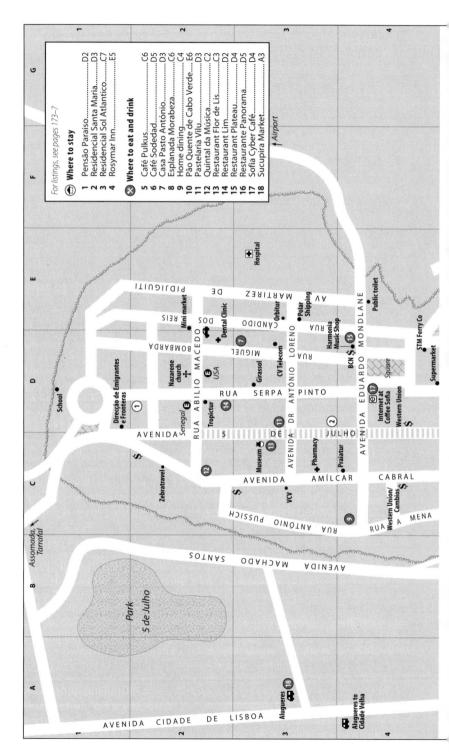

For listings, see pages 173–7

Where to stay

1	Pensão Paraiso	D2
2	Residencial Santa Maria	D3
3	Residencial Sol Atlantico	C7
4	Rosymar Inn	E5

Where to eat and drink

5	Café Pulkus	C6
6	Café Sodedad	D5
7	Casa Pasto António	D3
8	Esplanada Morabeza	C6
9	Home dining	C4
10	Pão Quente de Cabo Verde	E6
11	Pastelaria Vilu	D3
12	Quintal da Música	C2
13	Restaurant Flor de Lis	C3
14	Restaurant Lim	D2
15	Restaurant Plateau	D4
16	Restaurante Panorama	D5
17	Sofia Cyber Café	D4
18	Sucupira Market	A3

PRAIA
Plateau

AVENIDA CIDADE DE LISBOA

AVENIDA MACHADO SANTOS

Prainha

Football
stadium

RUA A MENA

Supermarket
Calu & Angela

Market

Supermarket

Palácio de Cultura

Farmácia
Moderna

Ministry of
Information

Alexandre
Albuquerque
Square

AV PATRICE LUMUMBA

RUA SERPA PINTO

Internet
Praia Ouro

TACV

Police

Air Senegal

Wine shop

CV Fastferry

RUA ANDRADE

Pano de Terra

AV CESARIO DE LA
CERDA

Post office

CORVO

Palace of Justice

Cathedral

Town Hall

Palácio da
República

Diogo Gomes Statue

Prainha

BATERIA

N

Bradt

0 100m
0 100yds

G F E D C B A

5 6 7 8

Santiago PRAIA

5

175

get chilly later on – take a jumper. $$$$

✕ Restaurant Flor de Lis Avenida 5 de Julho; ⏱ 07.30–23.00 daily. Friendly staff & a bright, renovated interior, plus some outdoor tables. Changing menu of meat & fish dishes. Breakfast *cachupa* is the one constant, a mere $150. $$$$

📺 Sofia Cyber Café ⏱ 07.00–23.00. This restaurant is one of the few places on the Plateau where you can sit outside under a parasol & enjoy watching life go by, with the added advantage that you can check your emails inside while your meal is cooked. Popular venue for chess matches. A reasonable menu & an assortment of desserts. Service has a reputation for being notoriously slow. $$$$

✕ Restaurante Panorama ⏱ 11.00–15.00 & 19.00–22.00 daily. Above the Hotel Felicidade on the Plateau but with an entrance in Rua Serpa Pinto, not Av Corvo. This rooftop restaurant is an escape from the noise & heat below, with plenty of seating including an open-air terrace at the back looking east. Popular with white-collar workers for its speed, conviviality & price rather than its cuisine. $$$

✕ Restaurant Plateau Av Eduardo Mondlane; ⏱ 08.00–21.00 Mon–Sat. Somewhat tatty exterior. Serves basic Chinese food & one of the few places in Cape Verde to serve tofu. $$

✕ Esplanada Morabeza ⏱ 09.00–23.00 Mon–Sat. In the middle of the square, an outdoor cafeteria-style option with decent daily dishes, pizzas & snacks. Free Wi-Fi. $$

📺 Café Sodade Rua Andrade Corvo. A pleasant establishment. Serves simple snacks, drinks & a well-priced plate of the day. $$

📺 Café Pulkus Av Amilcar Cabral, by the side of the main square. A newly renovated, stylish café with pleasant courtyard & live music every Fri & some Sat. Semi-permanent exhibition of local art. $$

📺 Casa Pasto António Rua Miguel Bombarda; ⏱ 08.00 –15.00 Mon–Sat. Bustling café serving cheap *cachupa*, pizzas & soup. $$

📺 Pastelaria Vilu Av 5 de Julho. Savoury snacks & cool drinks, served inside or out. $$

✕ Restaurant Lim Rua Serpa Pinto. Otherwise known as the 'Chinese Hole in the Wall' for reasons which will become obvious when visiting, this serves cheap Chinese food most of the day. A tiny entrance to a tiny restaurant may cause you to walk right past it. $$

✕ Nameless 'home dining' Rua Viscomte S Januario 3–5, next to the closed Tera Kafe, but with no sign; ⏱ 12.00–15.00 Mon–Fri. Daily dishes, including Cape Verdean specialities, served informally in someone's own dining room. Very inexpensive, unique ambience, communal tables. You may find other similar establishments in the city. $

Off the Plateau

✕ Atlântico [map page 172] Oasis Praia Mar Hotel; 📞260 8440. Accepts Visa. One of the most expensive restaurants in Praia, this AC restaurant is a good bet for quality & variety. $$$$$

✕ Gamboa [map page 172] Chã d'Areia; 📞261 2008. One of the places to be seen in Praia, highly rated by locals and popular for its levels of service & quality of food. Live music at w/ends. $$$$$

✕ O Poeta [map page 172] Achada Santo António; 📞261 3800; ⏱ 10.00–midnight daily. Go up the hill that leads from Chã de Areia to Achada Santo António & it is on your left, just before the Portuguese Cultural Centre. This old-fashioned restaurant is one of the oldest in Praia & remains a firm fixture despite the emergence of newer rivals. Its clifftop position gives its outdoor terrace splendid views over the port, the island & the coast; & the food is adequate. Accepts Visa. $$$$$

✕ Panorama Bar Oásis Praia Mar Hotel; 📞261 4153; Tucked away overlooking a little cove to the side of Praia Mar Hotel, this is a beautiful place to while away an hour or 2, particularly in the soft breezes of the evening. There is a limited bar menu, cocktails & occasional music. $$$$$

✕ Plaza Park [map page 172] Across from the Portuguese Embassy; 📞262 1080; ⏱ lunch & dinner Mon–Sat. One of the newer, smarter, place-to-be restaurants it has a choice of AC, non-AC & terrace seating. The food is good though the view, across a car park to the main road, is not its best feature. Accepts Visa. $$$$$

✕ Restaurant Alex [map page 172] Hotel Pestana Trópico; 📞2614200. With AC indoors, & a small outside area partly overlooking the pool, this restaurant has an excellent reputation for its food, especially its steaks. $$$$$

✕ Alkemist [map page 172] Located at Quebra-Canela, along the seafront west of the Praia Mar Hotel; Italian & traditional cuisine with a panoramic view of the sea. $$$$

✘ **Punto d'Incontro** [map page 172] Av Cidade de Lisboa, opposite the football stadium in Chã d'Areia; ☎ 261 7090. Italian bar & restaurant serving fine pizzas & pasta. $$$$ –$$$

✘ **Churrasqueiro Benfica** [map page 172] Achada Santo António; ☎ 262 2195. The place to go for piles of barbecued chicken, pork kebabs & beefsteak. Indoor & outdoor seating. It is a bit grotty to look at, and in a half-baked locality, but the grills are divine. $$$

✘ **Churrasqueiro Dragoeiro** [map page 172] Av UCCLA-Meio, on the west side of Achada Santo António; ☎ 262 3335. More piles of barbecued meats, popular at w/ends. $$$

✘ **Espace Kappa** [map page 172] ⊕ 18.30– late Tue–Sun. Indoor & terrace seating that overlooks a rocky wasteland that stretches down to the ocean. A hip & stylish vibe, with live music Thu & Sat. The shoreline itself is beautiful. $$$

✘ **Achada de Santo António** [map page 172] At night, buy grilled fish with salad on the street in this district for 100$ or try fried *moreia* (moray eel). $$

✘ **Sucupira Market** Great platefuls of cheap lunchtime eats can be found in the kiosks of the market, round the back in the covered area. $

ENTERTAINMENT AND NIGHTLIFE Several restaurants play live music, most notably the Quintal da Música (see pages 173–4).

♀ **Cockpit** Achada Grande, near the airport & Ponta Bicuda. A smart place frequented by anyone who is anyone. Well-established. Take a taxi to find it.

♀ **Fogo d'Africa** Tira Chapeu. Ask any taxi driver. Plays good music in a rougher & readier setting than Quintal da Musica. W/ends.

♀ **Discoteca Zero Horas** Achada Grande. On the road to the airport take the right turn past some warehouses & it is about 400m down on the right, a large purple building. For young clubbers: sweaty, crowded & loud. It plays a mixture of Cape Verdean, South American, American & European music. Entry 500$.

♀ **Tabanka Mar** Live music at the Hotel Praia Mar Fri & Sat evenings.

SHOPPING Sadly, the Palácio de Cultura [175 C6] on the main square on the Plateau (Praça Alexander Albuquerque), which previously sold a variety of music and artefacts is re-inventing itself as an arts 'laboratory' for locals only. It could be worth checking out, in case there's a change of heart. Music shops include Harmonia Music Shop [174 D4] and Quintal da Música [174 C2] (see pages 173–4) on the Plateau, and you can buy both genuine and fake CDs at Sucupira market.

If you are interested in the traditional weaving of **pano de terra**, visit Fatima Almeida at Pano de Terra [175 D6] (*Rua Andrade Corvo 18;* ☎ 262 3660), a successful designer who incorporates *panos* into her clothes designs. She achieved fame after a fashion show in 2002 and makes linen and cotton clothing adorned with *panos*, as well as ties, bags, lampshades and curtains. Over the years she has passed on her skills to students of all ages. Originally, the cloth was used as currency in trading on the African coast. Although the tradition was to weave the cloth only in black and white, now colour has been introduced to make it more marketable. Prices are high: weaving *panos* is expensive and so is the Italian linen.

There are many *minimercardos* on the Plateau for **food shopping**. There is also a large supermarket on the Plateau by the main square on Avenida Amílcar Cabral. On the same road heading north, a branch of Kalu e Angela also has a wide range of goods. The main branch of Kalu e Angela in the suburb of Achadinha is a megastore by Cape Verdean standards; any taxi driver will take you there.

OTHER PRACTICALITIES
Airlines
Many of the travel agents and tour operators around town will book flights for these airlines.
TACV [175 D5] Rua Serra Pinto; ☎ 260

8242/8200/261 8271; ⏲ 08.00–13.00 & 14.30–17.00 Mon–Sat
TAP Office at the airport; ✆261 5826; ⏲ 08.00–12.00 & 17.30–19.30 & 21.00–01.00 Mon–Sat Senegal Airlines Office at the airport; ✆263 5555; e praia@senegalairlines.aero;international.sn; www.senegalairlines.aero
TAAG Rua Dr Manuel Duarte, Prainha; ✆261 6915; office at the airport; ✆261 6715/263 2030; ⏲ 08.00–15.00

Banks
You will not walk far before passing a bank with an ATM. Some are listed below. On the Plateau: Banco Interatlântico and BAI Banco are both in Praça Alexander Albuquerque (⏲ 08.15–15.00 Mon–Fri); Caixa Económica (without ATM), Av Amílcar Cabral, at the northern end (⏲ 08.00–13.00 & 14.00–15.00 Mon–Fri); BCN, Av 5 de Julho, at the very northern end (⏲ 08.30–15.00 Mon–Fri). Most districts of Praia off the Plateau have several banks and ATMs and, back on the Plateau, there are various *cambios* along Av Amílcar Cabral.

Dentist
Dr Antoninho (✆261 5444) or Dr Olivio Pires (✆261 9899).

Embassies
For a full list of embassies and consulates in Cape Verde and abroad, see pages 56–7.

Ferries
🚢 **Polar Shipping** [174 E3] Rua Candido dos Reis, Rua Serpa Pinto, Plateau; ✆261 5223; e polarp@cvtelecom.cv. Operates the *Sotavento* to Maio, generally leaving on Fri & returning on Sun.
🚢 **STM** [174 D4] Rua Andrade Corvo, Plateau; ✆261 2564. Operates the *Sal Rei* to São Nicolau & São Vicente.
🚢 **Agencia Nacional de Viagens (ANAV)** Rua Serpa Pinto, Plateau; ✆260 3107; e anavpraia@cvtelecom.cv. Operates the *Djon Dade* to Sal & Boavista, once per week.
🚢 **Cabo Verde Fast Ferry** [175 D5] Avenida Andrade Corvo 35, Praia; ✆261 7552; e cvff.info@cvfastferry.com; www.cvfastferry.com

Hospital
[174 E3] Av Martirez de Pidjiguiti (✆261 2462). Situated at the northeastern edge of the Plateau, overlooking the airport road, this has a mixed reputation though it is well equipped. One recommendation is to use its facilities via a private doctor.

Internet
Wi-Fi is available on the two Plateau squares, free of charge and no code or password is necessary. Connectivity can be variable. Just keep security in mind when flashing your state-of-the art laptop/tablet.

Pharmacy
Various places throughout the city, including: Farmacia Moderna [174 C3] (*Av Amílcar Cabral;* ✆261 2719; ⏲ 08.15–12.30 & 14.30–17.00 Mon–Sat), on the main square; Africana (✆261 2776); Central (✆261 1167); Farmácia 2000 (✆261 5655); and Santa Isabel (✆261 3747).

Police
[175 D6] The office (✆261 3205) is located on Rua Serpa Pinto, close to the Palace of Justice.

Post office
[175 E6] On the Plateau, behind the Palace of Justice, and in various other districts, including Fazenda near the big roundabout (⏲ 08.00–12.00 & 14.00–18.00 Mon–Fri). For delivery services, contact DHL (Av OUA, Achada Santo António, CP 303A; ✆262 3124; e dhl_praia@vtelecom.cv).

Telephone
There are many booths on the Plateau from which to make national and international calls.

Tourist information
An information kiosk sponsored by Cabo Verde Investimentos has recently appeared on Praça Alexander Albuquerque, providing city maps and selling a small range of souvenirs.

WHAT TO SEE AND DO
Museum [174 C3] (*Av 5 de Julho, Plateau;* ⏲ 08.30–16.30 Mon–Fri; admission 100$, *students & children free*) Small but well laid-out display in a restored 18th-century

building on the Plateau, with some interpretations translated into English. One of the few places you will see the beautifully woven *pano* cloth that was so important in Cape Verde's history (for this, see also page 177). There are also relics from rural life.

Museu de Arqueologia (*Rua Cabo Verde Telecom, Chã de Areia;* ✆ *261 1528;* ⏱ *08.00–16.00 Mon–Sat*) Formerly the Centro de Restauracao e Museologia, now renamed the museum of archaeology. Tucked away behind the football stadium. Interesting though modest display of treasure retrieved by the company Arqueonautas from various shipwrecks around Cape Verde, with exhibits demonstrating the detective work done in piecing together the histories of the various wrecks and their painstaking restorative efforts. Information in Portuguese, English and French. (See also box, page 11.)

Main square [175 C/D6] On the Plateau, this houses the old Catholic cathedral, the old Palace of the Council, the Presidential Palace and the newest building, the Palace of Justice. In the centre, there is a pleasant café, Esplanada Morabeza, open early until late, daily, allowing you to take a drink, access the free municipal Wi-Fi and people-watch. Behind the square is the statue of Diogo Gomes, one of the two discoverers of the southern islands. Wander a little further and enjoy the views off the Plateau down to the sea.

Beaches Prainha is a pleasant little yellow-sand cove, popular with locals, between the Hotel Praia Mar and the Hotel Trópico in an upmarket part of town, but with no facilities.

To the west of the Hotel Praia Mar, you can find **Quebra-Canela**, which is larger and less busy. A decent bar perches above the sands, with a few restaurants nearby.

Other places of interest The wild and windswept **lighthouse** has a good view of the town; the caretaker should let you climb to the top.

The **Institut Francais** (✆ *261 1196;* e *contact@ifcapvert.com; www.ifcapvert.com:* ⏱ *08.30–13.00 & 14.30–18.30 Mon–Fri*) is opposite the French Embassy on Rua Manuel Duarte. Since relocating from the Plateau to Prainha it has lost its café, but has a library and organises cultural events such as art exhibitions and musical evenings.

Santiago has tentatively dipped its toe in the shopping mall pool with the Chinese-funded **Praiashopping**, perched rather incongruously on the shore in Prainha. It incorporates a cinema, a smart restaurant overlooking the water, a supermarket and a few shops. The VIP hotel is part of the same complex and under construction at time of writing.

CIDADE VELHA

This once-proud town, formerly known as Ribeira Grande, has had nearly 300 years to decay since the French robbed it of its wealth in 1712. Now there is just an ordinary village population living amongst the ruins of numerous churches, the great and useless fort watching over them from a hill behind. Its inhabitants are still poor but there have been efforts to develop some tourist potential in town and it is becoming a delightful place, with a café on the shore, bright fishing boats in the harbour and a tourist information office. It is magical to wander through the vegetation in the *ribeira* and in the surrounding hills to discover the ruins of what was once a pivot of the Portuguese Empire. It's popular as a Sunday destination for city dwellers.

HISTORY Ribeira Grande is where the history of Cape Verde began – where the first Cape Verdeans were born. It was chosen by António de Noli as the centre of his portion of Santiago and it flourished. It had a reasonable and defensible harbour that was the second safest in all of Cape Verde, Madeira and the Azores. It had ample fresh water and a stony landing beach. One of its early illustrious visitors was Vasco da Gama, in July 1497, who discovered India later on the same journey. Just 70 years after the *ribeira* was settled it was granted the status of *cidade*, and by 1572, some 1,500 people walked its streets (many of them slaves whose job was to till the plantations up the valley). They were watched over by a bishop, dean, archdeacon and 12 canons. Portuguese ships called there on their way to India and Brazil.

The upper valleys were planted with 'vast groves... of oranges, cedars, lemons, pomegranates, figs of every kind, and... palms which produce coconuts', according to one 16th-century account. Although there are still plantations in the valley it is hard to imagine such foliage there today.

But this was an isolated outpost, helpless under attack and victim of any country that happened to have a grudge against its colonial masters. In 1585, forces supporting the Prior of Crato, fighting for the succession to the throne of Portugal, attacked the town.

When Francis Drake's force landed in mid-November 1585, his 1,000 men found the city deserted. Everyone had fled into the mountains, where they remained for two weeks while the Englishmen were below. Drake marched 600 men inland to São Domingos but they found it too deserted. They torched the settlement, went on to Praia and did the same and then left, having acquired food and water but none of the gold they were after. Two weeks later a fever contracted on the island killed hundreds of Drake's crew.

Nevertheless Ribeira Grande continued to grow. By the end of the 1600s, it had a population of about 2,000. The grand cathedral was completed in 1693, but little did the people know that the demise of their city was imminent. The French raid of 1712, led by Jacques Cassard, began the drain to Praia and the city's fate was sealed by the decision of a new bishop in 1754 not to live at Ribeira Grande. Soon it was to be known only as Cidade Velha.

Cidade Velha today

Today archaeologists are trying to piece together what the city was like. They are finding a rich buried history that could shed light on the origins of Cape Verdean culture, the history of slavery, and Jesuit history as well. This, the first European city in the tropics, is more than just a national treasure. And, in recognition of this, in June 2009, Cidade Velha became Cape Verde's first UNESCO World Heritage Site. It seems that very little has changed since this status was bestowed, but the Ministry for Culture, together with Promitur, are promoting the benefits of preserving this historic site and have trained young people to work as guides for visitors.

Increased demand for new housing in the town could threaten future excavations. 'The whole area is potentially at risk – including the nearby town of São Pedro,' warns Konstantino Richter of Cape Verde's Jean Piaget University. Where new buildings are going up, potentially valuable data is being lost as basements are excavated before sufficient exploratory work is carried out.

GETTING THERE AND AWAY

Take the approximately hourly *aluguer* (30 minutes; 80$) from Sucupira Market or from Terra Branca in Praia. A taxi costs 1,000$ one-way. *Alugueres* depart from Cidade Velha from the tree in the centre of the square. Don't worry about finding one: it will find you. The road between Praia and Cidade Velha is new and smooth – apart from the occasional speed bump.

WHERE TO STAY All listings are located on the map, page 182.

 Hotel Limeira (31 rooms) ☎ 267 1104; e atendimento@hotellimeira.com. A fairly new hotel with a variety of rooms, suites & apartments, featuring AC, cable TV & minibar & a restaurant. Spread out along the side of the hill with great views & a few mins' walk to Cidade Velha. Bar & swimming pool. **$$$**

Pôr do Sol (8 rooms, 2 villas) Santa Marta, Cidade Velha; ☎ 267 1622; m 991 2136; e dama@ cvtelecom.cv; www.pordosol.com.cv. Some 2km west of Cidade Velha. A taxi from the airport costs 3,000$, or 3,500$ at night, if arranged with the proprietor beforehand. Pôr do Sol is a haven of white tiles, bougainvillea & terracing, currently in an isolated spot on the rocky coast north of the town. There's a small pool, a good restaurant & a super view. Spacious rooms are en suite with AC, TV, fridge. Wi–Fi & internet available. The owner, Xista Almeida, is developing the land & it will eventually (it is said) become a gated community with several privately owned villas. The restaurant serves delicious local dishes including its speciality, a seafood & bean dish (*feijoada de mariscos*). There is sometimes live music. The owner will organise excursions. **$$$**

Tereru di Kultura (4 rooms) m 918 3581/2. At the side of BCA bank, good value with simple but tasteful rooms. Adjoining restaurant has live music on Sat. **$$**

WHERE TO EAT AND DRINK There are several cafés, including **Kuska**, on the right as the road enters Cidade Velha from Praia, and **Casa Velha**, on the land-side of the square. There is also **Café Pelourinho** on the Esplanade, a great place to watch beach life. Or retreat to **Pôr do Sol** or **Tereru di Kultura** (see listing above). All listings are located on the map, page 182.

WHAT TO SEE AND DO
Key ruins in Cidade Velha
Fort Real do São Filipe (☎ 267 1681; e proimtur@proimtur.cv; admission 500$, students & children free; guided tours 10.00—18.00 daily) Most easily reached from the main road from Praia, from where it is an 800m walk; the tourist information centre offers multilingual information boards, 15-minute video and cold drinks.

The fort was built after the 1585 sacking and was intended to guard primarily against attack from overland. Its extraordinarily thick walls were built with brick from Lisbon; its turrets with their little windows give a wide view over the Atlantic and the village. Behind are long views over flat-topped hills and lonely, rocky moors, and also deep into the canyon of Ribeira Grande with its sprinkling of plantations spreading up the valley floor. Inside the fort are some of the old cannons.

Cathedral (*Enter through a gap in the fencing*) Inside are the remains of its 1m-thick walls, begun by the third bishop of Cape Verde, Francisco da Cruz, in 1556. After his initial impetus, the work was half-hearted and construction funds were diverted elsewhere. In 1676, the ambitious original plans were scaled down and it was proposed to build only a sanctuary about 24m long. But the energetic Bishop Vitoriano Portuense, who arrived in 1688, returned to the original design and it was completed in 1693. Its life was short, however: in 1712, it was attacked and virtually destroyed by French pirate Jacques Cassard.

Archaeologists have done occasional digs here and these have revealed the gravestones in the floor; the balustrade between the central nave and the

> **OTHER PRACTICALITIES**
>
> **Bank** Just east of the main square
> **Hospital** ☎ 267 1111
> **Internet** The main square has free Wi-Fi.
> **Police** ☎ 267 1132

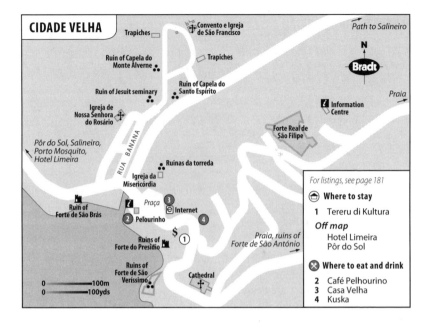

CIDADE VELHA

Trapiches

Convento e Igreja de São Francisco

Path to Salineiro

Ruin of Capela do Monte Álverne

Trapiches

N

Bradt

Ruin of Jesuit seminary

Ruin of Capela do Santo Espírito

Praia

Igreja de Nossa Senhora do Rosário

Information Centre

Pôr do Sol, Salineiro, Porto Mosquito, Hotel Limeira

RUA BANANA

Forte Real de São Filipe

Ruinas da torreda

Igreja da Misericórdia

For listings, see page 181

🛏 **Where to stay**

Ruin of Forte de São Brás

Praça

Pelourinho

Internet

1   Tereru di Kultura

Off map
    Hotel Limeira
    Pôr do Sol

Ruins of Forte do Presídio

Praia, ruins of Forte de São António

❌ **Where to eat and drink**

Ruins of Forte de São Veríssimo

Cathedral

0 ——100m
0 ——100yds

2   Café Pelhourino
3   Casa Velha
4   Kuska

---

transept; the baptistry, with red-tiled floors and the foundations of the font; and the tomb of António José Xavier, first bishop of Cape Verde. Once the cathedral had a gabled façade, a tower on either side and a flight of steps which led down to the square.

Pelourinho This 16th-century pillory was used for the punishment of slaves. It is not much more than a century since slavery was abolished in Brazil and the pillory is an arresting symbol of inhumanity – as long as it is there the memory will never slip away.

Igreja de Nossa Senhora do Rosário This is the earliest documented church in the tropics. This church served as the settlement's principal place of worship until the cathedral was built, and is still full on Sundays. Laid in the floor are 17th-century tombstones of noblemen from the time of the reign of Philip of Spain. For more information, see box opposite.

Igreja e Convento de São Francisco Built in about 1640, this was a monastery and later a cultural and training centre. Another victim of Jacques Cassard, it was destroyed in 1712.

A walk through Cidade Velha Start at the fort, then walk down into town either along the main road or via the zig-zag path down the mountainside. The **cathedral** is on the right of the main road, surrounded by high wire netting. Returning to the road and descending into town you will find the **pelourinho** at the far left of the square.

Leave the square at the pillory end, by the coastal road, and turn right into the wide and dry *ribeira*. This was once a great stream, which, before it reached the sea, formed a wide pool which was dammed at the mouth by a maze of pebbles through which the water trickled out slowly to the ocean. Fresh water was loaded from it into small boats and

TAKE THE HIKE

Hike No 9, page 198, finishes at Cidade Velha.

brought out to the ships, for which a huge charge was made. You can walk up the *ribeira*, turning left onto a track that joins it after about 100m, after the ruins. The track bends round to the right and peters out into the valley above after five minutes.

Up on the right is **Igreja e Convento de São Francisco**. The ruins of this church hide among the trees up to the right and include a bell tower. Returning to the track, walk up amongst the trees of the valley to reach, after 15 minutes, a small water tank in which the local people bathe and which used to supply water to Praia. You can return to town along the concrete water channel that leads from the water tank just below you. It follows a contour round the hill and affords good views of the town and the hills behind. When the channel turns to the right at a road, jump off it and follow the track back to the main road.

As you return to town, after 50m, you will see a narrow path between stone walls off to the left. This leads up and then to the right to the church of Santa Luzia. There's little left of it, but there's a good view up to the fort and the cathedral.

Before crossing the *ribeira* to return to town, take the road on the left which leads to Nossa Senhora do Rosário. Wander through the few little roads here: Rua Banana is a pretty one, as is its neighbour, Rua Carrera. If you have time you can also wander further up Ribeira Grande among the plantations. The road continues up the coast for about 20km as far as the small village of Porto Mosquito.

A CHURCH GIVES UP ITS SECRETS

When archaeologists first started work on the Igreja de Nossa Senhora do Rosário, all that was visible were some foundations protruding into the neighbouring track and some walls that had been incorporated into drystone terracing. Since then the team, led by Konstantino Richter of Cape Verde's Jean Piaget University, and Christopher Evans, director of Cambridge University's Archaeological Unit, has exposed the church's massive foundations and reconstructed its outline. It was 26m long and 11m wide with, on its north side, a Gothic-style side chapel (discovered to great excitement in 2007). They have found some very early 'relief-style' tiles dating from about 1500, nearby, which they believe were the first tiles used in the church. They have also uncovered an early 16th-century inscribed grave-slab set into the church's floor, and an enormous tombstone, dating to the mid 16th century, laid into the floor of the side chapel. They have found late 16th–17th-century tiles in the nave – which must have been the result of a later recladding job.

'All this indicates that we certainly have found a very early church here, one dating from at least the early 16th century,' say the researchers. It is even possible that there is an even earlier phase of the church still buried underneath: the archaeologists estimate that they have found the remains of over 1,000 people sealed below the church floor. This number is very high, given the population at the time, and demonstrates 'just how high the mortality was during the first half century of the settlement's history'. Isotope analysis of the teeth, which is only at an early stage, suggests that the remains are of two or three distinct populations, at least one of which seems to be of West African origin.

The researchers have found all sorts of objects on the site, too, including Chinese porcelain, Portuguese earthenware and what looks like West African pottery.

The main reason to stop here is for drives or walks up to the west into the hills. Look out for the Artesanatos of São Domingos and their pottery, *pano de terra* (literally 'bread of the earth'), and other local arts and crafts.

GETTING THERE AND AWAY *Alugueres* leave Sucupira Market all day for São Domingos (60$). Any Tarrafal or Assomada *aluguer* will stop there. They run back to Praia well into the evening. By hire car from Praia, take the road north, signposted São Domingos, Assomada and Tarrafal, passing through the urban sprawl and into the countryside. About 12km later there is a sharp bend to the right at which you take the main road to São Domingos.

WHERE TO STAY AND EAT There is little in the way of worthwhile accommodation and eating options in São Domingos itself, but nearby Rui Vaz offers a hilltop hotel; otherwise it is probably best to stay in Praia.

Quinta da Montanha (18 rooms) Rui Vaz; \268 5002/3; m 992 4013; e quintamontanha@ cvtelecom.cv; www.caboverde.com/ pages/685002.htm. Although subject to some mixed reviews, this enjoys an imposing position high in the mountains. With its dramatic view of the lush plantations below, this hotel is a good base for visits to the botanical gardens, hiking & birdwatching. If you don't want to stay in Praia, the Quinta will arrange the 30min taxi ride from the airport (€25). The owner, a returned Cape Verdean *emigrante*, is an agriculturalist, so the hotel grows its own produce including an array of vegetables &, in season, strawberries. There is a telescope for stargazers. Rooms are en suite with TV, hot water &, unusually for Cape Verde, baths. Internet is offered in the 100-seater conference room. FB possible; hiking excursions arranged. Its restaurant ($$$$; €14 for a whole meal) is often packed with day trippers from Sal so booking is advisable. It operates a buffet for groups, full menu for others. Take a jumper for the evenings. $$$

WHAT TO SEE AND DO At the **Artisan Centre** (*near the petrol station;* ⊕ *08.30–12.00 & 14.00–18.00 Mon–Sat*), Cape Verdeans are trying to rejuvenate old crafts, in particular the weaving of *pano* cloth and the production of ceramics. You can watch them practising their skills around the back. In the front is the craft shop selling locally made dolls, as well as attractive trinkets made from coconut and cow horn. Crafts imported from Senegal are also for sale. The centre waxes and wanes – sometimes there is not much there, but at time of writing displays were good – worth dropping in to see.

Rui Vaz and Monte Xota The road up into the mountains to this village and up to the peak is magnificent. Take a left turn amongst the shops, towards the end of São Domingos, then take the first right at an ill-defined roundabout. *Alugueres* go as far as Rui Vaz fairly regularly – the rest of the journey can be completed on foot. Alternatively, charter an *aluguer* in São Domingos (630$ one-way). At the top it is sometimes possible to enter the antennae complex and go up to the viewpoint for a panorama of the interior of Santiago. (See also hikes on page 193.)

Barragem Poilão Just before João Teves, in São Lourenço dos Orgãos at the roundabout where there is a large, new school, turn right and follow the road down. This dam, funded by the Chinese, was inaugurated in 2006, and is already altering the ecology in the area – there are anecdotal reports that birds are congregating to enjoy the environment there. It cost 38 million Cape Verdean escudos to build and has a potential capacity of 1.7 million m³. The dam wall is 26m high. Other dams are under construction on the island.

Botanical gardens and São Jorge dos Orgãos
Cool, verdant and pretty, this village is reached by going up the main road as far as the village of João Teves (*aluguer* from Praia 150$; one hour) and turning left a few hundred metres after the post office for São Jorge. Above you tower the mountains of the Serra do Pico do António.

Here, houses rise up the crevices between the mountains, all relying on a single little mountain spring for the watering of their many crops. The agricultural research station here, known as Inida, became part of the newly established University of Cape Verde in 2007. It is located near the blue church and has a national botanical garden (Jardim Botânico Nacional), which lies up a turning to the left just beyond its main buildings.

Here they are trying to study endemic species and conserve those threatened with extinction. The research station, meanwhile, selectively breeds plants in the quest for ever hardier species and develops more efficient irrigation techniques. If the researchers are not busy they sometimes show visitors around the garden, though entrance is free and you can visit on your own (*09.00—17.00*). Look out for *língua de vaca* (*Echium vulcanorum*), if they've managed to get this inhabitant of Fogo volcano to grow, and the purple flowers of *contra-bruxas-azul* (*Campanula jacobea*).

 Where to stay and eat Up in the high wilderness, half an hour's 4x4 drive from São Orgaos itself, you can stay in true isolation. Impossible to find it on your own, the owner will come and collect you from São Orgaos, or you can follow him up the bumpy track if you have your own sturdy 4x4.

Cabo Ned (2 rooms) 271 1500; **m** 921 0488; **e** info@caboned.com; www.caboned.com. For a true wilderness experience in the middle of the island, ideal for hiking. Built on the childhood home of the hostess. Activities also include birdwatching, photo-safaris & day trips. Can accommodate up to 5 guests, bookable daily or weekly, on a B&B, HB or FB basis. The guesthouse has 2 bedrooms, living area & stunning terrace with great views. English & Dutch spoken. **$$**

ASSOMADA
Recently granted the rank of *cidade* (city), Assomada nevertheless still feels like a country town and does not possess the infrastructure of the two other 'real' Cape Verdean cities, Praia and Mindelo. It is the capital of the region of Santa Catarina, the grain basket of Santiago. It is an ancient town, as old as Cape Verde's human history, and was often more highly populated than Cidade Velha.

GETTING THERE AND AWAY By public transport, the journey from Praia takes 1½ hours (250$). *Alugueres* leave all day from Sucupira Market, returning to Praia until late at night. Private taxis cost 4,000—5,000$ for half a day.

The drive to Assomada is spectacular, particularly after João Teves, when jagged clifftops rear into view and there are vistas into valleys on both sides of the road. A rock formation that looks like the profile of a recumbent face has been christened the Marquês de Pombal rock, after a statue of that nobleman in Lisbon. Other rocks are said to look like a man on a horse, though locals say that the resemblance depends on how much *grogue* you've consumed. Climbing out of the Pico you can, on a clear day, see the island of Maio to the east, before the descent into Assomada.

🏠 **WHERE TO STAY AND EAT** There are half a dozen places to stay in Assomada, from budget to smart mid-range. The two below are probably the best town-centre options. As there is usually a good wind blowing through town, the hotels' lack of AC is not a problem. The new Pousada Vassora provides an out-of-town alternative.

🏠 **Pousada Vassora** (5 rooms) ☎ 265 3800; e pousada.vassora@gmail.com; www.pousada-vassora@gmail.com. Countryside location, about 3km from town. Tasteful, spacious rooms have private bath & balcony, some with TV. French-owned, cooking is both Cape Verdean & international. **$$$**

🏠 **Hotel Avenida** (16 rooms) Av Amílcar Cabral; ☎ 265 3462; www.caboverde.com/pages/653462.htm. Clean, well-kept & bright with large rooms & good-quality bathrooms. All have TV & fridge, but no fans or AC. Not all rooms have views – ask for a top-floor room with a mountain view. The Avenida also has a decent rooftop restaurant. FB available. **$$**

🏠 **Hotel Cosmos** (9 rooms) ☎ 265 3738; e ccomercialcosmos@cvtelecom.cv. Up 2 flights of stairs. Opposite the market, right in the middle of town. Large rooms with fans, en suite (some with baths) & ornate doors. FB available. Very spacious suites available if you fancy a splurge. The top floor is a restaurant, with live music on Sat nights & panoramic views. **$$**

OTHER PRACTICALITIES
Airlines
Airline and other tickets are available from Orbitur (☎ 265 1767), left of the aluguer stop.

Bank
Many options, including BCA, Banco Interatlantico (both with ATMs), and Caixa Económica.

Car hire
🚐 **Garagem Monteiro** ☎ 265 1351
🚐 **Veiga Car** ☎ 265 4751; e veigacar.cv@hotmail.com

Hospital
There is a large, new hospital (☎ 265 1130).

Internet
Next to and opposite Hotel Avenida or free Wi-Fi in the main square.

Pharmacy
Farmacia Santa Catarina (☎ 265 2121).

Police
Near the Palace of Justice (☎ 265 1132).

WHAT TO SEE AND DO
Centro Cultural Norberto Tavares (*In the main square;* ☎ 265 2800) On the former site of the museum, this attractive cultural centre has a good selection of locally made crafts, including dolls, clothes, ceramics and modest jewellery. Named in honour of a well–known musician who was born in the town and died in 2010. A small display cabinet contains mementoes to him.

Museu de Tabanka This museum has now relocated from the main square to the village of Chão de Tanque, some 15 minutes' drive away. Ask directions at the Centro Cultural (see above). The museum covers the history of Assomada and Santa Catarina and gives extensive coverage to the musical form of *tabanka*. There are also interesting displays of pictures, instruments and other objects.

African market With all the mesmerising colours, smells and noise of a West African market, this is held in the town centre every day, but ramps up a notch on Wednesdays and Saturdays. You can buy a chicken, dead or alive, whole or in pieces; you can buy a dog, step on a dog or simply be barked at by a dog. On the two busy days, near the schools in the southernmost part of town, there is a livestock market. Pigs, cows, goats and the smell of freshly cooking *chouriço* makes this worth the trip. At the end of the day, logic is defied as small pick–up trucks are crammed to bursting (and beyond) with villagers and their purchases, before trundling off home.

On Saturday evenings, the hustle and bustle moves to the main square, where hundreds gather to hang out and chat – and to surf the free Wi-Fi.

Porto Rincão   This little fishing village is reached by turning west at Assomada (or catching an *aluguer* from beside the market or from the road junction) and following a fantastic road to the coast. There are deep red canyons and a stunning view of Fogo sitting on its cloud cushion across the water. Halfway along, the cobbled road turns to dirt. It's a 24km round trip, but if you have time for just one foray down to the west coast, we recommend the more northerly one, to Ribeira da Barca.

Boa Entrada   North along the main road from Assomada, just slightly out of town lies a signposted turning to this village, which lies in the green valley that meanders down to the east. You can walk down to Boa Entrada from Assomada. Dominating the valley is a magnificent, centuries-old kapok tree, in which nests one of the few known colonies of Cape Verde heron, known locally as *garça vermelha* (*Ardea purpurea bournei*). (For more on this bird, see pages 6 and 164) Another colony is at Banana de Ribeira Montanha, near Pedra Badejo and they can also be seen at the Serra Malagueta – see page 188. This tree might be the biggest you will ever see and is said to have been there when the island was discovered.

The valley can be reached by several obvious paths. One leads down to a white church with pinnacles and a green door and from there to the tree. There is also a

(see pages 6 and 164)

BADIUS AND REBELADOS

The Badius were at the heart of the Santiago peasant population. Whenever there was a pirate attack, or drought caused some social chaos on the island, some of the slaves would seize the opportunity and flee into the mountainous interior. There, though in exile in a restricted and infertile area, they had freedom. The Badius form the African core of Cape Verdean society, reflected in their music, which harks back to the African coast for inspiration, and in other aspects of culture. Because of this they have been despised by many. It was from the Badius that the Rebelados movement arose as a reaction against the arrival in the 1940s of the Portuguese Catholic priests of the Holy Spirit Congregation. They wished to purify Catholicism, eliminating the many native practices which were based on a clashing personal spiritualism. It is said that those who stuck to the old methods in regard to baptisms, marriages and other rituals were imprisoned or persecuted.

Ultimately the movement coalesced around practices such as the communal farming of land, the refusal to deal with money and a prohibition on killing living creatures. As their rebellion centred on treasuring traditions and rejecting change, they also renounced many of today's luxuries such as television and radio. When they thwarted an antimalarial campaign by refusing the fumigation of their homes, their leaders were arrested and dispersed to other islands. Some still live in the Santiago highlands in distinctive dwellings; their houses can be seen from the main road. They object to being photographed.

5

cobbled road that leads down from the main road about 100m further on, but if you are driving down, you'll need a 4x4 to get there – and back.

House of Amílcar Cabral
House of Amílcar Cabral National hero Amílcar Cabral lived as a child in a yellow-walled, red-roofed house set back from the main road that leads north from Boa Entrada, on the left-hand side. However, he spent most of his short life in São Vicente, Portugal and the African mainland. The house is not open to the public.

Ribeira da Barca and Achada Leite
Ribeira da Barca and Achada Leite It should be possible to reach this village by *aluguer* but there may be some long waits at the road junction. It's a 6km walk so it could make a pleasant day trip.

As you leave the vicinity of Boa Entrada start counting churches that possess separate bell towers. After the second one on the left there is a fork in the road – turn left and follow the cobbled track as it swings past a dramatic canyon on the left and continues past deeply carved *ribeiras* all the way to this beautiful beachside village. Sadly, most of the black sand that characterised the beach has long since been removed for house construction, but it still has character.

✗ Where to eat and drink
✗ **Restaurante Riba Mar** ✆ 265 9017; m 991 6764. About 200m up the *ribeira* to the right as you enter Ribeira da Barca town, this is a pleasant place for a meal of fresh fish or a drink. Live music most Sats. $

SERRA MALAGUETA

Situated in northern-central Santiago, Serra Malagueta is an important area ecologically and one of the last remaining forest resources on Santiago. It is the starting point for some classic Santiago hikes.

The heart of the area is now a natural park, which spans 774ha and reaches a height of 1,064m at the peak of Monte Malagueta. The park houses important threatened and endemic species (see page 164). There is even one local endemic, the *carqueja de Santiago*, a small shrub that lives between 500m and 800m. The ecotourist facilities offered are not as well advanced as those in Fogo or São Nicolau but the management has created a campsite and marked out (on a map and information boards) some suggested hikes covering in total 55km and with a wide range of difficulty and duration. There are no guides at present, though some may be available if you ask around in Tarrafal.

While hiking in the area, watch out for vervet monkeys and for the rare endemic Cape Verde purple heron or *garça vermelha* (*Ardea (purpurea) bournei*), which can be seen here in the trees near the Centro Ambiental. Santiago is its only home.

WHERE TO STAY AND EAT Unless you are making use of the campsite, it's best to stay in Tarrafal or Assomada. There is no other readily available accommodation.

WHAT TO SEE AND DO
Centro Ambiental (✆ 265 3707; e ecoserramalagueta@gmail.com; www.areasprotegidas.gov.cv) A renovated Portuguese house at the entrance to the park, reached by following a downhill track for 200m from the left side of the road to Tarrafal near the Serra Malagueta School. This is the place to get a pamphlet, available in Portuguese or English, have a drink, organise your camping or buy

handicrafts. Note that the 'camping' is in cabins, and tents are not allowed. The view down into the valley from the *centro* is spectacular.

TARRAFAL

A cobalt sea, a string of little coves and a flat land under the forbidding mountains are what make Tarrafal. Don't be deterred by the shabby entrance to town and the half-built villas between you and the sea. The beach beyond the main square is of lovely soft sand and there's a jumble of life going on there: fishermen, local sports fanatics, sunbathers and lots of dogs. This place becomes packed at weekends but is very quiet midweek. It can be a bit windy and depressing during the harmattan period from December to March.

It is a good base for doing some of the walks the island offers and it is easy to laze away a few days here – the beach is cosier and more lived-in than Santa Maria in Sal, though it has none of the awesome splendour of beaches on the flat islands. There can be quite a few mosquitoes at night.

Tarrafal's mention in the history books comes from its notorious prison, 3km before town on the main Praia road, on the west side (see page 192).

GETTING THERE AND AWAY The 80km trip from Praia along the central road takes two hours and *alugueres* leave all day from Sucupira Market (500$); you may have to change in Assomada. To return to Praia on the same, inland road catch an *aluguer* from where the Praia road joins the main square of Tarrafal. They run until early evening. To return along the coastal road find an *aluguer* behind the church in the main square along with women returning from their early forays to Tarrafal Beach to buy fish. *Alugueres* on this road rarely go all the way to Praia so you will have to change where necessary (200$ to Calheta; 250$ Calheta to Praia).

 WHERE TO STAY

🏠 **King Fisher Resort** (9 lodges & apts) ☏266 1007; e hrolfs1@gmx.net; www.king-fisher.de. In western Tarrafal, this is an imaginatively conceived set of lodges built into the rocky promontory of Ponta d'Atum, each with a terrace & its own surprises (one, for example, is built over a wave-washed grotto). King Fisher consists of apartments with kitchens rather than a hotel, & at many times of year there is a minimum booking period of 4 days. B/fast is available, though not included, & there is no bar. The German owner has plenty of information for guests, as well as a dive centre on site. There's a ladder directly into the sea, so guests can swim, but no beach. **$$$$**

🏠 **Hotel Cachoeira** (27 rooms) ☏266 1272; e reservas@hotelcachoeira.com.cv. Just back from Hotel Baia Verde. A smart new place, opened in 2012. Rooms are large, with cable TV, AC & minibar. Pizza restaurant attached. No sea view, but one suite has a terrace. **$$$**

🏠 **Hotel Baía Verde** (34 bungalows) ☏266 1128; e baiaverde@cvtelecom.cv. The chalets scattered in the shade of coconut palms on Tarrafal Beach are an appealing prospect but for some the dream is spoilt by the tattiness & the management's lack of interest in either the buildings or the guests. The chalets' isolation is an attraction but the beachfront location may actually create a feeling of insecurity. Each chalet has a TV, fridge & minibar. All have hot water, some have AC. **$$**

🏠 **Pensão Nôs Dôs** Modern accommodation in the centre of Tarrafal between the main square & the Mercado Municipal Artesanat Cultura. Most rooms have balcony & AC, some budget rooms without AC. No contact details available, so turn up & try your luck. **$$**

🏠 **Residencial La Marea** (4 rooms) ☏266 1700; m 920 3556; e residencial.marea@sapo. cv. Good, spacious rooms , en suite with ceiling fans. 100m northeast of the square. Hot showers. Restaurant & bar downstairs. Internet access. **$$**

🏠 **Hotel Sol Marina** (9 rooms) 📞266 1219; m 998 9721; e gilbertofvieira19666@hotmail.com. Located on the beach. 6 rooms have a nice sea view. A little run-down, but that's reflected in the price. Most of the rooms have a private terrace. B/fast is served on the roof terrace. **$**

🏠 **Pensão Mille Nuits** (12 rooms) 📞266 1463; e pensaomillenuits@hotmail.com. At the heart of town with respectable, budget-type rooms arranged around a bright atrium. The cheapest have shared bathrooms. All have fans, hot water. Has a restaurant serving lunch & dinner. **$**

🏠 **Pensão Tata** 📞266 1125. Simple guesthouse with smallish rooms in the centre of town. Has a restaurant serving lunch & dinner. Good budget value. **$**

✖ WHERE TO EAT AND DRINK

✖ **Altomira** 📞266 2251; m 996 3865. Through an unprepossessing doorway is a little courtyard with a bamboo roof in which is a very good restaurant run by a Frenchman, François. He serves mainly pizza & fresh fish. A hundred yards back from Baia Verde. Sometimes closes off-season (May) for vacations. **$$$$**

✖ **Baía do Tarrafal** Spanish restaurant, getting good reviews, between the Caixa Económica & the BCA. **$$$$**

✖ **Hotel Baía Verde** 📞266 1128 Open-air restaurant overlooking the beach, with main dishes starting at 950$ & sandwiches & snacks for less. The place of choice because of its location. Advance ordering is advised if there are more than a couple of people. **$$$$**

✖ **Maracuja** m 913 8854; e restmaracuja@hotmail.com. A Cape Verdean/French restaurant with excellent cuisine. Fresh fish, homemade ice cream, marvellous crepes. Local specialities can be ordered in advance. Tastefully decorated, this is highly recommended. **$$$**

✖ **Sol e Luna** m 997 9535/925 4061. Breezy Italian restaurant overlooking a small beach serving great fresh fish & pasta. Reasonably priced & good food. **$$$**

✖ **Boka Boka** 📞266 1999. Behind the church. Although it doesn't look much, it offers a variety of daily changing dishes at very good prices. **$$**

✖ **Dragoeiro** 📞266 2616. On the right-hand side of the old market, across the street from the Girrasol office. Fast service, a couple of *pratos do dias* & a chicken grill at the front. **$$**

🍽 **Bar Mama (Lanchonete Mira Mar)** 📞266 2097. Known for its excellent cakes, but also serving an inexpensive dish of the day. May also offer rooms. **$$**

🍽 **Bar Rosa** Head south from Hotel Tarrafal; only 2 tables but serves *cachupa* & good coffee. **$$**

✖ **Churrasqueira Mangui Baxo** m 994 1404. Also south of the Hotel Tarrafal. Pre-order your BBQ or be prepared to wait a couple of hours. **$$**

✖ **Sucupira Market** In & around the new market hall there are several small restaurants & snack bars that offer simple Creole dishes & cakes at very low prices. Probably the best spot to have lunch if you are on a low budget. **$**

✖ **Zenite** Main *praça*. Grilled chicken, hamburgers & chips, & a good place to watch local residents meeting in the square. **$**

ENTERTAINMENT AND NIGHTLIFE There are two late-night places: Discoteca Sagres, near the new market, and Discoteca Baía Verde, in the restaurant of the same name.

OTHER PRACTICALITIES
Bank
BCA & Caixa Economica, both near the main square & both with ATMs.

Hospital
(📞*266 1130*) On the main road to Assomada, on the left, opposite the football stadium.

Police
(📞*266 1132*) On the main road to Assomada, on the left.

Post office
(🕐 *08.00–15.30 Mon–Fri*) On the main road to Assomada, on the right.

WHAT TO SEE AND DO
Diving There are two diving outfits in Tarrafal, both operating from King Fisher Resort. For further details, see page 189.

Boating Local fishermen may take you out fishing or down the coast to Ribeira da Barca and on to Achada Leite (see page 188), if you ask at the beautifully painted Associacao dos Pescadores e Peixeiras, on the small beach at the side of Baia Verde restaurant. Negotiate, but expect to pay around 6,000$ per boat (not per person) for two hours.

Mercado Municipal Artesanat Cultura (⏲ 07.00–18.00 Mon–Sat) In a courtyard next to the main square, this houses a selection of stalls selling handicrafts and souvenirs. The number of stalls varies from day to day. Some of the wooden items, though attractive, are from mainland Africa rather than Cape Verde itself.

Surfing Before midday, the break to the west of the bay is good and extends all the way down to Ribeira da Prata. Many locals favour the water near King Fisher. There are no official places to rent boards, but if you ask around those breaking the waves, you should find a friendly local who will oblige for a fee.

Hiking Tarrafal is a good starting point for several hikes, including the short walk to the lighthouse and the walk down Ribeira Principal (see page 193).

OTHER PLACES TO VISIT

CALHETA DE SÃO MIGUEL There's no particular reason for stopping the night here, although it is a pretty enough coastal town. It is a useful starting and end point for some hikes to and from the interior. To get there from Praia take an *aluguer* from Sucupira Market that is travelling up the coastal road; from Tarrafal catch an *aluguer* from behind the church in the main square. From Assomada you can catch an *aluguer* that takes an interesting route down a cross-country road to Calheta.

🏠 Where to stay
🏠 **Villa Morgana** (24 rooms) ☎ 273 1628; m 996 9356; e contact@villamorgana.com, www.villamorgana.com. An interesting array of villas scattered around a central restaurant & pool. Claims to have a 'private' beach, though locals insist it is public. Each room has fan & outdoor space. Prices vary according to season: some clients report overcharging, so confirm & reconfirm price at the outset. **$$$$**

🏠 **Hotel Edu Horizonte** (32 rooms) m 994 4040/594 3003; e emanuelsantos_2@hotmail.com or hoteledu-horizonte@sapo.cv. Near the Shell petrol station as you enter town from the north. Spacious rooms, en suite, with TV & fan. Good, busy restaurant (**$$$**) downstairs. **$$**

🏠 **Mira Maio** (5 rooms) ☎ 273 1121; e info@miramaio.com. At the southern end of town, off a road leading down to the shore. Varied rooms, some large, some with balconies, some with TV & fridge. Rooftop terrace with coastal views. **$$**

✗ Where to eat and drink
✗ **Esplanada Silibell** Ponta Calhetona; ☎ 273 2078; e info@silibell.com; ⏲ 12.00–22.00 Mon–Sat. Situated at the southern end of Calheta, on the right as you head south, this is an open-air restaurant & bar with a sea view. It's the place to recover from the heat of the day & mull over what you have seen with Gerhard & Sibylle Schellmann, the German owners. The Schellmanns have been in Calheta for years & willingly offer tourist information as well as tour operator services, specialising in hiking in the hinterland (see also page 168). They will also give sound advice on local accommodation choices. **$$$$**

✗ **Loja Casa Tute and Bar Esperança** ⏲ 08.00–22.00 daily. Friendly, thatched open-air bar with good-quality local dishes made from fresh ingredients (order meals a day beforehand). **$$$$**

PEDRA BADEJO This growing settlement is located a little north of Praia Baixo along the northeast coast. Some people love this coastal settlement but it can be hard to see beyond the sprawl, rocks, litter and cement-block buildings, many unfinished. Admittedly, the large black-sand beach at the southern end is quite impressive. A collaboration between local community groups and the Austrian town of Leibnitz has resulted in a nature-guide service based at **Casa Ecotec** (m *989 5914;* e *geovision.boedendorfer@aon.at; http://ecotec.geo-vision.info/hikes_en.php; see below and opposite for more details*) in order to encourage sustainable ecotourism in this area. Multilingual guides will take you on birdwatching beach walks and more strenuous hikes all over the island as well as cultural tours.

Where to stay and eat

Palm Beach (16 rooms) 269 2888/594 5941 (multilingual line); e palm.beach.cv@gmail.com; www.capeverdehotel.no. A large yellow building on the coastal side of the main road, this is smart, vast & newish, if a bit soulless. Rooms have TV & AC, are spacious & finished to a high standard, though seem overpriced. There are very few alternatives nearby. There's a restaurant on the ground floor with terraces overlooking the beach, & 2 conference rooms. Wi-Fi access available. The hotel can arrange local excursions, for example in fishing boats. **$$$**

Casa Ecotec (3 rooms) 269 1064; m 989 5914; e geovision.boedendorfer@aon.at; http://ecotec.geo-vision.info/house_en.php. Simple accommodation in pleasant rooms overlooking a courtyard facing the sea, 2km south of Pedra Badejo in the village of Achada Igreja. The drive through the village is a little off-putting as there are no signs, so make sure you ask for directions. Part of an Austrian project to develop sustainable tourism in the area; guided walks, hiking & cultural tours can be arranged in many languages. The owner is an expert birdwatcher. Meals can be arranged. **$**

PRAIA BAIXO Located on the northeast coast of Santiago about 20km from Praia, this spot is noted for its safe beach. Sir Francis Drake is thought to have made a landfall here. Recent closures mean that there is now no accommodation here. The Restaurant Morabeza may re-open shortly.

SÃO FRANCISCO With superb beaches and deserted coves, this is the best place near Praia for a day in the sun. The on/off saga of the Sambala Resort rumbles on, with stories of Indian investors putting in the funds to complete a project that has stuttered since its inception. Perhaps within the lifespan of this guide, Sambala will transform itself from idea to reality.

Getting there and away *Alugueres* leave approximately every 30 minutes from Paul, behind Fazenda in Praia and cost about 80$. They drop you in the village of São Francisco from where it is a walk of several kilometres downhill to the beach. A taxi costs about 1,800$ each way.

✖ Where to eat and drink
✖ **Catumbela** m 991 5459. The only restaurant, with fish specialities & meat dishes. **$**

HIKES *Alexander Hirtle (AH); Aisling Irwin (AI); Colum Wilson (CW)*

1 SERRA MALAGUETA–HORTELÃO–RIBEIRA PRINCIPAL (LONGER ROUTE)
Distance: 13km; time: 4½ hours; difficulty: 3 (AH)
This is a beautiful walk, and the peak time for it is between mid-August and early December (late October is probably the greenest and most picturesque). Beware, though, that during the rainy season that usually starts mid–late July and ends mid-October, trails can be slippery and, in a good year for rain, wiped out with streams rushing through them. Visibility can also be limited due to cloud cover and the rain itself. The walks are mainly downhill, but continual downhill jaunts can be very stressful on knees and ankles. You need to get transport up to the area of Serra Malagueta. From Assomada, an *aluguer* costs 100$. Tell the driver to drop you off at the secondary road with the gate (*portão*), before the primary school (*escola*).

Follow the secondary road, which is clear and wide with generally good footing, up several hundred feet; it makes winding turns, some so sharp and steep you'll wonder how vehicles get up there. There are some excellent views of the *ribeira* off to the left. As you continue upwards, the flora changes. You'll see groups of pine trees, part of a continual reafforestation project in which the locals participate. It is a necessary programme, because local residents are always collecting firewood from the area (you may pass several people coming down the road carrying loads of wood on their heads). Continue up the road and it begins to level off. You are near one of the highest points on the island, **Serra Malagueta**. There are spectacular views to the right; you may even be above the cloud cover, depending on the day. Watch the sides of the cliffs though: a misplaced step will send you hundreds of feet down. Continue on the road, and past a small clearing where at times vehicles are parked.

5

This is highly recommended, as the interior of Santiago is a drama worth making the effort to see. It could be accomplished in one day but this would be pretty exhausting – it is better, if possible, to travel from Praia to Tarrafal, Assomada or another location with accommodation on the first day and return down the coast road on the second. If you have time take the left turn after Assomada (just before Fundura) and visit Ribeira da Barca for a vivid glimpse of the terrain leading to the west coast. There is a cursory description of the landscape below – for more information see the entries above.

The drive begins through the urban sprawl of Praia – ever expanding as people move from the villages to the city. As you reach the countryside you should see the long yellow flowers of aloe vera lining the roadside, along with, at the right time of year, maize and haricot beans. About 12km from the centre of Praia, where you take the left turn, you begin to gaze down into a green valley. The road passes through São Domingos and Assomada – springboards for visiting all the places described above. After marvelling at the Pico do Santo António and its surrounding craggy peaks you will later come to the Serra Malagueta – the other high point of Santiago.

From Tarrafal, the journey to Praia along the coast is 2½ hours. There is less to stop for than on the inland road but the drive is spectacular, tracing hairpin bends that take you into verdant creeks with compact black-sand beaches, waves crashing over brooding rocks and out again into the dry mountainsides. The houses have hay piled high on their flat roofs and sometimes goats live there too. Wires stick out of the top of every house in anticipation of the building of the next storey. Pigs forage round the houses and the dry landscape.

After Calheta the land becomes almost lush with great banana plantations, coconut trees and always the yellow of aloe vera poking up from cacti-like leaves.

Stay to the right, along the drop-off, but not too close to it. The paths to the left lead to somewhat dangerous wooded areas. You will begin to descend, as the path takes a left turn and leads you into very green and beautiful woods: thus begins the decline to Ribeira Principal.

The path switchbacks several times; it is important to stay on the main path that generally goes to the left of the ridge and eventually to the bottom of the *ribeira*. If you find yourself going down to the right of the ridge, you will need to retrace your steps and find the correct path again. You will descend to an area with some enclosed animal pens and houses. Most residents here are very friendly, but it's wise to respect their privacy and property as on occasion you may meet a local who is not always happy with foreigners passing by. After entering the first area of houses, continue through another area with sets of houses and, as the path veers to the right, walk along an area that is a small ridge where the drop-off is steep to the left, shallow on the right. You will reach an area where the path quickly drops down, makes a slight turn to the right, and then a sharp turn to the left. This place can be dangerous when it is wet, so take it slow and steady. The path then takes you along a lower terrace that brings you to the left side of the *ribeira*. You will descend further to more houses, again staying along the lower ridge that overlooks the *ribeira*. There are very good views here: you can see the terracing of the agricultural areas, and the isolated *vilas* below. In several places there are diverging paths, so you need constantly to ask the locals the way to Hortelão, the *vila* just past Ribeira Principal. You will come to a converging area that will bring you across to the right side of the *ribeira*. You may not notice it at first, but once you leave the more dense areas with houses, you will be following the lower ridge on the right side of **Ribeira Principal**.

Continue to descend, past some fantastic rock structures on the right including a keyhole in one part of the ridge. Your final climb down is full of tricky switchbacks. The path eventually takes you to the bottom of the *ribeira*, to **Hortelão**. Waiting vehicles can take you to Tarrafal, or Calheta, where you can change vehicles to return to Assomada, or Praia. Alternatively, you can walk the extra 30–40 minutes along the road to the main road, but it is not the most scenic part of the trip, and may take longer if you are tired and hungry.

2 SERRA MALAGUETA–RIBEIRA PRINCIPAL (SHORTER ROUTE)

Distance: 8km; time: 3½ hours; difficulty: 2 (AH)
The second, and shorter, way down the pretty Ribeira Principal starts from the *vila* of Serra, at the small market, or *mercearia*. The owner, Marcilino, can point out the path that starts your descent.

The first part is tricky: steep switchbacks where it is easy to slip. Take it slowly, and when you come to the first major fork (about 0.5km from the road) take a left.

This second path is much simpler than the first: the higher part of the walk stays to the left of the *ribeira* the entire time. The path levels off quickly as it leads you onto a lower ridge, again staying on the left side of the *ribeira*. You can see the beautiful terracing of the lower gorge, the isolated houses, and the forested view of the opposite side of the *ribeira* – the route for the longer hike to Ribeira Principal (see previous hike). The path follows the ridge and then cuts inward (to the right), descending towards the centre of the *ribeira*. It cuts back and forth but leads mainly to the right, ending up at the bottom centre of the *ribeira* in a lush oasis of mango trees and sugarcane.

This is a good area to stop and have lunch. You will probably see locals coming and going, carrying water from the tank, or maybe sugarcane: give them passing space with their heavy loads. As you follow the path, you will pass several *grogue* distilleries. Many owners enjoy demonstrating how their distillery operates; feel free to enquire, but you may find they are at a tricky moment and can't take a break just now. Follow the path that climbs just a bit to the higher area of the oasis and goes through several small *vilas*. The path continues a little longer, again descending slightly to the lowest part of the *ribeira* where it ends at a large *grogue* distillery. By showing interest in the facility, and some friendly rapport in Portuguese, Creole, or maybe limited English, you may be invited to sample some of their *grogue*. Nearby vehicles can take you onto the main Tarrafal–Calheta road.

3 CHÃO BOM–RIBEIRA DA PRATA–FIGUEIRA DAS NAUS

Distance: 9km; time: 3½ hours; difficulty: 2 (AI)
This is an attractive, if lonely, walk that begins on the level, following the coast as far as Ribeira da Prata. It then toils uphill along a remorselessly shadeless track, relieved by the drama of the canyons and the vista back towards the sea. The walk is on road and track and there are no problems with slipperiness or steep slopes, but the 1½-hour upward slog from Ribeira da Prata requires a certain amount of fitness if it is to be enjoyable. To get to the beginning of the walk at Chão Bom (pronounced 'shambome'), travel for about five minutes by *aluguer* from Tarrafal along the Assomada road. The turning to Ribeira da Prata is signposted, on the right, at the beginning of Chão Bom.

From the Tarrafal side of Chão Bom, take the road signposted **Ribeira da Prata**, passing initially through slums. Leaving habitation behind, the lonely road passes in and out of the coastal fractals for about an hour, revealing eventually the black-sand beach of the *ribeira* with acacia and coconut palms offering a bit of shade. The bottom of the valley is where people pause in the shade to rest. Follow the road out, up, into the village and out of the other side after which it will do a great loop backwards and upwards to ascend into the hills.

This is an extremely quiet road and, as it ascends, there are views back to Tarrafal, to the harshly bright sea and over the rocky ground that characterises the western side of Santiago. There is a huge amount of reafforestation here. Some 1½ hours after leaving Ribeira da Prata the track begins to pass through a series of villages, including Figueira Muite and Marmulano, most of which have bars tucked away – all you have to do is ask for them. Some 2½ hours from Ribeira da Prata you reach **Figueira das Naus** with its pretty church. Here the road divides and you can wait for an *aluguer* (there are three to four per day) to take you along the right fork and back to the main Tarrafal–Assomada road.

Alternatively, if you have a taste for more of this rocky, inland drama, you can walk the 8km to the main road. Just take the right fork and remain on the same track, ignoring a single right turn.

4 MONTE XOTA–PICO DO SANTO ANTÓNIO–MONTE XOTA
Time: 6 hours; difficulty: 3 (AI)
This walk is quite dangerous and only for the fit and sure-footed. Even then, the final ascent is up a dangerously steep and crumbling slope. All the rules of hiking apply (for health advice, see page 63), in particular that you should go in a group of at least three and wear boots with good grip. Take two litres of water for each person. Set off before 11.00. For the middle third of the journey the path is obscure or non-existent and one needs to trust to an understanding of the topography to find the way up the ridge to the top. Sadly, it is hard to find a competent guide. There are many local men who will agree to take you but few know the way or understand that most Westerners are less fleet of foot than they – so they may give you a false sense of security. The soldiers at the telecommunications station at the start of the walk work on rotation and may never have been up the Pico.

The walk begins at the telecommunications installation, on a path opposite its entrance. The path disappears into the vegetation and winds back behind the station. Almost immediately there's a view of the curved pincers of the Pico. Climb down the low wall ahead of you and follow the path that goes round the installation and then branches away to the northwest. You emerge on a little ridge and already the views are spectacular, with Fogo visible to the west and within five minutes, views of São Domingos and Serra Malagueta.

For the next half-hour the path is clear, descending through pleasant forest, past a couple of smallholdings and in and out of the valleys until you are in the position from which to begin the ascent up the spur that leads to the top.

The ascent will take two–three hours, depending on fitness and agility. After the first 1½–2 hours, you reach the lesser peak.

5 MONTE XOTA ANTENNAE–SÃO DOMINGOS
Distance: 5km; time: 2 hours; difficulty: 1 (AI)
Spectacular views accompany this downhill walk from the antennae station at the peak of Monte Xota to the town of São Domingos on the main road. The road is cobbled throughout and navigation is simple: just head downwards. If you become

tired at any point, you can just sit and wait for the next *aluguer* – these are fairly frequent from Rui Vaz downwards. To reach Monte Xota for the beginning of the walk either take a public *aluguer* as far as the Rui Vaz turning and walk, or charter an *aluguer* in São Domingos, which should cost around 700$.

Try to kick off the walk by gaining entry to the grounds of the Monte Xota telecommunications station and climbing the knoll to the right. The soldiers there may let you in if you ask nicely and they are not too busy. From the knoll you can see spread before you the heart of Santiago. Retracing your steps, join the road and enjoy the greenery and the sharply scented, cool air before it fades as you descend. The magnificent cobbled road takes you through sheer cliffs and craggy rock formations with occasional glimpses of Pico do Santo António, the canine tooth poking up behind them. Watch out for Pico de João Teves, one of many raw, majestic shapes, which looks like the top of a submarine. You will also pass the president's holiday home, on the left.

Further down the road descends towards the valley and travels parallel with it before a left and a right turn deposit you on the main road just in the north of São Domingos.

6 ASSOMADA–POILÃO–RIBERÃO BOI–SANTA CRUZ

Distance: 16km; time: 5 hours; difficulty: 1 (CW)

This is a long, gentle walk down a shallow *ribeira*. If you want to see rural corners of Santiago without tackling tougher peaks, this is a good walk to do, though it is not as interesting as many of the others. There are several active *grogue* distilleries along the route, where people will be only too happy to let you try some of the raw spirit, often still warm from the still. Your path is an easy, valley-floor track throughout. But if you want to avoid a one-off scramble down a rock face, you have to take a brief detour up the valley side.

The track out of Assomada is a little tricky to find – the best thing to do is to ask for **Poilão** (not to be confused with the location near the dam further south, of the same name), where there is a tourist-friendly distillery (or *trapiche*) (see box, page 78). The track to Poilão threads along the right-hand side of the head of the *ribeira*, and finally brings you down to the valley floor about 1.5km out of Assomada.

You will know you have arrived because you will pass two large concrete tanks on your right. Turn right along the *ribeira* floor – the beginning of the path does not look promising, but does improve.

After about 500m, you will pass the Poilão *trapiche* on your right. There is usually pressing or distillation in progress (except Saturday, when the week's produce is taken to market).

From the *trapiche*, follow the track along the valley floor. Before the track bears round to the east, you will pass the outskirts of **Boa Entrada** on your left. After about 3km of easy walking from the *trapiche* you will see a line of houses on a high crag which projects into the valley from your left. Just before the track cuts up to the left, stay on the valley floor by taking a small path down to the right at the point where the track crosses a riverbed. There is a small concrete-lined spring directly beside the track.

Approximately 1km from the turning you will pass another *trapiche* on your left. If you continue on at this point, the path enters a tight gorge, and you will have to scramble down a 2m drop that interrupts the path.

You can avoid this by turning right, out of the valley floor, opposite the *trapiche*. After about 15m, take a steep path leading up a ridge on your left. After about ten minutes, this path passes over the shoulder, and you can take a small steep path on the left which will bring you back down to the valley floor, on the other side of the 2m drop.

Continue along the track in the valley floor for another 6.5km (about one hour 40 minutes), and you will reach **Riberão Boi**. Just before you arrive, you will pass beneath a high cliff face on your left, where the rock has formed into dramatic faceted columns.

From Riberão Boi to the Calheta–Pedra Badejo road it is about 3.5km. On the road, you can pick up an *aluguer*.

7 CALHETA–FLAMENGOS DE BAIXO–RIBEIRETA–CALHETA
Distance: 11km; time: 3¼ hours; difficulty: 1 (AI)

This is a pleasant little walk with no great ascents or descents, although it is quite rocky underfoot. It is not a walk of great drama but it shows off plenty of Santiago rural life on the way: from *trapiches* to terracing, and water extraction to traditional stone housing. The middle of the walk, up in the verdant hills, is very pretty.

Walk south out of Calheta along the main road as far as the big bridge across Ribeira dos Flamengos. Descend the rocky track into the *ribeira* and turn inland, among the palm trees. Wander up the *ribeira* for 1½ hours, past three windmills in total, until you confront an earth road that crosses the *ribeira* and heads up to the right, becoming cobbled very quickly. Now you are walking uphill in pretty countryside. Some 15 minutes after joining the road, you reach a 'crossroads'. Go straight across, and then turn right, down the riverbed, disturbing clusters of butterflies as you go.

The descent down this second *ribeira* involves negotiating your way round several barrages. See the tiny, drystone terraces and hear the dogs, cockerels, goats and people, whose echoes help to make *ribeira* life a noisy experience.

Some 15 minutes after passing a pumping station on your right you will reach the main road. Turn right and walk for another 15 minutes through Calheta to reach the bridge again.

8 TARRAFAL–LIGHTHOUSE–TARRAFAL
Distance: 6km; time: 2½ hours; difficulty: 2 (AI)

Note: there have been muggings on this route; ask locally about safety and/or take a guide.

This walk will take you from the Tarrafal cove to the lighthouse at the foot of the big headland to the north of Tarrafal, which you can see from the beach. It involves a steep scramble at the end and there is no shade – take at least 1.5 litres of water and a hat.

Go to the north end of the most northerly cove of the beach and follow a little sand path up through the rocks and past the last of the holiday bungalows. You can see the path cut into the cliff side ahead. Keep an eye on it as it often disappears underfoot. After 30 minutes clinging to the headland, the path turns inland to face an inhospitable ravine strewn with huge boulders from a landslide. There is a path, though it turns to a scramble at times. When you have reached the end of it follow a path out along the big bulge of land, past deserted drystone walls built to keep cattle.

Instead of turning to the lighthouse you can continue up the coast and walk for hours, even as far as a distant cove (about three hours). It really is empty and there are exhilarating views down green stone canyons and up the coastline.

9 SALINEIRO–CIDADE VELHA
Distance: 4km; time: 1½ hours; difficulty: 2 (AI)

This walk plunges you from a dry, impoverished village up on the escarpment down into the verdant *ribeira* of Cidade Velha and past a few of the old city's important

Alex Alper

High along the jagged cliffs of Serra Malagueta Natural Park, green nets billow in the wind like a half-erected modern art installation. They are, in reality, fog collectors, harvesting water from the clouds that shroud the park in almost year-round mist. The technology is simple: water vapour condenses along the mesh surface, forming droplets that fall into a gutter below and on to a holding tank. How much water could that possibly provide? More than you might think. Fog contains 0.05–3ml of water per m^3. Serra Malagueta, which receives only about 900mm of rainfall per year, has a semi-permanent layer of 'stratocumulus' – low-lying clouds – pushed upwards from the coast by the mountains themselves. Thanks to these clouds, Serra Malagueta's 120 metres of netting (suspended on eight separate frames) produce approximately 1,440 litres per day, with production reaching 75 litres per metre of net per day in the rainy season. That's a big help for the park's 488 families, who rely principally on local springs, wells, and private cisterns for their water. Rainfall is decreasing and underground sources are drying up, but 80% of Serra Malaguetans still earn their livelihood in agriculture.

Fog water is free from the microbes that contaminate ground water, requiring no treatment. Construction materials – mesh, plastic tubing, and wood or metal poles – are cheap and readily accessible worldwide. The most challenging aspect is positioning the nets accurately, and scientists say that fog harvesting will not damage the microclimate.

Despite these benefits, fog harvesting does not constitute a major source of water in Cape Verde. While 1,133ha of Cape Verde's territory are considered suitable, fog is currently harvested only on Santiago (though efforts are currently underway to install them on São Nicolau). Yet potential national output is estimated at roughly 14 million m^3 of water per year.

ruins before depositing you in the main square. This *ribeira* is quite lush with a wide variety of trees and the canyons on either side are magnificently striated. It's not hard but the initial descent is steep and shingly underfoot.

Take an *aluguer* from the old town up to the village of Salineiro for 100$, or charter a taxi for around 500–600$. At the village, ask to be set down as close as possible to the *caminho* to Cidade Velha, a path that lies a little beyond the village's water source. The path is inauspicious, rocky, steep and rubbish-strewn, but persist as it winds into the canyon, and watch the greenery of the acacias and palm trees below.

After about ten minutes of descent you reach a T-junction of paths, more or less at the treeline. Turn right towards the sea. Some 5m later you will pass piping and a barrage across the *ribeira*: there are several ways down to the *ribeira* floor.

As with many *ribeira* walks, the path emerges and fades and walkers have to negotiate themselves around the great barriers erected against the rain. Here there are mango trees, a stream and an unusual sensation of humidity. Keep heading seaward, passing a mighty baobab, and finally the route becomes a track, about an hour after the start of the walk. Some ten minutes later you will round a bend and the fort will be in sight, and a few minutes later you will pass a *grogue* distillery on your left, the Pousada São Pedro on the right. After another 5m you will find yourself in the main square of Cidade Velha.

Santiago   HIKES

5

6

Maio

Huge heaps of salt like drifts of snow, and most fine and perfect in nature, the abundance whereof is such, and the daily increase so exceeding great, that they serve all countryes and lands about them, and is impossible to be consumed.

Sir Francis Drake, British sailor, pirate and slave trader, 1578

Maio was, and some would say still is, the forgotten island. Its quiet dunes and secret beaches have been overshadowed by the more boisterous Sal and beguiling Boavista. It has been waiting to be thrust into the tourist mainstream, and fleetingly it seemed that its time had come. But plans for a massive increase in accommodation have, at least for now, been thwarted and development projects stand gathering dust. How the transport and other infrastructure was ever intended to keep pace is unclear. For many, this is a blessing, as it leaves undisturbed this island backwater. With some uncertainty over Maio's future as a mass-market destination, restaurants and tourism-related businesses are susceptible to changes of ownership and closure.

Those who live on Maio or visit it frequently justifiably claim that the island is overlooked in other ways. Flight times are often changed, cargo boats fail to materialise and as a consequence, the shops sometimes run short of supplies. But visitors may revel in the authentic feel that Maio possesses, the genuineness of the island and the seemingly gentle and welcome indifference of the inhabitants to grabbing hold of your hard-earned holiday spending money.

HIGHLIGHTS AND LOWLIGHTS

Much of Maio is flat, desolate brown desert, broken by unexpected patches of acacia forest and, in the east, relief for the eye from the odd fertile valley planted with crops and palm trees. In the rainy season, the landscape is transformed into a carpet of green, *ribeiras* are full and roads can be washed away. The main town of Cidade de Porto Inglés (formerly Vila do Maio, and still often referred to locally as the *vila*) is charming and quaint with a slight spaghetti western feel, narrow cobbled streets and brightly painted houses. But it is not Clint Eastwood who will step out of the shadows, more likely a chicken or a dog. There is little traffic to run you over and few taxis to stalk you.

Maio lacks the development of Sal or as generous a supply of beautiful dunes and oases as Boavista. It has little gripping walking. But it is this quiet that attracts some people – there are some lovely, lonely white-sand beaches. There is the biggest acacia plantation of the archipelago – and the trees are mature and green although they make surprisingly little impact on the eye, perhaps because the soil itself remains dry and bare. For naturalists there are turtles in the summer and some interesting birds, particularly seabirds on Ilhéu Laje Branca off the north of the island. There are now a few options for diving and fishing, and several good and

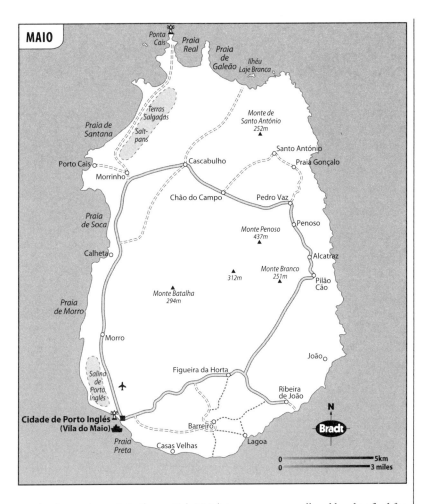

good-value restaurants in the capital. Maio's treasures are small and hard to find for the visitor, yet it remains an island with its own considerable charm.

SUGGESTED ITINERARY AND NUMBER OF DAYS There is little point in visiting Maio if your goal is to tick off the sights of Cape Verde. There's so little here, but combining it with a trip to Santiago could be the perfect combination of islands: Santiago for hiking and mountains, a strong African flavour and a bustling capital city, and Maio for the old Cape Verde, peace and tranquillity, beautiful empty beaches and a selection of reasonable restaurants. A day to visit the town and a day to undertake an island tour will be enough for most. Beyond that, Maio is really a place to flee to for a quiet retreat, a place with few distractions or competing demands. It's a destination for wandering and musing among the dunes and beaches. This could take half a day to a lifetime.

BACKGROUND INFORMATION

HISTORY Maio's one resource is its prolific salt and for this reason it was a bustling island from the late 16th century until the 19th. In a good year it exported 11,000 tonnes. Before this treasure was discovered, Maio was a grazing ground for cattle and goats, producing 4,000 head a year at its peak. But soon the fragile vegetation was eaten and there was little left to sell but salt and lime.

It was the English who commandeered the salt production because the Portuguese never had much interest in Maio. One Englishman even made a profit by loading salt at Maio and bartering it at Santiago. The salt was shovelled into sacks at the salt lake, fastened to donkeys and carried to the beach where it was loaded into boats specially designed to cope with the heavy swells in the bay. They would travel out to the boats belonging to the big ships which would themselves be anchored away from the shore.

The English ships, each laden with about 200 tonnes of salt, would leave for Newfoundland to pick up cod, salt it, and take it to Europe. Other ships took salt on journeys between Europe and the West Indies and between America and Africa. Maio's neat, tiny fort was built by English sailors left behind by Sir Francis Drake in 1588.

All through the 17th century, about 80 English ships a year called at Maio for salt; there was usually a battleship standing by to guard English interests. The Maio people were paid with some money but also with old clothes and food. It is said their houses were full of English ornaments.

By the 19th century, the principal market for salt switched to Brazil, where thousands of tonnes were sent annually. That business was killed when Brazil introduced protective tariffs at the end of the 19th century.

Maio did not escape plunder. In 1818, a pirate ship from Baltimore sacked the port, and a South American ship sacked it in 1827. In the 20th century, there were repeated droughts and emigrations.

Maio today Farming occupies about 15% of the population and fishing about 7%. The people use their now plentiful wood to turn to charcoal in underground ovens for export to other islands. There are large lime reserves and there is some gypsum. A co-operative, launched in 2003, gathers a little salt from the salina at Porto Inglés. Although several low-key holiday complexes have successfully opened in the last couple of years, sadly it is the half-built Salinas Beach that dominates the western part of the capital from the air giving the entirely false impression of a thriving beach complex. The premature publicity promised a hotel, apartments, restaurants, shops and even a golf course. Instead, there is a modern ghost town, perhaps in future destined to become an unusual tourist attraction in its own right.

But for some, the failure of the project is welcome, keeping Maio as the peaceful place it always has been, its character unchanged. The website www.maiocv.com has up-to-date news, maps and photos of what's happening on the island.

GEOGRAPHY Maio, like the other islands, is an old volcano that has slowly been eroded by the wind. But Maio is unusual because beneath the volcano that welled up out of the ocean floor was ocean sediment that ballooned up behind it. Subsequent erosion of the volcanic rock has exposed vast amounts of marine sediments that are 190 million years old, which is why some texts refer to it as the oldest island.

Maio is small, at 268km², with a population of about 4,000. It lies 25km to the east of Santiago. Its terrain is similar to Sal and Boavista with one big difference: it has been heavily reafforested in parts, almost exclusively with acacias, which can survive for years without rainfall. The highest peak is Monte Penoso at 437m. There are saltpans in the southwest and northwest and there is more fertile, agricultural land in the east.

NATURAL HISTORY Terras Salgadas, Casas Velhas, Lagoa Cimidor and Praia de Morro are natural reserves. Barreiro e Figueira is a natural park and the Salina de Porto Inglês, Monte Penoso, Monte Branco and Monte de Santo António are protected landscapes. A marine reserve stretches east of Praia Preta. For the natural history of Maio's great salina, see *Salina de Porto Inglês*, page 209.

Turtles Maio has the second-largest nesting population of loggerhead turtles (*Caretta caretta*) in the archipelago. Its long sandy beaches and limited amount of development have, in the past, made it an ideal habitat. Their survival, as elsewhere in Cape Verde, is threatened by the hunting of females for food, nest poaching and new beachfront development. There are programmes for their protection and in season it is possible to take a guided walk to see them nesting. Ask around for information when you are there.

HAZARDS Maio boasts that it is crime-free. Many northern beaches are unsafe for swimming, as is Praia Preta to the east of the capital. There is a strong current at Ponta Preta which has claimed the lives of the unsuspecting. Follow the advice, and more importantly, the actions of the locals.

A BIRD'S-EYE VIEW OF LOVE

Some birds stay faithful for life, some have a roving eye – and it was always thought that this varied according to their species. Now researchers have discovered that even within the same species you get different types of behaviour. Just as with humans, some look after their kids and some are too busy elsewhere. What intrigues scientists is what makes one bird's attitude to its eggs or chicks so different from the next. 'The classic situation is who (mother or father) should go to the disco and who should provide care for the young,' says Tamas Szekely, Professor of Biodiversity at the University of Bath, UK. 'If they both go to the disco then the babies die.'

Maio may be the place to answer this question because it is home to the Kentish plover (*Charadrius alexandrius*), the object of this research. Unlike elsewhere in the world, the Kentish plover stays in Maio all year round. Wander down to the salinas outside the vila and you might find Szekely or one of his students or volunteers manning their mobile hide, documenting behaviour, ringing birds, counting nests and taking genetic samples.

So far, it appears that the birds are remarkably good at varying their behaviour depending on what's going on around them. In Saudi Arabia, where they lay their eggs in the heat of the desert, it takes two parents to run the show: one to sit on the eggs to keep them cool and the other to fetch food. In less demanding environments like Maio two parents may not be so vital – might this liberate one, and if so is it mum or dad who gets to play around? Even more intriguingly, it looks as if even one individual bird may behave differently from one relationship to another. 'If you are a good mother in one family it doesn't mean you will be a good mother in a different family,' says Szekely.

Kentish plovers nest on the ground and start to breed after the annual rains (usually from September onwards). This is when Szekely and his team start their work. In addition to the plovers, the salina harbours breeding populations of cream-coloured courser (*Cursorius cursor exsul*) and the greater hoopoe lark (*Alaemon alaudipes*). It also hosts migratory waders and waterbirds. Protection of the salina is an issue, because both the research.and the habitat were briefly threatened by the massive new Salinas construction site right on the edge of the salina. The future of the two seem inextricably linked.

6

The religious festival of Santa Cruz on 3 May, and the saints' days in June, are the biggest celebrations. There is a music festival at the beginning of September.

2 February	Nossa Sra do Rosário
19 March	São José (Calheta)
3 May	Santa Cruz (Maio)
13 June	Santo António (Santo António)
24 June	São João (Ribeira de João)
29 June	São Pedro (Pedro Vaz)
26 July	Santa Ana (Morrinho)
1st week September	Music festival (Cidade de Porto Inglés)

GETTING THERE AND AWAY

BY AIR There's a ten-minute TACV flight from Praia, the frequency of which varies enormously. At time of writing, this had been cut to twice weekly, much to the disgust of the Maio inhabitants. Yet suddenly, and without warning, the frequency may accelerate to four per day – temporarily and without logic. Even more than the other islands, it is vital when travelling to and from Maio to check and recheck that your flight has not been rescheduled. Any sudden shortage of aircraft seems to target Maio first, before it impacts on the other more-frequented islands. *Hiaces* wait at the airport (✆ *255 1108/256 1370*) and can be chartered as taxis for the five-minute trip to town. It is easy to walk the few kilometres into the centre, though tiring if laden with luggage: facing the sea, the town can be seen to the left. Take the only road, towards the sea, and turn left at the T-junction. Pass the saltpans and in about 40 minutes you are in town. On departure, ask around the hotels for transport back to the airport or allow time to walk.

BY FERRY Ferries come and ferries go and Maio has suffered from their vagaries more than most. There is generally some sort of service from Praia, currently the Sotavento operated by Polar Shipping (✆ *261 5223*) who have an office in Praia. Usually it arrives in Maio on a Friday and returns on a Sunday. Sometimes it doesn't arrive at all. Check with the ferry companies on the Plateau in Praia. When you are ready to leave Maio ask around or keep an eye on the port – there is no booking office and the tour operators in town do not book tickets. Ferry travel is an option for those on a budget and without time constraints, costing around 1,500$ each way, but given the lack of comfort, frequency or reliability, cannot otherwise be recommended.

BY YACHT There is good anchorage in the rocky, sandy bay in front of the *vila*, but it can be difficult to disembark on the pier on account of the big swell. (After a few scary landings in Maio, even the CV Fast Ferry gave up its proposed route to the island, never – thus far – to return).

Clear all landing formalities with the police on arrival.

GETTING AROUND

BY PUBLIC TRANSPORT It is just about possible to do a circuit of the entire island in a day by picking up *alugueres* and hitching. But there is always the small chance of being left stranded and the desire not to end up in this situation will prevent you from exploring off the main road, especially given the lack of accommodation options. Hitchhiking is an option and if there is passing traffic it will normally stop for you.

Several of the good beaches lie within walking distance either of the *vila* or of Figueira da Horta, which is easy to reach by *aluguer*. For other sights take a chance, hire transport, or ask your hotel owner to come and look for you in his car (if he has one) late in the day if you haven't returned.

Alugueres depart from villages such as Ribeira do João and Alcatraz very early in the morning to come to the *vila*. From the little square northeast of the post office, they return to Barreiro at around 11.00, Figueira, Alcatraz and Ribeira do João around midday, coming back again from Figueira and Barreiro an hour later. For Morrinho, they leave the capital between 08.00 and 10.00, from the stop on Avenida Amílcar Cabral near the fish market. One-way fares are 100–150$.

BY CAR Find a 4x4 – a minibus or car will substantially restrict where you can go. A car can be rented for about 4,800–5,800$ a day, though Ellcar may have a Hilux pick-up (2-seater) for a bit less. A car plus driver will cost more – about 7,500$. Distances are short, but your average speed will be slow: you'll be driving on cobbles most of the way.

 Benvindo 256 1370; m 995 9713; e benvindomaio@hotmail.com. A *hiace* driver who can often be found at the airport when a flight is due, Benvindo has a good reputation for safe driving. As well as his *hiace*, he has a 4x4 to rent, with or without driver, & he offers a day-long, round-island excursion (7,500$ with driver).

Ellcar [210 A7] m 992 4273; e ellcar@ cvtelecom.cv. On the way out of town towards the airport.

MaioCar [211 F2] 255 1700. On the street continuing northeast of the post office building.

BY BICYCLE A great way to see Maio is by bicycle, but one would need a mountain bike for cushioning against the cobbled roads. You can rent bikes from the **Wolf Djarmaio Restaurant** (see page 208), which has two good-quality mountain bikes for €10 each for a full day. Take several litres of water and remember that every village has a shop somewhere, often indistinguishable from a private home – so ask.

WHERE TO STAY

There is a growing assortment of apartments and condominiums in the *vila*, some of which are very pleasant, as well as a few small hotels or *pensões*. There is little choice outside the capital, though.

ACTIVITIES

EXCURSIONS Maio is a place for resting and taking early-morning walks along the beaches and around the saltpans. **Benvindo** and others offer a round-island excursion (see above). Girassol Tours [211 G5] (255 1288; e reservas@girassol. cv; www.girassol.cv) may organise an island tour for you, but otherwise they are mainly useful for booking air tickets. Stephen and Janette (see details on page 206) organise excursions to see the island by vehicle and boat.

HIKING Maio is not really the island for hiking but it is possible to go for a couple of pleasant walks. In particular, you can head out from Morro towards Monte Batalha or try the more challenging walk to the top of Monte Penoso for which you almost certainly need a guide. Ask around in the *vila* for more information when you arrive.

BEACHES Maio has many accessible and inaccessible beaches, some of them breathtakingly deserted and remote. Near the *vila* are Ponta Preta and the delightfully named Bitcharocha. Up the west coast it is sandy way past Morro until just before Calheta. The beautiful half-moon-shaped Santana Beach, northwest of Morrinho, is usually deserted. Porto Cais, directly west of Morrinho, is a remote and beautiful beach. You will make your own enchanting and personal discoveries.

CAMPING If you are self-sufficient you will find many quiet places to pitch a tent. You can arrange with an *aluguer* driver to be dropped off and collected.

DIVING English couple Stephen Frankland and Janette Salem run the well-established Sunfish Scuba centre (𝄞 *255 1629;* m *954 9562;* e *crew@capeverdediving. com; www.capeverdediving.com*). Stephen is PADI certified and the centre is BSAC approved. They offer guided dives and try dives using local boats as well as snorkelling trips. Diving takes place in the marine reserve. There are also cave and wall dives suitable for all levels of divers. As well as the contact numbers above, information is available from Club Bitcha Rocha (see page 208 for details).

WHALE-WATCHING Winter and spring are the times when humpback whales pass by with their new-born calves. Ask around if there are any boats that will take you to see them – you may even be lucky enough to see them from the shore.

FISHING Maio Fishing Club (m *988 9160/971 0006;* e *michela@maiofishingclub. com; www.maiofishingclub.com*) offers various types of sport fishing, from the shore and on boats, including catch-and-release fishing trips for wahoo, dorado and sailfish. Big Game Maio (m *932 9002/970 1665;* e *biggamemaio@gmail.com*) organise both big-game fishing and options closer to shore.

Some locals report bad fishing practices, such as killing of protected species of shark to satisfy bloodthirsty clients. It is best to make enquiries as to the operator's policy before signing up.

QUAD-BIKE RENTAL Big Game Maio (see contact details above) can organise rentals. Quad bikes are not allowed on any beaches in Cape Verde. Expect to pay around €50 per day.

CIDADE DE PORTO INGLÉS (VILA DO MAIO)

Now officially renamed Cidade de Porto Inglês (it was previously known as Vila do Maio) and bestowed with city status, the capital has a well-kept and gracious town centre with a large square endowed with extra drama because it rises up a small but steep hill to a huge, white Baroque church, built in 1872. As the principal streets reach the edge of town, the *vila* becomes somewhat scruffy with half-built construction projects.

At the southeast edge of town is a pretty 18th-century fort, now restored and including some cannons. A nearby local may offer to get the key and let you in, but you can see as much from outside the locked gate. In front of the town stretches the long and wide expanse of pristine white sand of Bitcharocha Beach, with a couple of beach bars.

WHERE TO STAY There are no real stand-out hotels in the town centre, rather an adequate supply of mid-range options. The apartments and infinity pool at Stella Maris make it an attractive choice. All listings are located on the map, pages 210–11.

Hotels and pensãos

Hotel Marilu (10 rooms, 2 suites)
255 1198. Newly reopened in 2013,
a decent, central choice with good facilities.
$$$

Residencial Bom Sossego (14 rooms)
255 1365. A refurbished pensão with a
restaurant underneath. Rooms on the
upper floors have AC & are more expensive
$$$–$$

Casita Verde (2 rooms) 10mins' walk along
the road to Morro; m 996 0633; e info@casita-
verde.de; www.casita-verde.de/index_en.htm.
Overlooking the beach, this is a private house
owned by a German artist who offers 2 very
comfortable & beautifully conceived rooms that
are en suite with hot water, fan, mosquito net &
fridge. You are welcome to join in her
creative activities or sit on the shaded terrace
admiring the garden & the sea view. Excursions
offered. You can download a colourful &
informative brochure about Maio from
the website. **$$**

Jardim do Maio (5 rooms) 255 1199;
e giardinidimaio@gmail.com; www.
giardinidimaio.com. Friendly Italian host,
rooftop terrace facing the ocean, pleasant
courtyard. Restaurant is for guests only.
Wi-Fi. **$$**

Residencial Porto Inglês (7 rooms) 255
1698; e rpingles@cvtelecom.cv. A blue building
just northeast of the centre, this has some decent
rooms, All en suite with hot water & AC. Try for an
upper-floor room. **$$**

Apartments

Maio Fishing Club m 971 0006; e fulvio@
maiofishingclub.com or michela@maiofishingclub.
com; www.maiofishingclub.com. Offers to arrange
apartments & B&B which can be part of a fishing
package (see page opposite). It will organise
collection from the airport. **$$$**

Stella Maris (11 apts, 4 villas) m 983
4671; e maiocasa@yahoo.com; www.maiocasa.
com. Overlooking Ponta Preta Beach in the south
of town, Stella Maris offers a relaxing place to
stay with beautiful views in well-appointed &
well-managed villas & apartments. Friendly &
knowledgeable English management. There is a
clifftop infinity pool, a mini-market close by, & it's
near the vila's restaurants. All apartments have
sea views. Studios, 1- & 2-bedroom apartments
& villas have kitchen, sitting area, bathroom &
terrace/balcony. All available for short- & long-
term rental; villas can sleep 6 persons. **$$$**

Cape Verde Holidays m +44 (0)701 008
3058; e book@cape-verde-holidays.net; www.
cape-verde-holidays.net. UK-based agency which
has a number of private villas for rental throughout
Cape Verde, including Maio. **$$$–$$**

Ilha do Maio Imobilária m 993 7022;
e info@ilhadomaio.it; www.ilhadomaio.it. Agency
with helpful staff. They manage property & are
able to find you an apartment or villa to rent. Their
list of properties includes nearby Residencial Inês
and Residencial Solemar, as well as Stella Maris
& Santa Luzia. Will arrange collection from the
airport. **$$$–$**

WHERE TO EAT AND DRINK For a small, unfrequented island, Maio has some pleasant restaurants. Some of its expats claim they are the best fed in the archipelago. All listings are located on the map, pages 210–11.

Bar Tropical On the main beach,
Bitcharocha; 12.00–18.00 Wed, 10.00–18.00
Thu–Sun. This snack bar is popular for its beach
location. Homemade pizza, ice cream & snow
cones. It also serves sandwiches, hamburgers &
french fries. Picturesque because of its clear walls
which afford a super view of the sea. **$$$**

Kulor Rua 3 de Maio; m 981 1303;

e kulorcafe.maio@voila.fr; 10.00–15.00 &
18.00–late Mon–Sat. Towards Stella Maris, this
French-owned restaurant is popular, with a rooftop
dining area. The food is varied & good quality, &
may include fish kebabs, chilli, buzio, pork caramel
& various pastas. There are also some mouth-
watering desserts. Vegetarian dishes prepared on
request. **$$$**

✘ **Restaurant Tutti Frutti** ☎255 1575; m 997 9195. Along the main road towards the airport. Alberto & his wife serve excellent pizzas & other fine food. $$$

✘ **Bom Sossego** This *pensão* has a restaurant downstairs. Pleasant surroundings, but food has had mixed reviews. $$

✘ **Club Bitcha Rocha** m 976 4109. Next to the fish market, attractive beachside bar/restaurant with fish & shellfish (in season). Also offers snacks, cakes & homemade ice cream. Tourist & dive centre information available. First-aid post. English spoken. $$

✘ **Kabana Beach Bar** Also on the main beach; m 993 7270. Under new management, much improved. *Cachupa*, snacks & sandwiches as you watch the world go by. Live music on Fri & a disco on Sat. $$

💻 **Miramar Café** A small kiosk on the seafront near the phone booth, with plastic chairs & a beach view. $$

✘ **Restaurant Maresol** Well-kept, pleasant restaurant/bar, with the cleanest toilets in town. Usual fish & meat offerings, at reasonable prices. $$

✘ **Wolf Djarmai** ⊕ until late, closed Sat. A blessing in the heat. One of the few pleasant outdoor venues in the centre of town. Usual fish & meat menu, plus 'special' baked bonito if ordered in advance. Also has a snack menu. Occasional live music, Jun–Sep. Popular ex-pat hangout. $$

✘ **Senegalese Restaurante** ⊕ early–late. A small restaurant opposite the *aluguer* stop. Advanced ordering is advisable. $

✘ **Folgado** Basic fish & chicken dishes, no menu, simple surroundings & very cheap. $

✘ **Enzo's** Inside the market hall. Run by an amiable Italian, the place to run to if you've had enough fresh fish. Basic but tasty & inexpensive pizza, whole or by the slice. Espresso coffee. $

ENTERTAINMENT AND NIGHTLIFE

🍸 **Bar Esperança Disco** [210 C7] Av Amílcar Cabral.

✘ **Kabana Beach Bar** [210 D7] See listing above for details.

SHOPPING Whether the market has produce depends on when the last boat arrived from Praia, but there are several small shops: Pick Pay [211 H5] (close to Stella Maris); the Co-operative (north of Stella Maris, next to the distinctive beehive buildings); and Ramos [210 B7] (on the way to the airport), are the largest and probably have the best choice. There are a number of unmarked bakeries: one near Folgado restaurant [211 G4], one to the northeast [211 E2]. and another close to the market [211 G6]. The fish market [210 E7] is situated at the start of the main beach near Club Bitcha Rocha and the best time to buy fresh fish is when the boats return between 11.00 and midday. There is a tiny but well-stocked souvenir shop , Djarmai Souvenir, [211 E4] in the town centre.

OTHER PRACTICALITIES
Airlines

TACV [211 E1] (☎*255 1256*) To the northeast of town, beyond the Barreiro/Figueira aluguer stop. Office may be closed when flights are arriving, as the multilingual staff will be at the airport.

Banks

[210 C7, 211 E5 & E6] (⊕ *08.00–15.00 Mon–Fri*) A choice of three, all with ATMs and Western Union. One on the square, one close to the church and the third on Avenida Amílcar Cabral (Rua Principal).

Hospital

[210 A5] (☎*255 1130*) A new hospital lies just outside the centre, to the northwest.

Internet

In theory, the square with the TACV office has free Wi-Fi; in practice, it works only occasionally. This 'service' may relocate when the camara get their new office in front of the cathedral. Best to ask a local, Facebook-obsessed teenager playing with their laptop. Other options include Photo Neves [210 D5], on Rua da Liberdade, or Henry's, on the next street north [210 D5] (at the back of the hardware store) or another one by the water fountain [211 E5]. At Henry's you can plug in your laptop and/or make cheap international calls.

Pharmacy

Farmacia Forte [211 H5] (☎*974 4066*).

Police

[211 G6] (✆ 255 1132) Currently at the far end of Av Amílcar Cabral, with a new police station under construction near the hospital.

Post office

[211 E3] (🕑 08.00–12.00 & 14.00–18.00 Mon–Fri) North of the square.

WHAT TO SEE AND DO

Salina de Porto Inglês This extraordinary lake of salt is, at 5km long and 1.5km wide, the largest salina in Cape Verde, stretching almost as far as the village of Morro. It no longer produces the vast supplies it once did (see pages 201–2), but it is a poetic reminder of Maio's historical significance and thus an island treasure.

The salina is still in use: from April to June, endless little conical piles of salt appear around it as local women work to make salt for the local market – just 1.5 tonnes a year. Inside the small co-operative building at the salina's southern end, women sort the salt by hand before it is ground and packed. The United Nations funds the operation, providing local women with employment.

Between the pans and the sea is a raised beach over which the seawater rises during spring tides and at times of high swell. Seawater also infiltrates underground, while rainwater trickles in from mainland streams between August and October. For the rest of the time the intense heat, wind and lack of shade allow the water to evaporate, leaving crusts of salt behind.

But the salina is not just Maio's biggest piece of heritage and a source of local income – it has important natural history as well. As a wetland it is visited by migrant waders. Its situation, surrounded by dunes and desert, make it an important breeding and feeding habitat for a wide variety of birds, including the cream-coloured courser (*Cursorius cursor exsul*) and the Kentish plover (*Charadrius alexandrinus*) (see page 203). Alexander's kestrel (*Falco alexandrii*) and the Iago sparrow (*Passer iagoensis*) are

---

PROTECTING THE SHARKS FROM THE SHARKS? *Murray Stewart*

Sharks are not prone to attracting good publicity: they usually only make the news when they choose someone's leg for dinner. But in Cape Verde, it's far more likely that they will end up as someone's dinner – someone abroad, that is. According to Tommy Melo of environmental organisation, Biosfera I, sharks are in danger of disappearing from Cape Verdean waters. Under an agreement with the European Union, up to 75 boats from the EU are allowed to fish those Cape Verdean waters for tuna, but if other species are caught as a 'by-catch' (ie:, incidentally), then that is permitted, too. And as the fishing method is trawling, it is no wonder that other species are regularly netted.

What is a surprise is that in one year, over 12,000 tonnes of shark were caught…and only 600 tonnes of tuna, according to Melo, a man with a wise old head on his young shoulders. Ignoring the value of the shark meat, the annual revenues to the Europeans for just the fins of the sharks – a popular ingredient in some cultures' soup – are estimated at a staggering €200 million. And the annual price paid by the EU for the right to fish? Just €435,000.

The Cape Verde government are aware of the issue, but the threat if they don't sign up to such agreements is that Cape Verde fish exports will not be given access to the lucrative EU market. In the cut-throat pool of international negotiations, it seems that 'big fish eats little fish', while it seems that from the ocean around Cape Verde, those same big fish eat the big fish (the sharks) – and profit from it handsomely, as well.

6

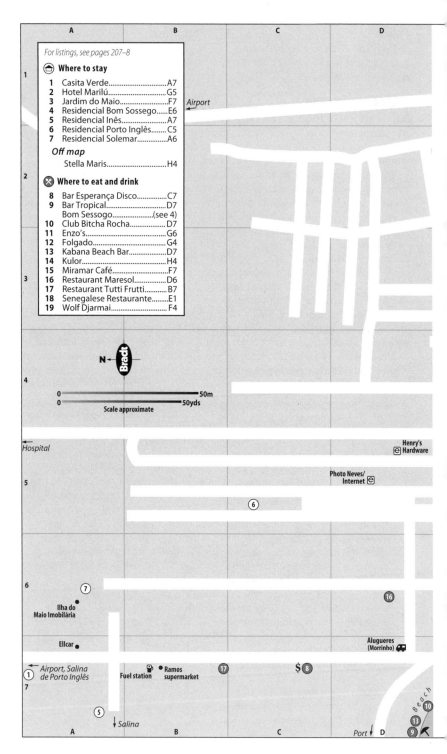

For listings, see pages 207–8

Where to stay

1 Casita Verde.................................A7
2 Hotel Marilú...............................G5
3 Jardim do Maio..........................F7
4 Residencial Bom Sossego......E6
5 Residencial Inês........................A7
6 Residencial Porto Inglês........C5
7 Residencial Solemar................A6

Off map
Stella Maris.................................H4

Where to eat and drink

8 Bar Esperança Disco................C7
9 Bar Tropical................................D7
Bom Sessogo.......................(see 4)
10 Club Bitcha Rocha.................. D7
11 Enzo's...G6
12 Folgado......................................G4
13 Kabana Beach Bar...................D7
14 Kulor..H4
15 Miramar Café............................F7
16 Restaurant Maresol................D6
17 Restaurant Tutti Frutti...........B7
18 Senegalese Restaurante........E1
19 Wolf Djarmai.............................F4

N

0 ────────────── 50m
0 ────────────── 50yds
Scale approximate

Hospital

Henry's
Hardware

Photo Neves/
Internet

Ilha do
Maio Imobiliária

Ellcar

Alugueres
(Morrinho)

Airport, Salina
de Porto Inglês

Fuel station   Ramos
supermarket

Salina

Beach

Port

Fuel station
TACV office

Alugueres
(Barreiro/Figueira)

18

Maio Car Hire

Mini supermarket
Bakery

Post office

Drogaria Central

The Cooperative

Souvenir shop

Stella Maris

19   12

Bakery   14

Largo António Évora

Pick Pay

Parking

Cathedral

RUA 3 DE MAIO

2 Girassol Tours

Pharmacy

RUA DA LIBERDADE

Water fountain

School

4   *Square*

11
Market

Bakery

CV Telecom

RUA 1 DE MAIO

New Town Hall

Music shop

Fort

$

Police

3

Nazerene Church

AVENIDA AMÍLCAR CABRAL

15

Fish market

E   F   G   H

6

the two endemic birds to be found in the salina. Loggerhead turtles (*Caretta caretta*) nest here, though in tiny numbers compared with Boavista.

The salina and its inhabitants face several threats. Firstly, sand extraction for building on both Maio and Santiago threatens to remove the barrier between the salina and the sea. Secondly, it was threatened by burgeoning tourist ambitions – though, as it is in itself a tourist attraction, one would assume that the salina will eventually be ring-fenced rather than destroyed and the town hall is developing a conservation plan.

Ponta Preta From the *vila* walk east along the coast, across the refuse tips and past the cemetery on the left – after about 15 minutes there is a small, pretty bay. A further 30 minutes will take you to the beach at Ponta Preta. Ask in town for further directions. This beach is not safe for swimming, due to a strong current. Behind the beach lies one of the island's two desalination plants, which use seawater and the process of reverse osmosis to provide water for the entire island.

Turtle walks Biosfera I (e *tommymelo@hotmail.com; http://sites.google.com/site/biosferaum/*) is working with the Câmara Municipal do Maio to protect and monitor turtles on Maio. It may be possible to arrange to see nesting turtles by contacting Biosfera in advance. It is not a good idea to go to the beach alone at night as you may disturb the turtles.

OTHER PLACES TO VISIT

MORRO Morro is a small settlement with very little going on, but its beach is worth a look. In common with many beaches in Cape Verde, it fluctuates in size with the season's changing currents; in winter about 3m depth of sand vanishes, and the sea as a result comes many metres further in. The beach is safe for swimming apart from the odd day when the waves come from the south. From the town of Morro it is quite a long walk to the beach, so make sure that you ask to be dropped off at the beach rather than in the village.

From Morro there is a two-hour walk up the nearby hill with good views at the top and a walk along the stunning beach to Calheta.

Where to stay and eat Although there were several tourist developments planned for Morro, at time of writing these were either closed or had been abandoned halfway through construction. There is a surprisingly large supermarket in the settlement, underneath the planned hotel, Casa Blanca. There is also a smaller shop and a bar hidden away behind the village's water fountain.

CALHETA About 3km north of Morro is Calheta, divided into the inland town which is clustered around the main road, and the pretty fishing village of Calheta, reached by turning left off the main road towards the sea. Unusually for Cape Verde, the small fishing community use sailing boats to bring in the catch, rather than the more common motorboats. At the end of its street, lined with red-tiled pitched roofs and white-painted stones, is the bay. You can swim here, though it is probably cleaner away from the settlement. Bashona Beach is one of the calmest on the island. This is also the place to buy locally woven bags.

Where to stay and eat There are no restaurants in Calheta but several small bars. You may find someone willing to cook for you if you ask around and give advance notice. In terms of accommodation, **Torre Sabina** (*2 villas;* \ *256 1299;* m *985*

5585; e *maiokapverde@gmail.com; www.inseltraum.bizan;* $$) is an unmissable establishment down on the seafront and the only official place to stay outside the capital. Quirky, but tasteful, one 'villa' is a tower, the other is a chapel. Each sleeps two people. The price includes the use of the owner's kayaks and fishing trips are possible with the local fishermen. Meals by arrangement for residents for 1,100$.

MORRINHO About 4km north of Calheta is Morrinho. A couple of local men manufacture souvenirs here, though you'll see no signs to help you find them. Stop on the main road in the village centre and ask for either Itelvino – who makes boxes and photoframes from *tamara* grass – or Wilbert, who uses banana leaves to make bags and other items. There is a rough track that leads from Morrinho west to Porto Cais – keep heading towards the already visible sand dunes. As you leave the village on this track, off to your left you may see a few smoking pits, covered over with arched metal covers and surrounded by upright plastic sacks. This is where local men make charcoal, using the plentiful supplies of replanted acacia. Much of this charcoal is 'exported' to the other islands and is sold there for twice the price it fetches in Maio, a valuable source of income. Continuing along the track, stop your vehicle on firm ground before the track becomes too sandy, and continue on foot. Look for the dune with the footprints on it. On the other side, is the beautiful beach of Porto Cais, popular with locals at the weekend and usually safe for swimming. Back at Morrinho, a further track heads northwest from town and takes you to Praia de Santana, a wild and desolate beach that remains invisible from the long road, hidden by a ridge of dunes. These endless, evocative dunes are well worth exploring. In the middle of them is a patch of palm trees which the locals think of as an oasis. It is possible to drive along the track by the beach for a few kilometres, after which it peters out: if you want to go further you must walk. Eventually, you reach Praia Real: bear in mind that northern beaches are not safe for swimming. There is a further track from the settlement of Cascabulho that leads north to Praia Real.

CASCABULHO AND PEDRO VAZ This area in the north is filled with more green and mature forest followed by a landscape that feels like an abandoned opencast mine. Pedro Vaz feels like it could be the end of the earth but it's not – there's another two rough kilometres to the beach, possible by car. This is perhaps the loneliest and wildest beach, enlivened occasionally by women who come to meet the returning fishermen. There is a bar and a shop in Pedro Vaz. Food may be available if you ask around and are prepared to wait. On the road north of Pedro Vaz, towards Santo Antonio, you can see a number of low-level dams, built to slow the flow of water in the rainy season and let the water penetrate the ground.

PENOSO This is an old village where all that remains is a little white church. They hold a service here on the last Sunday of each month. Just after the church you can walk up the slopes of Monte Penoso. Even a short stroll will be rewarded with good views.

ALCATRAZ The land between Pedro Vaz and Alcatraz feels increasingly isolated – abandoned stony plains and lifeless land. Alcatraz lies 4km from Pedro Vaz – a single wide and dusty street.

FIGUEIRA DA HORTA AND RIBEIRA DE JOÃO Ribeira de João is reached by a turning to the south, east of Figueira da Horta. It's a road past pretty oases, though take care as the road is sometimes washed away in the rainy season and not repaired in a hurry. On arrival, turn right off the main street, down a footpath, and it is a ten-minute walk past the football pitch and along an enormously wide *ribeira* to find a magnificent beach with unbearably turquoise water. Look behind you – the village nestles like some Arabian desert town on the top of the bare brown hills. There is a bar in the village which can serve food if given notice – order it before going to the beach, eat it on your return.

BARREIRO AND LAGOA Barreiro is a neat settlement built on two sides of a valley. It is possible to drive from here to Lagoa and onto the beach. Locals say they walk to the beach from the *vila* (about 9km along the coast).

MAIO'S MYSTERIOUS BEACH BOULDERS

On the beach at Praia Real are a series of boulders that have intrigued visitors for years because they do not originate from anywhere in the archipelago. One academic thought they harboured clues to the whereabouts of Atlantis – it was once argued that the islands of Cape Verde might be the tips of a submerged continent. The mystery was solved by a vulcanologist who demonstrated that the boulders were from Brazil and were used as ballast – thrown onto the beach when the boat was loaded with salt.

7

Fogo

It is all of it one large mountain of a good height, out of the top whereof issues Flames
of Fire, yet only discerned in the Night: and then it may be seen a great way at Sea.

William Dampier, 1683

Fogo rises steeply from the ocean, pokes through the clouds and towers above them.
From the coast of Santiago or the peaks of São Nicolau it looks as forbidding as a
fortress. Fogo is a volcano, still active, and inside the crater the latest eruption still
smokes gently.

To some visitors, Fogo is a menacing place: dark lava rivers from centuries of
eruptions reach down its eastern side to the ocean. But it has a soft heart. Amongst
the clods of cold lava that have covered much of the floor of the crater are fertile fields.
Spilling over its northeast side are woods of eucalyptus and cool valleys in which
grow coffee, fruit trees and vines. Inside the crater lives a resilient race of people
who have defied government orders to evacuate and instead live and farm below the
smouldering peak that last erupted in 1995.

HIGHLIGHTS AND LOWLIGHTS

The crater is a true highlight of the Cape Verde archipelago, a unique landscape
whose drama is matched only by the mountains of Santo Antão. Fogo is thus one
of the principal hiking islands, but it is also fascinating for its anthropology and
its natural history. From a base in the Chã das Caldeiras you could combine a few
days spectacular hiking with some time discovering about village life. This area and
other parts of Fogo have caves to explore. For your visit, you can engage one of the
established tour operators based in São Filipe, hire a vehicle, or simply use *alugueres*
or taxis to ferry you around.

The second attraction of Fogo is São Filipe itself, a neat and attractive island capital
peppered with handsome Portuguese houses. It has a small but lively market, a range of
quality restaurants and a new museum with some interesting exhibits.

There are only modest opportunities for swimming and no white-sand beaches.
Apart from fishing, there are no organised watersports.

SUGGESTED ITINERARY AND NUMBER OF DAYS Many visitors spend two nights
in Fogo, wandering round the pleasant town of São Filipe on their first afternoon,
spending their one full day travelling to the crater for an ascent of the Pico, and
departing the next day. The crater is rewarding enough to merit a little longer than
this. We suggest four nights: on the first day look at São Filipe and perhaps visit one
of Fogo's lesser sights such as its lagoon, at Salina. On day two head to the crater
and climb the Pico. Day three, another of the crater walks. Day four, a descent to
the northeast, to Mosteiros. After a night in Mosteiros an early *aluguer* should be

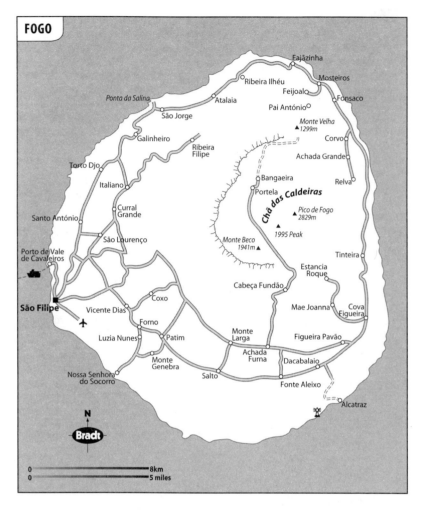

FOGO

Fajãzinha

Ribeira Ilhéu

Mosteiros

Ponta da Salina

Atalaia

Feijoalo

Fonsaco

Pai António

São Jorge

Galinheiro

Ribeira
Filipe

Monte Velha
1299m

Corvo

Achada Grande

Torto Djo

Italiano

Bangaeira

Relva

Portela

Chã das Caldeiras

Santo António

Curral
Grande

Pico de Fogo
2829m

São Lourenço

1995 Peak

Porto de Vale
de Cavaleiros

Monte Beco
1941m

Tinteira

Estancia
Roque

Cabeça Fundão

São Filipe

Coxo

Mae Joanna

Cova
Figueira

Vicente Dias

Forno

Monte
Larga

Figueira Pavão

Luzia Nunes

Patim

Monte
Genebra

Achada
Furna

Dacabalaio

Nossa Senhora
do Socorro

Salto

Fonte Aleixo

Alcatraz

N

Bradt

0 ————————— 8km
0 ————————— 5 miles

able to take you to your flight. If you are tight on time, you can arrange a day trip
from Sal (and sometimes from Santiago or Boavista) with several travel agents and,
although this won't allow you much time to get to know the island, it does, at least,
give you a flavour. The tours usually include a quick trip to view the crater and walk
around São Filipe.

BACKGROUND INFORMATION

HISTORY Geologists have done intricate work to piece together the volcano's
history by extrapolating from the directions of lava flows of different ages and
combining that information with literary descriptions of the appearance of the
volcano at different times.

Fogo erupted from the sea a few hundred thousand years ago, a single volcano
reaching a mighty 3.5km high. Its walls were steep and unstable and so, sometime
within the last 10,000 years, a great section in the east collapsed towards the sea –
reducing the height of its walls by about 300m in one giant avalanche. After the first

eruption there were numerous smaller ones, all making craters in the floor of the original large crater, which is now about 10km long and 7km wide.

Volcanoes are fertile places and Fogo's agricultural potential was harnessed from early on – it had acquired a population of 2,000 within the first 120 years of its discovery. It was the second island of the archipelago to be settled and was populated with slaves who grew cotton and developed the skill of weaving – the island was famed for its *pano preta*, or deep indigo cloth (see page 41). The cloth was shipped to Santiago, and because of this the island remained remote from the trans-oceanic ship trade. But it did not escape attack: the Dutch had a four-day spree there in 1655. Lisbon's response to the ensuing plea for more Portuguese settlers was to dispatch convicts. Fogo was regarded as a hardship posting and, though it is only 50km from Santiago, it was the threatened place of exile for the people of the greater island.

For much of this time the volcano in the background was growing: it appears to have put on several hundred metres between 1450 and 1750, and in the early 1600s, black clouds swathed its heights. An eruption in 1680 was savage and gave the island its name, which means 'fire' – before that it had been called, as usual, after the saint's day on which it was discovered. Much fertile land was ruined in that 1680 eruption and many people emigrated permanently to neighbouring Brava. From the end of the 1600s into the 1700s, the fire of Fogo could be seen from afar and was used by ships to aid their navigation.

It was into the open space left by the giant ancient collapse that, in 1785, Pico de Fogo erupted. Lava spewed down the northeastern slopes creating the bulge on which the town of Mosteiros is situated today, and the Pico became the highest point of the archipelago.

Against this tempestuous background the people of Fogo welcomed the crews of American whaling ships who came ashore in search of supplies and personnel, as they were doing on Brava. Thus began the **emigration to the United States** and the creation of the great Cape Verdean diaspora.

Since 1785, all eruptions have been inside the old crater. There was one in 1799 and three in the following century, in 1847, 1852 and 1857, after which there was a century's gap. Each eruption leaves cones in the crater floor, which is how it earned its name, Chã das Caldeiras or Plain of Craters. In 1847 there were fatalities caused not by lava flows but by the associated earthquakes. The eruption of 1852 created the cone known as Monte Preto de Baixo.

In the 20th century there were two eruptions. Lava spewed from one of the two chimneys on the southern side of the volcano in 1951, and also created cones to the north and south of the Pico – such as Monte Orlando, Monte Rendall and Monte Preto de Cima. These eruptions all began along a line of volcanic fissures extending from the flank of the Pico de Fogo summit cone across the floor of Chã das Caldeiras. The lava flows that issued from these vents spread over the northern and southern parts of Chã das Caldeiras and down the eastern flank of the island.

The latest eruption occurred comfortably within living memory for many inhabitants, on the night of 2 April 1995. For a week before, the villages had been shaken with small but increasingly powerful earthquakes. Just after midnight the flank of the Pico split apart as a line of fissures opened. It was as if the Pico had been 'cut by a knife', said one villager. The eruption began and a curtain of fire issued from the volcano and poured down into the crater. Thousands of inhabitants fled. By daylight the whole island was covered by a thick cloud of dark ash extending 5km into the sky; lava bombs up to 4m wide landed half a kilometre from the eruption and a day later lava fountains were spurting 400m high: it is estimated that at its height the volcano ejected between four and 8.5 million m³ of lava per day.

One month later the lava had thickened but was still flowing at 15cm per hour. It was another month before the flow stopped. Miraculously nobody died; perhaps the luckiest escape was made by two guitarists who are said to have climbed the Pico the day before the eruption, to make music and enjoy the view.

The 1995 eruption was different from the others. Unusually, it occurred southwest of the Pico, through a system of fissures that lay in a broadly south-to-west orientation. As a result the lava flows spread west and then north, covering an area of fertile volcanic soils and ultimately much of the small village of Boca Fonte. Today, shells of its houses remain, invaded by monstrous clumps of lava as high as their roofs. One house was even spun around on its axis by the lava flow, but remained standing.

Alternative housing was quickly built on the southern slopes – it can be seen from the road as you ascend to the crater. It was assumed that the people would move there permanently but most of them have defiantly returned to their crater homes to cultivate whatever land escaped the lava flow. The road across Chã has been rebuilt.

For most of the duration of the eruption (from 10 April to the end of May) the only active vent was at the northeastern end of the fissure system and it is here that the largest volcanic cone of the eruption grew – the yellow-streaked, smoking black slope that lies at the foot of the Pico de Fogo. You pass it on the right soon after entering the crater by road.

Fogo today Today Fogo has been boosted by development work, much of it funded by Germany. It has a new harbour, still under development, and acres of terracing, catchment dams and reafforestation. A newly asphalted road leads most of the way up to Chã das Caldeiras, before giving way again to cobbles..

Agriculture is the main activity, though fishing occupies a small number of people. There's plenty of water underground but hoisting it to the surface is expensive, and directing it higher – to the slopes that carry much of the agriculture – is even more costly. Some rainwater catchment tanks have been built to address this, with every village now possessing at least one of these communal tanks. The islanders grow coffee and – to the delight of many a visitor to Cape Verde – produce wine. The coffee is grown on the outer northern slopes near Mosteiros. Grapes are grown in the crater by digging pits amongst the little black pieces of basaltic rock known as *lapilli* and planting a vine in each: at night the moisture condenses on the rock and dribbles into the holes. As well as the crater's sporadic vines, there is a slightly more traditional vineyard near São Filipe and another co-operative in the far north. The results are some really very quaffable wines, and there is also production of juices and various liqueurs.

Fogo is thought to have potential for geothermal energy for electricity production, though the investment needed to kick-start this would be enormous. Rainwater filters through the permeable volcanic rock and reaches underground reservoirs. The water samples taken during investigations have reached as high as 200–300°C. Some of the more progressive commercial establishments are installing solar panels to harness the 320 days of sunshine.

GEOGRAPHY The fourth-largest island, with an area of 480km², Fogo's highest point is the Pico de Fogo which reaches 2,829m. Fogo has a population of about 39,000. São Filipe is the third-largest town in Cape Verde.

NATURAL HISTORY

Flora There are eight plant species endemic to Fogo. Two to watch out for are *língua de vaca* (*Echium vulcanorum*), a white flower with a broad leaf, which is confined just to Fogo volcano and might be encountered on a Pico ascent; and *cravo-brabo babo* (*Erysimum caboverdeanum*), a delicate pink flower with long pointed leaves, which is found only inside the crater.

Birds The crater is designated an Important Bird Area by BirdLife International. Fogo is one of four islands in Cape Verde where the endemic Fea's petrel (*Pterodroma feae*) is known to breed, and it likes the inner walls of the crater best. There are perhaps 200 of these in the crater. The Cape Verde little shearwater (*Puffinus assimilis boydi*) breeds on the outer slopes of the crater and it has the largest population of Alexander's swift (*Apus alexandri*). Other breeding species include the grey-headed kingfisher (*Halcyon leucocephala*), the spectacled warbler (*Sylvia conspicillata*), a small population of the Cape Verde cane warbler (*Acrocephalus brevipennis*) and probably the Cape Verde peregrine (*Falco madens*). (For more on birds, see *Natural history and conservation*, page 6.)

CONSERVING THE CRATER

The crater was deemed a natural park in 2003. The park extends over a large part of the landmass of the island: its 8,469ha include a margin around the south and north of the crater and a western section that extends quite close to the coast at some points. Some areas are under greater restrictions than others: for example any land use is banned on the Pico and on the inner wall of the crater, but some uses are permissible elsewhere. A project to conserve and develop the crater has been in progress, in one form or another, for some years. It is said that the true value of the crater is geological, rather than to do with its flora and fauna, and so the priorities lie with conserving its rocks. 'Geological tourism' is said to be the focus.

Since the crater houses two expanding villages, and there are increasing numbers of visitors, some activities threaten the crater while others do not. The areas where people are growing vines are just ash, and thus this causes no problems. Conversely, large quantities of ash and sand in the crater have been shovelled away and used in the construction boom. These are valued because, compared with sand from the shore, they have a low salt content. And lava stone is used for roof tiles. On a small scale this would be no problem, but the expansion of the crater population from 500 in the year 2000 to its current estimate of 1,500 has resulted in significant construction.

Conservation plans extend to the crater slopes. On the outer northern slopes of the volcano, there are eucalyptus, pines and acacias, planted during job-creation activities in the 1940s after the famine. In an area of the southwest, the project has planted fruit trees watered by drip irrigation and by reservoirs which fill over two–three months and then are used over the rest of the year.

To deal with the goat problem, the original project did a deal with local people: they were given 'beautiful, big' goats from the Canaries that produced a lot of milk, if they agreed to build stables for them and prevent them roaming the countryside.

The end of April is the time for Fogo's big party, Bandeira (Flag) de São Filipe. There is horse racing, held (incredibly, given its size) on the black sandy terrace outside Hotel Savana, dancing and processions. Special dishes are made. The island has a distinctive music known as *pilão*, a bit like *batuko*, a chanting and beating of drums that forms the background to the grinding of corn in the run-up to the festival. Accommodation during this festival is scarce and prices rise steeper than a volcano. Up in the crater, there are said to be an annual 45 days of festival – for one reason or another!

20 January	São Sebastião
Late April	Bandeira de São Filipe
24 June	São João
29 June	São Pedro
2nd Sunday in July	Santa Rainha de Cabo Verde (Chã das Caldeiras)
5 August	Nossa Sra do Socorro
10 August	São Lourenço
15 August	Municipality Day (Mosteiros)
24 November	Santa Catarina (Cova Figueira)

Turtles   As with all the Cape Verdean islands, Fogo is home to nesting loggerhead turtles (*Caretta caretta*) from June to October. Contact SOS Tartarugas (e *info@turtlesos.org*) for advice.

HAZARDS   You should take care if **swimming**: the land drops steeply away and the removal of vast quantities of sand for construction has not helped this. Take local advice. **Hikers** should be aware that the Pico is pretty challenging and some walks, like the crater rim, are dangerous without a guide.

GETTING THERE AND AWAY

BY AIR   Flying over the flanks of the volcano and landing on a sliver of flat land between the grey slopes and the blue sea is one of the most spectacular experiences you will have on the archipelago. Coming from Praia, sit on the right-hand side. There is a daily flight with TACV from Santiago, which takes 30 minutes.

There are also well-established day trips from Sal (advertised all over the island of Sal) in chartered planes owned by Cabo Verde Express. Fogo's airport has a café, serving drinks and welcoming slices of cake.

It's 2km into the capital, a 20-minute walk downhill into town. A shared *aluguer* from the airport to São Filipe should not cost more than 100$ (taxi 300$). Some hotels collect their guests if they have booked in advance. There is at least one *aluguer* for Mosteiros which meets every São Filipe flight. On Sundays, the taxis that have been stalking you all week can mysteriously disappear, so if you have a flight to catch, organise your trip to the airport in advance.

BY FERRY   The situation with ferries to Fogo, once volatile, has now been stabilised with the arrival of the CV Fast Ferry (*www.cvfastferry.com*) which has replaced the previously slow and somewhat haphazard service of yesteryear.. At the time of publication there was a daily connection with Brava and somewhat less frequent connections with Praia, though the timetables are published weekly and it is essential to check the website beforehand – or better still, check with one of the tour operators, as they are often more reliable. This is especially true if you are relying on returning to Fogo (from Brava) or to Santiago (from Fogo) by ferry to get an onward flight. Fogo's port (Barca Balêro) lies a few kilometres to the north of São Filipe and a taxi to or from town costs 400$. At present, ferry tickets can be bought in advance from the CV Fast Ferry office or via many of the tour operators listed. The port itself is in a process of constant reconstruction. A new terminal building with smart waiting room has been built, though there are few facilities as yet.

BY YACHT Fogo is bathed in a swell that can only be avoided by anchoring at the harbour to the north of the capital, the development of which has improved matters greatly for yachtsmen and women. Nevertheless, lack of funds has led to some lingering doubts as to the user-friendliness of the port and further improvements are still required. The approach of any vessel will be noted by the Delegaçao Maritimo (Port Authority) and you will be required to present the usual identification documents.

GETTING AROUND

BY PUBLIC TRANSPORT *Alugueres* leave Mosteiros, the villages in the crater and other outlying villages between 04.00 and 05.30. They generally head north, travelling anticlockwise around the coast, and arrive in São Filipe about an hour later. They depart from São Filipe mid-morning and also at midday and at 14.00 for the crater (500$): don't get stranded. There are no communal *alugueres* to and from the crater on a Sunday, so a private hire is the only option. An *aluguer* leaves São Filipe for São Jorge sometime between 09.30 and 11.00 and one returns to São Filipe at 13.00.

Alugueres for the crater and for Mosteiros leave from beside the block that houses the town hall (*câmara municipal*) and the market. Those for São Jorge, Salina, the airport and the port leave from outside Pousada Belavista.

BY TAXI The bright yellow taxis or chartered *alugueres* will go most places. The taxi rank in São Filipe is now down behind the market. In practice taxis also roam the streets incessantly and are likely to find *you*, except on Sundays. Fares are relatively fixed – for example, to the crater 5,000$; around the island 8,000$; to Mosteiros 6,000$; to São Lourenço 800$; to Curral Grande 1,200$. You will struggle to find an English-speaking driver, though Valdemiro (**m** *958 7707*) does passable French..

BY CAR The going rate is around €65 for a one day hire. Mileage limits may apply, but you can't really go too far on this small island. The usual deposit will be requested, by credit card or cash. Most tour operators will find you a car, or you can try the agencies below.

 Aliance Grupo São Filipe; ✆281 1050; **m** 918 2539; **e** comercial@rltur.cv
 BBAS São Filipe ✆281 1089

 Intercidades São Filipe, ✆281 3334; **e** www.intercidadesrentacar.cv

WHERE TO STAY AND EAT

Almost all the major accommodation is in São Filipe where you have a choice between the relatively upmarket Hotel Xaguate and Colonial House as well as a full range of *pensãos* of varying quality, some of them tastefully renovated and situated in traditional *sobrado* houses and some with views of the ocean. There are a few options on the outskirts of São Filipe town. The other major place to stay is in the crater, where the choice is between homestays, humble *pensãos* and the slightly more upmarket Pensão Pedra Brabo and Casa Marisa.

ACTIVITIES

EXCURSIONS AND TOUR OPERATORS The operators listed below are established, experienced and usually multilingual. They more or less offer the same kind of tours. Sample prices are: trip up to the crater, with a guide, lunch, trip to the winery, a walk between the two villages, return transport, plus stops on the way– €60 per person (minimum two people), €50 per person (group of four). Note these prices do not include a climb to the top of the volcano. A trip to Salinas for one to four persons would cost a total of €90.

You may well be approached by unofficial 'guides' in São Filipe. Use your own judgment as to whether to engage their services. In the absence of any tourist office, it is difficult to know who is who. One English- and German-speaking town guide is Fabio Goncalves Dias (m *952 1507*), but whoever you use, agree exactly what the tour will include and the price, in advance.

If you prefer to plan your own day trip, speak to a taxi or *aluguer* driver – they'll be happy to oblige.

Dja'r Fogo [225 F6] Rua Dr Costa, São Filipe; 281 2879; m 991 9713; e agnelo@djarfogo. net; www.djarfogocv.net. Descended from an old Fogo family, Agnelo, the proprietor, is deeply interested in the traditional Fogo way of life & this is reflected in his tours. Specialising in small groups & individuals, he can arrange any itineraries to suit, including a visit to his country house, the interesting Quinta das Saudades. Dja'r Fogo also sells crafts, maps & Fogo coffee which Agnelo roasts & grinds himself, & he is active in promoting cultural events.

Qualitur [225 E6] Praça Câmara Municipal, São Filipe; 281 1089; m 997 1142; e qualitur@ sapo.cv/qualitur@gmail.com; www.qualitur.cv. An efficient outfit organising mainly group trips to Chã das Caldeiras, the salina, Monte Genebra, & a variety of walks in & out of the crater, with guides.

English spoken.

vista verde tours [225 F6] Close to the blue church, in a square-towered building, São Filipe; m 993 0788; e office@ vista-verde.com; www. vista-verde.com; ⊕ 10.00–12.00 & 15.00–17.00 Mon–Fri. Well-established, efficient travel agency specialising in socially & environmentally responsible tourism. Arranges small-group tours or tailor-made holidays incorporating accommodation, flights, hiking & excursions. Also offices in Sal & São Vicente. See ad on the inside back cover.

Zebra Travel [225 D5] On the main square; m 991 4566; e info@zebratravel.net; www. zebratravel.net. Can arrange flights, tours & excursions. It also rents cars. Connected to Colonial B&B & Fogo Lounge (see page 227). Business centre also available.

HIKING This is the great activity of Fogo. As well as the big hike up to the Pico in the crater, there are several delightful, and arguably more rewarding, walks from various points in and around the crater (see *Hikes*, page 234).

FISHING The game fishing around Fogo's waters is high quality, with plenty of blue marlin, sharks and tuna. Zebra Travel are currently the only operator who organise fishing trips, though you could always try and strike a deal with one of the local fishermen, if you are happy with smaller fish. Cost will depend on the number participating.

CYCLING Fogo is steep and cobbled, and cycling anywhere but along contours or downhill can be unbearable without a good, comfy, mountain bike. Only for true lovers of discomfort.

BEACHES AND SWIMMING It is often dangerous to swim off Fogo, but when the sea looks really calm it is safe at the beach at the port, and at Praia Nossa Senhora. The best place to swim, however, is Ponta do Salina – a stunning cove with black rock formations smothered by white seaspray and riddled with grottos and reefs. It can be reached on the São Jorge *aluguer* – ask to be dropped off there and check what time the *aluguer* is returning.

CAVES There are at least three volcanic tubes to explore on Fogo and the Parque Natural do Fogo is opening more to visitors. The tubes are lava flows that solidify on the outside, after which the inner liquid flows away leaving them hollow inside. Inside they are beautiful, with frozen lava in streams down the inner walls like melted chocolate.

Two of the caves lie on an imaginary line drawn roughly between Pico de Fogo and São Lourenço, on the slopes of Fogo a bit higher than the roads. To reach them ask one of the tour operators or check with the park office. You should be taken to Ribeira de Aguadinha, to a large concrete water tank and then on to the caves. Access to one involves a 5m crawl before it opens out into a larger area. Bring a good head torch and don't go alone or if you are not an experienced caver. The floors of the caves are uneven.

CULTURE The *sobrado* architecture of São Filipe is the main draw, plus a visit to Casa da Memória and the recently established museum. The Casa has occasional outdoor screening of films in its courtyard. Live music can usually be found around São Filipe and up in the crater, especially at weekends.

SIGHTSEEING BY VEHICLE The volcano crater's grandeur is eminently appreciable from a vehicle if you don't mind a slightly hair-raising ascent to the crater. Once that has been done it is pleasant to trace other roads, enjoying the gentle western slopes and visiting a few further sights, all accessible by vehicle (see *Other places to visit*, page 234).

SÃO FILIPE

São Filipe is a large and pretty landslide of a town, with its houses seemingly tumbling down steep cobbled streets towards the narrow black-sand beach and the ocean below. It is on the 'tentative' list as a UNESCO World Heritage Site, hardly surprising given its many Portuguese squares, esplanades and *sobrado* houses (see below) – some of them collapsing, some lovingly restored. Generally, it has a well looked-after feel to it, the buildings are pastel with terracotta tiles, and vegetation springs from pots on every fragile wooden balcony. Bougainvillea abounds and trees are a healthy size.

The town could do with some more outdoor cafés from which its architecture and the views of Brava could be enjoyed. Until then, there is a promenade, adorned with busts of Portuguese heroes, which lines the clifftops and from which you can gaze down the harsh drop to the black sands and the occasionally violent sea below. There's also a large terrace on which to sit, halfway up the hill at the top of a flight of steps (marked on the map). Cafés with views are mentioned in the following listings. on page 227.

SÃO FILIPE

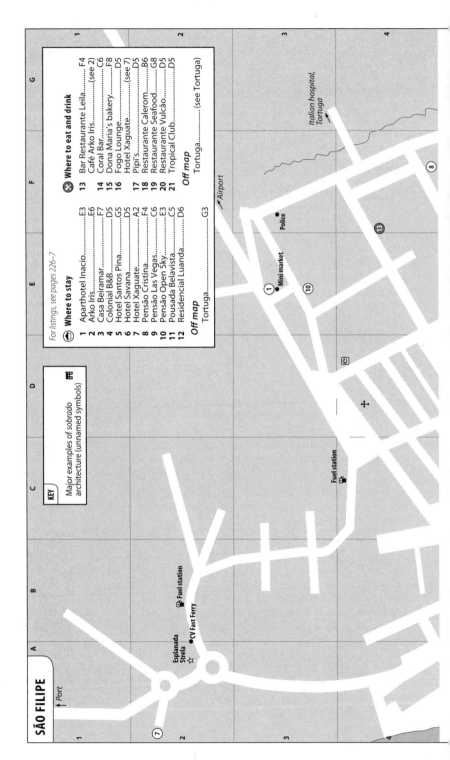

KEY

🏛 Major examples of sobrado
architecture (unnamed symbols)

For listings, see pages 226–7

🛏 Where to stay

1	Aparthotel Inacio..............E3
2	Arko Iris........................E6
3	Casa Beiramar..................F7
4	Colonial B&B....................D5
5	Hotel Santos Pina.............G5
6	Hotel Savana....................D5
7	Hotel Xaguate..................A2
8	Pensão Cristina................F4
9	Pensão Las Vegas..............C6
10	Pensão Open Sky................E3
11	Pousada Belavista.............C5
12	Residencial Luanda............D6

Off map
Tortuga..............................G3

✖ Where to eat and drink

13	Bar Restaurante Leila..........F4
	Café Arko Iris............(see 2)
14	Coral Bar........................C6
15	Dona Maria's bakery............F8
16	Fogo Lounge....................D5
	Hotel Xaguate...........(see 7)
17	Pipi's.............................D5
18	Restaurante Calerom...........B6
19	Restaurante Seafood...........G8
20	Restaurante Vulcão............D5
21	Tropical Club...................D5

Off map
Tortuga..............(see Tortuga)

↗ *Airport*

Police

Mini market

Fuel station

*Italian hospital,
Tortuga*

Esplanada
Strela
☆   ● CV Fast Ferry

🅿 Fuel station

↑ Port

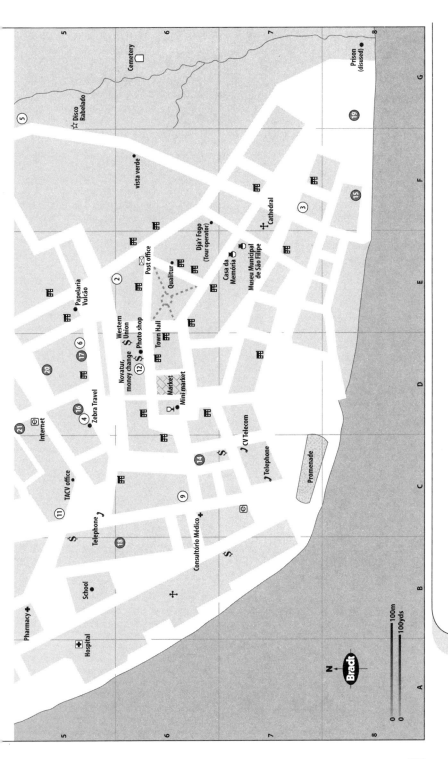

WHERE TO STAY Some hotels raise their prices threefold in April to capitalise on the island's annual festival. An interesting new development a few kilometres out of town is the Cerrado Resort, which will give visitors the chance to stay out in a rural setting whilst enjoying good-quality facilities and having opportunities for encounters with the locals and nature. The resort is being developed by Zebra Travel (see page 222), to whom enquiries should be directed. When complete, it will feature accommodation (including camping), bar, restaurant, swimming pool, yoga, meditation, nature walks and many other facilities. All listings are located on the map, pages 224–5.

Colonial B&B (9 rooms) Part of Zebra Travel (for contact information, see page 222), this tastefully restored & undeniably beautiful colonial building has a small swimming pool & great views. It also offers use of a jacuzzi & massages at extra cost. A pleasant & peaceful top-end place to stay. Price includes airport transfers. **$$$$**

Hotel Xaguate (38 rooms) ☎281 5000; e reservas@hotelxaguate.com; www. hotelxaguate.com. The hotel is set in a spectacular position on the headland, which can be enjoyed from the balconies of some of the rooms, or from the swimming pool terrace. This is the smartest hotel in town, with AC, satellite TV & most mod cons. Free Wi-Fi. Not all rooms have a sea view: it is worth paying the extra for this. Offers massage & organises excursions. Non-residents may swim there for a reasonable fee. **$$$$**

Casa Beiramar (3 apts, 1 room) ☎281 3485; m 913 8931; e info@cabo-verde.ch; www. cabo-verde.ch. Opposite the cathedral, this was formerly the Casa Renate & is a beautiful, restored *sobrado* with views of the ocean. Rooms are simple but en suite & have access to a shaded courtyard, where breakfast is served. **$$$**

Hotel Santos Pina (20 rooms) ☎281 4225; e hotelsantospina@gmail.com. Brand-new (2013), European-style hotel. Good facilities, though lacks the character of the converted *sobrado* hotels. Swimming pool under construction. Rooms have AC, TV, minibar. **$$$**

Tortuga (4 rooms) m 994 1512; e casamarelacv@hotmail.com; www.tortuga-fogo.eu. To the east of town, down a steep & rough track past the Italian hospital, this is a stunning retreat in a quiet & beautiful location looking out on the black-sand beach of Nossa Senhora da Encarnação. Beautifully planted with a large, shady terrace, the Italian proprietors grow their own vegetables & produce a lot of their own food, including marmalade, fish roe & cheeses. Rooms are en suite, & there is hot water & electricity

courtesy of solar panels. FB available & the restaurant is of very good repute. Internet access. You will need to take a taxi or the owner can arrange pickup. Often closed in May. **$$$**

Aparthotel Inacio (15 rooms) ☎281 2746; m 991 7917. A newish *pensão* in the orange building just off the airport road. An airy place, with lots of windows & shared veranda offering views either of the sea or of the volcano; fitted with most of the mod cons. There are better places for the same price but this one is convenient for the airport. **$$**

Arko Iris (8 rooms) Walk past the town hall & turn right; ☎281 2526; e arkoiris.fogo@ gmail.com; www.caboverde.com/pages/812526. htm. Don't expect stunning views here; just a good-value, modest hotel. Vibrant & colourful with modern fixtures & cosy atmosphere. Rooms have AC, TV & good storage. Rooms are above the café of the same name. Portuguese owned; English spoken. **$$**

Hotel Savana (16 rooms) ☎281 1490; e reservasavana@yahoo.com; www. hotelsavanafogo.com. A beautifully restored traditional *sobrado* house with great sea views in a quiet location. AC, TV, hot water & fridge. Plunge pool in courtyard, new restaurant & bar. Good value. **$$**

Pensão Open Sky (10 rooms) ☎281 2726/2012; m 991 4595; e majortelo@yahoo. com. At the top of town east of the main square. Some rooms are down at heel with internal windows, others are bright, offering views of the volcano or the sea. Pleasant rooftop terrace, restaurant for residents only. **$$**

Pousada Belavista (11 rooms) ☎281 1734/1220; e p_belavista@yahoo.com; www. bela-vista.net. Around the corner of the same block that houses the TACV office. This friendly, excellent-value hotel is a popular choice in an immaculately kept *sobrado* house. Rooms are en suite & vary in their equipment: some have AC, some have fans;

some have fridge & TV; all have hot water. Front rooms have balconies but can get a little noisy because *alugueres* stop in front. **$$**

🏠 **Residencial Luanda** (6 rooms) Near the town hall; ☎ 281 1181; e reservasavana@yahoo.com. Connected with Savana Hotel, this small residencial has comfortable clean rooms with AC & TV, hot water, some with balcony. **$$**

🏠 **Pensão Cristina** (4 rooms) ☎ 281 2623. On the east side of town, the rooms are basic but en suite & there's a small restaurant. It is linked with the hotel in Mosteiros & may be closed off-season when the owner concentrates on that hotel. **$**

A Pensão Las Vegas (12 rooms) ☎ 281 2223. The Las Vegas has friendly management & a variety of rooms, some with balconies giving sea views to Brava. Not the best, but often the cheapest acceptable option in town. **$**

✖ WHERE TO EAT AND DRINK

Find freshly made bread, cakes and warm ginger biscuits at Dona Maria's bakery on the edge of the cliff, just up from the old prison. It's around the back in an alley next to the sea wall. There is also an established *pastelaria* in the north of town [224 F4] and a new one next to Fogo Lounge [225 D5].

Fresh goat's cheese, fruit and tomatoes can be found in the municipal market in the middle of town, in the same block as the town hall. All listings are located on the map, pages 224–5.

✖ **Hotel Xaguate** Has a good-quality restaurant, normally with seating on the terrace overlooking the ocean – otherwise it's the rather soulless AC interior. **$$$$**

✖ **Fogo Lounge** ☎ 281 3373; m 918 5430. Off the main square, courtyard with large umbrellas & serving a variety of food including some local specialities & varied b/fast options. **$$$**

✖ **Pipi's** Next to Hotel Savana. ⏰ 07.30–03.00 daily. Cape Verde native Gerard & his Senegalese wife have created a stylish, spacious bar/restaurant next to the Hotel Savana. Tasty Senegalese specialities, snacks, drinks & ambience on the shady terrace. **$$$**

✖ **Restaurante Calerom** An excellent open-air place for breakfast *cachupa*, barbecued chicken & other tasty delights. Live music Sat, sometimes till 02.00 or later. **$$$**

✖ **Restaurante Seafood** ☎ 281 2623; e seafoodalmada@cvtelecom.cv; www.seafoodfogo.com; ⏰ for b/fast, lunch & dinner. Down near the prison with a good view of the sea, & receives good reports. **$$$**

✖ **Tortuga** (for contact details, see *Where to stay*, opposite) ⏰ daily. Highly rated as one of the best in town…though it's not actually in town. It's essential both to book & to arrange transport to this inaccessible spot. **$$$**

✖ **Tropical Club** ☎ 281 2161. Popular choice with an outside terrace. Claims to be the best in town and some locals agree. Good range of fish dishes & seafood. Often has live music at weekends. **$$$**

✖ **Bar Restaurante Leila** ☎ 281 1214. Consistently good reports about the food in this unpretentious basement restaurant. **$$**

✖ **Café Arko Iris** ☎ 281 2526; ⏰ all day daily. European-style menu, mainly burgers & pizzas served in a modern & colourful setting. **$$**

✖ **Coral Bar** A watering hole & good-value eatery in the centre of town, with outside tables in inner courtyard. **$$**

✖ **Restaurante Vulcão** Copious local fare & inexpensive. **$$**

ENTERTAINMENT AND NIGHTLIFE

☆ **Esplanada Strela/Casa de Cinema** [224 A2] On the roundabout to the northwest of town. Good reputation for traditional music most Fri nights, plus a venue for other cultural events. Unusually, events start punctually! Admission can be around 1,200$, but this may include buffet dinner. On the roundabout at the northwest of town.

🍷 **Pipi's** [225 D5] A great, tasteful place to chill out into the wee small hours (see listing above for more details).

🍷 **Tropical** [225 D5] Traditional music every Fri night (see listing above for more details).

☆ **Discoteca Rabelado** [225 G5] Lem de Baixo, São Filipe; ☎ 281 1468; ⏰ w/ends.

Fogo   SÃO FILIPE

7

OTHER PRACTICALITIES
Airlines
TACV [225 C5] (✆ 281 1340/1701; ⊕ 08.00–13.00 & 15.00–17.00 Mon–Fri) Novatur agency sells national and international air tickets.

Banks
BCA and BCN (both with ATM); Caixa Economica.

Ferries
CV Fast ferry [224 A/B2] (✆ 261 7552; ⊕ 08.00–18.00 Mon–Fri) North end of town. Tickets can also be booked through tour operators such as Qualitur or Zebra.

Hospital
[225 A5] (✆ 281 1130) The main hospital is on the same road as the BCA bank, further up on the left. A previously private Italian hospital [224 G3] which has an operating theatre and a good reputation, located to the east of town, has been donated by Italy to Cape Verde.

Internet
Free Wi-Fi is available in the praça in front of the town hall, if you have your own laptop. Internet also available at Restaurante Calerom and a few other places around town.

Pharmacy
[225 B5] Near the main hospital, head up the hill east of the main praça.

Police
[224 F3] (✆ 281 1132)

Post office
[225 E6] (⊕ 08.00–15.00 Mon–Sat) Down in the town hall square.

Shopping
Souvenirs, including Fogo wine and coffee, and crafts, are on sale at Qualitur [225 E6], Dja'r Fogo [225 F6] (see page 222) as well as the museum. Food supplies can be found at the various small mini-supermarkets.

Tourist information
None, but the tour operators (see page 222) are very helpful. There is a very helpful information kiosk in Chã das Caldeiras.

Water use
Water is a very scarce resource on Fogo, so be sparing with your usage.

WHAT TO SEE AND DO
Architecture Wander the streets admiring the *sobrado* architecture. About 100 of these houses remain – built by the rich and decorated with fine woods and tiles imported from Portugal and West Africa. If you can peek into one of them take the opportunity: a central courtyard planted with trees and vines gave coolness and shade and around it, on the ground floor, were the working rooms. The next floor was more beautiful, lined with an inside balcony that overlooked the courtyard on three sides – this was the floor for the master and his family. On the street side there was a balcony of carved wood. It is said that slaves did not ascend to the first floor except once a year, on the festival of Santa Cruz. During the summer the town house was closed and the family went inland to oversee the farming. See map (pages 224–5) for the location of some more prominent examples.

Casa da Memória [225 E7] (The 'House of Memory') ✆ 281 2765; e moniquewidmer@yahoo.com.br; www.casadamemoria.com.cv; ⊕ 10.00–12.00 Wed–Fri or by prior appointment; free) A private museum in a restored family house, run by a Cape Verdean team together with Monique, who has lived in Cape Verde for over 30 years. Through its exhibits, it depicts the history of Fogo from the early to mid-1800s. Full of photos, domestic objects and a patio in which there was Fogo's first cinema, now restored and with a programme of films showing in the open air. Cultural events are held there, as well as some conferences. The Casa also has a library packed with interesting literature about the islands, including a handful of books in English. Although admission is free, donations which go towards the upkeep will be gratefully received.

Museu Municipal de São Filipe [225 E7] (*São Filipe Municipal Museum;* ⊠ *281 1295;* e *camaramunicipal@yahoo.com.br; admission 100$, children & students free*) A welcome addition to the city's cultural scene. Here you'll find some excellent displays explaining the everyday life of Fogo's inhabitants including their gastronomy and wine, festivals and agriculture. There is a reconstruction of a *funco*, a traditional Fogo house made out of volcanic rock. A café is planned. Information boards are only in Portuguese. A selection of crafts and Fogo wine are available for purchase.

The beach and swimming A walk down the grotty *ribeira* road to the black beach is interesting, if not a conventional tourist attraction. This is a poor part of town, with goats foraging and pigs tethered in makeshift shelters. Below lies a strip of black sand under the ominous Fogo cliffs, lashed by Atlantic breakers. As you begin your descent you will see the prison. Perched on the cliff, with a view of both the ocean and the cemetery, it must have afforded many a prisoner an inspirational setting in which to reflect on his misdemeanours. Take a cue from the locals as to whether swimming is safe – currents can be strong.

Take a swim at the Hotel Xaguate [224 A2], which has an enjoyable poolside terrace. Admission for non-residents is 1,500$, but that includes lunch.

CHÃ DAS CALDEIRAS

The road to the volcano passes first through pleasant countryside dotted with abandoned Portuguese farms, and old volcano cones, and filled with cashew, banana and papaya trees. Just after a left fork, where the sign says '14km to Parc Natural de Fogo', is the 1951 lava spill down the right-hand slope.

Later the road becomes a series of terrifyingly steep hairpin bends with views down the massive ancient lava spills to the coast. Then it enters the echoing silence of the crater. Its sinister dark walls, and the vast clods of lava scattered over it, make one feel very small.

Some of the people are of a different race – light skinned, straight haired, some of them even blond and blue eyed. These are the descendants of the fecund Duc de Montrond (see box, *The Duke of Montrond*, page 233), a French nobleman who came here in the 19th century and brought the vines that began Fogo's wine production. Clearly he planted his seeds in more ways than one as currently more than half of the Chã villagers bear the Montrond name!

There are attempts to improve the crater's fragile ecology and geology, and develop an economy (see box, page 219). One step has been to define the crater as a natural park; another has been to set up small-scale tourism. The park office is at the entrance to the crater and a new visitor centre is due to open in 2014.

The town is traditionally split into two villages: Portela (upper) and Bangaeira (lower), though there is actually very little to distinguish them from each other. Nevertheless, that does not diminish the rivalry when the two meet in local football matches, in a stadium which must be almost unbeatable for its stunning volcanic backdrop.

In many places in Chã das Caldeiras the power is turned on in the early evening and off at 22.00.

GETTING THERE AND AWAY There is a midday *aluguer* from São Filipe (500$). The return journey starts very early: listen for the horn which sounds loudly in the village at about 06.00. Let your *pensão* proprietor know the night before that you want transport, and they should make sure that the *aluguer* doesn't leave without you. For a small supplement, you can ask to be dropped at the airport first. Pedra Brabo has its own vehicle for daily transfers, though these cost more.

If you prefer to walk some of the way to the volcano, then catch an *aluguer* from town to Achada Furna; it takes three hours to cover the steep road from there.

A day trip to the volcano is tricky by public transport, though there are cars in the crater which can be chartered as taxis for the trip back to São Filipe for several thousand escudos. Many people organise their visit through Qualitur or Dja'r Fogo.

⌂ WHERE TO STAY

You will not find luxury up in Chã das Caldeiras. But the locals don't live in luxury and the minor hardship of a cold shower and part-time electricity is a small sufferance when set against the stunning landscape and unique ambience. Things are constantly improving however, with increased availability of hot water and installation of solar panels. Book in advance, as accommodation can be full in busy season.

⌂ **Casa Marisa** (10 rooms) ☏ 282 1662; e info@fogo-marisa.com; http://fogo-marisa.com/ or book through Pedra Brabo. Basic but newly built en suite rooms in a lava-brick style similar to Pedra Brabo, plus a restaurant & bar. Solar power will soon provide 24 hour electricity. Hot water. **$$**

⌂ **Pousada Pedra Brabo** (12 rooms) ☏ 282 1521; e pedrabrabo@cvtelecom.cv; www.pedrabrabo.net. A single-storey lava-brick guesthouse, its rooms arranged around a pretty courtyard – it manages to be both basic & tasteful at the same time. With or without private bathroom. The food is excellent, the view stunning. There is electricity from a generator, but solar power may be installed by the date of this book's publication. **$$**

⌂ **Sirio Bed & Breakfast** (6 rooms) ☏ 282 1586; e chatour@chatourfogo.com; www.

chatourfogo.com. A newly constructed B&B at the foot of the volcano. Some rooms have private bathroom. **$$**

⌂ **Casa Fernando** (11 rooms) ☏ 282 1531. Mountain guide Fernando offers rooms adjacent to his family's house. Separate bathroom & no hot water, reflected in the lower price. **$**

⌂ **Homestays** Accommodation is either in the houses of local people or in rooms they have built alongside especially for tourists. Best to ask in São Filipe or at the visitor centre when you arrive in Chã. Accommodation is pretty basic; within people's houses it is sometimes just a windowless room made of lava blocks. But the best are clean & careful preparations are made for visitors, who are received with great delight & good spirits. Range of prices.

✗ WHERE TO EAT AND DRINK

✗ **Casa Marisa** (see listing above) **$$$**

✗ **Pousada Pedra Brabo** (see listing above) ⊕ for lunch & dinner, though it can be chaotic in the busy seasons with day trippers at lunch. **$$$**

✗ **Bar Restaurante Antares** ☏ 282 1528; m 994 9128. Serves traditional food, Italian food & pizza. **$$**

ENTERTAINMENT AND NIGHTLIFE There is often wine, music and dancing into the small hours at Casa Ramiro, the grocer's store/bar at the midpoint between the two villages. An evening there is unforgettable, and in quiet times you may be invited by the musicians to someone's house to continue the party. No payment is expected for the entertainment.

WHAT TO SEE AND DO

Hiking The highlights are the walk up and down the Pico (which can take anything between three and six hours depending on your fitness and your proficiency at

The music is due to start at Ramiro's at 18.00, so we joke that it should be underway by 20.00. But an unexpected busload of Cape Verdeans has turned up mid-afternoon from São Filipe, hell-bent on having a party, and the occupants are already jammed into the tiny space in front of the grocery store's counter when we arrive at 17.00. It's chaos as the party-goers clamour to buy more wine: it's clear from the swaying and clapping that these are far from being their first bottles.

Behind the counter, Ramiro is combining some mournful violin-playing with customer service, putting down his instrument to sell a packet of biscuits or some olives. Antonio strums his tiny *cavoquinho* one-handed as he passes over a bottle of red wine; in charge of the till, Jose is playing percussion while taking money and handing out change. An old man in a distinctive white cloth-cap and probably in his eighties, who keeps asking me if I am from '*A-mer-ee-ca*', is playing an acoustic guitar.

In the corner sits Kevin, son of an emigrant to Massachusetts and visiting the land of his roots for the first time at the age of 25. He tells me that he is fluent in *kriolu*, despite never having been here, but that does not prevent him being relentlessly teased by the locals for not knowing the words to the songs, which tumble out from behind the counter one after the other.

'Soon, we go to my brother's house. He is returning to America. Soon. We celebrate!' the octogenarian in the white cap tells me earnestly.

And sure enough, as the smiling, waving bus party depart for the vertiginous trip back to the island capital, their happy and somewhat blurred faces pressed against the windows of their crowded *aluguer*, Ramiro's grocery store/music venue is closed up and we pile into a dual-cab pick-up for the short drive down towards the only light left shining in the village. Inside the house are maybe 20 people, most of them seemingly living there; three generations, maybe four. I am introduced to the 'brother', a man in his seventies with a Boston Celtics sports cap on his head.

'So,' I enquire, conscious of the stated reason for this party, 'is it tomorrow that you're leaving for the States?'

'No,' comes the reply, as he picks up his guitar 'I'll be going back in about 35 years.' I estimate that, by then, he'll be about 110 years old. Perhaps these volcano-dwellers have discovered the secret of immortality.

At this point, the electricity goes off, but the wail of the violin, the frenetic strumming of the guitars and the tinny resonance of the *cavoquinho* have only just begun. These guys might still be playing in 35 years.

A pot of food is produced by the womenfolk of the house, a delicious stew accompanied by some rice. We are encouraged to eat, the Fogo wine flows a lot quicker than lava.

Towards midnight, we say our thanks and leave, despite protestations that we stay. Amazingly, it is us who are thanked profusely, and we depart feeling as if we have done these incredibly warm, generous people some kind of favour. Outside in the cold and the dark, the giant, brooding volcano seems to point upwards to a star-spangled sky.

running back down through the lava powder – see page 235), and the walk down to Mosteiros. Many visitors walk up the smaller, 1995 peak for a much less demanding hike or in order to limber up for the big one. New trails are being developed by the park offices, and it should be possible to traverse the crater rim, which will be a major attraction, and also to enter the crater over the rim from Ponte Alto do Sul, in the southwest. Some of these walks are described in *Hikes*, page 234.

For some walks it is essential to have a guide and the use of one is strongly recommended. An example is climbing the Pico de Fogo, because the path shifts with the movements of the ash. The crater rim, to be negotiated at times by clipping oneself to a cable handrail, should also involve a guide.

There are several guides conversant with the natural history of the volcano, having worked with botanists and geologists. The guides have recently formed themselves into an association, organised by an energetic and passionate Turkish/German, which should guarantee a good level of training and regularise pricing. At present, a list of prices is published by the association and is on display in Pedra Brabo and should also be available from the information centre. In 2013, a guide cost 4,000$ per group of four to ascend the big Pico, 2,000$ to ascend the 1995 peak. If not booking through an operator, try English-speaking Jose Lopes dos Santos (m *952 7093;* e *jose.doce@yahoo.com.br*), who has had good reports. For walks where a guide is not essential, you might still consider employing one to embellish the experience and contribute to the local economy.

Wine It may seem extraordinary to most visitors to the crater that anything is grown here at all. But as you walk from the village towards the Pico, depending on the time of year, you'll quickly encounter apparently randomly planted vines. Each of these belongs to someone, however. Each year the planting of the vines creeps higher up the mountain. The humidity is trapped by the ash and a bit of animal manure is used to encourage the vines' growth. There is no watering of the vines, the trapped humidity and any rainfall providing the only moisture. Harvesting takes place in June.

As you walk towards Bangaeira from Portela, the winery is on your left. It is a cooperative with 96 members and six staff and currently produces between 50,000–100,000 litres per year. The grapes grown are muscatel and touriga and examples of its reds, whites and rosés can be found in restaurants throughout Cape Verde. The production is all consumed domestically, though the odd bottle or two might be 'smuggled' back to the United States by homesick emigrants after their holidays in the archipelago, says the co-operative's president. All the wine from the co-operative is sold under the 'Cha' label, and given the seemingly hostile conditions, is very good indeed. In addition to wine, liqueurs made with pomegranate and herbs are sold here.

Casa Ramiro and other outlets sell wine with the Manecom label (homemade by Adriano Montrond, who also has his own tasting shed down towards Bangaeira). Some of the unlabelled wine does not have the same quality as the Chã brand.

Information centre (☉ *08.00–12.00* & *15.00–17.00 daily*) Almost in the centre, between the two villages, this rondavel is the place for booking rooms, hiring guides and finding out about crater life through some exhibits. There is for example an exhibit on the genealogy of the Montrond family, including profiles of some of its more colourful characters; there are also displays about endemic species, and old and new photographs of the landscape, through which you can trace its changing topography.

An architecturally stunning new visitor centre, located at the entrance to the villages, was structurally complete as of June 2013, but waiting to be kitted out and due to be fully functional by 2014. The intention is that it will house a theatre, museum, laboratory for scientists and be used for other purposes such as foreign language lessons for the guides. With its sinister, sleek black walls, it blends beautifully into the surroundings. Once it is opened, the guide bookings will still be based at the rondavel in town.

Shop On the Bangaeira side of Portela a little shop sells an array of Fogo wines as well as Manecom wine (homemade by Adriano Montrond), various spirits, fruit juices and simple crafts.. Pedra Brabo also sells some local products and you may also be approached in the dusty streets by children selling articles made from the few materials locally available. Arte Tarzon, on the left side as you head for Bangeiro, sells masks and other crafts made out of lava rock. Prices are very modest.

Spa A relaxing massage may be just what you need and deserve if you have climbed to the summit of the Pico. The recently opened **Spa Natura** (⏲ *987 7037*) is run by a returned emigrant and offers inexpensive massage, reflexology, manicures and pedicures. The setting is very rustic, situated on the main road near the Pedra Brabo.

Fogo MOSTEIROS

MOSTEIROS

The town, also known as Igreja, is a useful stopping-off point during trips around the island but otherwise is not really worth a visit. It has a pretty centre, squashed between the mountain and the sea, and a depressing suburbia of black, lava-block houses built on black lava rock.

GETTING THERE AND AWAY The southern *aluguer* run to and from São Filipe is a fantastic journey along the precipitous eastern slope of the island but since the opening of the road around the north, that is the direction that most of the public transport goes. The proprietor of Pensão Christine will arrange for one of the drivers to call at the hotel for you at about at an invigorating 04.45. *Alugueres* leave São Filipe for Mosteiros at about midday.

WHERE TO STAY AND EAT

Pensão Restaurante Christine e Irmãos (7 rooms) ☎283 1045. In a green building on the main road through town; it has lovely, airy rooms & a big restaurant with recommended food. **$$**

Pensão Tchon de Café (12 rooms) ☎283 1610. Rooms are pleasant, en suite with hot water in this *pensão* nestled at the foot of a hill. There's a small restaurant with courtyard. **$$**

OTHER PRACTICALITIES

Airlines
TACV (☎283 1033; ⏰ 08.00–12.00 & 14.00–16.00 Mon–Fri) In Mosteiros's main square.

Bank
(⏰ 08.00–14.00 Mon–Fri).

Hospital
(☎283 1034) In the same square as the TACV office.

Post office
(⏰ 08.00–12.00 & 14.00–16.00 Mon–Fri) In the other square.

OTHER PLACES TO VISIT

Nothing else on Fogo matches a crater visit, but all of the visits below are pleasant alternative ways of filling spare days on the island.

SÃO LOURENÇO A large church and a peaceful graveyard – clusters of white crosses all with stunning views of Brava. Visiting it is a pleasant way of enjoying the green Fogo lowlands. It is a 12km round trip but you will probably find lifts for parts of the way. Leave São Filipe from the roundabout opposite the Hotel Xaguate, and, with your back to the hotel, take the second turning on the left (the first leads down to the port).

MONTE GENEBRA AND NOSSA SENHORA DO SOCORRO Find an *aluguer* to Forno and from there walk to the village of Luzia Nunes, then take the left fork to Monte Genebra. German development workers helped to build these gardens in 1976. Pumping stations take hundreds of cubic metres of water from a natural spring near the sea, to water tomatoes, potatoes, cabbages and fruits. You can go to the top of Monte Genebra, while down towards the sea is the little chapel of Nossa Senhora do Socorro.

PONTO DO SALINA This is one of the few possible swimming creeks on Fogo where the lava here has formed a natural pool. It is located close to São Jorge north of São Filipe. Take an *aluguer* to São Jorge and walk down to the sea. The walk there and back takes about two hours.

HIKES

Colum Wilson (CW); Aisling Irwin (AI); Hannah Cruttenden (HC); Murray Stewart (MS)

1 THE PICO

Distance: 7km; time: return trip between 4 and 7 hours; difficulty: 2 (MS)
Note that it requires energy and fitness particularly because there is no easy way of

going back: to return halfway along requires a guide, but so does continuing to the top and there is generally only one guide per group.

Walking from Portela towards Bangaeira, the walk starts by taking the wide track to your right after Sirio's B&B. First there is a gentle, flat meander through scattered fig trees, vines, apple and pear trees, as well as mustard plants and the odd lavender bush. To the uninformed, it seems incredible that anything grows here at all, but the cultivation is healthy if unusual. After ten minutes, the route goes off the main track and you face the volcano head-on. For the following half-hour, the slope is gentle, before ramping up steeply through ash and then onto a shoulder of stones, where occasionally you may have to scramble on all fours. Walking in ash is often a case of taking two steps forward and one back, making the calves protest. From the village to the summit will take most climbers between three and five hours. You may well come across examples of *lingua de vaca* (cow's tongue), an endemic plant, but you may be too focused on avoiding a fall. You will be grateful for any breeze. Away to your left, you will see the sea, bordered by the white of waves crashing onto the shore. At around two-thirds of the climb, you may catch the first whiff of sulphur, then it's gone on the wind, only to return again, this time perhaps stronger. From the summit, gazing down into the crater, the twin villages are like dust specks below. Marvelling at the crater in front of you and pondering the *via ferrata* for the more adventurous, you will no doubt conclude that all the effort has been worthwhile. This is one of the steepest and most spectacular volcanic cones in the world and you have just conquered it. Now, the real fun is about to begin.

The first part of the descent involves fifteen minutes of picking your way back down over the stony descent. Then, your guide takes you across to the top of the slope of ash scree. Staring down maybe 600m of steep descent, off he sets with giant strides, each ending in his front leg sinking knee-high in *lapilli*. Perhaps tentatively at first you follow him, but quickly you realise that you can't fall and your confidence and speed increase accordingly. You have to focus on what's in front of you, as the odd rock will appear, threatening to de-rail you and halt your rapid return to the villages. This is simply better than any fairground rollercoaster, surely. Your guide will have done this many times before, so is likely to be more fearless and quicker than you, however much of your inner daredevil you release. Eventually the ash becomes thinner and you have to return to a more conventional descent, as the depth of ash is no longer enough to cushion those giant strides. As long as your knees have held up, you'll have a giant smile on your face. As well as dirty black legs, you will have socks that will need several washes and boots that will be spewing out bits of ash for weeks to come.

2 PORTELA–1995 PEAK–PORTELA

Distance: 7km; time: 2 hours 10 minutes; difficulty: 2 (CW)

You will never have done a walk like this. Walking through this lava field is like walking through a nightmarish black sea that has frozen in mid-storm. Slabs of dark rock rest at jagged angles like buckled plates of ice; elsewhere, rivulets of molten rock have hardened in place. Beyond the lava field, you crunch across a glittering black landscape of *lapilli* that seems to muffle sound and life. The tricky bit is to find the rough path that takes you across the lava field up towards the peak.

From Portela, take the cobbled road that leads to São Filipe. After about 40 minutes you will pass just beyond the 9km² lava field that flows down in an ever-widening river from the 1995 peak and reach a point that is directly between Pico Beco on your right, and the 1995 peak on your left. Looking up at the cone you will see it is made of black, chilled fragments of lava, known as *scoria*. These have been turned a rusty red by exposure to the hot sulphur dioxide that poured out in the first few years after the eruption. The yellow patches are sulphur, precipitated from the gas as it cooled.

A few hundred metres before the road does an obvious turn to the left followed directly by an obvious turn to the right, strike out from the road to the left across the black sand (there is no path) towards the 1995 peak. About 600m from the road, you should join the edge of the lava field, and immediately start ascending on a rough path. This path takes you in a northerly direction across the side of the Pico for a few hundred metres before starting to bear northeast.

The crater of the 1995 peak is a gash a few hundred metres long running in a northeast direction. You are approaching the crater at the point where the lava spilled out and down the side from the southwest end. Twenty minutes after leaving the road, you will be at a low rim within the open southwest end of the crater. If you are prepared to scramble over loose rock and lava for another 50m, you will be able to look into the very eye of the crater, a jumble of massive yellow-streaked boulders and lumps of lava.

You must return the same way you arrived, which should take about 40 minutes.

As an alternative, you can approach the northern rim of the 1995 crater from the northeast, where there is no path.

3 BANGAEIRA–CRATER RIM–BANGAEIRA
Distance: approximately 14km; time: 5 hours; difficulty: 2 (AI)
This trip takes you up to the rim of the volcano for a stunning bird's-eye view of the crater. Parts of the path are steep and slippery.

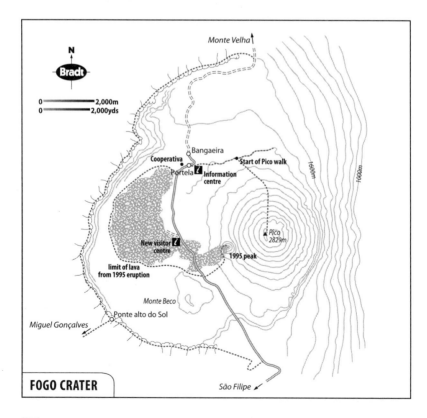

From the *Cooperativa* walk the 5km north along the road to the barrier that marks the protected forest. Continue down the road for 15 minutes to a fork. The road to the right leads to Mosteiros. Follow the left-hand road which becomes a dirt track, quite precarious in places. It winds its way up the side of the volcano. Soon you find yourself above the low cloud, gazing at a superb view of Santiago. The road eventually climbs steeply upwards to a large white building used to store rice and grain: this is where cars must stop. Walk past the front of the storehouse and on to a path running along the left-hand side of the building and up towards the volcano rim. It's a steep climb and the path is slippery in places but it shouldn't take longer than half an hour to get to the top.

This part of the crater is very green and you will see women from the villages gathering firewood. Recent eruptions are 'mapped out' in the vast area below, covered by lava, which pushes right up to the edge of the villages of **Bangaeira** and **Portela** to the right. The darkest lava is from the most recent 1995 eruption. Closer to you, the slightly lighter coloured lava is from 1951; the lightest-coloured lava, directly in front of you, is oldest of all. It is possible to continue walking round the rim – take a guide.

4 COOPERATIVA–PORTELA–1995 LAVA FLOW–BOCA FONTE–COOPERATIVA

Distance: 6km; time: 2 hours; difficulty: 1 (HC)
This two-hour walk starts at the *Cooperativa*. Head back towards the village of **Portela**, but as you leave the village, turn off to the right following the car tracks in the grey soil. The track leads you towards the west walls of the crater and continues round the edge of the 1995 lava to the former village of Boca Fonte – now destroyed except for the colonnaded façade of a *Cooperativa* which still stands at the edge of the flow. About 100m further on, climb up on to the lava and clamber across it to get a view of a house marooned in the flow. A short walk later you arrive at the vineyards – the vines look almost pitiful, straggling along the ground like weeds. Next, after curving round to the left and on to the southern side, you'll see several small agricultural and fruit farms. Their produce goes to the market in São Filipe. Shortly afterwards there's a chance to turn back towards the Pico and the main road back to Portela.

5 CRATER–MONTEBARRO–PAI ANTÓNIO–MOSTEIROS

Distance: approximately 10km; time: 4½ hours; difficulty: 2 (AI)
This delightful walk takes you out of the crater and down the volcano's steep northeastern side, with views across the sea to Santiago, and a host of pretty plantations, in particular oranges and coffee. The hike involves some steep descents likely to produce aching and shaking knees, and those who find such descents difficult could find the walk takes five hours. Navigationally it is pretty easy.

Begin with a 5km walk north along the road through the crater which takes you out, past a road barrier that marks the protected forest and on past a road to the left that goes to **Montinho**. Two minutes after this turning there is a steep little path down to the right. You can stick with the road or follow this short cut, in which case you will rejoin the road after ten minutes, turning right. Some 15 minutes past this point you arrive in Monte Velho. The road bends to the right over the bridge where there are a few small houses. After crossing the bridge leave the road and turn right, down the right-hand side of the first house. The path takes you down the side of a ravine, across which can be seen the president's house. Giant *carapate* plants stack the sides of the path. Descend through **Pede Pranta**, after which the ban on farming expires. You enter little valleys planted with coffee, mango and orange plants.

Mist drifts upwards and the view of the ocean through the vegetation is beautiful. After a while, descending past little dwellings built on terraces of lava rock you reach the first region of Mosteiros – **Montebarro** – and the air is filled with the scents of oranges and fires and the noise of children and cockerels. Three hours into the walk you reach **Pai António**, with a steeply cobbled street, from where it is a 40-minute walk down the cobbled road (ignoring the left turning to Feijoal) to the centre of Mosteiros. Alternatively, it should be possible to pick up a lift in Pai António to save your knees that last steep descent.

6 THE CRATER RIM

This is probably the longest walk available as it could take as long as two days, but a shorter version is possible. Stretches of the rim are so precarious (Ponte Alto de Norte and Ponte Alto do Sol are the worst sections) that the park staff have erected cable handrails to which you can clip yourself with a hoop available from the park offices. It is essential to have a guide.

7 MOSTEIROS–FEIJOAL–MOSTEIROS

Distance: approximately 5km; time: 2 hours; difficulty: 2 (AI)

There are various strolls up into the lower slopes of the volcano. To walk up to **Feijoal** for a drink, leave Mosteiros on the south road and, a little after the big Delegação de Fogo, take the cobbled road on the right (ignore a turning up to the left just before Feijoal). After a drink at the *mercado*, find a little footpath (*caminho para Igreja*) back into the centre of Mosteiros: with your back to the *mercado* turn right and the path is a few metres along on the left, running between two buildings. It's a bit slippery and the less sure of foot may prefer to return by the road.

8 CAVES

Distance: approximately 1km; time: 1 hour; difficulty: 1 (JC)

A simple walk to see some caves that you can look inside but would need a guide to go into. The caves are quite deep.

WALKING ROUND THE NORTH From the Mosteiros end, the first 2km north along the coast are dismal – save your legs and hitch if you can. Just before the disused airport, there is a left turning uphill. This is the beginning of a spectacular road, which goes up to Ribeira Ilhéu and then continues as a 9km track to São Jorge. From there you have to try and hitch back to São Filipe – there is supposed to be an *aluguer* at 13.00. The better alternative is to take a mid-morning *aluguer* to São Jorge from São Filipe and walk in the other direction, staying in Mosteiros at the end of the walk.

TRAILS UNDER DEVELOPMENT

The path up to the crater rim from **Miguel Gonçalves** is shingly and unpleasant in places, and there are plans to rebuild it. However, once you have reached the crater rim (at Ponte Alto do Sol), the crater trail to the southeast is easy and ends at the road that enters the crater.

8

Brava

Swallows of the wide seas
What wind of loyalty
Brings you on this bitter journey
To our land of *Sodade*
Eugénio Tavares, quoted in Archibald Lyall,
Black and White Make Brown (Heinemann, 1938)

Brava is the most secret of the islands – a volcano crater hides its town, rough seas encircle it and the winds that buffet it are so strong that its airport has been closed. Brava lies only 20km from its big brother, Fogo, but many visitors to Cape Verde will merely glimpse it from the greater island's western slopes.

Brava – or 'wild' island – appears at first to live up to the meaning of its name. Approaching by boat, the dark mass resolves itself into sheer cliffs with painted houses dotting the heights above. A few fishing hamlets huddle at sea level.

But its unpromising slopes hide a hinterland that is at times fertile and moist, filled with hibiscus flowers and cultivation. At least that is how it was: today, after years of drought, its flowers are less visible and its food more likely to be imported than grown.

This tiny, westerly island, dropping off the end of the archipelago into the Atlantic, seems to hide from its companions and look instead towards where the sun sets – it is dreaming of the wealth of the USA. Perhaps that is no surprise. For Brava is the island where the great 19th-century American whaling ships called to pick up crews and spirit hopeful young men away to new lives in another continent (see box, page 257). The legacy is an island full of empty houses waiting for the return of the *Americanos* who have built them for their retirement. Meanwhile, a big container ship from Boston visits several times a year and American goods appear in the streets. Brava Creole is peppered with American expressions, those who speak English do so with a transatlantic twang, their words emerging from beneath a Boston Red Sox baseball cap. For some visitors and the few expats who have chosen to live here, Brava is the most 'authentic' of the islands. There are few concessions to tourism and the inhabitants get on with their everyday lives regardless. Having said that, those visitors who choose to engage with the locals will find a friendly, welcoming and gregarious people, more than willing to share their time and space with tourists. At times you may feel that *you* are the real attraction.

HIGHLIGHTS AND LOWLIGHTS

Go for the walking, for the peace and for the sheer authenticity and intrigue of a place that is so out of the way. Don't go for beaches or watersports, don't expect any conventional tourist attractions, and don't go if you are pushed for time. If you have

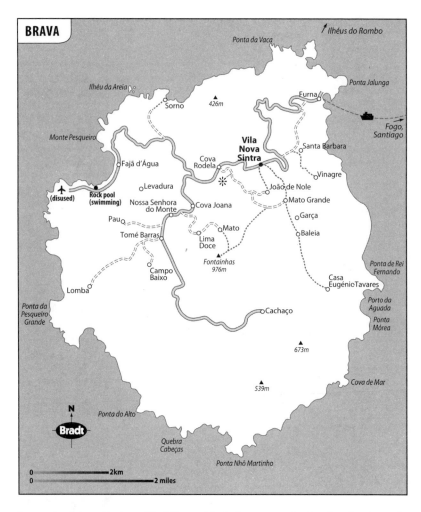

BRAVA

Ilhéus do Rombo

Ponta da Vaca

Ponta Jalunga

Ilhéu da Areia

Sorno

▲ 426m

Furna

Ponta Jalunga

Fogo, Santiago

Monte Pesqueiro

Fajã d'Água

Cova Rodela

Vila Nova Sintra

Santa Barbara

Vinagre

✈ (disused)

Rock pool (swimming)

Levadura

Nossa Senhora do Monte

Cova Joana

※

João de Nole

Mato Grande

Pau

Tomé Barras

Lima Doce

Mato

Garça

Baleia

Fontainhas 976m

Ponta de Rei Fernando

Campo Baixo

Casa Eugénio Tavares

Porto da Aguada

Lomba

Cachaço

Ponta Mórea

Ponta da Pesqueiro Grande

▲ 673m

N

Bradt

Ponta do Alto

Quebra Cabeças

Ponta Nhô Martinho

▲ 539m

Cova de Mar

0 ————2km
0 ————2 miles

just arrived from Praia or São Filipe, with their comparative bustle of taxis gently tooting their horns for your business, you will find Brava's capital, Vila Nova Sintra, to be a quiet alternative. With little traffic, cobbled streets and a sense of space, it is a pleasant town in which to stroll, though with few outright attractions as such.

SUGGESTED ITINERARY AND NUMBER OF DAYS
Brava is small. Someone who wants to just grab the sights and go could see the island in less than a day by vehicle. That would be a shame, as Fajã d'Água is a beautiful place to relax for a few days, perhaps taking a fishing trip, and keen hikers will find several days' worth of enchanting walks to undertake.

BACKGROUND INFORMATION

HISTORY Brava is, geologically speaking, part of Fogo. The channel between them is just a few hundred metres deep – shallow compared with the ocean floor that surrounds the rest of Brava, whose cliffs plunge 4km down beyond sea level. The oldest rocks of Fogo lie on the side that faces Brava and are very similar to Bravan rock, which is how their relationship has been deduced.

There are no volcanic eruptions now, but the land is not completely calm – clusters of earthquakes shake it, although most are too gentle to be noticed. Yet its active history was recent and its volcano cones are all less than 10,000 years old.

There is a legend about the first settlers of Brava. A young Portuguese aristocrat fell in love with a girl well below him in social class. To prevent their marriage, his parents banished the girl and her family to Fogo, but he pursued her on another ship and escaped with her to the haven of Brava. There they settled in the valley of Fajã d'Água, living with some of the loyal sailors who accompanied them.

Brava was discovered on 24 June 1462, on the saint's day of St John the Baptist (São João Baptista), after whom it was originally named. Settlers arrived in 1573 and included many fishermen from Madeira and the Azores. This, and the fact that Brava never really took part in the slave trade, is held to be responsible for there being a greater proportion of white skins on Brava than anywhere else.

When Sir Francis Drake's mariners passed by in 1578 they found only one of its 100 inhabitants – a hermit who looked after a small chapel. They probably never discovered the villages hidden in the volcano's crater. By the 1620s, there was a proper community there, which swelled 60 years later with desperate boatloads of refugees from Fogo fleeing volcanic eruptions on their own island. Many of them never returned.

By this time the island was owned by Luis de Castro Pereira, who also owned Santa Luzia near São Vicente. In 1686, the population was sufficiently large to merit a pirate attack in which its governor was killed.

Yet Brava remained a relative secret and took almost no part in Cape Verde's thriving 17th-century businesses. Its first major dabble with trade was in 1730 when the Englishman Captain George Roberts bought the rights to the *urzela* lichen that covered its slopes. The population was to double in the following 50 years to 3,200.

It was not until the end of the 18th century that Brava became of much interest to the outside world. It was the springboard for the great emigration of Cape Verdeans to the USA: an exile that was to be an important shaper of the whole economy of the archipelago.

That was when the whalers of New Bedford and Rhode Island, venturing further south and east, discovered in Brava a place where they could replenish their ships and recruit eager new crews. English whaling boats recruited there as well – it was easy for the ships to land in Brava's small but secluded harbours. Many of the young men disembarked at New England and set up new lives there (see box, page 257).

Withstanding an attack in 1798 by the French, who were trying to oust the Portuguese from the islands, Brava continued to prosper into the first decades of the 19th century. Intellectually, Brava became the place to be. The parish of Our Lady of the Mountain was created, an American consul arrived in 1843 and a secondary school opened in the 1850s to which students came from throughout the archipelago and from Guinea-Bissau. It was into this environment that the poet Eugénio Tavares was born in 1867 (see box, page 247).

By the late 19th century, Brava was considered one of the most pleasant islands in which to live and its population peaked at 9,200. Income surged into the 20th century, as American *emigrantes* sent their money home. But the prosperity was not to last. The depression came; remittances from abroad dwindled and, confident that the rainy years of the 1930s would continue, many *Americanos* returned home.

It was a mistake. A drought was looming that was to prove the worst catastrophe in Brava's history. It squeezed the island just as World War II caused foreign remittances to dry up completely. Hundreds died in the ensuing famine.

Brava's ageing population rose to 10,000 in the 1960s and then fell back to 7,000. A recent disaster was Hurricane Beryl, which destroyed much of the infrastructure in 1982.

Brava today On the surface little has changed in Brava and the march of developers and property speculators has, as yet, made few ripples. Nevertheless land prices have surged. This may partly be in anticipation of what has happened on other islands, or because Cape Verde's prosperity is attracting more *emigrantes* from Brava to return. Also, there is anecdotal evidence that the building of schools in Brava has combined with general optimism about the future to reduce the flow of emigration. The population is now just over 6,000. Nevertheless, many people depend on government aid and the island relies heavily on fruit and vegetables imported from Fogo, Praia and Portugal. Maize is planted every year but often turns brown and dies. In better times the islanders grow coffee, sugarcane, cassava, maize, potatoes and bananas, as well as papayas, mangoes and other fruits. Fishing is the base of the economy.

GEOGRAPHY The archipelago's smallest inhabited island, Brava is 64km² and just 10km across at its widest point. Much of the coastline is steep cliffs, which rise to a dry central tableland with some mountains rising out of it. In the west there is a

FESTIVALS

The festival of São João is held on 24 June and many emigrants return for it. Several days before the festival the women begin a ritual pounding of the corn, joined by others who sing with a high-pitched chanting and clap to a complex beat until the preparation is finished. Another preparation for the festival is the dressing of the mast of *Cutelo Grande* – decorating it with intricately woven breads and also cakes, fruit and drinks and guarding it against pilfering by children. On the day, the mast – all greenery and red flowers and edible ornaments – is raised with a pulley. At the right moment the pulleys are cut, the mast comes plummeting to the ground and the children run to grab what plunder they can. In Vila Nova Sintra, a number of temporary bars are constructed in a designated space opposite the market, and music, drinking and dancing take over. The heaviest imbibers can be seen sleeping off their excesses in the streets. Other festivals are as follows:

5 January	Twelfth Night
20 January	São Sebastião
1 May	São José /Labour Day
24 June	São João (main festival: see above)
1st Sunday in July	São Paulo
2nd Sunday in July	São Paulinho
Last Sunday in July	Santaninha
Last Sunday in July	Santa Ana
1st fortnight in August	Nossa Senhora do Monte (Fuma)
15 August	Nossa Senhora da Graça

spectacular valley – Fajã d'Água – which previously enjoyed the benefits of a small, semi-permanent stream, now long gone. Nevertheless, it is still green in parts. The valley between Lomba and Tantum is fed by a stream which creates something of an oasis. Offshore in Fajã's beautiful bay, photo opportunities for visitors are presented by the many jagged, wave-battered rocks and stacks. The highest point of the island is Monte Fontainhas at 976m, and often swathed in mist. Even a little lower down, within the crater, there is generally moisture and coolness.

NATURAL HISTORY Brava hosts none of Cape Verde's 47 protected areas but the adjacent Ilhéus do Rombo are a protected reserve. There are 24 endemic species on the island. The Cape Verde warbler (*Acrocephalus brevipennis*) once made Brava its home but is thought to have gone now, with dwindling agriculture. However, it was also thought to have disappeared from São Nicolau but was later rediscovered, so keep a lookout. The previously endangered Cape Verde shearwater is most famous for its occupancy of Ilhéu Raso, but also dwells within the Ilhéus do Rombo. Up in the valleys above Fajã d'Água and Lomba, carefully nurtured crops of fruit can be swiped by the mischievous monkeys who live there. Wild goats also pose a problem. Offshore, you may spot a pod of dolphins or the occasional whale passing by.

Flowering garden plants found on Brava include plumeira, bougainvillea and jasmine. Vila Nova Sintra abounds with planted dragon trees (*Dracaena draco*). It is cold between December and April in the *vila* and in higher zones and the rains fall from late June to September.

HAZARDS Swimmers should ask locals about any hazards before taking a dip. The natural rock swimming pool near the disused airport is a good bet and reasonably accessible.

GETTING THERE AND AWAY

Historically, Brava has been very hard to reach. There is no air service to the island because of dangerously strong crosswinds. The history of the ferry service to Brava has also been patchy, with ferry companies appearing and disappearing, amidst cancellations and delays due to bad weather. The arrival of the Cabo Verde Fast Ferry has made a huge difference to the previously unreliable service. The ferry is comparatively comfortable, but is still susceptible to significant delays and cancellations. It is always necessary to confirm departure times in advance, either at the local CV Fast Ferry office or one of the travel agencies, as the schedule seems to change weekly. Be sure of your exit strategy because trying to leave Brava with an international flight looming in Sal or Santiago is stressful and also fairly certain to end in trouble. It is advisable to give yourself at least a day's leeway to get back to Fogo, though if bad weather persists, even that may not be enough. Take seasickness tablets and accept the offer of the plastic sick bags cheerfully handed out on board by the ferry staff!

BY FERRY Ferry tickets to Brava can be bought in São Filipe either from the CV Fast Ferry office or from Qualitur, Zebra or other travel agencies (see *Activities*, page 222). In Vila Nova Sintra on Brava, go to Novatur in the main square (✆ *285 2278*), or Qualitur or Zebra just off it. You can also enquire at the CV Fast Ferry office in Praia (see page 166) or check www.bela-vista.net/Ferry.aspx, which keeps reasonably abreast of ferry information. The price should be around 1,550$ one-way, though some agencies advise purchasing return tickets in advance.

BY YACHT Some of the best anchorages in the archipelago are here. Fajã d'Água is secure and beautiful and Furna is secure, except during southeasterly winds.

GETTING AROUND

On arrival at Furna get to Vila Nova Sintra either by chartered *aluguer* (1,000$) or shared *aluguer* (200–300$). Alternatively you could walk the steep 3km up the old road, the reverse of the hike described on page 258, though with luggage it will seem a long, long way. From Vila Nova Sintra to Nossa Senhora do Monte a charter is around 1,000$ and from Vila Nova Sintra to Fajã d'Água a charter is about 1,500$.

The island's road network is so small that even one day's car hire is barely necessary. There are no official car-rental agencies in town, but you might get a car by asking at one of the tour operators or at O Poeta Restaurant (see page 246).

 ## WHERE TO STAY

There are a few options scattered around the island, but Vila Nova Sintra, has the biggest range of modest but acceptable accommodations. The opening of the Djabraba Eco-Lodge has arguably raised the standard of what's available in the capital. For something even more relaxing, a stay in beautiful Fajã d'Água is recommended, or there are a few other options west of the Vila (see page 246).

ACTIVITIES

EXCURSIONS These are best organised on Fogo with **Dja'r Fogo** or **Qualitur** (see page 222). Once on Brava, Carlos (m *978 1934*) is an English-speaking driver and known for island tours and is recommended, with four hours costing around 6,000$ for an individual or small group.

HIKING Brava is a superb hiking destination, with numerous circular walks, many of which can start and finish at the *vila* (see page 251). Again, hikes from Fajã d'Água or Cova Rodela are plentiful.

SIGHTSEEING BY BOAT From Fajã d'Água, it is possible to hire a fisherman and his boat, for a trip along the coast, a spot of fishing, or both. (See *What to see and do,* page 249.)

SIGHTSEEING BY VEHICLE You could probably see Brava in half a day by vehicle.

SWIMMING Brava is not really a place for swimming, but there are a few safe lagoons, including a natural swimming pool between Fajã d'Água and the disused airport.

FURNA

Furna is the main port and lies in an extinct volcano crater, encircled with rocks on three sides. The bay is just a few hundred metres in diameter – sailing ships used to find it easy to get in but trickier to escape. It is more bustling than the *vila* but not as attractive.

From Furna the road winds up the slopes of the mountain. The sea and the harbour sink far below until, about 0.5km above and after endless hairpins, it drops suddenly over the rim of a small depression and into Vila Nova Sintra.

There are modest restaurants and bars near the waterside in Furna, should you get stuck waiting for the ferry, but there is no real reason to linger here.

… an enchanted garden hanging by invisible cords from the clouds

Archibald Lyall

Named after the Portuguese town of Sintra, the *vila* is 520m above sea level. For weeks it can labour under a *Brigadoon*-like fog, inspiring melancholy in the visitor. On a clear day, though, there is a view across the ocean to Fogo: it is said that if you have good eyes you can see the women in São Filipe cleaning rice.

Nova Sintra is a quaint town, with a lived-in but well-kept feel to it, nestled among the volcanic rocks. Hibiscus trees line many of the streets, scarlet against the ancient cobblestones. In wet years its gardens are jumbles of blue plumbago and bougainvillea, almond trees and jacaranda. The houses of the town – all Portuguese whitewash with red tiles – are covered in flowering vegetation, and fruit trees intersperse with fields of corn and cabbage. There is a fair bit of renovation work going on, but fewer half-built construction projects than elsewhere in Cape Verde.

The *vila* is very quiet and sometimes you can be the only person in the pretty square. But before mealtimes the fish vendors are there, crying '*Nhos cumpra peixe*' – 'You all buy fish'. Each of the three fishing communities has its own signature cry so that potential customers will know where their dinner is from before they buy it.

VILA NOVA SINTRA

Red Cross

Police station

Nazarene church

Catholic church

Post office

Shell garage & shop

Square

Qualitur

Novatur

Hospital

Town hall

Pensão Paraizo, Fajã d'Agua, Nossa Senhora do Monte

Pharmacy

Ka Netcha

Outdoor public gym, church, Stone boat, Djabraba's Eco-lodge, Furna

TACV office

House of Eugénio Tavares

Market

School football pitch

School

João de Nole

N

For listings, see page 246

Where to stay
1 Casa Silva
2 O Castelo
3 Pousada Vivis
4 Residencial Nazareth

Off map
Djabraba's Eco-Lodge
Pensão Paraizo

Where to eat and drink
5 Kananga
6 O Castelo Restaurant & Bar
7 O Poeta
8 Restaurant Bar Pôr do Sol
9 Sossego

Brava VILA NOVA SINTRA

8

WHERE TO STAY All listings are located on the map, page 245.

Djabraba's Eco-Lodge (8 rooms) **m** 979 4934/970 5292; **e** marcogiandinoto@gmail. com; http://hoteldjabrabasecolodge.jimdo.com. New in 2013, smart Italian-owned place east of town, overlooking Furna. Good en-suite rooms, hot water. Also has 2 suites. Bar & restaurant. Organises treks & car hire. **$$**

Pensão Paraizo (3 rooms) **** 285 2646; **e** gerdadepina@live.nl; www.hotelkaapverdie.nl. In rural Cova Rodela, 15mins walk from Vila Nova Sintra. Dutch/Cape Verdean owned; hot water in shared bathroom. Great views from the spacious terrace over banana plantations & surrounding hills. Can arrange hiking & fishing excursions, visits to local houses. FB available. **$$**

Pousada Vivis (formerly Municipal) (8 rooms) **** 285 2562; **e** pousadavivisplace@hotmail. com. Looking tired, probably now a last option if everywhere else is full. Off the road with the town

hall on it, it remains a friendly enough place with a communal veranda & bar. B/fast included & evening meals available. **$$**

Residencial Nazareth (11 rooms) **** 285 2589; **e** joeravi27@cvtelecom.cv. Peaceful & spacious. Some of the Nazareth's rooms have TV & minibar. Hot water. There is a family apartment with 2 bedrooms, kitchenette & separate bathroom/shower. **$$**

Residencial O Castelo **** 285 1063. Close to the main square. English-speaking owner. A comfortable B&B, some rooms with private bathroom. Hot water. Rooms in the owner's house are the best. Bar & restaurant downstairs. **$$**

Casa Silva **** 285 1349; **e** velnastar@ hotmail.com. (Ask for Johnny Silva's place.) To the south of town, these are a good standard of room though not en suite. **$**

✗ WHERE TO EAT AND DRINK

Fresh bread can be bought from various tiny bakeries around town: just ask someone for the nearest *pastelaria*. Or follow your nose. Fruit and vegetables, if available, can be bought at the market. All listings are located on the map, page 245.

✗ O Poeta One block west of the main square. Standard chicken & fish. Pleasant interior, outdoor seating & occasional music. **$$$**

✗ Restaurante Bar Pôr do Sol The blue building on the main square. Also known as Casa Mensa, this is a pleasant old building with a couple of outside tables serving decent food including cheap platefuls of fish or beans, beef & potatoes. **$$$**.

✗ O Castelo Restaurant & Bar One block north of the main square. Pleasant setting, both

inside and out, limited choice but reasonable standard and good value. **$$**.

✗ Sossego Off the main road. Dingy inside but a good reputation for its food. Order in advance. **$$**

ENTERTAINMENT AND NIGHTLIFE

♀ Kananga ⊕ some Fri/Sat nights & the occasional Sun afternoon; admission: 300$ for men; free for women.

OTHER PRACTICALITIES
Airlines

TACV (**** 285 1192; (08.00–15.00 Mon–Fri) In the same building as Residencial Nazareth. Can book tickets and reconfirm flights, though no flights operate into Brava.

Banks

(⊕ 08.00–15.00 Mon–Fri) BCA or BCN banks are both close to the main square, both with ATMs. A new Caixa Economica is due to open in 2014.

Hospital

(**** 285 1130) Brava's health post is on the Furna road out of the square, on the right. There is no capacity for complex interventions like transfusions or surgery.

Internet

Wi-Fi is free and available in the main square. For internet, Ka Netcha is next to Bar Pôr do Sol. The Shell shop provides a faxing and photocopying service, as do a few other places around town.

Pharmacy

Look for the well-stocked Farmácia Irene (📞 285 1223), set back from the main square.

Police

(📞 285 1132) On the main road located west of the main square.

Post office

(🕐 08.00–16.00 Mon–Fri) On the main square.

Shopping

Minimercados are often better stocked than those in Fogo because of the American connection.

Postcards are on sale in the post office. For Fogo wine, grogue and certain food and drink products unavailable elsewhere try the Shell shop (🕐 07.00–21.00 daily), on the road leading from the square. The papelaria off the main square sells books on Cape Verde (in Portuguese).

Tourist information

None, but staff at the town hall (*câmara*) (📞 285 1314) are very helpful to visitors looking for guidance.

EUGÉNIO TAVARES

Eugénio Tavares was born in 1867 and spent his life writing music and in particular developing the art of the *morna*. He wrote in Creole rather than Portuguese, which was one reason for his immense popularity. Tavares lived on Brava where the sense of parting was particularly strong. Perhaps his most famous work is 'Hora di Bai' (Hour of Leaving), which was traditionally sung at Furna dock as relatives boarded the ships bound for the USA. The first verse is as follows:

Hora di bai	Hour of going
Hora de dor	Hour of pain
Dja'n q'ré	I wish
Pa el ca mantché	That it would not dawn!
De cada bêz	Each time
Que'n ta lembrâ	That I remember thee,
Ma'n q'ré	I would choose
Fica 'n morrê	To stay and die!

Translated in *Atlantic Islands* by Bentley Duncan (Chicago, 1972)

'Hora di Bai' is traditionally the last song, played at the end of the evening. You need the music and the dancing to appreciate the morna. As Archibald Lyall wrote:

> Properly to appreciate the work of Eugénio Tavares, it is necessary to see the humble people for whom he wrote gliding close-locked round the whitewashed, oil-lit room and to hear them, drugged for a few hours by his genius into forgetting their sorrows, singing softly to the strains of fiddle and guitar.

Tavares was primarily a composer – the words, it is said, took a couple of hours to invent after he had finished the music. But his lyrics struck deep in the hearts of his countrymen. Famous *mornas* of his include 'O Mar Eterno' (inspired by his love for an American woman who visited Brava on a yacht; her horrified father whisked her away one night and he never saw her again), and his lullaby, 'Ná ó menino ná'. When Tavares died in 1930, the whole of the island went to the funeral.

Brava   VILA NOVA SINTRA

8

WHAT TO SEE AND DO A house once occupied by Eugénio Tavares is at the top of the town just off the main road and has now been transformed into a *very* modest museum. Improvements to the content are expected and necessary, but at least a start has been made in honouring one of Brava's favourite sons. In the square is a kiosk with a plaque commemorating Tavares. In English it reads:

There above in planetary spheres
Shine brilliant and amazing stars:
But here on earth, one shines
For ever: Eugénio Tavares

FAJÃ D'ÁGUA

This is probably the most beautiful bay in Cape Verde – a little village at the foot of the mountains, sheltered from the northeast winds and always with a bit of green, at least in parts. Above the bay, mango and papaya trees sway in the almost constant and welcome breeze. There is not much to do in the village, though options are increasing and swimming and fishing are possibilities. The surrounding area is great for hiking. This is a great place to relax, with your peace and quiet disturbed only by the bleating of a goat or the laughter of children playing. Or by what the locals refer to as 'the old-fashioned telephone,' which is known elsewhere in the world as 'shouting to each other', a handy way of communicating across the *ribeira*.

Fajã is where the whaling boats used to anchor and here lies a monument to the passengers of the *Mathilde*. In 1943, a group of men – some American emigrants on a visit home, others young men who had never been out of Brava – bought the 55ft sloop. They all wanted to flee famine and go to New England. The *Mathilde* was in bad shape but this did not deter them; they made a few repairs and set sail on 21 August 1943.Their voyage was a clandestine one because there were wartime restrictions on maritime travel. To make matters worse, they had chosen the beginning of the hurricane season.

Just after the boat left the harbour, a 12-year-old boy on board noticed that it was leaking. He took fright, jumped overboard and swam for the shore, half an hour away. 'There,' says Ray Almeida, an American Cape Verdean, 'he wept as he watched the sloop disappear over the horizon, carrying his compatriots to what he knew was certain death.' It is believed that the *Mathilde* went down in rough weather near Bermuda.

GETTING THERE AND AWAY Look out for the one communal *aluguer*, which leaves Fajã for the *vila* at 07.00, returning at 12.00 (200$). It is supposed to do an afternoon journey as well, leaving Fajã in the early afternoon and arriving back at 18.00, and occasionally there will be others. To charter an *aluguer* there or back costs around 1,500$. Fajã to Furna costs 2,500$. Your accommodation choice will be willing to help with your transport needs.

WHERE TO STAY

Pensão Sol na Baia (5 rooms) ☎285 2070; e pensao_sol_na_baia@hotmail.com. A beautifully refurbished traditional house overlooking the sea, run by artist José Andrade, who speaks French, Italian, Spanish & Portuguese & makes his own high-quality grogue. Rooms are attractive, simple & en suite with hot water. FB available. **$$$**

Kaza di Zaza (2 apts) ☎285 5032; e kazadizaza@gmail.com; www.kazadizaza.com.

Set back up the hill, directly behind Motel Burgo, 2 apartments among fruit trees with commanding views over the bay. Roof terrace with hammock. Wi-Fi. Guests can opt to eat with the hosts, Dutch couple Erik & Marijke Katsburg, or use local fish & fruit & cook for themselves. The hosts will organise boat & fishing trips with locals or guides for hikers. **$$**

🏠 **Casa de Julia** (1 room) 📞 285 1431. A brightly painted *casa* perched high above the bay, in the middle of the village. Quaint & inexpensive. **$**

🏠 **Motel Burgo** (3 rooms) 📞 285 1321. About midway along Fajã's only road, the hotel consists of 3 rooms, very basic but usually clean with a communal balcony gazing directly over the ocean. Sleep to the sound of the waves, the breeze will keep you cool. Manuel will collect you from the port & entertain you with his stories of Brava. En suite, cold water only. In the bar below, the friendly local grogue drinkers pass the time. **$**

✗ **WHERE TO EAT AND DRINK** The key to eating *anything* here is to order it in advance. Much of what is on offer is fresh fish, and with small visitor numbers, nothing is bought in either hope or expectation. Call in at one of the places below the night before to order your lunch, or at lunchtime to order your dinner.

✗ **Pensão Sol na Baia** Fresh Cape Verdean produce with French style. **$$$$**
✗ **Bar Sodade** At the entrance to the village. Pre-ordering should bring you the catch of the day. Has outdoor tables, but you might be asked to eat in the owner's dining room, with its impressive range of ceramic chickens! **$$**
✗ **Motel Burgo** May serve snacks (cake, bananas & coffee) plus meals of fish or meat. **$$**

WHAT TO SEE AND DO

Hiking A gentle stroll is to continue on the road beyond the village to the abandoned airport. This allows you a close look at some of the impressive rocks jutting out of the sea and a chance to swim in the natural pool just before you reach the airport itself. The pool becomes crowded at weekends, when trucks from other parts of the island arrive to take advantage of one of Brava's few safe swimming options. For other hikes involving the village, see page 256.

Fishing and boat trips A different and less strenuous way of seeing Brava's coastal scenery is to engage one of the local fishermen for a half-day or longer to cruise the rocky coast or even go fishing. This is perhaps best arranged through Marijke Katsburg (see *Where to stay,* page 248) as she speaks English, Dutch and Creole and may find you an English-speaking boatman. Expect to pay about 6,000$ per boat, which includes the fuel and the time of the boatmen (usually two). Each boat can take four passengers, plus the crew.

A coastal trip will take you down past the airport and on to Tantum, where there is a single building and a beach with up to 30 fishing boats. Above the beach, you'll see a zig-zag path which leads to the village of Lomba, a settlement perched high on the ridge. Spare a thought for the village womenfolk, who every day have to carry up the heavy loads of fish so they can be collected and taken to sell in Vila Nova Sintra.

If you decide to do a bit of fishing, all the fish caught from the boats on Brava is by hook and line. A reasonable catch might include grouper, snapper and tuna, plus a few other varieties.

OTHER PLACES TO VISIT

VINAGRE This village derives its name from the mineral water which still bubbles up here from deep below the mountains. There is not much going on here now – a few broken-down donkeys and some ancient farmers, and an air of faded glory. The elaborate stone irrigation system and the extensive terracing are crumbling and largely overgrown. At the heart of the village is a bridge and a huge bougainvillea – a welcome splash of vermilion against the greys and browns.

On the left before the bridge is a majestic old water tank, fully equipped with gargoyle water spouts and large oval windows. Take a look inside to see how the water used to course through a carefully made tunnel under the road. To sample the water yourself, turn left just before the bridge, and follow the cobbled path down to where the piped spring water issues from a wall.

Further round on the left is the shell of a magnificent old house, inhabited within living memory. There are as many as four lime kilns around the settlement, once used to make whitewash for the houses – look out for their tall brick chimneys.

You can reach Vinagre by following a hike, or part of a hike (see pages 255–6).

NOSSA SENHORA DO MONTE This village was founded as a place of pilgrimage in 1826 and, within a decade, had become a bishop's palace. Earlier in the last century travellers said that the road from Nova Sintra to Nossa Senhora do Monte was as thickly populated as the Thames Valley. Now emigration has left just a couple of tiny villages.

DRIVES

Brava is very small, so small that in just half a day you can cover all the driveable roads by car or guided tour. This is well worth doing if you are pressed for time, but also to get a feel for the island – from its plunging mountains scored with deep *ribeiras* above Fajã d'Água, to the lively village at Lomba, and the dusty poverty at the end of the road in Cachaço.

Take the road west out of the *vila*. A sharp hairpin in the first kilometre takes you out of the *caldeira* and through the pretty village of **Cova Rodela**. Just past the telephone box in the heart of Cova, the road forks – the left-hand fork takes you round the rim of the crater, past **João de Nole**, to where the road ends at **Mato Grande**. It is worth a brief detour along this road: after about 700m, there is a viewing point (*miradouro*) looking out over Vila Nova Sintra towards Fogo.

Continuing from Cova, bear left at a second fork (the right fork will take you to Fajã d'Água) and descend beneath a hill where there is a large water tank – this is one of a series that serves all of Brava. If you look down the *ribeira* to your right at this point, you will see Fajã d'Água nestling in a bay far, far below. Below the water tank, you pass through the attractive village of **Cova Joana**, where one aspect of Brava's economy becomes apparent: while émigré money has allowed many of the houses to be restored, the others are just left to crumble away.

A hairpin bend brings you up out of the valley into **Nossa Senhora do Monte**. A turning to the left on the hairpin below the school will take you into the labyrinthine tracks and pathways that make up the villages of **Lima Doce** and **Mato**, further south. Standing over Mato is **Fontainhas** peak, which you will see if the mist is not down. At 976m, this is the highest peak on Brava. Nossa Senhora do Monte is a winding cobbled street between whitewashed houses, where the red flowers of the cardeal bushes spill down the walls. The village commands spectacular views down the *ribeiras* to the north, with the sea beyond. The village is more or less continuous with Tomé Barras, where the road divides. Take the left fork to continue on to Cachaço. At this point, the countryside seems to change, and it starts to feel wilder, emptier and drier. As the road weaves in and out amongst the ridges, note the rows of acacia trees – planted to maintain a semblance of green during the dry season.

Cachaço is where the road stops – less than 10km from Vila Nova Sintra. It is a poor place, and epitomises the economic problems besetting rural communities in many parts of Cape Verde. Dependent exclusively on farming, it has been reduced almost to a ghost village. Although the volcanic soil is very fertile, increases in the price of seed and labour, and the unpredictability of the rains over a number of years are factors that have been felt keenly in Cachaço. Look about you and you will see traces of old field markings and terracing high up the slopes – all abandoned now – and shattered farmhouses left to the elements. However, perhaps the new goat's cheese factory offers some hope for the future. The tiny production is usually exported to Praia, hence the presence of passengers clutching cool boxes on the ferry. It is possible to visit, before 11.00 being the best time.

Returning from Cachaço, take the left turning at Tomé Barras. After about 900m, a small turning on the left goes to the small settlement of **Campo Baixo**. Carrying straight on, you will arrive at the fishing settlement of **Lomba**, after about 3km. Although the cobbled road surface stops after about 1km, this journey is worth making just to marvel at the road engineering – in places the track has been cut through ridges of solid rock.

The village of Lomba is strung out along a thin, exposed ridge. Bravans have remarkably limited access to the sea because of the steepness of their volcano. If you have a good head for heights, and are prepared to crane your neck, you will see the fishing boats drawn up hundreds of metres below. Mid-morning, the women carry the fish in basins on their heads up an interminable zig-zagging path back up to the village, then climb into pick-up trucks to go and sell the catch in Vila Nova Sintra. Depending on the season, they may be carrying bright orange groupers, or swordfish and tuna which, from far off, look like slabs of silver. There is a single shop in the village, selling cold beers. Lomba is a great place to watch the mist rolling down the *ribeiras*, or just to sit on the crumbling white rock of the ridge and try to see where the sea meets the horizon. The fisherwomen have become something of a tourist attraction in their own right, though visitors should avoid being too intrusive.

Returning along the road, pass the turning to Cachaço on your right, go through Tomé Barras, into Nossa Senhora do Monte and on towards the *vila*. Winding up out of Cova Joana, you will come to the turning to Fajã d'Água on your left. This is another spectacular road – completed only in 1989 – cut through living rock. Down to your right you will see several abandoned farms. You will reach Fajã after about 4km. It is a wild and beautiful place, a well-protected harbour where yachts frequently drop anchor beneath mountains which seem to stretch upwards for ever.

A few houses line the waterfront, where, on really windy days, you will be wet by the spray. At 1km beyond the village there is the ill-fated Bravan airport, wedged in between the mountains and the sea. Fickle crosswinds and a runway that is not quite long enough conspire to make the airstrip unsafe – one of the last planes to land here almost ended up in the sea. Talk of a new airport abounds, and some tentative ground-clearing has taken place near to Vila Nova Sintra.

On the road back out of Fajã look out for a turning on your left after about 3km. This road is not for the faint-hearted. After just over 2km, you will have to abandon your car, and continue to **Sorno** by foot, but it is well worth it (see *Hikes*, page 258, for a description of Sorno).

HIKES   *Colum Wilson (CW); Aisling Irwin (AI)*

Several of the hikes below pass through Mato Grande, and hikers can therefore mix and match parts of routes.

1 VILA NOVA SINTRA–MATO GRANDE–MIRADOURO–COVA RODELA– VILA NOVA SINTRA

Distance: 5km; time: 1½ hours; difficulty: 1 (CW)

This walk takes you up a steep path and then around the ring of hills to the south and west of Vila Nova Sintra on a well-surfaced road. You are always in sight of the *vila*, but you pass through the picturesque village of Mato Grande, clinging to the hillside, and you get some excellent views of Fogo. The *miradouro* (viewing point) is the highlight of this walk, giving an amazing view of the *vila*, spread out beneath you like a map.

From the southeast corner of the main square, take the diagonal road out past the building labelled **Casa Teixeira**. After about 100m you will come to a crossroads, where you go straight on. Continue straight ahead again at a fork after a further 20m. After another 40m, the cobbled road turns sharp left. Go right on an unmade path that heads down to the bottom of the valley. After about 100m you will reach the valley floor.

Almost directly, go past a turning on your right leading up to a white house. After another 50m, turn right up a steep cobbled path in a gap in the stone wall. This is a steep climb between houses that seem to be built on platforms carved out of the hillside. After about five minutes, the path bears left and you go round a rocky outcrop with a ruin below you on your left. From this point, and if the mist is not swirling around you, you get your first uninterrupted view of Fogo.

The path winds on around the hillside, passing houses in various states of repair. After another five minutes, it crosses a small valley and, directly, you reach a T-junction in front of a two-storey house. Turn right, following the path uphill. As you get higher, you will get glimpses down into the neat courtyards of some of the houses, where bougainvillea spills across ancient walls.

Five minutes later you cross a second small valley, and then bear left at a fork. Several minutes after that there is a white cross standing on a wall on your right beside a white house. Pass in front of the house on your right, and immediately turn right up beside the house, following the path uphill. Within a couple of minutes you will reach a telephone box, and a larger cobbled path through **Mato Grande**, which is spread out below you on your right as a maze of little paths between crumbling houses. Turn left at the phone box, and after five minutes of ascending, you will reach the Centro Social de Mato Grande (the social centre) on your left. Opposite, there is a table-football table, and a small bar selling fizzy drinks and *grogue*. Inside the shop, the youth of Mato Grande gather to while away the time with a pack of cards.

Looking south (with your back to the social centre), you will see the village of **Garça** down in the valley (look for the bright-green house) and, close by, the white outline of one of a series of stone ships dotted around the mountainside. On the far ridge is the village of **Baleia**, and at the east end of the ridge you will see a further ship.

A few hundred metres down the slope to the left of where you are standing, there is a third ship. If you would like a close look at one, ask at the bar for directions to the *barco*. On 24 June, it is these boats that are decorated with leaves and fruit to celebrate the festival of São João (see *Festivals*, page 242).

From the Mato Grande social centre, take the road that leads up to the left of the tapstand, with the *vila* visible on your right. Follow the road around the ridge, past old houses and small areas of cultivation squeezed in amongst the folds of land. After 1km (about 20 minutes), you will reach a T-junction in the road, where the right turning leads down to **João de Nole**. Turn left to continue to the *miradouro*.

Just 100m beyond the T-junction is a small, rough and steep path down on the right. (If you trust your knees, this is a quick way to descend to the *vila*.) The *miradouro* is another 200m beyond this, and gives a breathtaking view over the *vila*.

Continuing beyond the viewpoint, another 600m will bring you to a second T-junction, in the pretty, often misty village of **Cova Rodela**. Turn right here and follow the winding road back down to the *vila*. You will reach the western end of the main street after about ten minutes.

2   VILA NOVA SINTRA–MATO GRANDE–BALEIA–CASA EUGÉNIO TAVARES–BALEIA–MATO GRANDE–VILA NOVA SINTRA
Distance: 10km; time: 4 hours; difficulty: 3 (CW)

This walk south of the *vila* is a demanding sequence of ascents and descents, with spectacular views of Fogo out to the east. For much of this walk, the path is unmade and rough, and, particularly on the final steep zig-zag descent to the *casa*, care needs to be taken. Baleia is an attractive, if remote, spot to pause and gaze down vertiginous *ribeiras*. If you want to experience the unspeakable desolation of Brava's dryness, look no further than the *ribeira* where Tavares built his house.

Walk from the *vila* to Mato Grande (30 minutes) using the directions in the first five paragraphs of the previous walk.

In Mato Grande, looking south (with your back to the social centre), take the small path directly in front of you, which leads down in the direction of **Garça**.

At Garça, you can take a detour along the ridge to visit the stone boat (*barco*), which looks like it has been stranded at the end of the ridge in some cataclysmic flood. The path continues up to **Baleia** on the next ridge, about 1km from Mato Grande. Immediately on entering the village, you will see a house on your left that sells biscuits and *grogue*.

Baleia has the feel of a bird's nest perched high on a windswept ridge. The village comprises a single cobbled street and a few houses huddled together against the mist and the ceaseless purring of the wind.

It takes two hours to get from here to Casa Eugénio Tavares and return. People in Baleia will readily point you towards the path to the *casa*. Follow the cobbled path along the ridge through Baleia. Just before you reach the last two houses, turn right and immediately start to descend on an unmade path.

After about five minutes, the path branches. Going left will bring you in a few minutes to Baleia's stone boat. Bear right for the *casa*, down the side of the ridge. After about 20 minutes, you will reach a few scattered houses, mostly ruined. At a fork in the path bear left. You will see some rudimentary crosses on a cairn some tens of metres up the right turning. This is a homemade chapel, and means that the locals do not have to hike over to Mato Grande every Sunday.

You are heading towards what looks like a ruin (but is actually inhabited). Watch out for the dog, which may make you feel less than welcome. Cut close past the right side of this building (where the locals will point you in the right direction for Tavares's house), and descend a few hundred metres along the next ridge. If it is the dry season, you will enter a lunar landscape at this point, where there is nothing but rock and sand. The ruined huts look as if they have grown out of the landscape, rather than been built by human hand.

After less than ten minutes from the inhabited building, the path passes to the right through a small notch in a rocky ridge a few metres high. From here you will see the *casa* a long way below you on the other side of the valley. After a further five minutes, you will pass a ruin on your left. About 50m beyond this, there is a small (and easy-to-miss) turning on your right down the side of the *ribeira*. It is a very rough zig-zagging path, so watch your step. It will take you about ten or 15 minutes.

The ruin of Eugénio Tavares's house is reached by a five-minute scramble up from the floor of the *ribeira*. His house is surprisingly big – there are two storeys and outhouses. There is also a patio, and what looks like a small swimming pool, but was probably a water tank. In the dry season, you look out across a mind-numbing grey and brown panorama of splintered rock. But it clearly inspired Tavares and, apparently, a host of latter-day scribblers, who have left their poetic offerings all over the walls of the ruin.

Retrace your steps. For the return from Mato Grande to the *vila*, you can either go back the way you came (30 minutes) or go via the *miradouro* as described in the last part of the previous walk. The latter route takes about one hour.

3 VILA NOVA SINTRA–MATO GRANDE–MONTE FONTAINHAS–MATO– NOSSA SENHORA DO MONTE–COVA JOANA–VILA NOVA SINTRA

Distance: 9km; time: 3 hours 10 minutes; difficulty: 2 (CW)

This walk takes you to the heart of Brava, to its highest peak, from where you will get superb all-round views if you are not shrouded in mist. It is a steep ascent to Mato Grande, followed by a further steep ascent (on a cobbled path) from near Mato Grande up to the Fontainhas Plateau, where it is cool and green, and the air is heavy with sharp pine scents. Note: Mato Grande and Mato are different places.

Walk from the *vila* to Mato Grande (35 minutes) using the directions in the first five paragraphs of the Vila Nova Sintra–Mato Grande–*miradouro*–Cova Rodela walk.

For the 50-minute walk to **Fontainhas**, begin from the social centre in Mato Grande and take the road that leads up to the left of the tapstand. You will see Vila Nova Sintra below you on your right. After about 400m, you will pass a green church on your right, and, cresting a rise, you will see the path you are to take leading up from the left of the road about 200m in front of you. This is the beginning of a steep ascent onto the Fontainhas Plateau.

The path ascends the right side of a small valley. After about 200m, a path joins from the right. Your path bends round to the left at the top of the valley, and zig-zags upwards. Some 15 minutes after leaving the main road, the path flattens out and you pass to the right of a small peak with a large antenna on top. Directly after that, a small path joins on the left.

Five minutes after passing the antenna peak, take a right fork, and pass along the right edge of an undulating plateau, where the mist trails through spiky aloe vera and among the red flowers of the cardeal bushes. There are some farming huts, and occasional cattle grazing on the coarse grass. The air is sharp with the smell of pine.

After another ten minutes, you reach a T-junction. The right turning heads down to **Mato**. Turn left, and very shortly you will pass a whitewashed house on your right. Bear right at a fork shortly after this. Follow the path upwards, and after less than ten minutes, you will reach the peak. To get to Mato, which takes about 45 minutes, go back to the T-Junction before the whitewashed house, but instead of turning right to retrace your steps, head straight on. After about seven minutes of descending from the T-junction along a winding path, you will emerge on a low saddle, and will see the upper end of Mato down on your left.

Continue along the saddle for another five minutes, and then take a deeply worn path leading down on your left. After five minutes, this path will lead you past a concrete water tank on your left.

After another few minutes, the path becomes cobbled, and you are descending through the first of the houses in Mato. Five minutes later, you reach a T-junction with a telephone box on the right. From here, your aim is to reach the main road through Mato. Mato is criss-crossed by any number of small paths, and the best way to the main road is simply by asking.

Once on the road, follow it to the right, descending past a school on your left, and joining at last the main road to Nossa Senhora do Monte at a sharp hairpin.

Turn right onto the main road and walk for an hour, passing through **Cova Joana**, **Cova Rodela** and eventually reaching Vila Nova Sintra.

4 VILA NOVA SINTRA–SANTA BARBARA–VINAGRE–MATO GRANDE– JOÃO DE NOLE–VILA NOVA SINTRA

Distance: 5km; time: 2 hours 20 minutes; difficulty: 3 (CW)

In this walk, you descend almost to sea level by a steep zig-zagging cobbled path, and then climb back up again by a very rough (and in places precipitous) ridge path. It is not a walk to undertake if you have dodgy knees or don't like getting out of breath. Vinagre – a village nestling in the mouth of a *ribeira* – is the highlight of the walk, with its old lime kilns and air of decayed grandeur. The mineral waters that flow from a natural spring taste like a mild mixture of lemon juice and soapsuds, and have given the village its name. It is said that those who drink of the waters will never leave.

For the 40-minute walk to Vinagre, set out on the road east from the main square of the *vila*. After five minutes, you will reach the stone boat looking out towards Fogo.

Take the little cobbled path down to the left of the boat, and after just a short distance you will join the main road snaking its way down to Furna. Cross the road, and double back a few metres to pick up the cobbled path continuing its descent on the other side. Your path is actually the old road to Furna – watch out for the stray vehicles that still use this road. After five minutes descending, take a cobbled turning on your right towards **Santa Barbara**, which you will reach after another few minutes. About ten minutes from the turning, staying on the same path, you will round an outcrop, and catch a glimpse of Mato Grande above you on the hill.

At this point, you will begin a series of sharp zig-zags down towards **Vinagre**, which you will reach after about 25 minutes.

The one-hour hike from Vinagre to Mato Grande is a scramble, and some may prefer to turn round and retrace their steps up to Santa Barbara. The undaunted should cross over the bridge in Vinagre and follow the main path past a white house on the left with a brick kiln behind it. Immediately bear right up a rough path that looks as if it ends in a small rock quarry a few tens of metres from the main path. Pass through this area of broken rock, and, after a few minutes pass a ruin and follow the path as it doubles back up a ridge.

About five minutes after leaving the main path, you will pass an inhabited house on your left, and directly ascend past a ruin. The path is indistinct at this point, and does not look promising, but turn directly left behind the ruin, and you should be able to follow it.

This is the beginning of a very steep ascent on a rough path, where you will sometimes be looking for handholds. After about 20 minutes of arduous zig-zagging, you will emerge at a T-junction on a more major path, where you turn right along a contour. Following this path around the side of the hill will bring you to a small settlement after about ten minutes. From here, you can see Mato Grande on the hill on your left.

Follow the path as it doubles back on itself through the settlement, and then follow the path up the hill under the phone line. After about seven minutes, you cross over a small ridge, and your path improves. Three minutes later, you pass a water point with taps, where you turn left uphill.

After another two or three minutes, a path joins you from your right in front of a white, two-storeyed house. Go straight on, following the path uphill. Five minutes later, you cross a small valley, and then bear left at a fork. Two or three minutes later there is a white cross standing on a wall on your right beside a white house. Pass in front of the house on your right, and immediately turn right beside the house, following the path uphill. Within a couple of minutes you will reach a telephone box, and a larger cobbled path through Mato Grande. Turn left at the phone box, and after five minutes of ascending, you will reach the Centro Social de Mato Grande (social centre) on your left.

To get back to the *vila*, via **João de Nole**, takes about 40 minutes. From the social centre in Mato Grande, take the road up to the left of the tapstand. After about 1km, turn right at a T-junction.

After a further 400m, turn left down into João de Nole. After 100m, go straight across a small T-junction. After this, the cobbled path gets smaller as it starts to zig-zag sharply down towards the *vila*. About ten minutes after the small crossroads, the path emerges on a cobbled street at the edge of town. Turn left onto the street.

5 VILA NOVA SINTRA–LEVADURA–FAJÃ D'AGUA

Distance: 6km; time: 2 hours; difficulty: 2 (Al)

This is a classic, downhill Cape Verde *ribeira* walk, with your destination sparkling beside the sea during the brief glimpses you snatch as you descend. Before you reach it you have to negotiate a lot of superbly crafted cobbled paths, ghostly villages and the echoey sides of the harsh valley walls. There is a short patch towards the end where there is no clear path and the going is slippery.

The first 25 minutes of the walk is on the road. From the town square head west on the town hall road. At the end of the street turn right up the Nossa Senhora do Monte road. Follow this for just over 20 minutes, passing through the village of **Cova Rodela**, with its superb dragon tree, on the way. Stop at a fork in the road: the high road continues to Nossa Senhora do Monte; to the right is the road to Fajã d'Água.

Walk for two minutes along the high road, then take a track to the right beside a sizeable tree. Follow this for about five minutes, ignoring another track up to the left, until you reach a crossroads of paths. To the right a track leads to a few houses on a nearby peak. Take the middle path, downhill, which leads you swiftly into a hidden valley of stark cliffs and, beyond them, the sea. Some 25 minutes from the crossroads you reach a water tank around which the path forks. The left path goes to the village of **Tomba Has**: take the right one instead. You are in a deep valley world of steep, stone-wall terracing and startling echoes.

Within a couple of minutes of leaving the water tank you will have your first proper view of Fajã d'Água, the archetypal nestling village, snug and green between the hostile brown Bravan mountains. Keep going, past two water tanks, through a settlement and, 15–20 minutes after the first water tank, past the quiet village of **Levadura** (to see it take a small detour on a path to the left). Now you are deep in the valley and the path is steep and winding.

Some 15 minutes from Levadura, when you are about level with a wood and a few houses on the other side of the valley, the path crosses a watercourse (generally dry) and a small dam, often full of water. Don't take the little path down to the left but go straight on, crossing, after a few minutes, a concrete barrier and following a path up through the houses ahead. In this jumbled settlement you will find someone who can lead you through to the other side where there is a well-trodden path the villagers all take down to Fajã d'Água. Beware: it is gravelly and slippery. For half an hour you descend on a path that is a mixture of rock, landslide and gravel, criss-crossing water channels, dams and stream beds and passing a big water tank, until you arrive at the road through Fajã d'Água.

6 VILA NOVA SINTRA–SORNO–SÃO PEDRO–VILA NOVA SINTRA

Distance: 9km; time: 4½ hours; difficulty: 2–3 (AI)

This spectacular walk encapsulates the essence of Brava: the remote valley hamlet of Sorno making miraculous use of its little stream to farm extensive green terraces up the mountainsides; the vivid, slightly menacing sea; the barren mountains; the ghost villages that are testament to livelier times; and, periodically, big brother Fogo looming from across the sea. The walk is suitable for any walker of average fitness, with just a very small slippery stretch to be negotiated. There is a two-hour walk downhill, mainly along a road, and 2½ hours on a remote path that is steep but not difficult. There are no facilities in Sorno.

From Vila Nova Sintra walk for 25 minutes to the fork, as described in the first two paragraphs of the walk from Vila Nova Sintra to Fajã d'Água.

WHALERS AND THE PACKET TRADE

For a young man with nothing but a peasant's struggle against hunger ahead of him, the prospect of a job on one of the New England whaling ships that pulled into Brava provided excitement and escape.

The first such boats arrived towards the end of the 18th century. Throughout most of the 19th century, a new vessel would arrive perhaps every three days so that the crew could resupply, drink and deposit their genes in the ever-absorptive pool. Crucially, the whalers would also be searching for crew – as replacements for obstreperous crewmen who would be abandoned on Brava. The Cape Verdeans were disciplined and took lower wages than their American counterparts, and developed great skill in the arts of whaling.

Stories of life aboard the whalers are full of excitement, courage and horror. The shot of the harpoon sinking into a 30m-long beast; the cries as the men rowed frantically to escape the thrashing of the whale's tail; the speed with which their little boats were towed through the ocean by the fleeing animal until they won control and sank a killer harpoon home. Men frequently died during these battles.

Some used the whaling ships as brief stepping stones to jobs in the USA – manual labour in the ports, in the cranberry bogs of southern New England and in the textile mills of New Bedford.

As steam replaced sail, the schooners and whalers could be bought or even 'inherited' for nothing. Cape Verdeans in the USA took them over, did them up and began the era of the Brava Packet Trade – a regular link between the USA and the islands. The boats would take Bravans to work in the cranberry bogs and return loaded with goods and with *emigrantes* visiting their families. The Packet Trade became an independent link by which Cape Verdeans could keep in contact with their families without depending on the transport system of another country.

There are plenty of dramatic tales about these ships – of charismatic captains, of tussles with disaster and of tragedy. The *Nellie May* was the first to begin a regular journey between the continents, in 1892. One of the longest recorded journeys of such a schooner was 90 days; the record for the shortest crossing was claimed to be 12 but was probably longer. World War II halted the trade, but afterwards one of the most legendary of the packet trade captains, Henrique Mendes, resurrected a sunken schooner and named her *Ernestina* (see box, page 21).

There is also an easy path from Fontainhas to Cachaço; and there is said to be a path from Cachaço to Casa Eugénio Tavares: enquire locally.

Take the right fork (the Fajã d'Água road), passing a big white water tank on the right after 20 minutes and, after a further 15 minutes, reaching a turning to the right. This road on the right is of much poorer quality and takes you past a small quarry and various houses. You may pass the odd person harvesting grass or loading it onto a donkey but soon you will leave even these few behind, and there is just you, the sea and the odd hawk. The dull brown of the mountains makes a huge contrast with the rich blue and harsh white of the sea.

Eventually one of the road's twists will reveal **Sorno** below, improbably tame below the ominous Brava slopes. The Sorno road takes 1½ hours to cover, dwindling to a path – slippery in places – some 20 minutes from the village and, all the while, the ingenious village reveals itself in the form of irrigation channels, neat water tanks and endless squares of tended terraces. Follow the path round to the front of a square white building and then follow your nose, and a set of stepped irrigation channels and water tanks, to the sea.

After a break on the beach, it is time for the ascent out of Sorno. Finding the path, which winds out of the other side of the valley from the side you entered, takes a little care. Use as your guide Sorno's first (more southerly) bay. With your back to the water and its twin-peak stacks behind you, gaze up the valley and look for the little path that mounts its left side. For the first five minutes it is a small dirty track, but it then becomes paved and walled, if old and crumbly, soon crossing a concrete water channel and tank.

As you leave Sorno its colours dull and, after a good 20-minute walk, you turn to see its vivid greens already merging with the dull surrounding browns, its charm retreating. Half an hour of climbing out of Sorno brings you round into the next bay, a new set of jagged peaks ahead of you and, after entering a little wood, a turning to the right past a stack of dry stones. Take this and, in less than five minutes, you pass another prehistoric old home on the left – the path goes up and round behind it.

You are now entering the loneliest part of the walk, its stark remoteness made more poignant by the carefully crafted path, with its implication that someone once thought it would be useful. Some 50 minutes from the right turning at the stack of stones below, you reach the ghost village of **Tez Cova** – decaying old piles of stone houses from which folk used to try to farm the now-abandoned terraces. One half-expects the ghost of an old Bravan crone to emerge from one of these hovels and share a thought on the fate of the island.

At Tez Cova you should walk through the village, broadly following the contour, rather than heading upwards and inland. The path dips shallowly and then climbs gently, passing on the left No 26, a building with a pale pink door. At the edge of Tez Cova, the final house is inhabited and you pass it on the left and go over a saddle, which reveals the vista of **São Pedro**, the busy overflow from Vila Nova Sintra. From here, it is half an hour to the *vila*, initially through a maze of paths (keep asking for the *praça*).

7 VILA NOVA SINTRA–FURNA

Distance: 3km; time: 50 minutes; difficulty: 1 (AI)

This walk follows the old, little-used cobbled road from Vila Nova Sintra to Furna. It is an easy descent, steep in places, and is a good alternative to being rattled around in the back of an *aluguer* when you are descending to the port for home.

Set out on the road east from the main square. After five minutes, you will reach the stone boat looking out towards Fogo. Take the little cobbled path down to the left of the boat, and after just a short distance, you will join the main road snaking its way down to Furna. Cross the road, and double back a few metres to pick up the cobbled path continuing its descent on the other side.

After five minutes descending, you pass a cobbled turning on your right towards Santa Barbara. Some 25 minutes later, the old road briefly joins the new road, but leaves it again after a short distance.

Just before entering Furna, you rejoin the new road for the last time.

THE ILHÉUS DO ROMBO

These islands have been nature reserves since 1990 and are protected by law. The smaller ones are Ilhéu Luiz Carneiro, Ilhéu Sapado and Ilhéu do Rei.

The islets are, along with Raso Island near São Nicolau, the only home for the Cape Verdean shearwater (*Calonectris edwardsii*). Bulwer's petrel (*Bulweria bulwerii*), known locally as *João-petro*, breeds here as well as on Raso. And the Madeiran storm petrel (*Oceanodroma castro*), known locally as the *jaba-jaba* or the *pedreirinho*, breeds only here and on Branco, Raso and islets off Boavista. For descriptions, see *Birds*, page 7.

Until 2007, it was possible to visit the islets on a fishing boat from Fajã or Furna, which would do the round trip for about 2,200$. Most people chose to camp overnight, taking their own water and eating fish that they caught and grilled there. However, in 2007 the government tightened up on access to protected islands. Written ministerial permission is now required for foreigners, together with a modest fee, and is unlikely to be given. Fishermen could get hefty fines if discovered taking a tourist to the island. The restrictions may be relaxed sometime so it is worth checking.

ILHÉU GRANDE Some 2km², Ilhéu Grande's highest point is Monte Grande, at 96m. It has a rounded shape. Seabirds used to breed here – the island is covered in thick layers of guano.

ILHÉU DE CIMA This long and narrow rock of 1.5km² is famous for its seabird colonies. It has a big lump sticking out of its southern end, 77m high, and some smaller rocky outcrops.

9

São Vicente

Four o' clock in the dawning
São Vicente folk are there
To cry their sorrow
For sons who are sent away
To São Tomé
> Mindelo lament

For many people Mindelo, the island's capital, *is* São Vicente. It's a fine city, full of life and a certain grace. In some ways it is one of the most pleasant cities in West Africa. Mindelo's buzz contrasts with a dead hinterland – as dry as Sal but more extraordinary, as it has died at a younger age, while still covered in sweeping hills and mountain ranges. Hemmed in by mountains on one side and the ocean on the other, Mindelo has only one option: make music and party! The British called São Vicente the 'cinder heap'.

Wander outside the capital and those haunting questions evoked by the flatter islands return once again: 'How did people end up here? How have they survived?'

HIGHLIGHTS AND LOWLIGHTS

Many Cape Verdean writers and thinkers were educated at the São Vicente *liceu* and Mindelo is proud of its intellectual and artistic tradition. It has a liveliness: visit for the music, for the occasional performance, for hanging around in the bars. Mindelo also houses a number of characterful restaurants. Cape Verde's two most exuberant annual festivals take place on the island: the exotic Carnival, a miniature Rio, in mid-February, and the beach music festival in August.

Also go for watersports, in particular windsurfing (if you have your own gear) but surfing and fishing as well. If you love desolate rocky coastlines and deserted beaches you will enjoy wandering here.

If you love greenery, avoid São Vicente. For most of the year, much of the island is a desert. If you are on a tight schedule and long for the mountains you may regret having allocated time here. Swimming is treacherous on many beaches. There are some sandy beaches but, at present, only one actual beach hotel of an international standard.

SUGGESTED ITINERARY AND NUMBER OF DAYS Wandering around Mindelo, including going up to the fort, takes about half a day, as does a trip by vehicle to the top of Monte Verde and back. If you want to make the most of the music, you may need to plan on a late, late night, with perhaps the following day to recover. A tour of the island taking in Baia das Gatas, Calhau and São Pedro also takes a day. If the landscape appeals to you there are a few hikes or wanderings that could occupy another day or two. If you just have a day in São Vicente, for example from a cruise

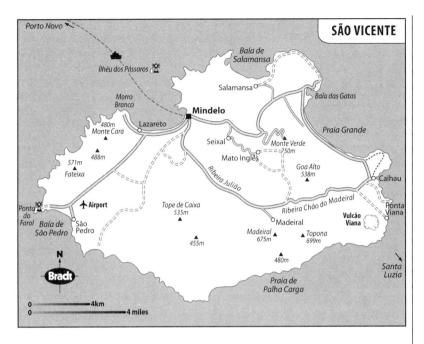

Porto Novo

Baía de
Salamansa

Ilhéu dos Pássaros

Salamansa

Baía das Gatas

Morro
Branco

Mindelo

480m
Monte Cara Lazareto

Seixal

Monte Verde
750m

Praia Grande

488m

Mato Inglês

571m
Fateixa

Goa Alto
538m

Calhau

Ribeira Julião

Ponta
do
Farol Baía de
São Pedro São
Pedro

Airport

Tope de Caixa
535m

Ribeira Chão do Madeiral

Madeiral

Vulcão
Viana

Ponta
Viana

N

455m

Madeiral
675m Topona
699m

Bradt

480m

Santa
Luzia

Praia de
Palha Carga

0 ──── 4km
0 ──────── 4 miles

ship, and you arrive early enough, visit Santo Antão, across the channel, instead, and enjoy its glorious scenery by taking a trip along the mountain road to Ribeira Grande and back. Otherwise, if it is a clear day, then a walk or drive up to the top of Monte Verde is the most scenic activity; failing that go for a drive up Fortim for a grand view of Mindelo. For a day on the beach jump into a taxi and go to São Pedro (for details, see page 281).

BACKGROUND INFORMATION

HISTORY This rock in the ocean was of little use to anyone before the end of the 18th century. After its discovery on 22 January 1462, and the traditional release of goats to prey on its delicate vegetation, humans forgot about it, except to land there occasionally with dogs and spend a night goat hunting. An attempt to populate the island was made in 1795, but it failed and just a few people remained, at the top of Monte Verde.

But São Vicente has one superlative natural resource. The island's harbour is a sweeping curve formed by a crater rim over whose northern side the sea has breached. A headland to the northeast of the harbour completes the protection while the ring of hills blocks wind from almost any direction. Thus Mindelo is a fine stopping point for ships crossing the Atlantic. When coal replaced wind as the main propellant, Mindelo became the ideal place for refuelling mid-journey.

It was the British, by then the lords of the Atlantic and creators of the steam engine, who began to realise Mindelo's potential. By the early 1800s, they had established a consulate and depot there. One John Lewis, a lieutenant, brought coal and set up a refuelling station for ships crossing from Europe to South America or to southern Africa. His arrival was followed by the Royal Mail in 1850. Soon Mindelo was busy, and in its heyday thousands of ships a year would pause in its harbour to load with coal brought from Cardiff to São Vicente. At any time 5,000 tonnes were waiting in lighters ready to load onto ships – part of the constant reserve of 34,000 tonnes. A 100,000-gallon tank was kept in the harbour, filled with water ferried over from Santo Antão.

John Rendall, one of the British involved in the coal business, reported of São Vicente in the 1850s:

> There is space sufficient to anchor 300 vessels. Two steam packets run to and from England with the Post Office Mails, calling here every month for a replenishment of coals. The place is improving daily, and will no doubt, in a short time, become the wealthiest of all the islands.

São Vicente was also chosen, in 1875, as the site for the submarine cable that allowed telecommunications across the Atlantic, and it filled with British employees of the Western Telegraph.

Yet the trade did not bring much prosperity to ordinary people. Cape Verde earned some money by charging for water and anchorage and exacting coal taxes, but the refuelling was in the hands of foreign companies and many locals scratched a pittance from the sale of rum and from prostitution and dingy guesthouses, though some earned livings heaving coal. For their part the authorities made little attempt to develop São Vicente: there was no investment in a proper pier to ward off competition from Dakar, and little thought was given to the possibility of taking advantage of world events rather than being their victim.

When Alfred Burdon Ellis visited in 1855, he wrote at length about the antics of the characters in his bawdy and squalid lodgings. On leaving, he concluded:

> Taken as a whole it is, perhaps, the most wretched and immoral town that I have ever seen; but what can be expected of a colony which is rated at such a low value that the salary of the governor is only four shillings and sixpence a day?

Thus, at the same time that it was the fourth-greatest coaling station in the world after Egypt's Port Said, Malta and Singapore, the city became a place of beggars, prostitutes, starving invalids and smugglers.

Unfolding world events dealt São Vicente a series of blows. The opening of the Suez Canal between the Mediterranean and the Red Sea in 1869 diminished the port's activity, though it bounced back after a while. Technology advanced and the cable connection became mechanised, so the employees of the Western Telegraph returned home. Ships' bunkers were built larger so they could carry enough coal for their entire journeys. Finally, oil replaced coal, drastically cutting the amount of labour required for refuelling. Drought and famine bit viciously and in 1941, the British consul at Mindelo, Captain J L Sands, reported on Mindelo's inhabitants:

> A large number are emaciated, worn out and have lost both heart and hope... the starving seem to accept the situation with an oriental fatalism. They do not press their claims to live, they scarcely beg, may ask you for alms once or twice, and then simply stare at you as if resigned to what is to happen.

It was from Mindelo at that time that the *contratados* were recruited in their thousands to go and labour on the plantations of São Tomé and Príncipe, islands to the south. But the conditions there were akin to slavery and few ever returned.

Mindelo was the intellectual capital of the archipelago, so it was here that despair and education came together to create the idea of revolution (see pages 22–3).

PORTO ANTIGO
CABO VERDE

Beautiful Residence Porto Antigo enjoys an unrivalled location, directly in front of the old fishing port on the seafront in Santa Maria, a short stroll from the town's bars, restaurants, music venues and water sports centres. For those visitors looking for the independence of their own, elegant self-catering apartment - but with some real hotel-style comforts - Porto Antigo is the perfect solution. It has been thoughtfully built from attractive stone, planted with lush vegetation and in perfect harmony with its surroundings.

The Residence consists of 148 stylishly furnished studios, apartments, houses and villas, sleeping up to six persons. You will find everything you need for a perfect holiday: fully-equipped kitchen, living-room, bedroom(s), bathroom, satellite TV, air-conditioning, Wi-Fi and either a porch, terrace or even garden.

Guests have the use of a stunning swimming pool with terrace and sunbeds, as well as a pretty white-sand beach. The Porto Antigo's renowned Papaia's restaurant, with a fantastic setting overlooking the harbour, serves tasty buffet breakfasts, homemade cakes and diverse lunchtime and evening meals, including choices for vegetarians and children.

If you are looking for perfection, then at Porto Antigo you may well find it!

You may enjoy your stay so much that you decide that you want to buy an apartment here, either as a holiday home or investment property. If so, we would be delighted to talk to you! Compared with Europe and elsewhere, purchase prices are low and rental incomes are good. This is a fast-growing tourist destination – become a part of it.

PORTO ANTIGO
CABO VERDE

Tel : +238 242 18 15
portoantigoreservas@hotmail.com
www.portoantigo.com

Ana Monteiro, Alex Alper and Murray Stewart

As any visitor to Cape Verde will quickly realise, these are islands which encounter plenty of strong breeze. Sweeping across the Caribbean and Africa, the *alize* tradewinds have for centuries brought ships to Cape Verde's shores and unwanted dust into newly swept homes each summer. The vagaries of wind have rendered the airports on Brava and Santo Antão inoperable. On the credit side, most visitors will have welcomed the cooling breezes when the African sun is burning down at midday. Now, the same winds look set to be a rich source of clean, renewable energy.

Wind energy technology made its debut in Cape Verde in the 1970s, but until recently, only about 2% of Cape Verde's energy was provided by its wind. But with high average wind speeds and electricity demand increasing by roughly 10% per year, wind has been increasingly seen as the solution, or at least a large part of it. The massive annual cost of importing diesel fuels has been a major driver in finding an energy solution closer to home. The mid-1990s saw the first large, grid-connected wind turbines being donated by the Danish government, to be managed by Electra, the Cape Verdean utility company. Eight turbines, each with a capacity of 300kW, were provided to three wind farms on the islands of Sal, São Vicente and Santiago.

Fast-forwarding to July 2012, and a step-change in the importance of wind energy had been experienced. By then, Cabeólica SA, a public/private enterprise, had brought into commercial operation four new wind farms in Sal, São Vicente, Santiago and Boavista. With an installed capacity of 25.5MW (30 turbines of 850kW each), an incredible 20% of Cape Verde's electricity production is now generated by the farms, making this one of the highest wind energy penetration rates in the world. On Sal and São Vicente, over 30% of these individual islands' requirements are met by their wind farms and on some days on São Vicente this figure has been as high as 50%, with no technical problems being experienced. Overall, greenhouse gas emissions have been cut by 70,000 tonnes CO_2e, and the bill for importing diesel has been reduced. The incidence of power cuts has decreased.

Of course, wind is highly erratic – changing direction and intensity – and thus is an 'intermittent generator'. Its guaranteed output is therefore zero, and diesel capacity must be able to meet 100% of demand. The wind's intermittency is what has traditionally prevented it from supplying more than 25% of any country's total energy, but with technological advances and increased know-how, this perceived limit to wind power's capability is now clearly being challenged in Cape Verde. Further improvements to the wind-generating infrastructure, such as storage systems or an automatic dispatching system, could see more drastic advances in wind power's penetration.

At least part of the answer to Cape Verde's energy demands, it seems, is indeed 'blowing in the wind'.

São Vicente today Mindelo, the capital, has an air of importance about it these days and is growing wealthier. *Emigrantes* are returning and there is inward migration from other islands. A marina has been built, as well as a new international airport. Currently there is only one direct flight a week from Portugal with TACV and two with TAP but there are hopes that São Vicente will make great strides, with talk of French and Dutch charter flights operating soon. There is a scenic new road from Calhau to Baía das Gatas.

Much of Mindelo's terrain feels like a potential vast natural building site and, unsurprisingly, the island has not escaped the ubiquitous talk of mesmerising, huge foreign development plans. But talk and plans are cheap and development is not. The grandest plan was the brainchild of investors from Dubai who wanted to build the Cesaria Resort, a €1.5 billion tourism and real-estate development at Praia de Palha Carga and Calheta Grande in the south of the island. It seems unlikely now that this will go ahead.

Resorts planned for Baía das Gatas, São Pedro and Calhau all appear to have ground to a halt, leaving a few hopeful constructions either half-complete or lying empty, waiting for the retreating economic tide to turn. As for Alto Fortim, in town – this was supposed to have been transformed into the Nikki Beach Village and Casino Resort. In all, five international golf courses were planned. In total there are supposedly plans for four more marinas in São Vicente in addition to the existing new one in Mindelo, but there's no sign as yet of these actually leaving the drawing board.

GEOGRAPHY The island is 227km² and lies about 14km east of Santo Antão. It is extremely dry. Its highest peak, Monte Verde, is 750m. There is irrigation in some of the principal valleys – Ribeira de Calhau and Ribeira da Vinha. Earlier this century there were irrigated plantations in Ribeira Julião. The population is around 80,000, overwhelmingly living in Mindelo. There have been many attempts at reafforestation, particularly along the road to the airport. The onset of the rains in July and August transforms the desert to green, before the island gradually begins to dry out again.

NATURAL HISTORY São Vicente has one protected area: Monte Verde, which is a natural park.

Turtles used to nest prolifically on São Vicente's beaches and one of their last remaining beaches, Praia Grande, runs between Baía das Gatas and Calhau. Here, as everywhere, hunting is a serious threat, as well as the illegal removal of sand for construction. The new road running alongside the shore has storm drains running directly onto the beach and the rain will most likely sweep away any nests in their paths. The island does not harbour any bird specialities but there are plenty of interesting waders and migrant birds on the wet sand towards São Pedro, 1km from the airport, and on the sewage ponds 2km from the centre of town (reached by going south along the coastal road until just after the Shell oil storage terminals and following a track inland on the left).

FESTIVALS

22 January	Municipality Day
February	Carnival
3 May	Santa Cruz
24 June	São João (St John)
29 June	São Pedro
8 August	Nossa Senhora da Luz
August full moon	Baía das Gatas music festival
September	Mindelact theatre festival

HAZARDS In terms of **crime**, begging by street children and indeed adults can be a nuisance and verging on the aggressive. Some beggars have a habit of attempting to help themselves to the contents of your pockets before you are quite sure that is what you want them to do. They are most common in Praça Amílcar Cabral and along the coastal road. Watch out in general for pickpockets and don't go up to the fort on your own. Like many port cities the world over, Mindelo has an 'edge' to it, but in truth it is far safer than many cities in the 'developed' world. Taking a taxi after dark is advisable.

Many **swimming** areas are dangerous: take local advice.

GETTING THERE AND AWAY

BY AIR There are several flights a day with TACV to and from Sal and Santiago. Mindelo has the benefit of a smart new international airport, receiving a few international flights a week from Lisbon, the rest being domestic. Named after Cape Verde's late and great cultural icon, Cesária Évora, it has a café, tourist information booth (not always open), TACV sales office, gift and music shops, ATM, car-hire agency and free Wi-Fi to while away time waiting for your flight. For guidance on arriving at a Cape Verdean airport from overseas see *Red tape*, pages 55–6.

Taxis to town from the airport (\ *232 3715*) cost 800$ (1,000$ at night). It is 10km to Mindelo and 1km to São Pedro.

BY FERRY There is, theoretically, a regular ferry connection between São Vicente, Praia and São Nicolau but this needs to be checked just before the trip with one of the ferry agencies: try STM, which operates the *Sal Rei*. The journey takes at least 16 hours and currently costs around 3,800$. At time of writing, the ferry company Santos e David were operating the *Ribeira do Paul* from Sao Vicente to São Nicolau, then onward to Sal. However, knowing that these journeys can take up to 12 hours, and looking at the size of this vessel and its apparent state of repair, these journeys can't really be recommended.

Cargo ships regularly go to Praia from São Vicente and, less regularly, to other islands. To find a place on one of these ships try the agents up towards the port and on Rua Cristiano de Sena Barcelos. To get to Santo Antão take the usually reliable daily ferries from Mindelo port to Porto Novo. For further details see page 287.

BY YACHT There is a modern marina at Mindelo, and the harbour and anchorage are excellent, offering protection from the northwest winds through to eastern and southern winds. In Mindelo, there is fuel and water at the Mindelo Marina (*www. marinamindelo.*com) and ship repair is the best in the archipelago – they should be able to repair instruments here and are authorised for warranty work. There is also a chandlery with a range of equipment suitable for crossing the Atlantic.

Whether or not this is your first port of call in Cape Verde, the procedure is to tie up at the marina and then walk to the Porto Grande and identify yourself to the *capitania* who will guide you through the other necessities such as the maritime police and the immigration police. Mindelo Marina has a floating pontoon with a pleasant bar/restaurant. The other possible anchorage is at Baía de São Pedro, where it is best to anchor off the eastern end of the beach. Winds can occasionally be difficult there and there are no facilities.Watch the channel between São Vicente and Santo Antão, where winds can gust to up to 40 knots, particularly between December and May.

For yacht services try BoatCV (see *Sailing*, page 267)

GETTING AROUND

BY PUBLIC TRANSPORT Transcor buses journey around Mindelo and its outskirts (25–30$), visiting Baía das Gatas during July and August. Buses and taxis gather at the square to the west of the Presidential Palace. *Alugueres* gather in Praça da Independéncia.

BY TAXI

There are plenty of marked taxis cruising around town. The municipality publish official fares, so if in doubt, ask your driver to show you the list. A typical journey within the city will cost about 150$. Taxis charge about 2,200$ for a return journey to the top of Monte Verde, 1,800$ return to Baía das Gatas and 2,000$ return to Calhau. It's 800$ to the airport. Taxis can be hired for about 1,000$ per hour. Fares at night are about 10% more than the daytime equivalents.

Victor Hugo m 991 5940
Dilson's Taxis m 995 7976

Taxi 2000 231 4564

BY CAR There are many car-rental agencies in town. Many close for lunch between 12.30 and 14.30. In addition to those listed, any half-decent hotel receptionist will have rental agency details. Prices start at around €45 per day for something basic. You might consider whether it is really worth hiring a car. After all, the island's mainly cobbled road network is hardly extensive and taking taxis to Baía das Gatas and Calhau at one side of the island, and São Pedro at the other, will probably work out cheaper.

Alucar [271 D8] On Monte Sossego, southwest of town; 232 1295/5194; e alucarsv@cvtelecom.cv, alucarstrc@cvtelecom.cv
Atlantic Car [270 F2] 27 Rua Baltazar Lopes

da Silva, Mindelo; 232 7465
Joel Evora Madelrazino; 230 0303
Rentauto [271 G5] 231 9664

WHERE TO STAY AND EAT

Virtually all hotels are in Mindelo. There's a resort in São Pedro, a hotel in Calhau, and a couple of budget places in Baía das Gatas.

ACTIVITIES

EXCURSIONS There are several operators in Mindelo offering a variety of tours. The tourist information kiosk in front of the Pont d'Agua complex has details of boat trips and other excursions.

Atlantur [274 C3] Rua d'Antonio Aurelia 231 2728; m 918 7336; ; e saovicente@atlantur.com; www.atlantur.com. Tours, tickets & hotel bookings.
Barracuda Tours Rua de Coco, 28-A; 232 5592; e geral@barracudatours.com; www. barracudatours.com. Established family-owned agency that can organise inter-island travel & excursions.
Cabo Verde Safari m 991 1544/2721; e caboverdesafari@cvtelecom.cv. João specialises in taking you off the beaten track with boat trips,

snorkelling & trekking. A variety of island tours, full-day excursions by Land Rover from €90pp, based on 2 passengers. Cheaper as the group increases.
Mindelo Inside Out m 911 0016; e info@cabocontact.com. Can be organised via the tourist information at Pont d'Agua. Mimi will take you to see the everyday lives of Mindelo's inhabitants, meeting the beach gym instructor, explaining the challenges of water shortages, shoe repairs (!), before giving you a taste of grogue & dining with

her family in her home. With a group of 2 or more, the 3-hour walking trip costs €18pp.

vista verde tours [270 E3] ✆ 232 6671; m 993 0788; e office@vista-verde.com; www.vista-verde.

com. Well-established multilingual agency. The office is located just off the Praca Nova, next to the Syrius dance club, behind Hotel Porto Grande. See ad on the inside back cover.

WINDSURFING AND KITESURFING São Vicente could be one of the world's greatest windsurfing and bodyboarding destinations. World windsurfing speed records have been set in São Pedro Bay. The wind there, at the southwest corner of the island, is the result of an unusual quirk in the landscape: the long straight valley behind the bay acts as a funnel concentrating the wind – a phenomenon known as the Venturi effect. The result is an unusually steady and strong breeze. There are some good surfing spots around Calhau, including Praia Grande, around the headland to the north of Calhau, and Praia Branca, just south of Calhau and Sandy Beach. Frustratingly, however, the market for renting equipment has not yet developed, but there may be kit available to hire at São Pedro from the Foya Branca Hotel.

Itoma ✆ 00 43 699 195 28111; m 991 2852; e info@itoma.at; www.itoma.at. This 23m motor catamaran is based in Mindelo & is booked mostly by groups from Europe for week-long windsurfing (winter) or diving (summer) trips. This comfortable boat carries a range of sails & boards & offers a way to windsurf in places few people ever see.

Comfortably takes 12 passengers. Charters from €600 for 3 days' diving to €12,900 for one-week's windsurfing.

Kitesurf NOW m 987 1954; e ola@kitesurfnow. eu; www.kitesurfnow.eu. Offers lessons from its base between Mindelo and Baia das Gatas.

SAILING As with much of Cape Verde, but especially between São Vicente and Santo Antão, the seas can be rough and the winds very strong. Trying to anchor in Porto Novo, Santo Antão's harbour, in a strong offshore wind can be very hairy and there is not the same level of support as can be found in the Canaries.

⚠ **BoatCV** (Kai Brossmann & Cesar Murais) Av Marginal; ✆ 232 6772; e info@boatcv.com; www. boatcv.com; ⏱ 09.00–12.00 & 15.00–18.00 Tue– Sat. German & Cape Verdean operation offering yacht support services & hiring out a variety of yachts, bare boat or captained. Mr Brossmann can

often be found at the Mindelo Marina.

⚠ **Sailcapeverde** Mindelo Marina Berth C2; m 991 9431; e c.santos@sailcapeverde.com; www.sailcapeverde.com. Can organise island tours on the *Perseverance*.

São Vicente ACTIVITIES

9

Murray Stewart

Mindelo was formerly one of the staging points for the OnDeck Atlantic Adventure, a race from Europe to Barbados. Crews were able to sign on for any of the individual legs, starting at Portsmouth and continuing to Lisbon, Madeira, São Vicente and Barbados. The São Vicente to Barbados leg – invariably the most popular leg – took around two weeks and was staged each November. The boats were half a dozen Farr 65s, sleek, thrilling ocean racers, with massive amounts of wind available to fill the spinnakers all the way downwind to the Caribbean. Creature comforts were not what these boats were about, yet crew members still had to pay around €2,000 for the adrenalin rush. Sadly, the race seems to have died out a couple of years ago.

But new for 2013, a spin-off from the Arc Rally, another long-running yacht rally, was announced, with a Cape Verde stopover. Fifty yachts taking part in the Arc+ rally to St Lucia will draw breath at Mindelo and it is hoped that the city will become a regular fixture in the yachting calendar for many years to come.

FISHING The waters around São Vicente have international renown for their blue marlin. **Centro de Pesca do Mindelo/Cape Verde Big Game** (m *995 1546;* e *biggamecaboverde@gmail.com; www.biggamecaboverde.com*), based at the Residencial Alto Fortim, runs fishing-and-accommodation packages, taking visitors out on its Bertram 33 and Pace 40. A day's fishing on these boats, for a maximum of four passengers, costs from €700–950, depending on which boat you choose. Try also Residencial Jenny. Fishing trips are also organised at the Foya Branca Hotel.

DIVING Diving on São Vicente is undeveloped, but the Foya Branca Hotel (*www. foyabranca.com*) in São Pedro currently hosts the Deep Dive Nautical Center. *Itoma* is a 32m catamaran that offers dive charters in the summer (for contact information, see page 267).

SWIMMING The best swimming is probably at the semi-artificial lagoon at Baía das Gatas and also at Baía de Salamansa. Then there's Praia da Laginha, just north of Mindelo, usually safe and sometimes manned with a lifeguard. The Hotel Porto Grande and the Mindel Hotel both have swimming pools, the latter a little small but with great views from its rooftop position. The Foya Branca Hotel in São Pedro has a pool that opens to non-guests (for a fee of 700$), but the beach there has a vicious shore break and swimming is not advised. There is a swimming pool at Mindelo's new marina, use of which costs around 500$ for the whole day, including hire of a sunbed.

HIKING São Vicente is not one of the hiking islands but there are several rewarding walks. It has a few small mountains and a breathtaking coastline of black rocks blasted by white foam, and white- or black-sand beaches.

You can walk up to the top of Monte Verde (following the cobbled road), or all the way along the coast from Baía das Gatas to Calhau. There are several walks in Calhau (see page 280), ranging from 45 minutes to three hours. You can also walk from the Hotel Foya Branca, in São Pedro, to the lighthouse at the end of the point (2hrs round trip).

CULTURE One very good reason for lingering in São Vicente is the music. At times it seems to simply pour out of very bar and restaurant, and the choice is wide. There is regular live music in many of the restaurants, especially at weekends and events going on at the various cultural centres in town. There are currently no museums, although there are still murmurings about developing one at the fort and reopening the museum on Praça Amílcar Cabral. There is also the Centro Cultural do Mindelo which often has exhibitions on, shows occasional films in its impressively sized auditorium and hosts music and other events. Wandering around looking at the old colonial architecture is also a satisfying occupation.

SIGHTSEEING BY VEHICLE Several operators offer round-island excursions. Cabo Verde Safari offer off-the-beaten-track Land-Rover safaris (for further information, see *Excursions*, page 266). Another good option is to hire a taxi with driver. They will happily wait for you as you stop to take photos or visit places of interest. Quad bikes can also be hired from a number of operators, such as the Sao Vicente Quad Center (m *939 6098*) from around €60 for a day's hire. A driving licence is required. Outside Mindelo there is not much traffic and, with a good map, it should not be problematic to guide yourself around the main sights. Go to Baía das Gatas, Calhau, Monte Verde and São Pedro.

MINDELO

The wide streets, cobbled squares and 19th-century European architecture all contribute to the sense of colonial history in Mindelo. Most facilities lie not on the coastal road but on the next road back, which at the market end is called Rua de Santo António and, after being bisected by the Rua Libertadores d'Africa (also known as Rua Lisboa), becomes Av 5 de Julho. Most road names in the centre of town have changed, but many of the old signs linger and firms vary as to which street name they use. Like most towns in Cape Verde, street names are of limited use, and mentioning them when talking to locals will often draw a blank stare!

WHERE TO STAY There are many hotels in Mindelo at a range of standards and prices: only a selection is given here. As with the Plateau in Praia, some Mindelo hotels are in old colonial buildings with central atriums, which means that some of their rooms may be internal, with windows opening only onto a shaft. It's worth checking the room before signing up. All listings are located on the map, pages 270–1, unless otherwise stated.

Casa Azul (10 rooms) Lameirão; 231 0124; e casaazul@cvtelecom.cv; www.casa-azul-mindelo.com. Some 4.5km out of Mindelo off the road to Baía das Gatas, this is an artistic & beautiful place to spend a few days, perched on a hill in splendid isolation amidst spectacular views. Each of the rooms has a different theme & is tastefully decorated. Swimming pool can be filled on request. Only breakfast is provided, so you'll need transport to find other meals. The French owners are often out of the country, so check the hotel is open before you go. **$$$$$**

Hotel Don Paco (44 rooms) Rua de Cristiano de Sena Barcelos; 231 9381; e info@donpacohotel.com; www.donpacohotel.com. A relatively new arrival (2011) with a business-hotel feel. Smart, spacious rooms, all facilities, including Wi-Fi (chargeable). Guests have free use of the pool at Pont d'Agua. Good restaurant with live music & dinner evenings on Sat. **$$$$**

Hotel Porto Grande (50 rooms) Praça Amílcar Cabral; 232 3190/91/92; e portogrande@oasisatlantico.com; www. oasisatlantico.com/en/portogrande. The large yellow building on one side of the square, this is a pleasant hotel of international standard in a long-

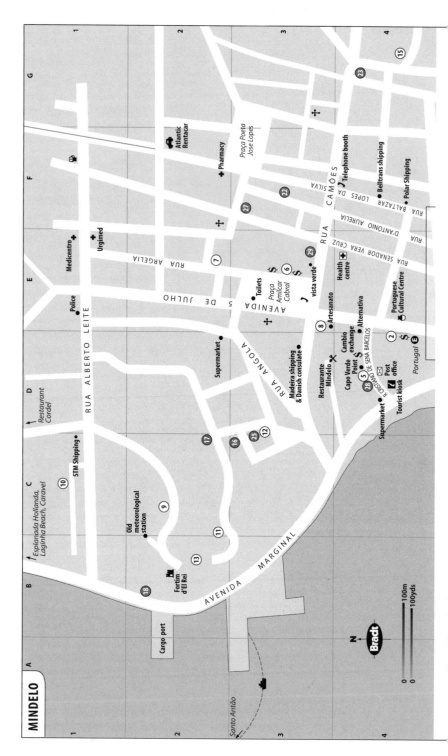

MINDELO

A **B** **C** **D** **E** **F** **G**

Santo Antão

Cargo port

AVENIDA MARGINAL

Esplanada Hollanda,
Laginha Beach, Caravel

Restaurant
Cordel

RUA ALBERTO LEITE

STM Shipping ●

Medicentro ✚

Police ●

Urgimed ✚

Atlantic
Rentacar

✚ Pharmacy

Old
meteorological
station ●

Fortim
d'El Rei

Supermarket ●

RUA ARGELIA

5 DE JULHO

AVENIDA

Toilets ●

Praça
Amílcar
Cabral

✚

vista verde ●

Praça Poeta
José Lopes

✚

RUA CAMÕES

⑩ ⑨ ⑬ ⑱ ⑰ ⑯ ㉕ ⑫ ⑪

RUA ANGOLA

Madeira shipping
& Danish consulate ●

Restaurante
Mindelo ✖

Capo Verde
Point
$

Cambio
exchange
$

⑤ ㉘

R CRISTIANO DE SENA BARCELOS

Post
office

Supermarket ●

Tourist kiosk

Artesanato ●

⑧

⑥ $
$

Alternativa ●

Health
centre ✚

RUA SENADOR VERA CRUZ

RUA D'ANTONIO AURELIA

RUA BALTAZAR LOPES DA SILVA

Belltrans shipping ●

Telephone booth

Polar Shipping ●

Portuguese
Cultural Centre ●

② $

Portugal

Ⓔ

㉗ ㉒ ㉓ ⑮ ㉙ ⑦

N

Bradt

0   100m
0   100yds

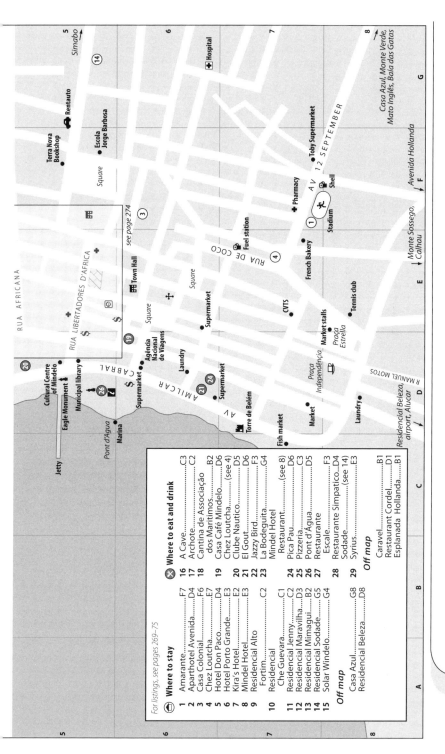

São Vicente MINDELO

9

For listings, see pages 269–75

Where to stay

1 Amarante......................F7
2 Aparthotel Avenida........D4
3 Casa Colonial.................F6
4 Chez Loutcha.................E7
5 Hotel Don Paco..............D4
6 Hotel Porto Grande........E3
7 Kira's Hotel....................E2
8 Mindel Hotel..................E3
9 Residencial Alto
   Fortim.........................C2
10 Residencial
   Che Guevara...............C1
11 Residencial Jenny..........C2
12 Residencial Maravilha....D3
13 Residencial Mimagui......B2
14 Residencial Sodade........G5
15 Solar Windelo................G4

Off map

   Casa Azul.......................G8
   Residencial Beleza..........D8

Where to eat and drink

16 A Cave...........................C3
17 Archote..........................C2
18 Cantina de Associação
   dos Maritimos..............B2
19 Casa Café Mindelo.........D6
   Chez Loutcha..........(see 4)
20 Clube Nautico................D5
21 El Gout..........................D6
22 Jazzy Bird......................F3
23 La Bodeguita..................G4
   Mindel Hotel
   Restaurant............(see 8)
24 Pica Pau.........................D6
25 Pizzeria..........................C3
26 Pont d'Água....................D5
27 Restaurante
   Escale............................F3
28 Restaurante Simpatico....D4
   Sodade...................(see 14)
29 Syrius............................E3

Off map

   Caravel...........................B1
   Restaurant Cordel...........D1
   Esplanada Hollanda........B1

271

established building, with terraces & swimming pool, children's pool, gym & entertainment. Rooms have AC, satellite TV. Abundant buffet b/fast. Wi-Fi available at extra charge. **$$$$**

Kira's Hotel (11 rooms) Rua de Argelia; 230 0274/5; e kiras@kirashotel.com; www. kirashotel.com. A new boutique hotel, created out of an elegant family home. Just off the main square, each room is different & is equipped with AC, ceiling fan, TV, internet, mini fridge & safe. Each named after one of the islands. Pleasant indoor & outdoor spaces. **$$$$**

Mindel Hotel (70 rooms) Av 5 de Julho; 232 8885/6; e mihotel2011@gmail.com. Just off the main square (Praça Amílcar Cabral) this is a smart, international hotel with all the trimmings, including satellite TV, hairdryers & AC in good-sized comfortably furnished rooms. Abundant buffet b/fast. Free transport to airport. Visa & MasterCard accepted. **$$$$**

Aparthotel Avenida (20 rooms) Av 5 de Julho; 232 3435; e aparthotel@sapo.cv. On the road that heads south from the main square (Av Amílcar Cabral) into the centre of town, this is a rather characterless but adequate middling hotel with rooms that have AC & hot water. There are good views of the harbour from one side. **$$$**

Casa Colonial (9 rooms) Rua 24 de Setembro; 231 8760 m 999 5350 e casacolonialmindelo@gmail.com; http://www. casacolonial.info. A tastefully restored old colonial house, near the centre. Rooms are twin or double, though extra beds may be added & single rates are available. All rooms en suite. Inner courtyard with plunge pool, roof terrace with city views. **$$$**

Chez Loutcha (24 rooms) Rua de Côco; 232 1636/1689; e chezloutcha@sapo.cv www. chezloutchacv.com. Just off the vast Estrela Square, Chez Loutcha is one of the old faithfuls of Mindelo, with a rabbit warren of rooms that are nevertheless of an acceptable standard, though some have interior windows. Rooms are en suite with hot water, AC & fridge. The restaurant below has a very good reputation, sometimes has music & receives tour groups. The proprietor offers free transport to his beachfront restaurant in Calhau where they have a large buffet, live music & dancing every Sun. **$$$**

Residencial Mindelo [map page 274] (11 rooms) Rua de Lisboa; 230 0863; e m.residencial@gmail.com. Attractively

decorated in white & dark wood, this is a centrally positioned hotel with good en-suite rooms with AC, hot water & fridge. Excellent b/fasts are served upstairs in a delightful, rooftop room with views over the harbour & inland over the mountains. Front rooms are lighter but noisier, some back rooms only have internal windows, however. There's a lounge with TV. Free Wi-Fi. **$$$**

Residencial Jenny (23 rooms) Alto São Nicolau; 232 8969; e hstaubyn@cvtelecom.cv. If a view of Mindelo Bay is what you are after you can't do too much better than this hotel which towers up one of its hills. It has some rooms with large balconies from which to enjoy the sunset over Santo Antão & the mountains that fringe Mindelo. Rooms without view are cheaper, but gloomy, though all rooms are comfortable & spacious with AC & TV. There are internet terminals & fishing tours. English spoken. **$$$–$$**

Residencial Sodade (30 rooms) 38 Rua Franz Fanon; 230 3200/7556; e residencialsodade@hotmail.com. Up the hill behind the Presidential Palace, the renovated Sodade commands perhaps the best view over the town & the bay from its rooftop terrace & restaurant. The architecture is pleasant. Rooms are highly variable, from depressing budget basement hideaways to excellent-quality upstairs rooms & even spacious suites – check when booking. More expensive rooms have fridge, TV & AC. All have hot water. **$$$–$**

Solar Windelo (9 rooms) Alto Santo António; 231 0070; e windelocapvert@gmail. com; www.windelo.com. Located up a steep, short hill in the Praça Nova area, this is the former home of musician & composer Vasco Martins. Offers smart self-catering studio flats, rooms, suites & family rooms that can accommodate 6 guests, on a B&B basis. All with private baths, hot water. Some suites have balconies & great views – recommended. Will arrange excursions & give advice about wind- & kitesurfing. Dinner available on request. Free Wi-Fi. Rooms get cheaper the longer you stay, no charge for children under 5. **$$$–$**

Hotel Gaudi [map page 274] (10 rooms) 231 8954; m 953 4259; e hotelgaudi@ cvtelecom.cv www.hotelgaudimindelo.com. A good location for some of the music bars/ restaurants. Small rooms, all with private baths & hot water. Some with TV & mini bar. Booking via the website is cheaper. **$$**

🏠 **Residencial Alto Fortim** (10 rooms) ☎ 232 6938; e altofortim@hotmail.com; www. biggamecaboverde.com. Up towards the fort, on the right. Run by a Frenchman & his Cape Verdean wife. Spacious rooms, some with limited sea view, all have AC, fridge & hot water. Fishing & boat trips offered. Lunch & dinner available. **$$**

🏠 **Residencial Beleza** (21 rooms) Rua Oficinas Navais; ☎ 232 4094; e geral@rsbeleza.com; www. resbeleza.com. To the south of the centre. Pleasant accommodation with a terrace, bar & restaurant. Rooms have TV, AC, hot water & Wi-Fi (extra cost). Buffet b/fast included. Internet café & bar next door. There is also a second hotel, Laghina Beleza, currently under renovation, beyond Laginha Beach. Contact details are as above. **$$**

🏠 **Residencial Che Guevara** (12 rooms) ☎ 232 2449; e cheguevara@cvtelecom.cv. A pleasant spot, located in the north of town along Rua Alberto Leite. Rooms all have private bathrooms with hot water. Also has triples & family rooms. **$$**

🏠 **Residencial Maravilha** (12 rooms) Alto São Nicolau; ☎ 232 2203/230 0094; ☎ 955 9693; e maravilha@gmail.com. Large, tastefully renovated house with rooms & suites just off the main coast road. **$$**

🏠 **Residencial Mimagui** (5 rooms) Alto São Nicolau; ☎ 232 7953; www.residencialmimagui. com. Near Residencial Jenny, the Mimagui's studios & apartments offer the same great view of Mindelo Bay & Monte Cara, the iconic mountain of São Vicente. This little residencial has large living areas & a terrace. All rooms have kitchens. No meals available. AC & TV. English spoken. **$$**

🏠 **Amarante** (18 rooms) Av 12 Septembre; ☎ 231 3219; e gdamarante@cvtelecom.cv. Very basic budget choice, without breakfast. Rooms are en suite, but no hot water. **$**

🏠 **Pensão Chave d'Ouro** [map page 274] (16 rooms) Av 5 de Julho; ☎ 232 7050. Centrally positioned on the corner of Rua Libertadores d'Africa & Av 5 de Julho. Supposedly at 80 years, the oldest hotel in Mindelo. The better rooms still have huge shuttered windows & are equipped with ewers & pitchers. Stuffed with character, but a budget option. Top-floor singles are little more than cupboards with warped chipboard partitions. First-floor rooms retain a sliver of old colonial charm. No en-suite bathrooms. There's also a restaurant. **$**

❌ **WHERE TO EAT AND DRINK** Mindelo is packed with restaurants, bars and cafés so only a selection is given here. The excellent Morabeza bakery is on Rua Baltazar Lopes da Silva; there is a good bakery on the Rua Senador Vera Cruz, around the corner from Katem Musique. There is also a French bakery opposite Chez Loutcha, which does its version of *pastel de nata*, but don't expect croissants. The Fragata supermarket opposite the marina also has a bakery. All listings located on the map pages 270–1 unless otherwise stated.

❌ **Archote** At the northern end of town, this is a good choice, popular with locals. Decent food & live music almost every night in high season. **$$$$$**

❌ **Restaurant Cordel** Rua Dr Manuel Duarte; ☎ 231 6402. Won 'Best Restaurant' award in 2012 from the *Atlantico* newspaper. Smart interior with chic décor & a few outside tables. Booking advisable at weekend. Fish, seafood & meat dishes plus lobster specials. Up a hill behind the military HQ, take a taxi. **$$$$$**

❌ **Restaurante Simpatico** Rua Sena Barcelos m 910 3030/2527; www.simpaticocaboverde. com. A swish & chic European place, serving steaks, fish & chicken. Wines from Europe. **$$$$$**

❌ **Chez Loutcha** (see page opposite for details) ⏱ 07.00–09.45, 12.00–15.00 & 19.30–23.30.

Much-praised restaurant on the ground floor of the hotel of the same name. There is live music Jul–Sep Tue–Thu. **$$$$**

❌ **El Gout** On the seafront, Av Amílcar Cabral south end, in an old building; ⏱ Tue–Sun. African-themed interior. Has a good selection of meals accompanied by live entertainment after 21.00 Wed–Sat. Also a bar. **$$$$**

❌ **Mindel Hotel Restaurant** Outside on the west side of the hotel. Extensive regular menu & separate pizza menu. Open air & a popular place, live music at weekends. **$$$$**

❌ **Restaurante Escale** ☎ 232 4434. West of Praça Poeta José Lopes; ⏱ 11.00–14.00 & 18.00–23.00 Mon–Sat. Definitely not a snack bar, despite the signage. Delightful owner, pleasant interior. High-quality cuisine, bookings preferred. Menus in

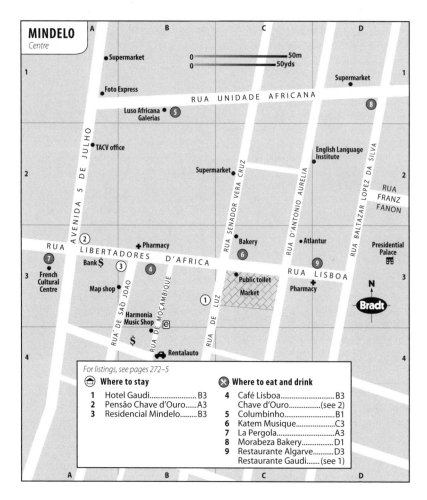

MINDELO
Centre

RUA UNIDADE AFRICANA

Supermarket
Foto Express
Luso Africana Galerias 5
Supermarket
TACV office
English Language Institute
Supermarket
Bakery 6
Atlantur
Pharmacy
Bank $ 3 4
French Cultural Centre 7
Map shop
Presidential Palace
RUA LISBOA
Public toilet
Market
Pharmacy
Harmonia Music Shop
Rentalauto
Bradt

RUA 5 DE JULHO · AVENIDA 5 DE JULHO · RUA LIBERTADORES D'AFRICA · RUA SENADOR VERA CRUZ · RUA D'ANTONIO AURELIA · RUA BALTAZAR LOPEZ DA SILVA · RUA FRANZ FANON · RUA DE SÃO JOAO · RUA DE MOÇAMBIQUE · RUA DE LUZ

For listings, see pages 272–5

🛏 **Where to stay**
1 Hotel Gaudi..........................B3
2 Pensão Chave d'Ouro......A3
3 Residencial Mindelo.........B3

🍴 **Where to eat and drink**
4 Café Lisboa............................B3
  Chave d'Ouro.................(see 2)
5 Columbinho..........................B1
6 Katem Musique....................C3
7 La Pergola.............................A3
8 Morabeza Bakery................D1
9 Restaurante Algarve...........D3
  Restaurante Gaudi.......(see 1)

French & English. $$$$

✗ **Restaurante Gaudi** [map above] Below the hotel of the same name, a pleasant interior & staff. Fish, seafood & spaghetti dishes. Live music Thu–Sun in low season, every night in the peak. $$$$

✗ **Pont d'Água** The new marina houses shops selling surf gear, an upmarket hairdresser, a brasserie & this stylish restaurant. The short menu includes salads, meat & seafood as well as sometimes a vegetarian option. Live music at w/ ends. $$$$–$$$

✗ **Cantina da Associação dos Marítimos** Av Marginal, towards Laginha Beach; ☎ 231 9348; m 996 2922; ⏰ 09.00–01.00. Specialities include steak with green peppercorn sauce, & profiteroles. $$$

🍷 **Caravel** At the northern end of the Laginha

Beach, just before the road bends away from the coast, this is a slightly windswept esplanade but worth going to for its beachside location. Live music at weekends, becomes a disco later on. $$$

✗ **La Pergola** [map above] (see *French Cultural Centre*, page 278). $$$

✗ **Pica-Pau** Rua Santo António 42; ☎ 232 8207; ⏰ 19.00–23.00, closed Sun. A bit of a Mindelo institution. Tiny & eccentric. If the restaurant is quiet, octogenarian Antonio will regale you (in broken English) with tales of the coal trade days. If it's busy, you can read the notes of praise from previous customers from across the globe. Specialising in seafood, it is most proud of its lobster & *arroz de marisco* (seafood risotto). $$$

✗ **Restaurante Algarve** [map above] Rua Libertadores d'Africa; ☎ 231 8921. Just down from the Presidential Palace, it has a vine-covered outside terrace from which to watch the world go by. $$$

✗ Sodade This rooftop restaurant offers an escape from the bustle of town, with an excellent panoramic view that is best before dark. Above the hotel of the same name. $$$

▭◠ Casa Café Mindelo A high-ceilinged café, in one of the old colonial buildings of Mindelo. A vibrant place. Excellent coffee, fruit juices, muffins & croissants, lunches, snacks, drinks & *cachupa*. $$

✗ Chave d'Ouro ⏱ 12.00–13.00 & 19.00–23.00 daily for reasonably priced, decent meals. An old-fashioned restaurant upstairs in the hotel of the same name. This is Mindelo's time warp. $$

✗ Clube Nautico ⏱ 08.30–00.30 Mon–Sat, 17.00–00.30 Sun. A vast space in a building

beside the old customs house on the coastal road, decorated on a nautical theme & with sails for shade. Live music at weekends. Has developed a slightly dubious reputation. $$

✗ Pizzeria ⏱ 12.00–15.00 & 18.00–23.00. Next to Residencial Maravilha. Serves excellent pizza & pasta dishes. $$

✗ Esplanada Hollanda On the land side of the coast road at Laginha Beach. Mainly drinks, but random food served in the evenings. Best for its weekend live music, which gets going at midnight & finishes around 04.00. $$

▭◠ Columbinho [map opposite] Inside the Luso Africana Galerias, Rua Africana. Tucked away along a passage that opens out into a courtyard, this is a café with other amenities such as a public toilet, boutiques & internet café. $$

ENTERTAINMENT AND NIGHTLIFE Live music abounds in Mindelo. For those who don't fancy a really late night, most of the visitor-orientated restaurants have at least one Cape Verdean evening with music. Try Esplanada Hollanda and other venues at Laginha Beach, the Archote or Gaudi (all listed above) or the French Cultural Centre, among others. For hardcore nightbirds, the clubs in Mindelo tend to open at about 22.30 or 23.00; people start arriving about midnight and they get lively by about 02.30, emptying at about 05.00. On a Sunday, people generally stop somewhere for some well-earned *cachupa* on their way home. Entry to most clubs costs 200–500$. Laginha Beach is also a happening spot, located just a little outside the very centre of the city. For a discussion of Cape Verdean music and dancing, see pages 40–6.

♀ A Cave [270 C3] ☏ 232 7802. In Alto São Nicolau, close to the Hotel Maravilha, it caters to an older, 30+ crowd.

♀ Café Lisboa [274 B3] A tiny, atmospheric bar full of character & characters, ideal 'people-watching' venue. Sip on some grogue or a cold beer. Famous musicians & singers drop by to chew the fat. Once you've been twice, you're a regular.

♀ Caravel [270 B1] ⏱ weekends (see page opposite for details). Entry fee varies.

♀ Jazzy Bird [270 F3] ⏱ weekends. Local musicians often meet here for informal sessions.

A good place for chilling out & maybe catching a 'big name'.

♀ Katem Musique [274 C3] (previously Café Musique) Opposite the municipal market; ⏱ from about 23.00 Thu–Sun. A very popular venue that mixes reggae & hip hop with traditional music.

☆ Praça Amílcar Cabral [270 E3] At 19.00 on Sun, a different type of music: the municipal band plays here.

♀ Syrius [270 E3] ☏ 232 3190. Under the Hotel Porto Grande, it is free to hotel guests & 300$ to everyone else. Tends to be under 30s.

SHOPPING A good array of Cape Verdean products can be found at a stall inside the Centro Cultural do Mindelo (see *What to see and do*, below). The craft shop to the right of the Centro Nacional Artesanato on Praça Amílcar Cabral [270 E3] stocks a good range of products made only in either São Vicente or Santo Antão, including drums, fabrics and other crafts. Also try walking up Avenida 5 de Julho, heading north from its junction with Rua Cristiano de Sena Barcelos. There are several places, such as Alternativa (on the first corner). Crafts, mainly from mainland Africa, can be bought in many shops around town. For music, and music-themed T-shirts, try Harmonia, in front of the town hall. Also try Terra Nova on Rua Franz Fanon. Supermarkets are common; try the many branches of Fragata , for example opposite the marina or on Avenida 5 de Julho, which are open over lunch and late at night. There are several good-sized mini-markets including one near the Shell station on the way to Calhau.

OTHER PRACTICALITIES
Airlines
TACV [274 A2] Av 5 de Julho (✆ *232 1524;* ⏰ *08.00–12.00 & 14.30–17.30 Mon–Fri, 09.00–11.30 Sat*). Agência Nacional de Viagens, Av da Republica (✆ *231 1115;* ✆ *08.00–12.30 & 14.30–18.00 Mon–Fri*). For most internal and international flights.

Banks
There are many banks in the centre, nearly all with ATMs. Caixa Económica, Av 5 de Julho, near Aparthotel Avenida (⏰ *08.00–15.00 Mon–Fri*). Banco Cómercial do Atlântico, Praça Amílcar Cabral (⏰ *08.00–14.30 Mon–Fri*). Also on Rua Libertadores d'Africa and Avenida Amilcar Cabral, by the Pont d'Agua. There are also ATMs at the banks next to the Porto Grande Hotel.

Hospital
The Baptisto [271 G6] at the southeast corner of town (✆ *232 7355/231 1879*). There are two new private medical centres, both near the police station at the northern end of town and with good reputations: Urgimed (✆ *230 0170*) and Medicentro (✆ *231 8515*) [both 270 E1].

Internet
There are many internet cafés, including one beside the Hotel Porto Grande on Praça Amílcar

Cabral, and Global Net on Rua de Moçambique. There is free Wi-Fi in the main praças.

Pharmacies
Several marked on the map, including a large one at the top of Rua Libertadores d'Africa [274 B3].

Police
[270 E1] (✆ *231 4631*) At the north end of town on Rua Alberto Leite.

Post office
[270 D4] Rua Cristiano de Sena Barcelos (⏰ *08.00–12.00 & 14.00–17.30 Mon–Fri*).

Tourist information
Rua Cristiano de Sena Barçelos [270 D4]. Here there is a kiosk (⏰ *09.00–13.00 & 15.00–18.30 Mon–Fri, 09.00–14.00 Sat*), which may have information and definitely sells maps and postcards. There is another cabin in front of the swimming pool at Pont d'Agua. Bear in mind that these are not municipal kiosks, so they may be focused on selling you excursions.

Public toilets
[270 E3] In the square in front of the Hotel Porto Grande.

WHAT TO SEE AND DO Sturdy English architecture, with sloping roofs and the odd bow window, is pervasive in Mindelo. There is the old **Miller and Cory's building**, now the ferry ticket agency; the old residence of the employees of Shell, now the **Portuguese consulate**; and the **Western Telegraph building**, beside TACV.

A wander through the city should begin with a stroll up to the fort, **Fortim d'El Rei** [270 B2], on the headland to the east of town (Alto São Nicolau). Be aware that there have been muggings in this area. From there you can understand the layout of the city. This hilltop fortress became a prison in the 1930s. In 1934, the militia descended from Fortim onto a food riot incited by a famous carpenter, Ambrósio, who led the looting of the food stores in the customs house. His story is the subject of plays today. Many of São Vicente's notable rebels, including resistance fighters, were imprisoned in the fort in the 1960s before being deported to Angola.

Now the headland affords a more peaceful scene: the busy port and Mindelo beyond it, the hills curling round the magnificent harbour; the strange stump of **'Bird Island'** poking out of the harbour; and Santo Antão. **Monte Cara**, or Face Mountain, on the other side of the harbour, is one of several places in the archipelago where the sharp erosion has sculpted a remarkable human profile out of the mountains. Beside the fort is the radio station, Mira D'Ouro.

On your return along the coast road, just after the port, is a **monument** surmounted by an eagle, commemorating the first air crossing of the southern Atlantic in 1922 by Sacadura Cabral and Gago Coutinho. They stopped here after their leg from the Canaries.

Follow Avenida Marginal south with its shady trees down the centre of the road. You will pass some fine old storehouses dating from the height of the shipping days: many of them have been transformed for new uses. Opposite the pier is the handsome **Old Customs House**, built in 1858 and extended in the early 1880s. It is now the Cultural Centre of Mindelo.

Keep going and you will pass, on your right, the **Torre de Belém** [271 D7], built in imitation of the monument of the same name in Lisbon and which housed the Portuguese governor from the 1920s. It was restored, thanks to the Portuguese, in 2002.

Ahead and in to the left lies the market and the vast **Estrela Square**. One half of the square has been filled with permanent market stalls, and on the wall at the end of each row an artist has depicted a scene from the history of Mindelo, painted onto ceramic tiles. The pictures are lifted straight from photographs taken in the early 1900s. They allow us to imagine Mindelo at its economic height: great wooden piers, cranes and rail tracks forever hauling coal onshore to the storage bunkers; the grand and busy customs house; the ships' chandlers lining the front street. Old men wandering Mindelo today will reminisce about the golden time in their youth when there was plenty of work, abundant food, ships jostling for space in the harbour, coal piled up high – and it always rained. From there, head north towards the Presidential Palace, passing through the **Pracinha de Igreja**, the oldest part of town where the first houses were built and where there is a pretty church, constructed in 1862.

After the church you will pass the **town hall** (*câmara municipal*) [271 E6]. Built between 1850 and 1873, it initially housed the Aguas de Madeiral water company founded by John and George Rendall.

In front of the town hall and facing onto Rua Lisboa, is the **municipal market** [274 C3], a beautifully light and airy two-storey building begun in 1874, and extended in the 1930s with Portuguese influence. It was restored in the 1980s.

In the middle of town is the spotless, pink **Presidential Palace**, which is not open to the public. The ground floor was built in 1873 as a venue for official receptions. In the 1930s, the second storey was added as well as the frothy white bits – and it became the Presidential Palace. It is now the Supreme Court (Tribunal Judicial).

Behind the palace (ie: to the east) is the **Escola Jorge Barbosa** [271 F5] which has served a variety of purposes since its construction began in 1859. It has been an army barracks (the square was for parades), governor's office, army hospital and then, in the early 1920s, the influential grammar school, Liceu Nacional Infante D Henrique, important in fostering Cape Verde's independence movement.

Just out of town you can walk to **Morro Branco**, 10km there and back along the shore road to the west. This is not scenic – probably only worth it if you have exhausted every other possibility on the island. First you pass the Shell oil terminal, and then rusting shipwrecks close to shore. The settlement of Lazareto, which you pass on the way, has two hotels, but there is no particular reason to stay here. Do not attempt to take photographs as you approach Morro Branco, as the soldiers in the barracks at the end of the road get jumpy.

Beaches Beyond the fort, to the north, is the narrow sandy beach of Laginha, popular with the locals, safe for swimming and with an outdoor gym and a collection of bars and restaurants. It is also the venue for some lively nightlife at weekends, with both live music and a disco.

Biblioteca Municipal [271 D5] (🕐 *09.30–12.30 & 15.00–19.00 Mon–Fri, 09.30–13.00 Sat*) On the first floor, the Municipal Library has a collection of books on the history of Mindelo, including some on the British presence.

Centro Cultural do Mindelo [271 D5] (🕐 *08.00–12.00 & 15.00–19.00 Mon–Fri, 08.00–12.00 Sat*) Located in the Old Customs House on the coastal road, it houses an auditorium, souvenir shop and has exhibitions of photos and a café. Occasional films and music events are shown here.

French Cultural Centre [274 A3] (*Alliance Francaise de Mindelo;* 🕐 *07.00–19.00 Mon–Fri, 08.00–14.30 Sat*) Has a library and pleasant courtyard café, La Pergola, with a limited menu ($$), where there is live music on Fridays. Also occasionally hosts wine-tasting and other events.

OTHER PLACES TO VISIT

Baía das Gatas and Calhau are the settings for weekend parties: vibrant on Saturdays and Sundays in high season, abandoned during the week. Monte Verde is stunning on a clear day but rather unexciting otherwise. A trip round the island is not a conventional aesthetic experience but it is a profound one.

MONTE VERDE A taxi costs 2,000$ return. To walk to the summit take a taxi or *aluguer* along the Baía das Gatas road for 8km as far as the right turn to Monte Verde's summit. A good cobbled road zig-zags up the north and east sides of the mountain to the top. You will see a big tank on the way up, on the left, a relatively young project to gather the Monte Verde mist to irrigate the crops on the terracing below.

At the summit the mist may be down, in which case there is little to see but the radio antennae, guarded by three soldiers and a cat.

On a clear day, however, the view is of a forest of black, misshapen crags, and the harbour beyond. Sunset beyond the forbidding peaks of Santo Antão is fabulous.

SALAMANSA Only ten minutes' drive from the capital, in São Vicente terms, this is a thriving place – people actually live here, drawing their livelihood from the sea, and there is a shop. But there is really no reason to visit other than to walk on the beautiful beach and muse on why this fishing village exists at all: it's too exposed for launching boats and the fishing fleet is drawn up some 5km away on the other side of the peninsula. The beach is not always safe for swimming but often has good conditions for kite- and windsurfing. Kitesurf NOW (e *ola@kitesurfnow.eu; www. kitesurfnow.eu*) offers lessons on this beach and others.

BAÍA DAS GATAS This resort is 12km from Mindelo town. During the week it has the feel of an English seaside resort out of season. In front of rows of boarded-up bungalows, a pack of smooth-haired dogs trots along the wind-whipped sand. There's a children's play area with gaunt metal swings and slides reminiscent of gallows, and at the extreme end of the bay, a low pier with powerful waves. However, it's a brilliant place to fish where you can easily pull in two-pounders from the shore and then light a fire and grill your own supper. It's also great for swimming because of a natural barrier that creates a huge lagoon. At weekends the place is much more colourful, with families and groups of friends pitching their tents and playing football.

During the full moon of August people descend on Baía das Gatas for a weekend of music, dancing, eating and general revelry. The festival began as the best of them do – just a few musicians gathering for all-night jamming sessions. Now bands come from all over the archipelago and from abroad and there is horse racing and watersports.

As you drive back out of the village there is a ruin on the shore on your left. This is the old fish-processing factory – it is here that the Salamansa fishermen draw their boats up. If the wind is in the right quarter you may be lucky enough to see them running home under full sail. They venture as far afield as the uninhabited island of Santa Luzia, returning with cold boxes full of snake-like moray eels, squid and grouper (like giant, bloated goldfish but more tasty).

Getting there and away At weekends there are *alugueres* from Mindelo which cost 100$ one-way. A taxi costs 1,800$ return.

 Where to stay and eat
Most people come on a day trip, so accommodation is limited. You can pitch a tent on the beach – not too close to anyone's barbecue, though, for fire safety reasons.

THE BRITISH IN CAPE VERDE

Golf, cricket and a smattering of English vocabulary were some of the lighter legacies left by the British in Cape Verde. Their involvement with the archipelago was sporadic but widespread. It included the dominance of Maio in the heyday of its salt-collecting years; the brief 'ownership' of Santo Antão (see page 285); the drastic sacking of Santiago by Francis Drake; and the monopolising of the orchil trade in several islands including Brava.

The British have also contributed much to understanding the natural history of the islands. Charles Darwin spent three weeks recording fauna and flora here (see page 170) – his first initiation to the tropics on the famous voyage of the *Beagle*. Since Darwin, there have been others. T Vernon Wollaston visited in the 1870s and 1880s, and collected numerous beetles, moths and butterflies which are stored at the Natural History Museum in London. But it is in Mindelo that the British are now best remembered. They left a golf club that claims to be one of the largest non-grass courses in the world. Founded in 1893, it is the oldest sports association in Cape Verde and hosted the first international golf championship, in 1906. It is situated just outside Mindelo, accessible from the road to Calhau. The turning is (badly) signposted on the right, a few hundred metres after the large cemetery on the left as you leave town. The clubhouse is fairly spartan, with a layer of dust and few facilities.

They also left a feisty cricket team, which continued for many years. English-derived words that have entered the Creole language were gathered by Frank Xavier da Cruz in 1950. They include: *ariope* (hurry up), *blaquéfela* (black fellow), *bossomane* (boss man), *cachupa* (believed to have been derived from ketchup), *chatope* (shut up), *salongue* (so long!), *ovataime* (overtime), *tanquiu* (thank you), *fulope* (full up) and *ovacote* (overcoat).

Residencial Atlanta (9 rooms) `232 7500/6684; m 991 6211. Rooms have TV, most have private bath with hot water. Best to make enquiries at the Takeaway Átlanta, below. **$**

✗ Archote `232 3916; m 994 2751; ⊕ weekends for buffets & live music. Look out for the sign on the left as you enter town. Another branch of a Mindelo favourite. **$$$**

✗ Foya Grill ⊕ weekends only. On the left as you enter town. **$$$**

✗ Restaurante Loyd `232 6868; m 995 6112;

[12.30–16.00 & 19.30–23.00. Turn left onto a dirt road before the fishing boats & follow the road for 200m. The restaurant is on the left. International cuisine served outdoors under covered pergolas. **$$$**

✗ Takeaway Átlanta `232 7500/6684; m 991 6211. Occupying 2 blue & white buildings, this restaurant (it's not just a take-away) is the better of the 2 seafront options while the residencial is a little further back. **$$$**

CALHAU

Getting there and away There's a more-or-less hourly bus for the 20-minute journey from Mindelo to the seaside town of Calhau (150$). A taxi will cost 2,000$ for a round trip. You could also walk there from Baía das Gatas, along the coast (two hours).

A drive along the 18km road to Calhau is like a guided tour through all the ecological problems facing both the island and Cape Verde as a whole. The road follows Ribeira Calhau, and takes just 25 minutes.

First the road passes through an area where there is a reafforestation programme. Then, as you continue southeast, you will see Monte Verde on your left. The little village on its western slopes is **Mato Inglês**. Lack of water has driven away all but one or two people.

A few kilometres further on is a right turn for **Madeiral**, a small village in the shadow of Topona Mountain. Old folk claim that the village was once supplied by water running down from the green slopes of the mountain above. Now the mountain has the same scorched, dusty aspect as the rest of São Vicente. Madeiral, like the island's two or three other inhabited villages, is dependent on desalinated water, tankered in from Mindelo.

Past Madeiral the *ribeira* opens out and the valley floor is scattered with small squares of green. This is agriculture under siege – strong stone walls keep marauding goats out. The water that the windmills draw from the ground is becoming progressively saltier. In the search for sweet water, wells are pushed deeper, and windmills require stronger winds to keep the water flowing. In such precarious conditions, water-storage tanks are indispensable. Meanwhile the search for water goes on: the piles of earth across the valley floor mark the places where boreholes have been sunk but have struck only dry earth and rock.

It takes a particular kind of personality to like Calhau. The village is a windswept wasteland of gravel and brown sand, protruding from which are the grey carcasses of half-finished breeze-block buildings. Brown peaks tower behind it while, in front, desperate waves obliterate themselves against the black, rocky coast. Nevertheless its proximity to the city makes it a reasonable place to base yourself if you don't like the hustle and bustle of Mindelo, and from here you can explore the rest of the island, occupy yourself with some interesting walks or just relax for a while. The land between the mountains and the sea is just asking to be built on. Down the southern part of the bay optimists have indeed built apartments and there is a high-end hotel.

A roundabout joining the new tarmac road to Baía das Gatas tells you that you have reached the village. People live here still, and fish, but as with every other village, water is the problem. Calhau is alive and bustling at weekends, however, with city folk coming to their seaside retreats.

Where to stay and eat

 Residencial Goa (10 rooms) Turn right at the roundabout on the new road; ☏ 232 9355; m 996 2696; e goacalhau@goa-mindelo.com; www.goa-mindelo.com. This French-owned hotel has stark, minimalist architecture that fits well with the surrounding landscape. The panoramic view encompasses Santo Antão, São Nicolau, Santa Luzia, Raso & Branco. Rooms are huge, striking & of a high quality, with balconies on the first floor overlooking the sea. With its living area & quiet location the hotel is good for families. Breakfast is served on either the seaside terrace or the inside courtyard, & dinner can be arranged. Free Wi-Fi. Charming hosts Stan & Rafael are very knowledgeable & will arrange some excellent walks, excursions & fishing. Prices are on a sliding scale depending on length of stay. **$$$$**

✗ Chez Loutcha ◷ 13.00–16.00 Sun only. Clearly signposted down a rough track on the right as you enter Calhau (after the turning to the volcanoes), this is run by the proprietor of Chez Loutcha, the *pensão* in Mindelo, who opens up on Sun. There is a buffet spread, with around 20 dishes, you can eat as much as you like for 1,400$, & there is live music. **$$$$**

✗ Bar Restaurant Hamburg m 983 0916; ◷ lunch & evenings daily. A spot of colour on the landscape. Turn left after the telecom tower & look for a blue building with black-&-white pebbles on the walls. Famous for its simple but good food, this little spot gets busy at the weekend. **$$$**

What to see and do There are various good fishing spots within easy access of the village, as well as surfing spots on Praia Grande, Sandy Beach and Topim Beach in the south. In summer turtles nest on the beach directly in front of Residencial Goa (do not go to the beach at night without asking advice as it is illegal to disturb them). There is a natural swimming pool at the foot of the volcano, offering some pleasant snorkelling.

There are also several walking trails. It takes about an hour to walk up to the Calhau volcano, to the north of the village. It takes three hours to do a circuit of the headland to the north (Panilinha). **Vulcão Viana**, to the south, can be ascended from a track that runs down its eastern side: the round trip from the track takes about 45 minutes. The oasis of Santa Luzia Terra can be reached in around two hours (you can arrange to be collected). You can also walk to Baía das Gatas, which also takes about two hours.

From Calhau you have a great view of uninhabited **Santa Luzia** and also the islets of Raso and Branco, and even São Nicolau in the distance. See the São Nicolau chapter (page 341) for more information on Raso.

SÃO PEDRO An *aluguer* from Mindelo will cost 100–200$ to São Pedro, which is just 1km past the airport. It is a little fishing village with a shop and a bar, colourful fishing boats drawn up on the beach and an air of tatty quaintness.

Where to stay and eat

🏠 Foya Branca Resort (68 rooms, 6 villas) ☏ 230 7400; e geral@foyabranca.com; www.foyabranca.com. This is on the other side of the bay The first (& currently the only) beach resort hotel in São Vicente, it is dedicated to seclusion with white walls and well-maintained gardens. The restaurant is very good & caters for vegetarians. Rooms have spacious balconies: ask to be housed in the new complex, where they are bigger & have a better view. The hotel is quiet during the week & more vibrant at weekends when local families come down for the day. There's a regular, free shuttle bus to Mindelo. The hotel offers windsurfing, bicycle hire, diving, fishing & boat hire. There are 3 swimming pools, a gym, tennis & excursions. Free Wi-Fi. **$$$$$**

✗ Bistro Santo André ☏ 231 5100; m 971 1765. Located behind the Foya Branca resort in São Pedro Beach, this tiny restaurant opened by Swedish resident Per Tamm has a terrace where you can enjoy their famous suckling pig or Brazilian *feijoada*. Also specialises in lobster, seafood & the 'ice cream bomb'. **$$$$**

What to see and do The beach is the main attraction, but there are unexpected currents in the sea so take local advice and don't swim alone.

SANTA LUZIA The smallest island of the archipelago (anything smaller is an islet), Santa Luzia is 35km² and uninhabited. Its highest peak, Topona, is 395m. It is extremely dry and barren. It has a rugged north coast and a south coast of scenic beaches and dunes. No seabirds are known to breed there any more.

Santa Luzia lay uninhabited until the 17th century, when it was granted to Luis de Castro Pireira. It has mainly been used for livestock raising when there has been rain. In the 19th century, about 20 people continued these activities. A family of goatherds lived there until the 1960s. Although it was previously possible to visit the island, it now forms part of Cape Verde's largest marine reserve where projects are underway to rebuild the fragile eco-structure. Visiting is therefore forbidden, except for scientists and volunteers, though in the long term there is a possibility of an ecologically sound visitor centre being constructed.

10

Santo Antão

The rugged peaks and canyons of northeast Santo Antão are one of the world's great landscape dramas. Precarious roads trace the tops of its ridges giving sheer views on both sides down 1,000m cliffs. The people live in these deep valleys, their worlds enclosed by colossal volcanic walls. As you ascend the valleys on foot you discover in astonishment that their settlements reach high into the cliff sides, clinging to ledges and surrounded by banana trees and cassava. In the west of the island is an apocalyptic and inaccessible landscape of steep walls, jagged edges and harsh ravines.

There is a legend that Santo Antão's precipices defeated a bishop who, while visiting the more distant of his Cape Verde flock, tried to reach Ribeira Grande from Paúl across the mountains. It is said that halfway through the journey, having scaled a terrifying cliff, he lost his nerve and could move neither forwards nor backwards. And so the bishop remained, supplied regularly by the more sure-footed of the island who would arrive with tents, food and clothing for him. He waited in a crevice until a road was built to conduct him away in safety.

HIGHLIGHTS AND LOWLIGHTS

There is one overwhelming attraction: **hiking** the *ribeiras*. Non-hikers can also appreciate the landscape from the spectacular **drives** over the ridges and along the *ribeira* floors. The mountain road from Porto Novo to Ribeira Grande is one of the highlights of a visit to Cape Verde and is worth travelling along even if you must return immediately to São Vicente. There are several rare **birds** to watch out for and **fishing** is possible with the locals. In Tarrafal de Monte Trigo, remote but with its own stark beauty, there are newly established opportunities for diving and snorkelling.

Santo Antão plans to have a beach tourism industry but this has not yet taken off. There are black, sandy beaches but some are hard to access and others disappear during the winter, and swimming is generally only safe in the summer months. Watersports facilities are still scarce, though a dive centre now operates from remote Tarrafal and another is rumoured to be opening in Porto Novo. Accommodation, while perfectly adequate, clean and friendly, is not luxurious (apart from Santo Antão Art Resort in Porto Novo and Pedracin Village) but this is part of the island's charm.

SUGGESTED ITINERARY AND NUMBER OF DAYS If you are interested in hiking, allow at least three clear days in which to tackle some of the classic Santo Antão walks: you could easily spend more than this if you are set on really exploring the island. If you are determined to explore the west, allow plenty of time because roads are bad and transport infrequent. If you are not into hiking, you could still fill at least a couple of days with sightseeing by vehicle and wandering through the valley

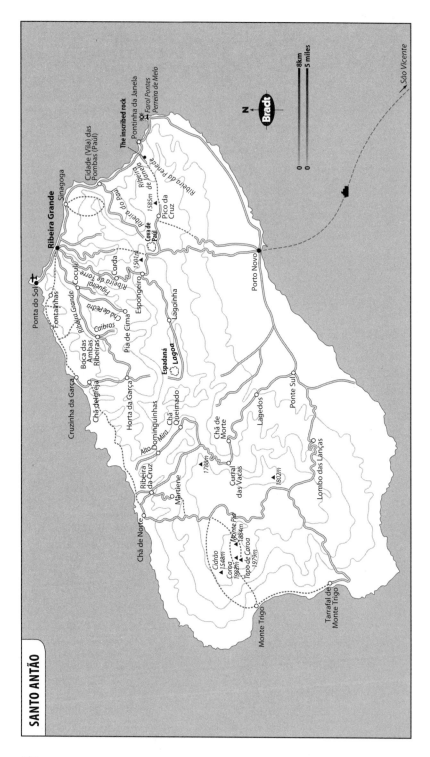

SANTO ANTÃO

of Paúl. A day trip is better than nothing, but ensure it is well organised beforehand to avoid wasting valuable time in negotiations with local drivers.

BACKGROUND INFORMATION

HISTORY Fertile and green but mountainous and inaccessible, Santo Antão remained without much of a population for the first 90 years after its discovery on 17 January 1462. If people knew it in the 15th century it was because of its use in the mapping of an imaginary line down the Atlantic that divided Spanish and Portuguese colonial rights. The Treaty of Tordesillas in 1494 agreed that this north–south line would pass 370 leagues west of Santo Antão. Land to the west of that line was to belong to Spain. Land to the east – including the islands themselves and Brazil, which protrudes quite far into the southern Atlantic – was to belong to Portugal.

A series of people leased Santo Antão from the Portuguese Crown, the first in 1548. In the 1600s, its administration and ownership were granted to the Count of Santa Cruz. It was the son of the fourth Count of Santa Cruz, the Marquess of Gouveia, who was to add brief drama to Santo Antão from as far away as Europe. In Portugal he kidnapped Mariana de Penha de França, the wife of a Portuguese nobleman, and escaped with her from Portugal to England where, having run out of money, he mortgaged Santo Antão to the English in 1732. This went down very badly back in Cape Verde and the Portuguese soon drove the English away.

After that excitement the 18th century granted Santo Antão a little more recognition. Ribeira Grande achieved the status of *vila* in 1732 and, two decades later, Bishop Jacinto Valente chose to settle there, having rejected the crumbling and unhealthy capital of Santiago. It was to be another 120 years before Santo Antão was made capital of the Barlavento – it was the richest, most populated and least malarial of the northern islands at this time.

Perhaps it was the effect of living between the high and menacing walls of the *ribeiras*, but the people of Ribeira Paúl and the people of Ribeira Grande had a major argument in 1894 about their representation in Portugal. The people of Ribeira Grande decided to make war on their cousins down the road, armed themselves with guns, clubs and sticks and roared down the coast.

The people of Paúl were ready, though, and destroyed the road so that no-one could cross it. None, that was, but an athletic horse which leapt across the opening, whisking to safety a lucky inhabitant of Ribeira Grande who had been on the wrong side of the road. The people of Paúl fared the worse in the conflict – many of their men were later imprisoned and spent a lot of money regaining their freedom.

The island lost its position as Barlavento capital in 1934, when the seat of government was transferred to São Vicente. It also recently lost its important role as supplier of water to its barren cousin across the channel, when a desalinisation plant was constructed on São Vicente. Santo Antão was plagued with an impenetrable interior and also the problem that its only good port – Tarrafal – was a long way from its agricultural area. In recent decades the port of Porto Novo and the new road between it and Ribeira Grande have improved the situation slightly.

Santo Antão today Santo Antão is a poor island with high unemployment and has its eyes fixed on tourism and agriculture as its principal routes to economic success. As a result there are great plans for this mighty island. A new road to Tarrafal is partially complete and there are promises of another stretching to Cruzinha da Garça, as well as rumours of an airport. Developers have been talking about turning the east of Porto Novo into a tourist area, centred on Escoralet (also known as Curraletes) Beach. Local leaders prophesise tourist developments all along the new road to Tarrafal, though there is little evidence as yet. In the east, there is extensive building in Cidade das Pombas (also referred to locally as 'Paúl' – see page 294).

Whether all the proposed development happens at all in the near future or can be achieved without blighting Santo Antão's appeal are moot points. As the co-owner of Pedracin Village (see page 299), businessman José Pedro Oliveira, told *Iniciativa* magazine: 'I believe Santo Antão is one of the jewels of tourism in Cape Verde, if we don't destroy it before. Building a big hotel in a valley or riverbed is the same as destroying it.' Perhaps it will be Santo Antão's very remoteness and current lack of airport which will serve to preserve its plentiful rustic charms for years to come.

GEOGRAPHY Santo Antão is second only to Santiago in size, at 779km², and second only to Fogo in the height of its greatest mountain – the volcano crater Topo da Coroa at 1,979m. It is the most northerly and the most westerly of the islands with a mountain range stretching from the northeast to the southwest.

The population is about 50,000 and the island is divided into three municipalities: Porto Novo, covering the west and centred on the port town in the south; Paúl; and Ribeira Grande, which includes the town of that name (also known as Povoação) and the town of Ponta do Sol. The fertile areas are in the northeast, where there is often moisture on the peaks and intense agriculture, making use of permanent streams in two of the *ribeiras* – Paúl and Janela. The rest of the island is barren apart from around Tarrafal de Monte Trigo to the southwest where there is some water, which is used for irrigation.

Santo Antão's annual rainfall has plunged over the last century by about 45%. Engineers have been considering making better use of the island's one abundant source of water: the annual floods during storms between August and November, which can run off the mountains and into the sea in volumes of millions of cubic metres. Conservation dams in the upper mountains could store the run-off and be used for irrigation lower down the valleys.

NATURAL HISTORY
Protected areas There are natural parks at Moroços, the area encompassing Cova, Ribeira Paúl and Ribeira Torre, and Topo da Coroa; there's a natural reserve at Cruzinha and a protected landscape at Pombas.

An old administrator in Santo Antão and captain of the Portuguese colonial army, Serafim Oliveira, introduced to Paúl a substantial number of plants and trees, most importantly *caneca* (sugarcane – the only ingredient of *grogue*), a type of mango tree and *jaqueira* (breadfruit tree), which grows to be very large and gives fruit all year.

Turtles nest here on the few remaining sandy beaches (almost all the sand has been removed illegally for construction), most notably in Cruzinha da Garça, where the small fishing community has started a conservation programme with the assistance of the fisheries research institute, INDP.

ECONOMY Fishing, agriculture and the extraction of *pozzolana* (a volcanic dust used in cement making) are the economy's mainstays. But the island, which has the largest cultivated area of Cape Verde, has in the past been frustrated in its desires to export agricultural products to the tourist islands of Sal and Boavista because of a 24-year embargo implemented as the result of millipede blight. This embargo has now been lifted for the majority of crops. There are small but growing industries producing *grogue* and its variants, herbs and jams.

HAZARDS The water is calm for swimming at some beaches in the summer months (May–September) but the ocean is wild with a powerful undertow for the rest of the year. Take local advice.

During the rainy season and for some time thereafter, some roads may become impassable and some possibly dangerous. The sea can be too rough for diving during some months and too cloudy during the rainy season (see page 309).

The west is very remote, waterless and hard to navigate. Hikers should be well prepared and it is essential to take a local guide. Elsewhere, the principal walks, though punishingly steep at times, are mostly on cobbled footpaths which can lull your mind should you decide to explore elsewhere on your own. These are high mountains, remote at the top, with racing mists. Paths can fade into pebbly gullies, demanding a scramble. Between December and February temperatures drop to 10°C above 1,000m.

The hospital in Ribeira Grande is oversubscribed and may not be up to dealing with your hiking injury, in which case you would need to get the ferry to São Vicente to find medical attention.

GETTING THERE AND AWAY

BY AIR There are currently no flights to Santo Antão. The runway at Ponta do Sol suffers from dangerous crosswinds and has been closed for years.

BY FERRY Almost everyone travelling to Santo Antão takes the ferry from Mindelo to Porto Novo. The hour-long crossing is beautiful, if you can avoid sea sickness: the view of São Vicente, with the forbidding mountains behind Mindelo, and its guardian rock erupting from the harbour, is stunning.

Porto Novo has a brand-new ferry terminal, with a café serving good coffee, an information centre hosted by multilingual Maria, a couple of gift shops, plus – very rare for Cape Verde – escalators to whisk passengers up to the waiting land transport.

FESTIVALS

The big festival of the year is São João Baptista on 24 June. It begins with a 20km procession of the cross from the mountains down into Porto Novo – done to the accompaniment of drumming. On arrival in Porto Novo, the people begin a party which lasts all week, with the statue of São João being paraded around town, accompanied by drummers. Paúl's Municipality Day on 13 June is also a great festival, with a month-long build-up, horse races and dancing.

17 January	Municipality Day (Ribeira Grande)
3 May	Santa Cruz (Coculi)
13 June	Santa António das Pombas (Paúl) (see above)
24 June	São João Baptista (see above)
29 June	São Pedro (Chã de Igreja)
15 August	Nossa Sra da Piedade (Janela)
15 September	Nossa Sra da Graca (Ponta do Sol)
24 September	Nossa Sra do Livramento (Ponta do Sol)
7 October	Nossa Sra do Rosário (Ribeira Grande)
29 November	Santo André (Ribeira de Cruz)

10

In Mindelo the two ferries to Porto Novo are run by different companies and are more reliable and punctual than many other Cape Verde vessels. Nevertheless, it's not unusual to find one or even both of them out of service. Buy tickets as early as you can in high season and at festival times when there isn't enough ferry space. There is no ferry to Tarrafal.

Mar d'Canal Mindelo–Porto Novo: 08.00 & 15.00 Mon–Sat, 8.00 Sun; Porto Novo–Mindelo: 10.00 & 17.00 Mon–Sat, 17.00 Sun; 800$ one-way per passenger. Car ferry built in Norway in 1970 & operated by Naviera Armas, carrying up to 450 passengers & 60 cars. Luggage & large hand luggage (more than 5kg & 25cm³) will be stowed, though this is not strictly enforced at quiet times. Boarding up to 20mins before departure. Ticket office in Porto Novo is in the brand-new terminal building.

Vicente Mindelo–Porto Novo: 07.00 & 16.30 daily; Porto Novo–Mindelo: 09.00 & 18.30 daily; 800$ one-way per passenger. Smaller ferry, run by Tuninha, in operation since 2012. Ticket office is signposted off the main road, 100m west of the terminal, though it may relocate inside the terminal building shortly. This boat seems to be out of service more than the *Mar d'Canal*.

BY YACHT The trip across from São Vicente can be hairy, with winds gusting up to 40 knots from December to May – they are channelled by the two islands, creating a Venturi effect. To anchor at Porto Novo, the only harbour suitable for yachts, requires permission from Mindelo beforehand. It may be preferable to visit Santo Antão by ferry, though leave a watchman back in Mindelo. Tarrafal is a possible anchorage, offering total shelter from the trade winds but with a constant swell, making it hard to land with a dinghy. Supplies on offer would only be basic (a few food items and water). Ponta do Sol is completely unsuitable for yachts.

GETTING AROUND

BY PUBLIC TRANSPORT *Alugueres* now use the new, fast coastal road, so to travel the scenic route across the mountains you will have to negotiate this with the driver. Expect to pay a much higher price for this route. *Alugueres* are regular between Porto Novo and Ribeira Grande but many drivers time their trips according to the ferry timetables, when there is a frenzy of vehicles scrambling for passengers. Elsewhere they follow the usual principle, leaving villages for the town early in the morning and returning at midday or early afternoon. To access the west of the island it is best to stay in Porto Novo for an early start.

Aluguer drivers in Santo Antão are unlikely to overcharge you but they are likely to insist you have missed all public *alugueres* and should therefore hire them as taxis. Be sceptical and hang around for a bit. Cost follows the usual rule of thumb: charters cost ten times the price of a shared *aluguer*.

BY TAXI Taxis are either cars or chartered *alugueres*. Two English (and French)-speaking drivers are Adelino (m *992 6770*) and Philip (m *996 6691*).

BY CAR If you intend to take on the not inconsiderable challenge of heading west to Tarrafal or other remote area, nothing other than a 4x4 will do.

Motacar 222 1021
Pegaso 222 2460

Protur 222 2895

Nowhere on Santo Antão could currently be described as touristy, but the main venue for visitor accommodation is Ponta do Sol, attractive for its coastal aspect and colonial architecture (though ruthless modernisation may eventually erode its charms). It also has a good range of restaurants and one or two tourist services. There are several modest *pensões* in the capital, Ribeira Grande (Povoação) and the more upmarket Pedracin Village Hotel is a few kilometres outside town. There is also accommodation, including the first international-standard hotel, in Porto Novo – not the beautiful side of the island but a good transport hub nonetheless. A few *pensões* dot the valley of Paúl – if simplicity, embeddedness, a love of hiking and a cracking view are what you're after, these are for you. There are also some one-off venues elsewhere in the island, which are most useful for those trying to accomplish long hikes between distant outposts. Tarrafal has a few *pensões*, as does Chã de Igreja, and you can stay in Cruzinha and Ribeira Grande (the *ribeira* rather than the town). Homestays can be arranged through Alfred (see page 297) or Casa das Ilhas (see page 296).

ACTIVITIES

EXCURSIONS

Alsatour Paúl ☎ 225 1213; e alfred@ alsatour. de; www.alsatour.de. Alsatour runs a variety of programmes, mainly hiking (see below).

Kasa Tambla Ponta do Sol; see page 302 for details. Kayak & mountain-bike hire are available, though only for its B&B guests. They also organise walking guides & issue maps.

Hotel Bluebell Ponta do Sol; see page 302 for details. The hotel has its own minibus & general guides with whom excursions can be arranged

Protur ☎ 222 2895; e aviagenprotur@gmail.com. Provide tourist information & also rent cars.

Santtur Travel Porto Novo; ☎ 222 1660/76; e emiterio.ramos@gmail.com. With the port behind you, it's straight ahead up the hill a little on the left. Walking & hiking, day tours of the island, hotel reservations & transfers.

Atlantur Porto Novo; ☎ 222 1991; e santoantao@atlantur.com. Excursions, car rentals, fishing & transfers.

Viagitur Ribeira Grande; ☎ 221 2794. Mainly for air tickets (TACV & TAP).

HIKING The obvious walks are the grand *ribeiras*. You can either take transport up the main road and disembark for a steep descent, or you can walk or take transport along the coastal roads for a steep ascent. After torrential rains these *ribeiras* fill – take local advice about how to ascend them because there is usually an alternative path (see page 287, for safety advice).

The west of the island is unfrequented, a hidden world of ravines and cliffs cut into bizarre shapes by erosive winds. There are craters filled with lava flows and looming boulders of white pumice. Interspersed is the odd pool of greenery where irrigation has allowed cultivation. Now that there is a map of Santo Antão (see page 70), and locals are opening their houses to guests, the west is slightly easier to explore. However, the area is lonely, the roads are sparse and the traffic is scarce. The landscape is full of hidden dangers – landslides, sudden cliffs and lack of water. Even paths shown on the map can disappear in the rains. Plan well and take a guide.

CYCLING With the right kit, mountain biking is a rewarding activity – but don't underestimate the steepness of the hills or the heat of the day. Biking can be arranged through Kasa Tambla (bed and breakfast guests only; for contact details see page 302). See also page 75, for the logistics of getting a bike to Cape Verde.

Praia de Escoralet To the east of Porto Novo.
Praia de Gi Between Vila das Pombas & Janela.
Praia Formosa In the south, inaccessible by road.
Sinagoga Black sand, popular for swimming.
Tarrafal The largest beach in Santo Antão (black sand).

DIVING There are canyons, lava tubes and tunnels, caves and rock bridges, all for exploration. For further information, contact Santo Antão Scuba Diving (see box, page 309).

BEACHES AND SWIMMING Many beaches on Santo Antão disappear under the rougher water between October and May, and emerge, magically, to be enjoyed during the summer months of June to September. Likewise, the water is calmer for swimming during the summer but once winter starts the ocean is wild and there is a powerful undertow. You may make your own serendipitous discovery of beaches but there are a few in the box above. Along the coast to the east of Cruzinha da Garça there are also several beaches (some black sand, some white).

FISHING From Cidade das Pombas, you can accompany local fishermen as they go out to catch sea eel, grouper, mackerel, octopus and lobster. In the west, Tarrafal offers similar possibilities.

CULTURE Some examples of traditional songs, generally inspired by toil, are 'Cantigas de Guarda Pardal' (Songs of the Sparrow Watchman) and 'Cantigas de Currais de Trapiche' (Songs to Encourage the Oxen as they Plod around the Trapiche). Cordas do Sol is a well-known Cape Verdean band specialising in traditional Santo Antão music and hailing from Paúl. Their most famous CD is *Linga de Sentonton*. In high season at least, a few restaurants in most towns feature traditional music, as do many of the festivals listed.

SIGHTSEEING BY VEHICLE A lot of Santo Antão's beauty can be seen by vehicle, and an itinerary should include crossing from Porto Novo to Ribeira Grande by the mountain road, taking a detour at the top to see the Cova de Paúl and Pico da Cruz; driving up Ribeira do Paúl as far as Cabo de Ribeira (refreshments two-thirds of the way up at O Curral); and driving up Ribeira Grande (the *ribeira*) through Coculi, Boca das Ambas Ribeiras, and round to Chã de Igreja and Cruzinha da Garça (refreshments at Pedracin Village or Chã de Igreja) . The road to Tarrafal is very poor in parts and better enjoyed in an *aluguer* driven by someone used to the route, allowing you to take photos.

THE EAST

Destinations are listed in an anticlockwise order, starting with Porto Novo.

PORTO NOVO In September 2005, this busy and windswept town was inaugurated as a city. As the sole entry and departure point to the island, its importance can't be disputed. It is full of smart new buildings paid for by Luxembourg as well as tended gardens and promenades overlooking the channel. The new ferry terminal is a pride and joy and there is an impressive new municipal headquarters to boast about. It is *the* place to be during the São João festival.

An enjoyable evening can be spent here watching the sun set on the distant mountains of São Vicente and the glowing harbour of Mindelo. You can even see São Nicolau, no more than a timid relative beyond. There are one or two good restaurants.

Getting there and away Most people's first experience of Porto Novo will be arriving by ferry. To get to Porto Novo from Ribeira Grande find an *aluguer* in the main street. They run all day (contrary to what the drivers will tell you) but the vast majority co-ordinate their trips with the ferry schedules. If you have a ferry to meet in Porto Novo allow plenty of time, as the last *alugueres* to leave Ribeira Grande either sometimes miss the ferry, or arrive to find all the tickets have been sold.

To get from Porto Novo to Ribeira Grande, choose from the many *alugueres* that queue up to meet the ferry from Mindelo. More likely, they will choose you – you may even be recruited as a passenger by a zealous tout on the boat. Outside ferry times, hang around outside the port, or keep your eyes open as they are generally driving around town trying to find passengers. Sometimes, during the rainy season, Ribeira Grande can become a lake, roads can be washed out and visitors can become stuck on the other side of the island for several days.

 Where to stay All listings are located on the map, page 292.

Residencial Yria (7 rooms, 1 suite) m 987 6604; e fonseca.marie@hotmail.com. Brand new, a bit out of the centre. All rooms have AC, good standard showers, excellent b/fast. French spoken. Price reductions for longer stays. **$$$**

Santo Antão Art Resort (73 rooms) Porto Novo; ☎222 2675; e santantaoresort@gmail.com; www.santantao-art-resort.com. The first upmarket hotel on the island, wildly different from any other accommodation on offer. Very comfortable, spacious rooms with all the services, well up to international standards, & many with balconies overlooking the pool. Set in a barren landscape just to the west of Porto Novo. Offers a restaurant, a disco, massage service, large swimming pool, gift shop & excursions around the island. Fri is music & BBQ night & there is nightly entertainment. FB available. English spoken, popular with French tour groups. Internet & Wi-Fi (chargeable). Good value, given the facilities on offer. **$$$**

Pôr do Sol (16 rooms) Fundo Lomba Branca; ☎222 2179; e pordosolpn@cvtelecom.cv. Yellow & grey building in the west of town. Bar & good restaurant. Rooms have AC & TV; most with private bathrooms. **$$**

Residencial Antilhas (17 rooms) ☎222 1193; e residencialantilhas@hotmail.com. Just facing the harbour to the right, & thus with the potential for great views, this residencial is good for the price, with renovated rooms, generously sized & variable in facilities. The complicated pricing structure confuses the staff, never mind the guests, but still good value. The best rooms have private baths, AC, fridge, balcony & panoramas of São Vicente. Restaurant below, also with a sea view. **$$**

Pousadas de Juventude (11 rooms, 2 dorms) ☎222 3010; e pousadasdejuventude@ gmail.com. Behind the new *camara*. Despite the name, it's not just a youth hostel – all are welcome. Basic rooms & the cheapest in town. Doubles & twins, plus 10-bed dorms which can only be hired out in their entirety for 5,000$. No b/fast included. Acceptable standard for a true budget option. **$**

Where to eat and drink Fresh goat's cheese and fruit can be bought outside the ferry terminal at boat arrival and departure times; vegetables are available from the modest market at the west end of the main road, beside the bank. All listings are located on the map, page 292.

Restaurante Antilhas ⏲ 07.00–23.00 Mon–Sat, 08.00–17.00 & 20.00–23.00 Sun. In the hotel of the same name, a breezy terrace restaurant with a slightly more formal indoors

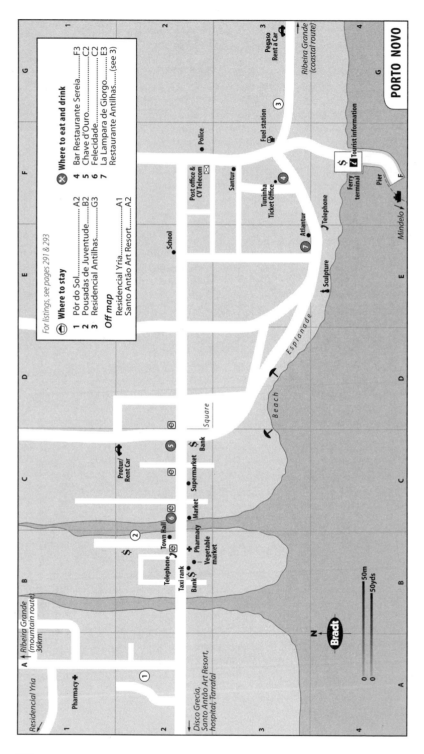

PORTO NOVO

For listings, see pages 291 & 293

⊙ Where to stay

1 Pôr do Sol A2
2 Pousadas de Juventude B2
3 Residencial Antilhas G3

Off map
Residencial Yria A1
Santo Antão Art Resort A2

✕ Where to eat and drink

4 Bar Restaurante Sereia F3
5 Chave d'Ouro C2
6 Felecidade C2
7 La Lampara de Giorgo E3
Restaurante Antilhas ....(see 3)

Residencial Yria ↖
↑ *Ribeira Grande (mountain route) 36km*

Pharmacy ✚

Disco Grecia,
Santo Antão Art Resort,
hospital, Tarrafal ↙

Telephone 📞
Taxi rank
Bank 💲

Town Hall 🏛
Pharmacy ✚
Vegetable market

Market
Supermarket
Bank 💲

Square

Protur/ Rent Car 🚗

School ●

Post office & CV Telecom ✉
● Police

Santur ●

Tuninha Ticket Office

Atlantur

Telephone 📞

Sculpture ♦

Esplanade

Beach

Fuel station ⛽

Pegaso Rent a Car 🚗

↑ *Ribeira Grande (coastal route)*

Ferry terminal
Tourist information 💲 ℹ

Pier

Mindelo ↙

N ↑

Bradt

0 ──── 50m
0 ──── 50yds

PORTO NOVO

venue. $$$$

✕ **Restaurante La Lampara de Giorgo** 📞222
1218; m 984 6277; ⏰ 08.00–23.00 Mon, Wed, Fri
& Sat, 08.00–15.00 & 19.00–23.00 Tue & Thu. Just
off the coast road, hospitable & characterful Giorgo
is proud of his renowned Italian–Cape Verdean
cuisine served on the terrace or inside. No menu –
just trust the owner to delight you! Lobster is often
available. $$$$

✕ **Bar Restaurante Sereia** A decent place to
while away an hour or 2, perhaps while waiting for
the ferry, gazing across the water at São Vicente. A
few yards west of the ferry terminal on the coast
road. $$$

✕ **Felecidade** 📞222 1167. Excellent food
including lobster, octopus & great cakes. Dishes of
the day are served quickly, but others take up to an
hour & are best ordered in advance. $$$

💻 **Chave d'Ouro** Snack bar serving donuts,
cakes & drinks. On the corner of the main square.
$$

Entertainment and nightlife

☆ **Disco Grecia** ⏰ Late until early. On the road
to Santo Antão Art Resort Hotel, weekend venue
for theme nights & revelry.

Other practicalities

Airlines
Try Santtur (see page 289).

Bank
[292 B/C2] (⏰ 08.00–15.00 Mon–Fri) One at the
west end of the main road through town, and
a BCN on the main square, both with ATMs and
Western Union. There's also an ATM in the new
ferry terminal.

Hospital
[292 A2] 📞 222 1130) Huge grey and yellow
building with an orange roof on the main road as it
goes west out of town.

Internet
On the main east–west road there are several internet
cafés. One is nearly opposite the market and another is
facing the little square. Free Wi-Fi in the main square.

Pharmacy
[292 B2] 📞222 1903) West of the main square. An
alternative one can be found on the mountain road
to Ribeira Grande [292 A1] .

Police
[292 F2] 📞222 1132) Near the post office.

Post office
[292 F2] (⏰ 08.00–12.00 & 14.00–18.00 Mon–
Fri) From the port follow the road north past the
petrol station and it is on the left.

Shopping
Souvenirs (*grogue*, punch and pottery), maps and
guidebooks, and postcards can be bought from the
two shops in the ferry terminal. The best-stocked
supermarkets are Casa Delgado's just off the square
and further along the main road, opposite the bank.

Tourist information
There is an office in the ferry terminal, though
it closes as soon as the ferries have arrived or
departed. It sells maps, postcards and souvenirs.
Staff at Santtur, the tour operator just up from the
ferry terminal, are also helpful.

What to see and do Visit the little grey beach in town and watch the fishermen
hauling up great tuna and the women selling it just a few feet away. Walk east
for 25 minutes to Escoralet Beach. Spend a night or two chilling out at the Santo
Antão Art Resort, and, if you're here during the São João festival, join in the party!

FROM PORTO NOVO TO CIDADE DAS POMBAS (PAÚL)
Pontinha de Janela This small fishing town has two points of interest about it:
the lighthouse and the inscribed rock.

What to see and do A 3–4km walk along a coastal track from the town, **Farol Pontes Perreira de Melo** is a great viewpoint from which, on a clear day, you can see the entire northeastern coast of the island, and over to São Vicente, Santa Luzia and São Nicolau.

From Janela, a path up Ribeira da Peneda leads, after about 0.5km, to the **inscribed rock**, Pedra da Nossa Senhora. This large, free-standing rock bears some mysterious inscriptions and a cross. Researchers have thought it to be Aramaic, Phoenician or archaic Portuguese – it bears little resemblance to modern Portuguese or to Arabic, Hebrew, Berber or Tifnaq. Richard Lobban writes in the *Historical Dictionary of the Republic of Cape Verde*:

> The most fruitful investigation rests upon a comparison with the Portuguese inscription of a similar appearance, on a stone at Yellala Falls about 150km above the mouth of the River Congo. This was almost certainly inscribed by Diogo Cão in 1485 [and] appears to have two types of writing systems which range from archaic Portuguese, as well as letters which are in a distinctly different style which is the only form of writing in the case of Janela.

It was also common for the 15th-century Portuguese explorers to mark their landings and passages with stone inscriptions, especially with crosses… In short, the Janela inscription was probably placed there by a 15th-century Portuguese. It is tempting to conclude that it was written by Diogo Gomes or by Diogo Afonso in the 1460s, or by Diogo Cão or his pilots in the 1480s.

CIDADE DAS POMBAS (VILA DAS POMBAS, PAÚL)

A 15-minute drive south along the coast from Ribeira Grande is Cidade das Pombas, which marks the beginning of the majestic valley of Paúl. It has recently gained city status, but is still often referred to as 'Vila das Pombas' or even 'Paúl', though the latter is actually the name of the district, not the town. It's a long, strung-out town along the coast, the site of ambitious building projects. There is a recently built bridge, funded by the Millennium Challenge Corporation.

Getting there and away From Porto Novo, the new coastal road is a spectacular introduction to the stunning scenery of Santo Antão. Following the cliffs and with a tunnel or two hewn out of the rock, you will reach Cidade das Pombas (the *alugueres* will be marked Paúl) in 20 minutes. In Pombas the *alugueres* for Porto Novo currently leave from beside the bridge. Instead of waiting in the minibus for it to fill up, you can go to a café and ask the driver to collect you there.

From Ribeira Grande, the journey to Cidade das Pombas is about 15 minutes and transport can be found around the mouth of Ribeira de Torre. In Pombas, it can be found by the road junction by O Veleiro restaurant. (50$). To Cabo de Ribeira (up the Paúl Valley) transport can be found along the *avenida* in front of the carpentry workshop (100$).

Where to stay

Hotel Paul Mar (19 rooms) ☎ 223 2300; e st.hotelpaulmar@gmail.com. Has undoubtedly raised the standard of what's available in town. All rooms have a high level of fittings, private bathroom, TV, good water pressure & hot water. Balcony rooms are right over the sea. Rooms without balcony are cheaper. Buffet b/fast served in O Veleiro restaurant next door. **$$$**

Aldeia Jerome (8 rooms, inc 2 suites & 1 apt) ☎ 223 2173; e aldeiajerome@gmail.com. Bright, clean, inexpensive *pensão*. All rooms are en suite with hot water & fridge. Includes a suite for up to 4 people. English spoken. **$$**

Residencial Takrida (6 rooms) ☎ 223

1129; **m** 995 6228; **e** damiaosilva@hotmail.com.
New place, take the first left after leaving bridge,
towards Porto Novo. All rooms with private bath,
hot water & fans. Terrace for b/fast. **$$**

🏠 **Residencial Mar e Sol** (6 rooms) \223
1294. On the coastal road, towards the Ribeira
Grande end of town. The owner, Noémia Melo,
offers home cooking, & simple but mainly spacious

rooms, nearly all with private bathroom (hot water
available), others with a balcony & uninterrupted
sea views. Prices vary accordingly. Courtyard for b/
fast. English spoken. **$**

🏠 **Residencial Vale do Paúl** (5 rooms) \223
1319. Simple budget rooms, some overlooking
the sea, shared bathroom. B/fast not included, but
available. **$**

✗ **Where to eat and drink** Several *mercearias* (small food shops) around the town
act as bars, where you can get a cold beer or shots of *grogue*. **Senhor Ildo's Trapiche**,
to the right of the petrol station has bottled *grogue*, *ponche* and *mel*. The *senhor*
has wised up to the tourist potential and now charges 100$ to view his handsome
trapiche, set behind some wooden doors in a courtyard of munching goats and
indifferent cats. There is a new municipal market opposite the *praça*.

✗ **O Veleiro** **m** 952 0364; ⏰ 08.00–23.00
daily. An offshoot of the well-established place
of the same name in Ponta do Sol, this restaurant
is light, bright & right by the sea, though lacks
character. Offers the usual fish & meat dishes, as
well as a few vegetarian options such as soup, plus
a pizza menu. **$$$**

✗ **Tillelo** **m** 920 3782. Opposite Aldeia Jerome.
Italian cuisine with excellent pizza prepared in the
open oven, bruschetta, spaghetti dishes. **$$$**
✗ **Atelier** Bar Opposite the Hotel Paul Mar. Nice
outdoor setting, with sun umbrellas. **$$$**

Entertainment and nightlife
☆ **Discoteca Beira Mar** ⏰ only occasionally on
Sat. To the left of the police station.

Other practicalities
Bank
BCA, next to Residencial Vale do Paul. Caixa
Económica, next to Hotel Paul Mar. Both have
ATMs.

Dentist
(\223 2230/1) On the main road.

Health centre
(\223 1130) In the central *praça*.

Municipality office
(\223 1197) Also in the central *praça*.

Pharmacy
(\223 2310) On the main road, to the right of the
police station.

Police
(\223 1292) On the main road towards the Ribeira
Grande end of town.

Post office
(\223 1397; ⏰ 08.00–15.30 Mon–Fri) Beyond
the central *praça* on the right.

What to see and do The main activity is to travel up Ribeira do Paúl (see
below) or to do neighbouring hikes such as that up Ribeirãozinho to Pico da Cruz.
The statue of Santo António at the northern edge of the foot of Paúl Valley is a
15-minute hike that will give you 180° views of the ocean and surrounding valleys.

RIBEIRA DO PAÚL A vast *ribeira* home to thousands of people and their
agriculture – sugarcane, breadfruit and bananas – Paúl is renowned throughout the
archipelago for its *grogue*, and one of its *trapiches* (sugarcane-juicing apparatus) is

10

still driven by oxen. Highlights include Passagem, with its charming municipal park nestled among impressive almond trees and bougainvilleas. Beyond the villages of Lombinho and Cabo de Ribeira, up a steep incline, a panoramic view of the valley and ocean opens out. The road ends at Cabo de Ribeira, but a steep cobbled footpath continues to Cova, an impressive ancient crater now filled with verdant cultivation.

Getting there and away *Alugueres* travel from Pombas all the way up to Paúl's Cabo de Ribeira for about 100$. Some *alugueres* do the full journey between Cabo de Ribeira and either Ribeira Grande or Porto Novo – the latter generally to meet the ferry from São Vicente.

Where to stay Accommodation is listed here in order of ascent up the valley. Most of the establishments below can arrange transfers from Porto Novo in which you are dropped off at the head of Paúl and walk down to your accommodation, your bags continuing by vehicle. They will also give you help planning hikes.

Casa Familiar (Sabine Jähnel) (4 rooms) Eito; 223 1544; e sabine.jahnel@gmail.com. This *pensão* can be found by walking up Ribeira do Paúl, beyond Eito, & turning left at the sign for Mercearia Brito. Sabine, who is German, offers rooms that feel like your bedroom at home & open onto a shaded roof terrace (shared bathroom). Excellent Cape Verdean meals *en famille*, & friendly hiking advice. English spoken. **$**

Casa das Ilhas (9 rooms) Lombo Comprido; 223 1832; m 996 7774; e casadasilhas@yahoo.fr; www.casadasilhas.com. This Belgian–Cape Verdean-run *casa* is made up of a series of little houses built on the steep terracing of the mountainside surrounded by fruit & vegetable planting – including sticks of sugarcane, from which their own grogue is made. It is worth staying here for the view alone: it is both panoramic & full of the detail of valley life. Rooms are simple & bare, but appropriate. 5 are en suite & there is hot water. At night great meals are served around a communal table where, during the day, the owners run a small local kindergarten – any contributions of children's clothes, pencils, etc, are welcome. Casa das Ilhas is reached by a 10min walk up a steep footpath (the owners will send someone down to carry your bags). HB basis only; vegetarians welcome. English spoken. **$$**

Aldeia Manga (5 bungalows) 223 1880; e info@aldeia-manga.com; www.aldeia-manga.com. Simply furnished bungalows perched on the side of a hill facing a steep cliff reaching up into the clouds, with spectacular views down the valley. The owner has made a great deal of effort to build in a sympathetic style & power is provided by solar panels. There is a natural swimming pool.

Water is purified by UV light. A substantial buffet dinner is provided for €10 (order in advance). Jams are made with fruit from the garden. From here at least 6 unguided hikes are possible, including straight down to Vila das Pombas. Collection from the ferry can be arranged in advance for 400$. Wi-Fi available. English & French spoken. **$$$**

Cavoquinho (4 rooms) Cabo de Ribeira; 223 2065; m 998 9919; e info@cavoquinho.com; www.cavoquinho.com. Run by a friendly Spanish couple, José & Belén, this house is wedged, vertiginously, into the mountainside & is easy to spot: it's orangey yellow & the path reaches it from behind the old village water pump. Rooms are simple & attractive, each with a window affording a stunning view down the valley. There is also a rooftop bar/restaurant with a spectacular view, though this may shortly be relocated downstairs, along with a library & Wi-Fi room. Rooms have private bathrooms with hot water. José also does guided treks & is very knowledgeable. There's a restaurant (◷ *evenings only*); vegetarians catered for. Food is excellent & dinner costs €11. English spoken. **$$**

Sandro's Hostel (2 dorms) Cabo de Ribeira; 223 1941; m 981 2478; e sandro_lacerenza@yahoo.fr. A French–Cape Verdean operation, this accommodation consists of 2 large, first-floor rooms, 1 with 3 bunk beds & 1 with 2, which share an en-suite bathroom & are accessed via a long balcony with a superb view. They are simple but bright, clean & attractively done. They are designed with hiking groups in mind, though the beds convert into loft beds with desk underneath. The shop below sells souvenirs: crafts & food produce, grogue & liquor. **$$**

✕ Where to eat and drink

✕ **Cavoquinho** (see page 296). Excellent & innovative cuisine. One day's advance notice required for non-residents. $$$$

▱ **O Curral** Chã João Vaz; ☎223 1213; ℯ grogue@alsatour.de; www.grogue.de; ◷ 10.00–18.00 Mon–Sat, 11.00–17.00 Sun. This café is perfect for taking a break from the long hike of Vale do Paúl. Try various kinds of grogue made by the owner, Alfred, who is passionate about it, buy some of his cheese & jams & chat to him about his latest ideas (see page 298). $$$

▱ **Sandr'Arte** Cabo de Ribeira Paúl, in the first village you come to after walking down from the *cova*. This is a good place to stop for a drink. They also sell local arts, grogue & coffee. The owner rents a few simple bedrooms (see Sandro's Hostel, opposite) & can do HB on request. $$$

What to see and do Walking up or down Paúl Valley is the chief activity and the sights along the way are described on pages 308–18. You can't fail to be fascinated by the everyday lives of the valley's inhabitants.

RIBEIRA GRANDE (POVOAÇÃO) The mountain road from Porto Novo to Ribeira Grande pulls away past the depressing outskirts of town where the inhabitants live amongst permanent, savage and sand-laden winds. It mounts through the cusps of the brown landscape. Already the achievement of the road builders seems extraordinary.

As it climbs higher and higher forest plantations begin to fill the higher valleys and a chill tinges the air. But you are still in the foothills – on and on you go until you reach the clouds and the eucalyptus and pine trees which thrive in the cold air. The road skates the ridges of the top of the island and sometimes there are breathless sheer drops on either side as you gaze down into the plunging *ribeiras*. Pinnacles, cliffs, and double bends around spires of rock, mark the descent into the verdant side of the island and you will see the puddle of Ribeira Grande long before you drop past the thatched stone houses to reach it.

The town, known to most as Povoação, is a muddle of cobbled streets crammed into the space between the cliffs and the sea, and overflowing up the mouths of the two *ribeiras*: Ribeira Grande and Ribeira de Torre. For a place in such an awe-inspiring setting, the town itself feels impoverished and run-down. It is strangely lacking in places from which to appreciate the view, and the idea of ending a hard day's hike sipping a quiet beer while gazing at some Atlantic panorama never quite materialises. Most people will pass through here without spending a night. Indeed, it is mainly a transport hub, and in low season you will be (gently) besieged by *aluguer* drivers ready to take you anywhere.

A church was first built in the town in 1595. Bishop Valente, who arrived in the mid 18th century, having abandoned Santiago, consecrated the large church of Nossa Senhora do Rosário in 1755. However, the transfer of the episcopal see to Santo Antão was never officially approved and it went instead, a while later, to São Nicolau.

> ### FROM CIDADE DAS POMBAS TO RIBEIRA GRANDE
>
> Sinagoga lies on the point between Mão para Traz and Paúl. It is where exiled Portuguese Jews settled in the early 19th century. There are Jewish graves here as well as in Ponta do Sol. Later it was turned into a leper colony. For more on Jewish history in Cape Verde, see pages 12–13. Sinagoga has a black-sand beach where people like to swim.

10

Ex-troubleshooter Alfred Mandl arrived in Santo Antão from Germany over 30 years ago and set up in Paúl, building himself a thatched home with walls made entirely from beer bottles. He started offering hiking holidays in Santo Antão – with his partner, Hans Roskamp, he specialises in remote adventures in which visitors reside with local people. But that's only a part of what Alfred is up to. Always interesting and always innovating he can often be found at a table in the café, O Curral (see page 297), which he runs with his wife, Christine, where he loves to philosophise with passers-by.

'When I started here everyone thought I was a little crazy,' he says, smiling. But with his thin form and long beard he retains the aura of eccentricity and the crazy ideas still flow thick and fast. One of his latest is his 'virtuous circle' of grogue production: using the leftovers from the milling of sugarcane to feed cows, whose dung is converted to biogas to power the grogue production. The remains of the dung, incidentally, are siphoned away for fertilising his vegetables. The cows also produce milk for cheese which he sells in his café.

One of his ideas, still on the drawing board, involves a new concept in tourism: not five-storey hotels and pizzerias but a site in Lagoa in the centre of the island where he has purchased 64ha of land and plans organic farming irrigated with harvested rainwater. He has planted nearly 20ha of trees there and plans to invite tourists to come not just in body but in mind too: webcams and media conferencing will mean that they can enjoy their holiday before it starts and continue it after it is over. Another ongoing experiment is the planting of hops, with which Alfred hopes to start brewing beer.

Alfred is exercised by the need to adapt to Cape Verde's altering demographics and educational levels. 'In 1982, 85% were illiterate; now 67% go to secondary school,' he says. He's trying to develop businesses that can utilise more educated people but he also wants to attract older foreigners to come and live on Santo Antão. 'Fifty per cent of our population is under 29. If you have a car you need a motor but you also need brakes.'

Getting there and away To get to Ribeira Grande from Porto Novo take an *aluguer* from the port. You have a choice between the old, mountain route and the new, coastal road but for the mountain road you will have to charter an *aluguer* or taxi, at ten times the price. It's worth doing, at least one-way – it's unmissable, though the coast road is also spectacular.

To travel towards Porto Novo along the coastal road, find an *aluguer* across from town, on the other side of Ribeira de Torre.

There is frequent transport between Ribeira Grande (from where the Ponta do Sol road enters town, near the food market) and Ponta do Sol (from the main square) (50$).

For destinations up the *ribeira* (Ribeira Grande) such as Coculi, Boca das Ambas Ribeiras and Chã de Igreja, wait outside the Caixa Económica Bank (walk up the road that goes parallel to that *ribeira* and you will see it on your left). To the more distant of these destinations the *aluguer* follows the usual pattern (into town early morning, out of town midday). On Sundays it may be impossible to find communal transport to more remote destinations.

Where to stay

All listings are located on the map, page 300.

Pedracin Village (32 rooms) Boca da Coruja; ☏ 224 2020; e pedracin@cvtelecom.cv. Out of town along Ribeira Grande (the *ribeira* rather than the town). Take the *aluguer* that is headed to Boca das Ambas Ribeiras – for a little extra the driver will ascend the steep 1km track from the ribeira & drop you right at the hotel. Pedracin is beautifully crafted, with an unusually sensitive sense of place. The accommodation is in chalets in a style evoking the traditional Santo Antão style of drystone walling & thatch, but with most of the mod cons. There's a small swimming pool, solarium, bar & good restaurant with a view. **$$$**

Divin' Art (3 rooms) 1km out of town, along the road that runs along the north side of the Ribeira Grande; ☏ 221 2832; m 992 2635; e divin_art1@hotmail.com. Tasteful, spacious rooms in a small guesthouse. Restaurant downstairs has live music at weekends. **$$**

Residencial Top d'Coroa (10 rooms) ☏ 221 2794; e topcoroa@hotmail.com; www.residencial-topcoroa.com. This accommodation is smart enough, though it doesn't have the restaurant back-up or centrality of the Trópical. Rooms are en suite with TV, AC, hot water & some have balconies overlooking its little square. **$$**

Residencial Trópical (15 rooms) ☏ 221 1129; m 993 4116; e rochatropical2011@hotmail.com. Although there's not much competition, still probably the most comfortable place in the town centre, with a restaurant & internet café below & a small terrace with some thankful shade (but no view). Most rooms are en suite with hot water & all have AC, fridge & TV. Some have a sea view, though no balcony. Accepts Visa. **$$**

Residencial Aliança (4 rooms) ☏ 221 2488. Very inexpensive, basic option with large rooms, 3 with great balcony views. Some are en suite with hot water. No b/fast. **$**

Residencial Bibi (5 rooms) ☏ 221 1149; e residencialbibi@cvtelecom.cv. Basic, clean rooms, some with balconies. Ring the bell at the first door to the left of the residencial's sign. Hot water available. **$**

Residencial Milfontes (8 rooms) ☏ 221 2234; m 595 3240; e cleomila@hotmail.com. Clean rooms, though no b/fast (as yet), nor TV or AC. Hot water. Pleasant Portuguese owner speaks many languages & has great plans. Good value. **$**

Where to eat and drink

Almost everything you need, including bread, can be found at the Shell station. There is a bakery, supermarket and fruit and vegetable shop on the road towards Caixa Económica Bank. For genuine Santo Antao souvenirs, Divin' Art (see listing above) sells a variety of crafts, wall-hangings, baskets and fridge magnets at reasonable prices. All listings are located on the map, page 300.

Divin' Art (see above for details). Pleasant & tasteful venue, usual range of fish, meat & seafood. Occasional live music. **$$$$**

Pedracin Village ⏰ 06.30–23.00 daily. Out of town (follow the directions under the listing above). Good restaurant; has a spectacular view. **$$$$**

Restaurante Trópical (see hotel listing above). With both terrace & indoor (AC) seating, it's a good choice for quality. **$$$$**

Cantinho de Amizade ☏ 221 1392. Near the petrol stations, a pleasant, spacious bar with restaurant & less formal area set in a courtyard. Fish, seafood, meat & goat dishes. A good place in which to while away an hour waiting for transport. **$$$**

Bar Pizzeria 3D Rua do Mercado; m 998 9150. Opposite the food market, this is a place for hamburgers & pizzas in a modern setting. **$$**

Café 5 de Julho ⏰ 07.30–15.00 & 18.30–23.00 daily. Basic, but good value, filling meals. Not a great setting, but definitely one place to find *cachupa*. **$$**

Churrasqueira Lêdêra d'Sentissima On the road that runs parallel with the *ribeira* (Ribeira Grande). Grilled meats. **$$**

Food market For a taste of real, local, traditional, basic food, try this daytime venue above the food market. There are just 2 tables & there's just 1 dish. **$**

Entertainment and nightlife

Not a music town, surprisingly, but Trópical has some on Saturdays, as does Divin' Art, out of town (see listing details above).

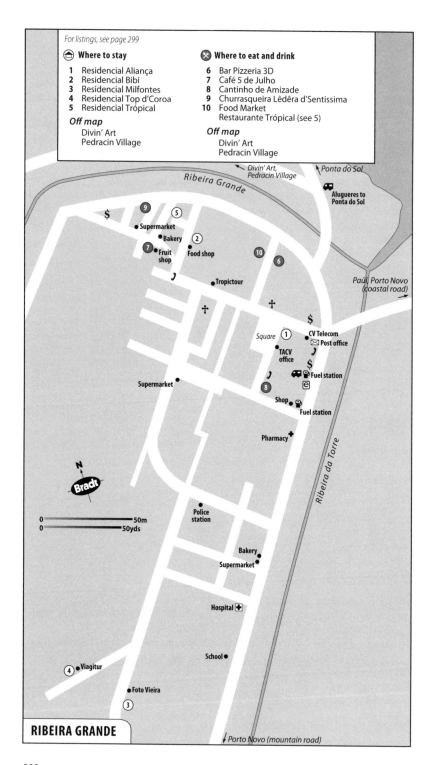

For listings, see page 299

Where to stay

1 Residencial Aliança
2 Residencial Bibi
3 Residencial Milfontes
4 Residencial Top d'Coroa
5 Residencial Trópical

Off map
   Divin' Art
   Pedracin Village

Where to eat and drink

6 Bar Pizzeria 3D
7 Café 5 de Julho
8 Cantinho de Amizade
9 Churrasqueira Lêdêra d'Sentissima
10 Food Market
   Restaurante Trópical (see 5)

Off map
   Divin' Art
   Pedracin Village

Divin' Art,
Pedracin Village

Ponta do Sol

Ribeira Grande

Algueres to
Ponta do Sol

$

⑨   ⑤

● Supermarket
   ● Bakery   ②
⑦ ● Fruit   ● Food shop
   shop

⑩   ⑥

Paúl, Porto Novo
(coastal road)

● Tropictour

✝   ✝

Square ① CV Telecom
              ✉ Post office
         ● TACV
           office
                    $

         ● ♪ 🚐 Fuel station
⑧   e
● Shop ●
         Fuel station

● Supermarket

Pharmacy ✚

N

Bradt

Ribeira da Torre

0 ——————— 50m
0 ——————— 50yds

● Police
  station

● Bakery
● Supermarket

Hospital ✚

School ●

④ ● Viagitur

● Foto Vieira

③

RIBEIRA GRANDE

Porto Novo (mountain road)

Other practicalities

Airlines
TACV (☎ 221 1184)

Bank
BCA Bank, opposite the post office at the crossroads on the edge of town (*08.00–15.00 Mon–Fri*). BCN, down the side Ribeira da Torre towards the hospital. Caixa Económica, Rua Ponte Lavad: follow the road up the side of Ribeira Grande for a minute or so and it is on your left (⊕ *08.00–15.00 Mon–Fri*). All with ATMs.

Hospital
(☎ 221 1130) Off towards the mountain Porto Novo road.

Internet
At the Residencial Trópical, and a couple of places in the centre.

Pharmacy
(☎ 221 1310) Near the hospital.

Police
(☎ 221 1132) Go along the mountain Porto Novo road and turn right before the hospital.

Post office
(⊕ *08.00–15.30 Mon–Fri*) At the end of the main street through town.

Tourist information
None, but try at Viagitur, next to Residencial Top d'Coroa.

PONTA DO SOL A gracious town, built on a breezy peninsula, this is one of the oldest Barlavento settlements. It has a neat main square, beautiful town hall, decent restaurants and a tiny but lively harbour. It is becoming increasingly popular with tourists and is undergoing a mini construction boom, with many new apartments springing up on the surrounding hills, many of which are owned by *emigrantes*, some which appear forlorn and unfinished. An entirely inappropriate six-storey hotel planned for the waterfront has progressed slowly, but all in all development in this little town has thankfully not made too much difference to its charm. From September to April, the numerous small hotels and restaurants can be full, so booking is advisable.

Getting there and away Ponta do Sol is nearly at the end of the road. It is a 15-minute *aluguer* trip from Ribeira Grande (50$), using transport that waits by the bridge over the Ribeira Grande itself. Transport leaves at times all through the day, but is most common in the early morning. A taxi from Ribeira Grande costs 500$. A private hire taxi from Ponta do Sol to Fontainhas is 700$; to Paúl 1,000$; to Porto Novo 4,000$; to Pico da Cruz 3,500$; to Corda 2,000$. Change at Ribeira Grande for transport anywhere else. Your hotel can book transport in advance, if you need it. Otherwise, Ponta do Sol's square is the place to find it, at any time of day. For an English- and French-speaking driver, Philip Delgado (m *996 6691*; e *filipeeloi@ hotmail.com*) is reliable and friendly.

 Where to stay All listings are located on the map, page 302.

⌂ **Pôr do Sol Arte** (4 rooms) ☎ 225 1121; e porsolarte@yahoo.fr. Basic, arty, friendly place. One room with balcony & private bath, others are cheaper. Also has a café, with food in high season. English & French spoken. Organises walking guides, transfers & picnics. **$$$–$**

⌂ **Coraçao da Ponta do Sol (previously Chez Luisette)** (7 rooms) ☎ 225 1048; m 924 9001;

e hilde_vg@hotmail.com, hildevangelder@gmail.com; www.hotelsantoantao.com. On the road into town from Ribeira Grande, before you descend into the square. Simple but good-sized & pleasant rooms, with many improvements underway, a rooftop conservatory where guests can have their b/fast & evening meals. A swimming pool & jacuzzi are planned by the Belgian owners. Rooms are en

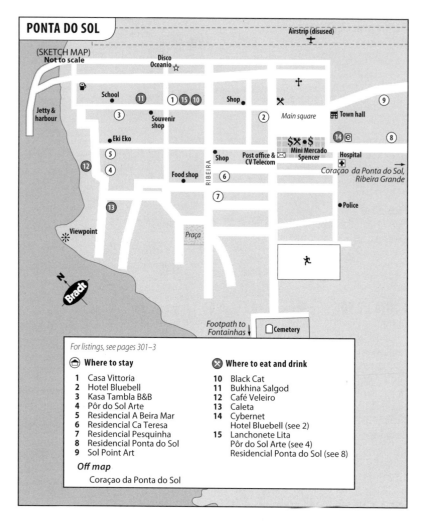

PONTA DO SOL

(SKETCH MAP)
Not to scale

Airstrip (disused)

Disco Oceanio ☆

School

Jetty & harbour

Souvenir shop

Eki Eko

Shop

Main square

Town hall

RIBEIRA

Shop

Post office & CV Telecom

Mini Mercado Spencer

Hospital

Food shop

Coraçao da Ponta do Sol, Ribeira Grande

Police

Viewpoint

Praça

Footpath to Fontainhas

Cemetery

For listings, see pages 301–3

Where to stay
1 Casa Vittoria
2 Hotel Bluebell
3 Kasa Tambla B&B
4 Pôr do Sol Arte
5 Residencial A Beira Mar
6 Residencial Ca Teresa
7 Residencial Pesquinha
8 Residencial Ponta do Sol
9 Sol Point Art

Off map
Coraçao da Ponta do Sol

Where to eat and drink
10 Black Cat
11 Bukhina Salgod
12 Café Veleiro
13 Caleta
14 Cybernet
      Hotel Bluebell (see 2)
15 Lanchonete Lita
      Pôr do Sol Arte (see 4)
      Residencial Ponta do Sol (see 8)

suite with hot water, balconies with sea views. English, French & Flemish spoken. **$$**

🏠 **Hotel Bluebell** (23 rooms) ☎ 225 1215; m 994 1153; e bluebell@cvtelecom.cv. Located near the square, this has all the facilities of a modest hotel. Rooms have TV, private bathroom & sea or mountain view. There is a roof terrace. There are 2 suites & some rooms have AC. The hotel offers transfers to & from Porto Novo & can organise walking & fishing excursions, with English-speaking guides. **$$**

🏠 **Kasa Tambla B&B** (10 rooms) ☎ 225 1526; m 982 5059; e kasatambla@gmail.com; http:// cap-vert-decouverte.over-blog.net. French-run establishment, offering excellent hiking & other

information (inc maps), plus kayak, mountain-bike hire & free snorkelling to residents. Rooms have private bathrooms. Communal library & satellite TV. Also luxury apartment with terrace available for rent. B/fast service, courtyard & bar. **$$**

🏠 **Residencial Ca Teresa** (3 rooms) ☎ 225 1532; m 982 2320. Rooms with private baths & hot water in a quaint building away from the square. One mini-suite with 2 balconies. **$$**

🏠 **Residencial Ponta do Sol** (14 rooms) ☎ 225 1238; e residencialpsol@cvtelecom.cv. On the road towards Ribeira Grande, a garish green & orange building. Thankfully, the large, bright, fairly modern rooms are not painted in the same colours. All are en suite with hot water & fans. Some have a balcony from which, for top-floor rooms, there is a sea view. There's also a restaurant which should be booked half a day beforehand. Can organise excursions. **$$**

🏠 **Sol Point Art** (8 rooms) ✎ 225 1080; m 951 8927; e construplex.construplex@gmail.com. Located down a dusty road behind the town hall. Brand new, smartly fitted & furnished. All rooms have TV & fridge, 2 have AC while the others rely on sea breezes. A restaurant & cultural space for music are under construction. **$$**

🏠 **Casa Vittoria** (5 rooms) ✎ 225 1075. Pleasant clean, spacious, well-lit rooms with AC, fridge & private bath, above Lanchonette Lita. The owner also runs a small shop next door. **$**

🏠 **Residencial A Beira Mar** (10 rooms) ✎ 225 1018; e chefatimaps@hotmail.com. Not far from the harbour, this has one of the best views of all hotels in the town. Each room has a private bath with hot water & balcony with sea view & there is a rooftop bar that has a panorama of the sea & the mountains. Rooms are clean, smart & cared for. Some French spoken. Good value. **$**

🏠 **Residencial Pesquinha** (7 rooms) ✎ 225 1091. Simple, good-value place up a side street. Rooms have private baths with hot water. Rooftop terrace. **$**

✖ Where to eat and drink All listings are located on the map opposite.

✖ **Black Cat** ✎ 225 1539. Catering to groups of hungry hikers (but all are welcome!), this lively place also has a *quintal fresca* (inner courtyard), & live music on Wed & Sun. The French-speaking owner offers a good range of dishes, including goat, meat dishes, pasta & fish. **$$$$**

💻 **Café Veleiro** Overlooks the sea & harbour – as close to the ocean as you can be, without getting wet. A good venue at sundown. **$$$$**

✖ **Hotel Bluebell** (see listing on opposite page) Indoor restaurant on the ground floor of the hotel, overlooking the main square. **$$$$**

✖ **Bukhina Salgod** ✎ 225 1068. Pleasant place with reasonably priced standard fish, meat & pasta dishes, plus a cheaper dish of the day. Occasional live music. French-speaking. **$$$**

✖ **Caleta** A tiny place on the seafront. Offers fish, seafood, goat's cheese dishes, plus cocktails. Indoor & outdoor seating with really good cooking & a fantastic view over the ocean. **$$$**

✖ **Lanchonete Lita** ✎ 225 1075. Serves *cachupa* & whatever else is fresh that day. **$$$**

💻 **Pôr do Sol Arte** This is a colourful little café, serving food only in high season. **$$$**

✖ **Residencial Ponta do Sol** (see listing on opposite page). **$$$**

💻 **Cybernet** On the uphill side of the main square, an atmospheric little internet bar. Live music every other Fri. **$$**

Entertainment and nightlife Not a lot of wild activity – look out for **Disco Oceanio**, in front of the airstrip, open late at weekends. Occasional live music at the Black Cat, Bukinha Salgod, Cybernet and others. Less traditional, but more thumping music often plays in the main square at weekends, to accompany the myriad, promenading teenagers.

Shopping An extensive range of crafts and food produce is for sale at the excellent Eki-Eko, affiliated to and located just behind the Kasa Tambla B&B. All products are sourced from Cape Verde. Sometimes staff will be making items in the shop. Lamps, clothes, jams and other souvenirs. Also sells maps. Some items at the Black Cat (see listing details above), plus a couple of Senegalese shops down towards the harbour, selling both Cape Verdean and African mainland products.

Other practicalities
Airlines
(✎ 221 1184) TACV, in Ribeira Grande.

Bank
BCA in the main square, with ATM.

Health centre
(✎ 225 1130) The colonial building with two sweeping staircases to the left of the post office. Limited facility, but there should be a duty doctor in town.

Internet

Try Cybernet (see listing on page 303). Free Wi-Fi in the main square.

Pharmacy

Only in Ribeira Grande.

Police

(☏ 225 1132) South of the main square.

Post office

(🕑 08.00–12.00 & 14.00–18.00 Mon–Fri)
Overlooking the main square, on the southern side.

Tourist information

Nothing official, but most accommodation will be able to organise excursions, transport, etc.

What to see and do

Ponta do Sol is the embarkation point for hikes along the north coast and it is close enough to Ribeira Grande to be a useful setting-off point for hikes up its *ribeiras* (Torre and Grande).

OTHER PLACES TO VISIT

Fontainhas Perched like a fairy-tale village on a high and precipitous spit of land above a deep *ribeira*, Fontainhas can be reached along a winding cobbled road from Ponta do Sol. Go up the hill, leaving the cemetery to your left, until you reach the cobbled road level with the end of the construction development, then turn right onto it. A spectacular walk on the road that heads west. It's about a 10km round trip.

Cruzinha da Garça This coastal village is more or less the end of the road that runs up Ribeira Grande, and can also be accessed on foot from Fontainhas (see *Hikes*, page 309). There is a small fishing fleet, but little else

🏠 Where to stay and eat

🏠 **Pensão Só Na Fish** (10 rooms) ☏ 226 1027; e sonafish@live.com. Large building in the centre, overlooking the water. Rooms are very simple & 1 is en suite. HB basis only. Bar & restaurant, available to non-guests, though choice may be limited. **$$**

CHÃ DE IGREJA This pretty village, with its smart white church and brightly painted houses, is built on a small promontory of land projecting from the west side of the *ribeira*. A good place to chill for a while, but if intending to hike between Chã and Ponta do Sol, you might consider doing the walk in reverse and spending the night in the latter, with its better choice of hotels and restaurants. To get there, take an *aluguer* up Ribcira Grande, through Coculi, Boca das Ambas Ribeiras, Horta de Garça and onwards. The best time to try for such transport is about 11.00–14.00. You are unlikely to find public transport back on the same day, as it generally leaves early in the morning. The road up from Ribeira Grande winds up and down through some spectacular scenery, with great photo opportunities.

There are beautiful, large beaches within 45 minutes of Chã de Igreja during the summer months (June to September) but for the rest of the year they are underwater.

🏠 Where to stay and eat

There is no official restaurant but meals can be obtained from the *residencials* listed below.

🏠 **Senhor Rodrigo** (5 rooms) ☏ 226 1019. A large building with a terrace & views over the ocean. HB only. Somewhat informal pensão. **$$$**
🏠 **Mite Residencial** (7 rooms) ☏ 226 1064; m 994 0759. Fairly basic rooms with shared bathrooms. Unmarked building, so enquire at the mini-market of the same name, just down from the church. HB only. **$$**

The western part of Santo Antão is dominated by one vast volcano which reaches a height of 1,982m. Within its crater stands a younger cone, with a height of 1,979m. To its east, and almost as high, is Monte Pia, at 1,884m.

The west is largely inaccessible and underpopulated, although, if tourism spreads along a new road west of Porto Novo this inaccessibility might gradually decrease. Currently there is a road from Porto Novo to Lagedos which runs northwest along a convoluted path through Chã de Morte, Curral das Vacas and on to Ribeira da Cruz in the northwest before heading west and then inland again, terminating at Monte Cebola. When the rains are bad, whole sections of road may be washed away.

However, a network of hikes has been put together in the AB Kartenverlag map series (see page 70), and there are local people at strategic points offering basic accommodation. So it is possible to explore, but not without some forward planning: either put yourself in the hands of a knowledgeable local operator such as Alsatour or make your phone calls to some of the people below to organise guides and accommodation (and don't forget to cancel homestays if your plans change as your hosts might otherwise waste a day's journey to purchase food for your dinner).

The views from the hike up and around Coroa are tremendous: down the steep western side of the volcano to Monte Trigo, and across to all the Barlavento islands when the weather is fine. The 1,000m ascent is not included in the hiking section because it's not the kind of hike that should be attempted without a guide. The paths are many and easily confused, there is no scattering of locals happy to put you right, and the landscape is hostile, with unexpected cliffs and no water.

TARRAFAL This isolated spot on the west coast is hard to get to but definitely worth the effort. The road up, then down, from Porto Novo is spectacular (see box, pages 306–7), with breathtaking views over to São Vicente, Santa Luzia, São Nicolau and even Fogo, on a very clear day. It may not be passable in the rainy season, as bridges can be washed away. Your *aluguer* driver will probably stop if you want to take photos – and you undoubtedly will. The approach from the sea is also beautiful – a small spot of green colour amongst the brown-grey massifs of the mountains gradually resolves itself into the whites and pastels of this sleepy town. Around the black-sand shore – the longest stretch of beach in Santo Antão – fishermen relax, fierce games of *oril* click away under the trees, women wash clothes; and hens, pigs, goats and dogs go purposefully about their business. Sea eagles are common here, so keep an eye open for them plucking their dinner from the ocean. This a great venue in which to do very little, a perfect place to relax at the beginning or end of a hiking holiday. Snorkelling and scuba-diving are both possibilities, as is fishing with the locals, which is best organised through the accommodation listed below. There is no electricity after 23.00 and no network coverage for phones, though internet access is possible. Improvements to the infrastructure are underway, for better or worse.

Getting there and away Several *aluguer* pick-up trucks leave Tarrafal at an unhealthy 05.00 or slightly later for Porto Novo (700$), departing on the return journey at about 11.00. If you notify your driver the day before, he will pick you up at your *residencial*. The journey takes about 2½ hours, and is uncomfortable and dusty, particularly when the cobbles run out on the half nearer Tarrafal. The trucks can be packed (a cushion is recommended, unless you manage to bag a much-coveted inside berth – reserve one with your driver the day before!). You could charter a 4x4 in Porto Novo instead for ten times the price. Generally they do not run on Sundays. There is also a Land Rover which can take eight passengers; ask your hotel for more information on this option. The *residencials* in Tarrafal will usually give you as much assistance as possible to plan your journey, including contacting the one or two local drivers on your behalf. To find the Tarrafal *aluguer* in Porto Novo, ask around at the ferry terminal amongst the assembled drivers.

Where to stay and eat
Be aware that hot water is not available in the village, there is no mobile-phone signal and electricity is available only some of the time. This may change – development is in progress. As accommodation is limited, it's best to book in advance. If you arrive without a booking, and everywhere is full, it's a long and expensive trip back to Porto Novo. For alternative accommodation options to those listed below, try www.bela-vista.net/accommodation-Santo-Antão-e.aspx for the odd tip on homestays.

Marina d'Tarrafal (3 rooms, plus 4 luxury tents) 227 6078; e info@marina-tarrafal. com; www.marina-tarrafal.com. Small coastal guesthouse in spacious grounds with charming

---

TO THE END OF THE EARTH AND BEYOND   *Murray Stewart*

The pick-up roars (briefly) out of town, but reaches little more than 40km/hour before the tarmac inevitably gives way to the more familiar, passenger-massaging cobblestones that are the trademark of Cape Verde's road network. Cobblestones do not encourage speed, and our vehicle duly slows.

For 30 minutes we wind upwards, our driver dropping through the gears until he can drop no more. We are now reduced to just above walking speed, and I am beginning to understand why it takes 2½ hours to cover the 26km from Porto Novo to Tarrafal de Monte Trigo. We come across a couple of cows, looking for something to munch: at an altitude of 1,200m, and at the end of the dry season, there's not much choice on their menu. In a month or so, the rains should come and the landscape will be transformed from desert to green. Life will be easier for the cows.

Higher up, the cows give way to goats. We seem to be eyeball to eyeball with the craggy peaks of São Vicente, away to the southeast and an hour's ferry ride across the ocean from Santo Antão. But we have not finished our climb, not by far. After another 20 minutes of funereal progress, we turn a corner and we are no longer looking *across* at São Vicente's peaks, but *down* on the whole island, as if we were in an aeroplane. Front, back and both sides of the neighbouring island are visible. I ask the driver to stop for some photos and when he obliges, I realise for the first time that we have acquired an extra passenger from somewhere. Perched on the back of the truck is a middle-aged man, his feet wedged between a crate of beer and some plastic barrels. As well as being the passenger transport, we are also the Tarrafal delivery vehicle. We continue. Left hand only on the steering wheel, with his right hand our driver is tossing up a sealed package of pills he has collected from the pharmacy in Porto Novo, to deliver to someone in Tarrafal. The package is lobbed upward, then neatly caught, the pills seemingly rattling in perfect time to the seductive music washing over passengers from the dusty radio. An unusual percussive aid, I think to myself, but my admiration at our driver's dexterity and sense of rhythm is tempered by my preference for a 'both hands on the wheel' policy, as we negotiate yet another hairpin.

hosts, excellent & innovative cuisine (available to non-residents, with notice) & simple rooms & views of the mountains, sugar cane fields & banana & coconut plantations. The owner used to be the ship's cook on the *Mar d'Canal*, & the cuisine is excellent. Luxury tents are cheaper & popular with children! Hiking & snorkelling trips arranged. **$$**

🏠 **Residencial Mar Tranquilidade**
(7 rooms) ☏ 227 6012; e info@martranquilidade. com; www.martranquilidade.com. Run by Frank & Susi, a German–American couple who arrived here on their yacht in 1999 & decided to stay, this is an artistically created little complex of high-ceilinged, stone & thatch cottages, echoing the

traditional architecture of the village. Most are en suite. There's a shady terrace in front in which to hang out, & also Praça Tartaruga, a terrace on the beach which they have built as a place for locals, & visitors, to congregate. They are very proud of their cuisine, which is available to non-residents with advance notice. Reservations are recommended as they are often full. **$$**

🏠 **Marie-Alice and Jaime da Cruz** (6 rooms) ☏ 227 6002. A very basic, locally owned *pensão* with a terrace overlooking the coast, on the main road uphill, north of the beach. No hot water, intermittent electricity, shared bathroom. Meals with advance notice. Reserve a room facing the sea & sleep to the sound of the waves. **$**

What to see and do Swim, dive, snorkel, fish from a local boat, play table tennis on the beach, chase a chicken, go by boat or walk to Monte Trigo. Bury yourself in

Our next stop, even higher, is for another passenger to buy some fresh goat's cheese from a precariously situated dwelling. The mother goat plays with her two kids as the transaction completes. At this new altitude, I also have another startling discovery, for beyond São Vicente, the peaks of São Nicolau – the 'next-door island-but-one' – are now visible above a distant layer of white cloud. My fellow passengers tell me that they have even seen the volcanic cone of distant Fogo, on a clear day.

At a junction, the cobbles pass over the baton to a rutted dirt track and the discomfort increases. At last we are heading downward, a line of lonely telephone poles to guide us. The *ribeiras* are dry now, though will not remain so for long and I marvel at the deep troughs the previous year's rainwater has carved in the ground as it headed seawards. Bridges are often washed away, I am told, making it necessary to send up a vehicle from Tarrafal to meet another from Porto Novo, transferring goods by hand from one vehicle to the other, across the gap, to keep the town supplied.

There is no other road in.

We stop again, this time at a squat building, and we edge nervously on foot towards the nearby cliff. Tiny Tarrafal is below, perhaps 1,000m of descent. Before the dirt-track road was completed in the 1980s, this building was used to store goods brought from Porto Novo and the townsfolk would have to carry everything down the steep cobbled path to town. It's actually quicker to walk from here, I am told, but I decline the opportunity. When our pick-up crawls for the remaining 30 minutes, I begin to believe it. I am looking at the sea ahead and wondering how we are going to descend so far in such a short distance. More hairpin bends provide the answer. Eventually we reach sea level and a wide black-sand beach is our reward as it ushers us into the town. For me, the journey is over. But our one silent passenger, a woman in her sixties, has yet further to go. Laden with fruit from Porto Novo, she has to wait for a boat to take her and her supplies up the coast to Monte Trigo, yet another hour away.

Or, if no boat appears, she has another three hours, on foot.

the sand, which is reputed to have medicinal properties. Hike with a guide. Read, sit and watch the waves.

OTHER PLACES TO VISIT
Norte This region is remote and inaccessible but the landscape is dramatic.

 *Where to stay*

🏠 **Casa Isabel and Luciano Neves** 📞222 3118. Simple accommodation with the family who also offer guided trips up to Topo de Coroa & have transport. Book in advance. **$$**

HIKES   *Colum Wilson (CW); Aisling Irwin (AI)*

For the manic, the fourth and fifth hikes can be combined so that the walker goes up one *ribeira* and comes down the next one.

1 VILA DE RIBEIRA GRANDE–COCULI–BOCA DAS AMBAS RIBEIRAS–CHÃ DE IGREJA
Distance: 12.5km; time: 5½ hours; difficulty: 2 (CW)

This is a spectacular walk, though not as green and cultivated as the other *ribeiras*. You can halve its length by taking transport from Ribeira Grande as far as Boca das Ambas Ribeiras. At the end of the walk you could turn round and walk back, or walk to Ponta do Sol (ie: the reverse of the next walk). Alternatively, you may be able to find an *aluguer* near the church that will take you to Ribeira Grande. If not, you may have to charter one.

Ribeira Grande is at the mouth of two *ribeiras*. The one that gives the town its name is the more northerly one. There's a wide, dusty track that leads up the *ribeira* from where the road to Ponta do Sol leaves town. The riverbed passes through scattered housing and cultivation and on the right, after about 20 minutes, an agronomy station. This was built by the Dutch under an aid scheme but is now run by the Cape Verdeans. A tennis court was included in the package.

Some 45 minutes after setting out there is a large windmill on the left and a small shop which sells drinks. After another ten minutes you reach the little village of **Coculi** with its prominent white church. This village marks the point where Ribeira Figueiral joins Ribeira Grande on the left. Bearing right at the fork just before the village, you will see that Ribeira Grande is joined almost immediately by another *ribeira* on the left, which leads up to **Chã de Pedra**.

The gentle ascent up Ribeira Grande continues and the land empties and becomes less lush, although a lot of sugarcane grows here. Two hours in, there's a slender aqueduct over the increasingly narrow *ribeira*. It was built by the Portuguese in 1956, and is still carrying water today.

Half an hour later is the small village of **Boca das Ambas Ribeiras**, or 'Mouth of Both Valleys' – the small valley of Ribeira dos Caibros leads up to the left. There are a couple of houses here and two prominent breadfruit trees. Breadfruit, which is in season in March, is considered a great delicacy. It has white flesh that is best cut into slices and boiled in salt water.

A cobbled road leads up the left side of Ribeira Grande, but the more interesting (and direct) route to **Chã de Igreja** is along a small path up the right (north) side of the valley.

You start climbing almost immediately, the path ahead repeatedly seeming to vanish as it curves steeply around the wrinkles of the sheer mountain face. Before long, the view of the valley floor far below is vertiginous, with farms and the

Snorkelling is possible with Marina Tarrafal (see listing on pages 306–7 for details). For diving, check out Santo-Antão Scuba Diving ☏ 591 2206; e santoantaoscubadiving@hotmail.fr; www.santoantaodiving.com). This is a new operation started in 2012, with brand-new equipment. PADI qualified, the owner is French, with naval and oil-rig diving experience and speaks English. Rough seas prevent diving at times during December to March, while visibility can be poor in August and September, due to the rains washing down into the ocean. Underwater volcanic landscape, with manta rays, occasional sharks and many others. Beginners welcome.

occasional vehicle spread out like toys on a carpet. In places, there is nothing but a knee-high drystone wall separating you from a sheer drop of 500m. It was the same in the 19th century, when Alfred Burdon Ellis was prompted to write:

Casualties… are not by any means uncommon, as the numerous wooden crosses that we passed on our way testified.

Watch out for Egyptian vultures (*Neophron percnopterus*) soaring on the thermals towards the head of the valley. They are unmistakable, with a black wing with a white leading edge, and a wingspan of up to 2m.

Finally, 1½ hours after leaving Boca, the path finds a nick in the mountain rim at a height of 830m. Over the saddle, look down on the tiny settlement of Selado do Mocho.

It is a hard descent (40 minutes) on a zig-zagging cobbled path to reach the edge of this remote village. Not long after passing around the head of a small valley into the village, the path cuts up to the top of a low ridge, where you find the village standpipe. Straight away, the path begins the descent into Ribeira Garça. Before long, you will catch your first glimpse of Chã de Igreja, on a small promontory of land projecting from the west side of the *ribeira*.

Descend into the deep cleft of the *ribeira*, and find a steep path up the seaward side of the village's promontory.

2 PONTA DO SOL–FONTAINHAS–FORMIGUINHAS–CHÃ DE IGREJA

Distance: 12km; time: 5 hours; difficulty: 2 (MS)

This coastal walk makes an interesting change from the *ribeiras*, passing through the village of Fontainhas, perched on a knife edge of rock, and with plenty of exposure to the sound and aroma of crashing waves. A lot of the walk is undulating with some steep parts and some level sections. Refreshments are available at all the places mentioned below and there are a couple of bathing opportunities along the way, though care should be taken if the ocean is rough. At the end of the walk you can either stay the night in Chã de Igreja, or catch the *aluguer* that runs from near the church to Ribeira Grande. If you are forced to charter an *aluguer*, it should be about 2,500$. Some may prefer to do the walk in reverse, dropping their luggage at a hotel in Ponta do Sol, then taking transport to Chã and starting the walk back to their hotel from there.

From Ponta do Sol, head uphill and go past either side of the cemetery until you reach the wide, cobbled road. Turn right onto it. The cobbled road winds in and out amongst the folds of the steep mountains and finally affords you a fantastic view of **Fontainhas**, perched like a fairy-tale village on a high and precipitous spit of land above a deep *ribeira*. Some 40 minutes after setting out you will be on its extraordinary main street, built on the spine of the narrow promontory. The houses lining this higgledy-piggledy street have a sheer drop of several hundred metres behind them.

As you leave Fontainhas, and as the path climbs back towards the coast, there is a good view of the *ribeira* with its intricate terracing and ingeniously engineered irrigation channels running across the slopes. On the valley floor the wooden structure is a traditional *trapiche* – a mule-driven contraption used for pressing sugarcane in the all-important manufacture of *grogue*.

In the next *ribeira* the path weaves back inland towards the well-watered village of **Corvo**, 40 minutes from Fontainhas. Another 20 minutes brings you to the prettier village of **Formiguinhas**, where you descend to the shore.

The next stretch of the walk is the most impressive because much of the path has been hacked out of the massive, ancient rock formations. It is a spectacular but

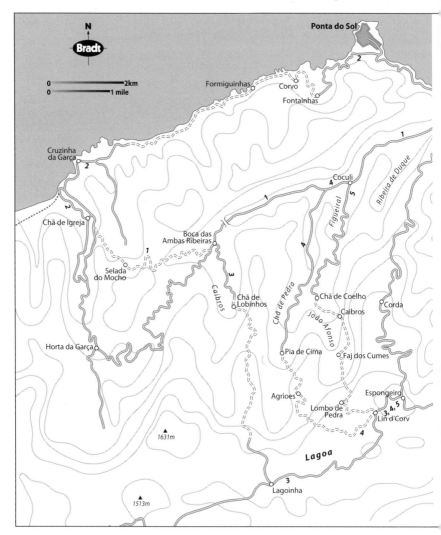

desolate walk, with the air full of the sound of the waves and the taste and smell of salt. At one point you emerge in a small, nameless settlement, where there are four houses and fields of rock. Here, there is no evidence of the passage of the centuries.

About 1½ hours from Formiguinhas the land opens out again and a broad *ribeira* leads up to the left. A small village (out of sight of the path) shelters in the mouth of this *ribeira*. After 15 minutes, cross a football pitch with metal goalposts and, 20 minutes later, you descend into the small fishing village of **Cruzinha da Garça**.

Pick up the cobbled road here and follow it for ten minutes out of the village, seeing a cemetery high up on a hillside opposite. There's a track leading into the *ribeira* on the left. Although this does not look very promising follow it inland. The *ribeira* is dry, desolate and dramatic. There is nothing but the rustle of parched leaves and the rattle of pebbles falling from the sheer valley sides. Some 40 minutes

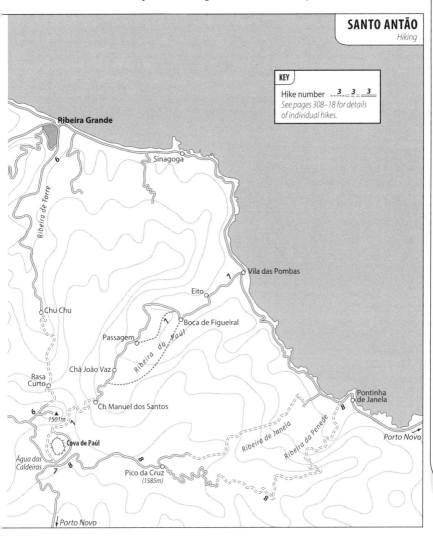

SANTO ANTÃO
Hiking

KEY
Hike number
See pages 308–18 for details of individual hikes.

Ribeira Grande
Sinagoga
Ribeira de Torre
Chu Chu
Vila das Pombas
Eito
Boca de Figueiral
Passagem
Ribeira do Paúl
Chã João Vaz
Rasa Curto
Ch Manuel dos Santos
Pontinha de Janela
1501m
Cova de Paúl
Ribeira de Janela
Ribeira da Penede
Porto Novo
Água das Caldeiras
Pico da Cruz
(1585m)
Porto Novo

When British merchant navy radio operator George Monk's ship, the *Auditor*, was torpedoed by a U-boat in 1941, most of the crew managed to escape into lifeboats. But what then? They had no navigational equipment, limited water and just a few cans of condensed milk to keep them going and they were bobbing up and down in the hostile Atlantic.

Monk, now in his nineties, happened to have a diary in his pocket with navigational charts from which the crew worked out where they thought the Cape Verde Islands might be. Then began traumatic days in which they rowed and rowed, all the time becoming fainter and more dehydrated. They rationed themselves to a few teaspoons of the milk each day.

Finally, one morning, dawn rose on a distant mountain. 'It was vertical black lava rock going straight down into the sea,' says Monk. 'We couldn't land. We rowed for another six hours until we spotted the little village of Tarrafal.

'As we got near they spotted us and two of their fishing boats came out with carafes full of water. We just sat there, drinking water.'

They eventually reached the beach and staggered into Tarrafal where they were cared for so kindly that Monk always yearned to return one day to say thank you.

His dream came true in late 2007 when his story caught the imagination of Ron Hughes of Cape Verde Travel. Ron organised a trip for him, and the Cape Verdean navy offered to take him to the remote village in western Tarrafal. As the ship approached the green puddle at the foot of the Tarrafal Mountains, Monk reminisced. 'I remember so well walking ashore here on this beach. It's so wonderful to come back,' he told me.

He walked slowly up Tarrafal's main street in the heat of the midday sun and the word quickly spread. Before long a man of similar age, Germano Delgado, was coming along the street to meet him. Delgado had been one of his rescuers. The two 90 year olds stood smiling at each other, nothing in common but a chance meeting 60 years before – and their age.

'I remember it quite well,' said Delgado. 'They were completely exhausted.'

Then Monk and Delgado put their hands to their chests in Cape Verdean greeting, shook hands like the British and went their separate ways.

after leaving Cruzinha, you arrive at a promontory projecting into the *ribeira* with a steep path up its side leading to **Chã de Igreja**.

3 BOCA DAS AMBAS RIBEIRAS–CAIBROS–CHÃ DE LOBINHOS–REAL–LAGOINHA– ESPONGEIRO

Distance: 14km; time: 5 hours; difficulty: 3 (Al)

This walk is a feast of ever more dramatic panoramas and, like the others leading from parallel *ribeiras*, takes you to an eerie, higher world away from the drama of canyons and terraces. No part of the path is tricky, but the unremitting ascent requires a certain degree of fitness. To get to the starting point, take an *aluguer* from Ribeira Grande (outside Caixa Económica) all the way to **Boca das Ambas Ribeiras**, a 20-minute trip. The last part of the hike is a 1½-hour walk along the road to Espongeiro – you may wish to arrange beforehand for transport to collect you from Lagoinha.

Entering Boca das Ambas Ribeiras from Ribeira Grande, you will find a turning to **Caibros** on the left, just before the cobbled main road ascends and bends to the right.

Follow this dirt track and, after about 15 minutes, you will begin to ascend the right-hand side of the valley. Five minutes later you pass a small, brick aqueduct on the left and the *ribeira* becomes more interesting, filled with palm trees and plantations. The track ends 30 minutes from the main road, after passing between two high buildings and reaching a little turning area. Continue in the same direction, on the footpath ahead, passing up a valley heavily planted with sugarcane, bananas and vegetables. After five minutes, at **Chã de Lobinhos**, there is a path up the hillside to the left which ascends in a hairpin for 20m. Less than ten minutes after beginning this path, you cross an irrigation channel and a public tap. The path ascends steeply and, after passing the last house for some time, you will see your route ahead, darting back and forth, its cobbled walls camouflaged by the rock.

Reaching a ridge, half an hour from Chã de Lobinhos, you can see into the next *ribeira* and you are already eye to eye with the first of the craggy peaks. The path dips slightly and there's a little path to the left: stay on the main path for the ever more spectacular views of the two *ribeiras* – and of valleys beyond – ample compensation for this breathless climb.

Some 1½ hours from Chã de Lobinhos, the path reaches a T-junction with a path of red earth. Here is the best panorama so far – you can see both the Chã de Pedra and the Figueiral roads. Turn right and arrive ten minutes later at the upper world, whose beginning is marked by a stone house and extensive terracing. The path is varied, sometimes through open agricultural land, sometimes along narrow ridges with cliffs plunging to either side.

Some 50 minutes from the last T-junction you reach another: turn right and go up the hill towards a green concrete water tank and tap. From here, the path becomes a road which, after 35 minutes meets a fork at which you turn right. Five minutes later you pass a graveyard, and five minutes after that the weather station at **Lagoinha**. Turn left after the weather station and begin the 1½-hour trudge to **Espongeiro**.

4 COCULI–CHÃ DE PEDRA–LIN D'CORV–ESPONGEIRO

Distance: 10.5km; time: 4 hours 20 minutes; difficulty: 3 (CW)

Parts of this walk are quite tough – particularly the long, steep and dramatic ascent at the head of Chã de Pedra on an uncobbled path that can at times be akin to rock climbing. The approach to Lin d'Corv is across gently undulating agricultural land. To shorten the walk a little, you can try to catch a lift to Coculi and onwards, as far up Chã de Pedra as possible (it is possible to get a lift as far as Pia de Cima, if you are lucky).

From Coculi to Chã de Pedra takes 1½ hours. At **Coculi**, take the right fork, passing Coculi's church on your left, and after about 700m, take a turning on the left. The first part of this road up to **Chã de Pedra** is flat and not particularly interesting. It becomes livelier when it leaves the valley floor as it approaches **Pia de Cima**.

Through Pia de Cima, the road twists itself into mind-boggling contortions as it tackles unnerving inclines; it then deposits you in a rare flat area at the top of the village. Your path leads up to the left by the low wall beside the shop.

Ascending from Pia, you pass houses and the school. Even at the peak of the dry season, water may be rushing down the sides of the path from the pine-clad slopes above. Some 25 minutes after leaving Pia, you will crest a rise and find yourself looking down on the small settlement of **Agriões**. From where you are standing, you can see the path you will take weaving to and fro across the ridge that rises up behind the village.

Ten minutes will bring you down amongst the houses of Agriões. Carry on around a sharp hairpin between two houses and continue down to a *grogue* still.

There are two forks here in quick succession: the first is of two narrow paths (turn left) and the second of two wider paths (turn left again). Your path crosses the valley floor, and after another few minutes leads you up the ridge. Ten minutes from the valley floor, the cobbled surface stops, and you will find yourself battling up a tough incline. To survive the next half-hour, up a steep and winding path, you need to be quite fit. The path will take you to the right at a fork, just above a small house. It is all worth it when you finally emerge on a breathtaking ridge, with a deep valley on either side, and Agriões behind and below you. There is a small farmer's hut nearby, with arguably the best view in Cape Verde.

Ten minutes from the ridge, turn left at a T-junction. From here, the path zig-zags up and up, affording great views to the north if you are lucky enough not to be caught in mist. Now you are facing the challenge of making your way up narrow paths of crumbling rock. At one point the path is so narrow and the walls so high that it is almost as if you are entering a cave. After 20 minutes, the path flattens out and, within a few minutes, goes up a shallow ridge towards a low thatched cottage. Bear right past the cottage and, after a few minutes, you will find yourself walking along the right side of a wide, low valley. Some 20 minutes beyond the thatched cottage you will emerge on a further, smaller ridge. Follow the path down towards the valley floor on your left.

After ten minutes bear left at a fork. You are now in a desert-like area barren of greenery, the path at the mercy of shifting winds. The path may be hard to distinguish so confirm the route that follows with passing locals.

Five minutes after the previously mentioned fork bear right at a second fork and start ascending towards the road at **Lin d'Corv**, which you will reach after just over ten minutes. There is not much at Lin d'Corv except a single house and a large area of the hillside concreted over and walled in to collect rainwater.

Turning left onto the road, it will take about 20 minutes to walk the 1.5km to **Espongeiro**. Wait here for a lift back down to Ribeira Grande. *Alugueres* run all day, though sometimes it can be an hour's wait.

5 ESPONGEIRO–LIN D'CORV–JOÃO AFONSO–CHÃ DE COELHO–FIGUEIRAL–COCULI

Distance: 10.5km; time: 3½ hours; difficulty: 3 (CW)

This hike involves a steep and spectacular descent into the head of João Afonso on a good, cobbled path. It can be shortened by getting transport to Coculi at Chã de Coelho. Get to the starting point by taking an *aluguer* along the Ribeira Grande–Porto Novo road as far as Espongeiro.

Standing on the main road from Ribeira Grande, take the turning at **Espongeiro**, known as the Lagoinha road. Walk for 1.5km until you reach **Lin d'Corv**, where there is a large area of hillside concreted over to collect rainwater. The path down João Afonso begins here. Be careful not to confuse it with the path to Chã de Pedra – the two paths meet at Lin d'Corv. It is important to pick up the right path, otherwise you will end up descending the wrong valley. Stand with your back to the tap at the bottom of the water catchment area, and then follow the path off to your right. The path will lead you down along the side of a low hill through a pine forest, and after about ten minutes you will see a cottage at the top of a small rise. Take a small turning down to the right about 15m before reaching the cottage.

After less than ten minutes you will reach a few houses at **Lombo de Pedra**. Pass through the settlement and, five minutes later, follow the white arrow painted on a rock to begin a series of zig-zags down the side of the mountain. From here, the path becomes dramatic, sometimes darting backwards and forwards, sometimes tracing down the knife edge of precipitous ridges, and sometimes carving across near-vertical slopes. After a vertiginous 35 minutes, you will pass a tapstand where clear water runs from the mountains above, and will be looking out over the village of **Fajã dos Cumes**.

Continuing the descent, another 30 minutes will bring you to the small village of **Caibros** (not to be confused with the *ribeira* of Caibros) and another 35 minutes beyond that, to **Chã de Coelho**. Passing through here and descending steeply for ten minutes will bring you to the valley floor in João Afonso. From the point where you hit the valley floor, it will take about an hour to reach **Coculi**.

6 ÁGUA DAS CALDEIRAS–RIBEIRA DE TORRE–RIBEIRA GRANDE
Distance: 10km; time: 4 hours; difficulty: 2 (AI)
Torre is the most beautiful *ribeira* of them all: a descent from empty, misty pine forest through the clouds, down a steep rocky path with just the jagged peaks and the more adventurous birds for company, and finally through greenery and cultivation to sea level. Navigation is easy but the path is steep. To get to the start of the walk take an *aluguer* along the old Ribeira Grande–Porto Novo road to **Água das Caldeiras**. From Ribeira Grande this takes 40 minutes, and you should disembark at the first sign for the village on the right-hand side of the road. (To do this walk the other way round, leave Ribeira Grande on the Porto Novo road, passing the petrol station, and then the hospital, on the right. Torre is the great *ribeira* on the left.)

Take the cobbled road to the left, fenced off with a chain, and follow it uphill for ten minutes enjoying the sharp coolness. Then take a wide stone track to the left and descend, always through forest. Pine trees were chosen for reforestation because their needles comb water from the clouds which drips down and moistens the soil.

After another ten minutes there's a clearing. A footpath leads out of the far end. Take it and emerge at a vista of high craggy mountains dropping way below to patches of vivid green, tiny houses and, even this high, the sounds of barking dogs and voices echoing towards you. Two *ribeiras* lie before you – Torre is to the left and after 15 minutes of steep descent you realise you are firmly destined for it as you see the teeth-like crags that now separate you from next-door Paúl. The view is infinitely interesting: crazy terraces inserted into crevices; intriguing local paths disappearing into rock faces.

After 1½ hours you reach the first cultivation. After this, just continue downwards, through coffee and banana crops and past shallow shelving built to capture water. Sometimes the path follows a terrace – there are lots of people around by now so just ask for the footpath (*caminho*).

Ahead is the strange pinnacle of Torre, a rock that has defied the forces of wind and water to rise out of the middle of the *ribeira*. As you descend you pass the extraordinary hamlet of **Raso Curto**, built on a ridge just wide enough for a row of one-room-thick houses and a footpath. Two-and-a-half hours from the beginning, the path meets **Chu Chu** village, green and damp, with dark cliffs on either side. It's another 1½ hours, or 6km, to **Ribeira Grande** along the road track down the *ribeira*. If you are lucky the *grogue* distillery 20 minutes down the road on the left will be in operation. Ten minutes before the end of the walk there is a glimpse of the sea through the crack in the mountains.

7 ILA DAS POMBAS–RIBEIRA DO PAÚL–EITO–PASSAGEM–COVA DE PAÚL
Distance: 9km; time: 4½ hours; difficulty: 3 (AI)
This is many people's favourite, in a huge, abundantly green valley cloistered among vast, cathedral-like cliff walls. It is so large that there are many villages on the way up, crammed onto every available ledge. Laughter, barks, clucks, arguments,

drunkenness, car horns and radios resound through the valley so that even when you have left them below, and the clouds have intervened, their sounds pursue you into the peaks.

The starting point is **Cidade das Pombas** but you can cut over 1½ hours (and a lot of sweating) from this walk by taking transport up the *ribeira* – the road persists as far as Cabo de Ribeira. Perhaps a good compromise is to take transport beyond Eito as far as the drop-off point for Casa das Ilhas and pick up the hike from there.

From Pombas turn inland at the stadium to enter the valley. Reaching an aqueduct after ten minutes, take the road up to the right, and leave the valley below, filled with cornfields and deep green trees. The road ascends through various villages including **Eito**, the biggest. Some 2.5km after entering the valley, and less than 1km after leaving Eito, the road bends back sharply to the right. Soon after this you will see a little sign, just after a shop, on the wall on the left, to the guesthouse Casa das Ilhas. Take this path, which leads you on a glorious route and cuts out a loop of the road.

You will pass Casa das Ilhas after about 15 minutes of steep ascent. Keep going, the only navigational challenge being a T-junction of paths with a wall in front of you, at which you turn left. The path continues, up and down, and eventually broadens into a road which takes you past flowing water, pools and verdant planting, up through Passagem. Half an hour after leaving Casa das Ilhas, you will reach the main road. Turn left to continue up the valley.

In **Passagem** there is a swimming pool newly filled with water every day during July and August (otherwise, with a day's notice, they'll refill it for you).

Keep going, through the villages of **Chã João Vaz** and **Chã Manuel dos Santos**. There are one or two places to stop for a drink (see listing on page 297). A couple of hours later you will finally leave the most vertiginous local house behind and follow the finely crafted cobbled path with its drystone walling, gazing upwards to wonder how it can possibly take you through the mountains above. Four hours from the start (assuming no stops), your lonely world of cold and cloud will push you over the top of the ridge and you will be gazing down into a fertile volcano crater filled with crops, orange trees, tomatoes and a few houses. Your exit from the crater is on the opposite side; reach it by following a stumbling path down to the right and into the crater, and then a track across it and out onto the road where, if you walk for a few seconds to the left, you find the final spectacle of the walk – the southern slopes of Santo Antão, Porto Novo and São Vicente beyond. Wait here for a lift back to town.

To go down the *ribeira* instead of up, take a lift along the main island road as far as **Cova**, which lies on the eastern side of the road and has two entrances – you want the one nearer to Ribeira Grande. As you enter Cova you will see the path you want leading up and out of the crater on the other side. Once you are on it, it's the same path down to the coast road.

8 PENEDO–RIBEIRA DO PENEDO–ESTÂNCIA DE PEDRA–PICO DA CRUZ–COVA
Distance: 14km; time: 5 hours 40 minutes; difficulty: 3 (CW)
Not for the unfit or faint-hearted, this long hike demands a high degree of fitness and takes you from sea level up to 1,600m in little more than 7km. After that, it is a less demanding one-hour walk to the main road.

Reach the starting point by taking an *aluguer* along the coast road as far as the little village of **Penedo**, which lies at the mouth of the *ribeira* of the same name.

You strike up the *ribeira* on foot and the climb begins almost immediately, weaving amongst sugarcane plantations and the scattered houses. Follow the path up to the head of the valley and round to where it begins a tortuous zig-zagging ascent up an impossibly steep mountain face. If, as you pause for breath, you look back towards the coast, you will see the smaller Ribeira de Janela running parallel to Ribeira do Penedo, and slightly to the north.

There are small paths that lead off to the right and left but, sticking to the main path, you emerge on a narrow shoulder about two hours after setting out from Penedo. As you continue to ascend, it turns into a narrow ridge with staggering views first down one side, then the other, and a fantastic panorama to the south, east and north. If it is a clear day, **Pico da Cruz** can be seen ahead.

Even at this height (800m), the vegetation has changed – it is much greener here than on the ridges that lead, like dry ribs, to either side. Higher up it becomes cold and alpine with a sharp, resinous smell among the trees.

Along the ridge there are several houses. People have erected frames stretched across with gauze to allow the mist that boils over from the *ribeira* below to condense. After 1½ hours of walking along the ridge, you pass one of these frames and, at the same point, see the cobbled main road that snakes up from the valley towards the Pico. The road is slightly down to your left. Keep to the path, and, after 15 minutes, you join the road, and emerge, after another 40 minutes of steep

LAST CHANCE TO SEE... THE CAPE VERDE RED KITE

When researchers travelled round the archipelago searching for the black kite (*Milvus migrans*) and the Cape Verde red kite (*Milvus milvus fasciicauda*) in 1996–97, they were startled to find fewer than ten of each across the whole of Cape Verde.

The black kite can be found elsewhere – it is a very successful African and European species, and Cape Verde is its westernmost outpost. But the Cape Verde red kite can be found only on Cape Verde (it may be a subspecies of the red kite or an endemic species in its own right).

Scientists returned in 2000 to search again for kites. As birds go, they are quite easy to spot because they soar away from the ground. After two months roaming the cobbled paths and waiting around potential feeding grounds, they produced their verdict: on Cape Verde there remain just one black kite and two Cape Verde red kites.

The red kites were seen on Santo Antão and the black kite was spotted on Boavista. The researchers, Sabine Hille and Jean-Marc Thiollay, say that this means they are 'technically extinct'. Indeed, they are now listed as such on the website of Birdlife International (*www.birdlife.org*).

No-one is sure why the raptors have disappeared. It may partly be persecution – they are known to be chicken thieves and so humans pelt them with stones. They eat rats and mice that, these days, have probably been poisoned as part of pest control. Finally, the days are over when goats roamed freely through the plains, leaving the odd goat carcass for raptors to feed on. Now livestock and vegetation are so precious that goats are kept penned up.

The researchers want to round up the two remaining Cape Verde red kites, plus any they have missed, and do a captive breeding programme to enhance their numbers. They would then release them and keep them alive through feeding stations and through a campaign to persuade the local people that raptors do a good job clearing fields of pests.

Santo Antão   HIKES

10

The bases of many of the *ribeiras* provide flat walks with mighty views up the canyons. The best such walk is up Ribeira de Torre as far as Chu Chu (see page 315). Ribeira Grande provides a less interesting flat walk. All the *ribeiras* can be ascended quite far by vehicle, at which point you can walk back downhill. Ribeira do Paúl would be a particularly dramatic venue for this option. Finally, it is worth travelling to Cova de Paúl and wandering around the crater (see page 290).

hairpins, at a small group of houses in the shadow of the summit. Turn right on the road to Paúl past the old, white-painted house. Directly behind the house follow the very rough path which cuts up to the right. It's a 15-minute walk to the summit.

Retracing your steps from the summit to the small settlement, rejoin the road you arrived on and follow it straight on towards **Cova** (crater) and **Água das Caldeiras**. Following this road as it gently descends you will get your first glimpse of the crater about 45 minutes after leaving the summit. Ten minutes later you arrive at a crossroads. This is a good place to wait for a lift, or an *aluguer* back to either Porto Novo or Ribeira Grande.

11

São Nicolau

> Mother dear
> I wanted to say my prayer
> but I cannot:
> my prayer sleeps
> in my eyes, which cry for your grief
> of wanting to nourish us but being unable to do so.
> Baltasar Lopes, born in São Nicolau, quoted in *Fire: Six Writers from Azores, Madeira and Cape Verde* edited by Donald Burness (Three Continents Press, 1977)

It was in the shady valley of Ribeira Brava in São Nicolau and along the civilised cobbled streets of its town that the seeds of Cape Verdean awareness were planted towards the end of the 19th century. São Nicolau was for over 50 years the intellectual centre of the archipelago. Yet by 1931, its educational buildings had closed and the scholars had vanished to neighbouring São Vicente. Now Ribeira Brava, the capital, has an air of quiet dignity like a university town in the holidays. For all the island's beauty, it receives just 0.6% of Cape Verde's tourists and its population is declining. It is a victim, as Maio has been, of being the neighbour of a busy centre of commerce. But this makes São Nicolau a joy to visit. The *vila* is pretty and quiet and there are several outstanding walks in the mountains, affording the visitor the opportunity to get close to village life.

HIGHLIGHTS AND LOWLIGHTS

This island has a little bit of everything the other islands have: a pretty main town with colonial architecture; long, deserted beaches; villages frozen in time; dramatic cliffside roads; and verdant mountains. Go for beautiful walks almost undisturbed by other tourists. Go for fishing: the island's waters are famed for their blue marlin. Go to enjoy the daily routines of the local people, maybe joining them in one of their festivals where you may be a focus of their friendly curiosity. If you are not a hiker, you can still access some of São Nicolau's beauty by road though you will not be able to penetrate the Monte Gordo Natural Park.

It is thought that the diving and surfing potential is high, but it is mostly undiscovered and there are few facilities at the time of writing. There are some accessible beaches but it is not a luxury beach destination (there are no resort or high-end hotels). The coast offers other joys such as rocky, wave-lashed dramas and the odd *lagoa* suitable for swimming. Culturally, São Nicolau's interesting history has not yet been gathered together for presentation to the visitor: there are no museums.

SUGGESTED ITINERARY AND NUMBER OF DAYS For hikers, the opening of the Monte Gordo Natural Park, with its facilitation of guiding and advice, has raised

11

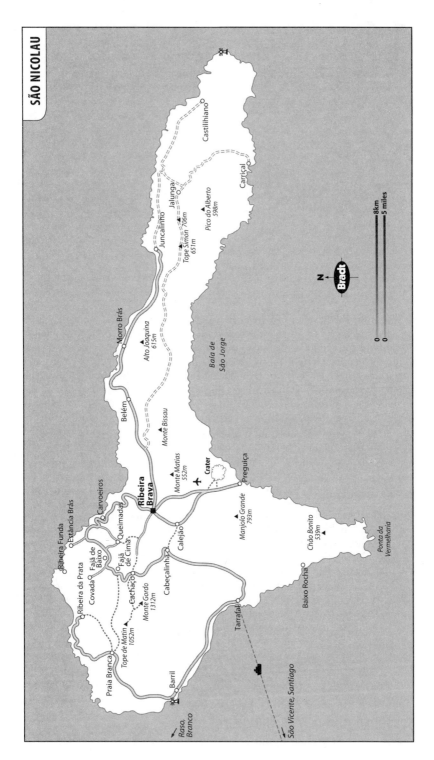

Castilhiano

Carriçal

Jalunga

Juncalinho

Pico do Alberto 598m

Tope Simón 706m
651m

Alto Joaquina 615m

Morro Brás

Baía de São Jorge

Belém

Monte Bissau

Monte Matias 552m

Crater

Preguiça

Ribeira Brava

Carvoeiros

Estância Brás

Ribeira Funda

Queimadas

Fajã de Cima

Calejão

Manjolo Grande 793m

Chão Bonito 539m

Fajã de Baixo

Covada

Ribeira da Prata

Cabeçalinho

Cachaço

Monte Gordo 1312m

Tope de Matin 1052m

Baixo Rocha

Ponta da Vermelharia

Praia Branca

Tarrafal

São Vicente, Santiago

Barril

Raso, Branco

N

Bradt

0   8km
0   5 miles

all sorts of interesting possibilities for hiking across the centre of the island over several days. One could easily fill two or three full days with hiking, with perhaps a day of sightseeing in between. If you are a really committed hiker, then you could comfortably spend a lot longer here. If you are not a hiker you could still fill two full days with perhaps a trip to Juncalinho's *lagoa*, and a drive through the island between Ribeira Brava and Ribeira da Prata, with many stops on the way.

BACKGROUND INFORMATION

HISTORY With a fertile hinterland and several almost permanent streams, São Nicolau was able to produce more agriculturally than the impoverished flat islands. It also has the widest bay of the archipelago, formed by the island's strange long finger that stretches to the east and affords a safe anchorage. Yet São Nicolau has always been overshadowed by others and so, apart from the brief flourishing of its seminary a century ago, it was never an island of importance.

It was discovered, along with the other windward islands, in 1461 – the date was probably St Nicholas's Day, 6 December. Families from Madeira and their Guinean slaves came to settle in the early 1500s. But the island was mountainous and inaccessible – indeed its lush interior is completely hidden from the outside – and so its **productive agriculture and livestock potential** did not attract more settlers until the 1600s. Even then, when the English sailor Dampier visited in 1683, he reported only 100 families on the island. He described the green interior, the vineyards producing good-quality wine, the abundance of wood and the great number of donkeys and goats. Even by 1731, there were only 260 inhabitants.

One great disadvantage of São Nicolau was the ease with which marauders could attack. Dutch, English and French pirates plagued the people, even after they retreated from their coastal settlement to Ribeira Brava, inland. It was not until a fortress was built in 1818 that security and a soaring population came to the island.

In 1805, the wealthy landowner who governed the island, José António Dias, had a son, Júlio José. He was a brilliant student but returned from his medical studies abroad to spend his life as a philanthropist on São Nicolau. Perhaps his greatest legacy came from his decision to move out of his large house in Ribeira Brava in 1866 and offer it to the three canons, three priests and three students who had arrived from Portugal to found a **seminary** on Cape Verde. This prevented them leaving for Santo Antão, having despaired of finding a building on São Nicolau.

The school attached to the seminary flourished, offering the same subjects as high schools in Portugal. Suddenly the brightest Cape Verdean children were able to learn subjects as varied as the classics, chemistry and political economy. This education groomed them for careers in either the Church or the Portuguese civil service. In this way Cape Verde became the centre for evangelisation of Portuguese west Africa.

The impact created by the generations that passed through this seminary should not be underestimated, for they spread abroad, used by the Portuguese as an interface between themselves and their west African territories. They were articulate and intelligent, wedded to the idea of Cape Verde being part of Portugal, but deeply concerned with the lot of their people. As teachers and administrators they had influence over the next generation, which took their ideas and moulded them into more radical form. The prime example of such a two-generation process was Juvenal Cabral, the seminary-educated teacher who fought for better conditions for Cape Verde and whose son was Amílcar Cabral, the leader of the revolution.

But the life of the seminary was all too brief. It was a victim of the difficult

11

relationship that emerged between the Catholic Church and the government in the democratic republic of Portugal after the Church was separated from the state in 1911. This separation led to the splitting of the seminary – its secondary school function was relocated to Mindelo.

The seminary closed in 1917, reopened in 1923, and shut for ever in 1931. Later, it was used to accommodate 200 political deportees from Portugal. The Bishop of Cape Verde, rumoured to be terrified by 'hordes of deported revolutionaries and anti-clericals', fled to São Vicente. All that remained was a highly educated peasant population. One visitor in the 1930s was astonished when a local boy, prompted by a reference in Creole to a rose, quoted: '*Rosa, vita tua diuturna non est.*' The 20th century brought desperate **droughts** to São Nicolau, in 1921, 1940 and the 1950s.

São Nicolau today Agriculture, and the port at Tarrafal, are the economic mainstays. Catching and canning tuna keeps the occupants of Tarrafal busy, though the second factory at the remote, eastern village of Carriçal is now closed. The island hopes to eventually develop ecotourism and beach tourism, though this has barely started.

GEOGRAPHY

At 343km², the island is mainly barren rock with a large semi-humid valley in its centre, cultivated with maize and beans on the higher slopes, and sugarcane and banana below. In the west is a range of mountains with the highest, Monte Gordo, reaching 1,312m. This peak is the meeting point of two ranges – one runs north–south and the other out to the northwest. The eastern finger of land is a long ridge of barren mountains. Between the central mountains and the western coast are stony plains. Desertification seems to have hit São Nicolau particularly hard – its orange groves and coffee plantations have gone and the old folk reminisce about verdant mountainsides that are now bare – in fact the lines of stone walls that used to divide fields can be traced impossibly high up the mountainsides. There is evidence of much reafforestation. The population is about 13,000.

NATURAL HISTORY

Flora There are 46 endemic species of plant in São Nicolau, of which 32 can be found in the Monte Gordo Natural Park. One of these, Macela do Gordo (*Nauplussmithii*), is native to Monte Gordo and 17 are on the list of endangered species for the island of São Nicolau.

The fairy-tale dragon tree (*Dracaena draco*), locally known as *dragoeiro*, is almost abundant on this island – this is about the only place in the archipelago where the

A CHANCE FIND

The endangered Cape Verde warbler (*Acrocephalus brevipennis*) was until recently thought to inhabit only Santiago. Then, in 1970, someone found a specimen of the bird stored at Centro de Zoologia, Lisbon. It was reported as having come from São Nicolau, so ornithologists decided to scour the island in the hope of finding some more. They were rewarded – by 1998, their surveys had identified eight territories in the northwest of the island although they believe the bird's long-term prospects there are poor. The bird is brown with a creamy throat, a long-pointed black beak and black feet. In São Nicolau it inhabits the forested areas of the park and nests in small, dense stands of cane (*Arundo donax*) along dry riverbeds.

Although there are 47 protected areas in Cape Verde, enshrined in law, all but Monte Gordo have an Achilles heel: their precise, mapped boundaries have not been legalised. This leaves them vulnerable. In Boavista, for example, there are several areas where land originally allocated for protection has been reallocated for tourism development instead.

In São Nicolau, however, the boundaries of its beautiful heart were officialised in 2007. Much work has been done and more is still underway to create a park that is pleasant for tourists and might enhance the prosperity of the people who live there.

The park occupies some 952ha in the northwest of the island, and includes the peak of Monte Gordo.

It's an important area ecologically because of its rich biodiversity. The unique conditions that have generated this interesting ecology set it apart, not just from the rest of the island but also from the rest of Cape Verde. At the heart of these differences is climate, which affects not just life in the area but also landscape. In the south and southeast there are humid and semi-humid regions. In the north and northwest it is arid.

A key aim of the park is to develop a thriving local economy predicated on conservation of the area: over 2,000 people live within the park boundaries. This is why a lot of thought has gone into training guides (who are salaried), and training local people to be useful to visitors, for example by making handicrafts. There is a good visitor centre where you can get information and purchase handicrafts made exclusively on the island.

For more information contact e pnmonte.gordo@hotmail.com, or see www.areasprotegidas.gov.cv, though the website is currently only in Portuguese. In Cachaço, you can get close to local life by booking a homestay, organised by the park office.

endangered species grows naturally. It can reach about 10m high and its flattened top and grey gnarled branches give the landscape the feel of an ancient world – it is said the trees can live for 1,000 years. The 'blood' of the dragon tree has been used in traditional medicines to relieve pain and is also used to colour *grogue*. The tree grows mainly on northeast-facing slopes at altitudes of between 500m and 900m, but the lazy way to see it at its finest is to walk up the path from the main road to the Monte Gordo Park office. Some fine specimens line the route. Conservationists are trying to use it more in reafforestation programmes. The dragon tree is an endemic species of Macaronesia – it grows in the Canary Islands and in Madeira, where it is also endangered.

Birds BirdLife International currently lists nine Important Bird Areas in Cape Verde, of which the central mountain range around Monte Gordo is one. This area, running roughly between Fajã de Baixo and Praia Branca, is an important breeding area for the Cape Verde petrel (*Pterodroma feae*); there were thought in 1998 to be about 30 pairs, making its status 'near-threatened'.

Other birds thought to frequent São Nicolau are the Cape Verde little shearwater (*Puffinus assimilis boydi*); the Cape Verde kite (*Milvus milvus fasciicauda*) – although there may now be none left; the Cape Verde buzzard (*Buteo 'buteo' bannermani*); the rare endemic Cape Verde peregrine (*Falco peregrinus madens*);

11

Festivals reflect the strong Cape Verdean tradition of music and dancing. The February Carnival, held at the same time as the famous São Vicente Carnival, is an exhilarating, exhausting three-day party (see box, page 325). New Year is also cause for big celebration, and there is a festival on 5 January. In April there is Pascoela, celebrated in Fajã – mass followed by games, horse races and processions. There are many festivals through the summer, including one lasting two days in Juncalinho, as well as São Pedro which is best seen in Ribeira Brava . Festival dates are as follows:

February (variable date)	Carnival
April (variable date)	Pascoela (Fajã)
13 April	Santo António (Preguiça)
Early May (variable date)	Nossa Sra do Monte (Cachaço)
24 June	São João (Praia Branca, with horse racing)
29 June	São Pedro (*vila* and Fajã Lompelado, with horse racing)
Sunday following 29 June	São Pedrinho (Prainha beach, near the *vila*)
August	Music festival (Praia da Telha)
September	Sweet Water festival (Ribeira Prata)
1st Sunday in October	Nossa Sra do Rosário (in the *vila*)
1st Sunday in December	São Francisco (Tarrafal)
6 December	Municipality Day

the spectacled warbler (*Sylvia conspicillata*); the blackcap (*Sylvia atricapilla*); and the endemic Cape Verde swift (*Apus alexandri*). For birds on Raso (such as the Cape Verde shearwater) see page 341.

HAZARDS Some of the walks in this chapter are steep, especially in and out of Ribeira Brava, and the descents can be hard on older knees, no matter how fit their owners are. We have indicated this in the text, but do heed local advice if you are concerned.

Swim in the *lagoas* only when the water is calm. Crime is almost unheard of, apart from the hunting of turtles.

GETTING THERE AND AWAY

BY AIR São Nicolau is served by TACV inter-island flights from São Vicente (via Sal) and Sal several times a week. In a land of dramatic scenery, the descent into São Nicolau is one of the best. As it nears land, the plane veers suddenly between a jagged ridge and a volcano cater. In winter, flights can be cancelled at short notice, due to high winds. The tiny airport (✆ *235 1313*) is a ten-minute drive from the main town.

From the airport to Ribeira Brava costs 200$ in an *aluguer*. You might be able to charter one as a taxi, which will cost 600$.

BY FERRY Currently the *Sal Rei* travels from São Nicolau (Tarrafal) to Santiago (around 13 hours), and from São Nicolau (Tarrafal) to São Vicente (about six hours) twice a week. It's much cheaper than the plane (3,500$ one-way – but it is not a comfortable boat so it is worth paying the extra 1,000$ for a reclining, padded seat). There is also the *Ribeira do Paul,* which plies its trade between Tarrafal and Sao Vicente and also Sal. This is a small boat and is also uncomfortable. Some cargo boats also take a limited number of passengers from Tarrafal to São Vicente. You can get more information about ferries from the agencies in Praia, or ask at the Praia d'Tedja agency (\ *236 1155*) in Tarrafal. Those in the know question the seaworthiness of some of these vessels and the schedules are unreliable.

BY YACHT The best anchorage is at the harbour of Tarrafal, and it's where you report to the marine police. There's no marina and there are no buoys. Should there be northeast winds rushing down the ravines towards you, it can be impossible to shuttle to land. There's also Preguiça – for a long time São Nicolau's main harbour – which is more exposed. Carriçal is a tiny, remote village with a pretty bay and shelter from the northeast winds. Anchor outside the cove.

GETTING AROUND

BY PUBLIC TRANSPORT *Alugueres* ply the road between the main square in Ribeira Brava and Tarrafal (50 minutes; 250$). They travel intermittently all day, but are more frequent leaving Tarrafal before 08.30 and leaving Ribeira Brava at 11.00–12.00. Near the check-in time for plane arrivals you'll find *alugueres* destined for the airport waiting in Ribeira Brava's square.

Alugueres also travel along the eastern ridge as far as Juncalinho (200$) and, very infrequently, on to Carriçal (700$). They go from Tarrafal north up the coast as far

---

SÃO NICOLAU'S CARNIVAL

If you ever catch yourself wondering how people on this quiet island entertain themselves then here is the answer: Carnival. It may last just three days but arguably the other 362 in the year are spent preparing for it.

There is the music, for a start. Songs are written specially for the festival, dispersed, learned and rehearsed. But that's nothing compared with the costumes. The Carnival King's and Queen's outfits cost around 100,000$ (€1,000) each to produce – and they look correspondingly spectacular. Anyone who wants to have a costume made, dance in the procession for all three days and get into the sponsored parties must pay 7,000$. The costumes are designed according to the theme of the year. Fittings are conducted blindfold so that the wearer has no idea what he or she is dressed as until the big day.

By the first day of the festival the island has divided into two rival groups who spend four or five hours dancing and singing their way along different routes into the main square. Festivities continue into the next morning – the two rival, post-procession parties don't begin until around 03.00. After sleeping until mid-afternoon, the second day of festivities begins: pretty much a repeat of the first. Then there is a day of rest. On the third day of the festival (Fat Tuesday), many onlookers emerge in their own costumes. Even outside Carnival times, the evidence of this giant party is there to be seen: you may suddenly be confronted by the figurine of a full-sized, papier-mâché elephant, starfish or even Donald Duck, abandoned in someone's garden – relics of the previous year's festivities. After all the work in creating them, it is sometimes too painful to destroy them.

11

as Ribeira da Prata. These follow the principle: into town in the early morning, out of town around lunchtime. Drivers are very keen for tourists to hire them as taxis, at roughly ten times the price. To avoid this, hang around nonchalantly until you are part of a group rather than approaching an empty minibus or truck, or simply insist that you will only travel *colectivo*. A new road has made travelling to Tarrafal much easier, although heavy rain can cause landslides in the wet season.

BY TAXI Taxis are mostly in the form of chartered *hiaces*: Ribeira Brava to Fajã 1,000$; to Tarrafal 2,000$; to Preguiça 800$. A day's hire might be 8,000$.

BY CAR To reach outlying places accessed by dirt tracks, it is best to enquire about a jeep and driver from the *aluguer* drivers or at the town hall. A day's hire will cost around 6,500$ without driver and a 4x4 is strongly recommended.

Monte Gordo Rent a Car Ribeira Brava \235 1280; m 992 8877; e montegordorentacar@ gmail.com. Based in an office upstairs in the Municipal Market.

Agência e Transporte Santos &

Santos Ribeira Brava; \235 1830; e fsantos57@ hotmail.com

Rotcha Scribida Tarrafal \236 1804; e rotchascribida1@hotmail.com

BY BOAT A fishing boat can take you from Preguiça to Carriçal and from Carriçal to visit caves down the coast, though you may have to bargain hard to keep the cost under 10,000$ for the two-hour journey.

WHERE TO STAY

The two main centres are Ribeira Brava (*vila*) and Tarrafal. Hikers tend to stay in Ribeira Brava and anglers in Tarrafal. There is a modest guesthouse in Preguiça and a decent one in Juncalinho.

ACTIVITIES

EXCURSIONS

Agência e Transporte Santos & Santos Ribeira Brava; \235 1830; e fsantos57@hotmail.com. Organises trips & offers car hire with or without driver.

Guides There are a few knowledgeable *aluguer* drivers on the island who speak English, can give advice on major hikes, can drive you here & there & be general fixers. 2 recommended guides are Paulinho (\235 2800; m 996 6191) & Toi d'Armanda, who does jeep excursions (\236 1804; m 994 5146; e toilopescv@gmail.com).

HIKING Hiking and fishing are the two big attractions of São Nicolau. Some walks are described below (see page 338). The mixture of verdant agricultural land, vertiginous *ribeiras*, craggy peaks and dry, arid landscapes all in such an unfrequented place is what makes São Nicolau so special. By far the most beautiful walks are in the mountainous interior, though we include one or two others as well. The walks can be divided, roughly, into two: those that are based on several steep and beautiful paths in and out of the *vila*; and those that lie west of the main road that runs through Fajã and Cachaço. Since this road runs in a horseshoe shape through the centre of the walking areas, you can alter some walks to suit: you can use local transport to shorten walks or to enable you to walk only downhill or only uphill – or you can sandwich several walks together.

The **Monte Gordo Natural Park** (see box, page 323) encompasses many good walks and its office, Casa do Ambiente, can be found in Cachaço (✆ *237 1582;* e *pnmonte.gordo@hotmail.com*). It is a white building about 200m uphill along a track from the main road. Here you can obtain information about the park and about hikes, collect a map, pick up a trained multilingual guide (no fee, though there are proposals to introduce charges shortly), and look at the little endemics garden, where they are trying to grow every plant that is special to São Nicolau. You can also arrange for lunch to be prepared for you at a distant village (500$ per person approximately), discover where the campsites are, and buy some artisanal products. The office also sells water, plant- and bird-identification books, as well as postcards. There are plans to increase facilities for tourists here, including setting up a café and shop, but at the time of writing these seem to have stalled due to a lack of funding.

The principal hikes are signposted. Staff can find you homestay accommodation in Cachaço. The park regards itself as a resource for the whole of São Nicolau. They may therefore be of assistance with walks that lie outside their boundaries.

DIVING São Nicolau's diving potential is untapped at the moment and currently the only facilities are through the Farinha de Pau Guesthouse (see page 333).

FISHING The quality of the deep-sea fishing is high, particularly for blue marlin and barracuda. Chartering a boat for blue marlin fishing requires a bit of planning because they generally have to come across from another island. It is best to book beforehand. In the UK, for example, Cape Verde Travel advertises deep-sea fishing off São Nicolau for €500 a day. The proprietor of Pensão Tonecas (see page 332) offers blue marlin fishing for €700–1,000 per day for a minimum of five days and a maximum of six people, though four is optimal. The season runs from March to July.

BOAT TRIPS Local fishermen can be hired at Tarrafal. At Preguiça, you could take trips down the coast, for example to caves, beaches or to the village of Carriçal.

BIRDWATCHING Birdwatching rates along with fishing and hiking as one of São Nicolau's prime attractions. For some of the birds that can be found on the island see *Natural history*, page 323.

One of the key attractions, however, is no longer available. Visits to Ilhéu Raso, to view, amongst others, the Raso lark, were banned in a 2007 clampdown by the government and as the island forms part of a marine reserve, this situation is unlikely to change in the short term. It is now possible only to hire a fishing boat for around €70 per day and circle the island, and its companion Ilhéu Branco.

As a consolation, it is worth visiting scenic Carberinho (see page 341) where many of the migratory birds found on Raso also visit, and which some ornithologists believe should be given protected status.

TURTLES Loggerhead turtles nest here and are particularly abundant on beaches north and south of Tarrafal, Porto da Lapa and Carriçal. The town halls in both Tarrafal and Ribeira Brava have turtle-conservation programmes in which you may be able to participate, though no 'turtle walks' are offered at present. Ask around at the town hall or email SOS Tartarugas for further information (e *info@turtlesos.org*).

BEACHES If you wander the coast of São Nicolau you may make some discoveries of your own. There are beaches up the west coast from Tarrafal – for example

Praia Grande, Praia Branca and Praia Francês. Porto da Lapa has a beautiful beach which is accessible either by fishing boat from Preguiça or by hiking from south of Juncalinho (you will need a guide). There's also a beach at Carriçal and Praia Baixo is a pretty cove and important turtle-nesting beach a one-hour walk south of Tarrafal. Be warned, however: beaches can temporarily disappear in bad weather.

SURFING There can be good surf on the coast north of Tarrafal, for example around Ponta Cascalhão. The potential is there, the infrastructure is in its infancy, but surfing can be organised through the Farinha de Pau Guesthouse (see *Where to Stay*, page 333 for details).

HORSERIDING

São Nicolau has a proud horse-racing tradition and horses are brought from other islands for the big races of the year at the festivals of São João and São Pedro. Organised through the Monte Gordo Park office, horseriding through Casa do Ambiente (*see details page 327 or contact Daniel Cabral;* m *981 6516*) takes place mainly within the park, though other options may be possible. Horses are fully equipped, but there are no riding hats, etc, for riders. Expect to pay around €10 per hour.

SIGHTSEEING BY VEHICLE One of the most spectacular roads in Cape Verde is the road from Ribeira Brava to Tarrafal. This 26km route pulls out of Ribeira Brava and negotiates a series of deep creeks cut into the mountainside of the northern coast before turning inland to the lush Fajã Valley. Mountain ranges spike the right-hand side and you ascend gently through Fajã de Baixo (Lower Fajã) and Fajã de Cima (Upper Fajã), almost completely encircled by a ring of mountains. Then the road turns to the southwest and you enter the stony plains that lead down towards Tarrafal. After Tarrafal the land is flat and brown but it is worth following the odd signposted track down to the coast on the left to witness the beaches or the striking rock formations. Finally the road bends inland to Praia Branca and out in a semicircle, finishing in Ribeira da Prata. Many sights to see on the way are described below.

RIBEIRA BRAVA

This is a pretty town with houses of ochre, green and blue, and neat gardens blooming with plants and flowers. It is wedged into the steep sides of a *ribeira*, leading to a charming chaos of steep, interlocking streets in some parts of town. Narrow cobbled streets lead away from the large square which contains a bust of the town's philanthropist and an imposing cathedral visited by the old ladies of the town every day. They have first claim to the wooden benches in the square, by the way. Lining the streets are surprisingly well-stocked, old-fashioned shops in dim, shuttered interiors. The *ribeira* – green even in the dry season – towers above and cuts the town deeply in two, its narrow floor functioning as an extra road for much of the year, and an impromptu racetrack for horses during festivals. There is a charming statue of the town's famous poet, Baltasar Lopes da Silva, in the smaller square to the west of the main *praça*. Especially in low season, there are few restaurant options and only a couple of places to enjoy a drink in the sun.

WHERE TO STAY Accommodation is limited and sometimes booked up in high season, so book ahead. All listings are located on the map opposite.

🏠 **Bela Sombra** (20 rooms) 🗎235 1830; e fsantos57@hotmail.com; www.belasombra.com. The biggest in town and fairly new. Rooms are fine, some with AC, all with hot water. Corridors are a bit gloomy. Room facilities vary, as do prices, so ask to see what you're getting. Will organiuse car hire. **$$**

🏠 **Pensão Residencial Jardim** (10 rooms) 🗎235 1117/1950; e pensaoresidencialjardim@hotmail.com. A sparkling white *pensão* up the hill at the southern end of town with some old-world charm, a friendly, helpful owner & a small degree of eccentricity. A terrace offers a shady retreat from which to gaze down on the pastels of the town below & muse on *vila* life. All rooms have AC, TV private bathrooms with hot water. There are 2 mini apartments with kitchenettes & options for families via interconnecting doors. Internet available & there is a rooftop restaurant serving lunch & dinner. It's in a steep part of town, & access is along a 20m, uphill alleyway. French-spoken. **$$**

🏠 **Pensão Santo António** (15 rooms) 🗎235 2200; e mcdossantos@cvtelecom.cv. Just east of the main square gardens, this has a bright, fresh, new feel with large rooms, some of which overlook the square, & a shared living room with TV. Rooms have private bathrooms with hot water, AC, TV & some have a fridge. **$$**

✖ **WHERE TO EAT AND DRINK** Finding *anything* to eat here can at times seem a challenge, especially in low season. Having said that, fresh fish arrives daily from the coastal villages, so it's well worth finding. Order several hours beforehand if you want something other than the dish of the day. The São Nicolau speciality is *molho* or *modje* – goat meat, potatoes and onions with cornmeal and rice. In addition to the places listed below, there are a few rough-and-ready places on the road up to the old seminary. Fresh bread can be bought from the bakery on a little road off the post office square; vegetables are available from the municipal market in a new building on the street running down from the bank to the *ribeira*. Ask around in the market and someone will find someone who will sell you some fresh goat's cheese. All listings are located on the map to the right.

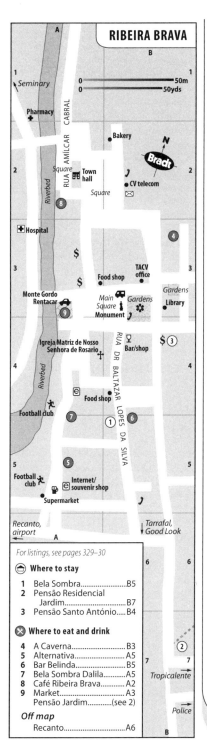

For listings, see pages 329–30

🏠 **Where to stay**
1 Bela Sombra..........................B5
2 Pensão Residencial
   Jardim.............................B7
3 Pensão Santo António.....B4

✖ **Where to eat and drink**
4 A Caverna............................B3
5 Alternativa..........................A5
6 Bar Belinda.........................B5
7 Bela Sombra Dalila............A5
8 Café Ribeira Brava.............A2
9 Market.................................A3
   Pensão Jardim............(see 2)

Off map
   Recanto................................A6

✗ **Recanto** 📞235 1689 Much-praised seafood restaurant. Just outside the *vila* on the road to Juncalinho, downhill on the right side of the road. Walkable but a taxi might be preferable, particularly if returning in the pitch dark with a belly full of wine. Advance ordering required. May have occasional live music at weekends. $$$$

✗ **Alternativa** In the south of town nearly opposite the petrol island. A pleasant little courtyard bar & restaurant. Good value. $$$

✗ **Bela Sombra Dalila** Down the narrow street that leaves the main square to the right of the cathedral, this serves good-value traditional plates of food such as *modje* & *cachupa*. Advance ordering required. $$$

✗ **A Caverna** Tiny entrance & dungeon-like corridor, leading up to smart dining room with elaborate, throne-like chairs. Belongs to the Pensão Santo António & standards are good. $$$

✗ **Pensão Jardim** ⏰ 07.30–22.00 daily; lunch when ordered, 19.00 onwards for dinner. Rooftop restaurant serving lunch & dinner, with a mostly traditional menu. Above the hotel of the same name. Lunch & dinner should be ordered in advance. $$$

🖵 **Market** Selling cheap pasteis & snacks, this café is located just inside the market building. $$

🖵 **Café Ribeira Brava** This bar has potential to be much better than it is. Outside tables are a good place for recovering from the heat of the day. It is beside the gardens of the *praça* opposite the old town hall. Occasional live music. $$

✗ **Bar Belinda** ⏰ lunch & dinner, popular with locals. Normally has a couple of good-value daily dishes. Covered courtyard & inside tables. $

ENTERTAINMENT AND NIGHTLIFE The population of Ribeira Brava is not generally sufficient to sustain the two Saturday nightclubs, so one is likely to swing while the other fades. Even the owners of the losing venue have been known to give up on a quiet night and go and party at the other one.

☆ **Clube de Ribeira Brava & Atletico** [329 A4 & A5] These 2 football clubs regularly hold parties. The first is almost opposite Restaurante Bar Bela Sombra Dalila, the other is further down the same road, opposite the petrol station.

☆ **Good Look** ⏰ Sat. It looks abandoned on the outside but is fully equipped inside. Follow the Tarrafal road off the map & it is about 50m up, on the left.

☆ **Praça** [329 B3] On Sat & Sun nights the town becomes very lively as people go to the *praça* (the gardens in front of the old town hall) to hang out & listen to a DJ or traditional music. In the old-fashioned way rarely seen on other islands any more, entire families arrive to chat, dance, play & socialise – young & old mixing & everyone keeps an eye out for everyone else's kids – a lively crowd.

☆ **Tropicalente** ⏰ Sat. In Chãzinha, out beyond Residencial Jardim. Open only occasionally.

OTHER PRACTICALITIES
Airlines
[329 B3] TACV 📞*235 1161*; ⏰ *08.00–12.30 & 14.30–18.00 Mon–Fri*) At the top of the central square. Agência Santos & Santos, for internal and international airlines.

Bank
BCN and BCA [both 329 A3], plus Caixa Economica [329 B4] all just off the main square and all with ATMs (⏰ *08.00–15.00 Mon–Fri*).

Hospital
[329 A3] 📞*235 1130*) A vast building on the hill past the Municipal Market and across the ribeira.

Internet
[329 A5] Cybercafé in the southern square that houses the petrol station; also on Rua Dr Baltazar Lopes da Silva. Free Wi-Fi in the main *praça*.

Pharmacy
[329 A1] Cross the *ribeira* from the old town hall, turn right and it's on the left.

Police
[329 B7] 📞*235 1152*) On the airport side of town, out beyond Pensao Jardim.

Post office
[329 B2] (⏰ *08.00–16.00 Mon–Fri*) Opposite the

back of the town hall.

Shopping

There's a mini supermarket on the road going north that has the BCA Bank on its corner. The internet shop on Rua Dr Baltazar Lopes da Silva sells Cape Verdean souvenirs and music. A few Chinese shops close to the square make up the rest of the options.

Tourist information

None. Try your accommodation choice or, for hiking, go up to the Monte Gordo park office.

WHAT TO SEE AND DO Igreja Matriz de Nossa Senhora do Rosário, on the main square, was built in the 1700s, and rebuilt between 1891 and 1898 to become the cathedral: the bishopric was in São Nicolau between 1866 and 1940. In the main square is a bust of Dr Júlio José Dias and also the library, in the building that was originally the birthplace of José Lopes de Silva, one of Cape Verde's major poets.

The **seminary**, the Liceu de São Nicolau, is on Rua Seminário, a little way up the road away from the pharmacy, on the right. You can ask the priest's permission to explore its rambling buildings and courtyards and one of the knowledgeable priests may explain some of the history. Part of it is under renovation, for use as a cultural venue, and further renovations are planned. Eventually, it could be restored to its former glory.

AROUND RIBEIRA BRAVA

FAJÃ DE BAIXO AND FAJÃ DE CIMA At the heart of the lush interior of São Nicolau, these villages have nothing specific to offer except some pleasant meandering.

CACHAÇO Here can be found more beauty, the office for the natural park, two viewpoints (*miradouros*) and two small shops, one of which sells a particularly fine goat's cheese: mild, slippery and with a salty crust.

Just down from the road to the park office is a tiny new Museu da Aguá (Museum of Water) which highlights the water deficiency problems facing Cape Verde. Entry is free, and displays – though somewhat limited – are in English as well as Portuguese.

Cachaço is the confluence of the main road, the track up into the natural park and two hiking paths, one from Fajã de Baixo and one from Ribeira Brava.

There's a small track to a viewpoint at the little church, Senhora do Monte. There's also another designated viewpoint just over 0.5km south down the main road, on the left.

Where to stay and eat Homestays can be organised through the park office (see page 327) including Pensão Arlinda ($) which has two rooms. Breakfast is included and other meals can be arranged.

TARRAFAL

This impoverished port town lies at the base of stony, barren hills that betray little about São Nicolau's lush interior. The town feels parched and can reach 40°C in the summer. It is strung out along a very long coastal road. At the southern end of this road is the port. A block inland from the port is the long, main square. Plans to turn Tarrafal into a marina have not progressed to date, though there is still talk of transforming not just the harbour but also the main street.

11

🏠 WHERE TO STAY

🏠 **Casa Aquário** (6 rooms) Alto Calheta; ✆236 1099; e info@casa-aquario.nl; www.casa-aquario.nl. Down in the south of town, by the beach, this is a Dutch-owned establishment with very simple rooms. The owner, Henny Kusters, prides himself on his cuisine & dining is communal. Excursions can be arranged, some to remote areas. HB accommodation only. Mixed reviews. **$$$**

🏠 **Pensão Tonecas** (12 rooms) ✆236 1040; e tonecas1959@hotmail.com. Large, en-suite rooms, some with AC & all with hot water. Restaurant upstairs for guests only. **$$$**

🏠 **Residencial Alice** (18 rooms) ✆236 1187. On the coast road, north of the port, this family-run place has been an institution in Tarrafal for over 20 years. Lots of old-world charm. Most rooms have a balcony with a view of the sea, & most have AC, private bathroom & hot water. Roof terrace. **$$**

🏠 **Residencial Natur** (7 rooms) ✆236 1178. Going north along the coast road, turn right just before the football pitch & then left – the hotel is on your right. Spacious, bright & simple, if a bit clinical, rooms have fans & private bathrooms with hot water. Hotel has tiled floors & a roof terrace. Great views both inland & seaward. B/fast available, but not included. **$**

✗ WHERE TO EAT AND DRINK

✗ **Buena Vida** ◷ 18.00–'the end' daily. At the southern tip of the harbour opposite the old processing factory. Italian food with a Spanish influence, pizza, tiramisu & ice cream. **$$$**

✗ **Casa de Pasto Alice** (see Residencial Alice; listing above) Thought by many to be the best eatery in Tarrafal, this is like a large living room in which guests feel like members of the extended family. Serves traditional foods. There is no obligation to order in advance but food other than the dish of the day may be slow to materialise. **$$$**

✗ **Golfinho** Opposite Pensão Tonecas. Standard fare, good-value dishes of the day. Shady & breezy terrace, pub-like interior. **$$$**

✗ **Felicidade** ◷ lunch & dinner daily. In the southeast of town, this is a good place for cheap local eats. Cuttlefish & octopus are the specialities. **$$**

ENTERTAINMENT AND NIGHTLIFE Tarrafal has a livelier nightlife than Ribeira Brava, with the **Disco Paradise** and **Bar-Restaurante Esplanada** (low blue building facing the water), the main disco in town, popular on Fridays and Saturday nights.

OTHER PRACTICALITIES
Bank
Caixa Economica and BCA, both with ATMs, both near the central mini-roundabout (◷ 08.00–15.00 Mon–Fri).

Ferries
Information and tickets available from agency Praia d'Tedja (✆ 236 1155) up near the *camara* building.

Hospital
(✆236 1130).

Internet
Follow the road inland from Pensão Tonecas. Cyberhebr@ico, further inland past Dorado Edileila.

Police
(✆236 1132).

Post office
(◷ 08.00–16.00 Mon–Fri) At the top of the main square.

WHAT TO SEE AND DO
Beaches A pretty and busy little beach, **Praia de Tedj**a is located just south of town. **Praia de Baixo Rocha** is a 1½-hour walk south of Tarrafal. A beautiful cove and an important place for nesting turtles – the sticks you will see in the summer are marking nests in the hope that people won't inadvertently destroy the eggs. It's a

lonely walk over a landscape like burnt fudge with dramatic views of the mountains beyond. Cross the town's southern cove (Praia de Tedge) and find the track leading south from it. You pass a yellow building on the left and a series of dumps as well as, perhaps, stone-breakers. You are making for a cove that lies between the furthest headland you can see and the second-furthest – a much lower, smaller headland. The trick is to avoid all the bulges of tiny headlands in between you and the cove and stick to the main track. The route is possible in a 4x4 or can be done in a fisherman's boat for around 7,000$.

NORTH OF TARRAFAL

The road northwest of Tarrafal follows fairly close to the shoreline until Barril, after which it cuts inland to Praia Branca, heads north out towards the coast again and then bends east, finishing in Ribeira da Prata. Along the coastal part of this road are several beautiful parts of coastline, including beaches (Ponta Cascalhão, Praia Grande (signposted) and Praia da Francês), and Caberinha with its spectacular rock formations.

PRAIA DA FRANCÊS A pleasant white-sand beach just south of Barril. It's signposted, and also rumoured to be a great surfing spot.

PRAIA BRANCA An attractive town on the hillside, said to be the birthplace of Cape Verde's iconic *sodade* music (see page 37), which has several quaint shops, bars, cafés and a new accommodation and activities option.

Where to stay and eat

Farinha de Pau Guesthouse
(6 bungalows) m 594 8630; e contact@ farinadepau.com; www.farinhadepau. com. Signposted from the main road, a new establishment with a variety of activities on offer. Bungalows all have fireplaces, private bathrooms with hot water. Restaurant, café bar.

FB &HB available. Airport transfers (extra cost), public transport available from airport. Activities include hiking, biking, surfing, fishing, snorkelling, introductions to Cape Verde cuisine, music, dance & Creole language. Island tours, English- and French-speaking guides. **$$$**

RIBEIRA DA PRATA Driving up from Praia Branca, the road ends in a bottleneck, where you have to leave your car and walk up cobbled streets to this beautiful scenic village – well worth the effort. Ribeira da Prata is an attractive place that will give you the feeling of having stepped back in time.

People visit mainly in order to see Rocha Scribida, the 'writing on the rock'. Ask for directions at the top of the village: it is a two-minute scramble up the other side of the *ribeira*. There you will see a stratum of rock where localised erosion has

São Nicolau   NORTH OF TARRAFAL

11

revealed some intricate darker lines – or, if you must, rock that bears words written by an ancient people who knew the island long before the Portuguese. Historians have plumped for the former explanation, some locals prefer the latter.

There is infrequent public transport between Tarrafal and Ribeira da Prata (250$ one-way). There are several shops selling water, biscuits, bread and *grogue*.

CABERINHA/PONTA BROUCO After Barril, turn left off the road and follow the signposted but dusty and desolate track over the rocks, stopping short of the coast. This is a stretch of dramatic rock formations and undulating expanses of smooth black rock on which to sit and gaze at the crashing waves and abundant white foam. There are some steps carved into sandy rock down to the drama below. To the right of them is a deep inlet with stunning rock formations (be careful walking its circumference on the high side as there is a sharp overhang). Well worth detouring off the main road for this experience. If, after descending the steps, you head south, you will find after a few minutes a little *lagoa* in which you can swim when the weather is calm.

SOUTH OF RIBEIRA BRAVA

PREGUIÇA From the road Preguiça does not look much – a few half-built houses, a football pitch, a signpost. The bulk of the village is out of sight, clinging to the steep slope above the shoreline. A precipitous cobbled street winds down amongst colourful houses past an old church, to a crumbling pier where sizeable boats used to berth with cargo from Mindelo. But Preguiça is a bit like the roulette player who puts everything on black only to see the ball come up on red: after independence, politicians favoured then tiny Tarrafal as the port of choice and as its western neighbour prospered, so Preguiça declined in importance. It now receives no cargo, and has to content itself with fish. To the right of the pier you can swim in the shingly bay where the bright fishing boats are drawn up on the beach. Fishermen used to dive from boats to catch lobsters by hand at a depth of 10–15m. They wore masks and breathed compressed air piped from the surface, allowing them to stay down for up to an hour at a time.

On the other side of the village is the Portuguese fort, built in the early 1800s, with several cannons. The two memorials (one erected by the Portuguese, the other by the Cape Verdeans) commemorate the voyage of Pedro Álvares Cabral, who in 1500 passed this point on his way to discovering the coast of Brazil.

Attempts by the Ribeira Brava town hall to protect turtles have been less successful in Preguiça than elsewhere. Those involved in the programme believe that much of the meat makes its way, either by boat or plane, to Praia, where it attracts a high price.

Getting there The town is a bit run-down and there's not too much to do there but it is a short journey if you have a spare couple of hours. To get there, take an *aluguer* from the main square in the *vila* – they leave intermittently (200$), or you can just walk and hitchhike the 8km. Before dark you will find *colectivo* transport back quite easily, though a chartered vehicle will cost 800$.

⌂ Where to stay and eat

⌂ **Maria do Ceu** (3 rooms) ☎235 1582; m 592 1870. The large pink house on the bend near the top of the village. Large rooms, simple but just about adequate; 2 have a good standard of en-suite bathroom though no hot water. Roof terrace

with some shade, giving super views of the ocean. The owner speaks Italian but no English. **$**

⌂ **Homestays** A small number of homes take paying guests. For example, the bright-blue house across the way from Maria's has rooms to rent with

a kitchen. Enquiries through Maria, above. **$**
🏠 **Maria do Ceu** 📞 235 1582; **m** 592 1870.
Maria's dining room is thought by some to present
the best food in São Nicolau, possibly because of
the influence of her 8 years in Italy. Because of this,
advance booking is essential. **$$**

What to see and do   Fishing with local fishermen; boat trips up and down the coast
to isolated beaches such as Porta da Lapa (a black-sand beach popular with turtles); or
to Carriçal; hanging out: some people love this fishing village as a place in which to do
very little very pleasantly.

THE EAST

The eastern part of São Nicolau is mostly an arid, boulder-strewn desert. It is hard
to believe that just 70 years ago it was well populated and farmed using dryland
techniques that yielded crops of corn and manioc. Now, however, just two populated
villages remain: Juncalinho and Carriçal. The area has a raw, desolate beauty that
will move some and depress others.

JUNCALINHO   Juncalinho lies along the eastern ridge which is almost entirely devoid of
vegetation, but which is characterised by jagged rock formations and deep *ribeiras*. The
effects of rain and the lack of it can be seen on the journey here. First of all, hundreds of
disused terraces and a scattering of abandoned dwellings bear witness to a time when
water and agriculture – and people – were far more numerous. Secondly, the damage to
the road caused by the heavy rains of 2009 and 2010 has yet to be properly repaired. In
places, it was entirely washed away. It is a very poor and humble village – some might
say desolate – on a plain littered with boulders, some of which seem to have randomly
assembled themselves into houses. Only the cemetery and the football pitch have been
cleared of stones. It has its charm, though. A dingy sign indicates the *lagoa*, which enjoys
top billing here as a tourist attraction, just ahead of the tiny volcano.

Getting there   *Alugueres* depart from Ribeira Brava for Juncalinho at around
10.00, taking about 25 minutes to get there. They depart from Juncalinho for
Ribeira Brava approximately between 14.00 and 16.00.

🏠 Where to stay and eat

🏠 **Jardim** (4 rooms) 📞 235 2800 (or through
Pensão Jardim in Ribeira Brava). A distinctive,
2-storey house with a tower-like construction
at the front, this is run by a branch of the Jardim
family who run the *pensão* in Ribeira Brava. Rooms
are pleasant, spacious & all have private baths with
hot water. Amalia & English-speaking Paulinho can
often be found in their restaurant, 100m further
into Juncalinho on the main road on the right. **$$**

🏠 **Homestays** These can be arranged via some
of the island's best guides, for example Toi (see
page 326).
🍴 **Jardim** ⏲ daily. A local eatery-cum-shop
on the right of the main road, this is owned by the
Jardim family (see page 329). **$$**
🍴 **Lanchonete Caminh d'Lagoa** Off the main
road on the route down to the lagoa, on the left.
$$

What to see and do

Lagoa   You can drive the five minutes to the coast, or walk for 15 minutes past
circular, stone pig-pens, and gaze down at the crater – black rock lashed with white
foam. On a calm day the *lagoa* lies just beyond the reach of the swell, full of beautiful
blue-green water, and is a pleasant place to bathe. If you are keen to swim, try to
choose a calm day by checking with the *aluguer* drivers in the *vila* who can judge
the state of the sea as they traverse the main road around the island. In August, the

lagoa is the somewhat unlikely but scenic venue for a well-established traditional music festival, with artists attending from all over the island. You can see the stage at the western end of the cliff.

Coastal walk and volcanic crater To the east of the *lagoa*, pick your way carefully along the cliff top to see some fine volcanic rock formations adorning the ocean inlets as the swell crashes against them. Down below, you may see some seasoned fishermen using a simple line, bait and stone-weight combination to haul in sizeable *pica* and other fish suitable for either supper or sale. Head inland, crossing the dry *ribeira,* and you can enter the distinctive crater of a modest volcano. Rather than scramble up the 100m or so of steep climb, circle around to its southern (inland) side where the crater wall has collapsed and you can gain effortless access. Afterwards, continue south for a few hundred metres to find the cobbled road that will take you back to Juncalinho after ten minutes' walk.

Hike to Carriçal There are two hiking routes to Carriçal. The first is along the road. It is a magnificent walk. The road turns right after Juncalinho and climbs in a series of precipitous bends high into the mountains inland, over the ridge and down to the sea again. The terrain is dark brown, with heaps of earth and rock, and a frothy coastline.

The second route is along a path that heads directly south out of Juncalinho village, climbing steeply into the mountains, traverses the heights for around an hour and then descends into Ribeira de Palhal and the abandoned village of Urzeleiros (named after the indigo lichen *urzela* which was farmed here – see box, page 41). The latter path takes around five hours and is known as the Caminho de Cinta. It is poor quality and hard to navigate in places. We suggest you either take a guide (who you could probably pick up in Juncalinho) or use the hike description given in the Goldstadt Wanderkarte 1:50,000 map of São Nicolau (see page 70). Not a place to be caught short of water. The road may be nearby, but traffic is sparse.

CARRIÇAL Carriçal is a poor but pretty village, probably one of the most isolated in the archipelago. Most families are crammed into two-roomed, concrete houses with hens, pigs, dogs and cats bustling outside. Below the houses lies a tree-filled

GREENING SÃO NICOLAU

Fajã and its environs are lush and green thanks to technology and a lot of effort. It began in 1980 when, with French help, the people built a 2km tunnel into the mountainside to tap into water there. The pipe did not just transform Fajã's agriculture but also became the source of water for outlying dry areas such as Juncalinho. Initially it gushed 1,000m³ per day but this has now subsided to 400m³. To see the tunnel ask for 'Galeria de Fajã'.

Engineers and educationalists have been working hard to introduce new farming techniques to the area. The key has been to expand the use of traditional irrigation channels (if you are interested, it's worth wandering around the heavily planted terraces of Fajã to see how endless terraces of crops are kept watered by the judicious opening and closing of channels). Some of the water is supplied by boreholes and pumped uphill from where it can descend to do its irrigation.

A second technique, microirrigation, or 'drip drip', is slowly gaining acceptance and can be found in the area too.

ribeira, a pretty beach and a cluster of boats. You can pay a fisherman to take you out to net a pile of moray eels and bright orange grouper, or to go up the coast to explore the coves and caves.

By the steps down to the shore is a deserted factory. Before it closed some years ago, huge pans of tuna were boiled on wood fires and then canned in tins pressed on the premises. Turtle hunting was popular and lucrative here until recently, but education programmes run by the Ribeira Brava municipality (see page 327 for information on turtles) have been largely successful in stopping this.

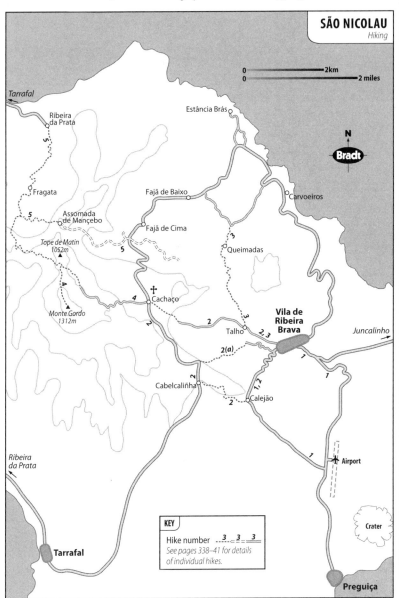

There is a small shop where you can buy drinks and snacks and it is possible to arrange a room for the night if you ask around.

Getting there In a 4x4, it will take another 35 minutes to get to Carriçal from Juncalinho. Check, however, that the road to Carriçal is open – it is sometimes impassable because of landslides. The road heads inland at Juncalinho, then continues east. When it is passable, it is spectacular, offering views all the way down the north coast.

Alugueres leave Ribeira Brava for Carriçal at around midday, and depart Carriçal for Ribeira Brava early in the morning. You might find a later one, depending on whether anyone has some fish to bring to town. If the road is impassable (which it often is in the rainy season) a fisherman might be persuaded to take you by boat from Preguiça to Carriçal.

HIKES   *Colum Wilson (CW); Aisling Irwin (AI)*

HIKES IN AND OUT OF RIBEIRA BRAVA
1 Ribeira Brava–Calejão–Ribeira Brava
Distance: approximately 4km; time: 2½ hours; difficulty: 1 (CW)
Leave Ribeira Brava on the airport road, ascending past the needles on your left. Bear right at the first junction (the left turn goes to Morro Brás and Juncalinho). After a short distance, bear right again on the road towards the cemetery, which you pass 25 minutes after setting out. The road winds for a short distance in the plantations in the bottom of the *ribeira* before leading you up the other side to rejoin the airport road. Follow it away from the edge of the *ribeira* to the airport, which you will reach 35 minutes after the cemetery.

Some 400m past the airport, there is a signposted turning to the right down to **Calejão**, which lies on the lower slopes of the mountain range.

It is a quiet village, strung out along the old road. After 3km you will pass a path on your left – the descent from Cabeçalinha (described in the next hike, below) which joins your path opposite a graffitied stone on the right. In the building on the corner, just after the path joins you, a craftsman manufactures ornaments from banana leaves. There's a shop selling water, biscuits and soft drinks. The impressive, ochre-coloured building on the left is the old orphanage and bishop's residence.

The road continues, straight at first, and then begins a superb descent into Ribeira Brava along a series of S-bends. There is an excellent view up the valley. The last section of the road is past impoverished suburbia and litter-strewn hillsides followed by some of the biggest houses in town. The track emerges in the São João area of town beside the old seminary.

2 Ribeira Brava–Cachaço–Cabeçalinha–Calejão
Distance: approximately 10km; time: at least 4 hours allowing for stops en route; difficulty: 2–3 (AI)
This is one of the best walks, at least four hours with a steep ascent and descent. Follow the cobbled road up the *ribeira* out of the *vila* – a fascinating walk through the villages. After an hour and 20 minutes of puffing you pass between some crags onto a small road leading to **Cachaço**. To the right the road winds up to a wonderfully positioned white church. Turn left to reach the busy main road of the island where there are a couple of shops selling biscuits and drinks (and, if you are lucky, goat's cheese – see page 331). Here the landscape is green, with plenty of perfectly shaped dragon trees. Turn left on the main road for a fantastic view of

Ribeira Brava. Peer down the gullies where vehicles have been known to tumble – and look up at the mountain on your right down which rocks often fall onto the road. There's a great view of the path you took up the *ribeira* and of the spine of mountains out to the east. Eventually the road turns to the right and you begin to see the gentler slopes that lead down to Tarrafal.

Some 35 minutes after leaving Cachaço the road takes a sharp right turn, just before a blue house. The track to the left (see (a) below) is an option for returning to Ribeira Brava, but you can also continue on the main road for another five minutes until you reach a white concrete water tank on the right – this is **Cabeçalinha**. Take the left track opposite this. For a good ten minutes the track ascends until you reach the third panorama of this walk – the southern mountains and sea. Now there's half an hour of steep, zig-zagging descent – not for bad knees – until you begin to sink into civilisation again, eventually reaching the dirt road. Turn left at the T-junction, opposite the graffitied stone. From here it is about 40 minutes back to town along the road described in the previous walk.

(a) An alternative is to descend down the first track to Ribeira Brava. On this track it takes about 40 minutes less to reach the *vila*. Leave the main road between Alto António Miguel and Morro Cone Rocha and go uphill for about 100m as far as the pass. Soon you will find yourself in Palso. Follow the path on the ridge to the *vila*.

3 Ribeira Brava–Queimadas
Distance: approximately 5.5km; time: 1½ hours; difficulty: 2 (CW)
Follow the cobbled road out of town and up the right-hand side of the *ribeira*. After 30 minutes you reach the small village of **Talho**. At the village standpipe (on a small concrete platform with a telephone box next to it), turn right up a small cobbled track. Very soon the cobbles give way to dust and the path begins to look far less promising. Keep following it up the hillside, resisting the temptation to take an easier, wider path which heads left after a few minutes.

As you ascend, the path swings to the left and, 30 minutes from the phone box, you emerge on a saddle. Looking back over the *ribeira*, Monte Gordo is to the right – the massive humpbacked mountain surmounted by radio masts. Turning around and looking over into the next *ribeira* you can see **Queimadas** in the valley. Fajã is through a gap in the range above it.

It is a pleasant, though steep, descent to the village. It is well worth (slightly) provoking any dog you see just to hear the extraordinary echo in this amphitheatre of a valley. At the T-junction by the old school turn left for Fajã to find transport back.

HIKES TO THE WEST OF THE MAIN ROAD
4 Cachaço–Monte Gordo
Distance: approximately 5km (return); time: 1½ hours; difficulty: 3 (CW)
This steep walk to the highest peak is also one of the most spectacular. You can lengthen it by walking from Ribeira Brava up to Cachaço first.

Take an *aluguer* to Cachaço (30 minutes; 200$). There is an obvious turning on your right, to the southwest, near the village standpipe (clearly marked *Água*). You ascend on a well-made path zig-zagging amongst lush plantations. It is attractive and shady, but this ascent is not for the unfit. After 40 minutes, the path flattens and skirts the right-hand side of a hill with radio antennae on top. After gently ascending amongst scattered houses and fields for 20 minutes, you reach a great view over Fajã on your right. Another 15 minutes takes you to a clearly defined saddle. On your right is the **Tope de Matin** (1,052m) and to the left is **Monte Gordo**

(1,312m). It may seem close, but don't be fooled – you are still at least 300m below the summit – which translates into a rough scramble of about 40 minutes. The ascent to Tope de Matin is about 30 minutes.

The view of the archipelago from the summits is the best you will find, including the uninhabited western islands – from left to right, Ilhéu Raso, Ilhéu Branco and Santa Luzia – as well as São Vicente and Santo Antão beyond. It is said that in exceptionally clear weather every Cape Verde island can be seen.

Floating around the peaks and saddle is the neglected kestrel (*Falco tinnunculus neglectus*), a small, brown bird common in the northerly islands. On the lower slopes you may disturb a flock of helmeted guineafowl. These birds, rather like grey,

TRAILS IN THE MONTE GORDO NATURAL PARK

With thanks to the Monte Gordo Natural Park office (www.ecosaonicolau.com)
These are three of the first trails delineated in the natural park:

SOUTHERN VIEW TRAIL This hike begins and ends at the entrance to the park. You begin by going along the main recreational trail, observing the plentiful endemic flora and fauna, the *caberinos* where local community members tend their fields, alongside the imposing peak of Monte Gordo to Assomada de Ribeira Calhaus. Here you encounter beautiful volcanic rock formations and have a splendid view of the valley below. You make your way down into the green, watery Ribeira Calhaus, and slowly begin to wind your way up the mountainside. You will see saio growing out of the rock walls. The hike is a bit steep and rocky, but well worth the effort for the views. After peaking, you come down along the cliffside and make your way to the village of Hortelão after passing more wonderful volcanic rock formations. In Hortelão, you can enjoy traditional foods for lunch, or continue to make your way back into the park.

RECREATIONAL TRAIL This hike takes you from the entrance of the park along the main recreational trail, past magnificent collections of *tortolhos*, through community farms, alongside Monte Gordo peak, winding your way to Assomada de Ribeira Calhaus. You then make your way down through volcanic rocks into a green oasis where you can sometimes see running water. Traverse traditional abandoned homes with views of the cliffs on both sides. You make your way back to Assomada and take the trail off to your left which winds down and along the edge of the farms in Cachaço, giving you great views of this rural village along with the valley below where Fajã lies. You end by making your way back to the park entrance.

WESTERN LOOP From Assomada de Ribeira Calhaus going westward, this loop passes over the top of Mont Desert with breathtaking views of Canto Fajã and the Fajã Valley. The ridge also passes over the mountain village of Fragata (where grogue is still produced in the traditional manner) before you descend past Tope de Matin and Tope Moka to the old settlement of Ribeira de Calhaus. Stay awhile to enjoy the freshwater spring and also enjoy shaded relief from the sun under the grand eucalyptus trees. Continuing along the loop you will make a climb back up to Assomada de Ribeira Calhaus along the old trail which was amazingly cut into the hillside. There are also spectacular views of the surrounding islands of Raso, Branco, Santa Luzia and, if you are lucky, you will be able to also see São Vicente and Santo Antão.

The park staff may be able to advise on other classic São Nicolau hikes. One of these runs north from Tarrafal, past Carberinho and on to Praia Branca, then turns inland towards Fragata, and on across the Monte Gordo Natural Park to Cachaço. Another is to descend from Hortelão to Tarrafal.

oversized hens, were introduced in the 1600s and are found on Santiago, Fogo, Maio and São Nicolau. They are very tasty.

5 Fajã de Baixo–Fragata–Ribeira da Prata
Distance: approximately 6km; time: 3 hours; difficulty: 3 (CW)
This is a magnificent walk with some steep ascents. The only problem is finding transport from Ribeira da Prata back to Tarrafal at the end of the walk: there are only two *aluguer* drivers resident in Ribeira da Prata and you may find yourself in a one-sided negotiation in which you end up chartering a vehicle for an exorbitant sum. Minimise hassle by beginning this walk early in the morning so you can try hitching back from Prata or picking up the mid-afternoon school run. Alternatively, take the midday *aluguer* from Tarrafal to Ribeira da Prata and do the walk in reverse. Take an *aluguer* to Cachaço. After Fajã and before Cachaço, there's a large sign on the right for Pico Agudo Canto Fajã. Take this and, after about 50m, bear left. You will see a prominent finger of rock in the saddle ahead. After about 15 minutes, you reach a T-junction with a small grave marked by a white cross on a mound nearby. Turn left and follow the track as it winds towards the saddle and then becomes a path which ascends steeply. You will reach the saddle about 50 minutes after setting out.

From the saddle, descend on a beautifully cobbled hairpin track. After about 20 minutes, you reach **Fragata**, with houses built on fantastic ledges and outcrops with sheer drops on either side. The track leads you round the head of the *ribeira* and then begins the descent towards **Ribeira da Prata**. From the saddle to the village is approximately a two-hour walk. Crops here include sugarcane, cassava, bananas and maize, and coarse tobacco (*erva*). It is smoked in pipes by the old folk, who spurn cigarettes as a lightweight invention.

RASO AND BRANCO

Just 7km², Raso has sheer cliffs, which rise out of the water to a plateau no more than 164m high. It has the traditional stony plains but also grassy areas. To the south there are colonies of sea petrels and shearwaters, red-billed tropicbirds and brown boobies – but Raso's most celebrated occupant is the Raso lark (*Alauda razae*), one of the rarest birds in the world, which lives only there and is rated 'critically endangered' on the international Red List of threatened species. There are fewer than 100 of these birds, known locally as *calhandra do Ilhéu Raso*; to the uninitiated, they can seem disappointingly small and brown.

The global population of Raso larks was estimated in January 2003 at 93–103 birds and in November 2003 at 76–87 birds. They cannot currently be encouraged to populate neighbouring Santa Luzia Island – though it seems to have suitable habitat – partly because there is a population of feral cats there.

Raso is also known for its endemic Raso lizards.

Branco is even smaller than Raso at just 3km². It is, however, taller, at 327m, and has one small water source. It is one of the most important sites in Cape Verde for breeding

A TASTE FOR BABY SHEARWATERS

Catch a young shearwater while it is still in the nest and eating mostly grass – and you have a creature whose ounce of flesh will fetch a lot of money. This was the reason for the annual hunt of shearwaters (*Calonectris edwardsii*), known locally as *cagarra*, on Ilhéu Raso, during which tens of thousands were harvested and, it is claimed, many were hidden amongst cargoes of fish and shipped to the Netherlands to satisfy the demands of the Cape Verdean community there..

It should have been easy to prevent. The fishermen who hunted the birds came from just one village, in Santo Antão; the cull happened during the same, predictable, short period each year, and it was strictly illegal. Yet it continued year after year, which eventually became a problem even for the fishermen because numbers started to plummet. In 2007, they managed to catch only 18,000 chicks compared with the previous year's catch of 27,000.

If left to their own devices, shearwaters live for about 40 years, according to Tommy Melo, founder of Cape Verde's first environmental organisation, Biosfera 1. But they lay only one egg annually.

Eating shearwaters was originally a tradition anchored in famine. During World War II, when imports were difficult, they became a food source. Later, they became a symbolic dish eaten during annual October celebrations to mark the end of famine.

By 2008, Melo was resolute that the hunting should stop and now, indeed, it has. He initially visited the fishermen to explain about the problem and gathered the resources to police the island during October. To convince the Cape Verde government that there was a problem, Melo even made a video about the cull, which can be seen on You Tube; it is not, however, for the squeamish or faint-hearted.

'My despair is knowing that the Cape Verde shearwater, the Raso lark and the Raso lizard are endemic species that exist nowhere else in the world and that in a matter of years they may no longer exist even in Cape Verde if we don't stop hunting them for food or raising them as pets,' said Melo back in 2007. Thankfully, thanks to the sterling efforts of Melo and others, the cull was stopped in 2008. During nesting season, a team stays permanently on the island, which is estimated to be home to 75% of the bird's total population, simply to protect them. It seems that the shearwaters have been saved.

---

seabirds and is white from their guano deposits. Branco was the unlikely host to 30 inhabitants in 1833 – prisoners who were dumped there and left to survive or die.

Branco was, until 1940, the last outpost of the Cape Verde giant skink, a delightful lizard-like creature coloured a mottled white and brown and with a big, heavy tail. It was the second-largest skink in the world, reaching 65cm in length and lived among the rocks eating the seeds of plants and occasionally augmenting this diet with bird eggs. Their numbers began plummeting when the prisoners arrived. After that they were the sporadic victims of local fishermen who trapped them to eat – and their skins were popular as shoe material. The final blow was the series of droughts in the early 20th century. A luckier creature is the giant gecko (*Tarentola gigas*). This lives in cliff holes and burrows on both islands.

The two islands were defined as nature reserves in 1990. Despite this, the island was swamped until 2008 with local fishermen to sate their desire for baby shearwaters (see box above).

Appendix 1

LANGUAGE

If you are serious about learning a language before going to Cape Verde then the big decision is whether to choose Portuguese or Creole. Creole is virtually impossible to learn outside the islands unless you have access to a Cape Verdean community, one of whose members might give lessons. On the other hand, if you plan to spend some time there and need to win the confidence of people other than professionals and officials it will be essential to learn Creole – learning Portuguese may turn out to have been a confusing waste of time.

In the absence of Creole, having some Portuguese is of huge help – every new word you learn will give you a little more access to people and be invaluable simply in helping you to get around. Most people speak no other European language. Ten minutes a day for a few months will double the satisfaction you get from your holiday. Combined with a smattering of French, to make what we call 'Fraughtuguese', you'll get by. English-speakers are becoming more common.

PORTUGUESE The biggest barrier to the swift acquisition of some Portuguese is pronunciation – it really takes several weeks to master it before learning any words. After that, the rudiments are reasonably simple and English speakers will recognise a large number of words, particularly when they are written down.

Pronunciation The following are basic rules, although there are a lot of exceptions:

- If a word carries an acute (´) or circumflex (^) accent then stress the syllable that carries it. Otherwise stress the second-last syllable.
- Vowels that carry a tilde (~) on the top, and vowels followed by 'm' are nasalised.
- Many vowels disappear, for example an 'e', 'a' or 'o' at the end of a word; and many 'e's at the beginning of words. Tone down unstressed vowels.
- Double vowels are pronounced as two separate vowels.

s	=	'sh' at the end of the word; 'z' in the middle; soft 'c' at the beginning
z	=	'sh' at the end of a word
c	=	soft 'c' if there's a cedilla underneath or if it's before an 'i' or an 'e'
g	=	soft 'j' if before an 'i' or an 'e'
j	=	soft 'j'
rr	=	rolled
r	=	only rolled at the beginning of a word
lh	=	'ly'
ch	=	'sh'
qu	=	'kw', before an 'a'; 'k' before an 'e' or an 'i'

nh = 'ny'
x = 'sh' or 's' – the rules are complicated – just take a chance
a = as in 'father' when stressed; as in 'air' when unstressed
e = as in 'jet' when stressed; as in the second 'e' of 'general' when unstressed
i = as in 'seen' but shorter
o = as in 'not' or 'note' when stressed; as in 'root' when unstressed
u = usually as in 'root'
h = don't pronounce

Grammar The most basic way of making something plural is by adding -s or -es to the end. The most basic verb endings are as follows:

I buy	*compr-o*	We buy	*compr-amos*
You buy (singular)	*compr-as*	You buy (plural)	*compr-ais*
You/he/she buys	*compr-a*	They buy	*compr-am*

Address all but intimates in the third person (literally: 'could he help me'). You don't need to bother with personal pronouns (I, you, he) unless you want to emphasise them (eg: *I* am talking to *you*).

Common compound verbs
be   *ser* (I am: *sou*/you are, he is: *é*/we are: *somos*/they are: *são*)
give   *dar* (I give: *dou*/you give, he gives: *dá*/they give: *dão*)
go   *ir* (I go: *vou*/you go, he goes: *vai*/let's go: *vamos*)
have   *ter* (I have: *tenho*/you have, he has: *tem*/we have: *temos*/they have: *têm*)
like   *gostar de* (I like = *gosto de*)

Greetings
good morning	*bom dia*
good afternoon (after midday)	*boa tarde*
good evening (after 18.00)	*boa noite*
goodbye	*até logo* ('until later')
how are you?	*como está?*
I am well/everything's fine	*estou bem* ('shtoe beyng')

Questions, answers and useful phrases
What is your name?	*Como se chama?*
Do you speak English?	*Fala inglês?*
Is it possible ...?	*É possível ...?*
How much does it cost?	*Quanto custa?*
What is this called?	*Como se chama isso?*
Can you help me?	*Pode me ajudar?*
Pardon?	*Como?*
Where?	*Onde?*
When?	*Quando?*
How?	*Como?*
Why?	*Porquê?*
What?	*Quê?*
Do you have a spare room?	*Tem um quarto vago?*
You're welcome	*De nada* ('it's nothing')
I am from London	*Sou de Londres*

My name is …	*Chamo-me …*
Where is …?	*Onde fica …?*
I don't know	*Não sei*
I don't understand	*Não compreendo*
Straight on	*Em frente*
On the right	*À direita*
On the left	*À esquerda*
More slowly	*Mais devagar*
I have to go	*Tenho de ir*
To have coffee	*Tomar café*
To have breakfast	*Tomar o café de manhã*
There is …	*Há …*
There is no …	*Não há …*
Too much	*Demais*
That's enough!	*Basta!*
More or less	*Mais ou menos*

Menus For basic words, see the list below – this list is of common dishes.

fish stew	*cozido de peixe*
grilled squid	*lula grelhada*
shellfish cooked with rice	*arroz de marisco*
generally wahoo, a white, hard fish steak	*peixe serra*
dried cod	*bacalhau*
dried cod and chips fried together	*bacalhau à Brás*
maize, beans, chicken, other meat	*cachupa rica*
maize, beans	*cachupa pobre*
a chicken dish	*djagacida* or *jag*
a soup	*conj*
corn bread	*gufong*
a milk pudding, rather like crême caramel	*pudim de leite*
sponge impregnated with coconut, like steamed pudding	*tarte de coco*

Food and drink

bean	*feijão*	cheese	*queijo*
beef	*carne de vaca*	chicken (as food)	*frango*
beer	*cerveja*	chips	*batatas fritas*
bread	*pão*	coffee	*café*
cake	*bolo*	dessert	*sobremesa*
cassava	*mandioca*	eel	*moreia*
eggs	*ovos*	shrimp/prawn	*camarão*
haricot beans	*congo*	spirits	*aguardente*
lobster	*lagosta*	sweet potato	*batata doce*
maize	*milho*	tea	*chá*
meat	*carne*	tuna	*atum*
milk	*leite*	turkey	*peru*
octopus	*polvo*	veal	*vitela*
potato	*batata*	water	*água*
rice	*arroz*	wine	*vinho*
rum (local)	*grogga*		

Days and months

Sunday	*domingo*	Wednesday	*quarta-feira*
Monday	*segunda-feira*	Thursday	*quinta-feira*
	(second day)	Friday	*sexta-feira*
Tuesday	*terça-feira*	Saturday	*sábado*

January	*janeir*	July	*julho*
February	*fevereiro*	August	*agosto*
March	*março*	September	*setembro*
April	*abril*	October	*outubro*
May	*maio*	November	*novembro*
June	*junho*	December	*dezembro*

Numbers

1	*um/uma*	16	*dezasseis*
2	*dois/duas*	17	*dezassete*
3	*três*	18	*dezoito*
4	*quatro*	19	*dezanove*
5	*cinco*	20	*vinte*
6	*seis* ('saysh')	30	*trinta*
7	*sete*	40	*quarenta*
8	*oito*	50	*cinquenta*
9	*nove*	60	*sessenta*
10	*dez* ('desh')	70	*setenta*
11	*onze*	80	*oitenta*
12	*doze*	90	*noventa*
13	*treze*	100	*cem*
14	*catorze*	1,000	*mil*
15	*quinze*	a million	*um milhão*

Other common words

aeroplane	*avião* ('avi-ow')		('pekaynalmoss')
after	*depois de*	brother	*irmão*
also	*também*	bus	*autocarro*
and	*e*	buy	*comprar*
at	*a*	candle	*vela*
bad	*mau, má*	car	*carro*
baggage	*bagagem*	casualty department	*banco de socorros*
bakery	*padaria*	cat	*gato*
bank	*banco*	change	*troco*
bathroom	*casa de banho*	cheap	*barato/a*
battery	*pilha*	chicken	*galinho*
beach	*praia*	church	*igreja*
beautiful	*lindo/a*	cinema	*cinéma*
bed	*cama*	city	*cidade*
before	*antes de*	closed	*fechado*
big	*grande*	condom	*camisinha*
boarding house	*pensão*	cow	*vaca*
book	*livro*	customs	*alfândega*
boy	*rapaz*	day	*dia*
breakfast	*pequeno almoço*	diarrhoea	*diarréia*

difficult	*difícil*	night	*noite*
dinner	*jantar*	nightclub	*boite*
doctor	*médico/a*	no	*não*
dog	*cão*	nothing	*nada*
drink (to)	*beber*	now	*agora*
drink	*bebida*	of	*de*
early	*cedo*	old	*velho*
eat	*comer*	open	*aberto/a*
English	*inglês*	path	*caminho*
enough	*bastante*	pen	*caneta*
exchange (to)	*trocar*	perhaps	*talvez*
father	*pai*	pharmacy	*farmácia*
fever	*febre*	pillow	*almofada*
film	*película*	please	*faz favor*
flight	*vol*	police	*policia*
girl	*rapariga*	post office	*correio*
goat	*cabra*	rain	*chuva*
good	*bom/boa*	rest	*descansar*
he	*ele*	restaurant	*restaurante*
heavy	*pesado/a*	road	*rua*
high	*alto/a*	room	*quarto*
hill	*colina*	room for a couple	*quarto casal*
hospital	*hospital*	room for one	*quarto individual*
hot	*quente*	room for two	*quarto duplo*
hotel	*hotel*	salt	*sal*
house	*casa*	school	*escola*
hurt (to)	*doer*	sea	*mar*
husband	*marido*	sell	*vender*
I	*eu*	send	*enviar*
ill	*doente*	she	*ela*
in	*em*	sheet	*lençol*
key	*chave*	shop	*loja*
lagoon	*piscina*	shower	*chuveiro*
leave	*partir*	sister	*irmã*
letter	*carta*	small	*pequeno/a*
light	*luz* ('loosh')	sorry	*desculpe*
little (ie: 'not much')	*pouco/a*	speak	*falar*
lorry	*camião*	spouse	*esposo/a*
low	*baixo/a* ('baysho')	square (town)	*praça*
lunch	*almoço*	sun	*sol*
magazine	*revista*	supermarket	*supermercado*
man	*homem*	swim	*nadar*
market	*mercado*	telephone	*telefone*
matches	*fósforos*	thanks	*obrigado/a*
money	*dinheiro*	(as in 'much obliged')	
mosquito net	*mosquiteiro*	that	*esse*
mother	*mãe*	they	*eles/elas*
mountain	*montanha*	this	*este*
much	*muito/a*	ticket	*bilhete*
never	*nunca*	to	*para* ('*pra*')
newspaper	*jornal*	today	*hoje*

toilet	*sanitário*	wind	*vento*
toilet paper	*papel higiênico*	with	*com*
tomorrow	*amanhã*	woman	*mulher*
town	*vila*	work	*trabalhar*
town hall	*câmara*	yes	*sim*
travel	*viajar*	yesterday	*ontem*
travellers' cheques	*cheques de viagem*	you (polite masc)	*o senhor*
very	*muito/a*	you (polite fem)	*a senhora*
village	*aldeia*	you (familiar)	*você*
visa	*visto*	you (polite masc pl)	*os senhoros*
we	*nós*	you (polite fem pl)	*as senhoras*

CREOLE *São Vicente Creole translations by 10th-grade pupils at the José Augusto Pinto School in Mindelo, São Vicente, with help from their teacher, Keith West. Santiago translations and introductory material by Steven Maddocks.*

The Creole language varies widely across the archipelago, to the extent that people from São Vicente profess not to be able to understand their compatriots from Santiago. Although every island has its own version, the greatest difference is between the Barlavento Creole spoken in the north of Cape Verde, and that spoken in the south (Sotavento Creole).

São Vicente Creole is slightly more Portuguese than Santiago, or Badiu, Creole – the latter contains more African words. Generally speaking, Barlavento Creole is more clipped and staccato, and Sotavento Creole is more open, with rounded vowels, and spoken more aggressively. There are differences in vocabulary, with each using its own slang. Among the biggest differences are subject pronouns, 'You' (singular) is *bu* in Sotavento Creole and *bo* in Barlavento Creole. 'You' (plural) is *nhos* and *bzot*, respectively.

An 'a' in Sotavento Creole often comes out as an 'o' in Barlavento, as in 'work' (*trabadju/trabodj*) or 'ill-mannered' (*malkriadu/malkriod*).

In Santiago they tend to pronounce the whole word. Consequently it is much easier for the beginner to understand what is being said. In São Vicente whole syllables – both in the middle and at the ends of words – may be left out. So for example the *-adu* at the end of words in Sotavento Creole becomes *-od* in Barlavento Creole – so *Kansadu* would be pronounced *Kansod*. In Santiago Creole, *v* changes to *b* and *lh* becomes *dj*, so the word for red – *vermelho* in the north – is pronounced *burmedju* in the south. For more about the rivalries between Creole and Portuguese, see box, pages 38–9.

Below, the Santiago translation is given first, followed by the São Vicente version. The two different versions of Creole have been represented as simply as possible for a novice. All of the sounds correspond roughly to their English equivalents. Peculiarities are as follows:

tx represents the 'ch' in 'cherry' j is the 'z' of 'pleasure'
dj represents the 'j' in 'Jerry' k is hard, as in 'kick'
x is the 'sh' of 'sham' s is soft, as in 'sick'

The only accents used here are to draw attention to stress. For verbs, in Sotavento Creole stress is always on the penultimate syllable, in Barlavento on the last syllable. This has been represented by an accented final a, e, or i.

Grammar 'You' has familiar and polite, singular and plural forms, as well as gender. It would be rude to address an elderly stranger with the familiar form.

	Sotavento Creole	Barlavento Creole
you (singular, familiar)	*bu* (except *bo e*, you are)	*bo*
you (singular, polite)	*nho* (masc), *nha* (fem)	*bosé* (masc and fem)
you (plural, familiar)	*nhos*	*bzot*
you (plural, polite)	*nhos*	*bosés*

Shopping

Excuse me, where is the shop?	*Undi ki e loja, pur favor?*	*Ondé k'e loja, d'favor?*
Do you have bottled water?	*Nhos tem agu di garafa?*	*Bzot tem agua d'garafa?*
How much does this cost?	*Keli e kantu?*	*Keli tonté?*
It's too expensive	*Kel e karu dimas*	*Kel e txeu kor*
I'm not paying that. It's a rip-off!	*N ka kre kumpra'l. Kel e robo!* (strong)	*N ka kre kompra'l. Bo ti ta ingana'm!*

Airport

What time will the flight leave?	*Ki ora ki avion ta sei?*	*Kazora k'aviau ta sei?*
Is there a telephone here?	*Li tem telefon?*	*Li tem t'lefon?*
I'm very upset because my baggage has not arrived	*N sta mutu xatiadu pa modi nha bagagem ka ben*	*N ta txeu xatiod mod nha bagagem ka ben*
I'm in a hurry	*N sta ku presa*	*N ta k'pres*

Taxi

Please take me to Hotel X	*Pur favor, leba'm ti Hotel X*	*D'favor, leva'm té Hotel X*

Hotel

Do you have a vacant room?	*Nhos tem kuartu?*	*Bzot tem um kuart?*
May I see the room first?	*N kre odja kuartu purmeru?*	*N ta gostá d'oia kel kuart primer?*
What time is breakfast?	*Ki ora ki e ora di kafé?*	*Kazora k'e kafé?*

Bank

Where is the bank?	*Undi ki e banku?*	*Ondé k'e bonk?*
Can I cash travellers' cheques here?	*Nhos ta troka'm travelxek?*	*Bzot ta troká travelxek?*
What is the exchange rate?	*Kal ki e kambiu di oji?*	*Tonté k'e kambiu?*
When does the bank close/ open?	*Ki ora ki banku ta fitxa/ ta abri?*	*Kazora k'bonk t'f'txá/ t'abrí?*

Hiking

Where is the path to the peak?	*Undi ki e kaminhu pa piku?*	*Ondé k'e kamin pa piku?*
Is this the path to get there? (hiker points)	*Ekeli ki e kaminhu pa la?*	*Keli k'e kamin pa la?*

Where can I buy water?	*Undi ki N podi kumpra agu?*	*Ondé k'n podé kompra agua?*
How far is it to the valley floor?	*Falta txeu pa nu txiga fundu rubera?*	*Tont temp kёgent t'levá pa txigá la na fund?*
How many hours to the road?	*Kantu tenpu falta pa nu txiga strada?*	*Tont temp k'falta'm pa'n txigá strada?*
Go left at the fork	*Na dizviu toma skerda*	*Na skina bo t'v'rá pa skerda*
Go right at the crossroads	*Na kruzamentu vira a direta*	*Na kruzament bo t'v'ra pa dreta Bo podé mostra'm li*
Can you show me on the map?	*Bu podi mostra'm li na napa?*	*na mapa?*
I need a guide	*N mesti um guia*	*N presiza d'um guia*
I want to go to the *grogue* distillery	*N kre ba ti trapixe*	*N kre bai pa trapixe*
No more grogue or I'll get drunk	*Si n toma mas grogu n ta fika moku*	*Se n tomá mas grog, n ta fuxká*
Is it possible to walk along that path? (point)	*N podi anda na kel kaminhu?*	*N podé anda la na kel kamin?*
I want to go to the crater	*N kre ba ti kratera*	*N kre bai pa kratera*
Is there public transport?	*Tem transport?*	*Tem transport?*

Restaurant

Could you bring me the menu, please?	*Traze'm ementa, pur favor?*	*Traze'm imenta, d'favor*
We've been here a long time	*Dja dura ki nu txiga li*	*Diaza k'nu ta li*
Could I have the bill, please?	*Traze'm konta, pur favor?*	*Traze'm konta, d'favor*
Do you have any change?	*Bu tene troku?*	*Bo tem trok?*

Personal communication

Hello	*Oi/Ola*	*Oi*
Goodbye	*Txau*	*Txau*
Yes	*Sim*	*Sim*
No	*Nau*	*Nau*
Do you speak English?	*Bu ta papia ingles?*	*Bo t'falá ingles?*
Which island are you from?	*Bo e di ki ilha?*	*Bo e d'kual ilha?*
What is your name?	*Modi ki e bu nomi?*	*Mané k'e bo nom?*
My name is...	*Nha nomi e...*	*Nha nom e...*
Can you help me?	*Bu podi djuda'm?*	*Bo podé isda'm?*
What is this called?	*Modi ki e nomi di kel kuza li?*	*Mané k'e nom d'es kosa?*
I don't understand	*N ka ta entendi*	*N ka ti ta entende'b*
Please speak more slowly	*Papia mas dibagar, pur favor*	*Falá mas d'vagar, d'favor*
I don't have any money	*N ka tene dinheru*	*N ka tem d'nher*
That's enough	*Dja txiga*	*Ta bom*

Miscellaneous

If	*Si*	*Se*
Often	*Txeu bes*	*Txeu vez*
Already	*Dja*	*Ja*
Still	*Inda*	*Inda*
Now	*Gosi*	*Grinhasim*
Other	*Otu*	*Ot*
Sorry	*Diskulpa'm*	*Diskulpa'm*
How are you?	*Modi ki bu sta?*	*Manera bo ta?*
General greeting	*Tudu bon? Tudu dretu?*	*Tud dret?*
Excuse me	*Kon lisensa*	*Ko l'sensa*
I'm here on holiday	*N sta li di feria*	*N ta d'feria*
I'm from London/ England/America	*Ami e di Londres/ Inglatera/ Merka*	*Mi e d'Londres/d'Inglater/ 'Merka*
Collective *aluguer* (often a Toyota Hiace)	*Ias*	*Ias*
Bad/damaged/broken/ill/ mistaken	*Mariadu*	no single word covers the same range
Good/excellent/cool/fine	*Fixe*	*Kul*
Good/tasty/delicious/fun	*Sabi*	*Sab*
That's not on	*Keli ka ta da*	*Keli ka ta dret*
There's a power cut	*Lus dja bai*	*Lus ja bai*
I don't eat meat	*N ka ta kumé karni*	*N ka ta k'mé karn*

Appendix 2

FURTHER INFORMATION

There is little about Cape Verde on the shelves of British bookshops. Two exceptions are Basil Davidson's history, and Mitchell Serel's book on Jewish history, both listed below. It's worth watching the secondhand books as they appear on Amazon, Waterstone's or the Book Depository websites, amongst others. Alternatively, the British Library (*www.bl.uk*) has many of the books below (membership is free and open to all, though you will have to register and obtain a library card. Books are generally for use in the library itself, not for borrowing. Its catalogue can be searched via the website. For the definitive digest of Cape Verdean literature in English consult the *World Bibliographical Series*, volume 123, Cape Verde, by Caroline Shaw (Clio Press, 1991).

BOOKS
Activities

Cabo Verde, Santo Antão, Guia dos Circuitos Turísticos. A beautifully produced guide to hikes in Santo Antão, each with a foldout, high-quality map to show the route. Although written in Portuguese, it is of great value even without the text. It might still be available on Santo Antão; otherwise try to get it from the agency Lux Development (*www.lux-development. lu*), which funded the project.

Hammick, Anne and Heath, Nicholas *Atlantic Islands: Azores, Madeira, Canary and Cape Verde Islands* Imray, Laurie, Norie and Wilson, 2004. An essential practical guide for yachties.

For more details on where to surf, get hold of *The Surf Report* or try www.surfermag.com.

Cape Verde library collections

The Arquivo Historico Nacional (*CP 321, Chã d'Areia, Praia, Santiago, Cape Verde*) was founded in 1988 and now comprises a large collection of historic and recent books as well as documents of the colonial administration concerning such issues as customs, emigration and church matters among many other subjects.

The Cape Verdean Special Collection is in the James P Adams Library, Rhode Island College (*600 Mount Pleasant Av, Providence, RI 02908;* ☎ *+1 401 456 9653*). In this collection you find books, newspapers, tapes of Cape Verdean television and radio programmes, photographs and various private Cape Verdean collections. There is about 40 linear feet of material.

Economy and politics For factual information on the country's economy there are two
reference books:

Africa South of the Sahara Europa Publications. A reference book that is updated every year.

Europa World Year Book, by the same publisher, where it is covered less extensively.

In addition, look for:

Foy, Colm *Cape Verde: Politics, Economics and Society* Pinter, 1988. A penetrating guide to the working of government in post-independence Cape Verde.

Health

Wilson-Howarth, Jane *Healthy Travel: Bites, Bugs and Bowels* Cadogan, 2009.

Wilson-Howarth, Jane and Ellis, Matthew *Your Child Abroad: A Travel Health Guide* Bradt Travel Guides, 2005.

History

Araújo, Américo C *Little Known: The European Side of the Cape Verde Islands* DAC Publishers, 2000. Documents European connections with the islands and includes translations of some poems of Jorge Barbosa.

Balla, Marcelo Gomes *António's Island: Missing Pages of History for Blacks and Hispanics* Braiswick, 2002. An idiosyncratic collection of articles about Cape Verde's history.

Berger Coli, Waltraud and Lobban, Richard A *The Cape Verdeans in Rhode Island: A Brief History.* On the same theme as Halter (see below).

Carreira, António *People of the Cape Verde Islands* Hurst, 1982. A detailed analysis of one of the fundamental forces of Cape Verdean society: emigration, both forced and voluntary. It is an academic work by a respected Cape Verde historian.

Davidson, Basil *No Fist is Big Enough to Hide the Sky: The Liberation of Guinea-Bissau and Cape Verde* Zed Press, 1981. A lively account of the armed struggle in Guinea-Bissau.

Davidson, Basil *The Fortunate Isles* Hutchinson, 1989. A one-volume history of the islands from start to finish by Britain's foremost historian of Africa. The book is a very readable, personal account of the emergence of a much-loved nation from the bonds of colonialism. There is also a rather detailed analysis of Cape Verde's socialist policies in the last third of the book. that makes for interesting reading.

Duncan, Bentley *Atlantic Islands: Madeira, the Azores and the Cape Verdes in 17th Century Commerce and Navigation* University of Chicago Press, 1972. A formidable mass of information about the slave and other trades, spilling over into other centuries and with plenty of interesting titbits.

Halter, Marilyn *Between Race and Ethnicity: Cape Verdean American Immigrants 1860–1965* University of Illinois Press, 1995. Written as part of a larger project to understand American immigrants from a variety of countries, this highly rated book is essential for a deeper understanding of Cape Verde, because emigration has played such a large part in moulding the country. As well as fascinating accounts of the lives of Cape Verdeans in the USA, it includes much history of the land left behind.

Lobban, Richard *Cape Verde: Crioulo Colony to Independent Nation* Westview Press, 1995. An excellent book with a broad sweep, by a seasoned Cape Verde-watcher.

Lobban, Richard and Saucier, Paul Khalil *The Historical Dictionary of the Republic of Cape Verde* Scarecrow Press, 2007. Very readable and up to date, this book is ideal for answering a broad spectrum of questions about Cape Verde.

Ludtke, Jean *Atlantic Peeks: An Ethnographic Guide to the Portuguese-Speaking Islands* Christopher Publishing House, 1989. Recommended, available secondhand.

Serels, Mitchell *The Jews of Cape Verde* Sepher-Hermon Press, 1997.

There are many fascinating accounts written by British sailors, civil servants and entrepreneurs who have passed through the archipelago. They include:

Burdon Ellis, Alfred *West African Islands* Chapman and Hall, 1855. Entertaining and irritating by turns.

Dampier, William *A New Voyage Round the World* Adam and Charles Black, 1937. This is an account of the sailor's visit in 1683, complete with pirates, bandits and a generally unfavourable impression of the Cape Verdean people.

Lyall, Archibald *Black and White Make Brown* Heinemann, 1938. An intelligent and highly entertaining account of the journey this journalist made to both Cape Verde and Portuguese Guinea.

Rendall, John *A Guide to the Cape Verde Islands* C Wilson, 1856. Frustratingly lacking in detail given the promise of the title, but fascinating nevertheless.

Roberts, George *Account of a Voyage to the Islands of the Canaries, Cape de Verde and Barbadoes, in 1721* can be found within *A New general Collection of Voyages and Travels, vol I*, collected by Thomas Astley Frank Cass, 1968 – another lively set of adventures.

Valdez, Francisco Travassos *Six Years of a Traveller's Life in Western Africa, vol 1* Hurst and Blackett, 1861. An unusually positive account by a Portuguese sent to report on the islands for the government.

Economy and politics For factual information on the country's economy there are two reference books:
Africa South of the Sahara Europa Publications. A reference book that is updated every year.
Europa World Year Book, by the same publisher, where it is covered less extensively.

In addition, look for:
Foy, Colm *Cape Verde: Politics, Economics and Society* Pinter, 1988. A penetrating guide to the working of government in post-independence Cape Verde.

Language
Gonçalves, Manuel da Luz and Andrade, Lelia Lomba de *Pa Nu Papia Krioulu* M&L Enterprises, 2003. A lively book that uses poetry, recipes and cultural articles to teach Creole to non-speakers, and teach Creole speakers how to read and write the language.

Literature
Burness, Donald *Fire: Six Writers from Angola, Mozambique and Cape Verde* Three Continents Press, 1977. This devotes some time to the exposition of Baltasar Lopes's novel *Chiquinho*.

Clew Parsons, Elsie *Folk Lore from the Cape Verde Islands* American Folklore Society, 1923. In British libraries. A fascinating accumulation of tales she collected from American *emigrantes* in the early 1900s.

Hamilton, Russell *Voices from an Empire: A History of Afro-Portuguese Literature* University of Minnesota Press, 1975. Includes an in-depth look at some of the leading Cape Verdean writers and poets.

Leite, Vicente Rendal *The Booklet (*A Caderneta*)* Instituto Caboverdiano do Livro. Translation of the story by Baltasar Lopes.

Strathern, Oona *Traveller's Literary Companions* In Print, 1994. Devoted to Cape Verdean poems, it is only worthwhile buying if you are interested more widely in African literature.

Classic Cape Verde literature, which does not seem to be available in English, includes:

Leite, Ana Mafalda, *Cape Verde: Language, Literature and Music* Portuguese Literary and Cultural Studies, 2002.

Lopes, Baltasar *Chiquinho* 1947. The seminal Cape Verdean novel and also a leader in the literature of Portuguese Africa. It is available in French, Spanish and Italian translations.

Lopes, Manuel *Chuva Braba* (Wild Rain) and *Flagelados do Vente Leste* (Victims of the East

Wind). The latter novel was the basis for the first Cape Verdean-produced feature-length motion picture, which has the same title and was shot on Santo Antão.

Pereira, Celia *Estória, Estória: Do Tambor a blimundo* (*www.tabanka.it*). A children's book and audio book, in Italian, Portuguese and English, including the story of the liberated ox, Blimundo, and an assortment of Cape Verdean sayings.

Natural history For birdwatchers, try these:

Aves de Cabo Verde This useful little orange booklet includes colour drawings of most of the important birds, their local and Latin names and a short explanation in English. Available from CVI (Cape Verde Investments) in Praia.

Bannerman, David and Mary *History of the Birds of the Cape Verde Islands* Oliver and Boyd, 1968. An entertaining book which combines distinguished ornithology with genial accounts of their times in Cape Verde.

Clarke, Tony and Orgill, Chris and Disley, Tony *A Field Guide to the Birds of the Atlantic Islands: Canary Islands, Madeira, Azores, Cape Verde* Helm Field Guides, 2006.

Garcia Del Rey, Eduardo, *Field Guide to the Birds of Macaronesia* Lynx, 2011. Includes Cape Verde.

Hazevoet, Cornelis *The Birds of the Cape Verde Islands* British Ornithologists' Union, 1995. Order from the Natural History Book Service (*2–3 Wills Rd, Totnes, Devon TQ9 5XN, UK;* ☏ *01803 865913;* e *customer.services@nhbs.co.uk; www.nhbs.co.uk*).

Hazevoet, Cornelis Sixth report on birds from the Cape Verde Islands, including records of 25 taxa new to the archipelago. Available for download from www.africanbirdclub.org/countries/CapeVerdeIslands/refs.html.

Plantas Endémicas A small guide to the country's vegetation, it has been translated into English and is also available from CVI (see above).

Portuguese titles

Carreira, António *Cabo Verde: Formação e Extinção de uma Sociedade Escravocrata* Archon Books. This is an important work on the Cape Verdean slave economy.

Germano Lima, António *Ilha de Capitães* Spleen, 1997. A Portuguese-language account of the history of Boavista.

Lopes, Jose Vicente *Cabo Verde: Os Bastidores da Independencia* Spleen, 2002.

MAGAZINES AND JOURNALS

Cimboa A journal of historical, cultural and political articles, published by the Cape Verdean consulate in Boston.

Fragata The in-flight magazine of the airline TACV, is worth picking up. The English translations of its articles are flawed, but the topics are interesting and there are good photographs.

WEBSITES

www.allafrica.com Regular news about Cape Verde is published here.

www.areasprotegidas.gov.cv Information about all of Cape Verde's protected areas.

www.asemana.publ.cv With a version in English, this Cape Verdean newspaper site has plenty of news from around the islands.

www.bela-vista.net A site for tourists written by a German and a Cape Verdean, with English, German, Italian and Portuguese versions. Includes accommodation listings and an update on ferries in the archipelago (not always up to date but worth trying).

www.bravanews.com Information and news about Brava, in Portuguese.

www.caboverde.com (or caboverdesmart.com) A huge, rambling site, one of the first devoted to tourist information on Cape Verde, with listings for accommodation and restaurants. Put together by Italian Eraldo de Gioannini, it is nevertheless a good first port of call for visitors to have a look and get a general idea of the place.

www.capeverde.com A well-organised website with plenty of information for planning a trip, with the occasional inaccuracy.

www.capeverdetips.co.uk Aimed largely at people who are buying or already own property on Sal. It includes plenty of advice about travel, life in Sal and can advise on wedding blessings on that island. Also has a useful link to British Embassy Information for British Nationals in Cape Verde.

www.expressodasilhas.sapo.cv Website for a Cape Verdean newspaper, only in Portuguese.

www.governo.cv The official government website, in Portuguese, but with some official documents in English.

www.macauhub.com.mo A news site that aims to link Portuguese-speaking Africa with the Great Pearl River Delta region of China in order to facilitate business, which regularly produces interesting news pieces about Cape Verde.

www.maiocv.com Information about Maio, with an emphasis on land development.

www.mindelo.info Information about Mindelo, in French.

www.oceancafe.com Ambitious website of the Ocean Café in Santa Maria features news articles about the islands.

www.rtc.cv Cape Verde Radio website allows you to hear the music and practise listening to the language before you travel.

www.sao-filipe.com A limited site about Fogo, in German with a few English links. Has property for sale and some nice pictures.

www.scvz.org Zoological Society of Cape Verde, with some English-language information.

www.tripadvisor.com Holidaymakers give post-mortems, mainly of package trips to Sal and Boavista.

www.umassd.edu/specialprograms/caboverde This site, though it does not seem to have been updated since 2000, nevertheless holds some interesting information and links. Aims to link Cape Verdeans all over the world and contains information about the islands.

www.virtualcapeverde.net A useful portal for those considering investing in Cape Verde, with links to the relevant bodies, and news from a wide variety of sources.

Index

Entries in **bold** indicate main entries; entries in *italics* indicate maps.

INDEX OF HIGHLIGHTED BOXES

INDEX OF ADVERTISERS